COUNTRY PEOPLE IN THE NEW SOUTH

JEANETTE KEITH

STUDIES IN RURAL CULTURE

JACK TEMPLE KIRBY, EDITOR

COUNTRY PEOPLE
IN THE NEW SOUTH

TENNESSEE'S UPPER CUMBERLAND

THE UNIVERSITY OF NORTH CAROLINA PRESS | CHAPEL HILL & LONDON

The paper in this book meets the guidelines for permanence and durability

of the Committee on Production Guidelines for Book Longevity of the

Council on Library Resources.

Library of Congress Cataloging-in-Publication Data

Keith, Jeanette. Country people in the New South: Tennessee's Upper

Cumberland / by Jeanette Keith. p. cm. — (Studies in rural culture)

Includes bibliographical references and index.

ISBN 0-8078-2211-6 (alk. paper). — ISBN 0-8078-4526-4 (pbk. : alk. paper)

1. Dayton (Tenn.)—Rural conditions. 2. Upper Cumberland Region

(Tenn.)—Rural conditions. 3. Scopes, John Thomas—Trials, litigation, etc.

I. Title. II. Series.

HN80.D314K45 1995   307.72'09768'834—dc20

94-39346 CIP

99 98 97 96 95   5 4 3 2 1

CONTENTS

A section of illustrations begins on page 91.

TABLES, FIGURE, AND MAPS

Acknowledgments

The people that I write about in this book survived by cultivating a web of family and community ties that sustained them in good times and bad. Like them, I have depended on family and friends to get me through hard times. However, unlike most country people, I have been unable to avoid debt. I am beholden to the following institutions and individuals:

Since I began work on this project I have been employed by three universities: Vanderbilt University, Tennessee Technological University, and Bloomsburg University of Pennsylvania. Vanderbilt provided a nurturing environment for a graduate student—and a much needed dissertation improvement grant. At Tennessee Tech a group of historians shared their research into the Upper Cumberland past; I thank them for their generosity. I am especially grateful to James Sperry, chair of the Department of History at Bloomsburg, who for five years scheduled my classes in such a way as to give me time for research and writing. His encouragement meant a lot.

Like all historians, I owe a debt to those individuals who preserved local history. In this work I cite the research of many local historians. Without their books this book would have been almost impossible to write. Of these historians, by far the best is Mary Jean DeLozier. Mrs. DeLozier, who taught Tennessee history for years at Tennessee Tech, was commissioned by Putnam County to write the bicentennial history of the county. Her book on Putnam County, carefully and exhaustively researched, is surely the secondary source I turned to most often. I owe her and other local historians thanks.

Historians are always in debt to archivists and librarians. I would like to thank the people at the Tennessee State Library and Archives; the Disciples of Christ Historical Society; the Southern Baptist Convention Historical Library and Archives; the National Archives in Washington and at the Record Center in East Point, Georgia; the Special Collections of the Hoskins Library at the University of Tennessee, Knoxville; the Jean and Alexander Heard Library at Vanderbilt; the Vanderbilt Divinity School Library; the Jere Whitson

Library at Tennessee Tech; and the Clara Cox Epperson Library, Cookeville, Tennessee.

Mr. and Mrs. Huber Butler of Carthage, Tennessee, spent an afternoon talking to me about Mr. Butler's father, John Washington Butler. I am grateful to them for their time, their information, and their gracious hospitality.

This book began as a paper in Don H. Doyle's social history seminar at Vanderbilt. At every stage of the long process by which paper became dissertation became book, Don's enthusiasm, encouragement, support, and guidance have been unfailing. I consider myself fortunate to have had such a mentor and to have worked with the excellent graduate students, among them Doug Flamming, Mary DeCredico, and Mel McKiven, who came to Nashville to study with Don Doyle. Collectively, in the Southern Social History Seminar, they critiqued major portions of this book; individually, they were extraordinarily kind and helpful to the older housewife in their midst. David Carleton provided useful criticism and help at each stage of the project. Paul Conkin read the dissertation as a historian and as a former farm boy from East Tennessee; both perspectives were immensely useful. Then he read it again as a writer and made me rewrite to avoid most (not all) passive voice. I also thank Dewey Grantham for his insights in southern politics and political culture.

Parts of this book first appeared as papers at various conferences. I am grateful for the comments and critiques offered by panel members and by audiences; special thanks to Cynthia Bouton for her comments at the 1990 Duquesne Forum, and to Jack Hurley and Mary Neth for their comments at the 1991 meeting of the American Historical Association.

Jack Kirby, acting as series editor for UNC Press, sponsored the book to the press when it was an unrevised dissertation. His suggestions during the revision process have been invaluable, as has his consistent support. Edward Ayers reviewed the book before publication. His criticisms sparked a chain of e-mail messages between the two of us and resulted in my making revisions that sharpened and focused my argument. I am grateful for his willingness to debate. Thanks also to Lew Bateman and the staff at UNC Press.

I am blessed with good friends beyond my due. I owe debts of friendship to Tom Furtsch, Linda Furtsch, Albert and Pat Wilhelm, Jesse B. Garner, Mike Birdwell, Calvin Dickinson, Larry Whiteaker,

Nancy Anderson, Anne Romaine, Mel McKiven, Anastatia Sims, Susan and Michael Carrafiello, Robert Hall, Paul and Bonnie Freedman, Nancy Gentile Ford, Susan Stemont, Michael Hickey, Margaret Gustus, and Vera Viditz-Ward. Over the past ten years these people have, respectively, taught me word processing, counseled me, bought me meals, provided me with places to stay while doing research, talked history with me, and fed my cats. As a group, they bear out the adage that friends will get you through times with no money. . . .

A special thanks to Tony Allen, most severe critic and best friend.

Any resident of the Upper Cumberland one hundred years ago would have known that family is the best support system of all. I owe more than I can ever repay to my son Ryan Denning; my sister and brother-in-law, Martha and Russell Brown; my brother and sister-in-law, Gary and Jenna Keith; and to my parents, Robert and Melba Keith. To my family, country people all, this work is dedicated.

COUNTRY PEOPLE IN THE NEW SOUTH

INTRODUCTION

THE SOCIAL BACKGROUND OF THE TENNESSEE MONKEY LAW

In the hot summer of 1925, a motley collection of people rarely seen in small southern towns shuffled along the dusty streets of Dayton, Tennessee. Professionally cynical big-city reporters brushed by Hebrew scholars. Scientists and Christian ministers of all denominations lined up next to famous criminal lawyers and local Democratic politicians for lemonade at the local drug store or stopped to listen to street-corner evangelists shouting their message above the crowd noise. They were all in Dayton for the trial of John T. Scopes for violating the Tennessee Anti-Evolution Law.[1]

Making his way through the crowds, the author of that law almost escaped notice. John Washington Butler, state representative from Macon County, was having the time of his life. Butler had expected to follow the trial from his home in the hills of Tennessee's Upper Cumberland, about 100 miles west of Dayton, but when a press syndicate offered to pay his way to Dayton, Butler jumped at the chance. He left behind in Macon County an indignant nineteen-year-old son, who suddenly found himself in charge of his father's wheat-threshing business in the middle of the summer harvest.[2]

Butler believed himself a participant in a highly important event; historians have agreed. The Tennessee monkey trial is one of the great set-pieces of twentieth-century American history, a story told in every textbook, with an agreed-upon symbolic meaning. With evolution as a pretext, modern, secular, urban, dynamic America confronted conservative, religious, rural America at Dayton. As the story goes, the forces of modernity lost in the Tennessee court but won in the national court of public opinion, and the trial signifies the emerging cultural dominance of urban secular values in American life.[3]

This book asks the reader to see the story from a different angle: not as the urban journalists and social critics who poured scorn on the "Tennessee anthropoids" that summer at Dayton saw it, but from the point of view of country people like J. W. Butler and his neighbors in the Upper Cumberland.

Although geography made the Upper Cumberland an isolated backwater, like many other southern hill-country regions, the area was not immune to the economic transformations that swept through the South in the late nineteenth century. However, the New South arrived in the Upper Cumberland several decades late. Until the 1890s the Upper Cumberland was a bastion of independent small farmers, still largely self-sufficient and dependent on family labor and local barter for sustenance. Traditionally folks in the region favored low taxes, minimal government services, and local control of institutions such as churches and schools. In 1890 a Nashville entrepreneur built a railroad through the region. By 1925 the Upper Cumberland had experienced three decades of economic development that radically changed the pace and the context of doing business in the region. During the early twentieth century, farmers and town folk fought repeated political battles over the meaning and the costs of progress and over who would control local institutions. These political divisions affected World War I mobilization in the region, pitting progressives against country people whose primary loyalty was to place and family. By the 1920s, men in the Upper Cumberland found their patriarchal control over wives and children threatened, as young women demanded a new dispensation in gender roles and young men left the farm for work in the cities. Improved transportation and communication began to integrate the region into the national consumer culture.

In this context, support for the Tennessee Monkey Law allowed Butler and his constituents to unite in affirmation of religious values at a time when politics, economics, and changing social mores increasingly divided people in the Upper Cumberland. Although people in the region belonged to diverse Protestant denominations, most could join in upholding the Bible as God's authoritative word. Indeed, as everything around them changed, religion became all the more important to country people, enabling them to maintain continuity with the world of their fathers. Thus religion facilitated adjustment to other aspects of modernity. Belief in the eternal Word of God offered shelter from the transient nature of twentieth-century life.

Even hill-country regions in the South have their history. But why bother looking closely at a place admittedly out of the mainstream of southern life, let alone the nation's? First, because such isolated regions all over the nation nurtured millions of people who migrated from the hinterlands to the cities in the nineteenth and twentieth centuries; it was in places like the Upper Cumberland that their values were formed. When people from the southern countryside moved into town, they brought with them their attitudes toward authority, gender issues, politics, and the proper way to live. These country ways still persist in southern ethnic enclaves from Cincinnati to Chicago to Bakersfield. (Southern immigrants also, of course, brought their music, their food, and their tastes in entertainment to town, with results still traceable in American popular culture.) To understand the mainstream, we need to know more about the history of the hinterland.

The Butler law indicates that the relationship between rural and urban in American culture also could benefit from a closer look. Conventionally we assume that mass culture (seen as urban, dynamic, secular, tolerant, fast paced, and consumerist) achieved national hegemony in the 1920s; ever since, rural ways have been under attack and in decline. But the present-day national culture wars echo conflicts about gender roles, parental control over education, and religion that were fought in remote Tennessee counties at the beginning of this century. In these earlier conflicts the people from the country often won: J. W. Butler's use of legislation to protect the Bible wrote the religious values of the countryside into the legal code of Tennessee and had a chilling effect on textbook publishers for decades. In short, the relationship between urban and rural in America is not a one-way street, with influence running from the cities out to the countryside. Rather, urban and rural participate in a dialogue.

This book focuses on the country voice in that dialogue and is concerned with rural life in one small region in Tennessee from 1890 to 1925. The Upper Cumberland in 1890 was a white farmer's world. Although the small farmer—legendarily self-sufficient and independent—is still a potent, if fading, American political icon, until recently relatively little historical research had been devoted to describing the farming world that was the common experience of the American majority until the twentieth century. In the past ten years social historians have begun the difficult task of describing the lives of people who lived on the land. In the past decade new studies have examined the economic strategies, politics, and family life of family farmers. Most of these studies argue that the advent of commercial farming transformed a relatively static farming economy in which each farming family was largely self-sufficient. Historians differ as to the precise impact of the market, but all agree that money—the substitution of a cash market for the old systems of barter and community interdependence—changed everything.[4]

This heavy concentration on the market sometimes leaves the impression that the disappearance of the self-sufficient family farm was predestined, that the market's effects were always, inevitably, corrupting to the traditional farmer. Let the market "appear" in an isolated rural region and offer profits, and farmers immediately jettison self-sufficiency and become agricultural capitalists. Sometimes the outcome is basically positive, as it was for the midwestern farmers described by John Mack Faragher. Sometimes yeoman farmers gamble on the market and lose. Stephen Hahn's north Georgia yeomen, pushed out of self-sufficiency by the necessity of recouping losses caused by the Civil War, plunge into the downward spiral of the cotton market, lose self-sufficiency, and often even give up their land.

Market choices were not predetermined, nor were they made in a vacuum. Instead, culture influenced economic choices made, for good or ill, and the same economic choices, made repeatedly over generations, became part of a cultural pattern, so that economic change would affect everything from religion to marriage to education. To understand the rural transformation, it is necessary to study the context out of which economic decisions emerged. What happened in rural America reflects market influences. But it also reflects the individual choices of millions of farm men and women, operating out of their own particular cultural context. In the Upper Cumberland the market came calling and was not welcomed with open arms. Market access did not lead to a transformation of agriculture: three decades after the railroad appeared, most Upper Cumberland farm families still valued their self-sufficiency and still produced the same crops their fathers had years before. However, the railroad brought other economic changes, which in turn affected regional politics and institutions.

The story opens with a geography lesson, since the history of the Upper Cumberland grows from its difficult, rocky, hilly terrain. First there are the rivers: the Cumberland rises in southeastern Kentucky, loops southeast into Tennessee, then flows off to the northwest to join the Ohio. When steamboats plied the river, the reaches northeast of Nashville were called the "upper" river, and the countryside along the banks shared the appellation, "Upper Cumberland." By strict application, the Upper Cumberland region includes counties in Kentucky. This work will focus on eleven counties in northeastern Middle Tennessee: Clay, Cumberland, DeKalb, Fentress, Jackson, Macon, Overton, Pickett, Putnam, Smith, and White. The area comprising these counties runs from the Cumberland Plateau in the east to the central basin in the west, from the Kentucky line in the north to the Caney Fork River in the south.[5]

The plateau, a wide ridge that runs from Kentucky to Alabama, divides East from Middle Tennessee. Upper Cumberland people call it "the mountain." The Upper Cumberland's tributary rivers, the Obey and the Wolf, Roaring River, and the Caney Fork, originate on the plateau. The Obey flows from Fentress County northwest to join the Cumberland at Celina in Clay County. Roaring River drains Overton County and unites with the Cumberland at Gainesboro in Jackson County. The Caney Fork, large enough to have as tributaries the Calfkiller and Falling Water Rivers, rolls down from Cumberland County on the plateau, west across White County and northwest across DeKalb, Putnam, and Smith Counties, to join the Cumber-

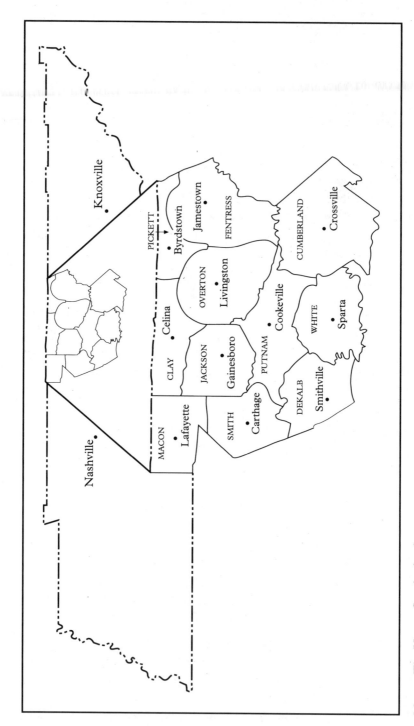

Map 1. The Upper Cumberland

land at Carthage. From their headwaters in the plateau, the region's rivers flow west through Tennessee's Highland Rim. There "the mountain" breaks down into ridges and valleys and finally into steep-sided hills and deep hollows drained by creeks that meander down to the Cumberland. The Cumberland itself cuts through the Highland Rim from Clay County on the Kentucky border, through Jackson and Smith Counties, and on out through the central basin to Nashville.

The region's geography prohibited plantation agriculture. Most early settlers were semisubsistence farmers. In the 1780s settlers moved up from the Nashville basin, following the river and its tributaries into the hills. The oldest communities in the region are in the west, along the banks of the Cumberland. In 1802 the east-west Walton Road was completed, linking Kingston on the Clinch River with Carthage on the Cumberland. The Walton Road crossed the plateau, but most settlers preferred to pass over the scrubby mountain land in favor of settlement in the fertile river and creek bottoms to the west. The plateau remained sparsely settled until the mid-nineteenth century.[6]

As the population increased, residents clamored for easier access to county governments, which had the all-important function of keeping land titles in order. Accordingly the state created new counties, roughly following lines of settlement and transportation, and tiny county seats grew around courthouse squares. Smith County was formed first, in 1799, and Carthage, at the juncture of the Caney Fork and the Cumberland, became the Upper Cumberland's first county seat. Jackson County, farther up the river, was incorporated in 1801, followed by Overton and White Counties in 1806, Fentress in 1823, DeKalb in 1837, Macon in 1842, Putnam in 1854, Cumberland in 1856, Clay in 1870, and Pickett in 1879.[7]

The settlers who moved into the Upper Cumberland in the first half of the nineteenth century typified that group of southerners Frank Owsley called "plain folk." Of English and Scotch-Irish ancestry, with a sprinkling of French and German, most came to the Upper Cumberland from Virginia, Maryland, and the Carolinas. Most farmers did not own slaves. Few regional slaveholders qualified as planters. Yet economic differences deriving from landownership did divide Upper Cumberland farmers. The early settlers who acquired property in the bottom lands beside the Cumberland and

Caney Fork had more productive farms than their neighbors "on the ridge." They were more likely to own slaves, to maintain business and social ties with Nashville, and to feel ties of loyalty to the plantation South. The farmers on the ridge, or farther east on the mountain, owned less productive lands, were less likely to own slaves, and often made their cash money by fattening cattle or hogs on the common range and driving them to market on the Old Kentucky Stock Road, which ran from Danville, Kentucky, to Huntsville, Alabama, through the plateau.[8]

When the Civil War came, the river counties favored the Confederacy; the ridges, the Union. In a June 1861 referendum on secession, Smith, DeKalb, White, Putnam, and Jackson Counties voted to leave the Union. Fentress and Cumberland Counties, off to the east, voted against secession, as did Macon County, in the extreme northwest of the region. Even within counties with Confederate or Unionist majorities, however, sizable minorities dissented. In Macon County, according to a local historian, the split reflected the "ridge" and "creek" divisions in the county: farmers who lived along the creeks favored the Confederacy; those on the ridges, the Union. But in DeKalb County the division followed political lines. Former Whigs, including some of the most prosperous slaveholders in the county, were Unionists, while the Democrats voted for secession. As the Confederate counties raised troops for the army, men slipped off to Kentucky to join the Union forces there. One Union general, Alvin C. Gillem, came from secessionist Jackson County.[9]

From 1861 through 1865 the people of the Upper Cumberland fought their own internal civil war. In Fentress County the war began with brawls on the assembly grounds on the day of the secession referendum; that set the pattern for the next five years. The region divided, Confederate against Unionist, county by county, farm by farm. The normal forms of governance disintegrated. Guerrillas, nominally in the service of the Confederacy or the Union, attacked supporters of the other side and used the war as an excuse for settling personal feuds. Mail deliveries stopped, schools closed, public offices shut down, and churches posted guards outside their services. In the Upper Cumberland the war would be remembered not as a glorious and gallant Lost Cause but as a time of hunger and fear. The guerrillas stole or destroyed food supplies and tortured and killed without regard to age or sex. For years after the war the violence lingered, occasionally erupting in revenge killings.[10]

By the 1890s, as memories of the war faded, the conflict could be safely cloaked in nostalgia. People in the river counties talked of putting up Confederate memorials, but nothing much came of it. Old soldiers of the Blue and Gray marched (in separate units) in Fourth of July parades. The war did have a lasting impact on politics. As a last resort politicians called on voters to be loyal to the memory of their illustrious ancestors. Confederates and their children voted Democratic. Unionists and their descendants voted the Republican tickets.[11]

After the war the area's black population, always small, began to dwindle. Although some freedmen stayed in the region and managed to buy land, many left for Nashville. By 1890 over 90 percent of the population of the Upper Cumberland was white. Only in Smith County did the black population exceed 10 percent of the total. (Just over 16 percent of Smith County's 18,404 people were black.) In Fentress and Cumberland Counties over 95 percent of the population was white. In Pickett County 99.7 percent of the population was white.[12]

Until the 1890s the river and its tributaries mediated the connections between the land and the people. Commerce traveled on the river, and the best farmland lay along the river banks. The region's terrain made travel by land difficult. Although the center of the region was only eighty miles from Nashville, the Upper Cumberland, like other southern hill-country regions, was outside the mainstream of the southern economy, existing on the periphery of the plantation South before the Civil War and on the periphery of the New South after.

The postbellum economic development that brought trains and towns, factories and mines, and accompanying transformations in social relations to much of the South did not reach into the hills northeast of Nashville until the end of the nineteenth century. The Upper Cumberland remained as it had been, a stronghold of small family farms. Though geographically close to Nashville, the region was isolated by its terrain. A land of steep hills and ridges, the Upper Cumberland had few good roads. Before 1890 the Upper Cumberland's only rail connection was a small branch line of the North

Carolina and St. Louis, built from McMinnville to the coal fields northeast of Sparta in White County. For most of the region the Cumberland River still served as the main thoroughfare for commerce with Nashville, and the river could not be navigated during dry seasons. Within the region, agriculture dominated the local economy. In 1890 only 467 of the region's 118,925 people were "operatives" in local manufactures. Over 90 percent of the population lived outside the towns. There were numerous artisans such as blacksmiths, carpenters, millers, and potters; there were sawmills, small coal mines serving the local market, and at least one cotton mill. But most people either lived on farms or were dependent on the farming community for business, and the New South remained only a promise.[13]

The persistence of semisubsistence farming in the Upper Cumberland grew from the culture of the region, which in turn reflects the region's geographic isolation. By 1890 the region's population was comprised largely of traditionalists, whose fathers and grandfathers had stayed in the Upper Cumberland while others moved to western lands where commercial farming would be the norm. It was a region populated by "those who stayed behind," to borrow Hal Baron's phrase. Residents in the region were, in effect, self-selected by their preference for traditional ways. Those ways included aspects of family life, education, governance, and religion that affected, and were affected by, economic choices.[14]

That culture and economy were inseparable in the region was well understood by the rural progressives who, in the early twentieth century, began a long series of campaigns aimed at regional transformation. As rural reformers understood it, progress included commercialized farming, better roads, better schools, and a more orderly society. Reformers believed that cultural reforms would lead to economic progress: good schools, good roads, and good (that is, commercial) farming were all part of the same reform agenda and were inseparable.

Rural progressive reformers had but limited success in the Upper Cumberland. They succeeded in modifying structures of governance so as to remove control of roads and schools from local hands. However, modernized structures did not transform local culture in ways foreseen by reformers. Locals took from reformed institutions what seemed useful for the maintenance of traditional culture and ignored those aspects of progress deemed irrelevant. Instead of transforming culture, rural progressivism had provoked a backlash against reform by the 1920s. The country people proved to be resilient, adaptable, and capable of co-opting for the service of traditional values techniques and institutions pioneered by progressives. Indeed, after twenty years of social conflict over development and progressive reform, traditional religious values, such as those expressed by J. W. Butler's antievolution laws, served to unify conservative country people—and their progressive neighbors.

This is not a story about uplift and progress: the progressives lost their battle to change Upper Cumberland culture. Neither is it a story about how the canny natives won out over misguided missionaries, kept their souls, and lived happily ever after. In a sense, nobody won the long battle between progress and tradition in the region—or the traditionalists lost by winning. In their assessment of the economic consequences of traditionalism the progressives were largely correct: in clinging to old ways, traditionalists inadvertently chose poverty.

1

MAKING DO

THE UPPER CUMBERLAND FARM ECONOMY IN THE 1890S

Upper Cumberland farm families, conditioned by years of poor access to distant markets, by 1890 had learned to provide for themselves. They grew most of what they consumed and produced a small surplus for sale or exchange. The necessity of supplying most family needs at home became the basis of a much lauded virtue—independence. Rather than change the operation of their farms in ways that might endanger family security and independence, members of farm families tried to make money through nonfarm enterprises or sought temporary or seasonal employment off the farm. This strategy involved no risk to the family's ultimate security, since the farm was always there to fall back on. Farmers tried to avoid debt. Being in debt constricted the economic choices open to farm families and might lead to modifications in farm operations that threatened family security. Debt also involved social relationships. Wealthy individuals, not institutions, made most loans. Debt thus threatened both social and economic independence.

In the 1890s the Upper Cumberland was on the periphery of a national exchange economy. Merchants and produce houses acted as middlemen between farmers and Nashville markets. Steamboats from Nashville provided stock directly for the shelves of stores in Carthage, Gainesboro, and Celina and pulled over at landings all along the upper river with cargoes for the waiting wagons of merchants from villages deep in the hills. The produce of the region—corn, wheat, hogs, poultry, hides, feathers, beans, fruit, and tobacco—returned downriver to Nashville. The river defined the economy as it did the region. Since the Cumberland was too shallow for navigation during the dry months of the year, commerce waited on the "tides," as business with Nashville grew only slowly.[1]

Upper Cumberland farm families tried to participate in the market economy without becoming dependent on it. The household economy of a hill-country farm interconnected, by necessity, with the national market. In order to buy land, the very basis of family security, families had to have money. In order to keep their land, families had to pay taxes. Farm families had to earn money. But the farms of the Upper Cumberland were not agribusinesses in the contemporary sense. They were households in which the primary goal was family survival, not profits.

Imagine the commercialization of agriculture as a spectrum. On one end is total family subsistence, with no commercial exchanges. (Examples of this are hard to find; even neolithic farmers traded some products.) At the other end of the spectrum are present-day highly specialized farmers who invest capital in farming with an eye to the world market and who produce crops as manufacturers produce widgets. These farmers sell their crops and buy their food in supermarkets, just like urbanites. On this spectrum the farm families of the Upper Cumberland in the 1890s were somewhere in the middle. They were accustomed to "trade." They bought and sold or bartered goods and services. Many prided themselves on their skill as traders. But they were not completely dependent on any market. Any Upper Cumberland farmers in 1890 who tried to live only by what they sold would have gone broke or starved in short order. The cost and the difficulty of transporting goods—the very slowness of commerce along the river—worked against agricultural entrepre-

neurship. Risk taking, in the form of diverting land and labor resources, might pay off; but it might not, and then how would the
family get through the winter? Given the region's isolation, placing family subsistence ahead .of market production made common
sense.

But self-sufficiency meant more than that. By the 1890s the Upper
Cumberland was populated by the descendants of generations of
farmers who had chosen to stay in a region where access to agricultural markets was difficult. This promoted the development and survival of a yeoman farmer worldview, in which economic independence was highly valued in and of itself. Throughout the nineteenth
century many people left the Upper Cumberland to farm lands in
the West. Local newspapers often ran letters from former residents
who described economic conditions in their new homes. Anyone
who really wanted to practice farming as a business had to know that
he or she could make better profits elsewhere. Out-migration acted
as a process of selection. In every generation, the more market-
oriented farmers, especially those who did not own land, left. Those
who stayed were basically satisfied with the status quo; they were
traditionalists and passed on their values to the next generation.[2]

Consider H. A. Whitefield, a Jackson County native who left the
region for Texas, where he became agent to a furnishing merchant.
In a 1906 letter to his hometown newspaper Whitefield undertook to
explain why western farmers had such a hard time. They bought too
much, he said, and of that too expensive a quality. In order to pros-
per, Whitefield opined, farmers should feed the family first. Then
they could save the money earned on market crops. As agent for
a furnishing merchant, Whitefield's own livelihood depended on
farmers buying rather than producing goods. Nevertheless, he
thought Texas farmers who bought syrup rather than producing sorghum were foolish. Whitefield expressed the conventional wisdom of
the hill country. In 1894 a correspondent to the *Cookeville Press*
attributed the hard times in agriculture to farmers' buying more than
they produced at home. He criticized the purchase of flour, bacon,
plowshares, axe handles, fencing, soap, garden seed, fertilizer, and
chewing gum. For the writer, as for Whitefield, household production was the key to survival, prosperity, and independence.[3]

The household economy of a small hill-country farm aimed at
security through production of both sustenance and a marketable

surplus. To see how it worked, we can use census materials, county records, and local histories to put together a picture of the economic choices available to the average farm family.

Family security depended first on owning land. In assessing the economy of a farm, one always has to make a distinction between landowners and tenants. But throughout the region a majority of farmers owned their land. According to the 1890 census only three Upper Cumberland counties, Jackson, Fentress, and Pickett, had landownership rates of less than 70 percent. The rate of landownership was highest in Putnam County, where 82.3 percent of all farmers owned land.[4]

Upper Cumberland farms tended to be rather small. The 1890 census divided farms by total acreage. The largest category in the Upper Cumberland was farms with more than 100 but fewer than 500 acres. But these farmers did not usually cultivate all this acreage. Farms often ran along a creek and up to the top of the ridge, or had small patches of relatively flat land on top of the ridge. Many acres of the typical Upper Cumberland farm would be too steep to plow. The average farm had only 45 acres of improved land. (According to the 1890 census the range was from 27 acres in Cumberland County to 62 acres in long-settled White County.)[5]

On a functioning hill farm, field crops, livestock, the kitchen garden, and even the unimproved forested acres contributed to family sustenance. On the typical cultivated forty acres the farm family might plant corn, oats, wheat, vegetables, and perhaps tobacco and even a small amount of cotton for household consumption. Most farmers would keep hogs, cattle, and chickens, while some had sheep, turkeys, and geese. A farmer would use either horses, mules, or oxen as draft animals. The proportion of each crop planted and the kinds of stock kept varied from farm to farm according to the needs, labor capacity, and land available to each family or, in the case of draft animals, individual preference. Some farmers liked mules; some preferred horses. For logging and breaking new ground, oxen excelled.[6]

Families, not individual farmers, worked farms. Work roles for men and women made both sexes responsible for family sustenance and the production of a marketable surplus. Generally speaking, men did the plowing, the heavy work during planting and harvest, the herding of cattle and hogs, and the first stages of butchering.

Women did everything else: kept house, cooked, put out gardens, tended chickens, and milked cows. Both genders were producers in the nineteenth-century sense, putting food on the table and money in the family's purse. As the family economy intersected with the market, marketable surplus was as likely to come from the wife's sector as from the husband's. In both cases goods produced for market did not require any significant diversion of resources from production for subsistence. Only one crop in the region, dark tobacco, was produced solely for market. In 1890 tobacco production was minuscule. Everything else Upper Cumberland farm families marketed was either surplus to family production, production that did not endanger family food supplies (hogs that had been fattened on the open range, for example), or wild harvests.[7]

Corn was the most important crop. Farmers in the Upper Cumberland devoted at least one-third of their improved acreage to corn. Farm families ate corn, fed it to their stock, and sold any surplus. They shelled the mature ears for hominy or meal. They stripped the stalks and bound the leaves for animal feed. They fed shelled corn to all farm animals and, in some cases, turned hogs into fields to "hog off" the crop.[8]

In addition to a large garden, farmers planted enough wheat to supply the family's needs, oats as a hay crop or to feed horses, and beans and field peas along the rows of field corn. The garden was traditionally the wife's responsibility. Upper Cumberland women cultivated English peas, tomatoes, okra, carrots, cucumbers, onions, lettuce, squash, hot peppers, cabbages, turnips (for greens and roots), melons, and Irish and sweet potatoes. Many farmers also kept small orchards. Apple trees were the most popular, followed by peaches. For sweetening, some farmers grew sorghum, which they rendered into syrup, locally called molasses, at small mule-powered mills. Others tended hives of bees.[9]

If corn was king of the plowed acres, hogs reigned supreme among stock. Hogs required little labor. Tennessee law made it the responsibility of farmers to enclose their gardens and field crops; stock ran free under this open range provision. A bill introduced in 1895 in the state senate that would have required enclosed pastures was denounced in Upper Cumberland newspapers; the *Cookeville Press* called it "nonsense." The bill was defeated, and the range remained open until after World War I. (Parts of the plateau were open range through the 1930s.) Hogs fattened on the mast in the woodlands. In 1890, according to the census, Upper Cumberland farm families had average herds of eight to twelve hogs and consumed four and one-half to six and one-half hogs a year. They slaughtered hogs in the late fall as soon as the weather turned reliably cold (a seasonal change referred to as "hog-killing weather"). They processed the meat into hams, shoulders, sides, ribs, backbone, sausages, and lard.[10]

Most Upper Cumberland farms also kept cattle. They ran beef cattle, like hogs, on the open range. Some of the wealthier farmers in the river lands drove herds to the plateau ranges for pasture and had cabins on the mountain for use during the summer grazing season. Beef was not a major component of the regional diet, since it could not be easily preserved. In some communities farmers took turns slaughtering cattle and shared the beef among several families. In other places one farmer might act as butcher for the community, selling or trading beef. Probably most farmers in the region sold their beef cattle. But Upper Cumberland families depended on milk cows almost as much as they did hogs for food, and it was a poor family indeed that did not keep a milk cow. The average Upper Cumberland family consumed 1.6 gallons of milk per day. Sweet milk, buttermilk, and butter were dietary staples, and a few families made cheese.[11]

Chickens provided the most reliable source of protein for the farm kitchen. Fried or boiled with dumplings, chicken was the centerpiece of "company" dinners. Eggs in some form boosted the food value of everyday meals. Eggs were fried or scrambled for breakfast, stirred into cornbread batter, or beaten into cakes or pies for dessert. Old recipes for regional favorites like chess pie or pound cake, which call for as many as a half-dozen eggs per pie or cake, seem clearly designed to use up a surplus of eggs. According to the 1890 census the number of eggs produced in the Upper Cumberland counties ranged from 64.8 dozen per farm in Cumberland County (or 1.2 dozen per week) to 198 dozen per farm in DeKalb County (or almost four dozen per week per farm household).[12]

Some farms also had geese, turkeys, and sheep. Farm women sold goose down or used it to stuff pillows and beds. Some farmers raised turkeys and drove turkey flocks, their feet tarred for protection, to market. Experienced turkey drovers warned neophytes that the birds would fly up to roost wherever they were at sundown whether or not that suited the drover's convenience. Some farmers raised sheep and sold wool. Although home textile production was fast becoming a curiosity, in the 1890s some women did process wool into yarn for knitting the family's stockings.[13]

Upper Cumberland farmers worked their land with horses, mules, and oxen. Horses outnumbered mules on hill-country farms two to one. Farm families preferred horses because they could be ridden or hitched to a buggy as well as to a plow. So could mules, of course, but riding a mule lacked status and was very uncomfortable. Unless they could afford to keep both, farmers chose horses over mules. Not until cars replaced buggies in the 1920s did farmers begin to switch from horses to mules for farm work. In 1890 some farmers still had teams of oxen, traditionally used, because of their great strength, to break new ground or for logging.[14]

The farm's unimproved acres also supplied food. Farmers and their sons hunted squirrels, rabbits, deer, and game birds. The biggest hunt of the season was at Christmas. Farmers hurried through their work so as to have two weeks in midwinter for hunting. For those who knew where to look, the woodlands provided a harvest of edible plants and marketable herbs such as ginseng.[15]

When it worked well, the farm economy combined diverse components and the labor of the entire family and produced subsistence and a marketable surplus. But the balance was always precarious. Farm life, far from being simple, required intelligence and attention. Lazy people could survive, but prosperity required hard work. Even the most industrious farmers lived at the mercy of nature. In any given year a crop could fail, cattle could die, or illness or death could reduce the family's labor supply. When that happened the family could quickly be reduced to misery. But if the household economy were sufficiently diversified, the family would scrape by. Generations of farming experience were summed up in the proverbial warning against putting all the eggs in one basket. Farm families made economic decisions cautiously and did not jump at "market opportunities" that would cut into labor and acreage needed for production for family sustenance.

Tobacco was the only cash crop in the region produced solely for market. The history of tobacco production in the Upper Cumberland illustrates the relationship farm families there had with the market economy. Just after the Civil War Upper Cumberland farmers grew dark, air-cured tobacco for market. Tobacco is a labor-intensive crop; farmers planted no more than the family could cultivate and harvest. Therefore tobacco patches tended to be small, and tobacco production did not consume land needed for food production. Because they were not dependent on the market, farmers could respond sensibly to market conditions. When the tobacco market plummeted in the 1870s, Upper Cumberland farmers got out of tobacco production. The aggregate figures available in the 1890 census indicate that in most counties tobacco was grown primarily for personal use. The amount of tobacco planted ranged from 7 acres in Pickett County to 1,154 acres in Macon County. The low volume of tobacco production in Pickett County could be attributed to transportation difficulties; Pickett, north of Fentress and Cumberland Counties on the plateau, was one of the most isolated counties in the region. Macon and Smith Counties, where sufficient acreage was planted in tobacco to indicate that farmers were growing it for sale, were close to a long-standing tobacco market in Hartsville; farmers there could have easily transported their tobacco to market. Macon County had no navigable rivers and no rail connections; for farmers there tobacco may have been attractive as a cash crop because it was much less perishable than most farm produce. Tobacco was cut, cured, and packed in baskets for transportation to warehouses for sale.[16]

When farmers did concentrate on market production, the family's standard of living often suffered. Sharecroppers had to produce primarily for market. Farmers who needed cash or had large debts probably also diverted a higher proportion of surplus to the market. The 1890 manuscript census for agriculture has been destroyed, so no detailed analysis of how farm owners' production differed from tenants' is possible. But some evidence indicates that landowners ate better than tenants. For example, a tenant farmer's son, as quoted in a history of DeKalb County, remembered that his family had to sell most of the milk and eggs they produced and that a fried egg and a hoecake was the height of luxury for him. On the other hand, local histories and memoirs are replete with references to substantial meals. How much produce became surplus for sale probably varied according to the cash needs of any farm family. The census of 1890 does not state what proportion of milk and eggs wound up on the market. However, the 1900 census indicates that more than three-fourths of all farm families had milk cows and that over 90 percent of all milk products were consumed at home.[17]

In the Upper Cumberland of 1890, work had social as well as economic functions. Like the antebellum farmers studied by Frank Owsley and, later, Stephen Hahn, Upper Cumberland farmers often worked communally. Log rollings, corn huskings, and various other "workings" (the local term for "bees") were still common. For a working, a farmer invited his neighbors and provided food and, sometimes, entertainment. As Calvin Gregory, a Baptist preacher and newspaper columnist, remembered in the 1920s, dinner for a working was a massive affair. Workers felt insulted if a host served dinner in the fields because such behavior indicated the host wanted to get as much labor as possible out of his "guests." Gregory, as a child, watched guests at a working retaliate for such bad manners by devouring all the food on the table (which had been carted out to the workplace in a wagon) before the host had time to fill his own plate. For the rest of the day the men teased their host, commenting on how much he had eaten for dinner and how hungry everyone else still was. Gregory commented that if the meal had been served in the house, the men at the working would have behaved much more decorously, in honor of the wife who had prepared the food. When people worked on community projects—building a school or church or repairing the local road, for example—men worked while women cooked; the meals produced were highlights of the local social scene. If a local fiddler came to a working, they could expect to close the day's activities with music. Workers also lightened the task at hand with contests of speed and strength, pranks, storytelling, and so on. John T. Oakley, a Baptist preacher who reminisced about his life for the Carthage newspaper in the 1920s, especially recalled two children (brother and sister) with phenomenal memories who upon request regaled workers at a wheat threshing with recitations of "The Boy Stood on the Burning Deck" and other declamations. Such festive occasions aside, farmers also swapped work when needed. When disaster hit a farm family, neighbors often contributed goods to pull the family through or worked the fields until the crisis was over.[18]

For farmers who owned land and were in good standing with the community, life on an Upper Cumberland farm offered a secure but cash-poor existence. In order to raise money, farmers could market surplus, go into "public work," or go into the logging business.

The family economy intersected with the national market at the region's produce houses and country stores. Produce houses marketed Upper Cumberland farm produce in Nashville. The regional newspapers listed local market prices. For example, the *Cookeville Press* of January 18, 1894, listed what the Cookeville Produce Market was paying for eggs, hens and chickens, ducks, cocks, guinea fowl, full-feathered geese, turkeys, prime and mixed feathers, wools, hides, beeswax, tallow, ginseng, goldenseal, dried apples, peaches, blackberries, beans, stock peas, and wheat. Produce houses sent wagons through the countryside to pick up goods that farm families had bartered at country stores. Although farmers could sell directly to produce houses, for most the store served as entry point to the national market economy.[19]

The relationship between farmer and merchant in the Upper Cumberland differed significantly from that described as typical of the cotton South. Although they sold farm supplies, Upper Cumberland merchants were not typically furnishing merchants. That is, farmers did not usually have to buy from them before they could start the annual crop, nor was the crop-lien system common in the region. The relationship between Upper Cumberland farmers and merchants was not that of client to patron. Merchants did "public work" and were dependent on farmers' trade. Credit went both ways: merchants owed to farmers, and farmers to merchants. Inventories of the estates of deceased merchants indicate that farmers kept small running tabs in country stores but rarely owed merchants large sums of money.[20]

For farmers, stores were as much trading posts as places to buy. Advertisements in Upper Cumberland newspapers indicate that most, if not all, stores took barter for goods. To the stores farm families brought eggs, poultry, feathers, beeswax, tallow, dried fruits, hides, wool, corn, peas, butter, meal, pork, potatoes, sorghum, furs, and ginseng. In exchange they got textiles, shoes, hardware, farm supplies, and food. How much food families purchased in stores is hard to determine. Certainly most families bought sugar, soda, coffee, and salt; a significant number also found it more practical to buy wheat flour. Grist mills in the region could grind corn meal but could not process wheat. If a farmer lived in an area far from a roller mill, he sold his wheat and bought flour.[21]

Stores varied by location. Merchants on the river carried raft supplies. Others in remote valleys ran trading posts for large areas. The store that operated in Fairview, a Fentress County community, was such a trading post. Opened in 1910 by John and Nancy Buck, the store operated in a way that would have been familiar to most merchants in the 1890s. The Bucks took in roots and herbs for sale to a Burnside, Kentucky, company and furs that they sold annually to a traveling agent for a Louisville furrier. The Bucks also bought corn, beans, peas, dried apples, eggs, and other farm produce, which they in turn sold in Jamestown, the county seat. They also bought chickens, accumulating a flock that they sold annually to a produce man.[22]

Upper Cumberland people lumped all work done outside the household under the faintly pejorative term "public work." In some parts of the South "public work" came to mean work for wages. However, in the Upper Cumberland professionals and self-employed businessmen were also said to do public work. The essence of public work was dependency. A public worker had to please bosses, customers, or clients and depended on them for wages, payments, or fees.[23]

Just as a security-first economic strategy on the farm allowed farm families flexibility in the marketplace, owning land—having the farm to fall back on—allowed farmers to make forays into the job market without becoming dependent on public work. Although Upper Cumberland people distinguished between public work and farm or household work, it was not uncommon for men to switch from one form of work to the other or to carry on both simultaneously. Doctors and lawyers kept farms; storekeepers raised kitchen gardens; farmers drove produce wagons; young men taught school and farmed. In one lifetime a man might move in and out of public work many times.

In the 1920s Bob Gwaltney, a Smith County farmer who was then in his sixties, wrote an autobiography for the local newspaper. Raised on a farm, Bob as an adolescent clerked in a store and worked as a carpenter, as a painter, and as a clerk in a railroad commissary. In 1890 he went back to farming, living with his parents. In 1892 he married a woman who had inherited a quarter interest in a neighboring farm. For a few years the young Gwaltneys lived with his parents; then they managed to buy out her brother and moved into her home place. From 1897 to 1899 Gwaltney worked setting up binders for the McCormick Harvester company. From 1900 through 1906 he farmed exclusively. In 1906 his family moved to Nashville so that his daughters could go to school. "We had most of our living for a year, and I knew I could get something to do to make expenses," Gwaltney recalled. He worked at odd jobs in Nashville (primarily fitting screen windows). According to Gwaltney, "My wife had never lived at any place, only on the farm, and had not been use [sic] to living out of paper bags and tin cans, and before the year was out she was about ready to move back home to live or die." Since 1906 the Gwaltneys had been living on the farm. Gwaltney also helped set up the local telephone exchange, which, he noted, "was my last public work of any kind." Gwaltney concluded, "And if I have made any success it has been from working hard, and having a good partner in the house and from studying an economical way of doing things and going them."[24]

Gwaltney's prosperity was based on his ability to be flexible in respect to the job market, and on the support he obtained from his family. During his youth he moved from manual labor to white-collar jobs to skilled labor and back again without ever, apparently, feeling that one kind of work was inherently superior to another. As he noted ruefully, his career as store clerk left him with nothing to show for several years of work once his board bill had been settled. That painful lesson did not leave young Bob in despair: he could go back to his parents' farm. As he matured, his personal life affected his economic life in the most direct manner. He married a woman with land. Mrs. Gwaltney also supplied labor: she was guardian of two orphaned nephews, who ran the farm while Gwaltney worked for the McCormick company. Gwaltney's farm background and family connections gave him security and flexibility.[25]

Farmers often raised extra cash by selling timber. In the 1870s farmers along the upper river began to send log rafts downriver to sawmills in Nashville. The timber business remained important in the region through the 1940s. Farmers sold timber for cash and raised crops for food. During intervals in the agricultural season farmers worked as loggers, harvesting their own woods and snaking logs out to the Cumberland's tributaries. According to folklorist

Lynwood Montell, "The key to understanding the timber industry of the Upper Cumberland lies in the term home-owned. While Northern entrepreneurs were grabbing up large acreages of forest lands and mineral leases in the Appalachian South for a mere fraction of their actual worth, the people of the Upper Cumberland, in the main, remained in charge of their own economic destiny."[26]

During the winter men formed logs into rafts on the Upper River. By spring flood the Caney Fork was jammed with rafts, each containing as many as 2,000 thousand logs. When the water got high enough, the loggers released booms along the Upper Cumberland, and the ungainly, 300-foot-long rafts swung out into the current. Raftsmen with oars steered according to shouted instructions from a pilot standing in the stern. After days on the river, raft and crews arrived in Nashville, where the logs were sold and the farmers-cum-raftsmen were paid. It was the return trip that earned Upper Cumberland raftsmen their notoriety. Although the Upper Cumberland river people interviewed by Montell recalled that the raftsmen were just good, hard-working folks, Nashvillians considered the upriver folk dangerous, drunken rowdies. It seems probable that at least some of the loggers who got off the upper river packet at the Hartsville ferry walked back to their homes far back in the hills without much to show for their year's work in the woods: they had spent it all in riotous living in Nashville or on the boat trip home.[27]

If the raftsmen did make it back home with cash, they probably did not have a bank in which to deposit it. Banks followed the railroads into the Upper Cumberland. Prior to the 1890s there were very few of either in the eleven-county area. A branch line of the North Carolina and St. Louis Railroad (NC&StL) reached White County in 1884; one year later the Bank of Sparta opened in the county seat. Putnam Countians established banks in the 1890s after railroads were built in the area.[28]

Farmers tried to avoid debt; nothing was more destructive of independence and security. In addition, because access to banks was difficult, farmers who wanted to borrow money had to apply to wealthy neighbors. The estate inventory books for Putnam County in the 1890s indicate that people who had money made loans secured by personal notes. Debt, therefore, like work, was a social as well as an economic matter. Rather than owing money to an anonymous institution, as might be the case today, debtors owed a neighbor (a situation fraught with potential embarrassment and humiliation). Although they often kept running tabs at local stores, Upper Cumberland farmers did not usually have mortgages. In 1891 a Crossville paper (operated by a land development promoter) criticized local farmers for their unwillingness to go into debt to make improvements, saying that "everywhere there are go-ahead farmers who make it pay, and they are not the men who are afraid of debt either." In an era when farmers often mortgaged their land to acquire capital to buy new farm machinery, Upper Cumberland farmers taught their children that "pay as you go" was more than an economic necessity; it was a virtue.[29]

Upper Cumberland farm families survived by economic diversity. The family economy provided sustenance. Marketed surplus, public work, or logging provided necessary cash. The system produced security; but it did not facilitate the accumulation of capital, nor did it foster the development of entrepreneurial attitudes toward farming. The margin between prosperity and disaster was just too small for risk.

For yeoman farmers in the Upper Cumberland of the 1890s, farming was not a business run by a (male) entrepreneur. Instead, farming was the economic component of family life. As Bob Gwaltney noted, his success had come from having "a good partner." Economic problems could not be distinguished from personal problems: coming from a poor family meant that a man would not inherit rich farmland; marrying a lazy woman meant he would lack that "good partner" necessary for economic success; but having relatives to rely on cushioned the blows of economic life. Family life formed the matrix in which economic decisions had to be made, and the family was the dominant institution in the Upper Cumberland.

2

FAMILIES AND COMMUNITIES

Old people in the Upper Cumberland sometimes ask children, "Whose girl are you?" It is not a casual question. *Whose* a child is, to what family the child belongs, is important information; a correct answer enables the questioner to fit the child into the network of blood ties that still matter a great deal in the region. But in the 1890s, family, more than anything else, determined an individual's life chances. As a transmitter of culture, the family had no rival within the region, since parents controlled schools. The helping professions then making their advent in urban America hardly existed within the region, and government and church were weak. In the Upper Cumberland, communities often consisted of collections of extended families connected by blood and marriage. Such communities fostered a powerful localism. Solitude was unusual, and privacy was unknown: everyone knew their neighbors' business.

The family, as dominant institution, figured in everything people in the region did. The extended family helped shelter people from the most dire results of mistaken economic choices. Families performed most of the welfare services now in the hands of the state. Social life revolved around the gathering of families. Family heritage often dictated political decisions. So interwoven was family with all aspects of life in the region that to change anything, from economics to politics to religion, would ultimately have repercussions on the family. To reform the culture, as progressives tried to do in the early twentieth century, would mean a symbolic rejection of the ways of the fathers.[1]

By law, custom, and religion, fathers dominated Upper Cumberland families. Patriarchy as a labor system operated undisguised by the sentimentalities of middle-class notions of woman's sphere or the nurturance of children. Although men, women, and children all worked to make money and to feed the family, Upper Cumberland farm families were not egalitarian partnerships. The husband owned the family farm, and money earned by family labor belonged to him. A man did not "support" his wife and children; they supported him, in the sense that their work contributed to wealth that he controlled. Not until 1913 did Tennessee institute the sort of married women's property acts northeastern states passed before the Civil War. Tradition and custom held that women controlled their earnings—their egg money belonged to them—but in fact married women legally held no property. Decisions about land usage, expenditures, or savings might be made by the couple in consultation, but if a husband wished to appropriate his wife's earnings, there was nothing in the laws of the state of Tennessee to prevent him from doing so. If men needed a justification for their authoritative position, they found it in religion: did not the Bible itself enjoin the submission of women and children to the head of the house?[2]

A young person coming of age in the Upper Cumberland of the 1890s had no reason ever to expect to live alone. In a random sample of 405 families drawn from the 1900 census, only 6 individuals lived by themselves. Most people lived with other members of their families. Young men and young women did not usually move out of the parental household until they were married. Most households were composed solely of family members; only 6 percent of the sample took in boarders, and only 6 percent had servants living in the household.[3]

The survey sample did not differentiate between families living in

Table 1. Household Types, 1900

Type	Number	Percentage
Single	6	1.5
Couple	32	7.9
Nuclear	253	62.5
Extended kin	114	28.1
Total	405	100

Source: Survey of 1900 census.

the region's small towns and families living in the countryside. However, of the 388 heads of household who did list an occupation, 72.2 percent were farmers, 7 percent were farm laborers, 4 percent were day laborers, and 16.5 percent were people with nonfarm occupations ranging from merchant to schoolteacher to coal miner. Some differences between country and town life could be detected simply by looking at the census rolls. People in town took in boarders, mostly single men, and were more likely to have house servants. If a farmer had either a boarder or a servant living in his household, it was most likely a farm laborer. Most of the time servants and laborers living with families were white.[4]

Most people lived in nuclear households composed of husband, wife, and children. However, the extended family was by no means unusual in the region. Of the 405 households surveyed, one-fourth sheltered relatives other than nuclear family members, usually orphaned grandchildren, nieces or nephews, widowed brothers and sisters, aged parents, aunts and uncles, or married adult children and their families. Some adult siblings shared houses.[5]

Men headed 91.6 percent of the families sampled. It may be significant that even when two or more families shared a house, census takers usually listed each husband as head of his specific nuclear family. When women headed a household, they tended to be widows or elderly single women who had inherited land and the care of young relatives. Divorce was rare. In the entire sample there was one divorced head of household, a forty-five-year-old black man living in Smith County.[6]

Statistics describing the different kinds of households may obscure the nature of life in Upper Cumberland families. For most people, family provided life's one unchanging constant. But household types evolved according to the stage in life of the family members. Households began with marriages, grew with the addition of children, were augmented when the primary couple took in additional relatives, and shrank again to the primary couple when the children left home. At the end of the cycle elderly parents either became part of the households of their children or retained their status as head of household while sharing a dwelling with younger family members. Moving through the cycle, each person had his or her prescribed role to play.

Households began with marriages. Within any neighborhood, everyone knew the eligible parties and those who were courting. Much of the courtship occurred either at public gatherings or in the young woman's home. In a family history William B. Hyder of Putnam County described how he courted Mary Jones, a Jackson County girl, in 1860: "Our Courtship was Short yess very Short but to the purpus their was know [*sic*] foolishness about it." Hyder first saw his future wife at a Presbyterian revival. Two years later he waited for her one Sunday at church and managed to cut out a rival and escort her home. They began to write to each other. After three months Hyder decided to pay a visit to Jones's family. If he liked them, their house, and the way the women of the family cooked, he would ask Mary to marry him.

Hyder rode to Jackson County and spent a night with the family. The next day, having made up his mind,

I went in and took a Seat by the Fire and a little to the left hand side Mr. Jones wright squair in front of the fire and Mrs. Jones to his Right Mrs.Jones was Smoking her pipe as most of the Old Ladys did in Tennessee *No* one was in the Room but the Two Old folks Mr. & Mrs. Jones and my self *and their* was a little Pause in the Conversation and all was as still as death except the smoke from the old Ladys pipe was Roaling up like unto a steam injain and all of a suddent Mr. Jones spoke up sayint How Old are you Mr. Hyder My First thought was Now is the time I anssered that I was 23 years old and that I thought I was about old enough to Marry *Well yes* said the old man if you can find anyone that you want I suppose you are old enough I then told him that I had found the one I wanted and the Old Lady took the Pipe out of her Mouth and shoved Her eye glasses up on to her Eye Brows looked at me as though she could go through me and her eyes fairly sparking she said in a sharp tone I hope you have no notion of taking our only daughter and I dont see how I can spair her But if nothing else will Do I suppose I shall haft to give her up to some one and the old Gentleman said if it is agreeable with you and our Daughter I shall not object.

William Hyder and Mary Jones were married that night by a justice of the peace and returned to Putnam County the next day.[7]

Other men took longer to make up their minds. Robert Gwaltney, whose memories of his early life were published in the *Carthage Courier* in the 1920s, in 1892 married a "little woman" who lived nearby and owned a quarter-interest in a farm. Gwaltney said she liked to talk, and he didn't mind listening; but they courted for some time before marrying.[8]

Country people often looked forward to weddings as major social occasions. Judging by newspaper stories and memoirs, weddings took place at the bride's home. The next day the wedding party rode to the groom's home for the "infare dinner." (The infare, a dinner supplied by the bridegroom's family, seems to have marked the passage of the bride from her family's home to that of her husband's family.) John T. Oakley, a Baptist preacher who married a fifteen-year-old bride in the 1870s, remembered the wedding procession. The "waiters" or wedding attendants, two men and two women, and the newlyweds rode horseback two and one-half miles to Oakley's family home, to be greeted by a crowd of relatives and friends. The infare dinner, cooked on the hearth, included corn dodger bread and biscuits, turnips and cabbage, backbones, chicken, dumplings, coffee and milk, pound cakes, ginger cakes, and sorghum molasses. By the 1890s the infare would probably have included more store-bought luxuries and would most likely have been cooked on a wood-stove rather than the open hearth. But many newspaper items indicate that the style of the wedding remained the same. A slightly more elaborate wedding story, from the *Crossville Times* of March 7, 1889, is fairly typical:

> The wedding of G. A. Haley and Miss Sarah M. Rose was the best we have witnessed for some time. The guests began to arrive at the home of the bride a few hours before the appointed time. . . . Shortly after the ceremony the bridal party were ushered into the

dining room where was spread a bountiful repast. Several friends remained over night, accompanying the new couple to their future home, where . . . they found another table groaning with the luxuries of the infare dinner. [The wedding festivities ended with] a grand serenade in the evening beginning about 8 o'clock with bells, pans, boilers and everything that a crowd of well-wishing boys could think of to send them on their way rejoicing.[9]

For most young people in the region marriage must have seemed the door to adulthood. There was no intermediate stage during which the young person acted as a primary individual. Instead, men and women went from their parents' household to their own. But within that household, life would be very different for husband and wife. The different expectations began with ages at marriage.

People in the Upper Cumberland married young, but women were significantly younger when they married than men were. Ten percent of the wives in the survey had married by the time they turned 16. Fifteen percent more had married before their 18th birthday, and an additional 25 percent were wed by age 20, which was, therefore, the median age at marriage. Seventy-five percent of the women in the sample were married by age 23. Extremely early marriage was not the norm for men: only 10 percent were married at age 19. However, 15 percent of the sample married between 19 and 22. The median age at marriage for men was 23. Seventy-five percent of the men had married by age 28.[10]

For men, marriage marked the transition to economic independence—of a sort. According to regional tradition, landowning farmers usually "gave" their sons farms. The census rolls indicate that if this was the case, the fathers usually retained title to the land. All the household heads under nineteen were renters, and almost 70 percent of those in their twenties were also. Obviously the census does not discriminate between renters living on their parents' land and renters whose relationship with their landlord was strictly economic. But evidence drawn from other sources indicates that fathers giving their newly married sons land was at least not uncommon. When John T. Grime, a Baptist preacher, married in the 1870s, his father gave him uncleared farmland and a horse, and his mother gave him a bed, bedclothes, and a new homespun suit. (He had $3.50 of his own.)[11]

The sons and daughters of landowning farmers could expect to inherit either a piece of land or its equivalent in cash. Wills filed in DeKalb County during the late nineteenth and early twentieth centuries most often order the executors to sell property and divide the proceeds equally. Such were the provisions made by C. C. Johnson of DeKalb County in May 1891. Johnson had minor children. He appointed his brother their guardian and left instructions that the children be given "a good English education" and a horse and saddle each. In compensation the brother was to have all use and profit from Johnson's farm until the youngest child turned twenty-one. Then, Johnson ordered, his land should be sold (unless the children agreed otherwise) and the proceeds equally divided between all his offspring, including his married daughter.[12]

On other occasions one child might be singled out for a larger share than siblings because that child had stayed at home to care for his or her parents. These "Benjamins," to use Hal Baron's phrase, were remembered and rewarded. Thus G. W. Puckett in 1900 left the largest portion of his estate to his daughter Lillie Cantrell for her kindness to her aged parents, with her brothers to serve as executors.[13]

Most people, however, divided their estates "share and share alike." Wills give no hint of any vestiges of primogeniture and very little indication of discrimination by sex. S. B. Sellers's will, dated 1892, balanced "advancements" on his estate to ensure that all his children shared equally: one daughter received a bedstead to compensate for what had already been given others. Perhaps S. H. Walker was most egalitarian. Walker, apparently dying when the will was recorded in 1902, had eight children and wanted the family to stay together. The will left all to them equally, with instructions: "mind Claud Walker my elder son . . . all the said children to share alike so long as they do right and if any of them gets mad and run off and want [sic] stay there and work just his clothes is all I want them to have and what he leaves is just for them that stays there."[14]

Most landowners did not bother with the formality of filing a will at the courthouse. Instead, like J. W. Butler's father, they divided their land while they were still living or trusted their children to do so after their death. In a handwritten will the elder Butler put the disposal of his Macon County estate into J. W.'s control and advised his children to settle any differences within the family and avoid going to the law.[15]

For white men, economic prospects improved with age. A sample of 397 households indicates that, while the percentage of the entire sample who were tenants was 39.6, household heads under twenty were uniformly renters. Of the men in their twenties, 68 percent were renters. But in the next age group, men in their thirties, just over half owned their land. The trend continued in the next group, with 70 percent of household heads in their forties owning their land. It seems likely that men who obtained land often either inherited it or married women who had. Robert Gwaltney's talkative wife controlled a quarter-interest in a Smith County farm; Gwaltney became a landowner in his own right when he bought out her brothers. Once men obtained land, they were loath to risk losing it. Very few landowners had mortgages—4.5 percent of the sample 397 households. All those with mortgages were white, and most were in the twenty to forty age group.[16]

For women, marriage meant a change in workplace, from parents' home to husband's, but no real change in the kind of work done. An adolescent girl in the Upper Cumberland of the 1890s carried an adult load of house and farm work. She would probably have a few years of schooling (the literacy rate for women in 1900 was 66.9 percent), but she would have been learning the housewifery trade all her life. J. T. Oakley's fifteen-year-old bride had been keeping house since she was twelve. Even the daughters of well-to-do farmers milked cows, cooked, cleaned, and sewed. Marriage for women did not mean the sudden assumption of adult responsibilities, nor did it mean the acquisition of adult independence. A woman went from her father's household to her husband's. The cultural assumption was that she was under male authority in either place.[17]

Farm women worked: as discussed in the previous chapter, they tended gardens, took care of cattle, kept chickens, and often sold vegetables, poultry, or eggs to bring in a portion of the farm family's cash income. However, in the Upper Cumberland women rarely did public work. A few daughters worked as schoolteachers or hired girls, and a few married women worked as teachers or milliners. One postmaster's wife worked as his assistant. In one Fentress County household Bertha Doss, a widow, listed herself as nurse. Her daughters were listed as, respectively, woolspinner, basketmaker, and servants. Doss was 64, and her daughters ranged in age from 49 to 34; but her 22-year-old son Robert owned the farm where they lived and was listed as "head of household."[18]

Marriage ushered in the years of childbearing. Urban American middle-class families by 1900 limited family size through various methods. By all signs the women of the Upper Cumberland did not control their fertility, producing extremely large families, with child following child every two years. The median number of children born to the women in the sample was four, but that is not an accurate measure of family size, since women with no children were included in the calculations. (Married women without children were either newly wed or, most likely, barren.) Completed family size—that is, the number of children a woman had during her childbearing years— is a better indication of fertility. The sample included 78 women over 50 years of age. Among those women, the median number of children borne was 6. Many of these old wives had given birth to 10 or more children. Only 5 percent of the sample had no children; 25 percent had 4 or fewer. For women in the region, the expectation must have been that, once married, they would continue to have a child every two years until menopause.[19]

They could also expect that some of their children would die young. Just over 40 percent of all the mothers surveyed had lost children. Although there are no death records for the region that extend back into the nineteenth century, it seems likely that the primary killer of young children was infant diarrhea caused by contaminated water. The second summer of a child's life was traditionally considered extremely hazardous (and is still thought to be so by old women in the region). By the second summer a newly weaned child would drink water with his meals, and his system would have to adjust. In some children impure water would cause diarrhea, dehydration, and death. Children also died of water-borne diseases like typhoid, of viruses and respiratory infections, and of accidents.[20]

The tiny lamb tombstones that dot old graveyards in the region indicate that the deaths of children did not go unmarked or unmourned. Parents who lost children expressed grief tempered with resignation, as in this obituary commemorating the death of one-year-old Willie T. Gaines, daughter of M. A. and Emma Gaines of Jackson County: "O how we all loved her, and prayed for her life to be spared! But we must submit to the will of him who 'doeth all things well.' Then, while the little body is laid away, silent in the tomb, to await the resurrection morn, we believe that the spirit of little Willie has taken its flight to God and the holy angels."[21]

What we expect, and do not find, is the kind of distraught grief parents now display when a child dies. In the Upper Cumberland of the 1890s the death of a child was ordinary—sad, but not likely to cause an emotional breakdown or the dissolution of a family. In any case, no matter how a grieving woman felt, she had no space in which to act out emotions. The other children had to be cared for, and the household would not run without her. Parents might exhibit frenzied grief at the graveside, but long mourning was a luxury the household economy could not support. This led to a kind of stoicism outsiders mistook for fatalism or apathy, and a dependence on the traditional solaces of Christianity, with a heavy emphasis on the potential for a family reunion in heaven.

Upper Cumberland folk lived in small houses packed with family members. The average household size in 1900 was 5.3; the national average was 4.76. Only 25 percent of the households surveyed had 4 or fewer persons living together. A married couple in their middle years usually had a house full of children. Canzada Lafever and her husband, of Putnam County's eighth district, married 27 years in 1900, had 9 surviving children, 8 still living at home, ranging in age from 26 to 3. Levy and Mary Wilson of Jackson County, married 22 years, had 7 children still at home, ranging in age from 22 to 2. (Mrs. Wilson was 38, had been married at 16, and had lost 2 children.) In addition, many families sheltered relatives. The Wilsons had living with them one of Mr. Wilson's cousins, a 50-year-old farm laborer. Fate and Sarah Roberts of Putnam County shared a house with their 4 children, ranging in age from 20 to 5; Sarah's mother, Elizabeth Sutton, an 82-year-old widow; and Martha Sutton, Sarah's niece.[22]

Single persons or childless couples seem to have been especially likely to augment their households by taking in relatives. G. and Martha Baker, a childless couple in their forties, lived with Mahulda Martin, Mrs. Baker's sister; schoolteacher William Kittrell, a cousin; and Charles Hennessee, Mr. Baker's nephew, who worked as a farm laborer. Rachel Upchurch, a 58-year-old Pickett County widow and mother of 6, lived with her 2 sons, ages 20 and 17; her 22-year-old widowed daughter-in-law; and 2 small grandchildren. Robert Gwaltney and his wife were childless, but they shared a home with Robert's father, Dawson, age 80; William Gwaltney, Robert's widowed brother; William's 3 children, ages 15, 13, and 10; and Ophelia Wills, 22, a niece.[23]

Houses in the region varied from the elegant to the barely adequate. By the late nineteenth century, wealthy townspeople built stylish homes in accordance with currently popular architectural styles from Queen Anne to Steamboat Gothic, lavished their homes with gingerbread trim, and sent to New York for Tiffany windows. Slightly less well-to-do merchants and farmers lived in comfort, if not in high style. In long-settled areas such as White County, style-conscious farmers often copied decorative details from the finer homes in the area, adding them to old farm houses. "On the mountain," builders took advantage of plentiful supplies of sandstone for foundations and walls. In Fentress County, a small colony of German immigrants at Allardt provided an unusual source of skilled artisans whose construction techniques influenced building throughout the surrounding area.[24]

The most common houses, however, were examples of regional folk architecture: cabins or tenant-style, one-room, double-pen, or dog-trot houses of log or frame construction. Visitors to the region described some houses as shacks, barely adequate to shelter the families who lived in them. Other houses started with a basic form such as the dog-trot, then were enlarged as families grew or as the owners' economic status improved. In the countryside even the better houses lacked indoor plumbing. Water had to be carried from wells or springs. Many farm families did not even have outhouses.[25]

When large families lived in small houses, each room had multiple functions. (One of the marks of gentility must have been the ability to set off a room for use as front parlor.) Every room in the house had at least one bed, and sleeping alone would have been as rare as living alone. In such an environment there was little privacy; however, physical modesty could be cultivated.[26]

Within these crowded households the region's children learned to play their allotted roles in life by working alongside their parents. Girls cared for younger siblings, cooked, and cleaned; boys began farming as soon as they were old enough to hold the plow in the furrow. Families still controlled their children's education and had no serious rivals as agents of socialization. Schools, weak institutions that offered little more than instruction in reading and writing, posed no threat to the cultural hegemony of the family. Local school directors set curriculum under very loose state guidelines and dominated the very young, untrained teachers they hired. If any teacher presumed to challenge the values of the community, parents could remove their children from school, since school attendance was not compulsory.[27]

Articulate but not literate, fond of telling stories but not of writing them down, Upper Cumberland folk left few of the letters and diaries historians mine for insights into the emotions of family relations. The sources available are of two sorts: those that prescribe ideal behavior (sermons and obituaries) and those that describe more earthy realities (folk tales and diaries).

Conservative Protestant churches of all types had definite ideas on how proper family life was to be conducted. Preachers urged their congregations to make their homes churches, and denominational papers, such as the Nashville Disciples-affiliated *Gospel Advocate*, ran essays on many aspects of family life. For Disciples, Methodists, Baptists, or Presbyterians, the ideal was modest, quiet, homebound wives, industrious husbands, and well-behaved children. As a *Gospel Advocate* writer put it, "No man who is a disciple of Christ can be an unworthy husband," although "Man was not born a good husband, nor is he such intuitively. It must be studied like making corn and cotton." A good Christian man should pay attention to his wife and "study her natural desires." He should also guard against the common belief that his wife was his possession in the same sense as a dog or a horse.[28]

Baptist and Disciples preachers sternly relegated women to the home, where their only power consisted of "influence," in the classic nineteenth-century manner. In an 1892 "Sermon to Young Ladies," J. C. Martin reminded readers that God gave women influence over men, to be exercised through the heart, not through politics or preaching: "An education that leads a woman to the ballot box, or even to as sacred a place as the pulpit, is a sin in the eyes of God." In 1894 women were warned that diseases, passions, and lusts were hereditary and that an unruly, "boisterous" mother could hardly raise a "gentle, modest, polite, refined, and quiet daughter."[29]

While relegating women to a restricted sphere, conservative Christians offered hope of a more elevated status within that sphere. Put simply, life on a pedestal might be confining, but it was better than being considered a possession like a dog or a horse. The *Gospel Advocate* in 1891 ran a short story in which a bride-to-be breaks her engagement when she finds out that her fiance's mother is a general household drudge. The young woman explains that a man who has little respect for his mother will treat his wife the same way, and concludes, "If the wife must do all sorts of drudgery, so must the husband; if she must cook, he must carry the water; if she must make butter, he must milk the cows." That described a more equitable division of work than what prevailed on many Upper Cumberland farms, where women (or children) did all the chores described above and did heavy farm labor as well. To such women a middle-class urban housewife's lot might have seemed an ideal to be aspired to, not a gilded cage.[30]

According to the religious press the first duty of parents was to "train up [the] child in the way he should go" so that "even when he is old he will not depart from it" (Prov. 22:6). In 1897 E. A. Elam, a popular *Gospel Advocate* contributor who often conducted revivals in the Upper Cumberland, advised parents to train their children to useful employment, to see that their secular education did not inhibit their development as Christians, but, above all, to teach the child early the difference between right and wrong. Children must be controlled, Elam said:

Line upon line, precept upon precept, instruction, correction, and some sort of chastisement are necessary to the proper training of children. We should not allow Satan to persuade us that we love our children too much to properly correct and chastise them. . . . It is not love, but selfishness, that keeps some parents from chastising their children. They will not take the trouble and endure the pain it causes them to punish their children. It is a source of pain, heart pain, to parents to deliberately chastise a child; and therefore, to spare themselves this pain, they spoil the child.

Elam noted that chastisement should not be applied in anger but in "coolness and love, when it will do the greatest good."[31]

The evangelical model for family life should not be confused with the reality. People living in the Upper Cumberland now cherish family legends that indicate how far the real diverged from the ideal. One family remembers the recalcitrant wife who lay down in the road in front of her husband's buggy because she did not want to visit other family members. A wife's trenchant comment on her life with her bootlegger husband has endured for three generations in another family: "When I was young, I was just like a butterfly in the sun, and

I had to go and settle on a dog turd." The same woman, disliking her husband's handlebar mustache, waited until he was asleep and shaved off half of it. Funerals seemed to bring out frankness in emotionally overwrought people. One old wife commented before her husband's bier, "Well, he's caused me a whole lot of trouble, but the old devil will never bother me any more." However, the Peyton Creek farmer who lamented the loss of his good woman, saying, "I had rather lost my best mule," meant well.[32]

Without these folk tales there would be a temptation to believe that the prescriptive literature described the real lives of men and women instead of reflecting the wistful hopes of preachers. In order to understand any culture, however, it is useful to know what people *thought* the correct behavior was, whether they attained it or not. Obituaries offer further insight into traits considered worth promoting, since obituary writers usually try to compliment the deceased.

Obituaries also remind us that for people in the Upper Cumberland in the late nineteenth century, death was not a hidden process but something that happened frequently and at home. People died surrounded by family. Women, either family members or neighbors, cleaned the corpse and prepared it for burial. Neighbors and relatives came to the home of the deceased to sit up all night with the corpse. Burial followed the next day in a church cemetery, a community graveyard, or a family plot on the farm.[33] After the funeral some family friend or preacher might pen an obituary for the press:

> Bro. Isaiah Mitchell died Jan. 12th after inexpressible suffering from consumption for many years. Comparatively an aged man, he has for the last ten or fifteen years of his life, consecrated himself to the love of Jesus. . . . Death's sting had no tortures for him, for his confiding faith in his savior gave him courage to stand all bravely. Never was there a more fit subject for the holy legend: Precious in the sight of the Lord, is the death of his saints. To the grief-stricken family we say with David, "I shall go to him, but he shall not return to me." No, for he is now securely sheltered in the bosom of Jesus.[34]

Obituary writers often emphasized the fortitude with which the subject met death. Perhaps the highest tribute was the comment made of Roland Terry of Putnam County: "He talked of dying as he would about going on a journey, and died in the triumph of a living faith."[35]

The great theme of obituaries in the region, however, is family reunion in heaven. Reading Upper Cumberland obituaries could lead one to believe that the point of heaven was to see all one's lost friends, relatives, and children again. The bereaved were often counseled, "We weep not as those who have no hope," and were reminded, as Mitchell's family was, that they could go to him.[36]

Obituary writers commended men for their success in life or their willingness to take on church work (an understandable emphasis given that the writer was often the deceased's minister). They praised women for their hospitality, cheerful attitude, hard work, fortitude, devotion to the Gospel, or character as mothers of large families (they were "mothers in Israel"). In an unusual accolade for a spinster, Elizabeth McKent, who died in 1895 after a long career as toll keeper on one of the roads leading to Gallatin, was held as an example for all. McKent was poor, unattractive, and without familial resources. Yet she stayed at her post as gatekeeper through the Civil War and took in several children to raise. She was brave, strong, independent, prudent, neat, and orderly. When she grew too old to work, the toll road company and her church arranged to care for her. Because of her character, "she never lacked friends, or food, or raiment, or home, or any necessary of life. And now she sits amid princes and kings, rich in the incorruptible inheritance of a ransomed soul."[37]

A rare diary provides insight into Upper Cumberland family and community life. Polly Draper, 21-year-old daughter of James W. Draper, a prosperous Smith County farmer, kept a diary during the fall and winter of 1888. The Draper household included Polly's mother, Lucy; her older sisters Mourning, 28, and Fannie, 24; her younger sister Betty, 17; and her brother Jim, 21. (Polly had other married siblings.) The Draper daughters, more privileged than many of their neighbors, apparently did not work in the fields, at least during the slack winter months. But they did do housework, cook, spin, knit, and sew. They were also unusual in being unmarried (Polly, Fannie, and Mourning qualified as old maids by Upper Cumberland standards) and in being literate enough to read for pleasure. James Draper took the Nashville *American* and the *Tribune*, and his daughters read novels. But the young women participated avidly in the community's social life. Polly's diary records a whirl of visits and parties. The following is a typical entry: "Sunday we shut up the doors and all went to meeting except B she was at Willies'. Perlina

Evans came home with us from preaching staid [*sic*] here until Saturday when she and Fannie went to Uncle Will. D. and from there Uncle Will W. staid until Wednesday and come home friday. Perlina and I went to see Eliza, McDonald came that night. Sunday Mr. Jessie Evins came after her and carried her to Mr. Winchester."

In December a quilting, a corn shelling, a rail splitting, parties, dinners, and constant visiting enlivened the social scene. Polly dressed up as "Old Chris" for some neighbor children. Two cousins showed up at 5:00 A.M. on Christmas morning to claim "Christmas gift," thus by custom obligating the Drapers to give them a present. Even washing turned into a social occasion: Fannie and Polly were "fixed to wash" when Miss Betsy G. came by to wash with them.

Although Polly chose to emphasize her social life, her diary also indicates the ways families carried on functions now relegated to other institutions. In December Mr. Draper fell and hurt his ankle. His daughters nursed him for several weeks. Hospitality was a duty. Dr. Howser of Macon County, detained past nightfall in Chestnut Mound, arrived unexpectedly at the Draper house after the evening meal. Polly cooked his supper, and he stayed the night. When relatives needed help, the Draper women went to their aid. In March 1889 Polly closed her diary with an account of how "Pa" was persuaded to take a four-year-old boy to raise. Although the details are not clear, the child was probably either orphaned or illegitimate, and in this case not apparently related to the Drapers.[38]

At the other end of the life cycle from gregarious Polly Draper, sixty-four-year-old Mary Malinda Kirkpatrick Tinsley used the diary she began in 1891 to keep an account of her most serious concerns: family, work, and weather. Tinsley, who lived either with or near her daughter Malinda Kuykendall in Clay County, recorded her income (mostly in the form of gifts from her son, who ran a shoe store in Nashville), her expenditures in the local country store, and items she owed in exchange to neighbors. In the back of her diary she listed her children and their children. She recorded the weather every day, an understandable preoccupation for a farm woman. A farm wife's place might be "in the home," but she worked mostly outside the house. Tinsley made soap; helped burn brush; kept a horse, a cow, and chickens; gardened; picked berries; put up preserves; and helped butcher hogs. She had a spinning wheel and spun and twisted wool yarn for stockings, which she knitted all winter. She also made brooms and bottomed chairs. In old age she was master of many household crafts and was a useful, productive member of the family and the community.[39]

According to Protestant mission workers in the southern highlands, the lives of women like Polly Draper and Mary Malinda Tinsley needed improvement. Missionaries looked at both family and community life in the Upper Cumberland and found it wanting. Missionaries funded by the American Missionary Association worked at Pleasant Hill Academy in Cumberland County. In 1903 H. Paul Douglass gave the New England missionary's view of southern hill people in *Christian Reconstruction in the South*, a book that contains a description of Pleasant Hill. Although Douglass's comments describe life in the southern Appalachians in general, not the Upper Cumberland in particular, they point up ways in which life in the region diverged from northeastern norms that New England folk thought were ideal for families throughout the nation.[40]

Douglass argued that the dominant form of social organization in the southern Appalachians was the clan. The regional economy still depended on household production and barter. Therefore people were not knit into communities by economic necessity: "There is an almost total absence of those more complex human relations, to express and control which social institutions are developed." The strongest tie was the "blood-bond." According to Douglass, mountain folk had "a feeble sense of the community," and although they were loyal to the nation, they were not citizens in the urban sense because they were not involved with institutions.[41]

Douglass, like many missionaries in the southern highlands, did not approve of the way the natives conducted their family lives. In particular, missionaries tended to feel sorry for farm wives. According to Douglass, men and women in the mountains lived separate lives, divided by gender roles that cast women as drudges in house and in field.[42] But, Douglass said, the mountaineers were good candidates for uplift. He cited as an example the great work being done at Pleasant Hill, where public school teachers were being trained in a community of "homes, much superior to those in neighboring settlements," where church services were "dignified and intelligent." The teachers educated at schools such as Pleasant Hill would, Douglass hoped, help the mountain folk assimilate and become Americanized.[43]

Map 2. Macon County, 1899. The map illustrates the plethora of small communities and the lack of roads in the county, as shown in an 1899 shipper's guide.

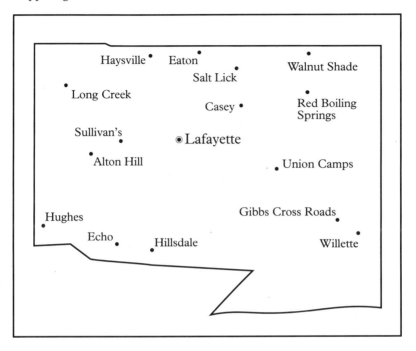

Douglass, like many well-intentioned outsiders of urban background, confused social institutions with community. The Upper Cumberland and other hill-country regions throughout the South did lack the sort of dominant institutions social reformers wanted. Missionaries who came to the region looked for leaders with authority who could be enlisted in uplift campaigns. They wanted to talk to the chief of the natives. But no such person existed. Instead, the (white, Anglo-Saxon, Protestant) natives were linked by blood, marriage, and long residence into an organic community.[44]

Upper Cumberland farm families created networks of kinship that acted as pre–welfare state safety nets. The Upper Cumberland family was expansive; even distant cousins counted as kin, and elderly friends of the family were accorded the respectful titles "Aunt" or "Uncle" when no blood tie existed. As a result, any long-settled neighborhood could take on the attributes of an extended family.

Every county in the Upper Cumberland abounded in small communities. People habitually identified themselves as being from some particular community. Newspapers reinforced this identification by running news supplied by county correspondents from many different small hamlets. Many of the larger villages had a store, a school, a community church building, a post office, and a justice of the peace who could hold trials for minor and civil offenses. In the early twentieth century some people living in Upper Cumberland counties had never found it necessary to make a journey to the county seat.[45]

Country people lacked a sense that some matters were private: correspondents to the county papers commented on who was visiting whom, who was courting or looking to find someone to court, who was buying or selling, and how everyone's crops were doing. When a wife ran off, they reported it, offered sympathy to the afflicted husband, and expressed hope that the couple would get back together. The *Crossville Chronicle* in August 1902 published a jocular story about a young man who wanted the county court clerk to marry him to one of the town's "lewd women." The clerk tried to dissuade the man, arguing that he was still in his teens and should wait, but when the young man insisted, the clerk performed the ceremony. The paper published the names of the man and his new wife—publicly labeled a prostitute.[46]

Communities fostered an intense localism. Residents of Defeated or Haydenburg Ridge or Genesis did not want to pay taxes to fund services to Difficult or Flynn's Lick or Grassy Cove, and the residents of those communities reciprocated the feeling. The outlying communities in all the Upper Cumberland counties resented attempts to centralize control of institutions in the county seat, let alone the state capital. Localism combined with familism to work against the development of a larger civic spirit that might focus on the county governing unit as an object of loyalty.

During the early twentieth century the primacy of family as the leading institution in the Upper Cumberland would be challenged as social reformers tried to create those dominating institutions that would link the population in community. To change the region's culture would necessitate a challenge to the region's patriarchal familism. In reaction traditionalists in the region reaffirmed their loyalty to the religious symbol that had justified the ways of the father: the Bible.

3

THE OLD-TIME RELIGION
CHURCHES IN THE UPPER CUMBERLAND

Next to families, churches mattered most to Upper Cumberland folk in the 1890s. Uniformly Protestant, religious people in the region brought to their churches the same habits of mind they exhibited in their secular lives: zeal for local control of institutions, egalitarianism (men were "brothers"; women, "sisters"), and patriarchal attitudes (fathers ruled the church family just as surely as they did the secular family). Most of the denominations popular in the region enrolled only adult believers willing to abide by stringent rules for behavior. Congregations provided social outlets for families, supported members in need, and established moral norms for their members. For believers the local congregations functioned as communities of faith. Small but zealous congregations had power disproportionate to their size. Upper Cumberland folk believed that personal morality as derived from religion formed the foundations of the home and the

Table 2. Selected Regional Religious Groups, 1890

Methodists		12,594
	Methodist Episcopal, South	8,976
	Northern Methodists	2,888
	African Methodist Episcopal	730
Baptists		10,408
	Regular	7,563
	Baptist Church of Christ	775
	Primitive Baptist	734
	General	406
	United	405
	Regular, colored	226
	Old-Two-Seed-in-the-Spirit Predestinarian	176
	Freewill	123
Presbyterians		4,720
	Cumberland Presbyterian	4,203
	Cumberland Presbyterian, colored	517
Disciples of Christ		4,455

Source: Department of the Interior, Census Office, *Report on Statistics of Churches.*

state. In a region without strong government, religion was a powerful bulwark against disorder.[1]

Conservative Protestants had dominated southern religion since the early nineteenth century.[2] The Upper Cumberland was not an exception to regional norms. Rather, the region apotheosized southern trends. The region had no Catholic churches and not even an Episcopal outpost. The most popular denominations were the Methodists and various kinds of Baptists, followed by the Cumberland Presbyterians and the Disciples/Churches of Christ.[3]

To a Catholic or a Jew, all the Baptist, Methodist, Presbyterian, and Disciples churches would have seemed very much alike. Indeed, all the churches had very similar styles of worship and expectations about behavior. But preachers spent most of their time pointing out the fundamental doctrinal differences among denominations on the most crucial topic: redemption and how it was to be obtained. With salvation at stake, arguments among denominations made religion a potentially divisive force in the Upper Cumberland. Yet, paradoxically, theological disputes reinforced belief in the Bible, the foundation on which all the regional denominations rested. The Authorized English (King James) version of the Bible supposedly held answers for all religious questions. Preachers created a world of discourse almost rabbinical in its concentration on the holy book. Any challenge to the truth of the Bible destroyed the basis for settling arguments. Quarreling denominations therefore venerated the Bible, which became a powerful symbol of an underlying unity of religious belief in the region.

Denominations also differed on issues of organization. The Methodists, with their centralized structure under the leadership of bishops, held the allegiance of about 40 percent of the churchgoing population. But 46 percent of those who claimed church membership in 1890 were Baptists of some variety or members of the Disciples of Christ and therefore belonged to groups with strong traditions of local congregational autonomy. Like the Lafayette Baptist Church, founded in 1849, they believed that "a majority shall rule in all cases."[4]

In the Upper Cumberland, older people often refer to "church houses." The phrase captures the way people thought about the structure in which they worshiped. For many there was nothing sacred about the structure itself; it was simply a building built along the same lines as a country store, without room divisions, in which people could gather to hear the Word. In the 1890s some people in the region remembered when worship took place in homes. In 1901 a Cumberland County resident reminisced about those days:

I seem to see the long two-roomed log cabin, with the open entry between, two immense stack chimneys, with great fire places, one at each end of the house.

On Sunday everything that could be turned into a seat was removed into the living room. The split and shuck concave bottom chairs were reserved for the grown folk, and stools and boxes were eagerly seized by the young people.

Finally the preacher came in, followed by the men in twos and threes, the boys bringing up the rear; one side especially reserved for them, and the women in sun bonnets sitting on the other, glanced anxiously around to see if husbands or sons were coming in and not off with the dogs for a squirrel hunt.[5]

When in later years Upper Cumberland congregations built church houses, those edifices were often spartan and undecorated. Some were poorly maintained:

The church is an unpainted one-room structure, propped up on piles, each of three or four rounded stones. The steps of the two doors, side by side at the rear end of the edifice—one originally for men and the other for women—are out of repair, and the little belfrey has lost part of its slates. Entering, we see a rectangular room with benches, a stove in the middle, and front, a platform having, besides a simple pulpit, two small square tables of the same height as the pulpit at the front corners of the platform. The walls are ceiled but unpainted, and the homemade benches are badly hacked with knives. Several window lights have been shot out by the guns of the older boys, who in this section frequently take this method of showing that they are grown up. Although the floor has evidently been swept, it is permeated by the red mud of the locality. There is no musical instrument, and there are no flowers.[6]

Although the battered building described above had been defaced more than normally for a rural church, it typified the small churches in the region in its size and lack of decoration. Many congregations shared church houses or simply worshiped in community schools.[7]

Some denominations in the region fostered social activism, while others held themselves aloof from the community as from the wicked world. The distinction made a difference for women in the various churches: the more outreach, the more expansive the definition of women's work in the church. The Methodists, the most inclusive, socially conscious denomination in the region, sponsored schools, involved themselves in long-term political projects such as the temperance movement, and raised money for missions. Town churches, whether Methodist, Cumberland Presbyterian, or Baptist, often supported youth groups, special Sunday School classes, and mission and circle meetings for women. Some Baptist congregations affiliated with the Southern Baptist Convention participated in missionary work and contributed to or ran local schools. These organized benevolent activities amounted to a shadow church in which women raised money and took responsibility for organizing events.[8]

However, men set the direction of denominational policy and decided how the money was spent. Upper Cumberland churches were egalitarian, but only within gender. Methodists and Cumberland Presbyterians agreed with their more conservative neighbors that women must, as commanded by the Bible, "keep silent" in the church. Only men could stand before the congregation as ministers, deacons, or elders. Still, the Methodist and Presbyterian women had a role in their churches that other denominations in the region denied to their women.[9]

In some Disciples and some Baptist congregations the very architecture of church houses indicated the status of women: there were two doors, one for men and one for women, and sex-segregated seating inside. Some intensely congregational churches refused to support missionary associations. Several of the Baptist sects fell into this category, as did most of the Disciples congregations in the region. Although churches opposed mission work for theological reasons, not because they wanted to deny women a role in the congregation, their opposition had that effect. Since women's work in Protestant churches often centered around raising money for missions, in antimission churches there was not much for women to do.[10]

The local Disciples of Christ, in the 1890s the fourth largest religious group in the region, believed in congregational control, scorned missionary societies, and denied any public role to women. In the 1890s the Disciples nationwide were in the process of splintering over such divisive policies as intercongregational missionary associations and the use of musical instruments in worship. Both were unwelcome innovations to Disciples in the Upper Cumberland. The major regional Disciples' newspaper, the *Gospel Advocate*, published in Nashville, thundered against what editor David Lipscomb called "offensive ecclesiasticism." Lipscomb reserved some of his most biting sarcasm for bossy women who "usurped" male authority by preaching or setting up societies for benevolent work: "The habit of women preaching originated in the same hot bed with easy divorce, free love, and the repugnance to child bearing." The "woman question" received more attention in the Disciples press than Darwinism or the higher criticism. Lipscomb in particular saw the issue in part as an issue of class: only wealthy women had time for benevolent societies, and, Lipscomb thought, they used their charity work as a means of indicating their superiority over less affluent women.[11]

The Upper Cumberland Disciples congregations, with rare exceptions, joined Lipscomb's conservative revolt and by 1906 called themselves Churches of Christ to distinguish themselves from the "digressive" brethren. In the midst of wrangling with each other over music, missions, and associations, the Churches of Christ in the Upper Cumberland surpassed the Cumberland Presbyterians in membership and, in some counties, became the dominant religious group. That this growth occurred at a time when Disciples preachers in the region emphasized the localistic, conservative, and patriarchal attributes of their church suggests that such attitudes had a powerful appeal in the region.[12]

Lacking the outward focus of organized benevolence or missionary work, Churches of Christ and Baptist sectarians concentrated on the congregation, creating a sort of extended family based on religious belief. Congregations, acting as a group, helped members in need and mediated disputes. But congregations also expelled members who violated the church's standards of belief or behavior. The records of the Defeated Creek Missionary Baptist Church in Smith County indicate how this disciplinary process worked. At the third Sunday business meeting in February 1889 the congregation took up a collection for an ailing member, raising $2.45 in cash, fifty pounds of flour, and a half bushel of meal. In May, Brother Kennedy accused Brother Witt of slandering him; Brother Witt retorted that Brother Kennedy had said bad things about him. The entire congregation appointed itself as a committee to reconcile the two men. By July, seeing that a reconciliation had not yet been effected, the church appointed an investigatory committee. Finally, in August, Kennedy and Witt agreed to get along and "forgive."[13]

Congregations excluded from fellowship members accused of heresy. However, churches brought heresy charges most often against men or women who had already left the congregation to join another denomination. Thus in October 1890 the New Bildad Primitive Baptist Church of Jesus Christ dismissed former members from the DeKalb County congregation for joining the Disciples of Christ, a group scorned as "Campbellites" who "call themselves Christians."[14]

For congregational sectarians, the local church, not the minister, held the ultimate doctrinal authority. In 1900 the Spring Creek Baptist Church ousted its minister for advocating a "theory" contrary to the belief of the majority of the members. About fifteen members ("all that took part in the racket today") were also expelled. The

Spring Creek church's action indicates the level of congregational control typical of Baptists or Disciples. In "Rules of Discourse" compiled in 1906 the Old Bildad Baptist Church of Christ summed up the attitude of at least half of the region's Christians: pastors and deacons elected by the church were not to "lord it [over] oure god heritage."[15]

Local Christians took it for granted that all agreed on certain moral standards: at the very least, Christians should keep the Ten Commandments and avoid drunkenness and dancing. The Bible specifically condemned drunkenness, while dancing was likely to arouse the lust of participants. Some congregations did not allow women to wear jewelry. But while Methodists and Old-Two-Seed-in-the-Spirit Predestinarian Baptists could agree that people who transgressed the moral code were sinners, they differed as to how sinners should be treated.[16]

Although Methodist and Cumberland Presbyterian congregations did expel transgressors, evidence indicates that they were less likely to do so than the smaller, sectarian groups. The Pleasant Grove Methodist Church of Putnam County, for example, had at one time 172 members on its rolls. While people left the church to move to other areas or to join other denominations, only two members were taken off the church rolls for immoral conduct, and the register notes that in both cases the church removed the guilty parties "by their own request."[17]

By contrast the New Bildad Primitive Baptist Church between November 1892 and January 1894 called up seven members for misbehaving and dismissed five. In November 1892 the congregation ousted a man for public drunkenness and disobeying the order of the church. In February the church preferred charges against a man for "gross immoral conduct" and in March dismissed him. In June two members faced similar charges. After acknowledging their errors, the two women were forgiven and reconciled with the fellowship. In December the congregation accused Hannah Griffith of dancing. As was the custom, a church committee went to visit Hannah to get her to confess her sins and ask forgiveness so that she could remain a member in good standing. The committee failed: in January 1894 Hannah lost her membership for cursing, dancing, and disobeying the order of the church.[18]

Hannah Griffith refused to act appropriately in the great drama of repentance and reconciliation that was so much a part of congregational life. Churches did not want to excommunicate members; they wanted sinners to confess and come back to the fellowship. The Spring Creek Baptist Church of Jackson County expressed the general attitude when they sent a committee to some members who had been missing church. The committee was to say to the delinquents, "if [you] are hurt at the church . . . come to our next meeting and show the church where it had done wrong and be reconciled."[19]

The churches of the Upper Cumberland made great demands on believers. In a region that tolerated public drunkenness and brawling, where men still operated out of a sense of honor and vengeance, predestinarian and free will congregations alike expected members to exhibit such behavior as would proclaim their status as nonworldly. They were to dress modestly, behave circumspectly, avoid frivolous amusements, and humble themselves to the discipline of their brothers and sisters in Christ.

Within the region the churches furnished the religious and moral standard. Even the young men who shot out church windows and disrupted church services could not escape being affected by the beliefs of their neighbors. They might rebel, but it was a specific view of religion and morality they were rebelling against. The standard applied to them also; in later years they might stand before a congregation and repent in tears the sins of their youth.

Preachers formed a large portion of the local intelligentsia. A young man in the Upper Cumberland of the 1890s who wanted to work with his mind more than with his hands could be a doctor, a lawyer, a teacher, or a preacher. For most families the cost of medical or legal training was prohibitive. Teaching was not a full-time occupation, since school terms were usually not over three months' duration. However, most denominations in the region required no special schooling for preachers. As a result, men with intellectual aspirations often went into preaching.

Upper Cumberland preachers could be divided into two types based on their relationship with their congregations. Denominational hierarchies placed Methodist and Presbyterian ministers in their posts. Their congregations expected these specially trained men to devote all their time to the church's service, and they were paid accordingly. Disciples and Baptist preachers were hired directly by their congregations or by the congregation's elected representatives, and the congregations could fire them the same way.[20] These men served as farmer-preachers in the Baptist tradition, supporting themselves and their families by working, and preaching on Sunday for a small stipend or for free. Some were well, if narrowly, educated; others were barely literate.[21]

When called to preach, most men made an effort to educate themselves. John T. Oakley, a Baptist preacher whose memoirs the *Carthage Courier* published in the 1920s, recounted that he had never been especially religious until he rather unexpectedly "got saved" and decided to be a preacher. At that point he was illiterate. He went to a denominational academy to learn simultaneously to read and to preach. John Grime, also a Baptist, was the son of Putnam County's only "planter." His father's antebellum library consisted of the Bible, a copy of Josephus, some readers, and some volumes of legal statutes. The Civil War disrupted young Grime's education. When in the 1880s he decided to preach, he went to school with his young daughter.[22]

Education did not translate into authority for Upper Cumberland ministers; in fact, many congregations suspected education might be incompatible with righteousness. Although the Southern Baptist mainstream had long since come to accept educated, professional preachers, rural churches persisted in their preference for farmer-preachers who were supposedly called by the Holy Spirit. The *Gospel Advocate* advised Churches of Christ to look for self-sufficient worker-preachers rather than professionals with seminary degrees. Hiring a theologian would "weaken the confidence of the people in their ability to read and understand the Bible."[23]

Like politicians, preachers in the region joined in religious debates. In debates they appealed to the intellect of an audience, which was expected to understand the terms of discourse and to be able to follow long, complicated discussions of points of doctrine. Crowds numbering in the hundreds and, occasionally, thousands attended religious debates between Baptists, Disciples, and Presbyterians in the Upper Cumberland in the late nineteenth century. The debates centered on the conditions for salvation and on the merits of each denomination.[24]

Although all the churches professed belief in justification by faith through grace, in practice they gave different emphases to the role of human choice and obedience. Thus when Elder D. Wauford of the (hyper-Calvinist) Primitive Baptist Church debated Elder O. P. Barry of the Church of Christ (an emphatically free-will sect) at the New Hope Meeting House in DeKalb County in 1895, the proposition for discussion was "All for whom Christ died will be saved in heaven." Elder Wauford took the view that Christ had died for the elect only. Elder Barry argued that Christ had died for all, but that some people "are damned not because Christ did not die for them. But because of *unbelief* and *disobedience*."[25]

Some arguments hinged upon the relative strength of rival denominations' Calvinism. In 1892 Baptist minister A. Malone debated Primitive Baptist S. F. Cayce at the Defeated Church in Smith County. For "the first two days" the two ministers discussed "instrumentality in the conversion of sinners." Cayce took the "high grounds" of extreme Calvinism, arguing that "the number of the saved and lost were fixed numbers and had been from before the foundation of the world." Malone argued for the necessity of preaching the gospel to sinners, citing human agency and instrumentality as God-ordained means of conversion. Cayce decried human instrumentality as useless, since the gospel was intended only for "the children of God."[26]

At the conclusion of such debates both sides would claim their denomination had won. A sinner saved was a matter for rejoicing, but a believer captured from a rival denomination was cause for jubilation: "Three came from the Methodists, and two Campbellites professed faith in Christ. Allow me to say in this connection that the backbone of Campbellism in this section is certainly broken. Many have already left the sinking ship and come aboard the old ship of Zion."[27] The debates underscored the ultra-Protestantism of the region. Regardless of denomination, preachers asked their hearers to make individual decisions based on the only authority to which all local churches owed allegiance: the Bible.

To understand the centrality of the Bible in regional religious life, it may help to remember the description of a typical church house quoted earlier. It had no flowers, no stained glass windows, no organ, and no pictures; the building itself was plain and barely functional and was treated with indifference even by congregants. In such a place the only sacred object was the Bible, and the sermon, the hearing of the Word, was the core of worship.

Consider, too, the power of the written word in a region where about one-quarter of the population could barely read and write. Writing was a trade skill for teachers, preachers, and, most importantly, lawyers. Writing anything down seemed to make it binding: laws were written, and land titles were inscribed in enormous, leather-bound volumes and stored in the courthouse. The seriousness of the secular uses of literacy could only have reinforced reverence for the Bible.

The Bible was often the only book in a household—*the* Book in reality. Regional folklore attributed to the Bible occult qualities. For some, to tear a page from the Bible was to risk premature death. Anything written in a Bible had an especially serious meaning. A person with a decision to make might open the Bible and read a verse at random for guidance. Some people even conjured with the Bible: by suspending scissors from a Bible and counting rotations, young girls could, it was said, divine the name of their future husbands.[28]

Argue as they might about scriptural interpretations, all the Upper Cumberland churches united to defend the Bible as authoritative. The very controversies that divided Upper Cumberland Christians increased the importance of the Scriptures; all arguments ultimately came down to rival interpretations of Bible verses. This was especially true of the Baptists and the Disciples, who had no official creed "but the Bible." However, Elisha Sewell's tribute to the Bible in the *Gospel Advocate* could just as easily have been written by Baptists, Methodists, or Presbyterians: "How thankful we should be that God has so plainly revealed to us our origin, our relationship to our divine creator, and our moral and intellectual capacities, and our obligations to him who gave us being. . . . Man must maintain the authority of the Bible in all its parts, or he is no servant of Christ Jesus or of God our Father."[29] Because of the Bible, men had knowledge of God. The Bible also established right relations for families. Most of all, the Bible offered a plan of salvation. Therefore all religious folk in the region joined to repel any attack on the Bible.[30]

Even people in the hills of the Upper Cumberland were familiar with some of the countercurrents in nineteenth-century religious and scientific thought. Some of the older generation remembered Tom Paine's *Age of Reason*,[31] and literate people knew of the controversies that had arisen over Charles Darwin's theories of evolution, as a letter published by the *Gospel Advocate* in 1898 indicates:

North Springs, September 26- Brother N. W. Proffit has just finished a protracted meeting at this place. Brother Proffit presented the truth as set forth in the gospel in a clear, comprehensive, and forcible manner, calculated to do much good for the salvation of aliens, the sanctification of believers, and the overthrow of skepticism, unbelief, and infidelity. We have a few infidels or skeptics in this section of country, styling themselves "Freethinkers" or "Liberals," exalting their opinions above God's word as set forth in the Scriptures given by inspiration. These men claim that the Bible should not be held up as a standard of morality to reform the world. They seem to think that scientific lectures on evolution, origin of species, astronomy, geology, and other scientific "ologies" will turn the people on Jennings Creek from their unlawful lusts. They claim that they cannot have faith without positive proof; they ridicule the Bible and stubbornly refuse to believe gospel facts as recorded by inspiration. A belief in the supernatural and those things pertaining to heaven and hell they call "credulity" and "superstition;" a belief in the Darwinian theory of evolution—that man is the offspring of a monkey—they call "s-c-i-e-n-c-e." Poor, deluded creatures![32]

This attack on the freethinkers of Jennings Creek says more about the faithful than about the (supposed) village atheists. For the author of the letter, belief in God depended on a belief in the "gospel facts recorded by inspiration." To doubt the exact truth of the Bible was to be an infidel. To be interested in all the "ologies" of science was to set up a rival belief system, in which lectures in science would substitute for sermons. Significantly, the author could not imagine any basis for moral behavior that did not derive from the Bible: how could science get people to turn away from their "unlawful lusts"? Taking his defining concepts from his own religion, the defender of the faith does not even understand his foes' terms of discussion.

In the 1890s conservative Protestantism held unthreatened hegemonic sway in the region. Churches created communities that supported, reconciled, and disciplined members. Whatever might change, the Bible was eternal; the values taught by religion, irreplaceable and immutable. Any threat to the Bible as the inspired Word of God would unify all the region's squabbling denominations in the book's defense, and that unity would cut across denominational, economic, and political lines. The Bible, then, was potentially a powerful cultural icon available for political purposes.

4

JEFFERSONIAN GOVERNMENT IN ACTION

POLITICS AND SOCIAL ORDER IN THE UPPER CUMBERLAND

When the family is the most important institution, what is the role of politics? In the Upper Cumberland of the 1890s, politics served as an outlet for the demonstration of familial loyalties. People followed national and state politics with passionate interest. Political contests entertained the public, and many men made politics their sport of choice. But allegiance to the Democratic or Republican party also formed an important element of intergenerational identification, linking men with their ancestors: *whose* boy one was normally determined how a man voted. In a system where family heritage mattered more than ideology or economic interest, politics had little to do with policy.

The hand of government rested very lightly on Upper Cumberland counties. Residents of the region could go a lifetime without ever having to deal with the power of the state as manifested from Washington or Nashville.

The county governments handled most matters of governance. But people in the region preferred to keep even county governments as weak as possible, resisting any attempt to concentrate power in the county seat: they wanted their tax dollars to be spent in their community, and they wanted local control over the spending. Therefore county governments acted with Jeffersonian restraint, collecting taxes, coordinating schools and road building, and doling out public charity.

County authorities also kept the peace, or attempted to do so. Men considered violence an acceptable means of settling differences and salvaging personal honor, and they considered private "difficulties" none of the law's business. People in the region expected that families would protect their own, using the courts as instruments of revenge when possible and using guns and knives when necessary.

Although Democrats formed the majority in most counties (Fentress, Pickett, Cumberland, and Macon were the Republican exceptions), both parties maintained organizations and competed for votes in state and national elections, sponsoring barbecues, "speakings," and rallies. Political contests offered free public entertainment for residents with a taste for debate and florid political rhetoric. During the 1890s the most popular politician in the region was Robert L. Taylor, an East Tennessee Democrat who was elected governor twice in the 1880s and again in 1896. The politics of "Our Bob" were short on content but long on rhetoric, both ornate and vernacular. Taylor could go from telling stories about his hound dog "Old Limber" to flights of purple eloquence. Underneath the hoopla of late nineteenth-century politics, however, lay the enduring antagonisms of civil war, put aside but hardly forgotten.[1]

In 1894 the Republican Party sent a speaker from Chattanooga to address a rally at Doyle, a community in White County, in support of Joseph Cliff, the GOP congressional candidate. The local Republicans built a speakers' platform and put up enough benches to seat a large crowd. "Col. Joe" Cliff had served in the Union cavalry, and people in White County well remembered his wartime expropriation of horses; indeed, among the crowd gathered for the GOP "speaking" were people who had lost horses to Cliff's troops. When the Chattanooga Republican rose to speak, Democrats in the crowd rose to heckle. The Republicans tried to stop the heckling. As the argument grew violent, people in the crowd saw the glint of gunmetal as men drew their pistols. Women grabbed their children and ran for safety. To avoid a slaughter of innocent noncombatants, some men in the crowd suggested that "both groups choose captains and that the groups fall in line according to military rules and 'shoot it out.' " Finally an elderly gentleman climbed up on the speakers' platform, talked the crowd down, and got them to go home.[2]

In the Upper Cumberland of the 1890s a child was born into a particular party. His adult political identification would stem from the choices made by his father and grandfather in 1861. Unionists raised Republican children; Confederates nurtured Democrats. (Politically mixed marriages were as difficult as religious mixes.) Cordell Hull, in 1890 a nineteen-year-old law student and son of a prominent raftsman in Clay County, recalled in his memoirs that the young men of his generation grew up on stories about the Civil War in the region, tales of murder and vengeance that "made a deep impression on us boys." Hull's own father, William, figured in one regional legend. Shot and left for dead by Union guerrillas, the elder Hull recovered but lost the sight of one eye and lived in constant pain from his wound. After the war William Hull tracked his assailant to Monroe County, Kentucky. As his son recounts the story in his memoirs, "When Father came upon him, [the assailant] tried to be friendly and said, 'Why, hello, Bill.' Father went straight to him and without ceremony shot him dead." Raised on such stories, young men in the Upper Cumberland were expected to be loyal to the party of their fathers. The men in Hull's family "were Democrats of the strictest sect." Some of their neighbors were Republicans. Voters were so loyal that, according to Hull, local politicians could calculate their chances to within three or four votes.[3]

Since party affiliation depended on family heritage and family memories, party politics united people with dissimilar economic interests and divided those whose interests were the same. Upper Cumberland Democrats included George Dibrell of Sparta, former Whig and coal field developer, who presumably shared economic interests with Republican John Wilder, also a coal field developer. But Dibrell had been a Confederate general, and Wilder had first come to Tennessee as a general in the Union army. Their wartime loyalties put them in opposite political camps and alongside small farmers. In postbellum Tennessee, disagreements about state or national economic policy had to be fought within either the Republican or the Democratic party; voters would not cross party lines even when doing so would have enabled them to vote for policies that furthered their economic interests.[4]

From the 1870s to 1890 Tennessee politics revolved around the state debt repudiation controversy. Antebellum governments had incurred most of the state debt by issuing bonds to encourage the building of railroads. Tennessee Republicans favored payment in full; the state's Democrats were divided on the issue. Would-be industrial promoters insisted that the state must pay in full to uphold its credit. The antipayment faction, known as the "low-tax" Democrats, held that the circumstances of war and a depressed economy precluded payment of the debt in full. As their name implies, low-tax Democrats were most concerned with keeping taxes down. Farmers generally favored the low-tax faction.[5]

Democratic Party leaders in the Upper Cumberland were divided over the funding issue. George Dibrell of Sparta led the "state credit" faction, while the main spokesman for the low-tax Democrats, John Savage, came from Warren County, just across the Caney Fork River. But while faction leaders played politics with the issue, Democratic voters in the region consistently supported the low-tax position. High land taxes were clearly undesirable to Upper Cumberland farmers, and the standing of the state's credit in northeastern bond markets mattered little to rural voters. For Democrats, intraparty politics allowed room for varied economic interests. Their Republican neighbors lacked such room. The Republican counties, Cumberland and Fentress, followed the Republican Party line and voted for the funding of the debt.[6]

Nothing more clearly illustrated how seriously voters in the region took crossing party lines. Republican farmers presumably had economic interests identical to those of Democratic farmers; but voting those interests would have meant repudiating history and identity, and most just could not do it. In the 1890s the Populist attempt to build a third party in the region also foundered on party loyalties based on family heritage.

The Farmers' Alliance organized locals in Upper Cumberland counties. It had its greatest success in White County, where the organization grew from five men in September 1888 to three hundred members by Christmas of that year. White County farmers organized several co-ops, and Alliancemen forced local merchants to lower prices. Upper Cumberland voters, in common with rural voters throughout the state, supported Alliance Democrat John P. Buchanan, who shocked party regulars by winning the primary and then the governorship in 1890. In 1891–92, as bemused regular Democratic factions scrambled to regain their normal control of the party, the Alliance Democrats began to leave the Democratic fold and organize the People's Party. In the Upper Cumberland, Populists fused with Republicans and ran tickets for local offices. (In Putnam County the fusion candidates for circuit court clerk, county court clerk, sheriff, and trustee won.)[7]

To beat off this third-party threat, Upper Cumberland Democratic newspapers accused Alliancemen and Populists of being turncoats, willing to sell out the old cause and join "the blackest black republicans" to gain public office. In White County fistfights disrupted a Democratic rally when the speakers attacked the Alliance for breaking up the "Solid South." The Democratic press in Sparta printed a letter (in dialect and rather obviously manufactured) supposedly from a poor deluded Democratic farmer who had attended an Alliance rally instead of accompanying his family to the Democratic barbecue scheduled for the same day. The "farmer" was ashamed when he heard a speaker reminisce about the good old days of Reconstruction, when Democrats were not allowed to vote: "when I heard him a talkin' that way I thought of my poor old father, now dead and gone, who fought through the war and wasn't afraid of anything, how the tears ran down his dear old face when he came home from the election and told my mother how they let niggers vote and drove him and Silas' father from the polls. I can't tell you how mean I did feel."[8]

In the Upper Cumberland evocation of family heritage carried more weight than any analysis of opposing party platforms. In 1892, when Buchanan ran for reelection, the Populists supported him and regular Democrats opposed him. Upper Cumberland counties that went to Buchanan in 1890 failed to do so in 1892: only in White County did he receive over 20 percent of the vote. The local Populist party dwindled. In 1896 when the Populists and Democrats fused behind William Jennings Bryan, the Upper Cumberland apostates came back into the Democratic fold and resumed their status as party regulars. Politics settled back into historical channels.[9]

To say that politicos in the Upper Cumberland followed state and national political contests with the fascinated attention reserved nowadays for organized sports is not intended to disparage either politics or sports. Men in the Upper Cumberland took their political contests seriously. Cordell Hull attested that he received his early political education by hanging around Upper Cumberland court-houses, listening to old men talk politics and dissect then-current issues such as the tariff. Certainly, throughout the 1890s Upper Cumberland newspapers ran columns of state and national news; some of this was boilerplate or patent outsides, but some was locally written and reflected editors' intense interest in the political scene. Politics, like sports, was intrinsically interesting. It mattered who won an election in the sense that victory matters in sporting contests; elections were contests of men or factions, of "us versus them," but rarely contests of ideas or issues.[10]

In 1908 Henry Rehorn, Jr., a miller in North Springs, a Jackson County hamlet, wrote a political satire for the county newspaper. Rehorn's article was an extended parody, supposedly of a speech by a Republican leader defending his party's tariff policies:

> The republican party hails with confidence the signs now ap-proaching of a complete restoration of business prosperity in all trade, commerce and manufacturing all over this mountainous country. . . . I have been told that Andrew Choat at the North Springs has started up his ax handle factory, and that Y. C. Clark, proprietor of the Star-Light Mills in Pine Lick has started up his large manufacturing plant. Mack Strode's saw mill is now in oper-ation on North Fork, a tributary of Jennings Creek not far from where the Anarchists had a candy pulling. . . . The woods are full of women digging ginseng and may-apple root, let us all sing for joy. Hams are worth 8 cents per pound at Mr. Kennedy's store by reason of protection to American industries.[11]

Although Rehorn meant to demonstrate the irrelevance of GOP politics to the everyday life of Jackson County farmers, his satire also indicates how distant the battles of national political parties were. What, indeed, did the tariff mean to Pine Lick? Existing on the periphery of the national market economy, Upper Cumberland residents were largely unaffected by tariff policies. And what impact did free gold or silver have on the barter exchange rates for eggs or ginseng? The state and national governments were a long way off, and representatives of their authority were rarely seen, except for judges, postal workers, and revenue agents. Technically the state general assembly created county governments and vested them with authority. In practice, once created, county governments functioned as autonomous units whose only responsibility to the state was to collect state taxes along with local taxes.[12]

The county courthouse symbolized the powers of civil government on the local level. The most imposing building in each Upper Cumberland county—built of brick or stone, two or three stories high, and often surmounted by a clock tower—the courthouse loomed over the false-fronted stores and wooden hotels built around the square. It was the physical center and focal point of the town. From the courthouse Tennessee counties ran school systems, built highways, doled out public charity, and enforced the law. At the courthouse, once every quarter, convened the basic governing body of the county, the county court.

County courts combined legislative and judicial functions. The courts were comprised of two justices of the peace from each county district. (The number of districts varied in 1890, from ten in Pickett County to twenty-two in DeKalb County.) As legislature, the courts set the county tax rate and appropriated county funds. However, each of the members was also a squire, a lower-level magistrate who could hear minor civil and criminal cases and marry people. The chief executive officer of the county was the chairman of the county court, the county judge.[13]

In addition to the county court Upper Cumberland voters elected a small slate of county officials: the county court clerk, who kept records of the court; the trustee, who collected taxes and kept the county books; the circuit court clerk; the register, who had perhaps the most important office in the courthouse, wherein was stored land titles; and the sheriff, who kept order and presided over the county jail.[14]

Usually the dominant party in the county, whether Republican or Democratic, controlled county offices. But there were notable exceptions. As the *Alexandria Times* editor complained in 1894, Democrats, being in the majority in the county, lacked party discipline and voted for candidates in the Democratic primary "on personal grounds, and from loyalty to a particular section," rather than choosing the best man for the party. This sometimes hurt the party in the general election.[15]

In local politics personal popularity or extensive family networks may have had as much impact on political success as good standing with party organizations. W. A. Hamby, Democrat, served as county judge in Republican Cumberland County for twenty-four years. The *Crossville Chronicle*, commenting on the prospects of a candidate for trustee, noted, "He has many relatives in the county and is well acquainted over the county. This with his personal character makes him a strong candidate." In addition voters had no compunction about returning popular men to office term after term. In 1902 the *Crossville Chronicle* noted that Hamby had grown gray in public service, the circuit court clerk was entering his third term of office, the trustee was retiring after holding office for three two-year terms, and the register, John Q. Burnett, was beginning his fifth four-year term. Of Burnett the paper noted, "When making the primary race the last time one of his opponents made the statement that 'in case he received the nomination this time the people had better make him a deed to the office for life and do away with the agitation over who shall be register.' Since such a course is impossible in fact the people have accepted it in spirit." Burnett's popularity stemmed from his personality: the paper called him "genial, generous" and "large-hearted" and noted that it had been "truthfully said, 'Every man, woman and child in the county has tasted salt out his smokehouse.'"[16]

If the courthouse proudly symbolized the power of government in any Upper Cumberland town, the way people in the region treated public buildings indicated their lack of interest in governance, as opposed to politics. Politics—the contest itself—fascinated county people. Governing, the business of maintaining institutions and supplying services, did not. Thus in 1915 the editor of the *Alexandria Times* complained about the DeKalb County courthouse:

The DeKalb County court house is a disgrace to the county. It is always dirty and if disease-breeding germs do not live there it is because they have not located the place. The doors are not only open, but are down and on the ground. Hogs make the court house a sleeping place and often walk about the lower floor through the day. There are holes in the ceiling[,] . . . in the floor, under the stairway and any number of windows broken. The walls are filthy. . . . DeKalb Co. is out of debt with money in the bank but one would never believe it to see its courthouse, which would not be a decent or sanitary place to milk a cow.[17]

Presumably Thomas Jefferson would have approved of the county governments of the Upper Cumberland; it is hard to imagine any governments that governed less. District justices' constituents only asked that taxes be kept low. Cash-poor farmers saw no need to fund extensive county services. Charged with maintaining schools, roads, and a minimal welfare system, county government often devolved authority to district level and acted more as coordinator than as governor. In the Upper Cumberland of the 1890s, local governments did only what local citizens would support. How this decentralized authority worked can best be illustrated by examining the three services operated by all the counties: school systems, road building, and charity.

As required by the state, all Upper Cumberland counties ran school systems offering free public education, paid for by a percentage of the land tax, a one-dollar poll tax, and monies received from the state. The county court appointed a superintendent of education, who was supposed to oversee county schools, but he had no control over hiring or budgeting. Each county was divided into school districts, and each district elected directors, who ran the local schools, hiring teachers and paying them with county warrants. Each school was basically a separate institution, reflecting community standards and needs. Schools ran for about three months a year, with the school term often broken for planting, harvesting, and bad weather.[18]

Teachers were part-time, ill-paid workers, not professionals. Most teachers received all their pedagogical training at county institutes held each fall. In 1893 Sam C. Brown, superintendent of Cumberland County schools, reported to a meeting of the state public school officers on a very successful institute held for two weeks in his county. Brown, who identified himself as representing "the 'hill country of Judea,'" where the children came to school when they got good and ready, was amazed and proud to report that all 106 teachers in the county had attended the institute and worked: "They stayed there for two weeks and answered at roll-call; answered every day." After such institutes teachers took a test. If they passed, they were licensed by the state, but the true requisite for employment was the goodwill of the local school directors. Young women taught school for a few years before marriage. Young men used teaching as a way-station to careers in business, law, or politics. Few teachers remained at any given school for more than one or two years.[19]

County education systems provided quantity, not quality, in education. Due to difficulties in transportation, counties tried to place a school within walking distance of all children in a county. As a result schoolhouses dotted the Upper Cumberland countryside; in 1920 Putnam County had seventy white and six black primary schools. There were only a few secondary (grades six through eight) schools in the region, and no public high schools. (It should be noted that although the schools were officially graded, in fact pupils studied at whatever skill level they could manage, and for as long as they pleased: a primary reading class might include children five to twenty years of age working their way through several different readers.)[20]

Few pupils continued in school past the primary level. Parents and students believed that education was supposed to prepare one for life. As a farmer and a citizen, one needed to be able to read and "figure," at least a little, although everyone knew people who managed to do without even minimal literacy. In 1902 the Southern Education Board reported illiteracy rates from 16 to 26 percent of the population in Upper Cumberland counties. Five years of schooling, it was believed, was enough time to learn to read, write, and count.[21]

The people of the Upper Cumberland did not exhibit hostility to education as such. Education was a component of status in the region. They admired people who could "write a pretty hand," do complicated arithmetic, or spell correctly. They especially admired the ability to turn an elegant rhetorical phrase in political or religious discourse. But these were special skills—social graces—not the kind of thing upon which a man's livelihood depended. For most of the farmers in the Upper Cumberland, education did not have a direct economic payoff. Consequently education past the primary level seemed a luxury, best paid for by the individual child's family and reserved for those who would be able to take advantage of it. Cordell Hull was one of five brothers attending primary school in the 1880s.

In 1885 the parents of students in Willow Grove school sponsored a series of debates (public speaking being one of the skills they wanted their sons to learn). Cordell's performance so impressed the community that his father decided to send him to school at a private academy. Hull remembered, "Generally the children of the section were given only a few years of free schooling and then were put to work on the farms. Only a few who showed outstanding promise were offered a chance to go on." One of his brothers was also deemed worth educating and became a doctor; two of his brothers were not, and while Cordell went on to political fame, they stayed in the Upper Cumberland and became raftsmen like their father.[22]

In the Upper Cumberland of the 1890s the state facilitated but did not control education. Communities ran schools and guarded jealously their local prerogatives. When a community had a particularly good school year—that is, when the teacher seemed competent and most of the local children attended most of the time—people in the community were wont to congratulate themselves in the local newspaper for putting on the best school ever and to exhort the community to bring it off again next year. School was not an institution but an impromptu performance, with the county inviting but not compelling attendance. Children still belonged to parents, not the state, and decisions concerning education were parental prerogatives. Since schooling was not compulsory, parents could—and many did—keep their children at home. If they chose to participate in public education, parents could exert much more control than would now be the case. In 1891 residents of Cumberland County complained that district school directors were too distant from the schools under their supervision and called for direct control of schools by the parents: "Why not give the people who have children to educate an opportunity to do it as they please?" one resident asked. What did the school board of a district, working without compensation, know of the needs of school patrons "perhaps ten miles or more from them"? Another correspondent, concerned that school districts were being consolidated (all "dumped into one") and thereby removed from direct parental control, said, "A school district is a neighborhood institution and next to the family circle in importance. Dear to us as children, and cherished by us as parents, we guard it with jealous care, and fight for it to the 'last ditch.' To put its affairs away from the control of the parents where children are directly interested, is contrary to the spirit of our institution, contrary to custom or precedent, contrary to right, justice or common sense."[23]

If counties educated their children in a decentralized and lackadaisical fashion, they built roads using methods that were authentically archaic. Well into the twentieth century, Upper Cumberland counties built and maintained their roads by the corvée, a labor draft with antecedents in medieval Europe. Each man owed the county a set number of days of labor per year (usually four to six days). He could work on the roads or pay a tax in cash. The county court appointed district road supervisors to enforce the corvée. In 1891 Cumberland County had fifty-eight supervisors. Unlike feudal lords, however, republican road supervisors had no real means to force work. Like revival preachers, they could exhort but could hardly compel; they could take a man to court for refusal to work the roads, but that cost money and time. They could count the days a man had worked on the road but had no way of making him work hard or efficiently. As might be expected, this system made for unreliable roads. Sometimes a community united for a road working day, complete with dinner provided by the local ladies. This was great fun, but more visiting and eating got done than actual work. Sometimes a farmer maintained the roads in front of his house, but most often roads were poorly built and badly maintained. As the *Cookeville Press* complained in 1895, "Generally speaking the public roads of this section are a disgrace to the people who are responsible for them. Many overseers believe a road has been thoroughly worked and repaired when a few decayed leaves are thrown into the wagon ruts, and old rotten chesnut [*sic*] bark is made to do duty in filling up and smothering over the many elegant hog wallows to be found in our highways."[24]

No farmer wanted a public highway bisecting his best fields. Accordingly, roads ran along fence lines or across patches of poor land. In places like Jackson County, roads ran along the edges of creeks or along the creek bed itself. In dry summers a creek bed was a level, graveled road, but in winter people prefaced promises to be somewhere at some specific time with "If the Lord is willing, and the creek don't rise." According to the columns in local newspapers, bad roads bothered people more than poor schools, but only rarely did folks call for an end to the corvée system. Rather, complaints tended to take the form of insistence that the system could work if people would just live up to their obligations.[25]

County governments also administered charity, making provisions for the care of paupers: persons too old, infirm, or handicapped to work. Counties took care of the poor by establishing poorhouses or county farms, where under the care of a county court-appointed overseer inmates put out crops and supported themselves as much as possible. Some counties also gave partial aid to people who needed a little help but were not so badly off that they had to be confined to the poorhouse. Since most families in the Upper Cumberland cared for their less fortunate relatives, the pauper population was quite small. In 1891 Cumberland County granted pauper allowances, ranging from $5 to $25, to twenty-one people, mostly female. In the 1890s Putnam County had, on average, ten paupers in the county poorhouse. In 1900 neighboring Cumberland County's poorhouse had only two inhabitants. According to county judge Hamby, "Other poor among their friends are well cared for and I know of no case of extreme destitution that our system of charity does not help to sustain." A year later, in 1901, the Cumberland County justices of the peace debated potential changes in the county charity system. Some wanted to abolish the poorhouse and return to the old system of "farming out" paupers, while others argued that all people on the county dole ought to be forced to live in the poorhouse because outrelief sometimes wound up in the hands of able-bodied but idle people and did not always benefit the unfortunates the court intended to help. The court decided to keep the mixed system as it was, convinced by arguments that confining all paupers would be too expensive and would mean that those receiving only partial aid would be cut off. The debate was remarkably free of any rancor toward the paupers; they were not seen as malingerers or as a potentially dangerous class but simply as unfortunate people to whom the county had a duty.[26]

Orphans under county care were farmed out. In 1901 the Cumberland County commissioner of the poor advertised "three children at the county house, one girl thirteen years old, one girl eleven years old, one boy eight years old. Any person that would like to adopt one or all of them for their board and clothes will please call."[27]

Elected sheriffs and district constables enforced the law in Upper Cumberland counties. The sheriff usually managed the county jail and often lived there with his family. District constables reported to district justices of the peace. Sheriff and constable alike received part of any fines levied on malefactors in magistrates' courts. The sheriff and constables were supposed to keep public order, a difficult thing to do in a country where alcohol was ubiquitous, most men owned guns, and violence in defense of honor was accepted as normal.[28]

Like the North Georgians studied by Edward Ayers, people in the Upper Cumberland were more prone to violence and disorderly conduct than to larceny. Circuit court and grand jury dockets printed in local newspapers indicate that most of the men who fell afoul of the law did so by fighting, gaming, drinking, carrying pistols, public profanity, and otherwise disturbing the peace. In 1896, when Putnam County built a new jail, the first two prisoners were charged with selling liquor and carrying a pistol, respectively. But using court records to judge the extent of violence prevalent in the Upper Cumberland in the 1890s and after will lead to an underestimation of violence in the region. County newspapers were full of complaints about disorder and stories about violent encounters, even killings.[29]

County law enforcement officials apparently did not ride out to apprehend lawbreakers unless invited to do so: in most cases the injured party, a friend, or a relative swore out a warrant before the sheriff got involved. In 1893 the DeKalb County grand jury complained that some parties had "committed offenses" but that "we know of no one who will agree or can be procured to become prosecutor." The grand jury called on the attorney general to file an indictment and prosecute the offenders.[30]

As an example of how the system worked, consider the case of Nat Hedgecoth. An elderly man, he was beaten and robbed by two young Cumberland County men, who also burned a shed belonging to a third man. A story appeared in the local paper detailing the crime and giving the names of the two assailants. No one would take action against the criminals, however, until Hedgecoth swore out a warrant. The editor of the local paper scolded Hedgecoth: "If Hedgecoth does not prosecute them vigorously he will neglect his plain duty as a citizen. He is a man as harmless, honest and inoffensive as anyone in the county, and is not made of the mould that would punish for mere revenge. Yet, in spite of all that, he has a duty that he owes to the community and himself, if he hopes to be safe from such abuses in the future."[31]

Drunken rowdies broke up evening church services in Putnam and White Counties and, the editor of the *Gainesboro Sentinel* complained, "monopolized" the public square in that river town, "cursing and blackguarding so that a peaceable man would hardly cross the square, and a lady could not without being insulted." At any public gathering one could expect that some of the crowd would be drinking, and most would be armed, if not with pistols then with knives. Volatile tempers fueled with illegal whiskey flared easily: men fought at elections, at parties, at school socials, over women, over money, and over insults. County newspapers called these brawls "affrays" or "difficulties" and carefully avoided indicating that any of the combatants were at fault for their participation.[32]

In 1903 the *Crossville Chronicle* printed a long, detailed murder story that indicates a great deal about public attitudes toward crime and law enforcement. Titled "Killed in Cold Blood," the story tells how Charles Turner, the twenty-one-year-old son of a poor Cumberland County farmer, got drunk and set out with a companion to avenge the theft of some chickens by John Rodgers, twenty-eight. Rodgers had supposedly threatened to kill Turner's father if any of the family had him indicted for theft. Rodgers was retarded, an amiable half-wit who worked for the Taylor family. Turner found Rodgers plowing at George Taylor's farm and, according to a witness, shot Rodgers while he dodged and circled around the mule and plow, pleading for his life. While the murderer fled, a coroner and jury came to the Taylor farm and viewed Rodgers' body where it fell; then the corpse was taken to the Taylor house and dressed for burial. The next morning the body was taken to the courthouse until burial the next day in the Crossville cemetery. Turner was arrested and charged with first degree murder. George Taylor hired a lawyer to assist the state prosecutor. Turner's father, the paper noted, had by hard work and economy "saved $200 cash. He gave this, his only horse, a one horse wagon and a mortgage on his farm as a fee to the lawyers" he hired for defense.[33]

The Rodgers case and the miscellaneous difficulties mentioned above illustrate the nature of justice in the region: it was personal, capricious, and uncertain. Sometimes men would be arrested for fighting, sometimes not. The jails held mostly men accused of misdemeanors. Arresting drunks was a reasonably safe way to earn the fees that made up most of law enforcement officials' pay. Sometimes a killing would outrage community sympathy, as in the Rodgers case, where the killer went too far by shooting a retarded man. Then public disapproval was immediate and vehement. Rodgers, surely one of the least powerful citizens of Cumberland County, was accorded high honor in his death and lay in state in the courthouse. The Taylor family, on whose land Rodgers was killed, acted as family members by hiring a prosecutor. This was a common expedient in the Upper Cumberland law courts, where justice was often revenge taken by legal means. On the other hand, if the person killed was someone people thought the community could well do without and if no one swore a warrant against the killer, the sheriff might ignore the whole matter.

The denouement of the Rodgers case also makes a point about Upper Cumberland justice: juries were inclined to be lenient. Despite public uproar over the killing and despite testimony that indicated the murder was premeditated, Turner was convicted of only second degree murder and was sentenced to fifteen years in the state penitentiary. Apparently the jury was moved by the fact that Turner had been drinking heavily when he killed Taylor and claimed he could not remember the crime. The verdict disgusted spectators and was condemned as contrary to the evidence by the trial judge, Cordell Hull. Nonetheless, the newspaper noted, no one blamed Turner's family for doing their best to get their relative acquitted.[34]

Families intent on avenging or protecting a member seem to have proceeded on the assumption that it would be easier to get forgiveness from the courts than justice for past wrongs. In the 1890s a Jackson County man, Isaac Jaques, was acquitted for the murder of his brother-in-law Si Anderson. Jaques moved to Cumberland County to get away from Anderson's family. Three years later Jaques, with his wife, came to the Putnam County fair. He was outside the fairgrounds talking horses with friends when two young men approached and asked him if he were the man who killed Si Anderson. Apparently Jaques did not recognize the young men as the brothers of the man he had killed. When he acknowledged his identity, "one of the boys behind Jaques immediately fired and the shot struck the man in the neck, breaking it and causing instant death.

Then both brothers emptied their pistols in his body, shooting him in all seven times, any shot of which would have been fatal. After the man fell and their pistols had been emptied, they then jumped off their horses and stomped the dead man in the face." The men were captured by the crowd, arrested, and sent to the jail in Lebanon. It was expected that in court they would "make a vigorous fight as their family is abundantly able to pay the expense."[35]

The Anderson family fulfilled that expectation and in such style as to become part of regional folklore. While they awaited trial in Cookeville, the young men entertained crowds that gathered outside the jail to hear them play fiddle and banjo in the jail cell. Their father, a locally famous Union cavalry captain, hired Henry Clay Snodgrass of Sparta to defend the boys. Snodgrass was renowned for his eloquence as attorney and his capacity as tippler: according to legend, during the trial Snodgrass kept a coffee pot filled with equal proportions of coffee and whiskey on the attorneys' table. Perhaps due to Snodgrass's skill, perhaps because the jury saw them as justly avenging the earlier murder of their brother, the Andersons were acquitted.[36]

County newspaper editors put the blame for violence on liquor and the practice of carrying weapons. In 1898 the editor of the *Gainesboro Sentinel* called for a law prohibiting the carrying of arms: "The practice is wholly indefensible, and to it is directly traceable many unprovoked murders." After such a law was passed, indictments for "carrying pistol" became as common in the Upper Cumberland courts as those for public drunkenness, with an equivalent lack of effect. Exasperated, Judge C. E. Snodgrass in 1907 concluded a Cumberland County carrying pistol case before him by taking the gun in question down to the local blacksmith's shop, where the judge had the weapon disassembled and beaten to bits. The editor of the Crossville paper applauded: "Make it as hard as possible to get whiskey and destroy every pistol that the law will permit to be destroyed."[37]

In 1901 a shooting affray in which one man was killed provoked the editor of the *Sentinel* to ask, "What value do we place on human life, is a question that has forced itself on our minds by the events of the past 12 months. Another life has been taken in this county, making six within a year." (The editor was careful, however, to make it clear that he was not commenting on the justification for any of the killings.) In that same year the editor of the *Crossville Chronicle* signaled a change in public acceptance of violence when he deplored the lynching of a white man (accused of raping a white girl) in Smithville on the grounds that "So gross disregard for human life is not only an infringement upon law and order, but *a menace to business growth and development*."[38]

The culture of the region, then, impeded business growth. Politics was so divorced from policy as to make the concept of using government to promote a social agenda alien to the culture of the region. Politics was a contest of families and factions, an affirmation of family heritage. People voted for candidates because of who they were, not what they promised to do. Few people seemed to want elected officials to do anything except keep taxes low and leave them alone. As a result local governments did very little, and local people liked it that way. They cherished local control; hated taxes; considered education a matter of family, not state, concern; and worked out their "difficulties" with knife and gun. Family mattered more than any other institution, and vengeance was more worthy than abstract notions of law and order. Lacking institutions of social control, people in the region depended on the morality of the individual to keep order. Small wonder, then, that religious folk, who derived morality from the Bible, insisted that to doubt the book was to strike at the foundations of society.

Such were the cultural biases with which the residents of the countryside entered the twentieth century. To work changes in the region, to do things as simple as building better schools and highways, would require an assault on the assumptions folk in the region had built their lives on for generations. In the early twentieth century rural progressives asked the people of the Upper Cumberland to do just that; the progressives had their work cut out for them.

5

RAILROAD DREAMS

CASH COMES TO THE CUMBERLANDS

In the 1890s the Upper Cumberland's long-standing isolation ended when a Nashville entrepreneur built a railroad through the hill country. Improved transportation had an immediate impact on the Upper Cumberland economy, facilitating intensive exploitation of the region's coal fields and timber stands. The pace of the economy quickened, since trade no longer depended on the "tides" of the river. The railroad also transformed the quality of economic exchange, introducing the cash economy to the region. The local people adjusted but not without confusion and violence.

The railroad whistle echoing through the hills did not signal the death of family-based, semisubsistence farming and the birth of commercialized agriculture in the region. Instead farm families added new activities to the patchwork of enterprises that traditionally furnished sustenance on a small farm. To acquire cash, farmers harvested their timber as if it were fields of wheat. Farm women marketed more surplus to regional produce houses. By making possible these new sources for income, the railroad, ironically, allowed small farms to survive longer than might otherwise have been possible. Rather than letting cash completely transform the local economy, Upper Cumberland farm families made the new economic opportunities fit into their old ways of life.

The railroad made both transportation and communication easier. Before 1890 a traveler headed from Nashville to Cookeville and points beyond had to take a stagecoach, one of the last in the state. By the early twentieth century, wealthy Cookevillians could send their daughters by rail to weekly music lessons at Ward-Belmont in Nashville and expect them home by supper. The world became smaller, and that had a profound effect. With increased communication came increased awareness of events—political, social, and intellectual—outside the Upper Cumberland's green forested walls. Thus in the early twentieth century the progressive movement came to the hills of Tennessee.[1]

> Come, let us sing together
> And Let Railroad be Our Theme
> Till, with hearts light as a feather,
> We shall realize our dream.
>
> . . . .
>
> Don't you hear that jarring rumbling
> Like young earthquakes out at play
> Tis the rocks and mountains tumbling
> To prepare the railroad's way.
>
> See the headlights dancing, flashing,
> Through the darkness down the vale,
> Hear the rattling, jangling, cracking
> Of the monster on the rail.
>
> And great God! what awful screaming!
> Surely 'tis the knell of doom!
> No, my friend, you're only dreaming
> That the railroad's surely come.[2]

This paean to railroads could have come from any Upper Cumberland paper. Throughout the region newspaper editors assumed that if a railroad were built through their town, prosperity would follow. On the plateau, land and development companies owned thousands of acres of forests that they wanted to harvest, and potentially rich coal fields could not be developed at a profit until transport in the region improved. For years the *Allardt Gazette* speculated each week about Fentress County's railroad prospects. In the *Smith County Press* a Cookeville correspondent wrote in 1884, "Let us all begin the new year, set aside resolutions that we will no longer be shut out from the outside world in these mountains, but cry aloud for a railroad."[3]

The first steel rails snaked through the steep hills east of Nashville in search of coal and timber. Capitalists had been talking about the potential wealth lying undeveloped under the Cumberland Plateau since the Civil War. The exploitation of the eastern part of the region began in the postwar period. But development of the western plateau, which ran through Cumberland, Fentress, Putnam, and White Counties in the Upper Cumberland, awaited rail access. The one major exception was the Bon Air coal field in White County, developed in the 1880s by George Dibrell of Sparta, a well-connected Democratic power broker and former Confederate general.[4]

To reach Bon Air the Nashville, Chattanooga and St. Louis Railway extended a spur line into White County. The economic effects of this one rail line foreshadowed what rail connections would do for the region as a whole. Between 1888 and 1904 coal companies built four towns on Bon Air Mountain. Bon Air Coal itself employed 600 men, including many county natives, who mined under the supervision of immigrant Scots. The spur line also accelerated the exploitation of the county's timber. By 1899 the county had twenty sawmills, an axe handle factory, and a spoke factory. Between June 1898 and June 1899 the county shipped by rail over 1,000 cars of wood industry products.[5]

A Pennsylvania iron manufacturer built the Upper Cumberland's next rail line. Alexander Crawford, having purchased thousands of acres of western plateau land without rail connections, began construction of the Nashville and Knoxville Railroad (N&K) at Lebanon (forty miles east of Nashville) in 1885. After his death the Crawford family interests continued the line, which reached Cookeville in 1890.[6]

The rest of the region languished without rail connections. The

Cumberland Plateau was in a neutral zone between the mighty Louis-ville and Nashville Railroad (L&N) (which owned the NC&StL) and the Southern Railway, which ran through East Tennessee. In letters, the presidents of the L&N and the Southern Railway referred to the "isthmus" separating their rival interests and agreed that neither would extend tracks into the region. To cross the isthmus might set off unwanted competition between the two great railroads.[7]

Nashville entrepreneur Jere Baxter crossed the isthmus, defying the L&N and making himself a legend in the Upper Cumberland with the construction of the Tennessee Central (TC) line between Nashville and Knoxville. Chartered in 1893 the TC reached Knox-ville in 1902, running through Smith, Putnam, and Cumberland Counties in the Upper Cumberland. To complete his line Baxter bought the N&K from the Crawfords, fought the L&N, suffered through the depression of 1893, and went into receivership. He res-urrected his company and went ahead, laying track across forested mountains and bridging deep river gorges.[8]

Baxter completed the connections through Cumberland County by September 18, 1900. Encouraged by "the promise of several kegs of beer," two crews, one working from Monterey and one from Har-riman, raced to complete this last stretch of track in the Upper Cum-berland. The TC reached Knoxville in 1902. Although the TC as a company never attained financial stability, the line's checkered finan-cial history made little difference to the people of the Upper Cum-berland. There, Baxter became a hero.[9]

The TC immediately changed the local economies of the counties through which it passed by introducing large quantities of cash. As a Cumberland County reporter noted in 1899, the TC paid out about $45,000 in one week, and "the spreading of this much cash once a month makes Klondike times over here." In the *Crossville Chronicle* another correspondent exulted that "conditions have changed since Col. Baxter has turned his herd of iron horses loose, running across the Cumberland Plateau. Today every man that wants work can get it at good wages and get his pay regularly. Mr. Editor, it almost looks incredible to see the progress made in this county since the advent of the T.C."[10]

The railroad paid, but it also expected people to pay to ride or to ship goods, a sentiment not necessarily shared by every native in the Upper Cumberland. In 1901 the TC announced that "no freight shall be delivered to any one, except persons who have made special arrangements with the company, until all charges are paid." The Crossville paper explained, "If you don't send the cash when you send for your freight, don't be surprised if the agent refuses to let it go. Such a course may seem too exacting to some, but it is only good business and no one should complain. Corporations do not conduct their business on the loose methods employed by most individuals."[11]

Sometimes the railroad's expectations and those of the natives clashed directly and violently. In 1894 three horsemen attacked an N&K train in Putnam County because the conductor had ejected one of their number who was riding without a ticket. According to the *Cookeville Press*,

> On the afternoon of Christmas day, as the evening train from Lebanon to Cookeville stopped at the water tank at the west end of the Caney Fork bridge, three toughs rode up on horseback and demanded that conductor W. B. Duke come out, as they wanted to be revenged for some imaginary wrong that he had done in putting some dead beat off a day or so before; they also accused the trainmen of confiscating a jug of whiskey that they supposed came up for them. When they found that Mr. Duke would not comply, they began cursing, yelling and shooting their revolvers in all directions. . . .
>
> The train pulled out, and the rowdies forded the river and arrived at Buffalo Valley, a mile distant, a few minutes later, and where the train had stopped to unload freight. Here they proceeded to repeat some of their former tactics. Not satisfied, they piled chicken coops, rail, etc., on the track under the coaches to prevent the train from pulling ahead. Finally one of the train crew, in a very perilous situation, succeeded in removing the obstacles on the track, and signaled the engineer to go ahead, and as the train started off at a brisk rate, the desparadoes [*sic*] threw another chicken coop under the rear coach, nearly wrecking it.[12]

Although the newspaper indignantly condemned the attackers, in fact their behavior was not unusual. Many Upper Cumberland men celebrated Christmas by going on an extended binge, and any public gathering might be disrupted by inebriated, pistol-carrying rowdies. The toughs had no reason to know that the railroad operated by different rules and that it was inappropriate as well as illegal to extract physical revenge for a commercial transaction.

Businessmen quickly understood the new rules. In 1903, three years after the TC came through Crossville, the county paper commented, "No one change that has come over the people of this country more broadly marks the advancement than the change in the business methods of the people. A few years ago if you sent a person a bill for what they owed they felt offended because they took it as a reflection on their integrity. Today there is scarcely a business man in the country who does not present bills to his debtors the first of each month, and no one thinks of being offended." It had also become common to turn accounts over to lawyers for collection. Perhaps as a result attorneys proliferated in the railroad towns. In the 1870s Crossville, then a village of 100 souls, had no resident lawyers. By 1906 the town's population had grown to 528, and the town had 15 lawyers.[13]

Banks followed the trail of cash the TC laid. Putnam County, bankless until 1889, by 1914 had two fiercely competitive banks in the county seat, and banks had been created in four outlying communities. In Cumberland County local merchants organized the Bank of Crossville in 1899. Deposits grew from $8,785 in 1900 to $88,000 six years later.[14]

As commerce in the region grew, so did towns. TC depots became nuclei for new communities. Baxter and Algood, in Putnam County, and Rickman, north of Cookeville in Overton County, began as TC depots. In 1893 members of the Cumberland Mountain Coal Company founded Monterey, by 1900 Putnam County's second largest town. From Monterey the coal company directed mining camps in Putnam, Fentress, and Overton Counties. Monterey also became a popular summer resort, offering a choice of eight hotels in which refugees from Nashville's summer heat could enjoy the cool plateau nights.[15]

After 1900 local transportation patterns gradually adapted to the railroad. The river still carried much trade, but the railroad was more reliable. As a result even areas well off the TC tracks often received freight and travelers via the railroad. Travelers to Macon County took either the L&N to Hartsville, in Trousdale County, or the TC to Carthage. Teamsters carted freight for Jackson and Clay Counties

Map 3. The Upper Cumberland, 1903. Note the completed Tennessee Central Railroad line.

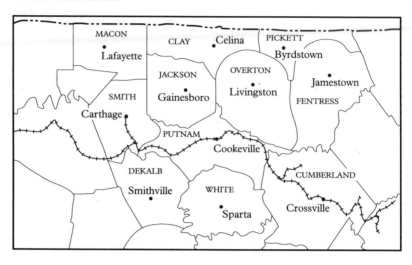

down from the railhead at Double Springs, in Putnam County. An independently owned spur line connected Livingston, the county seat of Overton, with the TC lines in Putnam County. (The spur line transported passengers on a steam-powered trolley, the only one in the region, affectionately called Phebe by the locals in honor of the line's female owner.)[16]

Because so much of the Upper Cumberland economy hinged on TC transportation, the railroad's reports to the Interstate Commerce Commission can serve as a rough guide to the state of the regional economy. The railroad ran from Nashville to Knoxville and from Nashville to Clarksville. The TC's reports list what the railroad shipped and whether the items originated on the line, but do not tell where on the line the shipments originated. The reports are therefore a crude source for information about any part of the territory served by the TC. Nevertheless they give a macrocosmic view of the economy of the region between Nashville and Knoxville, of which the Upper Cumberland was the principal western part. A comparison of the TC's 1905 and 1915 ICC reports also indicates how the regional economy developed in response to improved access to markets.

The Tennessee Central's ICC reports show a familiar picture: the classic extractive economy, in which raw materials drawn from a rural hinterland are shipped to urban centers for processing. Coal and forest products accounted for the greatest tonnage of shipping

Table 3. Tennessee Central Freight

	Tons Originating on the TC Line	
	1905	1925
Agricultural products		
Grain	10,892	35,088
Livestock	7,182	9,456
Poultry	412	4,656
Fruits and vegetables	341	1,831
Total	18,827	51,031
Extractive industries		
Coal	164,806	245,706
Forest products[a]	178,453	153,003
Total	343,259	398,709
Manufactures[b]	52,846	68,015

Source: Tennessee Central Railroad, Annual Reports to the Interstate Commerce Commission, 1905, 1915, Tennessee Central Railroad Papers.
[a]In 1905 this category included lumber, staves, logs, tanbark, and ties. In 1910 and 1915 the category included lumber and unspecified forest products.
[b]Manufactures included petroleum, sugar, naval stores, iron, machinery, metal, cement, brick, lime, agricultural implements, wagons, household goods, furniture, liquor, and beer.

originating on the TC lines. Exports of coal increased from 1900 through 1915. However, shipments of timber peaked in 1910 and began to decline thereafter. The manufactures on the TC tonnage charts mostly came from Nashville, Knoxville, or cities outside the region.[17]

After the TC came through, the development of the western plateau coal fields proceeded rapidly but unevenly. For three decades a variety of coal companies opened seams, built towns, exhausted their mines and moved on, or had financial troubles and sold out or disappeared, leaving few records behind. It is hard to determine how many companies operated in the Upper Cumberland and how many people they employed. However, the coal industry had two relatively stable centers in the Upper Cumberland: the Bon Air fields, at the southern end of the Upper Cumberland coal range, and the complex of mines at Davidson-Wilder, on the northern edge of the coal range in Fentress and Overton Counties.[18]

From the 1890s through the 1930s the coals towns illustrated most dramatically how the railroad had changed the Upper Cumberland economy. Coal miners depended completely on public work for survival; their fortunes rose and fell with the national market. But coal miners, greatly in the minority in the region, lived in isolated coal towns up on the plateau at the end of the railroad lines. In 1930, as in 1890, most people in the Upper Cumberland were not involved in the mining industry.[19]

The TC meant different things to coal company executives on the plateau and to the farmers who made up the region's majority. The railroad had been built to facilitate the extraction of coal and timber, and it did so. However, the line also made it possible for farmers to ship out increasing amounts of livestock and poultry. The tonnage of poultry originating on the TC is a feather in the balance of the coal tonnage carried on the railroad, but the wealth produced by the sale of agricultural products was much more widely distributed throughout the region.

The local economy depended on the labor of all members of farm families. The developing cash economy did not change that. Far from abandoning family self-sufficiency for market agriculture, farm families used newly available public work to add cash to the family economy. Rather than transforming Upper Cumberland agriculture, the railroad made it possible for farmers to persist in traditional ways and allowed young families to stay in the region and on the farm.

That better transportation did not transform local agriculture can be illustrated by comparing statistics from the 1890 and 1910 censuses. In those two decades the number of farms in ten of the eleven Upper Cumberland counties increased. Farm size in the region decreased. Tenancy increased in every county, with the greatest increase coming between 1890 and 1900. Farms shrank in size, and more farmers were tenants. Yet the way farmers in the region operated did not change. In 1910 Upper Cumberland farmers grew the same crops and raised the same animals as their fathers had in 1890. Corn was still the staple crop, and hogs, running loose to fatten on the mast in the forests, were still the most numerous farm animals. Upper Cumberland wives still put out big gardens and cared for flocks of chickens. Farm production did not grow to match the increased number of farms, however; the average acres per farm in corn and wheat and the number of hogs and cattle per farm all declined.[20]

Table 4. Tenancy Rates by County, 1890–1910

	1890	1900	1910
Clay	27.4	39.5	44.2
Cumberland	20.5	21.2	21.9
DeKalb	19.9	33	36.2
Fentress	33.5	30.5	32.6
Jackson	40.9	43.4	44.1
Macon	26.7	33.7	33.8
Overton	27.9	35.2	38.6
Pickett	32.6	32.3	32.5
Putnam	17.7	35	33.2
Smith	27.8	37.2	37.6
White	26.4	28.3	31.6
Regional average	27.4	33.6	35.2

Sources: 1890, 1900, and 1910 *Census of Agriculture.*

How was this possible? Farming in the same old way on smaller and smaller plots of land without significantly increasing production per acre, Upper Cumberland farm families should have been sliding into acute poverty. This may have been the case, especially for tenants, who had to pay rent and feed families with not much more than the proverbial forty acres and a mule. Yet reading the Upper Cumberland press for the period from 1900 through 1910 leaves the impression that farmers in the hill country, like others throughout the nation, were enjoying years of unusual prosperity, not suffering a decline in the quality of their lives.

The pattern makes more sense when examined in light of what is known about the family economy—family in this case meaning the extended, multigenerational family. Tenancy strongly correlated with youth. In 1900 just over half of all male farmers in their thirties owned their land; 70 percent of those in their forties owned land. Conversely, all the farmers under twenty were tenants, and almost 70 percent of those in their twenties were tenants. The increase in tenancy in the 1890s does not seem to have affected all age groups; this would suggest that the increase was not related to the national depression during that decade. Instead, fathers owned land, and sons (the generation coming of age just as the railroad came through) were tenants. The increase in tenancy may represent a decline in out-migration. For generations, pressure on the land in the region had led numbers of young men and women to leave the Upper Cumberland for lands farther west. If out-migration declined and more of the younger generation stayed home, the results would be just as outlined above: more families on the land and more tenancy.

But there would not necessarily be more poverty. Access to the railroad meant that as farm size declined, farmers could turn to a new cash crop: the region's abundant forests. For decades many Upper Cumberland farmers had worked part of each year as loggers, and they continued to do so after the TC came through. But rail access made it possible to open planing mills, spoke factories, and other industries that exploited the region's timber. Upper Cumberland men worked as loggers for companies that bought large tracts of plateau timber; they worked in sawmills and wood product factories. Many also interacted with timber companies as independent contractors, selling semiprocessed logs and wood blocks for staves and spokes.

For some farmers timber products became a principal "crop." In 1901 the Cumberland County paper noted that since the TC had come through, a stave mill and a planing mill had opened in Crossville: "The stave mill in particular is doing a good business and putting from $500 to $600 a week in the hands of the farmers of this county." A stave mill owner advertised that he would pay $16 to $17 per thousand stave bolts delivered to the TC depots at Crab Orchard and Ozone. The farmers responded. As a local man ruefully recalled, "We would take a load of timber to town and bring back a sack of corn and a bale of hay and have a little change to jingle in our pocket. We were so anxious to get a dollar that we cut much of our chesnut [sic] timber for tanbark." A Crossville reporter in 1901 found that all along the TC lines "thousands of feet of timber, handles, crossties, etc., . . . were stacked along the grade and standing on the side tracks and in the various stations." In 1903 the White County paper, assessing the farmers' economic prospects, listed the good cash prices being paid for spoke and stave timber along with prices for farm produce and livestock.[21]

These wood product industries fit, as logging had, into the old economy with minimal disruption. Farmers who sold stave bolts or timber to factory owners apparently did not think that they were doing public work. They were still farmers, supplementing the farm income with some work in the woods or at the sawmill, pioneers in the sort of dual employment now typical of the rural South. In many ways this was a conservative, safety-first strategy. Because they could get money by selling timber, few Upper Cumberland farmers found it necessary to try innovative agricultural methods or new crops.[22]

In 1901, just after the railroad came through Cumberland County, the newspaper editor there became concerned that the county's economy in general, and farmers in particular, were becoming too dependent on the timber industry: "Industries that utilize the timber of this section are very desirable, but not so much as those enterprises that tend to build up and assist the development of our agricultural resources. . . . Special effort should be put forth to secure these, as they may be made a permanent thing, whereas, woodworking plants can only be transitory at best."[23] In 1908 the paper urged farmers to return to the plow and warned that a minor depression made the future uncertain:

> For three or four years past, and to some extent, almost every year since the railroad was built through this county, there have been a goodly number of men who formerly made a crop each year, who have reckoned because they could go into the woods with an axe or with a team . . . and make from a dollar to three or four dollars each day, that they could afford to drop farming either in whole or in great part . . . and trust to buying corn. . . .
>
> This isn't an argument against taking all the jobs that pay, it is only insisting that a good field of corn is a very convenient thing from the time of roasting ears until the last nubbin and bind of fodder is fed to Pete and Bet, and that every ear raised doesn't have to be bought for corn at 70 to 80 cents per bushel.[24]

The Crossville editor sounded a note of warning that would become more common in Upper Cumberland papers as the years passed: what would happen to the local economy when the last marketable timber had been extracted? Editors and correspondents advised farmers to put more effort into new kinds of agriculture. Why not grow truck crops for shipment to the cities?

On the traditional Upper Cumberland farm, women produced truck crops. When farmers stopped growing corn and looked to the forests for a cash crop, their wives went right on feeding the family as they always had. Editors who wanted Upper Cumberland farms to ship more garden produce to Tennessee cities were probably talking to the wrong member of the family when they addressed the husband. The farmer's wife was already taking advantage of her new economic opportunities, marketing produce and especially chickens.

Produce men, operating out of towns on the TC or the river, sent wagons into the countryside. Farmers and their wives could also bring their goods to market in most county seats. In the 1910s the local paper in Overton County noted that "thousands of dollars worth of farm products, poultry, live stock, forest products etc. are brought here each week and sold or shipped to other markets." In 1899 White County had six dealers in produce as well as merchants who took "country produce" in barter. One merchant estimated that between January and June 1899 he had shipped out of the county 250,000 pounds of dried fruit, 160,000 pounds of hens, 52,000 pounds of frying chickens, 291,200 pounds of eggs, 81,000 pounds of hides, 2,400 pounds of beeswax, 2,000 pounds of feathers, and 300 pounds of ginseng. Of that quantity of farm produce, only the hides did not represent the productive labor of farm women.[25]

Putnam County became a center for the poultry trade. According to local historian Mary Jean DeLozier, "From 1890 to 1920 sales of chickens and eggs brought more money into Putnam County than any other farm product." Algood, a TC depot, billed itself as "The Chicken Capital of the World." In March and April the produce men announced chicken days. Farm families brought their spring chickens (young, tender fowl) to market. The birds went by rail from Cookeville and Algood to the Northeast.[26]

In 1905 Rob Roy, editor of the *Alexandria Times,* commented on the changes that the railroad had brought to his little town in DeKalb County. He found the greatest progress in the local produce business. Ten years earlier, "the merchants exchanged goods for . . . eggs, butter and other produce . . . because they thought they had to, and were glad to dispose of it to the first wagon passing through to Nashville." Now, Roy said, produce men paid out $75,000 annually for country produce and shipped eggs and dressed poultry by rail to far distant markets. Chickens from DeKalb County wound up on trans-Atlantic steamers, according to Roy, who marveled, "Did you ever think that the chickens you raise and sell from your yards would ever be eaten in mid-ocean?"[27]

Women raised chickens and garden truck, but who got the money? The profits could be sizable. In 1910 receipts for poultry and eggs ranged from $9,388 in Fentress County to $108,911 in DeKalb County. By law in Tennessee married women had no independent property. But local tradition indicates that in many families egg money was the rural equivalent of an urban middle-class housewife's pin money: hers to do with as she pleased. This was money earned by productive work, however, not received as an allowance.[28]

In the Upper Cumberland men and women responded to new economic opportunities by making those opportunities fit into traditional economic patterns and gender roles. Life on the farm continued much as it always had. Men supplemented farm incomes by selling timber; women sold chickens, eggs, and garden truck to produce houses. Barter continued to be very common, but families had more cash. Banks grew, and people learned that some forms of business transactions required money up front. The result, by the eve of World War I, was not a new kind of economy but an economy with new elements patched and fitted into old. In fact, like patches on an old quilt, the new elements helped to hold together the old and made possible the continuance of traditional ways of life.

Or, as rural progressives lamented, there was not much progress. The progressive movement's arrival in the Upper Cumberland coincided with the railroad's. In the Upper Cumberland, progressives attacked local culture, which was seen as impeding economic development. Progressives wanted less violence, less liquor, more order, better schools, better churches, and better roads. If they succeeded, they believed, the local people could take advantage of the opportunities the new economy afforded. If they lost, the progressives warned, the people of the Upper Cumberland would be left behind to become "hewers of wood and drawers of water."

From 1915 to 1974, the photographers of the Harding Studio in Cookeville, Tennessee, made pictures of the people around them. The negatives of their photographs wound up in the Tennessee Technological University archives, but no identifying information accompanied the negatives. The pictures on the following pages appear to have been made between the 1910s and the early 1930s. We do not know who these people are or exactly when the pictures were made, although surmises can be made from the content of the images themselves. Lacking the usual documentary information, we must rely solely on the images themselves. And in the images we see a fascinating record of country people, their surroundings, and their lives:

A young woman with her photo album and young men with their prized pistols and banjo.

The contrast of youth and age.

A family, complete with dog, ranged before the porch.

A school where the children have no shoes, but the teacher, hardly more than a child herself, stands proudly in her high-button boots.

A family making a record of its grief.

The brocade of a casket shining against wood and stone.

Men working in the log woods.

Chickens from Overton County.

Town merchants lounging nonchalantly in their gleaming hardware emporium.

A country store.

Fox hunters, guns, horns, kills.

In a home economics class, calm, clean domesticity.

A young woman with her Victrola (a gift? or did she buy it with money she earned?)

A young beauty, evidence that the Roaring Twenties reached rural Tennessee.

Finally, a couple, posed on their porch for the photographer, along with objects that must have had some special meaning for them— baskets of eggs, new-hatched chicks, an American flag—the man holding an autoharp and a bouquet of flowers, the woman with hands folded in (surely) Sunday repose.

6

PROGRESS AND RESISTANCE, 1900-1917

THE STRUGGLE FOR GOOD ROADS

From 1900 to 1917 Upper Cumberland progressives, often affiliated with national reform groups, organized reform crusades combining economic, religious, and social rationales for change. Progressives were future-minded, community-oriented reformers united by their attitudes and beliefs. Other than that, they were not much different from their neighbors. The region's most noticeable reformers came from the towns. They tended to be professionals or businessmen, or their wives. They were literate and could read local and state newspapers, write essays for the local press, and correspond with state-level reform groups. These qualities made some progressives more obvious but should not be confused with defining characteristics. Some farmers were progressives, and some middle-class, professional, educated town folk fought reform. Therefore, progressives must be defined by what they stood for, not who they were.

In the spring of 1900 a Gainesboro newspaper editor published a list of needed reforms for his town that could stand as a regional progressive agenda. Gainesboro needed, he said,

Less whiskey.
Less shooting on streets.
Better order.
Cleaner streets.
A good school.
A new courthouse.
Fewer loafers.
A Law and order League, and the backbone to support it.
No scandal mongers.
No drunkards.
No gamblers.
Harmony in social, religious and business life.
More industry.
The law enforced.
No walking saloons.
No "blind tigers."[1]

This list illustrates how progressive goals in the region combined the religious with the economic, and the social with the political. To succeed, progressives would have to reform the region's culture.[2]

Progressives wanted a series of interlocking reforms to create a more orderly, prosperous society in the region. Good roads would facilitate access to markets, churches, and schools; schools would teach good citizenship, proper consumer attitudes, and market-oriented farming; better-educated citizens would support law and order. To promote these ends progressives used secular and religious means. They wanted ministers to preach sermons in favor of good roads and education, and they wanted teachers to read the Bible in the public schools as an aid to public morality. They believed that orderly communities with good schools and socially minded churches would attract capital to the Upper Cumberland; conversely, local people needed to be educated to take advantage of the economic opportunities offered by increased access to markets. To attain this desirable future, progressives wanted local people to accept higher taxes now.

In many cases people who led reforms in the Upper Cumberland had vested economic interests in the outcome. Thus educators led the better-schools movement. The good-roads movement received its greatest support from merchants and farmers who hoped to benefit from better transportation. Like so many reformers, Upper Cumberland progressives hoped to do good (for their neighbors and posterity) and do well for themselves.

In many ways Cookeville businessman Jere Whitson exemplified the quintessential Upper Cumberland progressive. Whitson, a native of the region, went to work in 1869 at age sixteen as a clerk in a Cookeville store. For the next twenty years he operated stores in different parts of Putnam County. In 1890 he and his wife, Parizetta, daughter of a prominent Putnam County farmer, moved back to Cookeville in time to participate in that town's railroad-induced boom. Whitson became one of Cookeville's most prominent businessmen, running a general hardware and furniture store. He sold buggies and high-quality horses, was involved in the timber business, and opened the first funeral home in Cookeville.[3]

Whitson was "inseparably linked with the development and growth of the Upper Cumberland country," according to the local press. Active in Democratic politics, he worked for statewide prohibition and was a leader of the local Church of Christ, but he made his greatest contribution to his town in education. Whitson and other members of the Cookeville Church of Christ in 1909 chartered Dixie College, a private school for preachers that would also provide high school classes for local boys and girls. Whitson presided over Dixie College's board of trustees, and he donated twelve acres of land for the campus. The school opened in 1912 with 100 pupils and offered classes in Bible, science, literature, music, business, and agriculture as well as normal training for teachers. The city of Cookeville combined its Central High School with Dixie College.[4] Whitson wrote to the *Gospel Advocate* that the school was "solid" and "practical." He concluded by using the school to boost the town: "Many people have come and are coming to Cookeville, where they not only have the advantage of Dixie College for their larger and more advanced children, but also the opportunity to send their smaller children to one of the best public schools *free*, and where they find electric lights, city water, and nearly all the conveniences to be found in the city."[5]

In 1915 Whitson and other Cookeville businessmen, in combination with some of the Upper Cumberland's most powerful politicians, succeeded in getting Dixie College transformed into a state-supported college, Tennessee Polytechnic Institute. The college drew students from the entire region, many of whom settled in Cookeville (and, presumably, became customers for Jere Whitson and the other businessmen in town).[6]

Like other regional progressives Whitson had many interests that he could promote simultaneously. His support for a religious school helped his business, and his political abilities helped his town. As his town grew, so did his business, and so on. In 1922, when he and Parizetta celebrated their golden wedding anniversary, Cookeville political and business leaders praised them as "among the guiding spirits of the progress, citizenship and character" of the past fifty years.[7]

Under the leadership of regional progressives like Whitson, Cookeville and other Upper Cumberland towns became much more progressive than the surrounding countryside, willing to support good schools, highway building programs, and tighter law enforcement. But outside the towns, Upper Cumberland progressives had limited success, even though progressives insisted, with much justification, that the region's long-term prosperity depended on adoption of their program. They reacted to opposition by attributing venality, backwardness, and sheer wrongheadedness to their opponents. How else to explain resistance to progress?

Progressive reforms required that certain deeply held cultural values be modified or jettisoned. Most reforms would violate localist sentiment by transferring control of institutions to the county or even the state. School reformers contradicted ingrained familism by insisting that the child was an individual, due certain rights and privileges and existing in a relationship with the state that overrode a father's property rights to his or her labor. Progressive reforms would cost money, and the region's voters had a long-standing aversion to raising taxes. They also feared bond issues: public debt to small farmers was the same thing as private mortgage, and to be shunned. In addition, progressive reforms by their nature required a drastic readjustment of local attitudes toward government. Local governments in the region did very little. Progressives wanted government to act to better the lives of the governed—whether the governed agreed that their lives needed improvement or not. Finally, progressives called for the creation of a civic spirit in the countryside that would put the good of the whole ahead of familial interest.

Understandably, such efforts met intense resistance. Some people opposed change per se. Others agreed with many progressive aims but balked at the means. They might be for good roads but against the county government going into debt or raising taxes to finance a road-building program; they might be in favor of better elementary schools but against public high schools. Finally, some people's chief aim in life was to be left alone. They did not care for schools, churches, or sheriffs. Progress left them unmoved. They worked as hard as necessary to survive but were not motivated to accumulate much money or property. These people could be coerced into compliance with progressive reforms, but they could not be made to care: their indifference was their resistance.

Between 1900 and 1917 progressives and conservatives in the Upper Cumberland battled over roads and schools. To win, the progressives had to convince the conservatives to accept their socioeconomic reform package or take the decision-making process from conservative control. The progressives finally implemented most of their programs by using both methods. That is, progressives simultaneously courted public opinion through intense propaganda campaigns and worked with their allies throughout the state to transfer decision-making power (and control over tax monies) from the local to the state level. State government then mandated changes in local institutions and used the threat of withdrawal of state funds to compel local compliance.

By World War I this process was well under way, and local control over many institutions was rapidly eroding—at least on paper. Progressives wanted rational, efficient public administration of schools and roads, with control centralized into the hands of experts. But administrative structures adapted easily to old patterns of political patronage and local control. The gap between what reformers wanted and what they got was vast. When World War I began, neither the progressives nor their opponents had completely triumphed, nor had their conflict created a new synthesis. Instead, new institutions and old attitudes and values coexisted and sometimes conflicted.

The Upper Cumberland progressive effort and local resistance to progress can best be understood by examining two of the major reform campaigns in the region: for good roads and for education. As a local newspaper columnist said (somewhat facetiously) in 1921, "Let us ever remember that that blessed trinity good roads, good schools, and good churches are one and inseparable. We will be the nicest folks when we get them. Indeed charming."[8]

In 1917 Dr. May Cravath Wharton came to Crossville to join her husband on the staff of Pleasant Hill Academy. Wharton's first impressions of Crossville were not favorable. As she waited at the Tennessee Central station, "I became aware of four or five razorback shoats ambling over to a rich mudhole in the street just across the tracks. With gusto they wallowed in it." The doctor sat down and offered up a prayer for strength.[9] Roads in the Upper Cumberland in the 1890s had been very bad; as Wharton's experience indicates, by the eve of World War I conditions were not much better, despite years of effort by good-roads advocates.

As the twentieth century began, the Upper Cumberland lacked a system of roads connecting county to county. Instead roads usually ran from outlying areas to the county seat. In 1906 a correspondent complained in the *Celina Herald*, "No one thing conducive of real comfort to the people of Clay County is more neglected than our roads, our public thoroughfares. . . . No county can fully develop its resources and be brought in touch with the outside world with poor roads. If we had a first class road from Celina to Livingston, a distance of only about twenty miles, our condition would be much improved."[10] Many people complained about the quality of roads in the region but made no serious attempts at reform until after 1910.

After 1901, when good-roads advocates formed the United States Good Roads Association, good roads became the object of a national reform crusade aimed especially at rural areas. Southerners created the Southern Good Roads Association in 1901, and Tennesseans formed a state unit in that same year. Good-roads advocates saw highways as mediums of social and economic uplift for rural areas. With improved transportation would come better marketing facilities, better schools, better churches, and increased cultural opportunities. Good-roads promoters' strongest argument, however, was not ideological but mechanical: people who bought cars wanted better roads upon which to drive. Roads that were sufficient for horse or wagon traffic were often impassable for cars.[11]

To promote the building of extended highways that traversed states and entire regions, good-roads promoters established "named highway associations." The Dixie Highway Association, for example, lobbied in states and counties to get roads built that, link by link, would connect Michigan to Key West, Florida. (A section of the Dixie Highway, the Dixie Short Route, passed through the northern edge of the Upper Cumberland.) Tennessee had its own state-level named highway associations, such as Tennessee's Memphis to Bristol Highway Association.[12] The Memphis to Bristol group in 1910 staged a statewide rally by driving from Memphis to Bristol. Their route passed through Cumberland County, which in 1912 appropriated $40,000 for the local section of the proposed road. Putnam County lobbied for a section of the road also. But the state did not complete the Memphis to Bristol road until after World War I.[13]

In 1916 the federal government began to offer aid to state highway systems through the Federal Aid Highways Act. Anticipating the availability of federal monies, Tennessee in 1915 created a state highway department to funnel money to local construction projects but did not attempt to create a state highway system. The six men who comprised the state's first highway commission included the governor, the dean of engineering at the University of Tennessee, and the state geologist. In 1919 the state reorganized the highway department and put it under the direction of three commissioners, one from each of the three grand divisions of the state. The state legislature also authorized matching funds for county roads: the state would provide two federal-state dollars for each county dollar expended for state-approved highway projects.[14]

While the state and federal governments set up departments to encourage the building of highways, in the Upper Cumberland the clamor for good roads grew slowly in proportion to the number of automobiles in the area. Local folk considered autos to be rich men's toys and resented them as a danger to people and livestock. James N. Cox, who managed the Upper Cumberland's first telephone system, was one of the first in the region to have an automobile. On the way home from the Putnam County fair one night Cox was forced off a bridge by drunks who "protested the need for such a nuisance upon the public roads."[15] The resentment against autos and their wealthy owners in some cases inhibited good-roads campaigns, as the *Macon County News* acknowledged in a 1913 editorial. The editor began by saying that in all the years of time only one horse had been killed by a car in Macon County—but hundreds of horses and mules had been killed by bad roads: "Don't overlook that fact, when you are cultivating your prejudice against automobiles and good roads. When our PROGRESSIVE farmers make good roads, then good roads will make PROSPEROUS farmers who will no doubt own automobiles themselves, like Kansas farmers, and when that time comes there will be less prejudice against the other fellows who own them."[16] The prejudice the Macon County editor perceived remained in force, and automobiles remained relatively rare in the Upper Cumberland until after World War I.

Bad roads made cars impractical. A Cumberland County resident recalled that he and his brother bought a car in Sparta in 1918: "We had only a short road where it was safe to drive a car. Even then the first time we took it out we had a pucture [sic]. When we tried to take it down home in Walnut Grove, we would have to pull it out with the team. We didn't need that car and it never did us any good. When a sufficient number of citizens got as foolish as we were, the county court had to build roads."[17]

In 1914 a Monterey businessman hired the owner of an auto to go to Nashville and bring back his two young daughters, who had just completed a year at Ward-Belmont. The party left Monterey, east of Cookeville on the plateau, at 3:45 A.M. As the crow flies, Monterey was about 100 miles from Nashville. But no roads directly connected Monterey to Nashville or even Monterey to Cookeville, the county seat of Putnam. The people from Monterey had to drive south to Sparta, north again to Cookeville, then west to the bridge over the Caney Fork at Gordonsville. They had to stop to repair tire punctures thirteen times and finally bought one new tire. They reached Nashville after 9:00 P.M.[18]

Local reformers argued that bad roads were retarding the Upper Cumberland's economic and social development. In 1911 the *Crossville Chronicle* editorialized: "There can be no great development or prosperity in any rural community where the roads are inadequate to the demands of transportation, . . . nor do you find the same degree of happiness and intellectual development existing in sections cut off by inaccessible roads from communication with the rest of the world as you will find in communities more fortunately situated. Indeed lack of proper transportation and inability to market the produce of the farm at such a price as to render farming profitable is the great source of discontent in most all rural communities."[19] In 1915 the *Carthage Courier* editor stated that road improvement was crucial to the future of Smith County; upon it "depends largely the growth of our schools and churches, the increase of population, the enhancement of farm lands, and the welfare of our citizenry." In Overton County the local newspaper said that good roads would help farmers market their products and "improve their social, economic and religious standing." In Fentress County the *Gazette* editor hoped that good roads would help lure "more people and more capital" to the county and that new farms and factories would result.[20]

The struggle for better roads began with moral suasion, aimed at getting more work out of the men paying off their taxes on the corvée system. Newspaper correspondents frequently urged greater community efforts toward road building and praised communities that were doing a good job. Thus a report, "Big Road Working at Alpine," in the July 12, 1916, Overton County *Golden Age* commended the local men for their hard work and lauded the women for providing "a bountiful dinner of quality good enough for kings." The article concluded, "There was not a soul that was not happy in the consciousness of duty performed." To underscore the point, the superintendent of the Cumberland Mountain Presbytery preached a short sermon, taking as his text Nehemiah 4:6, "For the people had a mind to work."[21]

The corvée system, however, with its emphasis on local, amateur labor could not produce a regional highway system. Gradually Upper Cumberland counties began to look for a different way to build roads. The following editorial, published in the *Fentress County Gazette* in 1915, illustrates the different methods tried.

There are several ways of building roads. One of the old ways on which the County depended for many years, was the forced labor system. That was kept up for many years, but our roads got no better. For the past few years, we have been trying another plan. Under a special act of the legislature this County has a law provided for a direct tax of $2.50 on ever [*sic*] able bodied man between the ages of 21 and 45 years, also providing for three road Commissioners, composed of the County Judge, County Trustee, and a Road Superintendent. These Commissioners have had charge of the roads in the county for about three years and they have discharged their duty as well as men could under the circumstances; the roads have been improved to a great extent. But we must say to our great sorrow that Fentress County has no good roads. And the reason is not the fault of the men but is the fault of the system, as it does not and cannot bring in sufficient money to make good roads. The only way to get roads in this county is by bond issues.[22]

The corvée system was inadequate. Upper Cumberland counties could not or would not raise enough money by direct taxation to pay for good roads. The counties depended on property taxes, but property in the region was low in value and was assessed for tax purposes at even lower value. In 1915 the Overton County paper, noting that the county had the right to levy a tax of up to thirty cents per $100 of taxable property to pay for road construction, estimated that at that rate each district in the county could construct a few hundred yards of paved roads.[23]

Eventually Upper Cumberland good-roads advocates came to agree with the Fentress County paper quoted above: the only way to get roads was to issue bonds. Some counties moved to do so without great controversy, but in other Upper Cumberland counties bond campaigns faced strong opposition. The road bonds wars indicate much about what divided progressives from conservatives in the region.[24]

Bond issues, which in some counties had to be approved by local referendum, required Upper Cumberland voters to agree to invest in a future unlike anything they had ever seen. Good-roads advocates contended that all manner of good things, social and economic, would follow the building of highways; but to obtain that intangible future, voters had to put up money immediately. Some voters worried that a bond issue would "saddle a debt" on their children. Others distrusted local officials and expected that they would steal any money raised by bond issues. Some perceived bond issues as county mortgages: "Mr. voter, you are being called on by voting for these pike road bonds to mortgage your land and personal property to bondholders for one hundred and sixty thousand dollars to build a few patches of pike roads[,] . . . and if we fail to pay it when the mortgage falls due our land and property will be taken from us."

This Overton County voter clearly misunderstood the letter of the law in regard to issuing bonds; nevertheless he did understand the issue in essence. Taxes paid for bond issues, and if a farmer did not pay his taxes, he would lose his land.[25]

During a controversial drive for a road bond issue, the *Fentress County Gazette* mentioned a problem common to every county in the region: intense localism. The county issued bonds for highway work that would link Jamestown with the Dixie Highway short route. But people argued about how to sell the bonds and where to build the roads. A group of local citizens got an injunction prohibiting construction of one section of road, saying that the road was being built "just for the special benefit of a few reasonably prosperous citizens on the Wolf River." The paper complained that the people of Fentress County did not see themselves as citizens of the county but as residents of Pall Mall, Little Crab, Allardt, Wilder, and so on, and, apparently, all the outlying areas were suspicious of the county seat, Jamestown. The paper hoped that the day would "hasten when we all feel like pushing our county ahead, and may we soon pass this time when we will seek to place our community on top by putting some other community down." The injunction was dismissed, and by April 1916 Fentress County's connection to the Dixie Short Route was under construction.[26]

In Smith County, home of the president of the State Highway Association (a good-roads lobbying group), a bond referendum in 1916 failed by three to one in spite of a year-long good-roads campaign in the county and full support by the local press. The good-roads campaign began in February 1915 with editorials in favor of good roads: "Getting money with bonds to build roads is like buying a home or a business on the installment plan—we get them and receive the benefits from them while we are paying for them." On February 25 good-roads advocates held a meeting in the county, and the crowd voted in favor of a resolution asking the general assembly to pass House Bill 399, which would provide state matching funds for local roads. But voting resolutions in meetings and voting for bonds were two different things: in January 1916 Smith County voters rejected bonds 2,385 to 740. That summer a candidate for state senator from Smith County promised that if he were elected, he would work to repeal the very enabling act that allowed good-roads advocates to set up bond referendums, since it was clear that the people of the county were opposed to the issuance of bonds for roads.[27]

In Overton County, where voters repeatedly refused to authorize bond issues, the bond controversies indicated deep divisions between wealthy and poor residents and between the town, Livingston, and the surrounding countryside. Overton voters defeated a bond issue in 1913. In February 1915 good-roads advocates staged rallies in support of a proposed state highway department and drew enthusiastic crowds. As had been the case in Smith County, however, shouting "aye" for good roads and putting up tax dollars to build them were two different things. The local battle for good roads was joined in earnest on June 9, 1915, when the Overton County Road Improvement Association, the local branch of the state good-roads lobby, called for a bond issue to raise funds for a pike connecting the county with the Dixie Short Route. On June 16 the local paper printed the entire Road Bond Law. The law said that the bond money would be used to build roads linking Livingston with all the surrounding counties. In the upcoming referendum, the ballots for bonds would be marked "For Good Roads," and those opposed, "Against Good Roads."[28]

Opponents of the bond issue charged that if the bond issue passed, local folk would soon see taxes placed on horses and mules to pay for the bonds. In addition, they alleged, the county would get the state law exempting $1,000 of personal property from taxation repealed. Finally, the county would use convict labor to build the roads. Good-roads advocates countered by staging a rally in Livingston in early August. Speakers included Mr. Boykin, an engineer sent from the federal Department of Agriculture, who spoke for over an hour on the general advantages of good roads, and industrialist General John T. Wilder, then a resident of Monterey in neighboring Putnam County. Significantly, the speakers against the bond issue were from outlying communities, not the county seat. According to the *Golden Age*, local politicians, sensing that the voters were against the bond issue, took care to align themselves with the opponents.[29]

In August the bond issue lost by 285 votes. The *Golden Age* was cautiously optimistic; two years earlier a bond referendum had lost 412 to 1,260. The good-roads advocates immediately geared up for another referendum despite protests from opponents that to hold a second election so soon would be a waste of taxpayers' money. In

October 1915 the bond issue lost again, a defeat the local paper labeled "Another Road Bond Waterloo." This time good roads lost by 272 votes.[30]

At various times during the battle over the bond issue the opponents to bonds insisted that they were not opposed to good roads and would be willing to work more on the roads, but they opposed the county incurring debts. The diatribe quoted above comparing a bond issue to a farmer's personal mortgage appeared in the *Golden Age* as Overton County geared up for the second bond referendum in two months.

In January 1916 the county court rejected a proposal that the county join with local citizens in building better roads without issuing bonds. John C. Bilbrey, a Livingston manufacturer who had built the first flour mill, the first planing mill, and the first spoke factory in the town, and Burr L. Speck, merchant, lumber man, and coal operator, came with other prominent local men to offer the county court a proposal. They would put up $1,000 and labor to build a two-mile stretch of pike from Livingston toward Byrdstown if the county would match their funds. A member of the county court introduced a resolution that the court accept the offer and appropriate additional monies that would be available to any other community in the county that wished to build its own road. The court rejected the proposal by four votes.[31]

The local paper editorialized: "Those Justices of the Peace who stubbornly refuse to lend any encouragement to the improvement of the public roads of Overton County are going to realize their mistake some day. We are informed that the chief reason of some for voting down the proposition to appropriate $1,000 toward the building of two miles of pike was because this particular piece of road lies near the town of Livingston." The editor called such opposition unwarranted. The stretch of road in question was one of the most heavily traveled in the county. In addition, "the comparatively few people living adjacent to this piece of road pay about one-third of the total taxes in the county." The "big taxpayers" in all parts of the county, the editor said, were in favor of road building by this method.[32]

In April 1917 good-roads advocates tried once again to get bonds issued for roads. They failed again, this time by 300 votes. In reporting the latest failure, the editor of the *Golden Age* mentioned that he had been advised to drop the issue of good roads or face a boycott.

He was not worried because, he said, at least 90 percent of his advertisers and job work patrons and 75 percent of his subscribers were in favor of bonds: "In other words we find that a large per cent of the business men and heavy taxpayers favor bonds."[33] Overton County voters refused to invest in progress; however, the county was willing to take state largess. In July 1917 the state offered to build a road north from Algood through Livingston up to Pickett County if the county would pay for the survey, furnish the right-of-way, and maintain the road. To this, the county court agreed.[34]

The defeat of road bonds in Smith and Overton Counties points up the impediments to progress in rural Tennessee. Progressives often insisted that "the people" really favored reform and that the resistance of selfish politicians and special interest groups alone kept Tennessee from having good roads, good schools, and a more orderly society. But in areas where the people controlled the political system, they were likely to vote against items progressives assumed they should want. Overton County progressives could contend that the people wanted better roads, but the people did not want roads badly enough to pay for them.

The good-roads movement's success in the Upper Cumberland was less than overwhelming, as a 1926 state highway map indicates. At that date, over fifteen years after good-roads advocates began their campaign, there were four stretches of paved highways in the Upper Cumberland. One paved highway bisected Overton County. (It may be worth noting that an Overton County native, A. H. Roberts, was governor from 1918 to 1920.) A paved road linked Byrdstown, in Pickett County, and Jamestown, in Fentress, and two small patches of pavement ran from railheads in Sparta and Isoline (in Cumberland County) to coal fields on the mountain. By 1925 some counties had good graveled roads—Putnam, Jackson, and White were in the forefront—but those good roads often faded away into unimproved dirt tracks. The county road systems did not connect to form a transportation infrastructure. It would take state-level action to build good highways into the hill country.

The road campaigns in Overton and Smith Counties ran aground on traditionalism, localism (men from Nettle Carrier and Hilham opposed issuing bonds for roads that would not come within miles of their homes), suspicion of public authorities, aversion to debt, and resistance to higher taxes. In vain, newspaper editors in Carthage and Livingston claimed that the new roads would benefit the entire county; the vote against the road bonds indicated that the loyalty local people had to the county was not strong enough to override local or individual self-interest. In Overton County the county seat's most prominent businessmen were in favor of good roads, but that made no difference to the farmers who made up the majority of the county's voters. In fact the reverse may have been true: voting against road bonds may have been a way of expressing resentment against newly wealthy merchants and surely indicated a distinct lack of deference toward the town folk. The vote also signified that the progressive cultural agenda—good roads as a means of uplift—failed to stir Upper Cumberland voters. When progressives attempted to reform schools as a means to transforming culture, the reaction from the people was even more negative.

7

THE BATTLE FOR THE SCHOOLS

For Upper Cumberland progressives, school reform held the key to the future. Unlike road building, education directly affected culture. By reaching the children, progressives could raise a constituency that would support further reforms. As a Gainesboro editor put it in 1899, "It is all well enough to discuss the benefits of free silver and governmental reform, but the sum and substance of all that is the matter with us is ignorance and how to banish it is the problem of the hour."[1] Like Americans elsewhere, progressives in the Upper Cumberland expected a good dose of public education to cure all sorts of social problems, from alcohol abuse to pistol carrying to lackadaisical work habits. Education "eliminates crime, lawlessness, strife and builds up the church, the home and our welfare," stated a *Carthage Courier* editorial in 1915. Since, as it seemed, an uneducated populace impeded progress, an educated populace would naturally favor progress. Education would help farmers convert to market production. A good public school system would attract capital into the area. As the area prospered, the tax base would widen and more funds would be available for education, and the process would continue.[2]

School reformers in the Upper Cumberland found their task made harder by the fact that, in the region, levels of education had little to do with economic success or community standing. Being able to read and write would not make up for inheriting a hardscrabble hillside farm, although literacy might offer a way off that farm. Young men normally became farmers unless they made some special effort to do otherwise. The local phrase for such efforts was "making"— Tom was "making a preacher," while Joe was "making a lawyer." Unless a young man had ambitions to make something besides a farmer, however, education past basic literacy was immaterial to his economic success. If a young man wanted to be something besides a farmer, education might be necessary. Schooling—a requisite number of years in some educational institution—had not yet been confused with education: a young man could go to school or teach himself or apprentice himself to a mentor in his chosen occupation. This situation made it difficult for education reformers to argue that certain skills led to upward social mobility, much less that such skills had to be acquired in school. Anyone who looked at successful men in the region could see the falsity of that argument.[3]

In 1911 a Memphis publishing house put together a who's who for Tennessee. They solicited from each locality in the state the names of men deemed worthy of inclusion in their volume, and they did not ask for payment from the men they profiled. Biographies of 120 men from the Upper Cumberland appeared in the final book. The survey asked respondents to give details about their occupation, education, and family background.[4]

Among these members of the Upper Cumberland elite schooling and status had no clear correlation. Most of these men were at least literate; however, their positions did not depend on their having attending school. Thirty percent had attended high schools or academies; 15 percent had attended or completed college; just over 16 percent had professional degrees (45.5 percent of the professional category). Most teachers also did not have college degrees, with only 33.3 percent listed as graduates. Teachers and businessmen most often had attended local academies: 51.7 percent of the businessmen and 50 percent of the teachers had academy educations.

Farmers (and ministers) had the least schooling: 66.7 percent listed no schooling past the elementary level. These were not average farmers but "big farmers," major landowners, often politically powerful, wealthy men. But their position in the society was obviously not legitimized by their level of schooling.

The biographies of the eight men included in *Who's Who in Tennessee* from Gainesboro, the county seat of Jackson County and a Cumberland River port, indicate how little education had to do with status. Several men had only "common school" educations, which at that time would have meant that they had gone to school for no more than eight years, if that long. Others had college degrees. Richard Dennis, a farmer, had been educated in the local schools but apparently had no education past the elementary level. In 1911 he was serving as county tax assessor. Miles Dixon, a lawyer, had attended two different academies and worked as a schoolteacher before becoming an attorney, apparently by reading law with a local attorney. Robert Garland Draper, a lawyer, had a degree in law from Cumberland University in Lebanon. Ottis G. Fox, a farmer and politician, had attended an academy. Roscoe C. Gaw, circuit court clerk and businessman, had been educated in the common schools and began his work life by teaching school himself at the age of fifteen. Arkley F. Hix, who gave his occupation as public official, farmer, and sportsman, had been educated in the common schools. In 1906 he was the county registrar of deeds. G. Lee McGlasson did not give details of his education other than noting that he had taught school for ten years; in 1911 he was county court clerk. James A. William, banker and farmer, had only a common school education. He had been cashier of the Bank of Gainesboro for over twenty years and had represented the area in the Forty-fifth General Assembly.

As the example of the Gainesboro elite shows, parents in the region had little reason to think that their son's success depended on completing some regulated course of education. All these men presumably had sufficient education to perform their jobs; but most lacked any kind of certification of schooling, and no such accreditation was requisite for their positions in the community.

The lack of connection between schooling and success also explains Upper Cumberland school reformers' vagueness about what they expected better schools to do. Rather than arguing that schools were necessary to teach skills that would be needed in the new century, reformers repeatedly said that they wanted schools to instill attitudes, to change ideas—in other words, to change culture. They wanted to reform the people through the schools.

In their campaign to reform local schools, educationalists found allies in the Upper Cumberland's numerous academies. Academy principals often led the cause of education in their localities, serving as county superintendents for minimal pay. Mission school faculties understood that campaigning for better schools was part of the calling that brought them to the hills of the Upper Cumberland. Since local academies often educated members of the Upper Cumberland elite and served as local teacher training centers, the private schools had a greater influence in the region than their actual size might indicate.[5]

The Upper Cumberland had many academies, ranging from small, fly-by-night operations to well-staffed and enduring institutions. For example, in 1900 the Alden Rines College in DeKalb County had eight teachers and 241 pupils and had been in place for eighteen years. At Gordonsville, in Smith County, the Gordonsville Academy was twenty-five years old. Doyle College, established in White County in 1884, stayed in operation for forty years and produced a state supreme court justice, a railroad president, and numerous local lawyers and businessmen.[6]

Some of the best-known local academies were mission schools funded by northern Protestant denominations. Such was the case at Pleasant Hill in Cumberland County, supported by the American Missionary Association, and Livingston Academy, opened in 1909 and sponsored by the Christian Women's Board of Missions of the Disciples of Christ. Alpine Institute, in Overton County, had been founded before the Civil War by Cumberland Presbyterians. It was destroyed during the war, rebuilt, burned by the Ku Klux Klan, and reopened in 1880. It passed to the control of the northern Presbyterians after the 1906 partial merger of that denomination with the Cumberland Presbyterians. The board of education and the Central Tennessee Conference of the Methodist Church ran Putnam County's Baxter Seminary, which opened in 1908. Local presbyteries, churches, or associations funded other schools. The presbytery of Kingston sponsored Grassy Cove in Cumberland County.

Local Baptist associations helped fund Willette Academy, in Macon County. Members of the Church of Christ in Cookeville, Putnam County, established Dixie College there; classes began in 1912.[7]

The faculties of mission or denominationally affiliated schools varied. At Pleasant Hill, teachers were true missionaries, often of New England origins, sent by the American Missionary Association to uplift and Americanize the mountaineers. Livingston Academy's principal refused to employ Overton County natives as teachers unless they had college degrees. Since few did, in 1916 nonnatives with degrees from Columbia, the University of Michigan, Northwestern, various other midwestern colleges, and Kentucky Normal dominated the school's faculty. Baptist and Churches of Christ affiliated schools were less particular, however; they wanted teachers who were "consecrated Christian men and women, all of whom are specialists in their respective line of work," as Dixie College founder Jere Whitson put it.[8]

Local people often had ambivalent feelings about the mission schools, as the history of Overton County's Livingston Academy indicates. In 1909, hearing that the Disciples' Christian Women's Board of Missions (CWBM) planned to build a mission school in the Upper Cumberland area, Livingston's elite (businessmen, lawyers, and political leaders) offered the CWBM free land, an existing school building, and a residence as incentives to put the school in Overton County. Attorney A. H. Roberts, a Democratic political leader, went to Indianapolis to a CWBM board meeting and successfully presented Livingston's case. But as the CWBM began to solicit contributions for the new school, it embarrassed Overton County residents by describing them in the Disciples' missionary publications as worthy objects of Christian charity.[9]

Some residents of Overton County resented tax monies being used to fund a school controlled by outsiders. The academy would teach a five-month "free" public school course for the children of Livingston; local educational funds would pay teachers' salaries, and the CWBM would keep up the physical plant. In a mass meeting the first principal of Livingston Academy, an Ohioan with a degree from the University of Michigan, was advised to get out of town. After classes began, a teacher created a scandal by making disdainful remarks about the citizens of Livingston. One of the town's more imperious matrons wrote to the principal to demand that the teacher be sent back to Indiana immediately.[10]

To survive, mission schools had to become "naturalized" to the area, as an American Missionary Society publication put it. In a survey of religion in the southern mountains published in 1933 the author warned religious and social workers that the highlanders were proud, dignified, and sure of their own religious rectitude:

> To such people the idea that missionaries should be sent to them, as if they were heathen, is very galling. . . . Their pride, however, does not prevent the Highlanders from accepting temporal benefits offered by the missions. Indeed, a denominational official familiar with the region reported: "In some communities a mission school is looked upon as a fine cow for them to milk. They milk it, too. When the cow is dry they say, 'All right, it's not our cow.'" Yet, though in their extreme need they seize the gift, they do this with a sense of humiliation that in the course of time may turn them against their benefactors.[11]

Private academies, like mission schools, promised that children entrusted to them would be taught good morals. If any educator in the region thought that schooling should be purely secular, he left no record of that opinion. Instead local educators held that good character was as important a product of schooling as knowledge. In 1906 Professor W. B. Boyd, addressing graduates of Mont Vale in Clay County, urged his students to strive to be useful: "Enlightenment of mind and culture of heart are the only means by which a man can be lifted from the low and groveling plains of passion and sensuality and rendered truly useful to his God and his age."[12]

To build good character, common schools, mission schools, and private academies alike incorporated Bible reading and mandatory chapel attendance into their routines. On the state level the president of the state's Public School Officers' Association in 1904 urged that all public school teachers read the Bible to their pupils daily. Bible reading, he said, would help cultivate the good morals essential to the preservation of the state and the development of well-rounded individuals.[13]

At mission schools and at many private academies authorities designed routines to teach pupils to value work and to become orderly, law-abiding citizens. Pleasant Hill students worked their way through the academy by performing various chores. At Livingston Academy students earned academic credit for working in a store, bank, or printer's office; caring for an automobile; sewing; doing laundry; and participating in the local Corn or Tomato Club. Livingston Academy officials insisted that the children enrolled in their school (which was partially funded by local taxes) could not leave the school grounds without permission, could not have parties during the school week, and could not go to see vulgar traveling shows. Children had to attend Sunday School or face expulsion from the academy. The headmaster mandated an 8:00 P.M. curfew for children. Initially shocked by the severity of the school's rules, parents soon reported that their sons behaved better.[14]

In 1900 Ransom Hutchings, a White County native and a graduate of Pleasant Hill, founded his own college at his home in Grace community. Hutchings College operated from 1900 through 1925 and in its prime enrolled from 75 to 100 students each year. Hutchings's school routine indicates the influence of a mission school education reinforcing traditional farming self-sufficiency. Hutchings and his students constructed most of the school buildings and ran their own sawmill. They grew their own food on the campus farm, butchering two or three hogs each week to feed the students and faculty. Women attending the school prepared community meals in the college dining hall. Hutchings's tuition was quite low: fees ranged from $1 per month for primary students to $2 for students taking the most advanced courses. Housing cost $5 a month. Any student who lacked the money to pay Hutchings's fees could work out his or her tuition. Hutchings also employed the parents of families enrolled at his school.[15]

The school day at Hutchings College began with bells at 4:00 A.M. Breakfast was served at 5:00. Students then worked on the farm until 7:30, came in, cleaned up, and went to classes from 8:00 A.M. to 4:00 P.M. From 4:00 to 6:00 was another work period. Supper was at 6:00 P.M. Students filed into the dining hall and stood before their plates until grace was said. They were allowed thirty minutes to eat. They were then to go to their rooms for two hours of evening study. Lights went out at 9:30 P.M.[16]

Students who passed through such rigorous schools went on to become the region's literate elite: doctors, lawyers, and schoolteachers. Their schooling stressed methodical work habits and respect for manual labor. Farm boys who came to Pleasant Hill, Livingston Academy, or Hutchings College presumably knew how to work hard, but those schools also taught the importance of deploying time effectively and by scheduled increments. By demanding decorum at all times, mission schools separated their students from their non-educated neighbors. Finally, the mission schools made no distinction between religious and secular education; indeed, missionaries preached secular progress as well as literacy and good character.

The missionaries hoped that their students would be the yeast that would uplift a backward, ignorant rural area. Creating a constituency to support good schools and roads was part of the reason the mission schools existed.[17] But the very education that made the progressive agenda attractive to mission students often opened to them opportunities outside the region and set them apart from their contemporaries.

In 1924 Emma Florence Dodge, daughter of Pleasant Hill's first headmaster, published a souvenir history of the school complete with a list of alumni and their current addresses. Since its inception in 1888 Pleasant Hill had graduated 295 students. (Many more had attended but had left without completing the entire course.) Of the graduates 160 had left the region. Some had moved to Tennessee cities, but many others had moved to Texas or California. They had left to take jobs in business; to work as doctors, druggists, or nurses; to practice law; to preach or do social work; or to teach. Of the alumni who gave occupations, only twelve listed farming, and one of those combined farming with "rubber work" in Akron, Ohio. The souvenir edition closed by soliciting contributions for Pleasant Hill: "Pleasant Hill Academy Helps Mountain Boys and Girls Get a Practical Christian Education." The publication did not point out that one of the results of the education was that many of the boys and girls left the mountains.[18]

In 1916 a Fentress County student wrote an essay, "Some Dos and Don'ts for Boys and Girls," which suggested some of the pain and alienation an education could cause:

Don't think that you are better than other boys and girls because you can dress nicer than they. . . .
Don't think you know more than your mother and father be-

cause you have been in the big school. Always remember to honor your parents even though they have no education. . . .

Don't stick up your nose at your neighbor boy or girl that couldn't go to the big school as you did. . . .

Don't get it into your little bit of a head that you have "larnt" it all when you graduate from the big school. . . .

Above all, Don't make fun of other's mistakes who have not had the chance you have had.[19]

Available evidence indicates that the public or common schools as they existed at the turn of the century satisfied most of the Upper Cumberland populace. If the populace wanted better schools, they had within their power the capacity to raise taxes, set higher standards for teachers, build new schools, and so on. Some towns did so: Cookeville, for example, after 1903 established free (tax-supported) elementary and secondary schools and a two-year public high school. But outside the region's towns, children attending the common schools were taught in poor buildings by inadequately educated teachers who received very low pay. By the standards of progressive school reformers, or even in comparison with urban schools in Tennessee, schools in the Upper Cumberland and other rural areas in Tennessee were long overdue for reform.[20]

Young men and women who taught school were in many cases barely literate; rarely were teachers graduates of even a four-year high school. School terms were short—three months being usual—and school attendance, not compelled by law, was sporadic. Counties ran many small primary schools in an attempt to put public education within walking distance of all children; consolidation was almost impossible due to poor roads. (School reformers were among the strongest advocates of better roads.) Some counties had no secondary schools. In 1900 no county in the region had a publicly funded high school,[21] nor was there much need for one. Most children dropped out before finishing even the five-grade primary course.

Educators differed as to why children should go to school. A Jackson County educator, in a letter published in the *Gainesboro Sentinel* in 1904, made education a manner of filial honor:

Now parents, we owe a debt of gratitude to our forfathers [sic], not only for bequeathing to us a rich inheritance of pious precepts, but

Table 5. School Enrollment by County, 1900

	Grade 1	Grade 2	Grade 3	Grade 4	Grade 5	Grade 6	Grade 7	Grade 8
Clay	468	586	401	660	176	0	0	0
Cumberland	753	380	400	365	301	65	38	24
Fentress	579	318	233	161	210	7	0	0
Jackson	1,271	1,409	906	654	307	281	0	0
Macon	750	408	298	304	176	1	0	1
Overton	1,387	808	557	356	198	9	0	0
Pickett	654	426	221	117	19	0	0	0
Smith	1,507	786	763	896	576	191	134	79
White	814	540	456	425	400	410	325	320
Total	8,183	5,661	4,235	3,938	2,363	964	497	424

Source: Fitzpatrick, *Annual Report of the State Superintendent*.
Note: Statistics for DeKalb and Putnam Counties were not available.

for handing down to us and our posterity a free and a republican form of government. Only one way to pay this debt, and that is by taxation to educate our children, not only for the trials of life, but to perpetuate good government, which offers to everyone freedom of worship and to the press freedom of speech. But above all, it offers to every man the same opportunity of labor and commanly succeed [*sic*]. Therefore let us send our children to school, leaving off peavishness and petish [*sic*] whims; thereby availing ourselves of a God-favored opportunity.[22]

Contrast that sentiment with the views of Mont Vale College's correspondent in the *Celina Herald* in 1906: "Thought is the motive power of the world. He who cannot think and think fast, must soon give way to him who can. There are many young men from 14 to 20 years of age in this county who are failing to make the most of themselves. . . . Many of them will be doomed to be 'hewers of wood and drawers of water' for others of their contemporaries who have learned to think."[23]

If the Mont Vale educator was progressive, expecting his students to leave manual labor for public work, Jackson County's school superintendent W. L. Dixon was a strong advocate of social control: "Don't conceive the ideal that the only thing is for the child to know its lessons. While this is essential it is also very essential that it be orderly. We are all subject to government. The child must be taught that is [sic] must be governed and controled [sic], this should be done by mild means if possible, but if necessary you have the right to use coersive [sic] means."[24] The fate of Dixon explains why school reform in the Upper Cumberland was so sporadic. Less than a month after he wrote the letter quoted above, Dixon resigned as county superintendent when the county court refused to increase his salary; he was making $250 a year. Meanwhile 182 students had enrolled in school in the county seat, but not all attended classes. At least fifteen pupils did not come to school because they either could not afford or could not find the necessary books. Others had gone to work, and still more missed classes to help their families pick peas or gather corn.[25]

Like Dixon, county superintendents in the Upper Cumberland supervised schools but lacked control over hiring, curriculum, or budget. County courts elected superintendents, and the state certified superintendents' qualifications. But power in the schools rested with the district directors, elected by the people in each district. District directors were supposed to be able to read and write but needed no other qualifications. The state levied property and poll taxes for schools, but the county retained the money, combined it with county taxes, and sent funds to the district in proportion to the district's population. District school directors hired and paid faculty.[26]

A school superintendent's real job was to train local teachers in "county normals." The state required that would-be teachers attend training institutes held at varying intervals and for varying durations in all counties. At these sessions young men and women studied academic subjects and pedagogy. If at the end of the institute, which might run for as long as two weeks, the young prospective teacher could pass an exam on the subjects covered, the county licensed him or her to teach.[27]

In their reports to the state department of public instruction Upper Cumberland school superintendents complained that local people did not support the cause of education. Pickett County superintendent W. J. Chilton reported in 1900 that although his teachers were enthusiastic, "They do not, however, meet with much encouragement from the Directors, and with but little from many of the people. Some of the Directors and a great many of the people hang with stubborn tenacity to the old pioneer schools, with their primitive methods and old-time books. It seems well-nigh impossible to get them to fall in line with improvement and modern methods and ideas."[28]

In 1902 the superintendent of Clay County schools stated bluntly that instruction in his county was not satisfactory and was not improving. He found the teachers and directors apathetic, the schools ungraded, and of forty-nine teachers employed, only seven were experienced teachers back at the same school for another year. Less morose superintendents also reported problems with attendance and poor instruction. In 1902 the state was trying to introduce graded classes. The Upper Cumberland superintendents found that hard to do. Teachers were not prepared for graded classes. The books students had purchased were not suitable for graded work. Fentress County superintendent W. P. Little said simply that his county had not been able to grade the schools according to law because attendance was so poor and the school term so short.[29]

In 1905 R. L. Jones, state superintendent of public instruction, summed up the problems of Tennessee schools in an address to a convention of the state's teachers. Jones said that Tennessee prepared its teachers poorly and paid them poorly. The state did not coordinate education: in effect, Tennessee had ninety-five different systems. The ostensive professionals in charge of the system, the state and local superintendents, did not have any power. The local directors controlled finances and teacher hiring. Worse, Jones said, the Tennessee public did not care about the public schools: "With fewer than one-half the children in daily attendance in school, we can not say there is general enthusiasm for them." For this situation Jones blamed ignorant parents who kept their children out of school. The only solution, according to Jones, was a compulsory attendance law for Tennessee's children.[30]

When Upper Cumberland residents expressed discontent with their schools, which was rarely, their complaints centered on poor teachers and short terms, and the solutions they proposed did not require extensive structural reforms. Instead critics advised local school officials to hire better teachers and urged parents to do more to further their children's education. In 1901 a Fentress County correspondent from Little Crab commented that the local school session was going well:

The only trouble is it is not long enough—only two months. I think we could not do better than to employ Mr. Bertram to teach our fall school. . . . How much we need a good academy at this place. I wonder we do not have one. The only reason I can think of is that the men of young families have not thought of it as they should. As I see it, how much better it would be to spend a few hundred dollars in building an academy here and educate our children at home and thereby build up our community and also keep the money at home that it takes to send them abroad to educate them.[31]

In 1900 a correspondent from Livingston complained that school directors all too often hired unqualified friends, relatives, or anyone who would accept low pay, without regard for their qualifications:

It has got to be that we have men declaring themselves candidates for school directors and issues upon which they run. These candidates go among the people and press their claims, trying to convince the voters why they should vote for them. One of the issues is that they favor low-priced teachers. They are then touching their pocket-book, and this you know is a very strong and convincing argument with some. Directors of this kind are sometimes elected, and then the lowest bidder takes the school. His pupils soon learn that he is not competent to teach them and lose all respect for him.

The Livingston correspondent also criticized local school directors for refusing to hire women. He insisted that women often made better teachers and had better morals than many male teachers. The Livingston correspondent believed that "females should receive as much for teaching as men. The salary should be regulated by what she does and not by what some one else gets for doing different work." Apparently the problem with women teachers was not just that they might be paid as much as men teachers; it was the very idea that women in any occupation might make more than a male farmhand.[32]

In 1901–2, out of eight reporting Upper Cumberland counties, all but one county, Cumberland, had a majority of male teachers. In Clay and Macon Counties the number of men and women teaching school was almost equal. But in DeKalb and Pickett Counties four times as many men taught school as women, and Fentress, Jackson, Overton, and Putnam Counties employed twice as many men teachers as women. This suggests that in the Upper Cumberland in 1900 teaching had not yet become feminized and did not offer women a serious, long-term economic alternative to dependence on male family members.[33]

The people of Tennessee did not demand educational reform. Instead, after 1903 a talented group of educational reformers created a semblance of public support for reforms they wanted. These men worked for the state educational bureaucracy or as professors of education in state universities and colleges. University of Tennessee professor Philander P. Claxton led the group. Claxton, who worked for the Southern Education Board, also directed the Summer School of the South and ran the University of Tennessee's department of education before leaving Tennessee to become United States Commissioner of Education in 1911. Claxton, with his connections to the Peabody Foundation, was first-among-equals in a network of educators that included state superintendents Seymour A. Mynders (1903–7), Robert L. Jones (1907–11), and J. W. Brister (1911–13). The group, spurred by the Southern Education Board's critique of schooling throughout the South, attempted to modernize the state's educational system.[34]

The reformers concentrated on changes in organization, hoping to bring to rural Tennessee the administrative structures typical of northern school systems. The reforms they proposed included compulsory education laws, the reduction of local control over education, longer school terms, graded classes, the establishment of public high schools, the professionalization of teaching, higher pay for teachers, and the organization of a state educational bureaucracy. They had to sell this program to the state legislature and to the people. Since there was no great demand for school reform, they had to create it.[35]

From 1903 through 1913 Claxton and the state superintendents ran biennial summer crusades for school reform. Educators at the state level met and drew up a reform agenda, then took to the campaign trail. In 1902 Claxton formulated a plan of operation for the first crusade; later campaigns followed the same pattern. The reformers planned to inundate the state with educational reform propaganda aimed especially at "ministers, politicians, lawyers, editors and others who will make use of the facts in their speeches and writings." Claxton also did a mass mailing of educational propaganda to the state's preachers, who were asked to "preach one or more sermons on public education in their churches during the year." The school reformers used the minimal state school system as a vehicle for mobilizing people in favor of school reform. They asked county superintendents to get teachers to see that parents in their communities attended school reform rallies. At county rallies local politicians and educators, sharing platforms with representatives of state government, would be entertained by schoolchildren, who would get a day off from classes so that they could lend their support to education.[36]

Representatives of the state education lobby then presented to the crowd a cautiously worded resolution that avoided suggesting reforms would interfere with existing power structures or require higher taxes. For instance, educators wanted higher salaries for teachers, but they would not ask a rally crowd to approve that. Rather, they asked for approval of resolutions calling for better schools, a longer school term, or better teachers. As Claxton explained to a Conference for Education in the South in 1908, "Our people in the South here, with their blue eyes and soft hearts, can be moved, but after a time they will forget, so, while they are sympathetic the resolutions are read and are usually voted unanimously. . . . Those resolutions, or similar ones, were sent to all the women's clubs, to all the boards of education in the counties and in the cities, to the city councils, the Junior Order of United States Mechanics, [and] to the patriotic orders."[37]

Then, back in Nashville, the education lobby could tell the legislature and governor that the people wanted school reform, and that such reform meant higher salaries for teachers, structural reforms reducing local control, and so on. With this public support, education reformers could exert pressure at the state level for reform: by shouting "aye" in a public meeting, the people had indicated that they wanted better schools.[38] It should be noted that the resolutions offered to the crowds at education rallies were very general and (above all) made no mention of raising taxes.

As an organized pressure group the school reformers succeeded remarkably at orchestrating public opinion and pushing legislation through the general assembly. When the reformers held their last statewide campaign in 1914, they had already attained the most important of their goals. County school boards replaced district school directors in 1907, despite protests by representatives in the general assembly against this loss of local self-government. In 1913 the general assembly enacted a compulsory education bill and set up a state system of teacher certification. The state also increased its financial support for schools. The school reformers shrewdly avoided asking for higher taxes for schools. Instead they requested that the schools receive a higher percentage of taxes then being collected. In 1909 the school fund was supposed to receive 25 percent of the state's gross revenue; due to the efforts of the school reform lobby, that percentage was raised to 33.3 in 1913. From 1902 through 1914 state funds for education increased from $136,018 to $942,545, and county funds in most localities increased in a similar manner.[39]

The fate of educational reform in the Upper Cumberland, however, indicates that structural changes failed to work the sort of social transformation foreseen by the reformers. Although the people of the Upper Cumberland enjoyed the reform campaigns, the local reaction to the new school system ranged from mild approval to indifference to outright hostility.

During the years when he directed the state educational campaigns, Claxton visited the Upper Cumberland repeatedly. In 1902 he made a sweep through the region as part of a speaking tour promoting the reform package he hoped to get through the 1903 general assembly. He spoke in Macon, Smith, Overton, Putnam, Clay, Jackson, DeKalb, and Cumberland Counties to crowds of about 1,000 in each place. In 1903 Claxton addressed the Cumberland County teachers' meeting (following Bible reading and a choir's rendition of "Power in the Blood of the Lamb"). In 1906 he spoke in the county seats of each of the Upper Cumberland counties in behalf of the 1907 education bill. Apparently the blue-eyed southern folk of Cumberland County had longer memories than most: in January 1907 the county court adopted a resolution urging the passage of Claxton's program for that year. In 1908 the professor made another tour of the region, this time to rally support for county high schools.[40]

While Claxton campaigned to mobilize public support for state legislation, some local superintendents used the school rally as a means of arousing general interest in education. In 1907 the Clay County superintendent held four educational rallies in Spivey, Moss, Celina, and Willow Grove, respectively. A crowd of between 1,200 and 1,500 attended the meeting at Willow Grove, which culminated with dinner on the grounds. Overton County sponsored a school rally in 1916 at Pond Ridge, a very isolated community between Livingston and Monterey where students met in a log cabin. After an address by the local superintendent on the value of the school to the community, local people came forward to donate land and money for a new schoolhouse.[41]

Although local people flocked to school rallies, Upper Cumberland politicians balked at some of the school reforms. Most supported the compulsory education bill, as did much of the Upper Cumberland press. But the bill replacing the district director system with a county board of education passed the general assembly in 1907 only after attacks by rural representatives who defended the old system of local control. Most of the state representatives from the Upper Cumberland voted against it. The normally progressive editor of the *Golden Age* opposed what he called the "county unit rule" in education. He thought it unjust to take tax money from one section of the county and give it to another and believed that doing so was likely to "destroy local interest and pride in education work among any people."[42]

The 1907 bill passed and in theory should have restructured the system of school governance in Upper Cumberland counties. However, reform in theory turned out to be the same old system in practice. The bill established at least five school districts of equal size in each county, each of which would elect a school board member. These board members were supposed to run the school system. But the law also called for "advisory boards" of three men in each district. These advisory boards turned out to be the old district directors in new guise. According to the *Crossville Chronicle* their duties included "to visit schools of their respective districts and see that the house is in good repair, inspect the school work, see that water and fuel are provided, etc. To make recommendations to the County Board and recommend teachers for their schools. . . . The Advisory Board is to suspend pupils, subject to approval of County Board. Issue an order on the County Board for expenditures, or repairs and incidentals to an amount not exceeding $10." The editor of the *Golden Age* complained in 1915 that the district directors still ran the schools but with money now taken from other districts.[43]

Upper Cumberland politicians found most controversial House Bill 174, proposed in 1913, which set state standards for teacher certification. The legislation required teachers to attend state-approved county institutes, summer schools, or state normal schools and to take examinations before they would be allowed to teach. Teaching certificates were to be issued in two levels. One certificate would allow a teacher to work in the county in which he or she had been certified. The other, awarded after a teacher had passed a state-level exam, qualified the teacher for work in any county in the state. However, graduates of state normal schools obtained teacher's certificates good throughout the state.[44]

This law was a step toward the professionalization of teaching; moreover, it put the power of defining acceptable levels of professionalism in the hands of the state. The Upper Cumberland members of the state house of representatives, with one exception, voted against it. An editorial in the *Golden Age* in 1915 explained why: the bill invested too much power in the state board of education, opened avenues for favoritism and graft, and "will tend to discriminate against teachers in the rural districts who received their education in the private schools and in favor of the State Normal and other institutions supported by the state." The editor said that a law to take effect in 1917 would prohibit the employment of any teacher who had not received instruction at a state normal school, and he protested that "Livingston has a school that carries the student two or three grades beyond the free school course, and the state has no moral right to say that a boy or a girl who receives a diploma here shall not be licensed to teach until he or she shall have attended one of its favored institutions."[45] Upper Cumberland private schools countered by advertising that they prepared candidates for certification by teaching the "state course."

Upper Cumberland private school directors worried too soon: despite state laws giving preference to teachers with normal degrees, Upper Cumberland school boards went on hiring as they chose. In 1920 in the eleven Upper Cumberland counties 25 teachers had college degrees; 28 had normal school degrees; 96 had graduated from high school; 218 had only limited professional training, probably acquired in county institutes; and 247 had no professional training at all.[46] Once again, state law proved no match for local tradition.

In 1908 John W. Fox, chairman of Jackson County's board of education, had urged that only the best teachers be hired: "Don't recommend one whom you think might carry on the largest mercantile trade with you, thereby making him able to foot his bills. . . .

Don't recommend that fellow to whom you sold a horse last year in order that he might take in his note[, or relatives] because they are poor and need money."[47] After 1913, however, despite all state efforts toward professionalization, local school boards still gave preference to political friends, relatives, and above all, local people. In 1922 eighteen of the thirty-eight teachers hired in Pickett County were related to the county superintendent, to members of the county court, or to members of the school board. Twenty-four of the thirty-eight were natives of the county. As late as 1937 James M. Hatfield, who had been Putnam County superintendent from 1911 through 1921, wrote that his county hired "too many untrained and unexperienced teachers. . . . Too much political favoritism is shown in the selection of teachers, and not enough consideration given to fitness." According to Hatfield, the board of education had a policy of hiring "none but local teachers."[48]

The school reform campaigns apparently did help increase public interest in education. The 1909–10 county superintendents' reports sound a note of optimism and enthusiasm alien to the reports of a decade earlier. In Crossville, Cumberland County superintendent J. S. Cline presided over a new county high school, which was turning out teachers for the county schools. The school term was longer—five months. Two-thirds of Cline's schools had libraries. After eight years Cline's teachers were making progress at establishing graded classes. To help in this process Cline had copies of the school curriculum printed, mounted on a board, and hung in each classroom. Teachers were required to stick with the course, "putting the pupils into the grade as closely as possible; promoting from grade by grade to examination until they enter the County High School." Cumberland County schools now had new patent desks. Teachers decorated classrooms with mottoes and pictures. Cline's report reflected his pride in these accomplishments. In Fentress County the superintendent reported that new schools being built would be furnished with new desks to replace the old split-log benches. He wrote that the new county high school was doing a fine job of turning out better teachers: "We have several more teachers than schools." Smith County's superintendent reported that attendance was up, and so were teachers' salaries. Putnam County's superintendent, Ernest H. Boyd, a proponent of school reform, ran a model county school

Table 6. School Enrollment by County, 1912

	Grade 1	Grade 5	Grade 8	Grade 12
Clay	907	151	21	0
Cumberland	790	320	96	16
DeKalb	720	525	410	18
Fentress	738	272	6	0
Jackson	1,464	494	19	0
Macon	509	178	27	0
Pickett	489	156	0	0
Putnam	1,588	499	69	0
Smith	1,327	522	295	0
White	1,113	271	80	9
Total	9,654	3,388	1,023	43

Source: Brister, *Biennial Report of the State Superintendent, 1911–1912.*

district with institutes monthly, rallies throughout the county, graded courses, and teachers who read the educational journals and studied the books on pedagogy recommended by the state.[49]

The 1912 state statistics on enrollment, however, indicate that school reform did not reach the masses whose children attended country schools.[50] Enrollment remained high in the first five (primary) grades and sloped off by the eighth grade. In those counties that had four-year high schools, enrollment dwindled even further by grade twelve. Attending school past the first four grades was still not the norm in most Upper Cumberland counties.

In fairness it should be noted that in 1912 the new county high schools had not had time to process a class through four years of schooling. Smith County had no seniors but enrolled 99 freshmen; in White County, with 9 seniors, there were 96 freshmen. It should also be noted that Table 6 omits town schools and private academies that received public funds. However, in those counties that did provide free high school educations, only a tiny minority attended.[51]

J. W. Brister, the state superintendent whose office compiled the statistics quoted above, concluded his 1911–12 report with a call for a crusade against illiteracy in Tennessee. For that end, he said, a compulsory education law was essential: "Suffice it to say that parents who are indifferent to the interests of their children are enemies to the state; and, further, that the obligations of the state to the unfortunate children of such parents are such that all its power must be extended to educate them in spite of the indifference or unconcern of their parents."[52]

In 1913 the general assembly passed Tennessee's first statewide compulsory education law. The law made it a misdemeanor for parents to keep their children under age fourteen out of school, and it set fines of $2 to $20 for a first offense.[53] However, criminalizing the normal behavior of a large group of Tennessee citizens did not cause immediate changes in that behavior. The 1919–20 school statistics indicate that the dropout rate in the Upper Cumberland had not changed significantly in the seven years that compulsory education had been in effect. At best the compulsory education law meant that more parents sent their children to the first five grades of school. Most children still dropped out before completing the eighth grade.

Structural changes did not immediately translate into changed attitudes. The law was unpopular and laxly enforced in most of the region. In 1915 the editor of the *Carthage Courier* complained that less than half of the eligible children attended school. "This is not due to a lack of school houses and school teachers . . . but due to a lack of interest of the parents." In 1917 the Livingston newspaper said, apologetically, that the county board of education felt obligated to enforce the compulsory education law "until this law is repealed."[54] In 1920 as in 1915, 1910, 1900, and 1890 no clear economic or social payoff encouraged Upper Cumberland parents to keep their children in school. Understandably, then, many people in the Upper Cumberland could see no reason why they should be taxed to pay for anyone's high school education.

Historians of education debate the origins of public high schools in the antebellum North. Were public high schools created by town elites (the sort of people who would otherwise have sent their children to private academies) and imposed on unwilling taxpayers? Why were those taxpayers unwilling to fund high schools? Did working-class people resist the creation of high schools because they were ideologically opposed or because they lived too far from the proposed schools or because a high school education for their children simply did not seem practical to them? Once high schools were organized, what role did they play in facilitating—or deterring—individual social mobility?[55]

The experience of the Upper Cumberland suggests that elites did indeed impose public high schools on an unenthusiastic public. In 1909 the state made funding available for counties that opted to open high schools. Upper Cumberland counties were slow to take advantage of this opportunity. In 1912 only Cumberland, DeKalb, Fentress, and White Counties had public county high schools. In 1917 the state required counties to levy a high school tax and in 1921 mandated that all counties establish high schools. Attendance at high schools remained optional. In 1920 in the entire Upper Cumberland sixty-four pupils completed a four-year public high school course.[56]

In Cumberland County a proposal to build a public high school in the county seat, Crossville, sparked a controversy that pitted well-to-do farmers and merchants against less affluent citizens in the countryside. The long argument began in 1900, when citizens of Crossville founded a high school. In the fall of 1901 the new school had 129 pupils. In January 1903 the organizers of the high school requested that the county start funding it. Specifically they asked that the county levy one mill for the school. The county court defeated the motion.[57]

The measure's proponents argued that a high school would benefit the entire county by making it more attractive to new settlers. William Whitlock, a magistrate from outside the Crossville area, criticized his fellow members of the county court for opposing measures that would not benefit their own districts. In a newspaper article he wrote that Cumberland County must have good schools (and good roads) in order to attract settlers and capital. According to Whitlock the big taxpayers supported the high school.[58] The editor of the *Crossville Chronicle* agreed with Whitlock. Noting that the exploitation of the county's coal resources, then under way, would mean an increase in wealth, he argued, "The increase of wealth and business means an increase in business opportunities. If we do not fit our children by educating them for the business openings that come to us, people from a distance will come in and we will be forced to seek less profitable fields in which to earn a livelihood."[59]

Squire John Brown, who had voted against the high school, wrote to answer Whitlock. He argued that the county already had too much debt and that the high school would mean higher taxes. He contended that the belief that good schools would draw settlers was fallacious—the bad roads would keep them away. He stated that funding a high school was premature: "Give us a compulsory education law and in a few years we can begin to think about an institution like a High School." Brown questioned whether many citizens of the county could afford to send their children to a high school in Cross-ville, where they would have to pay board. He compared the proposed high school to a pauper begging for a county dole, and he asked why this school could not support itself as did the academies at Pleasant Hill, Grassy Cove, and Grandview. But most of all, Brown resented the town of Crossville: "Talk about its being our school. If brother Whitlock and I buy a gallon of good whiskey and I drink it all up myself, is it ours or mine? If the taxpayers of this county build a big school and Crossville gets it all, because the roads are so bad that we can't get there, is it ours or is it theirs?" In Crossville, Brown said, the country students would have to pay more for their board, and they would be corrupted by the town's ways: "How many genuine citizens would want their children turned loose in Crossville to promenande the streets . . . and be out after night until they saw fit to go in. How many?" Brown concluded by advising Whitlock that if he wanted the high school reconsidered, "Leave them ex-trustees, lawyers and congressmen at home. I think we can reconsider without them."[60]

In February an anti–high school squire sent to the newspaper a more measured defense of his position. J. S. Wyatt, magistrate from Newton, explained that his calculations of county revenues and expenses indicated the school fund would be so low that the common schools would only be able to run for two and one-half months in the coming year. Given the conditions of the primary schools in the country districts, Wyatt said, talking about a high school was greatly premature. Crossville might be able to operate such a school, but Cumberland County was not ready yet. Wyatt said, "Let us have better primary schools, better county roads and bridges, let us pay our county indebtedness. . . . I am with you then, and not until then will I be for taxing the people for a high school. That is as soon as we will need it for Cumberland County as a whole."[61]

Later that month a Crossvillian wrote to the newspaper on the subject of the high school. He said that he believed that two-thirds of the voters outside the county seat opposed levying a tax for the high school. The Crossvillian urged his fellow townspeople to mend their fences with the country folk, noting that the feeling "exists among our country friends that Crossville is composed largely of people who are every [*sic*] ready to sacrifice the best interest of the county as a whole to build up the county seat." The controversy raged on, but in March the county newspaper refused to publish any more letters on the subject. The county court did not levy a tax for the high school.[62]

Crossville got its high school in 1910, in part due to the influence of P. P. Claxton, who came to the county in 1908 to speak in favor of the high school. However, the claim that the high school would help fit the children of the county for competition in an expanding economic sphere apparently did not prove to be the decisive argument. Instead proponents said that the school would benefit the entire county by educating teachers for the common schools. In fact that came to be the primary function of the high school in Crossville. Cumberland County superintendent J. S. Cline, who doubled as high school principal, reported in 1910 that he had 86 pupils, "many of them teachers and others preparing to teach."[63]

School reformers hoped that education would be the first foundation stone of a whole series of reforms: by schooling the children of the Upper Cumberland, they hoped to change attitudes they believed were retarding the region's development. But before education could work its promised miracles, the reformers had to get the people of the region to accept changes in customary educational practices. The people accepted only those reforms that could be fitted into the traditional ways of schooling children. A decade of state legislation failed to transform the schools in the region. Students continued to come to school when they and their parents chose, and they dropped out when they were ready. High schools, rather than being an avenue of mobility for country youth, took over the private academies' role as teacher education institutes.

School reformers claimed success when they managed to put into place new structures: compulsory education, county school boards, tighter controls on teacher certification, and schools that taught an eight-grade elementary course. Such structures, on paper, qualified a county as progressive on education regardless of whether the structures made any substantive difference in the education of the region's children. On paper the new structures cut significantly into local control of local institutions; had some Upper Cumberland county court possessed the political courage to enforce the new school laws, schooling in the region might well have been transformed. Instead the new structures coexisted with county governments committed to Jeffersonian restraint. Without intervention by some more powerful governmental entity—the state government, for example—to force compliance with the spirit as well as the letter of school reform, new legislation was so much wasted paper.

The will to enforce reform in the region did not exist: progressives could not muster the local political power necessary to make real the letter of the new laws. But in 1917 regional progressives were handed power from above. They became the leaders of wartime mobilization.

8

SERGEANT YORK'S HOME FRONT

On April 20, 1917, schoolchildren and Tennessee Polytechnic Institute students rallied at the city school auditorium. Bands played patriotic songs, and local dignitaries addressed the crowd. At the end of the rally the crowd unanimously approved a resolution supporting the cause for which the rally was staged. The scene was familiar: it could have been a progressive rally for roads or schools. But this rally promoted local support for World War I. Instead of bureaucrats pushing state education or transportation, "several battle-scarred Confederate veterans" shared the stage with local progressives and civic leaders.[1]

Upper Cumberland progressives came to power in 1917, when the federal and state governments gave control of war mobilization to members of local elites. With this power the leaders of war mobilization could demand from local people their money, their time, and their very lives. They could create the sort of institutional community lacking in the region and require participation, with the force of the federal government behind them.

The First World War made an internationally famous hero of Alvin York of Fentress County, one of the Upper Cumberland region's many reluctant conscripts. The York legend appealed to the public because York appeared to be a figure out of the American past—a frontiersman from a simpler place and time placed in the middle of the hideous destruction of modern war. Ironically, the war brought the complexities of the modern world to York's home front and required people there to weigh the demands of patriotism against loyalties to family, church, and neighbor. Some reconciled such conflicts by assimilating all allegiances into a whole: for them, the boys in France were fighting to preserve the traditional farmers' world. Others, unable to achieve such a synthesis, put family and community loyalties ahead of the needs of the nation-state and paid a high price for their stubborn adherence to the values of traditional culture.[2]

The First World War brought unprecedented governmental intervention into the lives of the people of the Upper Cumberland through conscription, population enrollment, regulation, and incessant propaganda. As the state insinuated itself into what had hitherto been private matters, public reaction ranged from support to confusion to outright defiance. The Gainesboro paper found it necessary to run an editorial condemning people who said that the war had been started by Wall Street or by munitions makers. Mrs. W. E. Jared, the Silver Point correspondent for the Putnam County paper, wrote in April, "So I read everything I can get and read so much and I am tired reading that they have taken all of our young men to fight, and I can't see any use; our country was in peace."[3]

As Tennessee mobilized for war, a Putnam County progressive directed both civilian mobilization efforts and the selective service process in the state. Rutledge Smith, former Cookeville newspaper editor and longtime supporter of better roads and schools, worked for the Tennessee Central Railroad until 1917, when Governor Tom Rye appointed him to head the state branch of the Council of National Defense. As head of the state selective service, Smith held the title of "Major, Infantry, U.S.A. Executive Officer." Whichever hat he wore, Smith proved an efficient if somewhat heavy-handed agent of mobilization.[4]

Conscription brought the reality of the war home to Upper Cumberland families. Although some young men in the region fulfilled regional tradition by volunteering immediately, most did not rush to the colors.[5] In Overton County the leaders of a proposed volunteer company in June 1917 appealed to the patriotism of potential recruits, but they also warned that those who did not volunteer would be drafted, saying, "Ask any of the old soldiers what it means to be a conscript."[6] Prior to June 5, notices of the registration procedures appeared in Upper Cumberland papers and were posted throughout the area. In Putnam County Ernest H. Boyd, county attorney, was worried that some constituent might "get himself in trouble by failing to register," and asked that ministers, justices of the peace, millers, "and all others who come in contact with the public do their part toward fully informing the public as to this important matter." Boyd explained that all men aged twenty-one to thirty-one had to register, regardless of their plans to request exemptions.[7]

National authorities who remembered the draft riots of the 1860s looked toward registration day with some trepidation, but throughout the country young men registered without any major disruptions. The Upper Cumberland followed the national norm. In Cookeville registration day began as Rutledge Smith had planned:

> At 7 o'clock all the whistles in town were blown, and church bells rung, for two minutes. At 8 o'clock the band had assembled at the depot and headed a parade to the courthouse, where the registration took place. A large crowd was assembled in the courthouse during the entire morning, and several patriotic speeches made. A number of girls pinned a small American flag on each young man, after registering. The day was quiet, nothing occuring [sic] to mar the event or hinder the work. There was very little trouble anywhere in the county. Putnam County registered 1561 men.[8]

In country stores, schools, and courthouses young men filled out their draft cards without protest, participating in a ritual that united, however briefly, all men of their generation.[9]

Willingness to register, however, did not necessarily mean eagerness to serve. In this first of three World War I registrations, potential conscripts could indicate their intention to ask for exemption from service, and their reasons for doing so, on their registration card. The number of requests for exemption varied widely from county to county, as a sample of 330 draft cards from Clay, Cumberland, De-

Kalb, and Fentress Counties indicates. In DeKalb County 74 of the 122 men in the sample requested exemptions. In Clay and Cumberland Counties just over half the registrants requested exemptions. Only in Fentress County did the majority of registrants fail to ask for exemption. Fourteen men out of a sample of 72 requested exemptions. Perhaps patriotism prevailed more in Sergeant York's home county than in Cumberland County, adjacent on the plateau. But Fentress County registrars may also have discouraged requests for exemption: on one Fentress County draft card the registrar wrote that the man registering had no sensible reasons for wanting an exemption. On the other hand, registrars may have believed that listing dependents was the equivalent of asking for an exemption. Although most married men requested exemptions, 32 from Fentress did not.[10]

Ample evidence indicates that the majority of men called to the army in June 1917 would not have volunteered for service. In Clay, Cumberland, and DeKalb Counties 140 of 257 men whose draft cards were examined requested exemptions. A report from the *Carthage Courier* on June 7, 1917, noted that of the 1,463 Smith County men who had registered, only 296 did not request an exemption. The writer also estimated that "there is something like 100 who should have registered but failed to do so. Sheriff Dean says that he has received information concerning a number of the 'slackers' and that the government is going to require him to gather them all up within the next few days."[11] Proponents of conscription argued that the draft equitably distributed the burden of military service. If Upper Cumberland men's responses were in any way typical, another reason for conscription is immediately evident: without it the United States would not have been able to put an army into the field.

Most men who claimed exemptions cited poor health, dependent relatives, or some combination of the two. In DeKalb County a startlingly large number of young men had health conditions they thought should keep them out of the service; these afflictions ranged from serious disabilities to poor vision to "piles." Given that the median age of marriage for men in 1900 was 21, it is not surprising to find that many men who registered for the first draft, which took men 21 to 31, were married. Not all these men requested exemptions, but most did.[12]

Several Upper Cumberland men requested exemptions for religious reasons. Alvin York's draft card indicates that in 1917 he was 29, single, and employed as a farm laborer by R. C. Pile, who was also York's pastor at the Church of Christ in Christian Union, an unaffiliated holiness church with no connection to the more numerous Churches of Christ. As postmaster at Pall Mall, Pile served as registrar for the draft. York and two other Pall Mall men gave as their reasons for wanting exemptions, "Don't want to fight." In other counties, men wrote that going to war was against their religious beliefs. George Ray Lee, 21, of DeKalb County, said, "The Church of God, of which I am a member, forbids its members engage in carnal warfare." William Edward Hargrove, 30, of Clay County had a dependent family and a physical disability, but he also recorded his belief that "it [war] is not the teaching of the New Testament."[13]

Most of the conscientious objectors who stated a church affiliation belonged to the Church of Christ, by 1917 the third largest religious group in the region. Although the Churches of Christ had no official creed or any official denominational hierarchy, some young men requested exemptions from the draft on the grounds that "Church of Christ creed forbids." David Lipscomb, the long-term editor of the *Gospel Advocate*, for years preached strict pacifism.[14] After Lipscomb's death in 1917 his nephew, A. B. Lipscomb, urged members of the church to put aside thoughts of national vengeance and be prepared to be "cowards" for Jesus' sake. E. A. Elam, an evangelist popular in the Upper Cumberland, in July 1917 published an article insisting that no Christian could reconcile war with the spirit of Jesus. He and other members of the *Advocate* staff offered to sign conscientious objectors' petitions for exemption. In August Elam wrote that he would go with any young man requesting exemption before the local or district board or, if necessary, to "Washington City."[15]

Church of Christ ministers such as Elam and independent pastors such as R. C. Pile failed in their efforts to get church members exempted from military service. Members of churches without long traditions of opposition to war did not generally receive exemptions to the draft during World War I. Instead draft boards told the members of churches that claimed no creed but the Bible that the Bible could be interpreted in different ways. Like Alvin York, conscripted members of the Church of Christ or of holiness sects had to work out their problems of conscience with their commanders in army camps.[16]

After the first registration in June, the federal government organized regular draft boards. These boards could exempt men from the draft. If a man failed to get an exemption from his local board, he could appeal to the district board in Nashville; conversely, the district board could reverse exemptions allowed by local boards and order men to report to duty. Officially President Woodrow Wilson appointed draft boards; however, in most states governors exerted considerable influence on the choice of board members. In the Upper Cumberland as in the nation as a whole, "local commercial and professional elites" dominated the local draft boards.[17] In Putnam County the draft board included the county judge, a former sheriff, a Presbyterian minister, and a local physician. In DeKalb County a farmer/trader chaired the draft board, and a traveling salesman, two doctors, and an attorney also served.[18]

In Fentress County most of the members of the draft board had not been born in the county. Ohio native Ward Case, a lawyer then serving as county judge, headed the board. (His father had come to Tennessee in 1889 to teach at the utopian community at Rugby.) Other members included J. T. Wheeler, a native of Rhea county who was a pharmacist/lawyer specializing in "land law"; Dr. J. N. Chism, a native of Kentucky with a Vanderbilt medical degree who also operated a large farm; C. P. Garrett, born in California and resident in Tennessee since 1911, who was employed as a stenographer and as pastor of the Christian Church in Jamestown; and Dr. W. E. Mullinax, dentist and Pickett County native who also served as county superintendent of schools.[19]

In early August, as local draft boards prepared to examine the first group of draftees, Rutledge Smith put out a press release advising young men not to "shirk" the draft. Smith allowed that some men honestly did have dependents "necessitating their presence at home in order to provide support," but he warned of dire consequences for those who thoughtlessly asked for exemptions. "The man who does not bear his part of the burden in this awful conflict will sooner than he may imagine become a marked man and the finger of scorn will be pointed at him and his posterity forever. . . . As the United States is at war it must follow that a large majority of its citizens are in full sympathy and accord with the war . . . and the man who now shirks his duty may expect to feel the hearty hand of the righteous wrath of his fellow man. The man who does not shoulder his burden need not expect, nor will not [sic] receive, the sympathy or support of his fellows." Smith said that parents would not allow their children to be "instructed by school teachers not in sympathy with the order of the day." In the future, Smith said, no man who had requested an exemption would ever be elected to any public office. The affidavits requesting exemption would always be part of the public record and would be used as evidence against the good character of men should they be involved in lawsuits. As for businessmen, "If he, his sons or his brothers seek to escape military service, [they] will before they appreciate find their business wrecked and they themselves outcast from an indignant society." Smith suggested that thoughtless young men who filed for exemptions would find death on the field of battle preferable to their fate at the hands of a contemptuous public. As for the coward "seeking by exemption to escape," Smith considered such a man "more intolerable than the imperial enemy we face, and [he] deserves no more sympathy than to be shot as a traitor."[20] Such was the "order of the day" as seen by the man who directed conscription in Tennessee.

The overwhelming support for the war that Smith presupposed did not exist among his Upper Cumberland neighbors. When men drafted from the first registration reported to the local draft boards for physicals in August, newspaper reports indicated that many of those drafted did not want to serve. In Smith County almost all of the 350 men called in asked to be exempted. According to a report from Carthage, "There is a feeling of quiet submission on the part of those called, with no enthusiasm. In one section of the county, Pleasant Shade, it is said Tom Watson's Magazine has caused some discension [sic] and a fund has been contributed to test the validity of the draft act in the courts."[21] In Overton County 118 men passed the physical. A newspaper story noted that "out of this number about 100 are claiming exemptions, nearly all of them being married men with from two to five children."[22]

In the end it made little difference whether a prospective conscript came from a county where many claimed exemptions or from a county where few did. Taking the Upper Cumberland as a whole, 30,411 men registered for the draft, and 3,567, or 11 percent, were inducted into the army. The percentage of men registered who eventually wound up in the army varied slightly from county to county, from a low of 9 percent in White County to a high of 13 percent in Clay County.[23]

In September the first groups of conscripts began leaving Upper Cumberland counties, inspiring poignant public farewells. None were more painful than those in Livingston. In 1916 many of the young men of the town had joined Companies M and C of the Tennessee National Guard. As Charlie D. Smith recalled ruefully two years later, "When we boys signed our name to Uncle Sam's paper at Livingston Tenn., we didn't realize that the United States were at war. Of course we were called on to do some guard duty out on the Mexican border which was just a trip of sport."[24] Company M, back from guarding the border against Pancho Villa, was mustered out and thirteen days later was called back into service and sent to a training camp in South Carolina.

S. B. McGee, editor of the Livingston *Golden Age*, described the departure of Company C:

> All day last Sunday, and for days, a death-like pall has hung over Livingston and surrounding country as the members of Company C. paid their parting visits to loved ones. Many homes were like death chambers and religious services took on aspect of funerals.
>
> At 9:15 Monday, the hour for the train to carry them away, more than 2,000 people had gathered at the station. They came from far and near to bid the 100 young men Godspeed. . . . No brass band was there to thrill them with sweet music. No orator proclaimed aloud the inspiring words so common on such occasions. It was a quiet determined procession, showing at every breath and step the patriotism which prompted it to action. Strong men trembled and women wept as one by one these, our boys, boarded the train. . . . The signal was given and they moved away in breathless silence, save the waving of tear-stained handkerchiefs as the last act of encouragement.[25]

After September 1917, letters from soldiers became a regular feature in most Upper Cumberland papers. Some soldiers wrote directly to the editors, while family members forwarded other letters. Taken as a group the letters indicate that most soldiers, reluctant conscripts or not, adjusted well to army life. They quickly assured family members that the army clothed and fed them well. (Such assurances, repeated so often, seem to indicate that Upper Cumberland parents believed army life involved semistarvation; this assumption might have been based on the Confederate experience.)[26]

Other than homesickness ("I have heard several of the boys say they did not realize what home was until they were drafted"), Upper Cumberland soldiers had few complaints about the army. Many expressed amazement at the size of Camp Gordon and similar army posts, where 40,000 or 50,000 men might drill at one time—a pretty sight to Oscar Maggart of Jackson County. O. L. Green of Putnam County noted, "I used to think 12 or 15 was a large family. We are fixed here so that 250 can live in the same building."[27]

Upper Cumberland conscripts responded to military life according to their individual temperaments. Some acquired religion in the army or found their faith a comfort in their new surroundings. Others became proud of their prowess as soldiers. Edgar Gossage of Putnam County wrote to his mother, "Monday morning I was picked out of 350 men for a leader, and it made me feel good when he called me out to lead the company and the new men that have just come in. He gives me a bunch of them to drill, and I am going to make good in the army."[28]

By the summer of 1918 local papers printed cheerful letters from soldiers in France. Being farmers, the men from the Upper Cumberland noticed differences in farming practices in Europe, the most striking being the French tendency to live in villages instead of isolated farms, and the French habit of sheltering farm animals on the ground floor of the farmhouse. As always, the fact that the French did not speak English came as a shock to some men. Henry Trisdale told his mother not to bother sending him money: "Money wouldn't do me any good here, for the French talk like geese, and you can't tell them what you want, you have to go and get it." Trisdale added that French girls were pretty, but not as pretty as the girls back home, a sentiment with which other Upper Cumberland soldiers agreed, at least for publication.[29]

Some soldiers gained a new perspective on their home. A Smith County man, serving at Camp Jackson, South Carolina, said that home was prettier than the Carolinas but that Tennessee should emulate South Carolina's good roads. One Overton County man noted the good roads of France. I. F. Dillon, disturbed to find so many of his fellow Tennesseans illiterate, wrote from France to call for better and more "efficient" rural schools.[30]

The Upper Cumberland contributed its share of heroes in World War I. Alvin York was awarded the congressional Medal of Honor. Leslie Beaty of Fentress, a machine gunner, won the Distinguished Service Cross for carrying a wounded soldier to safety under heavy German fire. George Ashburn of Fentress County was said to be the first American serviceman wounded in France. Shot while digging a trench, Ashburn continued his task; for this he received the Croix de Guerre. Other recipients of the Distinguished Service Cross included Theodore Boyd of Carthage, Frank Y. Hill and Hugh B. Moorman of Sparta, John A. Mitchell of Livingston, and James H. S. Morison of Cumberland County. Milo Lemert of Crossville was awarded the Medal of Honor posthumously.[31] Two hundred and eight Upper Cumberland men died in the service, in combat or from diseases. Most Tennessee soldiers, however, survived and came home with stories to tell about their time in France.

Meanwhile, home front mobilization in the Upper Cumberland became the revenge of the town folk. Mobilization put considerable if unspecified power into the hands of members of the town elites, many of whom were veterans of thwarted progressive campaigns in the region. In counties where over 75 percent of the population worked in agriculture, the committees directing mobilization did not include farmers or the small-town merchants whose livelihood depended on the agricultural trade. Instead, people who had social, political, and commercial ties with their counterparts in towns throughout the state—society women, bankers, executives, lawyers, and physicians—ran war mobilization. Progressives, who had been unable to attain progressive goals through the democratic process, now had power handed to them.

Congress established the Council of National Defense in 1916 in an attempt to keep wartime mobilization decentralized. The national council was supposed to coordinate mobilization through state councils, which would in turn coordinate county and even school district councils. These councils would help with conscription, promote patriotism, and facilitate federal plans for mobilizing agriculture and labor. This emphasis on old geographic patterns of governance quickly proved inadequate to mobilizing an American economy that was organized by sector along lines of function, not locality. Federal agencies created later often bypassed or ignored the state and local councils.[32]

Tennessee's Council of National Defense, headed by Rutledge Smith, was the best in the South, according to William J. Breen's study of state councils. A memorandum in Governor Rye's papers, probably written by Smith, states that the Tennessee council should "assist in the enrollment of elligibles [sic]" for the draft and "make those who are thus selected to serve their country feel the responsibility and honor conferred upon them." The council would oversee raising subscriptions to the upcoming Liberty Loan. The memo called for "the highest service and the nobelest [sic] sacrifice," adding, "We are at war with German autocracy. Its people are the most warlike in the world. They are also the most industrious, most frugal and most highly educated. It is just as necessary that we match them in our every day life as on the battlefield and that our every action be as intelligent and as determined as theirs." Recognizing that Tennessee's primary economic contribution to the war effort would be agricultural, the memo suggested that the council require all farmers to furnish information as to their operations to Smith or to the commissioner of agriculture so that "those in authority may be able to estimate accurately the amount of agricultural products Tennessee can be counted upon to furnish during this year."[33]

Although the state paid lip service to agriculture's importance, it did not invite farmers to participate in wartime planning. Urban leaders dominated the council organized May 10, 1917. Of the sixteen men on the executive board, nine were from either Nashville, Knoxville, Memphis, or Chattanooga. The remainder were from Kingsport, Cookeville, Paris, Centerville, Clarksville, Humboldt, and Jackson.[34] This board established committees to deal with finance, legal questions, sanitation and medicine, food supply and conservation, industry, labor, military affairs, and coordination with county councils of defense. To reach the state's farmers the council planned to work through county agents, the state department of agriculture, and the presidents of farmers' institutes in the state's three grand divisions.[35]

The federal government conceived of the councils as democracy in action: decentralized and dependent upon public support rather than the coercive power of law for their effectiveness. In fact, war mobilization in the Upper Cumberland proved to be profoundly undemocratic. Appointed, not elected, councils could not be deposed by local people, nor did councils have clearly defined responsibilities or powers. The local councils' charge included promoting patriotism, encouraging compliance with wartime regulation of the local economy, and coordinating fund raising for Liberty Bonds and the Red Cross. To do so they combined appeals to community spirit and patriotism with threats of retaliation against slackers.

In Putnam County mobilization began with a food supply campaign in the spring of 1917. At a meeting in May at the city school, Cookevillians organized nine "teams" to take the message of increased food production and conservation to the countryside. The teams included Cookeville ministers, businessmen, Tennessee Polytechnic Institute professors, and their wives, many of whom would later have official status as council of defense committee members. Each team had a seven-point message to put across to meetings in each section of the county; the first point was "The crisis, or sounding the alarm."[36]

The spectacle of college professors, lawyers, and prominent members of the Cookeville Woman's Club telling farmers what to grow and how to conserve food prompted one farmer to write to the *Putnam County Herald*:

> When times are as exciting as now people sometimes almost lose their senses and go to extremes. . . .
>
> There is, in my opinion, much needless or useless advice being handed out to the farmers and farmers' wives by college professors, our city relatives and ministers, who are not experienced, telling how, what, when and where to plant. How to practice home economy, etc., when actually they had never seen a farm until this great cry for food became so popular.
>
> Why, we farmers are out with our lines over "Old Kit" and in the furrows long before they have been awakened from their sweet slumbers.
>
> We appreciate instruction but if we need it please may it be from those who have had enough experience to know gee from haw, and which cow gives the sweet and which the butter milk.
>
> Very few farmers have been invited to speak at these food meetings and this rather brings the impression that the speaker is some-

times more anxious to lower his own high cost of living than to save his country.

According to the writer farmers could best serve their country by planting crops that they knew could be successfully cultivated: "Don't be hoo-dooed into experimenting this year, for the season is late and cool and there is no time for experiments now." Instead farmers should "fight the weeds instead of each other, and look ever to the great God of all harvests, who has promised to never fail us if we do our part."[37]

When appointed, the local councils of defense did not include leaders in any way representative of the rural population. Instead members of the county seat elite and their wives staffed the council and its auxiliary committees and agencies. Many had worked for better roads and schools; most of the men were of the prohibitionist wing of the Democratic Party. Although mainstream Baptists and members of the Church of Christ belonged to local councils of defense and Red Cross organizations, and Methodist and Presbyterian ministers led local mobilization efforts, few members of the local-istic, sectarian denominations seem to have been involved in war work.[38] Ironically, while progressives throughout the nation made democracy a rallying cry and set up mobilization agencies that exemplified what government by experts could accomplish, on the local level in the Upper Cumberland who one was—or who one knew—seems to have counted more than either democracy or expertise in determining who directed mobilization.[39]

In Putnam County the Council of National Defense, the local board of the Red Cross, and the committees in charge of fund raising for "war work" formed a small club that excluded farmers. James N. Cox chaired the local council and also served as federal food administrator. Cox, the general manager of the Gainesboro Telephone Company and a well-known Cookeville civic activist, had by 1917 promoted good roads, Dixie College, and prohibition; he went on to be mayor of Cookeville and helped with local mobilization during World War II.[40]

The women's division of the council, especially active in Putnam County, drew its membership from town ladies who had gained organizational experience in women's clubs. In 1916 a state women's conference had been held at Cookeville; it featured speakers from the

Woman's Christian Temperance Union, the Parent-Teachers Association, the Daughters of the American Revolution, and the Federated Women's Club. The conference theme was "Organization and Education," and the local organizers of the conference noted that "organization is the only method of perfecting anything and education is fast coming this way." Many of the women who participated in the 1916 conference worked on war mobilization committees a year later.[41]

James N. Cox's sister Clara Cox Epperson, wife of merchant John A. Epperson, headed the Putnam County Women's Division of the council of defense. Clara Epperson, a member of the Church of Christ, a former teacher, and poet laureate of the Tennessee Federation of Women's Clubs, had campaigned for the inclusion of women on school boards. Her subcommittee chairwomen included women who, with their husbands, formed the core of support for progressive policies in the county. They or their husbands had worked for prohibition and education reform.[42] These men and women also served on the Committee for the United War Work Campaign organized in November 1918 to raise money for various agencies, including the YMCA and the Salvation Army.[43]

The county seat elite dominated war mobilization in other Upper Cumberland counties as well. In Jackson County B. L. Quarles, bank president, chaired the local council of defense. Nine of seventeen committee heads in that county were from the county seat, Gainesboro, which had a population of 408 in 1910, out of a county population of 15,036.[44] In Overton County religious and educational leaders, many not native to the region, shared control of mobilization with prominent local men and women.[45]

In addition to assisting with conscription, the Upper Cumberland councils of national defense had two other basic tasks: to "enlist" the population by getting various groups to register with the government, and to raise money for the war through Liberty Loan, Red Cross, and War Work campaigns. The county councils approached this work in the spirit of progressive reform campaigns. They tried first to arouse public support, using schools, churches, and public meetings as venues for disseminating propaganda. In general these methods sufficed to get people to cooperate with mobilization. However, when people did not cooperate, the councils threatened to shame them as slackers or to turn their names in to federal authorities for some ill-defined retaliation.

The councils began enrolling the population for war mobilization in October 1917 with two drives. Encouraged by the Council of National Defense, local councils tried to enlist all women sixteen and over. According to Governor Rye's proclamation, the government wanted "an accounting . . . of the women power of the state available for the several activities and occupations women are now pursuing and may be called upon to pursue during the war." The second drive, conducted by the women's councils on behalf of the food administration, had as its goal enrolling households in the government's food conservation programs. Both registration drives, following so closely on the registration of young men for the draft, stirred skepticism and suspicion among some residents of the region.[46]

Governor Tom Rye designated October 13 women's registration day and requested that all women come to register at the same polling places where men had signed up for the draft. Although the information furnished with the registration cards published in local papers emphasized that no women would be drafted, the process and the locale surely called up mental associations that were not precisely what the government intended. A statement by the council of defense printed in the *Jackson County Sentinel* did not seem designed to allay any woman's suspicions, being extremely martial in tone:

It is expected that every loyal woman in Tennessee will register on October 13th. . . .

It is true that the registration is not legally compulsory and those who fail to register will not be put in jail, but not for a moment can we conceive of Tennesseans failing to respond to the call of their country simply because they are under no legal penalty to do so. . . .

The diverting from industry and business of the thousands of men needed for the army and navy is already being felt throughout the country. There is to follow a general shifting of men and occupations, which with the curtailment of man power available for the civil pursuits can be regarded in no other light than a serious problem calling for the best thought of economists. It is therefore desired to register the women of America over 16 years of age, classifying them as to those who are trained and those who are untrained, and showing the work they are best fitted to do. . . . Opportunity will be given in many instances for the special training of those now untrained, and their eyes opened to the duty they owe themselves and to their countrymen to grasp the opportunity and add their bit to the sum total of national efficiency. It is hoped that American women will be mobilized as a mighty army, rising to the occasion from the patriotism in their hearts, and directed in their manoeuvers by the brains in their heads.[47]

Councils of defense insisted that women did not have to enroll but at the same time put intense pressure on them to assure that they complied with registration. Cookeville editor Elmer Wirt protested on October 11, 1917: "Whether or not a woman registers next Saturday is a matter left wholly to her judgement. There is no law on this question. Statements to the effect that those who do not register are traitors are false. People who make them apparently don't know what patriotism or treason are. The idea that a person who don't agree with you is a traitor is all tommyrot. And there is too much of this traitor talk."[48] Since the records of the state council of national defense are not available, there is no exact data as to how many Upper Cumberland women did register in October 1917. However, reports to the national council indicate that 66,000 of the state's 662,013 women registered; of those, 13,000 were from Nashville. The director of registration complained that German sympathizers in the state had discouraged registration by linking it to the suffrage movement.[49]

Registration signified that a woman's patriotic duty might outweigh her responsibility to her family, a highly novel and suspect notion in the Upper Cumberland, where only men traditionally held the prerogatives and responsibilities of citizenship. In addition, the registration form asked women to specify what line of work they did and what they wanted training in. In the Upper Cumberland many women had experience in poultry raising or child care, and a few had pink-collar occupations. But the idea that the government wanted women to be doctors, lawyers, pharmacists, or dentists and that women could learn to fly airplanes or ride motorcycles must have been a revelation. Through the registration the government intended to compile lists of women available for service. The last question on the form was "How soon can you start?" Small wonder women in the region feared signing up, even for volunteer work.[50] In February 1918 the Livingston paper found it necessary to assure women that the Red Cross was safe: "Some have not joined for fear of having to render other service. Such is a mistake, no obligation is incurred in joining."[51]

The food administration's Pledge Card Drive also began that same October. The county councils were told to canvass each community and get every head of household to sign a card pledging to conserve food. When the Overton County home demonstration agent urged all women to sign Hoover Pledge Cards to show their loyalty to the Wilson administration, the editor of the local newspaper ran her plea under the title "Ladies Enlist Now"—surely an unfortunate choice of words. In Jackson County the women's council called on all teachers, ministers, and club members to assist with the Food Pledge Drive and made signing the cards a test of patriotism. However, just before the drive began, the local paper ran a press release from Rutledge Smith denying reports charging the food administration and the local councils with getting rich on the high salaries they were drawing for war work. The press release warned that anyone who interfered with "pledge card propaganda, who seeks to obstruct it or who makes false statements with respect to it" violated the Federal Espionage Law. Despite these encouragements Jackson County did not make its quota of 3,200 cards. The campaign began October 29. By November 8 only 500 households had signed pledge cards.[52]

By 1918 local mobilizing agencies changed their focus from enumerations to raising money through Liberty Loan drives, Red Cross drives, campaigns to sell War Savings Stamps, and in November 1918 a final War Work Drive to raise money for seven quasi-independent charities, including the Salvation Army and the YMCA. To stimulate interest, fund raisers held frequent rallies. Like communities throughout the nation Upper Cumberland counties went "over the top" repeatedly, filling their quotas for these drives. However, by the summer of 1918 fund raisers began to threaten to label as slackers people who did not buy War Savings Stamps or one more issue of Liberty Bonds. Supposedly voluntary contributions to the war effort rapidly assumed the nature of taxes.

In several counties local officials issued public warnings that those not wholeheartedly supporting the war effort would wind up on the lists being compiled (by unnamed parties) of traitors and slackers. In June the mayor of Alexandria, in DeKalb County, told his constituents that they had to buy War Savings Stamps. The mayor said, "Our duty is as binding as [that of the soldiers] and we are required to take orders from our commander in chief." According to the mayor those who evaded this duty, those who failed to buy as many stamps as they could afford, and those whose attitude "smack[ed] of disloyalty" would be listed. The slacker list would go to Rutledge Smith; people suspected of disloyalty would be reported to the Department of Justice.[53]

In July 1918 the chairman of the Putnam County War Savings Stamps Committee ordered his district directors to report anyone who had not pledged or who had pledged only "a nominal amount." The chairman said that the names would be turned over to "Major Rutledge Smith, the highest military authority in the State." People who impeded the sale of War Savings Stamps would be reported to the Department of Justice. The chairman suggested that the recalcitrant be given another opportunity to contribute so that Putnam County could maintain its good record and go over the top for War Savings Stamps. Authorities made similar threats in other counties. In Smith County people were told that if they did not buy War Savings Stamps, their names would "be immediately forwarded to Washington and things will be made uncomfortable for them."[54]

When some districts of Jackson County failed to make their quota in the War Savings Stamps drive held June 28, 1918, the county had to repeat the drive. The local paper printed the orders sent to B. L. Quarles, the banker who headed the local council: "Call your Committee together for that District; assess each head of family, each wage-earner, and each employee living with family, the amount the Committee decides they are able to pledge and buy within the next six months." Quarles was supposed to summon all adults in the delinquent districts to a meeting to hear speeches about the War Savings Stamps program. The instructions warned, "Don't let the crowd leave without pledging the amount assigned to them."[55]

By August 15 the local paper could report that Jackson County had managed to reduce the number of slackers. More than 100 men who had been reported as slackers had come to the county seat with the committees from their districts, "and with only one or two exceptions every man pledged the amount the committee had assessed him." The paper attributed the failure of the first drive to a lack of understanding on the part of the public and expressed hopes that soon every district in the county would be slacker free and "100 per cent American."[56]

Did the public in the region support the war? If so, why did the government have to threaten people to get them to give to fundraising drives? These questions are difficult to answer, given the nature of the historical record. People could speak as much as they pleased in favor of the war, but dissenters faced federal prosecution. Most printed material dating from the period, therefore, is prowar. In the region local historians tend to accept as a given that Upper Cumberland men, as loyal scions of the Volunteer State, could hardly wait to get into the army. For example, a history of White County published in the 1930s says that "sentiment very quickly crystalized" in favor of the war. The same history goes on to note that a cavalry company was stationed at Sparta for a time to guard the railroad bridges and round up slackers.[57]

Public displays of support for the war rarely materialized spontaneously. Instead local war mobilizers, often acting on orders from their superiors, organized the rallies, parades, and meetings so profusely reported by Upper Cumberland newspapers. However, people in the region did occasionally exhibit unrehearsed enthusiasm for the war effort. In Algood, in Putnam County, the schoolchildren began daily military drills in December 1917. According to the Putnam County newspaper, the girls participated in the drills to show their patriotism, and "One girl stated that if she was a boy she would be wearing the uniform and shooting at the Kaiser's men."[58]

Some Upper Cumberland residents fervently supported war mobilization in an expansive version of traditional family loyalty. Regardless of whether people in the Upper Cumberland would have chosen to go to war with Germany in 1917, once the war began and American troops were committed, many felt obligated to help "the boys."[59] Thus Mrs. Ova McClain, a countrywoman of Putnam County, wrote to the *Putnam County Herald* in November 1917 to urge people to cooperate with the federal food administration:

Just why they are asked to eat less wheat, less meat and less sugar is not understood by many who have not taken the trouble to inform themselves on this war situation. They cannot see how eating more corn bread and less wheat bread only once a day will help. . . . There is a question now as to who will get the wheat bread, the comfortable folks at home or the boys at the front. I say the boys, always. Corn bread at your table will mean wheat bread for a boy at the front. Less sugar will mean less candy parties, and not so many cakes and cookies at home, but wouldn't it be much better for us to have less than the boys none.[60]

Or as Putnam County agent J. Jacobs said in urging farmers to produce more during the crisis, "No matter what you think of the present war policy, no matter if you think it is all wrong, it is your duty to feed your son and your neighbor's son, who are at the front protecting the land upon which you raise food for him."[61]

Some people in the region openly opposed the war by speaking against U.S. policies, by refusing to contribute to war bond drives, or by evading the draft. Slackers and war resisters came from all classes, from prominent merchants and political leaders to the poorest, most isolated farmers. Their motivations varied, as did the punishments their dissent provoked. Middle-aged, middle-class slackers whose indiscreet conversation got them into trouble rarely faced prosecution. Farmers who spoke too roughly were cited for sedition. Young men who evaded the draft risked more serious discipline from military authorities.

As far as can be determined from newspaper stories and court records, none of the Upper Cumberland men charged with sedition had foreign origins or sympathies. Simple farmers, most were guilty of impetuous, indiscreet, and often profane criticism of President Wilson. John Nard, a Warren County farmer whose arrest was reported in the DeKalb County press, typifies the group. In August 1917 authorities charged Nard with cursing the president and saying, "Any kink-headed negro in the South has more sense than President Wilson." Nard was bound over to U.S. District Court.[62]

People who had grudges against their neighbors discovered that they could use the federal authorities as instruments of revenge. In October 1917 a Fentress County farmer was denounced by two brothers who owed him a half bushel of corn. Si Stepp, the creditor, had loaned the Beatty brothers corn he could ill spare when they promised to pay him back quickly. When the brothers did not make good on the debt, Stepp remonstrated with them. In retaliation they informed federal authorities in Jamestown that Stepp had said, "Dad Gum the war- old President Wilson ought to be shot and stop this war. That there was no use of the war, that he was going to take his pistol and go to Washington and kill Wilson." On the basis of this testimony Stepp was indicted by the grand jury. In order to clear his name he brought to federal court in Cookeville depositions from his neighbors indicating that the Beattys had denounced Stepp as a means of getting even with him over the matter of the corn. Stepp denied threatening the president, saying that while he was a Republican, he had voted for Wilson in 1912. (He added that he suspected political malice on the part of the Beatty brothers, who were Democrats.) Stepp in effect threw himself on the mercy of the court, admitting that he was poor, illiterate, and ignorant of dealings at law; he said he had never even seen a railroad engine until he traveled from Fentress County to Cookeville to defend himself in federal court. Stepp was acquitted in June 1919.[63]

In May 1918, after Congress had passed a strengthened Sedition Act, Tom Carmack of Jackson County faced charges for criticizing the Red Cross. According to depositions filed in the case Carmack interrupted as a Red Cross volunteer solicited a donation from Henry Stafford, saying, "Uncle Henry, you had better keep that $5.00 and buy whiskey with it. It will do you more good. It won't do the soldier boys any good. When you give it to that Red Cross it goes to keep up a pack of God-damn whores." In prosecuting Carmack, federal attorney Lee Douglas stated that Carmack "well knew" that the Red Cross nurses were not prostitutes. According to Douglas the Red Cross was an agency of the government, headed by President Wilson. Since the Red Cross helped with the war, to criticize the organization hurt the war effort. Carmack made no statement in his own defense. His case dragged on until 1919, when prosecution was dropped.[64]

In May 1918 a deputy U.S. marshal arrested L. L. McDowell, superintendent of schools in DeKalb County, for sedition. McDowell, elected superintendent by the county court without opposition in the previous month, appeared before the U.S. commissioner at Cookeville, charged with "uttering language unfriendly to President

Wilson, and in opposition to plans and policies of the United States in the war with Germany." McDowell went free on $5,000 bond. Newspaper reports stated, "There are rumors that other arrests will be made on similar charges."[65]

In the spring of 1918 mobilization leaders encouraged public hysteria over loyalty issues and used that hysteria to help raise money for the war. The U.S. prosecutor for sedition cases issued a press release explaining the proper procedure for denouncing a neighbor: contact his office in Nashville, and be sure to sign the letter, as that would enable the government to contact the accuser to "secure the additional information necessary" to convict the person named.[66] In White County the local newspaper "exposed" the merchants Young and Boles, who ran a large store in the county seat, for their refusal to buy Liberty Bonds, sell thrift stamps, aid the Red Cross, or contribute in any way. The paper accused one of the people in the firm of insulting members of the Liberty Loan committee, which included a prominent woman. In its report the Sparta paper came close to calling for a boycott of Young and Boles. There is no record that any member of Young and Boles ever faced actual sedition charges. However, as a result of the exposure White County went over the top for the Liberty loans. At a rally, "The people, nervous over the sensational exposure" and feeling an added stigma in that the county had been slow in reaching its quota for the Liberty Loan, crowded in to hear politicians and a British army officer speak in favor of the war. The crowd, emotionally overwrought, cried and cheered the speakers. A reporter commented, "It is impossible to describe the emotions of one who was merely a looker-on of this event."[67]

Elmer Wirt, editor of the *Putnam County Herald*, used his editorial columns to point out the absurdity of aspects of war mobilization and got into trouble for doing so. Wirt published his paper in Cookeville, Rutledge Smith's hometown and the regional center of war mobilization, but he maintained a skeptical attitude toward the war and the measures being taken to prosecute it. Part of Wirt's opposition may have stemmed from old political grudges. In 1910, when Tennessee's Democratic Party split over prohibition, Wirt stayed with the party regulars. Putnam County council leader James Cox and Rutledge Smith had joined the prohibitionist Independent Democrats, who fused with the local Republicans to elect their ticket of county officers. Wirt had clashed with James Cox on at least one other occasion. Cox had offered to buy the city's electric power plant. Wirt, as city alderman, successfully campaigned to keep the city's plant in public ownership. Wirt had socialistic leanings that separated him from the elitist local progressives; although he often supported progressive reforms, he refused to consider himself a member of the group.[68]

During the spring of 1917 Wirt reproved people who casually labeled their neighbors traitors, and he exercised his right of free speech by publishing bad news about war mobilization in the *Herald*.[69] In July he criticized people who were overzealous in favor of conscription:

> Certain men in Cookeville are continually worrying themselves and their friends for fear that some man of the prescribed age failed to register and may therefore miss his chance of being drafted. We suppose their kind exist in all communities. We notice that these talkers are not of draft age, and generally have no sons who are. These facts probably account for the "gabfest." If they are so concerned about the Army getting men we suggest to these talkers that the door has been wide open for them to volunteer their own valuable services, and failure to do so constitutes them "slackers" as much as those who seek to dodge the draft.[70]

In October 1917 Wirt published an editorial supporting Senator Robert LaFollette, then under fire for his opposition to the war and to conscription. Wirt noted LaFollette's thirty years of public service and said, "He has always been for the people and against the big interests which no doubt accounts for the present bitter attacks on him." At this point Wirt had apparently gone too far; people he termed "braying patriots" denounced him to the government in an attempt to get the *Herald* suppressed. A local teacher told schoolchildren that Wirt, who had been born in Minnesota, was not a real American.[71]

Under fire, Wirt insisted on his own patriotism. He noted that his paper had "given over $200 worth of space to government and war matters over the past six months," for which the *Herald* had not been paid. In November 1917 he published an editorial titled "Super Patriots": "For one, I am tired of their yopping [*sic*] about their neighbors, and suggest they stop their self boasting until such time as they enlist in their country's army." Wirt said, "I have two sons and a son-in-law who are registered and another son who has several times sought to enlist in the navy. Personally, although 54 years of age I have offered my services as a soldier. Of this record I am proud, and deny the right of the yoppers to criticize me or question my loyalty, or that of any other man who must furnish sons for the army. Let the yoppers shut up or ENLIST."[72] After that outburst Wirt shut up for the duration, confining himself to publishing critical news stories.

Those who refused to serve in the army offered the most serious resistance to the war effort and suffered the most severe penalties. In World War I, military authorities considered drafted men who failed to show up for induction to be deserters as well as those who absented themselves from military camps. According to John White-clay Chambers II, approximately 2.4 to 3.6 million men evaded the draft by refusing to register. Of those 2.8 million men drafted, about 12 percent "deserted" by refusing induction. Chambers says that most of these deserters were poor men and members of ethnic minorities in the North, and poor whites and blacks in the South.[73]

Upper Cumberland deserters fit Chambers's description of the national norm. Members of the poorest class in the region, they became deserters by refusing to report for induction or by going AWOL. They did not desert or refuse service because of pacifism or principled opposition to the war; they refused to cooperate because they believed that no one had the right to force them into service, or because their loyalties to family and place were more important to them than abstract patriotism.[74]

Many Upper Cumberland deserters put family before nation. Take, for example, two DeKalb County deserters. Virgil Gentry of DeKalb County, twenty-seven, "uneducated and poor," lived near Alexandria "with his wife and two children and his aged parents in a little three-room log house." Conscripted for service, Gentry deserted and came back home and put out a crop. In May 1918 the government issued orders requiring local officers to pick up deserters. DeKalb County sheriff Puckett sent word to Gentry, offering him a chance to surrender. When Gentry refused to cooperate and let it be known that he "would not be taken alive," the sheriff and his deputies went to arrest the deserter. They arrived at Gentry's cabin shortly before midnight. The sheriff called to Gentry's father to "get up and light a lamp, they had come for Virgil." Virgil tried to escape and was shot. "Gentry yelled with pain and his wife and mother screamed saying 'he will do you no good now you have shot him.' "[75] The sheriff also arrested John Smith, who had failed to return to camp after leaving in March. Smith offered no resistance. According to the local paper, "Smith is married and has a wife and children. He lives with his parents and when arrested the screams of the old people could be heard for some distance."[76]

George Cox of Putnam County, who refused to come in for his draft physical, put up a fight when the Putnam County sheriff came for him. According to a telegram the Putnam County Draft Board sent Rutledge Smith, "in arresting him he shot the sheriff, two other men, one his brother, also arrested for assisting in resistance." Cox continued his battle in court until the war was over, fighting conscription and charges pending against him for shooting the sheriff.[77]

In July the government sent a squad of U.S. cavalry to capture deserters thought to be hiding in the hills along the southern border of the Upper Cumberland. Apparently stationed at McMinnville in Warren County, the troopers visited White and DeKalb Counties. As the *Alexandria Times* reported, "It is stated that the deserters will be given every opportunity to surrender but failing that they will be hunted down. Not only will the deserters be arrested but those who harbor them will be taken in charge and carried to Camp for trial by court martial." The paper noted, "The soldiers are fully equipped and their rifles and shining bayonets look like sure enough war."[78]

The friends of Rueben Walden, a DeKalb deserter, persuaded him to surrender rather than be captured by the soldiers. However, as "those to whom the surrender was to be made" approached his home, Walden went out to hunt squirrels in the woods. His family planned to blow a horn to signal him to come in and give himself up. "The officers came and the horn was sounded but the answer was the report of a gun that forever ended the young man's life. He had gone about the work of self destruction in a deliberate manner having cut the limb of a small bush in a way that the trigger of the shot gun could be pulled." According to the paper, "Walden leaves a wife and one child. He was a poor man and parties were at Smithville Monday collecting money to pay the burial expense."[79]

According to rumor, some sixty-five "slackers and deserters" hid out in the "Gulf" of the Caney Fork where Cumberland, White, and Bledsoe Counties met. The men, well supplied with arms, food, and money, had determined not to be taken alive. One, Thomas Walling, had been shot by soldiers after deserting from the army to be with his ailing wife.[80]

In late August mobilization authorities called a meeting of all "deferred classes" at Smithville, in DeKalb County. In response to the call 4,500 people came to the county seat—reportedly one of the largest crowds ever in the town. The meeting featured speeches by educators and home demonstration agents. The U.S. cavalry also attended, however, and took the opportunity to check the crowd for deserters, arresting one. Tom Jones, "a well respected farmer and good citizen of the 4th district, was also placed under arrest by the soldiers and carried away, charged with harboring a deserter." Failing to find a deserter they were hunting for, the officers of the cavalry troop located his wife in the crowd. She had been receiving an allotment from the army as the wife of a soldier. The cavalry officers took away her allotment scrip and tore it up. The local paper reported, "The crowd was very quiet but seemed to enjoy the occasion."[81]

When the war ended, the small towns of the Upper Cumberland erupted in celebration. In Gainesboro bells pealed, whistles blew, and "everybody rejoiced that the greatest war in the history of the world had come to a close." At a meeting at the courthouse over $2,000 was collected for the United War Work Campaign Fund.[82]

What legacy did the war leave in the Upper Cumberland? For the soldiers, serving brought pride and a wider view of the world. Conscription, however dreaded, took them from isolated rural communities, made them part of human assemblages larger than anything they had ever seen, and took them to places they would never otherwise have visited. As Cumberland County soldier Fred Dunlap wrote, "I have been to Paris and it sure is some place." Like Edgar Gossage of Putnam County, most Upper Cumberland "boys" took pride in making good in the army.[83]

What of the deserters and dissenters? Rutledge Smith warned in 1917 that a man's response to the crisis of war would mark his career for life. If that happened, it left few traces. Elmer Wirt continued to publish his newspaper, eventually selling it to a consortium headed by James Cox; Wirt and his family went on operating a print shop in Cookeville. Most of the region's sedition cases never came to trial; instead they were quietly dropped in 1919.[84]

The world war marked the first invasion in force of the modern state into the farmers' world of the Upper Cumberland. During the war the national government, acting through its agents in the region, required that men and women put their duty to the state ahead of their obligations to family and their religious beliefs. Many of the people in the countryside found that hard, if not impossible. Despite legal pressures, they resisted in language and in deed. More fortunate folk managed to merge potentially conflicting claims and to see the war as being fought to protect their own rural world.

Others brought to their confrontation with the U.S. Army the same obdurate refusal to accept authority that made the Upper Cumberland such a violent place. Some men in the region fought to prove that no one had the right to order them to fight. Many people reacted to the war as they had to progressive crusades for education reform: by complying as much as necessary and ignoring officious intrusions into family life as much as possible.

How much resistance was there? It is difficult to tell: free speech was suspended in 1917 and 1918. Wartime censorship casts a cloud over the historical record, a cloud that opens to give brief glimpses of what life in the region was like during the war. Through that cloud appear pictures that fit the official version of the World War I home front: prowar rallies, tearful but patriotic crowds waving goodbye to "soldier boys" entraining at mountain stations, and schoolchildren playing soldier at recess. But other pictures are more disturbing: men arrested for cursing the Red Cross, men carried off to military service while their families scream and wail, and that immense gathering of over 4,000 people at Smithville being very quiet as troopers on horseback weave through the crowd, stopping to question farmers suspected of sheltering neighbors now labeled "deserters."

In all, the war years in the Upper Cumberland worked an incomplete revolution. After the war, progressives had organizational experience and precedents on which to draw. They also had an enlarged constituency. Some people drew lessons from wartime cooperation that would lead them to cooperate with progressive reforms in the 1920s. However, progressives without federal authority to back them up still had hard battles for their programs in many Upper Cumberland counties. As always, the greatest impediment to progressive reform was not outright opposition but apathy on the part of the population. Without Uncle Sam looking over their shoulders, many residents of the region went back to being full-time slackers.

9

PERSISTENCE, POVERTY, AND POLITICS

People are already chafing under needless interference with their affairs.
Many people no longer look upon the rulers of the country as servants of
people as the old time rulers called themselves. But they almost regard
them as masters and many of them no longer regard them with respect and
confidence as formerly.—O. G. Fox, Jackson County farmer, 1920

During the 1920s Upper Cumberland folk resisted change and em-
braced it, working out their adjustment to the times in county politics, in schools, on road crews, and in their homes. Farmers faced the
agricultural depression of the 1920s, compounded by an enormous
increase in state taxes, and fought back. County politics increasingly
split along town/country lines as the economic interests and cultural
pretensions of the town folk were differentiated from those of their
country neighbors. Local conservatives opposed or co-opted state-
imposed progressive reforms in transportation and education. But

the greatest threats to tradition came from within the home, from children who might reject their fathers' ways and wives who might want a "new dispensation" in gender relations. In a world where taxes could be increased to pay for education that encouraged children to look down on their fathers' occupations, where public officials exhibited arrogance rather than deference to their constituents, where men criticized uppity women, and where women answered back in the county press or simply got into their cars and drove away, people in the region found unity in reaffirming their loyalty to the Bible. They did not always agree on what the book said, but as in the 1890s, they agreed that the Bible supplied the terms of discourse. When in 1925 Macon County representative John Washington Butler submitted to the legislature a bill outlawing the teaching of evolution in the state's public schools, his stand received almost unanimous support from people in the Upper Cumberland.

Upper Cumberland farmers began the decade by joining others throughout the state in a tax revolt aimed at the Democratic Party. War mobilization leaders, almost all Democrats, had alienated rural folk by their high-handed methods. As Jackson County farmer O. G. Fox noted, they seemed to see themselves as "masters" rather than as "servants" of the people. Democratic governor A. H. Roberts, a resident of Overton County, had been instrumental in obtaining Disciples of Christ funding for Livingston Academy. He was known well enough in the region to qualify as a native son. But when the Democrats, led by Roberts, raised land taxes, they provoked a voters' rebellion that swept their party from office and marked the resurgence of opposition to any kind of program that might call for an increase in the tax on land. The Upper Cumberland, always a bastion of low-tax sentiment, reaffirmed that tradition in the 1920s.

In 1918 Roberts was elected governor on the strength of his promise to reform the state's tax structure. The land tax, Tennessee's basic source of revenue, had been steadily increasing as the costs of state government rose. Roberts's plan, purportedly designed to alleviate the farmer's tax burdens, made the governor look either duplicitious or extraordinarily naive. Taxes would be placed on a sliding scale. Real property would be reassessed at its full market value by state, not local, assessors. Then the state's revenue needs would be projected for the next two years, and the tax rate would be set to meet those needs. As the total assessment of property increased, the state tax rate would theoretically decrease. Roberts assumed that owners of "intangible" property (stocks and bonds, for example) would voluntarily reveal those assets so that the state could tax them. The land tax could then be lowered. However, when owners of personal wealth did not rush to reveal their assets, Roberts's tax plan resulted in assessment increases of 260 percent on farmlands (just as agriculture slipped into its postwar recession), and the governor became one of the most unpopular men in the state's political history.[1]

In the Upper Cumberland, Cookeville editor Elmer Wirt forecast the results of the new tax law before it was fully implemented, warned of dire results for the Democratic Party, and even ran for governor himself in the Democratic primary in 1920. Local Democratic leaders, led by James Cox, eventually purchased Wirt's newspaper, apparently in an attempt to quiet his criticisms of Governor Roberts. Wirt's assessment of the situation proved accurate, however. As a Roberts supporter, a Cookeville attorney, wrote him in 1919, "All sensible people, and about the towns, know you should be renominated and they will do it in convention, but you remember that the old farmer has it laid up for you." The attorney feared that Roberts would be "butchered by these block-headed farmers when it comes to vote on the nomination for governor."[2]

When in March 1920 Jackson County farmer O. G. Fox wrote to the governor in protest against the new tax policy, his letter probably expressed the distress many of his neighbors felt at greatly increased tax assessments. Fox stated that as farm prices declined, the cost of labor had increased, as had the cost of everything farmers had to purchase. He disagreed with the policy of assessing farms at their market value. For Fox, farms were homes, not businesses that might be marketed: "There [are] many home owners who do not care to sell their homes. They are farmers and can not be anything else. There is no promotion for them. They will have to remain farmers. They can never be Judges and Governors but have to trudge along the 'even tenor of their way.' Now any condition that brings about dissatisfaction of the home owners or decrease the home owners of a country, will in the end be a disastrous policy."[3]

On election day Republican Alfred Taylor swept Roberts from office. Taylor, brother of former Democratic governor Robert "Our Bob" Taylor, won rural support by "arguing that farming land should be assessed and taxed more leniently than corporate wealth, since farming was 'not purely a profit thing.'" Taylor's victory was part of a Republican landslide that swept even the immensely popular Congressman Cordell Hull from office. (Hull was reelected two years later.)[4]

For the rest of the decade local politicians in the Upper Cumberland and in other rural parts of the state confronted resurgent low-tax sentiment and scrambled to disassociate themselves from any suggestion that they favored public expenditures that would lead to increases in taxes. Rural voters especially opposed appropriations for higher education. Thus in 1924 a candidate for state representative in Smith County maintained his support for local schools while proudly announcing that he had voted against appropriations for the University of Tennessee as a way of reducing state expenses. As he noted, no one from the county went to the university anyway. In 1926 C. S. Key, representing Smith County in the state legislature, courted voters by reminding them that he had kept his promise to vote against any measure that might increase the land tax. As a result, he had voted against appropriations for the University of Tennessee, the state normals, and Tennessee Polytechnic (in neighboring Putnam County).[5]

In 1926 Smith County farmer W. A. Scruggs explained the economic realities behind low-tax sentiment. In a letter to the Carthage paper, Scruggs protested the tendency of county government to get deeper in debt and then raise taxes. According to Scruggs, farmers had been in difficulties since the autumn of 1920. Men with good farms had been borrowing money to pay taxes for the past three years, "and we see from one to half dozen tracts of land advertised in this paper every week and then forced sales at that and bringing from 35 to 50 per cent of their purchase price. Is it possible that none of this makes any impression upon you with reference to the conditions of our county?"[6]

Scruggs's lament expressed what farmers in the Upper Cumberland faced in the 1920s. Comprising as they did the majority of taxpayers in all Upper Cumberland counties, farmers paid the bill for governance. Many farm families remained largely self-sufficient. To the extent that they produced for the market, farmers suffered from the national agricultural recession. They resented being taxed to pay for programs from which they could see no benefit. But such had been the farmers' lot for years. What produced the sense of embattlement that pervades farmers' letters to Upper Cumberland papers during the decade? In the 1920s farmers had to keep reminding themselves that theirs was an honorable, not a low, occupation. Farmers did not write that way in the 1890s. But by the 1920s literate men knew that their values no longer represented the national norm. The nation's dominant values had changed: the consumer economy of the 1920s did not honor self-sufficiency. What had been enough, a competency, in the 1890s was poverty in the 1920s, measured even by the standards of the region. By staying the same, by clinging to old economic patterns and old values, farm families in the Upper Cumberland became poor in comparison with their cousins in the towns.

As in the 1890s the typical Upper Cumberland man considered himself an independent farmer and controlled the labor of his wife and children. A survey of 313 households selected randomly from the 1920 census rolls indicates that of 453 workers, 254 were farmers and 80 were farm laborers, usually the sons of farmers. That in 1920 three-quarters of the working population could still be employed in agriculture is striking. Of the 313 heads of household in the survey, 214 were farmers, and 209 considered themselves to be "working on their own account." Only 54 heads of household worked for wages, on the farm or off. For men, being self-employed must have been synonymous with reaching adult status. As in the 1890s, the census did not recognize the labor of married women, whose occupation was usually given as "none." Frequently the census taker wrote in "housework," then scratched it out. Ironically, an old widowed woman with adult children living with her might be noted as an independent farmer, based on her ownership of land.[7]

The typical Upper Cumberland farmer of the 1920s was much more likely than his predecessors to be a tenant. Regional population increased from the 1890s to the 1920s, and the size of farms decreased. At the same time tenancy rates increased in all Upper Cumberland counties. In Putnam County, which in 1890 had the lowest tenancy rate in the region—17.7 percent—the tenancy rate rose to 29.5 percent by 1925. In that year Cumberland County had the lowest tenancy rate, 20.8 percent, and Clay County had the highest, 42.2 percent. However, as in the 1890s the tenant farmer was likely to be a young man. As Figure 1 shows, most heads of household in their twenties rented property. Owners outnumbered tenants in every other age cohort. The tenant was also more likely than his landown-

Figure 1. Tenure by Age, 1920. Source: Census Survey, 1920.

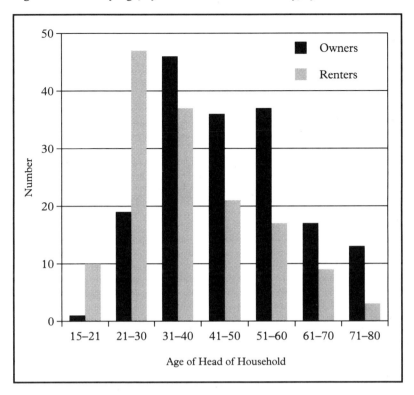

ing neighbor to be illiterate: 22 percent of tenants could not read or write, while only 8.9 percent of landowners were illiterate. Whether this reflects poverty or was one of the causes of it is impossible to tell from the data.[8]

As in the 1890s, farm families in the 1920s refused to divert resources from subsistence crops to market crops, maintaining traditional crop mixes. But by the 1920s this decision meant that the family had to depend, at least partially, on public work as a cash source. In the 1920s, farm families raised mostly hogs, grew mostly corn, and depended on the wife's chicken yard and garden for daily sustenance. But as the population grew (from 118,925 in 1890 to 152,857 in 1920), the number of farms increased (from 15,545 in 1890 to 24,204 in 1925) and farm size shrank. By 1925 23 percent of the farms in the region had less than twenty acres. Fifty-one percent had less than fifty acres of land. Such farms could barely support a large family, let alone produce crops for sale. A University of Tennessee economic survey of Overton County showed that in the

Table 7. Farms and Farming, 1890–1925

| | Regional Totals | |
	1890	1925
Population[a]	118,925	152,857
Tenancy	27.4%	32.9%
Number of farms	15,545	26,323
Livestock		
Horses	27,334	17,857
Mules	13,504	35,510
Milk cows	27,203	33,231
Other cattle	48,250	49,965
Chickens[b]	1,194,899	1,762,742
Crops (acres)		
Corn	263,844	329,850
Wheat	64,506	15,043
Tobacco	3,065	7,913

Sources: Department of the Interior, Census Office, *Report on the Statistics of Agriculture*; Department of Commerce, Bureau of the Census, *United States Census of Agriculture*.
[a]The population statistics are as given in the 1920 *Census of Population*.
[b]The data on chickens varies from census to census. The 1890 census counted chickens on the farm. The 1925 data is the number of chickens raised in 1924.

1920s, farm families there sold little, bought less, and ate what they produced at home. Farm families earned less than $400 annually from the sale of farm products; of that sum, poultry sales comprised one-third. Farm families produced their own meat (mostly chicken and pork). They bought wheat flour but grew their own Irish and sweet potatoes and still had corn ground into meal at local grist mills. In isolated Pickett County a 1924 study found that 97 percent of the farm families surveyed had gardens and noted, "The ordinary garden was considered as of paramount importance in the life of practically all the visited families." By the 1920s, as the University of Tennessee survey cited above noted, most farm families lived by a combination of self-sufficiency and part-time farming. Stated another way, farm families supplied most of their own food but made their cash in public work. The availability of part-time public work, mostly in wood product industries, allowed farm families to stay on the land as farm size shrank.[9]

Farm families did not cling to traditional ways because they lacked knowledge of market opportunities. During the 1920s merchants, bankers, and University of Tennessee trained farm agents busily promoted market agriculture. Merchants sponsored the production of new crops in the region, banks funded efforts to improve local farm products, and county agents acted as liaisons between farmer and market. Prior to the 1920s, Upper Cumberland county courts had been reluctant to hire county agents. However, when the state moved to tax counties to pay for agents regardless of whether their county hired one, most county courts hired agents.[10]

County fairs became vehicles for championing better-quality, marketable agricultural products. In the 1890s fairs in the Upper Cumberland featured frivolous contests (largest family, oldest couple, fattest couple, and greatest number of people on a farm wagon, for example). At an Independence Day fair in 1914, Overton County fair officials gave a prize for "most graceful riding by old soldier." Although fair organizers gave prizes for quality home and farm products, the emphasis was on having a good time. By the 1920s county farm and home demonstration agents ran local fairs and emphasized standard breeds and marketable quality. According to the Overton County paper in 1919, "Every prize winner has been an active student and followed the advice of the agent."[11]

In their search for a regional cash crop, farm agents and merchants often championed tobacco, but with limited success. As a cash crop, tobacco had distinct advantages: it was labor intensive but required little land; it could be easily transported; and the crop could be marketed nearby, at Carthage, on the Cumberland River. Despite these incentives and the promptings of county agents and would-be tobacco entrepreneurs, farmers in the region did not jump to adopt the new crop. In 1925 only 4,163 of 24,204 farms grew any tobacco. Of that total, 520 were in Jackson County, 1,884 were in Macon, and 1,130 were in Smith.[12]

Overton County offers the best illustration of local farmers' reluctance to adopt a cash crop. In 1914 W. C. Murphy of Hilham, a village in the county's third district, placed an advertisement in the county paper offering inducements for tobacco production. If 100 farmers would put in at least two acres of tobacco in 1915, Murphy would provide seeds free of charge, furnish a warehouse and press free for the first year, and offer a premium for the best crops. Murphy found few takers. Six years later the county agent pressed local farmers collectively to choose a money crop. Thirty agreed to grow tobacco, with the agent dispensing free seeds. Five years later Overton County produced only twenty-five acres of tobacco despite the efforts of the county agent, the agriculture teacher at Livingston Academy, and incentives offered by local merchants.[13]

Why were Overton County farmers so reluctant to seize this new opportunity? A statement in the local paper explains: "A so called money crop should not necessarily be something that the farmer and his family cannot use in case he fails to find a satisfactory market. It is of course grown for the purpose of selling in order to get funds to buy the things he cannot grow. But no money crop should take the place of other crops which are necessary for the support of the farm." According to the writer, the farmer's first goal should be to supply feed and grain for his stock and vegetables for his family. If he devoted all his time to a money crop, he would impoverish his soil and run the risk of not making enough cash to buy his necessities.[14]

Through the 1920s, Upper Cumberland farmers, with their traditional caution, made "support of the farm" the fundamental criterion for economic decisions and, like their fathers, did not take risks lightly. Despite invitations, most declined to participate in commercial agriculture if that participation seemed dangerous to the family economy. For them the cliché rang true: farming was not a business but a way of life. A primary concentration on the sustenance of the household precluded experimentation.

On the surface the types of households typical of the region had changed but little since the 1890s. Of 313 regional households surveyed (over 90 percent were in the country), 64 percent were nuclear, containing husband, wife, and children; 16 percent were extended, sheltering family members in addition to those in the simple nuclear family; 12 percent were composed of only the primary couple of husband and wife; and 7 percent were headed by single people, living alone or with family members. As in the 1890s, people rarely lived alone, and female heads of household remained uncommon. Since the 1890s the percentage of nuclear households had increased slightly (from 62.5 to 64 percent), the percentage of households headed by a single person had decreased slightly (from 10 to 7.4 percent), and more married couples lived alone, without children or other relatives (7.9 percent in 1890, 11.5 percent in 1920.)[15]

Family structure aside, one significant change had occurred: Upper Cumberland households averaged 4.8 members in 1920, down from 5.3 in 1900. Whether this decline in household size represents a decline in childbearing for women is impossible to tell, given the nature of census data. In 1920 the government did not ask women how many children they had borne. The only information available is the number of offspring living with parents in the home (including adult children). In 1920 the average number of children per household was 2.6, and the median was 2. Family size may have declined somewhat. But household size may have declined because young couples moved into houses of their own rather than living with parents. Given the increase in tenancy and the connection between tenancy and youth, and the increased availability of part-time work off the farm, this seems most probable.[16]

Country folk lagged far behind their town neighbors in acquiring modern conveniences. Many farmhouses lacked even outdoor privies, let alone indoor plumbing. Telephones were the most common item of modern technology on Upper Cumberland farms. To install a telephone did not require the expenditure of time and money that installation of electrical wires or indoor plumbing would have taken. In 1924 a University of Tennessee survey described the home of a typical farmer in one Upper Cumberland county as follows: "He lives in a three-room house, two rooms with a hall between in front, the kitchen behind, the house unpainted, unscreened, and with a lawn uncared for. He has a telephone, gets his water from a spring, uses kerosene lights, has built no toilet for the convenience of his family." In this house lived a family of six.[17]

Towns modernized much more rapidly than the surrounding countryside. By the 1920s railroad stops like Cookeville and Crossville, once sleepy, dusty market villages hardly distinguishable from the surrounding countryside, had grown into bona fide small towns with electric lights, paved main streets, drugstore soda shops and Ford dealerships, and aspirations toward urbanity. When Livingston put up hitching posts in 1926, the local paper noted that the facilities were for "the people from the country." In 1922 Carthage took a step toward refinement by requiring that chickens be confined and not allowed to run in the streets. In some towns the desire for urban amenities produced tangible results in the form of paved streets, municipal power plants, water and sewer systems, longer school terms, libraries, and civic clubs.[18]

Town folk, anticipating an end to the Upper Cumberland's timber industry, wanted to bring factories to the region. Inasmuch as they succeeded, they inaugurated a trend that would be increasingly significant in the region as the years passed: unlike the timber industry, the new manufacturing plants gave public work to women. By the end of the decade Putnam County had a "shirt factory," a hosiery mill, and a shoe factory located in Cookeville, and a textile mill in Monterey. In White County the local Civitan Club promoted the opening of a silk mill (which in this case actually processed imported silk). The Sparta-Welwood Silk Mills, built with capital furnished by town and county jointly, employed several hundred people.[19] But town boosters' limited success only pointed up the need for more social investment to make the region more attractive to industry.

Town boosters blamed "the people from the country" for opposing the necessary investment. As early as 1916 an irate citizen of Livingston, in Overton County, charged the county court with thwarting regional advancement. The old men on the court, he said, believed that "the sole function of the J.P. is to set tight on the lid" of the county treasury. Charitably, the writer excused the "ossification" of the "watchdogs," attributing their defects to hardening of the arteries. But the voters could not be excused: "The prevalent idea with the average voter is to select their justices of the Peace from the old staid conservative element. The idea of efficiency doesn't seem to play any part in the choice."[20]

Postwar campaigns for progress began with good roads. This time, after twenty years of propagandizing, progressives saw the tide turn in their favor. By reducing the amount of control counties had over road building, increasing the power of the state government, and sweetening the deal with state matching funds, progressives succeeded in obtaining authorization for road bonds in counties that had repeatedly voted against bond issues before the war. Perhaps progressives' analogies between Liberty Loans and road bonds convinced local voters. More likely, farmers began to see the necessity of good roads as Ford dealerships opened in Upper Cumberland towns. Voters in the Upper Cumberland had always suspected that money taken from them in taxes might be used somewhere else and, as localists, resented that prospect. Ironically, as the state assumed control of road building, local good-roads advocates could turn localism to their favor by arguing that to refuse to appropriate county

Map 4. The Upper Cumberland, 1926. The map shows the system of roads that had been constructed in the region by the 1920s. Adapted from a state highway map, Tennessee Department of Highways and Public Works, TSLA.

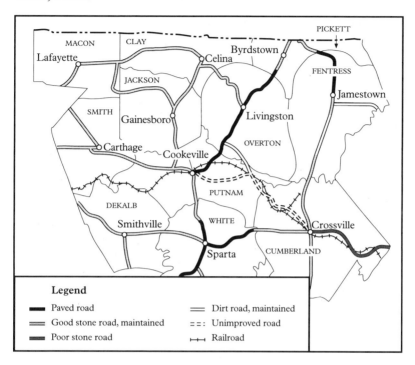

monies for roads simply meant some other area would get the benefit of state matching funds. With state money as an incentive, local opposition to road bond issues crumbled. By 1924 hundreds of miles of roads had been built in the Upper Cumberland. Road construction accelerated during Austin Peay's terms as governor from 1924 through 1927. Peay consolidated state control of road building, constructed the state's first modern highway system, and endeared himself to rural voters by doing so without raising land taxes.[21]

While good roads symbolized modernization to progressives, local people placed road building in the older context of local patronage. Building roads as cheaply and efficiently as possible was not their top priority. Local men considered road construction work a kind of tax-funded bonanza that should be available to all regardless of skill. In Smith County people criticized the road commissioners for paying workers too much and for paying supervisors more than workers (critics noted that supervisors did not know any more about building roads than the men they supervised). Harassed by public complaints, the road commissioners still rejected the idea of hiring a contractor to build the roads: "Our own people should build our own roads and get our money."[22]

Road building introduced hundreds of Upper Cumberland men to public work during the 1920s—a process not without its problems. When local men gathered, "difficulties" followed. In 1918 a road overseer and one of the workers nominally under his supervision got into a fight over a drink of water. The overseer was arrested for seriously injuring the worker by hitting him over the head with a shovel. In 1925 two men who had been fired from highway jobs set off twelve cases of dynamite in an Overton County contruction camp: the explosion shook buildings and broke windows in two counties.[23] Such fracases must have made state engineers' jobs unusually interesting. However, the chief problem with Upper Cumberland men was not their violence but their lack of familiarity with sustained, supervised labor, as construction supervisor W. H. Peebles explained in a 1920 letter to Governor A. H. Roberts: "We have a great many men working on this job something near two hundred and these people have never been used to working on public works and you have to train them up that we want a solid ten hour days work."[24] Road building caused squabbles but was ultimately accepted by the country people. More serious threats to traditional ways came from sources closer to home.

10

FOLLOWING THE OLD PATHS

THE FAMILY, RELIGION, AND POLITICS IN THE 1920S

Men tell us the farmers are the backbone of the nation but these same fellows are too proud to engage in such dirty work as plowing, hoeing, pulling weeds and grubbing bushes. I said too proud, I should have said too lazy.—J. W. Butler, Macon County farmer, 1920

The boys and girls of today are being educated to be above the common laborer. I heard a man say his boys were told in school, if they did not get an education they would not be anything but tillers of the soil, or something of that kind (like as if it was a low occupation).
—Robert Gwaltney, Smith County farmer, 1923

Well, the women have their rights at last. Now they can vote and hold offices. . . . How do you men think you will like the new dispensation? It is just like the doctor's medicine, you will have to take it whether you like it or not.—"Rolling Stone," Smith County man, 1920

Poor women they want to please the men. I have so little patience in trying to please them, because I know it cannot be done, so we women may just as well quit and rest and let them grumble. That is exactly what they will do, no matter what we do.—"X," Putnam County woman, 1923

Some of the old-timey women still think the only way to appeal to a man is through his stomach. This ideas keeps you over a hot cook stove when you might be holding a good position down town making a nice salary. Husbands are not worrying how to appeal to their wives. They won't let anything like a good cook interfere with their heart affairs, for the towns are full of good places to eat.

So, women, don your short skirts, bob your hair, get into your car, go to the polls and vote.—"Not An Old Maid," Putnam County woman, 1923

Men of John W. Butler's generation faced new challenges within the heart of the family. Women in the region adapted enthusiastically to new economic and educational opportunities; women in politics signified what one local man called a "new dispensation" in gender relations. In addition, parents found their authority over their children diminished when, in 1925, Tennessee progressives won their long battle to wrest control of schooling from local authorities. Schools impart culture and can be used to redefine success and failure. Men worried that education would lead boys to despise manual labor, leading them astray to what Butler called the "evils of the cities."

Under cultural attack, traditionalists like Butler tried various strategies for assimilating progress to traditional mores. Butler's Monkey Law itself illustrates one path taken by conservatives: the co-option of modernized structures (in this case, of schooling) for traditionalist ends. Others in the region ignored elements of reform and modernity that could not be incorporated into the service of tradition. When neither approach was possible, people in the region often reacted against modernity by making symbolic protests. The Butler Act, with its defense of the Bible, was only one manifestation of a new religiosity that cut across political, class, and generational lines to provide powerful unifying symbols.

The passage of the Nineteenth Amendment in 1920 provoked much discussion in the Upper Cumberland. Although suffrage itself did not make much difference in the lives of women, people considered the vote symbolic of a new dispensation in gender roles. In a sense Upper Cumberland farmers were ideologically unprepared to oppose woman suffrage. Having never placed women on pedestals as frail creatures in need of protection, yeoman farmers could not effectively use middle-class arguments that a woman's ladylike refinement would be soiled by her participation in the political world. Nor, having seen their wives and daughters do strenuous farm labor, could they argue that women were too delicate to do public work: anyone could see that sitting in an office typing was physically easier than hoeing corn. Since they had not prepared ideological bastions of male supremacy appropriate to the new world in which they found themselves, yeoman farmers had to fall back on simple patriarchal tradition, bolstered by the Bible.

Men in the region, like their brothers throughout the nation, debated the "woman question" without distinguishing between religious and secular issues. Methodists and Presbyterians, more liberal (or perhaps just less concerned) about women's issues, continued to encourage women to run benevolent associations. Although generalizations are difficult to make about denominations where congregational autonomy prevails, Baptist and Church of Christ leaders usually took the most conservative position, denying women leadership positions in worship and insisting that woman's true place was still in the home. When the Southern Baptist Convention began admitting women messengers (delegates) in 1918, conservative Baptists protested that this would lead to women serving on denominational boards and, ultimately, to women preaching.

In 1923 concerned conservatives published a collection of essays reaffirming their belief that the Scriptures prohibited women taking a public role in church affairs. In one essay, "The Menace of Feminism," the author argued that the Bible and nature combined to deny women the capacity for leadership outside the home ("Menstruation, is of itself, quite sufficient to produce mental peculiarities") and linked feminism with social anarchy, Bolshevism, infidelity, abolition, racial liberalism, promiscuity, divorce, a declining birth rate, an increase in women criminals, women working outside the home, and immodest dress. Conservative Baptists considered women's attire a serious matter, criticizing women who cut their hair and wore makeup. In 1917 the Enon Baptist Association, which included several Upper Cumberland counties, condemned the immodest clothing of "our women." Most Baptist men accepted the novelty of women messengers while maintaining their support of traditional gender roles. As one student of Southern Baptists notes, "Baptist men seemed more concerned about what women could not do than with what they should do." Upper Cumberland congregations were no exception. In some cases congregational leaders proved more liberal than the men and women in the pews. In 1927 when church leaders appointed women to serve as messengers from the Lafayette Baptist Church to their regional association meeting, the congregation rescinded the motion "sending sister delegates to the association" and appointed men to go instead. Sometimes women chose to limit their public role, as in 1919 when Sister Geneva Carr, superintendent of the women's work committee of the Bledsoe Missionary Baptist association, wrote a report on women's work for the association but asked a male messenger to read it for her. The Churches of Christ offered no public role for women at all, and the *Gospel Advocate* editorialized against woman suffrage.[1]

Political leaders scorned the idea that women should ever vote, and doubted that many of the good women of the region even wanted the right to do so. Some men in the region saw suffrage as a class issue: only idle rich women without children or husbands to care for were suffragists. *Their* women worked too hard to find time to play politics. In fact, although organized prosuffrage groups were unusual in the region, they did exist. In 1915 an equal suffrage league was formed in Dixon Springs, a crossroads community in Smith County; in 1917 a similar group was organized in Carthage.[2]

Once women obtained the franchise, political parties in the Upper Cumberland hurried (albeit reluctantly) to solicit their votes. Rather than attempting to appeal to women as an interest group, local politicians assumed that women would vote as their brothers and husbands had, in accordance with family heritage. Democratic politicians urged women to go to the polls to prevent a victory by blacks and Republicans. The chairman of the Smith County Democratic Party suggested that the ladies might want to meet and proceed to the polls together, to avoid embarrassment. In Putnam County the Democratic county chairman told men to take their wives and daughters to vote, lest the Republicans, always a strong minority in Putnam, win the upcoming elections. The Putnam ladies were urged to put aside their antisuffrage scruples and, in the fashion of true women from time immemorial, come to the rescue of the familial cause: "Surely the daughters and granddaughters of the Confederate soldiers of Putnam County will not desert the memories and traditions of the South."[3]

In the 1920s women began running for and being elected to county offices. County administration was obviously within women's physical capacity, as was suggested in 1922 by a Smith County woman in a letter to the local paper: she thought that women should have county offices and let the men who usually ran things get out and go to work. Upper Cumberland voters apparently agreed. In DeKalb County a woman became county judge; another was elected registrar. In Smith County a woman became registrar, and in Putnam County Mary Denny served two terms as trustee.[4]

Having the right to vote did not change the lives of women in the Upper Cumberland; however, men and women both understood the franchise as a symbol of women's changed status. In 1920 a Smith County man wrote an extended satire, "The New Dispensation," and signed it "Rolling Stone."[5] His lampoon is quoted at length for what it indicates about male attitudes in the region toward woman suffrage—and for what the author unwittingly reveals about acceptable male roles in the region.

> Well, the women have their rights at last. Now they can vote and hold offices; but they have had a time getting the right to vote. . . . While our old-time back number women were at home tending to the babies, canning fruit, keeping the house nice for father and the boys, while they were busy at work, some of our modern ladies were doing all kinds of stunts in order to gain the right to vote. They wanted to vote so bad they would dance barefooted in cold weather on the steps of the Capitol. Now they are allowed to vote and hold office, so I don't know what they will be dancing for next. Some one says let them quit dancing and go home. No use of that. They have no children to care for, they won't or can't cook or do other housework, they would not know which cow gave the sweet milk, so you must not blame them for wanting to vote, for they ought to learn to do something. The men are going to have to step down and let the women run the government machine.
>
> I look for them to strip the gearing the first thing, but they are going to have what they want if it makes the machinery of creation jump cogs. . . .

[In the future the news in the *Carthage Courier* will look like this:]

The winners in the August election were Sally Skinner, County Court Clerk, Mary Gossip, Circuit Court Clerk, Susie Shoofly, Register, Emily Goldbug, Sheriff. . . .

Several misfortunes happened on election day as usual. Jim Brown's baby was badly burned by falling into hot water while Mr. Brown was washing the dishes. Mrs. Brown, who had gone to the election, was phoned for but never started home until all the districts were heard from. The baby died before she got there.

Mrs. Rose Peppermint, constable of the 18th district, was seriously hurt while trying to arrest Mrs. Peggy Squash, who was trying to shoot some other woman in Grant.

While the sheriff, Mrs. Ida DeSpoof, was locating a wildcat still in the Carver Holler, Miss Spicy Hooknose, aged 46, enticed the sheriff's 16 year old son, Willie, away from home, going at once to Kentucky, where they were married. Miss Hooknose is fortunate in marrying Willie, as he is a splendid cook and a nice housekeeper. Mrs. DeSpoof will resume her work putting up telephone lines . . . as soon as the honeymoon is over. . . .

How do you men think you will like the new dispensation? It is just like the doctor's medicine, you will have to take it whether you like it or not.[6]

Rolling Stone unintentionally explained the rationale that lay beneath the region's patriarchal familism: women were considered mostly in terms of their usefulness in providing children, shelter, and clothing to men. They were not too delicate to meddle in politics, just too busy.

The satire provoked a response from an angry woman. She focused less on the right to vote than on the implications of the role reversal Rolling Stone had foreseen. Her letter provides a very unusual glimpse into what rural women in Tennessee thought about the "old dispensation." Women, she asserted, had been overworked and underappreciated: "Just imagine a home with a poor, hard-working woman, so tired that she is irritable, working in the field, planting corn, hoeing tobacco or anything else that had to be done, until sundown, then having the milking all to do, the supper to cook, and dishes to wash besides half a dozen children to care for, part of them crying, and you have the old dispensation well in mind." For this woman a complete role reversal was not desirable. Rejecting the notion that women wanted to be just as abusive and irresponsible as the men Rolling Stone described by implication, she suggested a true new dispensation in which marriages would be founded on respect.[7]

Was there a new dispensation for the country women of the Upper Cumberland in the 1920s? The kinds of sources that would give insight into intimate family relations are not available. However, some changes did occur in the region that seem to indicate an economic and social basis for a new dispensation.

First, by the 1920s Upper Cumberland farm wives could earn more money than ever. The railroad had made poultry the most lucrative form of livestock in the region, bringing in more cash to family farms than the sale of hogs or cattle. By tradition, chickens belonged to the farm wife, and "egg money" was hers to dispose of. If tradition held, and there is no reason to think it did not, then farm wives in the 1920s had much easier access to cash than their mothers had enjoyed in the 1890s. How that affected the familial balance of power cannot be determined from available sources.[8]

Second, the changing economy of the region created more jobs for women—and jobs that differed in ways that matter from those available for men. The census took note of wage- or salary-earning women; farm wives who did not receive pay for their labors were not listed as workers. Most women who worked for money in the Upper Cumberland in 1930, like most men, were employed in agriculture. A sizable minority of women (many of them black) worked as domestics. But the new jobs available for women in the 1920s differed qualitatively both from traditional female occupations and from new jobs available for men. While wage-earning men in the region worked in unskilled or semiskilled occupations, new jobs for women typically appeared in semiskilled factory work, service, pink-collar trades, or feminized professions such as teaching or hair dressing. The new women's work, significantly, required more education and enabled women to be geographically mobile. A beautician has a movable trade; a farmer does not.[9]

Third, women in the region were better educated than men. Perhaps because education opened employment to them, or perhaps because they were less needed as farm laborers, girls were more likely than boys to take advantage of the full eight grades of schooling offered by most Upper Cumberland counties. At the end of the 1919–20 school year, 340 girls had completed eight grades, compared with 285 boys. When four-year high schools opened in the 1920s, women were more likely to attend and complete the courses. By 1931 there were 1,663 white female students in the region's high schools and only 1,297 white males. More girls started high school than boys, and more girls finished.[10]

Young men did not begin to take equal advantage of the region's new high schools until late in the decade. Their new interest in education coincided with new requirements for factory work outside the region. In 1925 the *Carthage Courier* ran a notice that the Du Pont Fiber Silk Plant at Old Hickory near Nashville preferred high school graduates. Three years later the number of boys enrolled in the town high school equaled the number of girls for the first time. According to the paper, it had previously been customary for boys to drop out before finishing school.[11]

Teaching was the chief occupation education opened for women. In the 1890s men had held the majority of teaching positions in the Upper Cumberland. By the end of the 1920s that was no longer the case. The majority of elementary teachers in the region were female. Young women could obtain certificates to teach in Upper Cumberland primary schools if they completed the eight grades of elementary school.[12]

Upper Cumberland fathers complained in the 1920s that schools were educating their sons away from the farms. Few seem to have noticed (or perhaps cared about) the effects of education on women. However, women benefited most from the new school systems, as students and as teachers. If in those schools girls were taught what the state education authorities wanted them to be taught, and if the girls believed it, then their education should have made them exceedingly dissatisfied with the old dispensation. The further a girl's schooling proceeded, the more chances education had to spoil a good farm wife.

The state of Tennessee's 1921 *Course of Study* called upon all elementary schools to teach "Homemaking," starting in the first grade. Homemaking classes taught proper modes of consumption. Teachers were to discuss with their primary school pupils correct styles in shoes and clothing (showing pictures of suitable attire was recommended by the state). Fifth and sixth grade girls could put on a style show. Other topics included proper foods; etiquette (including table settings); good taste in house furnishings; proper cleaning of the dining room, bedroom, and bath; and correct color combinations.[13]

In 1924 Marie White, state supervisor of vocational home economics, issued "A Challenge" to high school home economics teachers via the state teachers' *Bulletin*. White criticized home economics classes that taught "merely" cooking and sewing. She suggested that "the girls of today" needed to be taught how to spend the family's income correctly: "Are we including in our class-room studies a working knowledge of the modern labor-saving devices in order that the girls may be able to determine which are really suitable to their needs. . . . In our clothing classes are we making clear the fact that it is as essential to the well being of everyone to be able to select and care for clothing that is suitable for seasons and occasions as it is to be able to make a garment?"[14]

What might the young rural women who attended high schools have made of such instruction? If they grew up on farms, their mothers had been producers, not consumers. Few could have lived in houses that fit the urban middle-class standards for tasteful decor inculcated in home economics classes. Nor did the farm economy typically produce enough cash to afford the sort of amenities the state home economics curriculum took for granted. Home economics classes, with their emphasis on rather prissy standards of correct taste and consumption, created expectations of living standards that life on the farm could hardly satisfy and surely encouraged the out-migration of many young farm women to the towns and cities during the 1920s.[15]

In the autumn of 1923 the editor of the *Putnam County Herald* set off a three-month-long controversy when he solicited letters on the topic, "Woman's True Place Is in the Home." Perhaps coincidentally, Mary Denny was running for trustee in the Democratic primary at that time. From late August through November (when Denny won renomination, tantamount to winning the office, by about 100 votes) Putnam County women filled the center columns of the semiweekly paper with letters discussing all aspects of the woman question, commenting on politics and religion and making comic asides about the foibles of men: "Without the help of the fair sex the men of our country would have to hide in caves, as the majority wouldn't have time to find their clothes and if they did, couldn't put them on by themselves." Starting with a discussion of suffrage, the letters spun off into arguments about the duties of married couples, the desirability of marrying at all, and the values of the older versus the younger generation. As one writer noted, "It seems we have almost left the subject and drifted into a mixup of politics and matrimony." These letters offer a rare glimpse into what rural women thought about their lives—and their men. They also indicate that women, like men, considered "woman's place" to be as much a religious as a political issue. Indeed, religion permeates the letters. Unlike men, however, they used religious discourse to demand changes in family relationships.[16]

The writers were divided over the question of women voting. A few (whose prose indicated a high level of education) expressed pride in modern women and supported the right of women to do whatever was morally correct: "Some prefer to be and are satisfied as home keepers, others prefer careers, which brings on severe criticism, and generally speaking, is unjust." Several thought voting was wrong and blamed men for dragging women into politics: "Why, I did not vote because I have read in the Book that was left for me to go by that he gave the man a stronger mind for them to rule, but they should rule righteously. I hope they will see their mistakes and ask us to forgive them for passing such a law over us." Others agreed that woman's place was certainly not at the polls, but having obtained the vote, women were duty-bound to use it wisely: "I think that should have been left to the men, but since it was not, I feel like it is our duty to vote for the right and try to outnumber those who vote for the wrong." Several women who had voted in past elections defended the propriety of their actions, noting that they went to the polls in the company of women friends. One woman commented, "They [men] thought we women could help them with their business affairs and said, 'Get your bonnet up and let's go vote.' So we did, and now such level heads were used it makes them ashamed to think we are wiser than they, so they would be glad if we would step down and out." Some women felt that voting was neither right nor wrong but an issue each woman would have to decide for herself. Several young women boasted that when they got old enough to vote, they would employ the franchise without asking their (future) husband's advice or consent: "When I get old enough I'll vote and the men won't hinder me."[17]

The letters reflect a generational conflict over proper behavior for women. Older women deplored sinful modern fashions and popular amusements such as "car riding." Bobbed hair violated God's laws for women as stated in 1 Corinthians, chapters 7 and 11: "I don't believe in short hair for the Bible teaches us that woman's hair is her glory, and it is a shame in the sight of God for a woman to wear short hair." Some of the young women seem to have been deliberately trying to shock their elders. "Not an Old Maid," whose refutation of the idea that men were attracted by good cooking is quoted above, addressed men: "God didn't make us equal in strength but he made us your superior in sense. . . . I vote for short skirts, short hair, Republicans and women's rights." Another joked, "I think girls ought to marry for money and work for love, its [sic] a much easier job."[18]

Most of these women found matrimony more interesting than politics. They expressed few romantic illusions about marriage or the home. Indeed, though some older women wrote affectionately about their husbands or counseled that both partners in a marriage needed to show consideration for each other, few expressed any great admiration of men in general—the more conservative, antisuffrage women being the most bitter. Single women wrote more favorably of men, but one wife warned, "Beware of the young man who is so nice and polite to you. That will not last when you marry him." Several writers advised women not to marry, thus provoking the most lively exchange of letters. The occasional bitter wife or timid young woman aside, most agreed that marriage was preferable to spinsterhood. They expressed contempt for old maids: "Just think how this world would be if it was filled with old sour maids. You would cry for the mountains to hide you." One single woman wrote, "I'm sure I won't be an old maid, for everybody to make fun of and to be a slave for my brothers and sisters." Older women warned young ones to choose a good man: "Marry just as soon as opportunity affords you the kind loving husband you wish. . . . It's not every man that wears breeches that's a man, an outright gentleman." Most, however, approved marriage for religious reasons: "Don't preach against marrying for the Bible teaches it. Read Ephesians 5:22–33."[19]

The letters indicate that the writers accepted their subordinate role in society and in the home. But respecting male dominance did not mean that women accepted the old dispensation in gender relations. One woman wrote that she agreed that woman's place was in the home, and therefore women should not work in the fields. Others praised affectionate husbands who spent time with wives and children, but they condemned wandering men who left their wives at home with the babies: "A man has just as much right to stay at home when he isn't at work and help care for the children as a woman has." A writer who signed her letter "A Happy Woman" contended that "a woman has just as much right to be out in company as a man has. A man should help care for the children just as same as she. I'm so glad woman slavery is a thing of the past." As one woman put it, "Why, if we get our work done, do you care if we have a little privilege?" Another commented, "Yes, indeed, a woman's true place is in the home—until she wants to get out, and another thing, a man's true place is at home with his wife." A few writers sounded a note of outright rebellion against patriarchy as a labor system: as southerners, they knew unfree labor when they saw it. One woman wrote from California to comment, "The majority of women in Tennessee are just slaves for the men. They work day in and day out tied down with a bunch of little ones, and never see anything but trouble." Another advised the young: "Girls, I say don't marry. You had as well be an old wrinkle faced maid as to be a slave for your husband and a house full of children."[20]

Religion is a two-edged sword. If country men could evoke the ancient texts of a patriarchal faith to justify their dominance over their wives and children, wives (good Protestants all) could read the text, too, and cite Bible verses back at the men in support of better treatment for wives within marriage. As one older woman advised, "The father should care for the children occasionally if they have no one else to do so, as well as assist her in housework. The wife should be a partner, not a slave. Girls, see that this partner is your equal." She justified her position by reference to 1 and 2 Corinthians. A deferential wife—"I don't believe in women voting. If I did and my husband did not want me to I wouldn't. This is love."—who always asked her husband's permission to go out nonetheless expected the same behavior from him: "My husband never goes off anywhere without telling me just where and why he is going. . . . You see the Bible teaches us to do unto others as you would have them do unto you." Others described as ideal marriages in which partners were united by affection and a shared interest in family life: "I can gladly say that each year finds my husband sweeter and kinder to babies and me, each year finds us happier with three little noisy boys, for the last two months he has only been away from us part of two Sundays. . . . Some men call it a sacrifice to spend a Sunday on an outing with wife and babies, when it should be a pleasure. He should be glad to help care for the babies. Our baby is three years old and cares more for daddy than for me." This letter was signed with pride by Rhoda Bush, who concluded, "Dear writers, sign your real name, don't be ashamed of what you are. If for Christ, stand firm at any sacrifices, ever watch, work, and pray."[21]

Operating within the same belief system, country men and women derived ideological justifications for positions that were contradictory. As economic and political developments challenged traditional gender roles in rural Tennessee, men could take comfort in their divine right to rule women. Women could use the same religious tradition to justify a restructuring of their place within the home, demanding that marriages be a union of equal partners based on love and companionship. This new dispensation threatened husbands' control over wives' labor (a woman's place was in the home, not in the field) and demanded a higher standard for husbands. Both sides justified their views by reference to the Bible. Both could unite in support of the Book.

The 1920s were a time of religious revival in the Upper Cumberland. Better roads made church attendance easier and led to the development of regional religious events. The churches changed, however, and in such a way as to deepen divisions between town and country, wealthy and poor, educated and illiterate. Meanwhile political forces such as the Ku Klux Klan appropriated religious symbols and created a bogus "old-time religion" that unified supporters in direct proportion to its lack of actual religious content.[22]

The increased vitality of organized religion in the Upper Cumberland reflects a deeper change: the acceptance of institutional community in the region. Thirty years earlier observers of mountain life noted the lack of organized community groups as a distinguishing attribute of the region. In the 1920s the social life of the region, while still less organized than a social worker might have wanted, blossomed into associations, groups, clubs, and institutions. Some of these groups were professional (the teachers' associations, for example); some were business oriented (Exchange Clubs, Booster Clubs, Civitan Clubs); some were organized by educators and progressive reformers (the Parent-Teacher Associations, the various agricultural clubs); and some were religious (men's Bible classes, Singing Conventions). A casual reading of Upper Cumberland papers of the decade leaves the impression that after World War I people in the region were more prone to participate in organized civic and social activities.[23]

Popular religious events reflected a change in attitudes toward religion. In the 1890s most regional churches had shared a certain style (plain) and the assumption that the reason for going to church was to save one's soul. Correct doctrine mattered most. Understandably, debates between different denominations were the most widely attended religious events in the region at that time. At those debates hundreds of people heard preachers contest points of doctrine. To follow the debates listeners were required to pay attention to the content of their religious beliefs.

Rural congregations clung to older religious forms. In the 1910s the Lafayette Baptist Church disciplined members for dancing, swearing, and drunkenness and excluded a young woman for bearing an illegitimate child. The Defeated Creek Missionary Baptist Church of Smith County continued to support and discipline its members in the old style—although the occasions for sin and discipline changed with the times. For example, in 1916 a sister was accused of having an "immoral picture" made. The photograph in question was passed around among the members of the church, who then promptly excluded the young woman from the fellowship. A year later three women were ousted from the church for having parties and "social plays." A decade later a young woman was put out of the church for bad conduct, with a member testifying that she had "become uncontrollable by her parents [and] would not heed her mother's advice," surely a complaint many parents could have made by 1927.[24]

The Methodist and Presbyterian churches in town, however, became less doctrinally oriented. Pastor Simon M. Ensor of the Livingston Methodist Church in 1920 invited the congregation—and the town—to consider his church a social center, noting that attending church was of social value. This emphasis on the social utility of religion could easily degenerate into outright Babbitry. By 1928 a men's Big Bible Class had been formed in Pastor Ensor's town. The group, which met at the courthouse, promised newcomers that they would study the Bible "and at the same time become part of an organization 'that means business.'" The class proposed to become a "body for civic improvement along all lines." Although the group boasted of its lack of class consciousness, the terms used in doing so clearly reflected a sense of social superiority. One might wonder how many farmers and working men were attracted by the assurance that the Big Bible Class did not make class distinctions: "The meaner the man the more we want him. The poorer the man the more we seek him. The more ragged the more we warm up to him."[25]

As vague religiosity replaced insistence on right doctrine, gospel singings replaced debates as popular regional religious events. The Macon County Singing Convention, founded in 1914, became the regional prototype. In 1927 4,000 people came to Lafayette to stand on the courthouse lawn, sing, and hear gospel quartets. Similar one-day events were held in other Upper Cumberland counties. Singings unified Christians across denominational lines, since gospel songs generally avoided doctrinal questions and focused on the desire for salvation, sentimental evocations of God's love, or that perennially favorite theme, the family reunion in heaven.[26]

Religiosity could be used politically as religion could not. When doctrine mattered, a politician who evoked religion took the risk of alienating as many voters as he won. In the 1890s religious leaders were more likely to use political metaphors than politicos were to talk about religion. By the 1920s a sentimentalized, secularized religiosity required only loyalty to certain symbols and was thus unifying politically across denominational, class, and town/country lines. To sing "The Old-Time Religion" did not require a person to define what the old-time religion was (other than good enough for Mama), nor did affirmation of belief in the Bible require that one had read the book. Religious symbols could now safely be politicized in a way new to the region.[27]

The state government linked patriotism and Protestantism. In 1915 the state mandated Bible reading in all schools. As control over education passed from parents and local government to the state, the emphasis on Bible reading and moral instruction in the public schools may have offered a reassuring sense of continuity for parents. Bible reading was not introduced into Tennessee schools due to any concerted public campaign. The state's public school administrators believed that inculcating moral culture was a proper part of a school's duty. This opinion was held not only by conservative evangelicals. In 1915 Episcopal bishop Thomas Frank Gailor, chancellor of the University of the South, was given space in the *Tennessee Educator* to make the case for teaching religion in the public schools. The bishop was quite blunt. Public schools, he said, must teach morality: "The only reason for their existence and continuation is the safety of the State. They are not public charities. . . . They are not intended primarily for the purpose of helping the individual to become more easily self-supporting and efficient for his own advantage. The success of the individual is an entirely secondary consideration." The government runs schools to teach children "respect and loyalty to our form of government." Gailor went on to say that the republic rested on Christian morality, which all states enforced by law. Moral instruction in state schools followed logically. For Gailor and, one suspects, for most of the readership of the *Tennessee Educator* the United States was a Christian nation; Christian virtues had built the republic and comprised the national heritage that should be passed on to future generations.[28]

By the 1920s, state-run schools emphasized the Bible and the flag more strongly than ever. In 1923 teachers in Smith County were warned via the local newspaper that "neglect to prominently display the flag on your grounds or in your building and to read or cause to be read not fewer than ten verses of the Bible in your schools will necessitate your answering to C. R. McClarin [grand jury chairman] at next session of court."[29]

In the 1920s organized reaction in the form of the Ku Klux Klan appeared in the Upper Cumberland. The Klan was something new in the region. While violence had always been common, it was personal or familial, and vigilante groups were not in the regional tradition.[30] However, Klan propaganda echoed progressive themes, and Klan activities often resembled the semiofficial coercion of slackers during the First World War. Klansmen in the Upper Cumberland chose moral reform rather than racism as their rallying cry, and local authorities accepted them as quasi-official agents of law. When in 1924 the foreman of the Smith County grand jury addressed an appeal "To the Law and Order People" of the county, asking them to inform on lawbreakers, he specifically requested the cooperation of the Klan. At a rally in Carthage in 1927 a Klan spokesman explained that his organization was for law enforcement and better moral conditions in the community and would especially attack "evils that could not or were not reached by the courts." Klansmen visited a house in Carthage, "captured" a man and woman together, and brought them to criminal court, where they were charged with "lewdness." Klansmen raided a still and delivered the moonshiners they caught to federal court in Cookeville. When the KKK paraded at the Putnam County fair in the 1920s, their floats depicted the local progressive icons, churches and schools.[31]

Progressives had worked to create organizations and structures of governance. Missionaries had hoped to instill within mountain children a sense of order and an appreciation for the books, music, and religious forms judged acceptable by New England. Good-roads activists had hoped that better highways would open the insular Upper Cumberland and help create a new, vital community life. But the people of the Upper Cumberland were not transformed into midwesterners. Instead local folk took over the structures and institutions reformers had created and used them in innovative ways derived from their own culture. They got in their cars and drove down good roads to "old time Gospel singings," not chautauqua lectures. Having learned the value of organization, they did not create rural community centers but Ku Klux Klan units. People who had fought the building of better roads and the creation of better schools now sought, like the Klan with its church and school floats, to capture and to co-opt the structures against which they had struggled so long.[32]

The schools were at the core of cultural conflict in the Upper Cumberland in the 1920s: to control the schools was to command the future. As the state took over education, traditionalists in the Upper Cumberland reacted—as always—by ignoring or co-opting the modern structures created by progressives and using those structures to further traditional cultural values.

In 1925 education reformers in Tennessee capped a generation of effort when the general assembly passed the General Education Act of 1925, which gave the state final sovereignty over most aspects of schooling in Tennessee. In order to obtain the passage of the general education bill, the state education lobby formed a political alliance with Governor Austin Peay and mobilized the state's teachers as a pressure group. Peay made better schools a major part of his successful campaign for reelection in 1924 and then worked for passage of the bill through the general assembly. As State Superintendent

P. L. Harned noted, the bill was controversial: it "would necessarily conflict with the local interest of certain communities and the personal interests of many individuals." The bill was amended 227 times before Peay signed it in April 1925 using a special gold pen purchased by the Department of Education. Under the General Education Act any county in the state that would levy a fifty-cent tax for schools would receive equalization funds for an eight-month school term—provided that the county complied with all state school laws. The bill also allowed the state to prescribe uniform courses of study for the entire state and established a state pay scale for teachers. After 1925 state authorities could assure local compliance in matters of taxation, hiring, and curriculum by threatening to cut state funding to counties in violation of state policies.[33]

By 1925 in the Upper Cumberland the school year was longer, more teachers were state-certified professionals, public high schools were being established, and better buildings were slowly replacing antiquated log schoolhouses. Schooling was now compulsory. However, the locals were not much impressed. A study of county statistics indicates that education failed to work the cultural miracles promised by reformers. The structures were in place, but the people remained unconvinced of the necessity of schooling. Statistics from the state education department indicate that the actual attendance at Upper Cumberland schools remained about 60 percent of the area's scholastic population from the 1890s to the 1920s. Of that 60 percent the majority were in the first five grades. The statistics available indicate that only a small group finished the eight-grade elementary course, and even fewer went on to high school. In the 1920s as in the 1890s only those interested in careers other than farming pursued education past the point of basic literacy.[34]

Upper Cumberland county courts indicated their lack of support for education by cutting funding or by refusing to levy taxes for education until forced to do so by the state. In Smith County in 1923 the county court cut taxes for all schools and eliminated two-year high schools in outlying areas. The county superintendent complained that "this was done mostly by magistrates from the communities where this high school teaching was being done." In Macon County a four-year high school was finally opened in 1926 as a result of mandamus proceedings against the county under the 1925 Gen-

Table 8. Pupils Starting and Completing Elementary School, by County, 1920

	Pupils in Grade 1	Pupils Completing Grade 8	
		Boys	Girls
Clay	936	8	10
Cumberland	791	32	40
DeKalb	1,202	40	58
Fentress	451	10	15
Macon	1,413	13	15
Overton	2,224		
Pickett	456		
Putnam	2,288	39	67
Smith	1,572	81	70
White	1,360	55	56
Total	12,693	278	331

Source: Albert Williams, *Biennial Report of the State Superintendent, 1919–1920*.
Note: Overton and Pickett Counties did not furnish statistics.

eral Education Act: the county was compelled to levy taxes to build and support the school.[35]

County courts refused to fund education. Parents refused to send their children to school. These actions may have arisen from more than indifference; they may reflect a widespread conviction that the new state-controlled school systems were teaching children values contrary to those traditionally held in the region. In Macon County J. W. Butler railed that schools were educating children "away from the farm," teaching boys to scorn honest labor. Robert Gwaltney, the Smith County farmer quoted above, agreed.

An examination of the state-mandated school curriculum suggests that critics like Butler and Gwaltney were right. If teachers followed state instructions, if they used the materials, examples, and texts they were supposed to use, and if the students paid attention to their lessons, Upper Cumberland children learned that urban life was the standard and that the lives they and their parents lived were deficient. In schools Upper Cumberland boys learned that success was having money, not being independent. Girls learned that the proper role of women was to consume, not to produce, and that social status depended on correct modes of consumption.

The 1921 state-recommended course of study for elementary schools statewide was clearly written with urban students in mind: the effect was to present urban life as the norm. Practical problems in arithmetic included figuring percentages of interest, taxes and insurance, the use of business forms, the cost of articles purchased, trips to movies, and other public amusements. Geography lessons included suggested field trips to grocery stores, cotton mills, farms, dairies, and sawmills to teach children where food, shelter, and clothing come from. Farming, when discussed, was presented as agribusiness. In fifth grade Tennessee rural students were supposed to study wheat farming in the Dakotas. Math students were given problems asking them to figure profits for various crops, taking into account labor, interest, and taxes.[36] Agriculture classes in Upper Cumberland high schools emphasized the market value of crops. At Livingston Academy a boy who took the vocational agriculture course (first offered in 1921) was required to choose a project and care for it "in such a way as to give him the biggest profit." The course also included training in keeping accounts.[37]

Farmers of J. W. Butler's generation believed self-sufficiency a worthy goal; as Butler said, they wanted the "right kind" of education for their children, the sort that would make youth "thankful that they live on a farm, where they can make what they eat and eat what they make."[38] Agricultural education tended to promote different values. A youngster who looked at farming in the Upper Cumberland as a business proposition would have quickly realized that other enterprises offered greater potential profits. As farm agent Hugh Childress told the Putnam County court, conditions on Upper Cumberland farms would "not permit a standard of living that will satisfy . . . the boys and girls on the farm. No wonder they are leaving the farm. I would and you would too if you could get away."[39]

Classes in civics became vehicles for progressive propaganda. In 1921 the state-suggested questions for eighth grade civics classes on public schools included, "Why cannot the family educate the children? Why should agricultural schools be developed? What is the need of high schools in your county? What does the school do that the parents cannot do?" Fifth graders were supposed to discuss good roads.[40]

Instruction in hygiene, while well intentioned, must have been profoundly embarrassing to many children in rural schools. Curriculum guides for health classes taught that sickness resulted from breaking the laws of health and was shameful. As another state publication put it, "A sick body makes a sick mind." After learning proper health habits in the lower grades, seventh grade students were asked to do a little diagnosis in class, checking for adenoids. They were also asked to study their classmates and suggest how their teeth could be improved. Finally, each student was supposed to discuss his or her weight with the teacher and make plans to bring weight up to normal.[41]

If the Tennessee Monkey Law held any symbolic meaning on the local level, it was as a regional reaction to decades of reform culminating in loss of local control over education. No one better articulated that reaction, coupled with a sense of frustration over the cultural depreciation of traditional agrarian values, than the author of the Monkey Law himself.

John Washington Butler was a middle-aged farmer from Macon County. In 1925 he lived on a 150-acre farm given to him by his father when he married, in a house built fifty years earlier by his grandfather. Mr. and Mrs. Butler and their five children grew most of what they consumed. Mrs. Butler raised chickens and bartered eggs for coffee and sugar. The family made its cash by selling millet seed to neighbors, who planted the crop for hay, and by selling dark, air-cured tobacco through the Hartsville warehouse. Butler, like his father before him, was also a thresherman, traveling from farm to farm in the summer to thresh neighbors' wheat. A genial fellow, Butler was something of a community organizer. When the Macon County farm agent convinced local farmers that fertilizer would help increase the yields from their upland fields, Butler took orders from his neighbors and arranged for a freight-load shipment of fertilizer to be delivered to the railroad depot at Hartsville. Butler was a member of the Primitive Baptist Church but was not "narrow-minded" about religious dogma. Since preaching was held only once a month at his church, Butler and his family attended other local churches in turn when they held services.[42]

Butler had a gift for writing clear and pithy if somewhat colloquial prose, which he had occasionally exercised by composing essays for the Macon county newspaper. He found much to mock in the world around him. For example, in 1920 he satirized proposals to outlaw tobacco as unhealthy, suggesting that pork, wheat, corn, milk, fruits, tea, coffee, and sugar could also be bad for one's health; mules and machinery had too much "kick"; water carried disease and air contained germs; and houses would have to go, as doctors agreed that outdoor life was more healthy. "I guess when they get through with us we will be allowed no clothing but a collar and tie, so then I suggest to complete the job we discard them and take to the tall timber and be ground hogs the remainder of our days with nothing to corrupt our morals or damage our health. This is prohibition to a finish. Do you want it?"[43]

Butler's most impassioned criticism, written two years before he ran for office, expressed his concern over education in Macon County. A former teacher himself, Butler remembered with nostalgia those days when teaching was unencumbered by bureaucracy: things got done and there was "no red tape about it." He opposed the loss of local control over teacher licensing and hiring and was also concerned about the quality of textbooks being used, which he considered far inferior to McGuffey's readers. But the heart of his complaint was that the children of rural Macon County were being educated away from the farms. In the old days, he noted, teachers themselves were often farmers. Now, however, education caused boys to want to move to the city. "They want to be clerks, bookkeepers and stenographers and wear biled shirts all the time and loud neckties and collars so high they have to jump up in order to spit over them." Then, the farmer said, these boys "want to get in what they call society (ever what that is) in the cities and marry some society belle." Nine months of schooling, as was being proposed, would only make the situation worse: "Have you ever noticed how lazy boys get when they go to school for awhile?" Butler's essay concluded with a call for education that would make farm children thankful to be where they were, not lead them astray to the "evils of the cities."[44]

In 1922 Butler's family doctor urged him to run for representative from Macon County. Butler was a Democrat, while three-fifths of his neighbors were Republicans. But Macon County was districted with Sumner and Trousdale Counties, which had Democratic majorities. Butler's threshing business had earned him many acquaintances throughout the three counties. Preparing to run for office, Butler turned his hand to writing political pieces. He promised his constituents that he would represent the farmers' interests, eliminate useless offices, and cut official salaries. He also wanted to change the law so that young men with common school educations could attend medical school. This proposal, which he never elaborated, probably grew out of his own frustrated ambitions: Butler had, in his youth, set out to study medicine, attending an academy in nearby Willette.[45] Elected representative from Macon County, Butler was reelected two years later.

Because he had been a teacher, the general assembly placed him on a committee that oversaw the operations of the schools (mostly for handicapped children) operated directly by the state. Part of the duties of that committee included inspecting institutions and curriculum. Butler discovered that the books used in state-run schools taught the theory of evolution. He had heard of children whose Christian faith had been destroyed by Darwinism. One night he told his family over supper that he intended to write a bill outlawing the teaching of any theory of evolution contrary to the Bible in any state-funded school. He added that he did not think the bill would get far.[46]

The Butler Act was championed by the Speaker of the senate, L. D. Hill of Sparta, and passed the general assembly, after considerable debate, with the overwhelming approval of representatives from all over the state, including the Upper Cumberland. O. G. Fox of Jackson County, the farmer whose protest to Governor Roberts is quoted in Chapter 9, voted for the bill, as did R. I. Hutchings, whose private academy in White County was described in Chapter 7. Governor Austin Peay signed the bill as a symbolic gesture: "a distinct protest against an irreligious tendency to exalt so-called science and deny the Bible . . . a tendency fundamentally wrong and fatally mischievous in its effects on our children, our institutions and our country."[47]

During the summer of 1925, as the bill he wrote became the center of an international media carnival, Butler followed events rather wistfully from his home near Lafayette. He wanted to go to Dayton but lacked money; besides, it was threshing season. Occasionally reporters from the national press came up to interview him. In July Butler picked up a *New York Times* reporter at the Hartsville station and brought him to the Butler place in Macon County. The *Times* man described Butler as a huge, bulky man, obviously sincere, with a kindly manner.

Butler explained that he believed the teaching of evolution threatened the family. In a prepared statement, Butler described an idealized Christian home in which a child grows up with a motto on the wall, "Christ is the Head of This House," the mother sings the baby to sleep with "Jesus, Lover of My Soul," and the father works on the farm while humming "I Am Bound for the Promised Land." This domestic harmony is threatened when children are taught scientific theories that cause them to doubt the Bible and thereby break the hearts of their parents.[48]

Butler also told the reporter that civil government rested on the Bible. The morality that made a republic possible derived from biblical authority. Therefore to teach evolution and so cast doubt on the Bible was to undermine the foundations of the state. Here Butler echoed old republican ideology in believing that the virtue of the individual was necessary for the survival of the republic. But his insistence on founding all morality in the Bible grew from his own cultural heritage: in the Upper Cumberland, where law enforcement was so weak and civic virtue all but nonexistent, religion was the only authoritative force available to turn people from their "unlawful lusts." Butler concluded by stating that the theory of evolution was a menace to civilization.[49]

Butler got his chance to go to the Dayton trial when three reporters from a press syndicate visited the family in Macon County. They offered to pay Butler's expenses if he would write articles for them about the trial. "Tickled to death," Butler packed his bags for Dayton, where he watched the trial and had his picture made with William Jennings Bryan, his political hero. He was somewhat disappointed when Darrow was not allowed to put on his expert witnesses on theology and science: secure in his faith, Butler wanted to know what the experts would say.[50]

Butler's bill was so popular among his constituents that it was accepted almost without comment. His neighbors "believed in the Bible" and supported his stand. Like Butler, people in the Upper Cumberland awaited the results of the Dayton trial with much interest. They mourned the death of Bryan. When the Enon Baptist Association, which included congregations in Butler's home county, met in September, they voted a special "Evolution Resolution" condemning Darwinism and asking that churches withdraw fellowship from anyone who believed in the theory. The meeting featured a singing of "The John T. Scopes Trial," a recently composed ballad then popular in the Upper Cumberland. In October the Stone Association of Baptists, comprised mostly of Putnam County churches and led by Cookeville Baptists, passed a resolution criticizing the Southern Baptist Convention itself for its Darwinistic leanings. Noting that the last convention had adopted a statement of faith and a message "in which there are certain statements which are distinctly pro-evolution in their expression and meaning," and that "some of our own trusted Baptist leaders and school men are suspected of being tainted with this heresy," the resolution asked that the statement of faith be rescinded and demanded that denominational support be withdrawn from any institution that employed anyone who would not repudiate proevolution dogma. The association affirmed its opposition to "the evolution dogma in every form: atheistic, agnostic, or theistic, and especially do we oppose it in either tax-supported or denominationally-supported schools."[51]

Butler's antievolution bill represented the consensus of a generation of Upper Cumberland citizens concerning the connections between Christianity, education, and the stability of the republic. Butler's constituents had learned in school that the Bible was as integral to American government as the Constitution. To be a good citizen was synonymous with being a good Christian, and both depended on believing the Bible. Everyone said so: local preachers, parents, the northern outlanders who taught at the mission schools, and even the state government. As education slipped from direct parental control, Bible reading in schools provided a reassuring constant in schooling for parents and children. To teach evolution threatened family unity, faith, and the very basis of civilization and government. To destroy faith in the Bible also destroyed one link binding generations together. Butler's constituents approved of his legislation. They did so across class lines, regardless of town/country divisions. By defending the Bible, Butler offered a symbol around which an otherwise divided population could rally. Progressives and traditionalists alike could agree on the Bible as a symbol of faith and continuity.

In 1925 education reformers triumphed in the passage of the General Education Act, which ratified and extended state control over schools. Education reformers hoped that schooling would work social and economic wonders in rural counties. But in the Upper Cumberland, attitudes toward education hardly changed, although the schools did. In the 1920s as in the 1890s, children in the region participated in schooling as they and their parents saw fit—and stopped coming to school when they chose.

The Butler Act represented another reaction to state control over schooling: a reaction that co-opted the very modern structures for which reformers had labored so long. To ensure that children in rural Macon County were not taught evolution, Butler had to resort to state legislation. Ironically, by creating a state system of education, reformers made it possible for people like Butler to influence education throughout the state and even the nation. For the Anti-Evolution Law, which remained on the books in Tennessee until 1967, had a chilling effect on the teaching of science in the state's rural schools. The law also had national repercussions, as textbook publishers hurried to protect their sales by removing discussions of Darwin's theories from elementary and high school texts.[52] Through the Anti-Evolution Law local tradition defeated modern structure; through their indifference to education people in the Upper Cumberland illustrated the futility of expecting school reform in and of itself to change customs and traditions.

Ultimately the Upper Cumberland traditionalists won their long battle for cultural hegemony in the region. Progressive reform did not transform the Upper Cumberland. Instead the traditional culture proved resilient, adaptable, and even expansive, capable of grafting new ways onto old or of co-opting new institutions to the service of old values. The family remained the region's dominant institution. Family connections mattered more than efficient administration or merit in determining who worked in institutions created by regional progressives. In the 1920s, family heritage still exercised a potent force in regional politics: witness the spectacle of Democrats in 1920 asking women to vote for their party to uphold family honor and the sacred memory of the Lost Cause. So ingrained was the region's familism that few authorities cared to enforce new compulsory education laws against the will of a child's parents. Highways, which were supposed to encourage the development of organized, institutional communities in the region and to bring in the "trinity" of "good roads, good schools, good churches," actually facilitated a resurgence of traditional culture; the "old time singings" created in the 1920s are an example.

Schools failed to reconstruct traditional culture along progressive lines. Instead state structures of administration were captured by traditionalists like Butler. The result was schools that were probably more conservative than the old mission schools like Pleasant Hill. Certainly the mission schools, with their "foreign" faculties, had attempted to teach pupils that the way things had always been done in the Upper Cumberland was not the only way. State schools, with their local teachers, many of whom were related to county officials, were hardly likely to lead students to question the regional status quo.

Although the rural progressives lost their battle to uplift the region, their work did encourage out-migration by holding up ideals and creating needs that the farm family economy could not satisfy. John W. Butler's oldest son, Huber, left farming to become a barber. Thousands of the sons and daughters of the region left the countryside for nearby towns and cities or migrated north to industrial work in Ohio and Michigan. For many years Upper Cumberland papers featured columns of "local news" from communities of the transplanted.[53]

Back home, life rested on the bedrock of farming, which had changed little since the 1890s. The roll of days and seasons went on as it had for parents, grandparents, and generations past. New farming techniques were introduced and adopted, new crops were planted, and new markets were opened. Farmers continued to make a little cash in part-time public work. But Upper Cumberland folk chose new ways only when those ways could be fitted into the traditional pattern of life, and they rejected change if it seemed to threaten traditional values.

The choices made helped doom the region's farmers to poverty and ensured that out-migration would increase. The progressives were right: semisubsistence farming, with its emphasis on security, was no way to become prosperous. By staying the same, farmers in the region fell behind. Ironically, however, their reluctance to trust the market or to go into debt helped most farmers in the region survive as landowners during the next decade. Self-sufficiency paid off during the depression and enabled farm families to provide refuge for relatives who lost their public work jobs when the market economy crashed in 1929.

For most people family, community, and church remained the constants of life, even though all three changed. By the end of the 1920s fathers like J. W. Butler could no longer expect their sons to take over the family farm. Wives gained spending money and power within the family economy, and daughters went out to work—or even away to work in the cities. Community life was more organized and more lively, as automobiles made public gatherings easier. Churches continued to discipline the wanton and support those in need as they had always done: the very continuity of religion was a glimpse of eternity. As a popular spiritual said:

Time is filled with swift transition,
Naught of earth unmoved can stand.
Build your hopes on things eternal—
Hold to God's unchanging hand.

As traditional ways came under attack, Upper Cumberland folk reacted by holding even closer to things eternal. The use of religious symbolism in the secular world proved a powerful unifying force within the region. They might not agree on what the book said, but most people in the Upper Cumberland believed that their salvation depended on the Bible and rallied to defend it. The Bible as cultural icon was particularly useful in the 1920s, appealing to people across political and class lines. Hidebound localist patriarchs, PTA activists, small-town progressive intellectuals, barely literate sectarian preachers—people who agreed on nothing else—could unite in support of the Bible. By the 1920s religiosity was the single most important cultural standard around which people rallied.

The history of the region from the 1890s through the 1920s is not a story of malevolent outside forces disrupting and destroying a traditional way of life. Nor is it the story of how a group of utterly benighted, backward people refused the blessings of modern civilization. Instead the history of the Upper Cumberland is the sum total of choices made by the participants, who included rural progressives as well as traditionalists. If in the end the traditionalists won—and won in such a way that their influence, reflected in the Butler Act, was extended nationwide—it is because for most people in the region traditional ways made sense. Country people clung to old ways through the 1920s because those ways worked, offering security and survival in an uncertain world.

EPILOGUE

One of the problems which any improvement program must take into consideration is that the people are in general satisfied with the present conditions under which they are living.—University of Tennessee educational, economic, and community survey of Jackson County, 1929

Hunters pursuing game through the Upper Cumberland forests sometimes encounter the ruins of small communities no one remembers. Chimneys stand sentinel over weed-covered hillocks that were houses; the vegetation grows in patterns that indicate a road once ran here.

I was born in Jackson County, Tennessee, in 1953. As a child I began formulating the questions that led to this book. Some arose from the incongruities between the Upper Cumberland of the 1950s and 1960s and the region of my family's memories. I lived in a place that was losing population, in a community that was losing its locus. North Springs could support a two-year high school when I was born; the staff dwindled to three teachers, then two teachers, and then the school was closed. But my parents and other relatives remembered a lively community with a sawmill, two stores, a diner, and a garage. They remembered a school large enough to support a basketball team and put on plays. They remembered people who now lived in Dayton or Akron, Ohio, in Detroit, or just in the Nashville suburbs.

I lived in a place that was poor, certified so by the federal government, which poured funds into the area during the 1960s. People in the area did not seem to know that they were "poverty-stricken." Indeed, I remember jokes being made about that phrase: "We thought we was just poor." Other questions arose from the dissonance between the Upper Cumberland and the world we all saw on television. No white married women on TV worked, but many of my female neighbors did, carpooling into town to their jobs in clothing plants, generically called "shirt factories." Most of the fathers of my friends did not wear suits to work.

I witnessed the effects of transportation improvements myself when Interstate 40 was built through the Upper Cumberland. I-40 accelerated the depopulation of the countryside; it was as if the towns on I-40, especially Cookeville, sucked up all the life and all the commerce from the rest of the region, leaving it a beautiful but empty place. Driving from Cookeville to North Springs late at night one can go miles without seeing any light but that of the moon.

As a child I did not know that I was living in a period of rapid transition. State economists knew, however, and were greatly worried by two trends: the rush of migration out of the region as agriculture withered, and the increased feminization of the work force. In 1940 65 percent of the region's work force worked in agriculture; by 1990 only about 3 percent did.[1] As state planners noted in 1967, "Male employment in subsistence agriculture, mining, and lumber manufacturing declined precipitously, and the increase in other employment sectors was unable to offset this decline in the primary sector. The employment decline led to high out-migration from the region." My home county lost 25 percent of its population during the 1950s.[2]

The young men who left school in the 1910s and 1920s were middle-aged men by the 1950s. Their poor educations fitted them to work as farmers, sawmill hands, or miners: "hewers of wood and drawers of water." Then in the 1950s and 1960s those jobs disappeared or did not provide enough pay or profits to support a family. The state planners saw the problem: moving to town and getting another job would not be easy for the average farmer, "usually past 50 years of age, poorly trained for urban employment, short on formal education, low on finances needed to resettle elsewhere, and probably strongly attached to his farm and rural community." The displaced farmer's hope lay in getting some sort of off-farm job to make ends meet.[3]

Meanwhile, Upper Cumberland women took up the slack. Women poured into the work force, finding jobs in the apparel plants that moved to the region in the postwar period. The state noted that "the drastic decline in male employment in agriculture . . . compelled many women to become breadwinners." They worked in low-wage, nonunion plants without many benefits or any hope of advancement. Nonetheless, while expecting the female work force to grow drastically in the next twenty years, state planners in 1967 did not concern themselves with the quality of work available for rural women. Rather, they believed that "the employment of males is the most important manpower need in the region today."[4]

Today the transition is complete, and farming as a way of supporting a family is no longer an option for most Upper Cumberland families. Although the local economy still varies from county to county, the largest sector of employment in the region is manufacturing, with 30.5 percent of the work force. Putnam County (population 51,373) continues to grow and to siphon off commerce from neighboring counties. Retail trade employs over ten times as many people as agriculture in Putnam. The college Cookeville progressive Jere Whitson started is now a university specializing in engineering; 2,765 people from all over the world work in educational services in Putnam County. Cumberland County, long one of the poorest in the region and previously dependent on extractive lumber and mining industries, has found its niche as a safe place to locate retirement homes for white northerners. The large retirement community built at Fairfield Glade affects the local economy in obvious ways. Cumberland has almost as many health services workers as Putnam County, which has 16,637 more people. The newcomers also pump a great deal of disposable income into the community. The median family income in the county seat, Crossville, is $18,958, while in Fairfield Glade it is $32,147. The individual poverty rate in Crossville is 28.6 percent; in Fairfield Glade it is 3.3 percent.[5]

Certain things have not changed much in the last 100 years. For most people, supporting a family still requires the work of both parents, as it did in 1890. Many rural women went from being farm workers to being factory workers without passing through the stage of domesticity described by women's historians as normal for middle-class women in the nineteenth century. Upper Cumberland women in the 1890s rarely were able to devote most of their time to child care and the psychological duties subsumed under the job title "angel in the house." In the 1950s their granddaughters' lives did not correspond to the models television and magazines offered for proper middle-class family life. Rather than being consumers, country women were producers, first on the farm and then in the factory. The kind of work changed, but the work went on. Today young women combine public work with raising families as their great-grandmothers combined farm work with child care. Throughout the region over 55 percent of the women with preschool children work; in some counties the rate for young mothers is higher than 70 percent. Even more women with school age children work: the range is from 68 percent in Fentress County to 82.8 percent in neighboring Pickett. Even with women working, incomes in the region are low. The median family household income in the Upper Cumberland Development District in 1989 was $24,060. In 1990 as in 1890 families do better than single people: the poverty rate in the development district in 1989 was 15 percent for families, 41.7 percent for "unrelated individuals."[6]

Upper Cumberland folk remain rather indifferent to education. In 1990 Putnam County had the highest proportion of high school graduates in the region: 63 percent of the population had finished a twelve-year course. It should be noted, however, that the presence of Tennessee Tech in Cookeville skews the data, as does the presence of Fairfield Glade in Cumberland County, where 59.8 percent of the population are high school graduates. Throughout the region between 40 and 50 percent of the adult population have a high school education. The percentage of college graduates is quite small, less than 10 percent in all the counties except Putnam and Cumberland.[7]

The rural transition that swept through the region when I was a child could not have been forestalled by the progressive attempts to reform the region's economy and culture. However, if those attempts had succeeded, Upper Cumberland folk might have been better prepared for the new dispensation. As an educator warned in 1906,

"Thought is the motive power of the world. He who cannot think and think fast, must soon give way to him who can. There are many young men from 14 to 20 years of age in this county who are failing to make the most of themselves. . . . Many of them will be doomed to be 'hewers of wood and drawers of water' for others of their contemporaries who have learned to think." The region's poverty today stems at least in part from decisions made at the turn of the last century. Refusing to make a social investment in a future they could not imagine, Upper Cumberland folk inadvertently doomed their children to chose between living on the verge of poverty or leaving the region.

If asked today why they stay, most people in the region would probably say that the Upper Cumberland is home. Most of all, it is where the folks are. Today as in the 1890s, families temper hard times for their members, help when needed, care for the sick, and mourn the dying. Such services cannot be quantified; nonetheless they exist and enable people to survive.

Religion continues to play an important role in regional life. As in the 1890s, local congregations provide emotional and spiritual support and a social outlet for their members—although one must wonder what the Baptists of the 1890s would think of Cookeville First Baptist Church's recreational center, complete with basketball court and billiard tables. Churches still schedule revivals in the autumn, as if people still had to wait for the crops to be laid by before attending night services. More conservative preachers still fulminate against Tom Paine and Voltaire, and Darwinist perspectives are scarce in Upper Cumberland schools. As they move into the next century, many people in the region cling to the ways of the fathers, at least in religion, and could agree with the sign posted outside one Cookeville church in 1988:

> Don't clip the wings of faith
> with the scissors of human reason.

NOTES

Introduction

1. Ginger, *Six Days or Forever?*, 84–88, 92–94, 125–28, 154, 162.
2. Butler interview.
3. This attitude is reflected in encyclopedias and textbooks. See "Scopes Trial," 971; see also Davidson et al., "The New Era," in *Nation of Nations.* Robert L. Dorman summarizes the conflict that produced regionalism in the 1920s as growing out of "the decades-long continental drift of values from producerism to consumerism, from Christianity to secularism, from the participatory to the bureaucratic" (Dorman, *Revolt of the Provinces*, 107).
4. See Wood, "Inventing American Capitalism," for a succinct statement of the arguments over the nature of rural society (was the economy "moral" or "market"?) and the origins of capitalism in England and in New England. George Fredrickson in "Down on the Farm" provides an overview of the literature to that date. See also Hahn and Prude, *Countryside in the Age of Capitalist Transformation*; Faragher, *Sugar Creek*; Hahn, *Roots of Southern Populism*; Jones and Osterud, "Breaking New Ground"; Osterud, *Bonds of Community*; and Kulikoff, "Households and Markets."
5. Montell, *Don't Go up Kettle Creek*. Montell, a folklorist, defines the region as follows: from Carthage north through Red Boiling Springs in Macon County to Edmonton, Ky.; east through Russell Springs to Somerset; south through Whitley City, Ky., to Crossville, Tenn.; down to Sparta in White County; and back west to Carthage. Montell believes that the Upper Cumberland is a "distinct cultural-geographic entity" and traces the use of the term "Upper Cumberland" to the early nineteenth century.

   Currently the term is used in the titles of numerous government agencies, ranging from the Upper Cumberland Development District to the Upper Cumberland Child Development Project; it also turns up in the names of local businesses. The Putnam County telephone directory alone has nineteen listings under "Upper Cumberland." In some cases the label "Upper Cumberland" includes counties not studied in this work. No claims are made here as to the distinctive nature of the region as defined; on the contrary, the author would expect that in culture the counties chosen are very similar to adjoining counties in Tennessee and Kentucky.
6. Ibid., chap. 1; Thomas G. Webb, *DeKalb County*, 9–12; DeLozier, *Putnam County*, 3–18.
7. DeLozier, *Putnam County*, 19–24; Blankenship, *Macon County*, 15–22; Foster, *Counties of Tennessee*.
8. Grime, *Recollections of a Long Life*. Grime's family moved into the Upper Cumberland in the 1850s. His father owned more than twenty slaves and was considered one of the most prominent slaveholders in Putnam County. Accord-

ing to his son, however, Grime's family worked in the fields with the slaves, and the family practiced the most stringent frugality. See DeLozier, *Putnam County*, 8–18; Montell, *Don't Go up Kettle Creek*, 39–43; Thomas G. Webb, *DeKalb County*, 1–2. See also Arnow, *Seedtime on the Cumberland*.

9. DeLozier, *Putnam County*, 36–46; Blankenship, *Macon County*, 171–74; Thomas G. Webb, *DeKalb County*, 29–30.

10. Whiteaker, "Civil War in the Upper Cumberland"; Blankenship, *Macon County*, 174–76; DeLozier, *Putnam County*, 46–47; Thomas G. Webb, *DeKalb County*, 30–34.

11. See the sources cited in n. 10 above. See also *Tennessee Times*, May 20, 1901.

12. DeLozier, *Putnam County*, 46–47; Blankenship, *Macon County*, 167–70; Thomas G. Webb, *DeKalb County*, 40–43; Department of the Interior, Census Office, *Report on Population*, tab. 15, 428–29. One of the few, brief, but fascinating glimpses of African American life in the region in the late nineteenth century comes from an unlikely source. W. E. B. Du Bois taught school at Alexandria in DeKalb County during summer vacation from Fisk University in Nashville, and he wrote about it in his autobiography. This was Du Bois's first real encounter with rural southern blacks. He enjoyed his stay in DeKalb County but found the quality of school facilities appalling. See Du Bois, *Autobiography*, 114–21; see also David Levering Lewis, *W. E. B. Du Bois*, 68–77.

13. See Ayers, *Promise of the New South* for a description of a bustling, dynamic New South. The Upper Cumberland's isolation from this transformation is reflected in Ayers's maps plotting various types of New South phenomena, from percent of families with member engaged in manufacturing to railroad lines. In most cases the Upper Cumberland is in the lowest percentile, and of course it was without a transversing rail line at all in 1890. See also DeLozier, *Putnam County*, 54–72; Montell, *Don't Go up Kettle Creek*, chap. 1; Krechniak and Krechniak, *Cumberland County's First Hundred Years*, 146–47; Thomas G. Webb, *DeKalb County*, 55–60; Seals, *White County*, 141–47; *Crossville Chronicle*, February 6, 1895; Department of the Interior, Census Office, *Report on Manufacturing Industries*, tab. 6, 594–96.

The region's towns were tiny, with populations as follows: Celina, Clay County, 223; Crossville, Cumberland County, 226; Smithville, DeKalb County, 572; Dowelltown, DeKalb County, 233; Jamestown, Fentress County, 84; Gainesboro, Jackson County, 462; Granville, Jackson County, 227; Lafayette, Macon County, 256; Livingston, Overton County, 320; Pickett County listed no towns at all; Cookeville, Putnam County, 469; Sparta, White County, 712. See Department of the Interior, Census Office, *Report on Population*, tab. 5, 317–28.

14. Baron, *Those Who Stayed Behind*.

Chapter 1

1. In 1899 the editor of the Jackson County paper complained that without locks to regulate the river the people of the Upper Cumberland "are almost cut

off from the world of commerce for nearly half a year" (*Gainesboro Sentinel*, June 8, 1899).

According to University of Tennessee agricultural specialists, farm production in Overton County was for home consumption until the turn of the century. See Allred and Robinson, "Significant Changes."

Montell, *Don't Go up Kettle Creek*, chap. 4; see also Douglas, *Steamboatin' on the Cumberland*, 207–46.

2. A typical letter in the *Gainesboro Sentinel*, November 13, 1903, from an outmigrant to the Indian Territory, urged renters to move west because in Jackson County rent was one-half the crop, but in Indian Territory rent was one-eighth the corn and one-fourth the cotton. On the other hand, he said, the moral tone of the community was low, and he urged any young man interested in migrating to bring with him a Jackson County bride, "one who can cook and help make a living." In a similar vein, an Indian Territory correspondent in the May 12, 1906, *Gainesboro Sentinel* advised landowners to stay in Tennessee, but those renting steep hillsides and "paying half what you make" should come out west.

3. *Gainesboro Sentinel*, March 24, 1906; *Cookeville Press*, May 17, 1984.

4. Department of the Interior, Census Office, *Report on the Statistics of Agriculture*, tab. 5, 180–83.

5. Ibid.; also, tab. 6, 227–28.

6. The 1890 census rolls were destroyed, so there are no easily available sources for information about individual farms. However, Estate Inventories in the attic of the Putnam County Courthouse give some insight into individual households. For example, when A. W. Byres died and left four minor children, their guardian made an inventory of the estate. As of February 1898 Byres's farm assets included 2 horses, 2 head of cattle, 4 hogs and 5 pigs, 3 geese, 6 ducks, 16 chickens, 40 bushels of corn, 75 binds of fodder, 75 binds of oats, 100 of bacon, 75 gallons of sorghum (and a sorghum mill), and a quantity of peas. An inventory of P. M. Hyder's estates in August 1899 showed that he had 10 hogs, 35 bushels of oats, 1 stack of hay, 1 cow, 1 calf and 1 heifer, and 40 bushels of corn. Hyder had numerous carpenter's tools and a "count book." He probably worked part time as a carpenter. Martha Henry, a Cookeville widow whose small estate, inventoried in June 1899, included household goods and furniture, also had a cow, which she willed to the Cookeville Methodist Church.

7. Montell, *Don't Go up Kettle Creek*, 23–28; DeLozier, *Putnam County*, 54–65; Department of the Interior, Census Office, *Report on the Statistics of Agriculture*, tab. 20, 450–51. Only Macon and Smith Counties produced significant amounts of tobacco. In Macon County 1,154 acres were planted in tobacco; in Smith, 1,202.

8. Department of the Interior, Census Office, *Report on the Statistics of Agriculture*, tab. 14, 384–38; Montell, *Don't Go up Kettle Creek*, chap. 1.

9. Montell, *Don't Go up Kettle Creek*, chap. 1. For statistics on various small crops in the Upper Cumberland, see Department of the Interior, Census Office, *Report on the Statistics of Agriculture*, tab. 16, 396; tab. 14, 384–85; tab. 22, 489–90; tab. 24, 529–30; tab. 12, 346–47.

10. Department of the Interior, Census Office, *Report on the Statistics of Agri-*

culture, tab. 12, 346–47. The number of hogs per farm was obtained by dividing the census total by the number of farms. See also Seals, *White County*, 62–63; *Cookeville Press*, February 21, 1895. The phrase "hog-killing weather" is still used by older persons in the region to describe very cold weather.

11. Department of the Interior, Cenus Office, *Report on the Statistics of Agriculture*, tab. 10, 306–7. Average gallons of milk per farm were obtained by dividing census total production by the number of farms. See also Seals, *White County*, 62–64; Blankenship, *Macon County*, 71.

12. Department of the Interior, Census Office, *Report on the Statistics of Agriculture*, tab. 12, 346–47.

A cake made with baking powder and soda will rise with no more than one egg. But traditional recipes for pound cake, such as the one printed in the *Jackson County Cookbook* (Jackson County PTA, 1950) indicate the need to use up extra eggs: Mix one cup butter, five whole eggs, pinch salt, one and one-third cups sugar, two cups flour, one teaspoon vanilla. In this recipe, eggs are the sole leavening agent, and the batter must be beaten vigorously for a long time if the cake is to rise. A recipe for chess pie in the same cookbook calls for five eggs.

13. Montell, *Don't Go up Kettle Creek*, 42–43; DeLozier, *Putnam County*, 109.

14. Department of the Interior, Census Office, *Report on the Statistics of Agriculture*, tab. 12, 346–47; Allred, "Economic Analysis of Farming in Overton County." The information about the relative merits of riding mules or horses came from Paul Conkin.

15. "Christmas in Cookeville 100 Years Ago Was—Well It Was Different," *Cookeville Herald-Citizen*, December 24, 1986. Ginseng grows wild throughout the area and is still collected, dried, and sold to local merchants.

16. Department of the Interior, Census office, *Report on the Statistics of Agriculture*, tab. 20, 450–51; Montell, *Don't Go up Kettle Creek*, 50; Killebrew and Myrick, *Tobacco Leaf*, 291. According to Killebrew, in the Cumberland River district (Smith, Trousdale, Macon, Clay, Jackson, and Putnam Counties) "tobacco is grown mainly on the low bottom lands and is coarse[,] . . . wanting in flexibility, deficient in oil, but having a good weight." Burley tobacco is grown in the region now.

17. Thomas G. Webb, *DeKalb County*, 53, 44; Census Reports, *Twelfth Census of the United States*, vol. 5, tab. 44, 620–21.

18. Owsley, *Plain Folk*; Hahn, *Roots of Southern Populism*; *Carthage Courier*, March 31, 1927, April 24, 1924; Montell, *Don't Go up Kettle Creek*, 23; Oakley, "Fifty Years in the Ministry."

In an obituary for a man who had moved to Cumberland County from Milwaukee in 1890, it was noted that his friends had planted and were working his corn for the family (*Crossville Chronicle*, June 19, 1901). In a story called "A Bad Fire at Dycus" a correspondent for the *Gainesboro Sentinel* (March 2, 1907) commented, "The people are donating freely of their means. This is everybody priveledge [*sic*] to help come forth those that haven't helped and do what you can and it will be appreciated."

19. *Cookeville Press*, January 18, 1894.

20. According to Montell, *Don't Go up Kettle Creek*, 48, commercial fertilizer was not used by most farmers in the area until the twentieth century. Although

some seed was purchased, many families saved their own garden seed. (The author's great-grandmother put garden seed in tiny cotton bags, which she suspended from strings attached to the porch roof. The idea was to keep rodents out of the seed.) The use of "trade" rather than "shop" to describe what one did at the store was still common in the 1950s.

Advertisements in the local papers for stores often indicate that there were cash prices and credit prices. Gainesboro had a Cash Grocery Store that offered lower prices, but no credit. The People's Store in Cumberland County gave a 5 percent discount for cash (*Crossville Times*, November 18, 1886). An ad in the *Crossville Chronicle*, December 24, 1902, for a store in Ozone called for cash "or its equivalent, such as good barter or credit with good security" instead of credit. This, the store owners insisted, would enable them to lower prices for all.

If the crop-lien system existed in the Upper Cumberland, it left no imprint in the memory of people in the region, and it faded before the 1920s. According to Allred, Robinson, and Luebke, "Rural Credit in Tennessee," in 1923 in Putnam and Cumberland Counties most people who borrowed money did so to buy land, and they borrowed from individuals by mortgaging the land they had. Those who had merchant credit used it for only small amounts; in Putnam the average was $14, in Cumberland $46. Merchant credit was secured by personal notes or chattel mortgages or was "open account," that is, simply a tab to be paid later.

Estate Inventories, books 4 and 5, indicate that merchants charged a "credit price" for goods but did not charge further interest on store tabs. People owing money to merchants were listed, but no rate of interest was recorded. On the other hand, when debts were secured by personal note, the rate of interest was usually (but not always) recorded.

21. *Gainesboro Sentinel*, May 4, 1899. The editor mentioned that the town shipped wheat to Nashville and brought flour from the mills at Lebanon, Gordonsville, Algood, Cookeville, and other neighboring towns. An ad for Hawks and Company General Store in the *Clay County Tribune*, December 30, 1899, is typical: the store would take "country produce" for dry goods, shoes, groceries, ammunition, and raft supplies.

22. Howell, *Survey of Folklife*, 112–13.

23. Butler interview. Mr. Butler, a retired barber whose father, J. W. Butler, wrote the 1925 antievolution law, said that some people did not like public work "because you always have a boss over you." Butler defined his own job as public work. Note also Robert Gwaltney's use of "public work," below, to describe helping form a telephone company.

24. *Carthage Courier*, April 9, 23, May 21, 1925.

25. Ibid.

26. Montell, *Don't Go up Kettle Creek*, 83–127; Schulman, "Lumber Industry of the Upper Cumberland Valley," 255–64.

27. Montell, *Don't Go up Kettle Creek*, 83–127; Doyle, *Nashville in the New South*, 36.

28. DeLozier, *Putnam County*, 67–69, 130.

29. Census Reports, *Twelfth Census of the United States*, vol. 5, tab. 10, 122–25. The percentage of farms "encumbered" per county was as follows: Clay 5,

Cumberland 2, DeKalb 4, Fentress 3, Jackson 9, Macon 11, Overton 4, Pickett 6, Smith 9, White 6.

The estate of Mrs. S. E. Wright, a wealthy widow, was inventoried in 1912, later than the period studied and twenty years after banks were opened in Putnam County. Wright herself had money deposited in the Bank of Cookeville, but she also had eleven loans due to her from various local men. The terms of the loans varied. Some were due at a specific date, and some were open-ended. Some were specified with interest; others were not. Some were secured with collateral (including one for $1,100 secured by mortgage), and others mention no collateral. Some notes were secured by the signatures of "co-signers," who guaranteed that the loan would be met if the principal borrower defaulted. Wright's estate indicates just how personal lending money was. See Estate Inventories, 1912.

"Mistakes on the Plateau," *Tennessee Times*, June 3, 1891. Grime, *Recollections of a Long Life*, 9. Grime was the son of Putnam County's largest slaveholder. The elder Grime owned more than twenty slaves, but the Grime family lived frugally. Grime's father worked in the fields beside his slaves, did blacksmithing, and made his family's shoes. Grime listed the economic rules by which his father operated in the 1850s: nothing wasted; no frivolity; no speculating; nothing for show; everything that could be made at home should be, with all family members contributing; little or nothing purchased.

Chapter 2

1. Banfield's *Moral Basis of a Backward Society* uses the concept of "amoral familism" to describe the culture of a particularly backward southern Italian peasant village. "Familism" describes Upper Cumberland culture, but "amoral" does not quite fit, perhaps because the extended family was much stronger in the Upper Cumberland than in Banfield's village, economic conditions were not as dire, and the class structure was completely different.

2. The word *patriarchy* carries heavy political freight; nonetheless, it better describes the labor system of the Upper Cumberland than such phrases as "family labor system," which implies that the family as a unit controlled its own labor. The situation in the Upper Cumberland in the 1890s was not dissimilar to that of eighteenth-century Britain, where the work of women in agricultural production was accepted, even assumed, as long as they were under the authority of a male "head of the family" to whom their wages were paid. See Seccombe, "Patriarchy Stabilized," 53–96.

The overriding paradigm in American women's history is based on bourgeois sources. Nancy A. Hewitt has pointed out the limited applicability of the concept of "woman's sphere" to the lives of working-class and black women in "Beyond the Search for Sisterhood." Rural women's history, long neglected, has flowered in the past few years. See "American Rural and Farm Women in Historical Perspective," an *Agricultural History* symposium, which includes Osterud, "Gender and the Transition to Capitalism in Rural America." See also Jensen, "Rural Women in American History," and "The Role of Farm Women in American History: Areas for Additional Research," in Jensen, *Promise to the Land*; Jones and Osterud, " 'If I Must Say So Myself' "; Sturgis, " 'How're You Gonna Keep 'Em down on the Farm?' "; Neth, "Gender and the Family Labor System"; McMurry, "Women's Work in Agriculture"; Kulikoff, "Households and Markets"; Fink, *Agrarian Women*; Sachs, *Invisible Farmers*.

In 1913 the state legislature enacted House Bill 2, removing the common law coverture of married women. It became law without the signature of the governor. In 1919 House Bill 2 was repealed, and a more carefully worded bill was passed, this time with the overwhelming support of both houses of the legislature and Governor A. H. Roberts. Chapter 126, passed in 1919, was "an Act to remove disabilities of coverture from married women, and to extend to them the statutes of limitation and to exempt to them a homestead." The act allowed married women to make contracts, hold property, and sue in court as if they were single. See *Public Acts of the State of Tennessee*, 1913, 59–60; *Public Acts of the State of Tennessee*, 1919, 406–97, 524.

3. These and other statistics presented in this chapter were derived from a sample of 405 cases drawn from the manuscript of the 1900 census rolls by taking down information on every sixty-sixth case on the rolls. A sample size of 405 should yield results 95 percent likely to be accurate within 5 percentage points. Where the sample size is less than 405, that is indicated in the note. Generally the subsets of the sample are large enough to produce a confidence level of 95 percent with a 5 to 6 percent limit of tolerated error. Estimates of confidence and error levels from Charles H. Backstrom and Gerald D. Hursh, *Survey Research* (Evanston, Ill.: Northwestern University Press, 1963).

The manuscript of the 1900 census rolls lists each member living within a household by his or her relationship to the head of household. Therefore, it is more useful for family studies than some earlier censuses. It also contains data on literacy and occupation for all persons listed. However, it does not contain information pertaining to the wealth of the household, other than noting whether the head of household owned or rented his or her house or farm and whether the property was mortgaged.

4. The regional population was over 90 percent white.

5. The sample for household type was the entire sample of 405. In actual frequency 32 households were composed of husband and wife alone; 253 of husband, wife, and children; 18 of nuclear family augmented with people from an older generation; and 23 of nuclear family augmented with people from a younger generation. Six households contained individuals living alone; 13 households were augmented with relatives of the same generation as the household head (brothers and sisters); 35 were headed by a single person living with family members; 19 sheltered more than one complete nuclear family; and 6 contained multigenerational families combining uncles, cousins, etc.

For servants and boarders the sample size was also 405. Twenty-six households took in boarders and 25 had servants.

6. Of the 405 families, 371 were headed by men.

7. Hyder's narrative of his courtship is found in DeLozier, *Putnam County*, 87–88.

8. *Carthage Courier*, April 9, 23, May 21, 1925.

9. John T. Oakley's memoirs ran as a column, "Fifty[-one, -two] Years in the Ministry," in the *Carthage Courier* from 1921 through 1924. The Haley-Rose wedding ended with a charivari (shivaree); this was common and did not necessarily indicate any ill feeling toward the newly wed couple. Although most weddings apparently took place in homes, in the 1890s area newspapers reported elaborate church weddings, complete with Mendelssohn and "O Promise Me," in the region's towns. Sometimes all the wedding gifts were listed. See *Crossville News Democrat*, December 21, 1898.

10. Note that this statistic was obtained by subtracting the years married from the age of the husband and wife, respectively. The census rolls do not indicate whether either partner had been married before. Therefore these median ages may not accurately reflect the ages at which people married for the first time. In particular, the median age at first marriage for women may have been lower than twenty. According to Robert V. Wells, in 1880–89 the median age at first marriage for American women was 21.6. See Wells, *Uncle Sam's Family*, 155.

The higher age at marriage for men may reflect a tradition that held that men should not marry until they could provide a separate home for their wives. Merged households, as noted earlier, were unusual in the region.

The sample sizes vary in this case due to blanks in the census and cases omitted because of quirks in the way the original data was collected. The sample number for wives was 340. The mean age at marriage was 20.6. The age ranged from 54 to 10. For men, the sample number was 347, the mean age was 25, and the age ranged from 68 to 13.

According to the thirteenth census, 18.3 percent of all Tennessee women aged fifteen to nineteen were married, while only 3.1 percent of the men in the same age group were married. See Department of Commerce and Labor, Bureau of the Census, *Thirteenth Census of the United States*, tab. 1, 594–611.

11. Grime, *Recollections of a Long Life*, 1–20.

Of men in their twenties, 67.5 percent were tenants. In this case, the sample size was 397, and the percentages were computed by running a cross-tabulation of tenure by age.

Throughout this chapter the source on "regional tradition" is the author, unless otherwise specified. See also Wharton, *Doctor Woman*. Wharton, a native of Minnesota, came to Cumberland County in 1917 as the wife of a teacher at Pleasant Hill Academy, a school for mountain whites operated by the American Missionary Association. When her husband died, Wharton stayed on and eventually opened a clinic at Uplands. According to the doctor, it was common for parents to give married children a portion of their farm and help the young couple build a house.

12. DeKalb County Will Books, roll 77, C. C. Johnson's will, May 27, 1891, 256.

13. Ibid., G. W. Puckett's will, July 25, 1900, 310. Hal Baron, in *Those Who Stayed Behind*, uses "Benjamin" to describe a youngest son who inherits the family farm. The term derives from the Bible: Benjamin was the last, best-beloved son of the patriarch Israel.

14. The will left by Thomas Bane in 1892 was a rare exception to the egalitar-

ian rule. Bane left everything to his wife, with the provision that upon her death his land was to be divided between his sons Harrison and Lemuel, with his daughters to receive $25 each. See DeKalb County Will Books, roll 77, Thomas Bane's will, September 8, 1892, 269; S. B. Seller's will, April 25, 1892; S. H. Walker's will, April 4, 1902, 11.

15. J. W. Butler's father's will, handwritten on lined paper, is in a scrapbook kept by his son and daughter-in-law, Mr. and Mrs. Huber Butler of Carthage, Tennessee, who allowed the author to see it during an interview in June 1987.

16. *Carthage Courier*, April 9, 23, May 21, 1925.

The survey number in this case is 397 because not all of the 405 households in the original survey indicated status of landownership. This computation lumped all heads of household together, regardless of race and sex. But 94 percent of the heads of household were white, and almost 92 percent were male. Of the thirty-four women who headed households, 76.4 percent were owners. This probably reflects the fact that most women who headed households were widows who may have inherited land from their husbands.

Blacks (5.8 percent of the sample) were more likely to remain tenants for life. The tenancy rate among blacks as a group was 65 percent, and the rate of tenancy in that group declined only slightly with the age of the head of household.

17. Oakley, "Fifty-one Years in the Ministry"; Langford Diary.

The female literacy rate was computed from a sample of 360 cases. Ten percent of the women were partially literate, being able to read, and 23 percent were totally illiterate.

18. The number of married women who listed occupations was too small to bother quantifying. Bertha Doss and her daughters were listed in the Fentress County census rolls, 24 A-1, case number 5.

19. In the United States the total fertility rate dropped from 7.04 in 1800 to 3.56 in 1900, as couples limited births through various means. Historians have argued that making the decision to limit one's family to a certain size (usually for economic reasons) is one of the markers of modernization. If this is so, modern attitudes were rare in the Upper Cumberland. See Degler, *At Odds*, 178–209; Wells, *Uncle Sam's Family*, chap. 2.

In 1900, census takers added a category of inquiry not present in earlier years. They asked women, "Mother of how many children?" and followed up by asking how many children survived. In a survey sample of 363 women, the median number of children borne was 4, and the mean was 4.6. The completed family size was calculated on a sample of 78 women past the age of 50. The median number of children was 6, the mean was 6.34, and the range was from 0 to 14. Although 78 is not a large enough sample to ensure statistical accuracy, it seems probable that a larger sample would produce similar results.

20. The sample in this instance represents women who had children, an N of 355. Of that number 41.7 percent, or 148 women, had lost at least one child.

21. "Gaines," *Gospel Advocate*, August 19, 1897.

22. Census Reports, *Twelfth Census of the United States*, vol. 1. Details of households taken from the manuscript of the 1900 census rolls for Tennessee.

23. See sources cited in n. 22 above.

24. "Final Report, Fentress County"; Dickinson, "Our Fathers' Houses," 77–88.

25. See sources in n. 24 above; Wharton, *Doctor Woman*, 1–52; Social Survey of Putnam County, Tennessee. This pamphlet states that of 200 houses inspected in the Putnam County countryside in 1918, not one had an indoor toilet. According to a survey of Pickett County in the 1920s, the "typical" farmer there had not bothered to construct an outhouse for his family. See Sanders, "Educational and Economic Survey of Pickett County, Tennessee."

26. In August 1904 Samuel Young, a wealthy merchant/farmer in Putnam County, died at the age of eighty-nine, leaving a large and complex estate. His son inventoried Young's home, which was large and lavishly appointed, listing furnishings room by room. With the exception of the parlor, the dining room, the front hall, and the kitchen, every room in the house had a bed in it. The family room (so named in the inventory) had a bedstead and dresser as well as a sofa-lounge, two rockers, and several split bottom chairs. The upstairs rooms all had at least one bed and were outfitted as sitting rooms as well. The fact that Young had a parlor set him apart from his less affluent neighbors, but even in his house most rooms had more than one function. See Samuel Young estate, Estate Inventories, book 4, October 4, 1904, 179; *Putnam County Herald*, August 24, 1904.

27. Schooling as an aspect of governance is dealt with in greater detail in Chapter 4.

28. The *Gospel Advocate*, a Church of Christ paper published in Nashville by David Lipscomb and Elisha Sewell (himself an Overton County native with friends and relatives throughout the Upper Cumberland), provided essays on many aspects of family life, and inspirational stories and poetry. The *Gospel Advocate* also ran a "Queries" column that answered questions from readers on the basis of the authors' interpretation of the Bible. The paper had many readers in the region, judging by letters to the editor. Within the region, the Churches of Christ grew during the 1890s and the first decade of the twentieth century to emerge in 1906 as the third largest denomination in the region, following the Baptists and the Methodists. See "Husbands Love Your Wives," *Gospel Advocate*, April 1, 1891; "The Apostolic Church," *Gospel Advocate*, October 25, 1894.

See Vickers, "Woman's Place," 59–60. Vickers describes how Baptist leaders continually preached that woman's place was in the home, stating their message in the most conservative and limiting terms. Porter, *Feminism*, is a collection of essays, some dating from the late nineteenth century, giving the conservative Baptist perspective on woman's place. See also recent works on evangelical churches and their influence on family life and gender issues: Ownby, *Subduing Satan*, and Friedman, *Enclosed Garden*. Ownby describes religion as a feminized domain in conflict with the hearty masculine world of the rural South. While this is true to an extent, he underestimates male supremacy in southern religion.

29. "Sermon to Young Ladies," *Gospel Advocate*, January 12, 1893; "Like Mother, Like Daughter," *Gospel Advocate*, April 19, 1894. In this regard the conservative southern Christians who ran the *Gospel Advocate* echoed antebellum northern creators of the "cult of true womanhood."

30. "She Resigned," *Gospel Advocate*, March 25, 1891.

31. E. A. Elam, "Training Children," *Gospel Advocate*, June 17, 1897; Ownby, *Subduing Satan*, 5–7.

32. Gregory, *Cal's Column*, n.p. Baptist Elder Calvin Gregory of Macon County, born in 1891, was a preacher and a newspaper columnist in the 1920s. In the 1940s he wrote a series of nostalgic columns. The funeral stories were published January 23, 1947. Gregory did not indicate the date when the events he described occurred. The other stories were told to the author in confidence by natives of the region.

33. Rogers, *White County*, 106–7.

34. *Gospel Advocate*, March 3, 1892.

35. Ibid., June 8, 1899.

36. The hope of a family reunion in heaven is a perennial southern evangelical theme. See Ownby, *Subduing Satan*, 7–9, and Friedman, *Enclosed Garden*.

37. *Gospel Advocate*, April 11, 1895.

38. Langford Diary. Miss Draper made weekly entries in pencil on a school tablet. James Draper's entry in the 1880 agricultural census, Smith County eighth district, p. 9, line 5, indicates that in 1880 he owned 150 acres of improved land, 20 acres in meadows, and 50 acres of forest. His land was worth $2,500. Mr. Draper hired white labor 45 weeks a year; kept cattle, hogs, chickens, and sheep; grew wheat and corn; and had 4 acres of tobacco. (Four acres is a large "tobacco patch" for the Upper Cumberland; the labor Draper hired was probably employed tending tobacco, an extremely labor-intensive crop.) The Draper family's entry in the manuscript of the 1880 census rolls (vol. 31, p. 15) lists as living at home at that time children Mary J., 22; William W., 20; Mourning, 18; Fannie, 15; Polly, 13; James, 12; and Elizabeth, 9.

39. Tinsley Diary.

40. Douglass, *Christian Reconstruction in the South*.

41. Ibid., 318–320.

42. On the other hand, according to Douglass, old women were often the true and respected heads of families because they were experts at the "home industries" that made life bearable.

43. Douglass, *Christian Reconstruction in the South*, 320–22, 352–53.

44. A map of the Oakley area of Overton in 1923 gives names of landowners. Of 53 farms, 23 were owned by people who had the same last name as one or more neighboring landowners. There were 4 Martins, 2 Mathewses, 3 Maynards, 2 Dennises, 2 Savages, 3 Spicers, 2 Smiths, and 5 Sellses. See Perry, "Eastern Part of Clay County."

45. The county correspondents are invaluable sources for general information about lifestyles and attitudes. The *Gainesboro Sentinel*, on July 10, 1902, took note of Sam York of the fourth district, in town for the first time in his life for jury duty. In the June 19, 1902, edition of the same paper it was noted that Uncle Solomon Wilson, who was sixty, had never been to the county seat. He had lived his entire life on Haydenburg Ridge, with the exception of three months spent in Illinois during the Civil War.

46. "Wanted to Marry," *Crossville Chronicle*, August 6, 1902.

Chapter 3

1. Department of the Interior, Census Office, *Report on Statistics of Churches*, 80–81, gives the number of church members per county, and the percentages of members in proportion to the county population were as follows: Clay, 974, 13.4 percent; Overton, 3,064, 25 percent; Cumberland, 1,720, 32 percent; Pickett, 4,736, 24 percent; DeKalb, 4,196, 27 percent; Putnam, 2,120, 15 percent; Fentress, 5,226, 18 percent; Smith, 7,453, 40 percent; Jackson, 3,608, 27 percent; Macon, 2,620, 24 percent. The religious census has notorious flaws: some groups list everyone who was baptized into the denomination, while others list only members in good standing, and still others refuse to cooperate with the census taker at all. However, there is no other comparable source for denominational membership in the 1890s.

As Edward Ayers indicates in *Promise of the New South*, chap. 7 and 497–500, religion permeated southern culture in the late nineteenth century. The actual proportion of the population belonging to a congregation varied, however, from 40 percent in the Black Belt to 24 percent in the mountains. This relatively low percentage of membership may seem strange, given the acknowledged influence of religion in the rural South. However, churches in the region had high standards for membership (as will be demonstrated later in this chapter). Also, many southern Protestant groups do not baptize infants or count children as church members.

2. "Conservative" Protestantism seems a better term than "evangelical" to describe the denominations in the region; technically, groups like the Primitive Baptists and the conservative Churches of Christ are not evangelical. Many of the churches in the region would today be called fundamentalists; however, as a recent study of fundamentalism noted, "Fundamentalism . . . differs from traditionalism or orthodoxy or even a mere revivalist movement. It differs in that it is a movement in conscious, organized opposition to the disruption of those traditions and orthodoxies" (Ammerman, "North American Protestant Fundamentalism," 14). In the 1890s Upper Cumberland Protestants held complete hegemonic sway over religion in the region; facing no opposition, they did not find it necessary to affirm support for fundamental beliefs that were not being challenged.

3. Department of the Interior, Census Office, *Report on Statistics of Churches*, Baptists, tab. 3, 164–65; Baptists, tab. 4, 175–76; Baptists, tab. 7, 187; Baptists, tab. 9, 195; Baptists, tab. 11, 197; Baptists, tab. 12, 198; Baptists, tab. 13, 204–5; Baptists, tab. 14, 210; Presbyterians, tab. 2, 642; Presbyterians, tab. 3, 662; Presbyterians, tab. 4, 672; Presbyterians, tab. 7, 686–87; Disciples of Christ, by Counties, Tennessee, 351–52; Methodists, tab. 2, 517; Methodists, tab. 4, 549; Methodists, tab. 9, 588–89. According to the census, there were no Catholics or Episcopalians in the Upper Cumberland (Protestant Episcopal Bodies, tab. 2, 717; Catholics, tab. 2, 245). However, there was a Congregational presence in Cumberland County (Congregationalists by County, Tennessee, 338.) The Congregationalist Church surely drew most of its members from the missionaries at Pleasant Hill.

Although there may not have been any Lutheran churches in the region in

1890, there were Lutheran settlers in Fentress County, at a small German colony named Allardt. However, the Lutheran presence in the hills seems to have had no effect on local Protestants.

4. The quotation continues: "except in the reception of members in that case unanimity is required" (November 1854, statement of organizational rules, records of Lafayette Baptist Church).

5. *Crossville Chronicle*, August 28, 1901.

6. The description is taken from Hooker, *Religion in the Highlands*, v, 82–91. The survey included churches in Overton and Cumberland Counties. Although it was conducted a full generation after the period now being discussed, the survey described churches and conditions that would have been familiar to congregations in the 1890s. Indeed, the first Southern Baptists described by Rhys Isaacs in *The Transformation of Virginia* would have felt at home. Today in the region one occasionally comes upon derelict, abandoned churches and schools built along the pattern described, with one large meeting room and two doors, one for men and one for women.

7. Hooker, *Religion in the Highlands*, 82–91. As late as 1923 89.6 percent of the rural Southern Baptist churches in Tennessee were one-room structures, with 92.3 percent being built of wood. At that late date only 76 percent of rural Baptist congregations had their own meeting houses. See Alldredge, *Southern Baptist Handbook*, 84.

8. Ayers, *Promise of the New South*, 169–70.

9. In *Subduing Satan* Ted Ownby describes a gender-based split in southern culture, with women and their allies, Protestant ministers, opposing what might be called the "Good Old Boy" way of life: drinking, carousing, hunting, and general rowdiness. There is plenty of evidence for Ownsby's point of view: young men often did act in a disrespectful way toward religion and toward churches, and more women than men went to church. However, I think it is a mistake to picture southern Protestant churches as feminized spaces. Men ran the churches on the local and denominational level, overseeing all women's work, hiring and firing preachers, and making all decisions of import. Inside most churches or outside, women were less than equal. In some denominations women could create and run societies and mission boards, but even in their own institutions they functioned under the supervision of the male church hierarchy. Ironically, only "outsider" churches, such as the early Holiness congregations, allowed women leadership roles in worship itself. (See McDowell, *Social Gospel in the South*, and Ayers, *Promise of the New South*, 169–70, 398–408.) As a southern woman, I must add that I am flattered by Ownby's description of southern women as gentle, noncompetitive creatures, but in my experience what appears to be cooperative behavior (cooking a church supper, for example) often occasions the kind of subtle but serious social warfare only a Jane Austen could do justice to.

Hooker, *Religion in the Highlands*, 82–91. In the Upper Cumberland, Pleasant Hill Academy in Cumberland County was funded by the American Missionary Association (supported by northern Congregationalists), and Grassy Cove in the same county was run by the Kingston Presbytery. The New Salem and Enon Associations of Baptists owned Willette Academy in Macon County (see *Baptist and Reflector*, August 28, 1890); Alpine Academy in Overton County was a Presbyterian school. In the early twentieth century the Disciples of Christ funded Livingston Academy in Overton County, and the Methodists supported Baxter Academy in Putnam County.

For an overview of the southern Methodist Church's social role, see Farish, *Circuit Rider Dismounts*, and McDowell, *Social Gospel in the South*. See also Norton, *Religion in Tennessee*, 84–87.

It is very hard to generalize about Baptist churches. As Table 2 indicates, Baptists in the Upper Cumberland were divided into many different sects. Moreover, all Baptist congregations zealously maintained control over their own affairs. One congregation affiliated with the Southern Baptist Convention might have Ladies' Missionary Circles and contribute to the convention's mission funds; the next SBC-affiliated church down the road might not do anything but meet one Sunday a month. Present-day Southern Baptists are among the most gregarious American Protestants, organizing their congregations' social lives and providing activities for all age groups. But one should not assume that tiny rural congregations in the 1890s did the same. A 1923 survey of rural Southern Baptist churches found that even then 63.6 percent of the rural churches had not organized women's work and that 86.3 percent of rural female congregation members were "unorganized." The survey noted, "The missionary and benevolent organizations among women of the local churches, particularly among the rural churches, were comparatively few in number and varied in form down to the year 1900." Prior to that date there were only 706 Ladies' Aid Societies and mission societies in rural churches in the entire South. See Alldredge, *Southern Baptist Handbook*, 116–17.

10. On the southern religious scene, see Harrell, "Religious Pluralism." Harrell says that the Disciples were the most separatist wing of the antimission movement that was especially strong among Southern Baptists. According to Harrell, antimission sentiment cut across denominational lines and was often a reflection of class differences, with poorer people being antimission. See also Harrell, "Seedbed of Sectarianism."

11. Lipscomb located that hotbed north of the Mason-Dixon line and noted that southern Methodists, Baptists, and Presbyterians shared problems in dealing with their northern brethren. See "Should Women Preach Publicly?," *Gospel Advocate*, August 5, 1891; "The Way to Break Up a Church," *Gospel Advocate*, February 8, 1894; "What Is Woman's Work in the Church (Again)?," *Gospel Advocate*, July 22, 1897; "Woman's Real Position in the Church," *Gospel Advocate*, July 22, 1897.

12. Applying a political metaphor to a religious question, Lipscomb compared missionary societies to trusts, which restricted labor and enriched the few at the expense of the many. Large combinations of people tended to produce evil, Lipscomb said; similar combinations in religion would "combine the influences of religion and place them under the control of a few selfish leaders." Besides, the missionary men were "a set of foreigners . . . proposing to come in and take possession of the churches and put in their own men at high salaries." See "Method of Work," *Gospel Advocate*, January 7, 1891; "Fundamental Principles," *Gospel Advocate*, August 26, 1891; "The Convention," *Gospel Advocate*,

October 29, 1891. When the Disciples split, most of the "progressives" were north of Kentucky, and most of the "conservatives" were south of the Ohio. However, the split also divided urban from rural congregations. As early as 1891 the *Gospel Advocate* called for spiritual warfare against the towns and cities, "where the 'dear Pastor' and his parishioners are holding high carnival" and laughing at "true, loyal, God-fearing men and women" as "chronic growlers, anti-everything" ("Perilous Times," *Gospel Advocate*, June 24, 1891). See Harrell, "Religious Pluralism," 822–23; Alstrom, *Religious History of the American People*, 822–23; Department of Commerce and Labor, Bureau of the Census, *Religious Bodies*, tab. 4, 354–57. The census showed 5,760 members of the Churches of Christ in the region and only 123 Disciples. In Clay and Jackson Counties the denomination had more members than any other.

13. Defeated Creek Missionary Baptist Church Records.

14. New Bildad Primitive Baptist Church of Jesus Christ Records.

15. Spring Creek Baptist Church Records; Old Bildad Baptist Church of Christ Records.

16. The Ten Commandments prohibited taking the Lord's name in vain, murder, theft, adultery, lying, covetousness, idolatry, and Sabbath breaking. As Link notes in *Paradox of Southern Progressivism*, chap. 2, southern Protestants created a new consensus on values in the latter half of the nineteenth century: drinking, which had been acceptable even for ministers, became taboo for Christians, as did dancing. Methodists, usually the most liberal denomination in the region, in the late nineteenth century crusaded against alcohol and dancing, according to Farish, *Circuit Rider Dismounts*. The Disciples frowned on drinking, dancing, "reveling," and wearing jewelry; see *Gospel Advocate*, January 14, February 4, April 21, 1892, January 21, August 12, 1897. E. G. Sewell, in "Wearing Gold," March 31, 1892, held that the Bible forbade the wearing of costly jewelry.

17. Pleasant Grove Methodist Church Records.

18. New Bildad Primitive Baptist Church of Jesus Christ Records.

19. Spring Creek Baptist Church Records. Disciples were urged to forgive repentant sinners but to withdraw from those who did not repent and shun them socially as well. See *Gospel Advocate*, January 21, 1897.

20. In 1902 while Methodist churches like McKendree in Nashville paid pastors $3,000 annually, the Lebanon Circuit paid $453, the Monterey Mission paid $159, and the Sparta-Bon Air ministry received $600; see Carter, *History of the Tennessee Conference*, 307. Baptists and Presbyterians were ordained by congregations before they began their careers as preachers. However, any male could constitute himself a Disciples preacher simply by preaching.

21. Grime, *History of Middle Tennessee Baptists*, 433–536. Grime's book includes a ministerial directory. Some ministers in the region had college degrees, while others had common school or academy educations, and still others noted their education as "very limited." Elder John Patterson of Salt Lick, Macon County, commented that he had "been to school just enough to read in the Testament when I entered the school of Christ for life."

As late as the 1920s a Southern Baptist Convention survey showed that most rural Southern Baptist churches had "part-time" ministers who visited the church once a month; 54 percent of rural Baptist ministers had no college or seminary training. See Alldredge, *Southern Baptist Handbook*, 49–50, 72.

22. Grime, *History of Middle Tennessee Baptists*, 481. Oakley said that before he got the call to preach, he followed laziness on the farm each day and coon hunting at night. Oakley's memoirs appeared in the *Carthage Courier* from 1921 through 1924. See also Grime, *Recollections of a Long Life*, 1–20; Roach, "Grime, John Harvey." Grime was thirty-one when he went back to school. By the 1890s he was a field editor for the *Baptist and Reflector*. Josephus was a first-century Jewish historian.

23. Flynt, "One in the Spirit," and Harrell, "Seedbed of Sectarianism." In the early 1930s a survey found that almost half of the preachers in the Southern Highlands had not finished elementary school; one-third had completed high school, and about one in five had graduated from a college or seminary. Primitive Baptists referred to educated preachers as "factory-made," while untrained ministers were "God-made." See Hooker, *Religion in the Highlands*, 160–63. The proportion of uneducated ministers must have been much higher in the 1890s. No statistics are available from that decade, but examination of *Who's Who in Tennessee* indicates that over half the ministers listed in Upper Cumberland counties had no schooling past the elementary level.

24. The Methodists rarely debated. Mathews notes in *Religion in the Old South* that while antebellum Baptists, Presbyterians, and Disciples liked to argue with one another, Methodists preferred to concentrate on mission works rather than doctrine. These denominational temperaments endured: in the Upper Cumberland in the 1890s the Methodists were the most socially active denomination and the least doctrinal and combative.

25. "A Debate on the Atonement," *Alexandria Times*, April 3, 1895.

26. J. H. Grime, "Malone-Cayce Debate," *Baptist and Reflector*, April 21, 1892.

27. G. A. Ogle, "Victory at Sycamore," *Baptist and Reflector*, August 21, 1890.

28. In 1914 the widow's portion allotted to Mrs. Sallie Walker of Putnam County included "1 Bible and Hymn Book and all books used in school" (Estate Inventories, 1914, 100–101). The estate inventory of Mrs. S. E. Wright, a wealthy Putnam County widow, mentions eight books, two New Testaments, and one large Bible (Estate Inventories, 1912, 58–59). The superstitions cited are familiar to the author; see also Hooker, *Religion in the Highlands*, 154. Using the Bible as a help in decision making is a very old practice, as is divining the future with the aid of the book; see Thomas, *Religion and the Decline of Magic*, 45–46, 118, 214.

The owner of a Cookeville bookstore once told the author that many people in the region believed the Bible was originally written in King James's English, and they resisted modern translations. The author's mother, as a young schoolteacher, angered a parent by reading the state-prescribed ten Bible verses daily from a modern translation: the parent was offended by a text that substituted *you* for *ye*.

29. E. G. Sewell, "Read the Old Testament," *Gospel Advocate*, January 14, 1892.

30. David Lipscomb, "God's Order, or Man's Wisdom," *Gospel Advocate*, May 13, 1891. For biblical justification for authoritarian families, see Chapter 2.

31. From an obituary for Julia Clark of White County: "She held God's word in profound reverence. Brother Clark and I were once discussing in her presence the reply of Bishop Watson to Tom Paine. She requested us not to mention any of the Paine blasphemies against the blessed Bible she could not bear to hear it" (*Gospel Advocate*, May 13, 1891). Conservative churches in the region still crusade against Tom Paine and Voltaire as arch-infidels.

32. Henry Rehorn, Jr., in *Gospel Advocate*, October 6, 1898.

Chapter 4

1. DeLozier, *Putnam County*, 136–37; Robison, *Bob Taylor*. Although Fentress and Cumberland Counties were reliably Republican, other counties in the region did turn in GOP majorities in some gubernatorial elections during the 1880s and 1890s.

2. Rogers, *White County*, 81–82.

3. Hull, *Memoirs*, 3–9. Joe L. Evins of DeKalb County, who served as U.S. congressman from the fourth district for decades, was the product of a mixed political marriage. His father's family were Democrats; his mother's, Republicans. When they married, Mrs. Evins "converted" to the Democratic Party, and Mr. Evins joined his wife's church. Young Evins, born in 1910, made his decision for the Democratic Party at age twelve. See Graves, *Evins of Tennessee*, 21, 31–37.

4. Rogers, *White County*, 90–91; Samuel C. Williams, *General John T. Wilder*, 40–51; Hart, *Redeemers, Bourbons, and Populists*, 85. Dibrell was part owner of a coal mine, president of a railroad, a five-term congressman, and a candidate for governor in 1886. The Dibrell family, according to Hart, was in itself a kind of political machine in White County.

5. Hart, *Redeemers, Bourbons, and Populists*, 28–55; Robert B. Jones, *Tennessee at the Crossroads*.

6. According to Hart, *Redeemers, Bourbons, and Populists*, 38, in 1879 there was a referendum on funding the debt at fifty cents on the dollar and 4 percent interest. The low-tax leader, John Savage of Warren County, opposed this compromise funding position and suggested that the state might pay as much as one-third of the debt, just to be nice. All of the Upper Cumberland counties but Fentress and Cumberland voted against the funding proposal. A map in Robert B. Jones, *Tennessee at the Crossroads*, 116, shows that in the 1880 gubernatorial election all the Upper Cumberland counties voted for the low-tax candidate except, again, Fentress and Cumberland.

7. Hart, *Redeemers, Bourbons, and Populists*, 122; *Tennessee Times*, February 12, April 22, 1891; *Sparta Expositor*, September 12, 1890; Seals, *White County*, 28–30; *Cookeville Press*, August 9, 1894. The Democratic *Cookeville Press* acknowledged that the fusion ticket was composed of men of good character but warned that they would be carefully watched by the local Democracy. See *Cookeville Press*, May 10, June 7, 1894.

8. Hart, *Redeemers, Bourbons, and Populists*, 176–77.

9. *Cookeville Press*, June 28, July 26, 1894; *Tennessee Times*, September 2,

October 7, 1891; Hart, *Redeemers, Bourbons, and Populists*, 176–77, 199; De-Lozier, *Putnam County*, 135–37.

10. Hull, *Memoirs*, 16–17. The *Cookeville Press*, in particular, ran a front page of state and national news and commented on that news in locally written editorials. Patent outsides were preprinted pages supplied to newspapers by advertisers. They contained news and ads for patent medicine—hence the name.

11. *Gainesboro Sentinel*, March 28, 1908.

12. Greene and Avery, *Government in Tennessee*, chap. 22.

13. Ibid.; Department of the Interior, Census Office, *Report on Population*, tab. 5, 317–28.

14. Greene and Avery, *Government in Tennessee*, 334–38.

15. *Alexandria Times*, April 11, 1894.

16. Allison, *Notable Men of Tennessee*, 331–32; *Crossville Chronicle*, September 3, January 2, 1902. Blankenship, *Macon County*, 151–59, lists county officials and their years of office. Some officials served for very long terms. From 1874 to 1923 Macon County had only four county court clerks, and two of the clerks served sixteen years each. One register of deeds held office for twenty years.

17. *Alexandria Times*, July 14, 1915. The Crossville *Tennessee Times*, February 12, 1981, commented that the courthouse needed cleaning: "It doesn't impress strangers to see our principal public building untidy." Public places throughout the Upper Cumberland tended to be messy. A letter to the *Crossville Chronicle*, August 5, 1903, complained that the peace of the town was disturbed by "the nightly bedlam of cow bells and bellowings, and the unctious grunts of omnipresent hogs. . . . The situation calls to mind the remark of a stranger, who, getting off the train not a thousand miles from here asked: 'What sort of a d—d place is this?'" The editor commented that it was impractical to shut cattle out, since they had free range to feed, but "the hogs that roam the streets at will and scatter fleas in superabundance could be dispensed with at little cost to anyone." In Livingston, the county seat of Overton, a "lake" on the main street between the square and the depot served as a refuse dump for the produce houses and the livery stables. The editor of the local paper complained that the hole was full of dead chickens and rotten eggs, and "strangers are taking note of it and talking and writing about it" (*Golden Age*, March 24, 1915).

18. Annual Reports of County Superintendents; see Holt, *Struggle for a State System*, for details on Tennessee schools in the 1890s.

19. *Proceedings of the Seventh Annual Public School Officers Association of Tennessee*; Annual Report of the County Superintendent of Public Instruction, 1901–2, record group 51, roll 85, Department of Education Records, Tennessee State Library and Archives, Nashville. Of 47 teachers in Clay County only 7 were repeaters, back in school for another year. In Jackson County there were 12 repeaters out of 88 teachers; in Macon County, 20 of 66; in Pickett County, 12 of 31; and in Putnam County half of the 87 teachers were repeaters.

20. Fitzpatrick, *Annual Report of the State Superintendent*, 56–58.

21. In 1891 the county enrollments per grade were as follows (starting with first grade): White, 961, 846, 796, 681, 535, 30, 25, 20; Putnam, 805, 900, 406, 600, 875; Overton, 2,302, 926, 700, 307, 209; Fentress, 526, 305, 227, 196, 77;

DeKalb, 1,300, 1,200, 950, 875, 700, 540, 450, 400; Clay, 1,000, 1,200, 750, 589, 400, 518, 265.

The other Upper Cumberland counties did not furnish suitable statistics. See Annual Reports of County Superintendents.

According to the Southern Education Board's report, *Educational Conditions in Tennessee*, in the Upper Cumberland counties the percentages of illiteracy among native white voters were as follows: Clay, 22.6; Cumberland, 16.1; De-Kalb, 18.4; Fentress, 26.4; Jackson, 22.7; Macon, 25.9; Overton, 19.9; Pickett, 25.1; Putnam, 16.2; Smith, 18.6; and White, 17.2.

22. That education, or at least a command of rhetoric, was seen as a social grace is indicated by Upper Cumberland newspapers, which often featured "literary" pieces written by locals. Political and religious debates were popular in the area and were reported with relish in local papers. See Hull, *Memoirs*, 14–15, 116. Like Hull, gifted children were often sent to private academies. See Chapter 7 for a discussion of academy education in the region.

23. *Tennessee Times*, November 20, 1890, February 19, March 6, 1891; *White County Favorite*, September 17, 1897.

24. *Crossville Chronicle*, January 24, 1900; *Cookeville Press*, June 27, 1895; Crossville *Tennessee Times*, January 8, 1891.

25. See sources in n. 24 above and *Gainesboro Sentinel*, October 26, 1899. The proverb quoted is common throughout the rural South.

26. "County Court Proceedings," Crossville *Tennessee Times*, April 8, 1891; *Crossville Chronicle*, April 4, 1900; "County Court Proceedings," *Crossville Chronicle*, January 16, 1901; DeLozier, *Putnam County*, 156.

27. "Notice," *Crossville Chronicle*, February 27, 1901.

28. Greene and Avery, *Government in Tennessee*, explains the constitutional structure of county law enforcement and the fee system. The author's understanding of community attitudes toward law enforcement, violence, and honor has been influenced by Ayers's *Vengeance and Justice* and Wyatt-Brown's *Southern Honor*.

29. "Court Proceedings," *Cookeville Press*, January 23, 1896, indicates that the majority of cases involved either "tippling," carrying a pistol, or both. See article on the opening of the county jail, *Cookeville Press*, January 9, 1896; see also "Circuit Court," *Gainesboro Sentinel*, November 17, 1898; *Tennessee Times*, February 5, 1891.

DeKalb County Circuit Court Clerk's Office lists indictments before the grand jury in November 1893. Most of the crimes listed involve violence, liquor, or disorderly conduct; few were crimes of property. The only women before the court in DeKalb County were apparently prostitutes, charged with keeping a bawdy house.

Not much had changed by 1914, judging by the "Court Notes" in *Bill Fiske's Bugle* (July 2, 1914), a Celina paper noted for straightforward reporting. Fiske listed the true bills found by the Grand Jury: Public Drunkness [*sic*], 30; Gaming, 9; Carrying Pistol, 8; Liquor Cases, 5; Lewdness, 4; Frequenting Bawdy Houses, 4; Disturbing Worship, 3; Assault and Battery with Deadly Weapon, 2; Dog Law Case, 1. (The "dog law" was the state's attempt to tax dogs. The idea was to reduce the number of dogs in country areas and give the farmers who raised sheep a chance; dog packs decimated Tennessee sheep flocks. But, as the *Crossville Chronicle,* June 19, 1901, noted, for the most part people ignored or laughed at the dog tax.)

30. DeKalb County Circuit Court Clerk's Office, Report of the Grand July, November 1893, 31.

31. "Old Man Assaulted" and editorial, *Crossville Chronicle,* December 5, 1906.

32. *Cookeville Press,* February 14, 1895; *White County Favorite,* January 23, 1903; *Gainesboro Sentinel,* January 1, 1903. In a shooting affray at Double Springs in April 1894, a long-standing feud climaxed in a battle during which W. J. Lewis shot and killed Ras Alexander and injured Alexander's son Tim. No mention was made of any arrests. See *Cookeville Press,* April 19, 1894. From June to October 1895 the DeKalb County *Alexandria Times* reported the following: a brawl in which one man called his neighbor a liar and was beaten over the head with a singletree for his trouble, a fight between two men at New Hope Church that resulted in the stabbing of one man and the shooting of a horse, miscellaneous episodes of disorderly conduct at the county fair, and a horrific report from a county correspondent reporting the near-decapitation of a man in a "difficulty" plus an incident in which a woman threw a pitchfork at her stepson. In the latter episode, the fork lodged in his head, and he was expected to die. The correspondent noted blandly that Mrs. Pinigan was "a very stout woman," "stout" in Upper Cumberland usage meaning strong. See "Singletree for a Weapon," June 19, 1895; "Bullets and a Knife," June 19, 1895; "Here and There," September 25, 1895; and "Correspondence," October 5, 1985.

33. "Killed in Cold Blood," *Crossville Chronicle,* June 10, 1903.

34. "Great Surprise in Turner Case," *Crossville Chronicle,* February 10, 1904.

35. "A Horrible Murder," *Alexandria Times,* October 2, 1895.

36. Kemp, "To Humanize Local History," 45–58.

37. *Gainesboro Sentinel,* December 15, 1898; "Pistols and Whiskey," *Gainesboro Sentinel,* October 26, 1907, story reprinted from the *Crossville Chronicle.*

38. *Gainesboro Sentinel,* August 15, 1901; *Crossville Chronicle,* August 28, 1901 (emphasis added).

Chapter 5

1. *Tennessee State Gazetteer and Business Directory,* 210. The information about taking the train to Nashville for music lessons came from Dollie Williams of Cookeville.

2. *Allardt Gazette,* September 1, 1892.

3. Land and development companies were much more common on the plateau than in the Upper Cumberland's river counties. In the mid-1890s W. F. and F. G. Neidringhaus and Jos. B. Johnson organized the Cumberland Coal and Coke Company, which bought about 500,000 acres of plateau land by paying delinquent taxes. The company sold most of the land but kept a 50,000-acre tract and an office in Crossville for over sixty years. The company's name varied

during that period. See Krechniak and Krechniak, *Cumberland County's First Hundred Years*, 67–89. Parts of Pickett and Fentress Counties were included in a 200,000-acre tract owned by the Sterns Lumber Company of Michigan. The Sterns family ran logging camps in the region from 1900 through the 1940s. The company also opened mines and built a company town at Sterns, Kentucky. The area of the company's operations is now part of Big South Fork National Recreation Area. See Birdwell, *Sterns Coal Company*, 15–37. The Cookeville correspondent is quoted in DeLozier, *Putnam County*, 94.

4. During the war, Union general John Wilder had been so impressed by the region that he returned south in 1866 to buy and develop coal fields and help found several Tennessee towns, including Rockwood in Roane County. There Wilder opened coal mines and built a blast furnace; he shipped iron and coal via the Tennessee River to Chattanooga to the Roane Rolling Mills. From the 1860s until his death in 1917 Wilder promoted the development of the coal and iron industries in Tennessee; by the end of his long life he was involved in the development of the coal fields in the Upper Cumberland. See Samuel C. Williams, *General John T. Wilder*, 40–51, 95–100; DeLozier, *Putnam County*, 106–7, 116. According to the 1890 census, in 1889 Cumberland County had ten local coal mines and produced 124 short tons of coal; the mines made $155 from the sale of coal. Fentress had five local mines that produced $30 worth of coal. Overton and Putnam Counties each had two local mines.

Dibrell, a politically powerful conservative Democrat, owned 15,000 acres of plateau land in White County. In 1882 Dibrell chartered the Bon Air Coal Company, with former Tennessee governor John C. Brown as president and Dibrell himself as vice-president and primary stockholder. See Huehls, "Life in the Coal Towns," 4.

5. When, exactly, Sparta was connected to the NC&StL line is unclear. George Dibrell was president of a "Southwestern Railroad" that was supposed to connect Sparta to Tullahoma; whether this line was built is unclear. White County historian Seals says that the NC&StL reached Sparta in 1884. At any rate, the NC&StL controlled the line into White County by the late 1880s and built the spur line up Bon Air Mountain to the coal fields. See Seals, *White County*, 60, and Huehls, "Life in the Coal Towns," 1–2.

Between 1889 and 1899 the Bon Air mine shipped an average of thirty-five cars of coal per day, according to "Report of Committee to Chamber of Commerce of Sparta, Tenn.," dated June 17, 1899, in the Tennessee Central Railroad Papers. Statistics on wood industries in the county come from the same report, which was compiled by the chamber and sent to the Tennessee Central in an attempt to get the railroad to build a spur line into White County. The chamber's committee complained that rates for shipping on the NC&StL were excessive.

6. DeLozier, *Putnam County*, 93–97.

7. Doyle, *Nashville in the New South*, 20–22; Burt, "Four Decades," 99–130.

8. DeLozier, *Putnam County*, 97–98; "History of the Tennessee Central Railway Company"; Doyle, *Nashville in the New South*, 20–32; Sulzer, "Three 'Tennessee Centrals,'" 210–14.

9. In 1898 Baxter mounted a successful railroad bond campaign in Cumberland County. For details on the campaign and on Baxter's business practices, see

the following sources: *Crossville Chronicle*, August 3, October 19, 1898; "Tennessee Central Railway Bond Campaigns," box 21, file 1, Tennessee Central Railroad Papers (included in the file is a map of Cumberland County showing when and where proponents and opponents of the bond issue made speeches); Doyle, *Nashville in the New South*, 24–32; Krechniak and Krechniak, *Cumberland County's First Hundred Years*; "History of the Tennessee Central Railway Company"; DeLozier, *Putnam County*, 97–98; Sulzer, "Three 'Tennessee Centrals,'" 210–14.

10. DeLozier, *Putnam County*, 93–116; Ozone correspondent to the *Sparta Expositor*, reprinted in the *Gainesboro Sentinel*, July 13, 1899; *Crossville Chronicle*, July 30, 1902.

11. *Crossville Chronicle*, March 17, 1901.

12. "Toughs Tackle a Train," *Cookeville Press*, January 4, 1894.

13. *Crossville Chronicle*, November 25, 1903. Cookeville had grown from a village of 150 in the 1870s to a small town of 1,500 by 1906; the population of lawyers had increased from 4 to 15. By contrast, Carthage, the long-standing political and commercial center on the Cumberland in Smith County, had 7 lawyers in the 1870s and 10 lawyers in 1906. See *Tennessee State Gazetteer and Business Directory*, 1873–74, 45, 171, 205; *Young and Company's Business and Professional Directory* 35, 107–8, 113.

14. DeLozier, *Putnam County*, 130; Krechniak and Krechniak, *Cumberland County's First Hundred Years*, 248–49. *Crossville Chronicle*, September 25, 1910, lists officers of the bank, which opened March 19, 1900. J. W. Dorton, president, had been the leader of the local bond campaign. In White County, the Bank of Sparta was organized in 1885, and the People's Bank opened in 1900. See Seals, *White County*, 58–60.

15. DeLozier, *Putnam County*, 93–116.

16. On transportation into Macon County, see Denning, "History of the Resort Business"; DeLozier, *Putnam County*, 98–99; "Nashville Woman the President of a Tennessee Railway," *Golden Age*, January 17, 1915.

17. Wright, in *Old South, New South*, summarizes the long debate over the South's purported colonial economy and notes that the most important manufacturing industry in the region until the 1920s was timber products. As Wright observes, the timber industry is rarely studied because it was so ephemeral: "Logging camps were isolated, temporary affairs. . . . The work force was even more temporary and did not build up either the self-identity or the social visibility of the cotton mill people" (161–62). According to Wright a majority of timber industry workers were black. In this respect, again, the Upper Cumberland was unusual: there the work force was overwhelmingly white and mostly local. See also Ayers, *Promise of the New South*, 123–31.

18. For a more detailed look at the Upper Cumberland coal mining industry, see Huehls, "Life in the Coal Towns," and *The Davidson-Wilder Story*.

19. U.S. Department of Commerce, Bureau of the Census, *Fifteenth Census*, tab. 20, 908–19. In 1930, according to the census, the number of workers employed in "extraction of minerals" in each Upper Cumberland county was as follows: Clay, 10; Cumberland, 255; DeKalb, 8; Fentress, 454; Jackson, 7; Macon, 14; Overton, 328; Pickett, 4; Putnam, 79; Smith, 1; and White, 354. The

totals in Cumberland, Overton, Putnam, and White Counties were probably higher during the period from 1910 through World War I than in 1930.

20. See Table 7 for statistics about crop and livestock production from 1890 to 1925.

21. Krechniak and Krechniak, *Cumberland County's First Hundred Years*, 159–60, 111–20, 223–24 (the Krechniaks refer to wood products as the Cumberland County farmers' first cash crop); *Crossville Chronicle*, January 30, February 27, April 17, 1901, July 24, 1910; *White County Favorite*, reprinted in *Crossville Chronicle*, December 30, 1903. The April 10, 1901, *Chronicle* summarizes business development in Cumberland County since the TC "Became an Assured Fact."

22. By the 1930s the percentage of Upper Cumberland farmers reporting that they worked part time off the farm ranged from 10.7 in Smith County to 50.2 in Fentress. See U.S. Department of Commerce, Bureau of the Census, *Sixteenth Census*, County Table IX, 236–39.

23. *Crossville Chronicle*, April 17, 1900.

24. "Let's Farm More," *Crossville Chronicle*, January 29, 1908. According to the chamber of commerce report cited above, White County farmers shipped large quantities of corn to Cumberland County.

25. DeLozier, *Putnam County*, 108–13; *Golden Age*, May 3, 1916, December 5, 1917. The latter paper had an advertisement from A. J. Mofield, Overton County produce man, who would buy eggs, chickens, hens, geese, ginseng, turkeys, yellow root, hides, wool, beeswax, dried apples, feathers, animal pelts, peas, beans, oats, millet seed, soybeans, corn, and scrap iron. The beeswax and ginseng operations could be the work of men or women. Figures attributed to J. D. Stewart, merchant, White County, in "Report of Committee to Chamber of Commerce of Sparta, Tenn.," Tennessee Central Railroad Papers.

26. DeLozier, *Putnam County*, 110–13. Produce men also bought eggs. According to DeLozier, "In the spring of 1900 produce dealers estimated that they had exported thirty-five carloads of chickens and 75,000 dozen eggs from Putnam County." The *Cookeville Press*, reprinted in the *Gainesboro Sentinel*, March 30, 1899, noted that on a recent chicken day about $7,500 had been paid to about 1,000 families. Chickens also left the region by boat, shipped south to Nashville or up the Cumberland to Burnside, Ky., to make a connection with the Cincinnati, New Orleans, and Texas Pacific railway; see Montell, *Don't Go up Kettle Creek*.

27. *Alexandria Times*, January 11, 1905.

28. Department of Commerce and Labor, Bureau of the Census, *Thirteenth Census*, tab. 3, 645–53. The "Married Women's Emancipation Act," giving married women property rights equal to those of single women, was passed during Governor Albert Roberts's administration, 1918–20. See Folmbee et al., *Tennessee*, 451.

Chapter 6

1. *Gainesboro Sentinel*, May 24, 1900.

2. My treatment of progressive reform in the Upper Cumberland will remind

some readers of Link's 1992 work, *Paradox of Southern Progressivism*. Like him, I think the southern progressive movement tried to transform regional culture. Like him, I see southern progressivism as paternalistic, more concerned about order than democracy, and only marginally successful, with progressive reforms often winding up being either co-opted or ignored by the southern population. My own research had led me to those conclusions, at least in regard to the Upper Cumberland, by 1990, when this work first appeared in the form of a Vanderbilt dissertation. Although I was not influenced directly by Link's work, my research independently confirms his thesis on every major point. Judging by my own research, *Paradox of Southern Progressivism* is the most accurate depiction of the nature of southern progressivism we have and is likely to be the historiographic standard for years to come.

3. Mrs. Rutledge Smith, "Mr. and Mrs. Jere Whitson," *Putnam County Herald*, March 30, 1922; E. C. Rogers, "Whitsons Pioneered Area Lumber Business," *Cookeville Citizen*, January 29, 1963; "Early Funeral Customs Changed," *Cookeville Citizen*, May 5, 1964. Whitson Funeral Home still exists in Cookeville but has changed greatly since its establishment. Jere Whitson sold coffins in his hardware store. He built a chapel for mourners and had a black hearse for adults, a gray hearse for children, and one team each of black and white horses. Mrs. Jess Barnes was Cookeville's first embalmer.

4. Mrs. Rutledge Smith, "Mr. and Mrs. Jere Whitson," *Putnam County Herald*, March 30, 1922; Jere Whitson, "Dixie College," *Gospel Advocate*, August 29, 1912; advertisement, *Gospel Advocate*, August 22, 1912; DeLozier, *Putnam County*, 180–82.

5. Jere Whitson, "Dixie College," *Gospel Advocate*, August 29, 1912.

6. DeLozier, *Putnam County*, 182–85. Today Tennessee Polytechnic Institute is Tennessee Technological University. Jere Whitson Memorial Library honors the founder of Dixie College. A street and an elementary school are also named for Whitson.

7. Mrs. Rutledge Smith, "Mr. and Mrs. Jere Whitson," *Putnam County Herald*, March 30, 1922.

8. "Yuby Dam, U.S.A.—The Elbow Road," *Carthage Courier*, June 9, 1921. "Yuby Dam" was a locally written humor column that appeared in many Upper Cumberland papers.

9. Wharton, *Doctor Woman*, 1–30. Wharton had grown up on a Minnesota farm, so she was no stranger to rural ways. Although conditions in the Cumberlands often shocked her, Wharton spent the rest of her life at Pleasant Hill and eventually founded a clinic, Uplands, there.

10. *Celina Herald*, June 7, 1906.

11. Tindall, *Emergence of the New South*, 254–84; Allred, Atkins, and Hendrix, *Human and Physical Resources of Tennessee*, chap. 15; Keith, "Lift Tennessee out of the Mud."

12. See sources cited in n. 11 above and *Fentress County Gazette*, April 16, 1916.

13. Krechniak and Krechniak, *Cumberland County's First Hundred Years*, 114; DeLozier, *Putnam County*, 156–57.

14. Allred, Atkins, and Hendrix, *Human and Physical Resources of Tennessee*,

chap. 14; Tindall, *Emergence of the New South*, 254–84; DeLozier, *Putnam County*, 157.

15. E. G. Rogers, "First Autos Here Caused Stir," *Cookeville Citizen*, January 21, 1964.

16. *Macon County News*, August 8, 1913.

17. Krechniak and Krechniak, *Cumberland County's First Hundred Years*, 159–60.

18. DeLozier, *Putnam County*, 209.

19. *Crossville Chronicle*, February 3, 1911.

20. *Carthage Courier*, February 18, 1915; *Golden Age*, August 19, 1914; *Fentress County Gazette*, December 30, 1915.

21. *Golden Age*, July 12, 1916.

22. *Fentress County Gazette*, December 30, 1915.

23. *Golden Age*, August 18, 1915.

24. According to the *Golden Age*, June 30, 1915, Pickett County had voted to issue bonds to build a road connecting the county to the Dixie Highway, and Cumberland County had issued $200,000 in road bonds. White County issued road bonds (*Golden Age*, January 19, 1916), as did Putnam. See DeLozier, *Putnam County*, 156–57.

25. *Golden Age*, September 29, 1915. In the *Macon County News*, January 21, 1916, the editor addressed fears that a bond issue would leave a debt to future generations or that county officials would steal the money raised. Trust for local officials may have been critical in determining how men voted in bond referendums.

26. "Highway Commission Enjoined," January 20, 1916; "Our Position," February 3, 1916; "Demurrer Sustained, Injunction Dismissed," March 2, 1916; "Better Times in Fentress," April 16, 1916, all in *Fentress County Gazette*.

27. *Carthage Courier*, January 21, February 11, 1915; "The Courier Favors Bond Issue, but Will Support Any Plan to Get Good Roads," *Carthage Courier*, February 18, 1915; "Good Roads Meeting Recommends Passage of State Highway Bill," *Carthage Courier*, February 25, 1915; "Good Roads Proposition Fails by Three to One," *Carthage Courier*, January 6, 1916; statement by L. B. Mathews, candidate for state senator, *Carthage Courier*, June 8, 1916.

28. "Rousing Good Roads Meeting," *Golden Age*, February 17, 1915; "Bond Election Endorsed," *Golden Age*, June 9, 1915; "Road Bond Law for Overton County," *Golden Age*, June 16, 1915. The editor of the *Golden Age*, G. B. McGee, chose the name of his paper to express his hopes for the coming age. McGee was very much in favor of the entire local progressive agenda; however, he also worried about what he saw as erosions of local autonomy. He criticized proposed state roads legislation because it would "take our road work out of the hands of the county" (*Golden Age*, May 19, 1915).

29. *Golden Age*, July 14, 1915; "A Jolly Crowd Indeed" and "The Future, What Shall It Be?," *Golden Age*, August 4, 1915.

30. *Golden Age*, August 11, 1915; "Another Road Bond Waterloo," *Golden Age*, October 27, 1915.

31. "Against Good Roads upon Any Terms and under Any Conditions," *Golden Age*, January 5, 1916; *Who's Who in Tennessee*, 256–58.

32. *Golden Age,* January 19, 1916.

33. "We Are Ruled by Reason," *Golden Age,* April 25, 1917.

34. "Everydoby [*sic*] Says, Aye," *Golden Age,* July 4, 1917.

Chapter 7

1. *Jackson County Sentinel,* June 22, 1899.

2. *Carthage Courier,* January 21, 1915. The editor also cautioned parents that their uneducated children would not be able to compete with educated people in the "struggle of life." A *Gainesboro Sentinel* editorial (April 17, 1902) proposed that educated youth would have minds "occupied with things higher and nobler [*sic*]" than carrying pistols; therefore, the state legislature should pass compulsory education laws. A correspondent to the *Crossville Chronicle,* July 25, 1906, linked good roads and good schools as incentives that would draw "good American citizens" to settle on the Cumberland Plateau.

3. Critics of American education such as Samuel Bowles, Herbert Gintis, and Michael Katz argue that in modern America education legitimizes a class system. Schools in effect sort people and fit them into niches in society. Education legitimates the position of middle-class Americans in society. Education relates directly to economic status for most people, and possession of a diploma at a certain level certifies one for a certain level of employment. See Katz, *Class, Bureaucracy, and Schools*; Bowles and Gintis, *Schooling in Capitalist America.* The author agrees with this analysis but contends that the sorting machine was not yet in place in the Upper Cumberland of the early twentieth century.

4. *Who's Who in Tennessee.* The survey lists prominent men by community. The survey includes a few men from Trousdale County, the state's smallest, which is on the edge of the Upper Cumberland. Of the 120 men, 25 percent were businessmen, 36.7 percent were professionals, 5 percent were educators, 2.5 percent were ministers, 15.8 percent were farmers, and 15.8 percent held a miscellany of jobs ranging from politician and newspaper editor to engineer.

5. A. J. Taylor, superintendent of schools in Overton County in 1911–12, believed that "more than ordinary interest" was shown in schools in his county in part because "our teachers have, almost to a body, attended the Livingston Academy school, and by so doing prepared for better service" (Brister, *Biennial Report of the State Superintendent, 1911–1912,* 525). In 1917 the associate principal at Willow Grove Academy, B. C. Ledbetter, was also superintendent of public schools for Clay County (see *Golden Age,* December 5, 1917). Rev. Warren E. Wheeler, principal of Pleasant Hill Academy for twenty-three years, was also county superintendent for part of that time. See Dodge, *Pleasant Hill Academy,* 1–62.

6. In 1900 the state superintendent's report to the governor included a list of all private schools in each county. Clay County had 3; Cumberland, 2; DeKalb, 6; Jackson, 3; Macon, 2; Overton, 6; Pickett, 1; Putnam, 4; Smith, 5; and White, 6. See Fitzpatrick, *Annual Report of the State Superintendent,* 80–95. Doyle College alumni included D. L. Lansden, state supreme court justice, and J. B. Hill, who became president of the L&N railroad. See Seals, *White County,* 33–39.

7. Wharton, *Doctor Woman*, 1–30; Douglass, *Christian Reconstruction in the South*, 352–53; Dodge, *Pleasant Hill Academy*; *Crossville Times*, November 18, 1886; *Golden Age*, April 7, 1915; Whitaker, "Livingston Academy"; Jere Whitson, "Dixie College," *Gospel Advocate*, August 29, 1912; Stratton and Stratton, *And This Is Grassy Cove*; "Alpine Mountain History"; Carter, *History of the Tennessee Conference*; "Dots by the Way," *Baptist and Reflector*, August 28, 1890, 5.

8. Wharton, *Doctor Woman*, 1–30; Douglass, *Christian Reconstruction in the South*, 352–53; Dodge, *Pleasant Hill Academy*; Krechniak and Krechniak, *Cumberland County's First Hundred Years*; Whitaker, "Livingston Academy"; Jere Whitson, "Dixie College," *Gospel Advocate*, August 29, 1912.

9. Whitaker, "Livingston Academy," 23–58; *Golden Age*, April 7, 1915. According to Whitaker the local promoters of the mission school included Roberts; Attorney General W. R. Officer; County Judge Bohannon; John Estes; A. J. Taylor, principal of the local academy; and J. C. Bilbrey, manufacturer. According to *Who's Who in Tennessee*, Roberts was a lawyer, chancellor of the fourth district, and for five years president of the Farmer's Bank. He had attended high school in Kansas and had taught school at Alpine Academy, a Presbyterian mission school in Overton County. Officer had been educated in the common schools, taught school, and apparently read law. He was elected district attorney general in 1902. He had also served as president of the Farmer's Bank and in 1911 was president and general counsel of the Overton Coal and Coke Company. Roberts was later governor of Tennessee. John Bilbrey had a common school and academy education. He was Livingston's foremost manufacturer, owning a sawmill, a planing mill, a flour mill, and a spoke factory. He had served as county court clerk from 1898 to 1906. Roberts owned stock in Bilbrey's manufacturing enterprises.

10. Whitaker, "Livingston Academy," 1–58; *Golden Age*, April 7, 1915.

11. Hooker, *Religion in the Highlands*, 209; Douglass, *Christian Reconstruction in the South*, 352–53. According to Douglass, Pleasant Hill had become "naturalized" to the region.

12. *Celina Herald*, May 24, 1906.

13. Wharton, *Doctor Woman*, 1–30; Whitaker, "Livingston Academy," 23–58; Brandon, "President's Address." Hutchings College, a private school in White County, had Bible reading, grace before meals, etc. All information about Hutchings College provided by Michael Birdwell of Cookeville, who wrote a brief history of the school as part of a petition to get a historical marker placed on the site. See Birdwell, Hutchings manuscript.

14. Dodge, *Pleasant Hill Academy*, 1–60; Whitaker, "Livingston Academy," 23–58; "Course of Study for Livingston Academy," *Golden Age*, September 13, 1916. The school also gave credit for "installing three electrical instruments in home" and for military service.

15. Interviews with Treva Hutchings Miller, Marie Hutchings Howard, and Tillman Hutchings, conducted by Michael E. Birdwell and Calvin Dickinson, June 5, 1989, in White County; see Hutchings family interviews.

16. Ibid.

17. See Hooker, *Religion in the Highlands*, 203: "The mission schools . . . raised popular standards of what schools should be. They trained teachers and

other leaders. . . . Further, they constituted centers of progressive leadership in the fields of economic prosperity, of health, of social life and especially of education."

18. Many of the 135 alumni listed with Upper Cumberland addresses may not have been living at those addresses. A number of addresses were marked "Forward." Not all alumni listed their occupations. Where occupations were given, the breakdown was as follows: farmers, 12; merchants, businessmen, and staff, 36; lawyers, 9; physicians, druggists, and nurses, 13; ministers, missionaries, and other religious workers, 11; teachers, 31; miscellaneous occupations, ranging from housewife to machinist, 29. See Dodge, *Pleasant Hill Academy*.

19. *Fentress County Gazette*, April 27, 1916. The newspaper does not indicate what school the student was attending.

20. In 1902 the Southern Education Board estimated the illiteracy rate in the Upper Cumberland among white men of voting age as follows: Clay, 22.6 percent; Cumberland, 16.1; DeKalb, 18.4; Fentress, 26.4; Jackson, 22.7; Macon, 25.9; Overton, 19.9; Pickett, 25.1; Putnam, 16.2; Smith 18.6; White, 17.2. See *Educational Conditions in Tennessee*, 3–16.

21. Some of the private academies received public funds. However, there were no county high schools per se in the region.

22. *Gainesboro Sentinel*, January 28, 1904.

23. *Celina Herald*, September 20, 1906.

24. W. L. Dixon, "To the Teachers of Jackson County," *Gainesboro Sentinel*, September 22, 1906.

25. *Gainesboro Sentinel*, October 13, November 17, 1906.

26. *Educational Conditions in Tennessee*, 3–16.

27. The county institute remained the major form of teacher education in the Upper Cumberland from 1900 through World War I. However, institutes varied widely in curriculum, personnel, and duration. (Teachers could also study pedagogy at many local academies.) Institutes were often held at the county seat and were for many young teachers the height of the social season. For two weeks they left their outlying rural communities and gathered with people their own age for classes and social events. Many institutes concluded with a program of recitations, to which the townsfolk were invited. These were popular events and allowed educators to propagandize in favor of public education. For information on institutes, see Fitzpatrick, *Annual Report of the State Superintendent*.

28. Ibid., 225.

29. Annual Report of the County Superintendent, 1901–2.

30. R. L. Jones, "Obstacles in the Way of Progress in Our Schools," in *39th Annual Meeting of TSTA*, 32–37.

31. *Fentress County Gazette*, February 14, 1901.

32. Ibid., June 14, 1900. A Jackson County correspondent in 1904 commented that school directors often hired the cheapest teachers. He contended that the schools could be improved if terms were longer and teachers were better paid; however, he advised against trying compulsory education, which would only fill classrooms with malcontents. See "Highland," *Gainesboro Sentinel*, September 15, 1904.

33. Annual Report of the County Superintendent, 1901–2.

34. The standard source on educational reform in Tennessee is Holt, *Struggle for a State System*. Holt's book is dedicated to his mentor, J. W. Brister, and includes detailed analyses of the reform campaigns and the legislation produced. See especially "Part II: The Campaign Era." See also Charles Lee Lewis, *Philander Priestly Claxton*, 112–69; Eigelbach, "Rise and Fall of a Summer School," 16–19.

35. Holt, *Struggle for a State System*, 93–116. According to Holt, "Lack of tangible opposition was one of the main difficulties encountered by Tennessee's educational campaigners. Expressed opposition would have given them something definite toward which to level their attack. The complacency and indifference which existed in its stead afforded a far more elusive and difficult target." Holt said that the teachers of the state were "little concerned about Tennessee's educational plight" (113).

Historians of education Jonathan P. Shea and Stuart A. Rosenfield argue that the intent of rural school reform was to replicate urban educational norms, whether such were truly applicable to rural areas or not. Reformers concentrated so much on organizational and structural change that, according to Shea and Rosenfield, they neglected substantive reform. Also, "by inculcating rural children with urban values, urban aspirations, and urban skills, the reformers encouraged out-migration while discouraging the preservation and improvement of traditional rural schools and communities" (Shea and Rosenfield, "Urbanization of Rural Schools, 1840–1970," 113).

36. Holt, *Struggle for a State System*, 209–25; materials concerning the Education Campaign in Tennessee, files F and G, box 14, Claxton Papers, MS-278. The quotation is from a campaign plan written by Claxton in 1902.

37. *Proceedings, Eleventh Conference for Education*, 1908, 80–81, quoted in Holt, *Struggle for a State System*, 209–56.

38. Holt, *Struggle for a State System*, 209–56.

39. According to Holt, the school lobby was also fortunate in that the state was unusually prosperous from 1900 through World War I, and the gross revenues, from which the school fund was taken, were generally high. See Holt, *Struggle for a State System*, chap. 7.

40. Claxton Papers, box 14-F; "Reports of P. P. Claxton as High School Inspector," box 15-1, contains Claxton's reports to the president of the University of Tennessee on his activities as educational propagandist, including a list of places visited each year. "Teachers Meet," *Crossville Chronicle*, December 9, 1903, January 16, 1907. Claxton and Superintendent Mynders spoke at Mont Vale College, a private school in Clay County, in September 1906. See "Mont Vale College," *Celina Herald*, September 13, 1906.

41. "Much Enthusiasm Is Displayed at Educational Rally," *Celina Messenger*, September 26, 1907; "School Rally at Pond Ridge," *Golden Age*, September 13, 1916.

42. *Golden Age*, September 15, 1915; Tennessee General Assembly, *House Journal*, 1907; Holt, *Struggle for a State System*, chap. 7.

43. "New School Law," *Crossville Chronicle*, May 1, 1907; *Golden Age*, September 15, 1915. In 1909 the Cumberland County school board added directors for each school. These directors were to "look after the local interests," provide

supplies and fuel for the school, and keep the building in repair. See "School Directors," *Crossville Chronicle*, August 4, 1909.

44. *Public Acts of the State of Tennessee*, 1913, 102–10.

45. Ibid.; Tennessee General Assembly, *House Journal of the Fifty-eighth General Assembly of the State of Tennessee*, 705–6. Of the seven state representatives from the Upper Cumberland area, five voted against the bill. It may be significant that the two men who voted for the bill listed their occupations as, respectively, farmer/merchant and merchant/lawyer. The other five men were farmers; two of them also taught school. The front pages of *Public Acts of the State of Tennessee*, 1913, list representatives and occupations. *Golden Age*, September 15, 1915.

46. Albert Williams, *Biennial Report of the State Superintendent, 1919–1920*.

47. *Gainesboro Sentinel*, February 1, 1908.

48. Hatfield, "History and Educational Survey of Putnam County, Tennessee," 95–98; Sanders, "Educational and Economic Survey of Pickett County, Tennessee," 45.

49. Robert L. Jones, *Biennial Report of the State Superintendent, 1909–1910*, 394–95, 402–5, 414–16, 471–72, 500–501.

50. Upper Cumberland towns customarily had their own schools; town schools ran longer terms, hired more qualified teachers, and in general were more modern than county schools. Since the majority of Upper Cumberland children did not live in town, the author has chosen to concentrate on the county school systems.

51. Brister, *Biennial Report of the State Superintendent, 1911–1912*.

52. Among the counties that already had compulsory education laws in 1912 were Cumberland, Clay, Fentress, Macon, Pickett, Smith, Overton, and White. See Brister, *Biennial Report of the State Superintendent, 1911–1912*, 61, 400–401.

53. Most Upper Cumberland representatives voted for the bill, which passed the House with only seven "nay" votes. However, of those seven two came from Upper Cumberland counties. See *Public Acts of the State of Tennessee, 1912*, chap. 9, House Bill 53, 19–24; Tennessee General Assembly, *House Journal of the Fifty-eighth General Assembly of the State of Tennessee*, 357–60. The law mandated school attendance to age fourteen. After that a working child was exempted, but a child without a job was required to attend school until age sixteen.

54. A few parents were arrested for failure to send their children to school. See "Failed to Send to School," *Golden Age*, October 11, 1916, reprinted from the Celina (Clay County) *Bugle*; *Carthage Courier*, January 21, 1915; "Official School Notes," *Golden Age*, July 4, 1917.

55. The controversy began in 1968 with Katz's *Irony of Early School Reform*. In 1985 Maris A. Vinovskis, in *Origins of Public High Schools*, attacked Katz's contention that the opposition to the Beverly, Massachusetts, high school was based on class. Katz, Vinovskis, and professor of education Edward Stevens, Jr., discussed the issue in "Forum: The Origins of Public High Schools," in *History of Education Quarterly*. See also Reed Ueda, *Avenues to Adulthood*. Ueda studied the Somerville, Mass., high school from the 1850s through the 1920s. He argues that although access to the high school was relatively difficult for working-class youths, those who did attend found the school an avenue to white-collar work.

Most of the students in the high school, however, came from middle-class backgrounds. For them the high school provided a springboard for geographic as well as social mobility: they tended to leave Somerville (thereby opening up white-collar jobs for their working-class classmates).

56. Albert Williams, *Biennial Report of the State Superintendent, 1919–1920*, 50–51; Holt, *Struggle for a State System*, 246–50, 261, 293–95.

57. "The High School," May 15, 1901; "High School," September 4, 1901; "County Solons," January 14, 1903, all in *Crossville Chronicle*.

58. "High School and Other Matters Discussed by a Justice," *Crossville Chronicle*, January 21, 1903.

59. *Crossville Chronicle*, January 21, 1903.

60. "More Discussion of the High School in Which Esq. John Brown Takes a Fling at the County Seat," *Crossville Chronicle*, February 4, 1903. Whitlock replied in the next paper. He resented the imputation that he had been bought in some way by Crossvillians and had betrayed the people of his district. He pointed out that the academies Brown cited as self-supporting were in fact funded by major religious denominations. Whitlock said that he was sure his taxes were higher than Brown's and that he was willing to pay more yet for the high school. See "Whitlock's Reply," *Crossville Chronicle*, February 11, 1903.

61. Wyatt discounted Whitlock's argument that the payers of the highest taxes wanted the new school: "The amount of tax paid has little to do with the necessity of a high school." See "Needs and Demands," *Crossville Chronicle*, February 11, 1903.

62. "Redistrict the County," *Crossville Chronicle*, February 25, March 4, 1903.

63. Robert L. Jones, *Biennial Report of the State Superintendent, 1909–1910*, 402–5; *Crossville Chronicle*, October 7, 1908.

Chapter 8

1. "Rousing Patriotic Meeting," *Putnam County Herald*, April 26, 1917.

2. Birdwell, in "Making of the Movie *Sergeant York*," describes how the York legend evolved and was used for political ends by diverse people.

3. "Cookeville," and "Gladdico," *Jackson County Sentinel*, February 16, 1917; "Why We Went to War," *Jackson County Sentinel*, April 19, 1917; "Silver Point, Route 2," *Putnam County Herald*, April 26, 1917.

4. Smith's enthusiasm grated on State Superintendent of Education S. W. Sherill. In March 1918 Smith complained to Governor Rye that Sherill's response to a request that April 1 be made a patriotic rally day in the state's schools "not only fails to give co-operation but the letter has no soul or heart to it and I really fear that it will do more harm than good." Sherill had asked teachers to hold a one-hour program emphasizing how pupils could help the war effort. Rye apparently forwarded Smith's complaint to Sherill, who retorted in an April 13, 1918, letter to Smith that Tennesseans did not take to commands without authority but would comply with requests. See box 21, folder 3, and box 37, folder 6, "Correspondence Re Registration of All Male Citizens of Spec. Age for WWI," Rye Papers.

5. "Jackson County Boy Willing to Die for His Country," *Jackson County Sentinel*, October 11, 1917. In Cumberland County people assumed that if a sufficient number volunteered, the draft would be forestalled. When a company was formed at Crossville, the editor of the local newspaper published "This County Has Furnished Quota," *Crossville Chronicle*, July 25, 1917. Later the local paper boasted that Cumberland was one of the few counties that had furnished its quota by enlistment rather than by conscription; but by April 1918, men from Cumberland were being drafted too. See "Our Quota Drafted," *Crossville Chronicle*, April 17, 1918.

The debates in Washington over conscription during April 1917 attracted local attention. On April 26, 1917, the editor of the *Carthage Courier* summarized the arguments, saying that those in favor of conscription believed that the law would put equal burdens on all men and would send "loafers" to the army; those opposed said the law was unfair to young men. The editor favored conscription. However, other rural Tennesseans shared with Champ Clark's Missouri constituents some attitudes about the draft. In his speech before the House opposing conscription, Speaker Clark said that in Missouri people considered a conscript not much different from a convict. Although Clark was exaggerating, conscription did carry a stigma. See Chambers, *To Raise an Army*, 165.

6. "Help Wanted, Quick!" *Golden Age*, June 27, 1917.

7. "Registration Requirements," *Putnam County Herald*, May 31, 1917.

8. "War Registration Day," *Putnam County Herald*, June 7, 1917.

9. Upper Cumberland draft cards are found in U.S. Selective Service Act Enforcement Records. World War I draft cards are stored in cardboard boxes, by county, with registrants in alphabetical order. There were three registrations during World War I. The first call-up registered men ages 21 to 31. The next, held in June 1918, enrolled the much smaller number of men who had turned 21 since the last draft. The final registration, in September 1918, was for all men 18 to 45. Although all the cards contain useful information about the men drafted, only the June 5, 1917, cards provided a space that men could use to state their request for an exemption and their reasons for doing so. Only these cards, therefore, indicate anything about the feelings of the men concerning the process of being drafted.

10. Ibid. The draft cards are not separated by date of registration. In order to locate the June 5, 1917, cards, it is necessary to turn over each card for each county. Approximately 30,000 men from the Upper Cumberland registered. No attempt was made to look at cards from each county in the region. Instead, cards were examined from the first four counties in the region, in alphabetical order: Clay, Cumberland, DeKalb, and Fentress. A sample was taken of every tenth card of the first registration, to produce an *N* of 330.

11. *Carthage Courier*, June 7, 1917.

12. Again Fentress County is an exception. Most married men in that county did not specifically request an exemption on the draft card.

13. U.S. Selective Service Act Enforcement Records. See also Lee, *Sergeant York*, chaps. 1–3. In the movie *Sergeant York*, Pastor Pile was a venerable old man; in fact, he was about the same age as Alvin York. See Birdwell, "Making of the Movie *Sergeant York*."

14. See draft cards of Fred K. Craighead, Walter Buel Craighead, Sidney Baily Craighead, Henry Martin Blankenship, Avery Newton Clark, and Lexie Gray Ray, all in Jackson County; Henry Jefferson Carey, Macon County; Louis Ruffin Langford, Martin Millard Dale, and Henry Luther Smith, Clay County; all cards on file by county, in alphabetical order, in U.S. Selective Service Act Enforcement Records. See also *Gospel Advocate*, March 10, 1910.

15. However, not all members of the paper's staff, let alone all members of the Church of Christ, were pacifists; in some counties Church of Christ members led mobilization efforts. See A. B. Lipscomb, "Why I Am a Pacifist," *Gospel Advocate*, March 8, 1917. On March 22 Lipscomb reported that the paper had received letters agreeing with his position. One writer blamed the war on the nation's monied interests. Others pledged to try to avoid military service. See "What Course Would Jesus Approve?," *Gospel Advocate*, April 19, 1917; in this article Lipscomb noted that many religious leaders were urging their congregations to enlist and that a "bitter screed" titled "Swat the Pacifists" was being passed around in the newspaper office. Despite the growing unpopularity of pacifism, the *Gospel Advocate* continued to publish articles like "Being a 'Coward' for Jesus' Sake," May 3, 1917, and E. A. Elam, "What Must We Do?," July 5, 1917. In an article by the same title published July 26, 1917, Elam said that Christians should ask for a draft exemption, but if they were not exempted, they should refuse service anyway. On August 9, 1917, H. Leo Boles wrote to commend Elam's articles, which, he said, expressed the feelings of many people in Alabama, Kentucky, and Middle Tennessee. See E. A. Elam, "Submit to the Powers That Be," *Gospel Advocate*, August 16, 1917.

16. Lee, *Sergeant York*, 17, and chap. 3; Kennedy, *Over Here*, 163–65; Peterson and Fite, *Opponents of War*, chap. 12; Chatfield, *For Peace and Justice*, 68–87.

17. Boards usually consisted of doctors, local officials, lawyers, and businessmen, according to John W. Chambers's study of conscription in World War I. Chambers sees draft boards as "an indication of the predominant influence of local commercial and professional elites" (Chambers, *To Raise an Army*, 182).

18. In Putnam County the draft board included county judge Sam Edwards; G. W. Alcorn, a former sheriff; Rev. A. J. Coile, a Presbyterian minister; and Zeb Shipley, a local physician. Edwards, a Republican, had come to office in normally Democratic Putnam County in 1910 when the local Democratic Party split into "Independent" (prohibitionist) and "Regular" factions. The Independents included most of Putnam County's progressive Democrats. See De-Lozier, *Putnam County*, 143, 156, 158.

In DeKalb County Guy Davis, a farmer and trader from Alexandria, chaired the draft board. Other members included J. Edgar Evins, traveling salesman for the St. Louis Coffee and Spice Mills; two doctors; and an attorney. See "The Men Who Are Selecting D'Kalb's Quota for New Draft Army," *Smithville Review*, August 23, 1917. The DeKalb board was larger than normal and included some members whose responsibility seems to have been to report directly to Governor Rye. Given the very large number of exemptions requested by potential draftees in DeKalb County, it seems likely that extra board members were appointed to process the overload. (J. Edgar Evins was the father of long-term congressman Joe L. Evins of Smithville; Edgar Evins State Park was named for him.)

19. Hogue, *Fentress County*, xviii, 80, 90, 149, xxx, 121–22.

20. "Young Men Advised to Not Shirk Draft," *Jackson County Sentinel*, August 9, 1917.

21. "Examination of Drafted Men Begun in Smith County," *Jackson County Sentinel*, August 9, 1917. Tom Watson's paper, *The Jeffersonian*, condemned the war and urged resistance to conscription of troops for use overseas. The post-master general held *The Jeffersonian* to be seditious material; in August 1917 the post office began to refuse shipment of the paper. See Woodward, *Tom Watson*, 451–63.

22. "Examination of Men Finished in Overton County," *Jackson County Sentinel*, August 23, 1917. Local draft boards apparently varied in their attitudes toward allowing exemptions. In DeKalb County thirty-nine men had been called for physicals. Most accepted the draft. There, only four tried for exemptions, and they were turned down (see "30 Rookies Ready to Fight," *Smithville Review*, August 23, 1917). Exemptions were forwarded to the district board in Nashville. In October forty-eight Putnam County men who had been exempted by their local draft board received word that the district board had reversed that decision (see "Exemption Denied Many," *Putnam County Herald*, October 25, 1917).

23. *Historical World War Data*.

24. *Golden Age*, May 15, 1918.

25. "Companies M and C Gone," *Golden Age*, September 12, 1917. In Jackson County 3,000 people crowded into Gainesboro to "say goodbye to the soldier boys" (see "Soldiers Leave for Camp Gordon," *Jackson County Sentinel*, September 27, 1917; "In Honor of Drafted Men," *Putnam County Herald*, September 6, 1917). As these newspaper articles indicate, most draftees from Tennessee went for training to Camp Cordon, Chamblee, Ga. Tennessee National Guard regiments were sent for training to Camp Sevier, near Greenville, S.C.

26. From November 1917 through 1918 Upper Cumberland papers ran soldiers' letters in every issue. The conclusions in this paragraph are drawn from extensive reading of those letters. See especially *Putnam County Herald*, October 25, November 8, December 6, 1917, May 16, 1918; *Jackson County Sentinel*, November 8, 22, 1917, June 13, 27, July 4, 11, 25, August 15, October 10, December 15, 1918; *Golden Age*, January 1918–January 1919.

27. O. L. Green, letter, in *Putnam County Herald*, December 6, 1917.

28. "A Soldier to His Mother," *Putnam County Herald*, May 16, 1918. See also letters from L. O. Burroughs, "Camp Sevier, S. C.," October 25, 1917, and "Camp Jackson," November 8, 1917, in *Putnam County Herald*; letter from Dillard Nivens, *Putnam County Herald*, December 6, 1917; "From Our Boys in Khaki," letter from Henry Trisdale, *Jackson County Sentinel*, November 8, 1917.

29. Letter from Henry C. Trisdale, *Jackson County Sentinel*, July 25, 1918; letter from J. W. Draper, *Jackson County Sentinel*, July 11, 1918; letters from soldiers in *Golden Age*, July, August, September 1918; "Sunny Letter from Sunny France," *Alexandria Times*, October 9, 1918.

30. *Golden Age*, July 31, 1918; letter from I. F. Dillon, *Golden Age*, September 25, 1918; letter from H. H. West in *Carthage Courier*, May 16, 1918.

31. "Tennesseans Awarded Distinguished Service Cross," *Historical World*

War Data. See also "Unknown Heroes," typescript written by A. R. Hogue, sent by G. W. Conaster to Governor A. H. Roberts, in Roberts Papers.

32. Kennedy, *Over Here*, 114–17.

33. "Re: Council of National Defense," box 33, folder 2, Rye Papers; Breen, *Uncle Sam at Home*, 71, 98, 99, 100, 109, 110, 111.

34. See sources in note 33 above.

35. Farmers' institutes did not exist in every county of the state.

36. "Great Food Supply Campaign," *Putnam County Herald*, May 3, 1917.

37. "The Farmer's View," *Putnam County Herald*, May 17, 1917.

38. Here the participation of members of the Churches of Christ in the region is an exception. It may be worth noting that the author has found no instance in which a Church of Christ preacher assumed a leadership role in war mobilization.

39. According to the Records of the Council of National Defense, State Council Section (record group 62, 14-E), the chairs of local councils of defense were, in Clay County, W. L. Brown; in Cumberland, C. E. Snodgrass; in DeKalb, J. E. Drake; in Fentress, G. G. Foskett; in Jackson, B. L. Quarles; in Macon, H. H. Houser; in Overton, S. A. D. Smith; in Pickett, John Lacy; in Putnam, J. M.[*sic*] Cox; in Smith, W. W. Brandon; and in White, Edgar Pearson.

In Tennessee the state council of national defense was created and appointed by the governor without any "statutory recognition" (see "Report on Organization and Activities of the State Councils of Defense," June 18, 1917, Records of the Council of National Defense, Committee on Women's Defense Work, General Correspondence File, record group 62, 13A-A1). Workers for the council in its Nashville headquarters were paid with monies raised by private subscription. See Confidential Reports on State Councils of Defense, Records of the Council of National Defense, State Council Section (record group 62, 14-D1).

40. DeLozier, *Putnam County*, 116, 133, 134, 143, 149–50, 157, 162, 180, 181, 193. Cox owned one of the first automobiles in Putnam County; he was once forced off the road by an angry, drunken mob who denounced his car as a public menace.

41. "Program Woman's Conference," and "Parent Teacher Association," *Putnam County Herald*, July 27, 1916.

42. Mrs. J. M. Hatfield, the wife of the school superintendent who had aroused the ire of outlying communities by consolidating rural schools, chaired the draft registration assistance committee. Mrs. O. K. Holladay ran the committee on food production. Oscar Holladay, a member of the Methodist Church, then serving as Cookeville's mayor, had as state senator written Tennessee's 1909 prohibition law. A lawyer, Holladay had been a teacher as a youth and promoted public secondary education in Putnam County; he also helped secure Tennessee Polytechnic Institute for Cookeville. Mrs. Robert Farley, a member of the Church of Christ and wife of a local banker and manufacturer, also served on the women's council. Mrs. Walter Carlen, whose husband was clerk and master and vice-president of the Citizens Bank and the Coca-Cola bottling plant, was herself an education activist who organized the local PTA in 1915. Mrs. A. J. Coile, a WCTU member, was the wife of the Presbyterian minister who served on the draft board. Mrs. W. A. Howard's physician husband founded Cookeville's first

hospital. Mrs. Zeb Shipley was married to the doctor on the draft board. Mrs. B. G. Adcock's husband was a prominent attorney; Mrs. Adcock, a member of the Church of Christ, had been president of the Cookeville WCTU in 1915. Mrs. Thomas A. Early was the wife of the president of Tennessee Polytechnic Institute. Mrs. Clarence Wilson, as president of the Women's Club of Cookeville, was a civic leader in her own right. Mrs. David Lansden, a Presbyterian, was married to a state supreme court justice. The secretary, Mrs. George Guthrie, was the wife of a dentist who was the son of a prominent Gallatin politician and lawyer. See DeLozier, *Putnam County*, 160, 162–63, 165, 171, 133, 134, 143, 149–50, 157, 158, 162, 189–91, 180, 182, 209–10; Hale and Merritt, *History of Tennessee and Tennesseans* 1757–58, 1787, 1793, 1785, 1781; *Who's Who in Tennessee.*

43. See sources in n. 42 above. Members included Oscar K. Holladay, James Cox, and Charles D. Daniel, dean of Tennessee Polytechnic Institute. Many of the women serving on the committee were also members of either the council or the Red Cross. Among the women serving were Mrs. O. K. Holladay, Mrs. Walter R. Carlen, Mrs. A. J. Coile, Mrs. William Shanks, Mrs. John A. (Clara Cox) Epperson, and Mrs. Charles D. Daniel.

44. "County and District Chairmen Appointed. Leading Men and Women of Jackson County Appointed to Responsible Positions," *Jackson County Sentinel,* September 26, 1917; Department of Commerce and Labor, Bureau of the Census, *Thirteenth Census,* tab. 1, 574–85.

45. The chairman of the Red Cross was Rev. E. C. Sanders, pastor of the local Methodist Church; vice-chairmen were Rev. N. K. McGowan, a Disciples minister and teacher at the Disciples-funded Livingston Academy, and T. M. Burgess, a teacher at the academy. The Red Cross secretaries were, respectively, natives of New York and Kentucky. Local businessmen and their wives served as committee chairs. See "History of Overton County Chapter American Red Cross at Livingston Tenn.," *Golden Age,* July 23, 1919. Mrs. S. O. Kennedy, wife of the owner of the Livingston Power and Light Company and a native of New York, was secretary until May 1918. She was succeeded by Miss Alice Johnson, a secretary, public stenographer, and court reporter employed by a local law firm, and a native of Kentucky. W. K. Draper, a lumber dealer, and J. T. Lansden, who was partner in a hardware store in Livingston, served consecutively as treasurers. A. J. Mofield, owner of the Morgan Produce Company, was chair of the committee on extension. J. H. Myers, a merchant in Livingston, was in charge of the membership committee. I. E. Garrett, president of Livingston Academy and a native of Virginia, was head of the publicity committee until May 1918, when he was succeeded by newspaper editor G. B. McGee. The chair of the finance committee was T. B. Copeland, cashier at Citizens Bank. Mrs. Harry Adkins was in charge of women's work. Mrs. Adkins, the wife of the manager of the branch line railroad that ran from Livingston to Algood in Putnam County, was a native of Iowa. When she resigned in 1918, her successor was Mrs. J. W. Henson, "the wife of . . . a very prominent and highly respected citizen of Livingston." Miss Linnie McCormack, who owned a millinery store in Livingston, was chair of the nursing committee. Miss Gertrude Officer, daughter of Chancellor W. R. Officer and a teacher at the academy, was head of the commit-

tee on canteen service. Mrs. J. H. Myers, whose husband was chair of the membership committee, was herself chair of the committee on civilian relief. W. H. Estes, cashier of the Farmers Bank, was chair of the "Main Committee."

46. "Women Chairmen Will Meet Saturday, Oct. 6," *Jackson County Sentinel,* September 13, 1917; "Women to Enroll for Service October 13," *Jackson County Sentinel,* September 13, 1917; "To Register Women," *Putnam County Herald,* October 4, 1917. *Herald* editor Elmer Wirt was skeptical about the value of registering women. His general attitude toward the war made him the Upper Cumberland's most prominent dissenter. His role as such will be dealt with below.

47. "Registration of All Women Expected," *Jackson County Sentinel,* September 27, 1917. In Tennessee the governor's proclamation served as the registration's only legal sanction. However, in Louisiana the state legislature enacted compulsory registration. See "Report of the Activities of the Women's Committee," Records of the Council of National Defense, record group 62, 13A-C1.

48. *Putnam County Herald,* October 11, 1917.

49. The state-level councils of defense were agencies created for the war and expired shortly after the war ended. In most states the councils' papers are available at the state archives. After an extensive search the staff at the Tennessee State Library and Archives was unable to locate the Tennessee council papers. They are not in the National Archives, Washington, D.C. However, some information can be obtained from state reports to the national council. (See "Charts and Maps of the Work of the Departments of the State Divisions of the Women's Committee," Field Division, Records of the Council of National Defense, September 1917–July 1918, record group 62, 13A-D2.) The complaints of Sue White, director of registration, are in the General Correspondence of the Committee on Women's Defense Work of the Councils of National Defense (record group 62, 13A-A1).

50. The Jackson County paper printed the registration card. See "Registration Card for Women," "Objects of Registration for Service," *Jackson County Sentinel,* October 11, 1917.

51. "Work in Livingston Red Cross Chapter," *Golden Age,* February 27, 1918. Note that both women who served as Red Cross secretaries in Overton County were from outside the region.

52. Other than newspaper stories there is no data as to how successful the various enrollment drives were on a local level. The stories quoted above suggest that the enrollment drives may not have been as successful as the later fundraising drives. See "Ladies Enlist Now," *Golden Age,* August 29, 1917; "Women Chairmen Will Meet Saturday, Oct. 6," *Jackson County Sentinel,* October 4, 1917; "Food Card Campaign to Begin Monday, Oct. 29," *Jackson County Sentinel,* October 25, 1917; "Food Campaign Lags," *Jackson County Sentinel,* November 8, 1917; "Food Pledge Cards," *Putnam County Herald,* October 4, 1917.

53. "Those Slacker Lists" and mayor's statement, *Alexandria Times,* June 26, 1918.

54. "Report Your W.S.S. Sales," *Putnam County Herald,* July 25, 1918; *Carthage Courier,* June 20, 1918. Similar orders were given in DeKalb County (see "To the People of DeKalb County," *Smithville Review,* June 27, 1918). In Octo-

ber 1918 people in Putnam County who failed to buy Liberty Bonds were also threatened with having their names put on the "Slackers List." See *Putnam County Herald*, October 10, 1918.

In Cumberland County, fund raisers found it hard to explain to residents of outlying areas the necessity of contributing; see "Over the Top for Cumberland County," *Crossville Chronicle*, November 21, 1917. By September 1918 the county was far behind in its War Savings Stamp quota, and noncontributors were threatened with having their names turned in to authorities. See "War Savings Stamps," *Crossville Chronicle*, September 4, 1918.

55. "Slacker List to Be Wiped Out," *Jackson County Sentinel*, August 8, 1918.

56. "Jackson County to Be Free of All Slackers," *Jackson County Sentinel*, August 15, 1918.

57. Seals, *White County*, 79–80.

58. "Patriotism and Loyalty Were the Keynotes of the Meeting," *Carthage Courier*, April 14, 1918; "Over the Top with Liberty Bonds," *Carthage Courier*, May 2, 1918; "Big Red Cross Parade Saturday," *Alexandria Times*, April 10, 1918; "Liberty Loan Campaign" and "War Bond Parade," *Putnam County Herald*, April 18, 1918; "Important WAR Meetings," *Jackson County Sentinel*, November 15, 1917; "Liberty Chorus Work," *Putnam County Herald*, February 14, 1918; "Military Drill at Algood," *Putnam County Herald*, December 13, 1917.

59. In the Upper Cumberland press, soldiers were most often referred to as "soldier boys" or just "the boys." In fact, no one under twenty-one was drafted in World War I.

60. "Monterey Route 3," *Putnam County Herald*, November 8, 1917.

61. "Why We Have a Great Country," *Putnam County Herald*, November 15, 1917.

62. "Curses President and Is Arrested," *Smithville Review*, May 23, 1917.

63. Si Stepp, docket number 304, U.S. District Court, 1918, Records of the Federal Court, Northeast Division of Middle Tennessee.

64. Tom Carmack, case 365, box 13, U.S. District Court records.

65. "$850 for Red Cross in DeKalb," *Alexandria Times*, April 3, 1918; "Supt. McDowell Arrested," *Carthage Courier*, May 23, 1918; *Alexandria Times*, May 15, 1918; "Federal Officers Here," *Smithville Review*, May 9, 1918. The author was unable to locate the court records of the McDowell case.

66. "U.S. Attorney Explains Scope of Espionage Law," *Jackson County Sentinel*, June 6, 1918.

67. "Sensation at Sparta," *Smithville Review*, May 2, 1918.

68. DeLozier, *Putnam County*, 157–58, 193. When the war in Europe war began in 1914, Wirt saw it as a manifestation of Old World corruption, not as a battle between the forces of good and evil. His attitude did not change significantly when the United States entered the war. In May 1917 Wirt reported that a peace conference in Stockholm, Sweden, was being planned by Socialists from many different countries. He noted, "According to news dispatches only two larger nations have no representatives, Germany and the United States. In Kaiser-ridden Deutchland and free America the governments refused passports

to the peace convention delegates. Here is food for thought, brother" ("A Peace Conference," *Putnam County Herald*, May 31, 1917).

Wirt was the most outspoken critic of the war among Upper Cumberland editors. The *Jackson County Sentinel* during the war filled its pages with government press releases and letters from soldiers. The editor of the *Crossville Chronicle* was against American involvement in the conflict but, once war was declared, did not make further negative comments. The *Chronicle*, however, was very subdued in its coverage of war news and of mobilization on the home front. (See "Our Position," *Crossville Chronicle*, April 11, 1917; *Crossville Chronicle* April 18, 1917.) Editor McGee of the Livingston *Golden Age* supported war mobilization with much free publicity, but in October 1918 he criticized a Liberty Loan speech by John Trotwood Moore, saying that the claim that soldiers who died in action would go straight to heaven was "Not Bible Doctrine." McGee also said that "the statement of the soldier speaker . . . that 'the Germans are not human beings' was also far from being rational." See *Golden Age*, October 16, 1918.

69. In the *Putnam County Herald*, May 24, 1917, Wirt featured "War Notes" that mentioned food riots in Paris and criticism of British military policy. In the same paper he criticized President Wilson for demanding the power to censor the press, saying that Congress had no right to endow the president with unconstitutional powers. In a February 21, 1918, editorial Wirt criticized government orders regarding food conservation that were unintelligible to the average person.

70. *Putnam County Herald*, July 12, 1917.

71. DeLozier, *Putnam County*, 157–58. *Putnam County Herald*, October 11, 1917; January 23, 1919. After the war, Wirt published an editorial noting the attacks on LaFollette and on himself, concluding that LaFollette had been exonerated and "the Herald is yet being published every week."

72. "Super Patriots," *Putnam County Herald*, November 8, 1917.

73. Chambers, *To Raise an Army*, 211–13.

74. "Arrested as Deserter" and "Shot by Sheriff Carr," *Putnam County Herald*, February 14, 1918; "Deserter Is Landed in Jail" and "Rounding Up Deserters," *Carthage Courier*, May 23, 1918; "Deserters," *Smithville Review*, January 17, 1918; "Slacker Arrested," *Smithville Review*, May 2, 9, 1918; "DeKalb County Deserters Are Captured," *Smithville Review*, May 16, 1918; "Deserter Surrenders," *Smithville Review*, June 20, 1918; "Sheriff Dean Captures Deserters," *Alexandria Times*, May 29, 1918; "Seven Deserters in This County," *Alexandria Times*, April 3, 1918.

75. "Deserter Shot by Officers," *Alexandria Times*, May 15, 1918. Gentry was one of several deserters rounded up in DeKalb County. The local newspaper noted that the sheriff was reportedly under orders from higher authorities. In arresting Gentry, Sheriff Puckett apologized, "reminding him that he had repeatedly sent word that he would not be taken alive and that he and the other officers were only doing their duty."

76. "Deserter Is Landed in Jail," *Alexandria Times*, May 15, 1918.

77. U.S. District Court records, Cookeville, Criminal Case 308.

78. "Soldiers on Trail of Deserters," *Alexandria Times*, July 3, 1918. Very little

information was published about the squad. However, a story in the *Smithville Review* (August 29, 1918) refers to them as U.S. cavalry. The people of Liberty, a small town in DeKalb County, entertained the "soldier boys" with a dinner and a musical program. See "Liberty Locals," *Alexandria Times,* July 3, 1918.

79. "Deserter Ends Life with Gun," *Alexandria Times,* July 3, 1918. Walden and other DeKalb deserters had gone AWOL from Camp Sevier, S.C. In April the army offered a $50 reward for information leading to their capture. However, Walden was still at large until he shot himself.

80. "Many Deserters in Gulf," *Crossville Chronicle,* July 24, 1918.

81. "4,500 People Here Saturday," *Smithville Review,* August 20, 1918.

82. "Greatest Day in History of Jackson County," *Jackson County Sentinel,* November 7, 1918. The news being celebrated was German acceptance of the Allied peace terms, not the actual armistice.

83. Fred Dunlap, letter, "From Sunny France," *Crossville Chronicle,* February 5, 1919.

84. U.S. District Court records.

Chapter 9

1. Thorogood, *Financial History of Tennessee since 1870,* 100–121; Macpherson, "Democratic Progressivism in Tennessee," 22–30; Reichard, "Republican Victory of 1920 in Tennessee," 10–14.

2. Letter from B. G. Adcock to Governor Roberts, August 1, 1919, box 5, folder 1, Roberts Papers; *Putnam County Herald,* May 13, July 22, 29, October 14, 1920; James N. Cox, letter to Governor Roberts, June 2, 1919, box 6, file 3, Roberts Papers.

3. O. G. Fox to Governor Roberts, March 9, 1920, box 19, folder 4, Roberts Papers. Sam M. Foster, clerk and master of DeKalb County, warned Roberts in a June 18, 1920, letter, "The farmers are very much up in the air and they seem to blame no one but you, the tax question here at this time is causing more talk than when we were in war and these people will not listen to reason" (box 8, folder 2, Roberts Papers).

4. Reichard, "Republican Victory of 1920 in Tennessee," 112.

5. "I. D. Beasley Calls Attention of People to His Record," *Carthage Courier,* July 31, 1924; "To the Democratic Voters and Taxpayers of Smith County," *Carthage Courier,* July 22, 1926.

6. *Carthage Courier,* March 11, 1926.

7. The sample was randomly and proportionally selected from the 1920 census rolls for the Upper Cumberland counties and was analyzed using Quattro Pro for Windows. In some cases the sample size is the entire database, 1,503 individuals. The number the percentages are based on will be given in the text. The survey will be referred to hereafter as Census Survey, 1920.

8. Statistics on tenancy, 1890–1925, are from Department of the Interior, Census Office, *Report on the Statistics of Agriculture,* and Department of Commerce, Bureau of the Census, *United States Census of Agriculture.* Other data from Census Survey, 1920.

9. Department of Commerce, Bureau of the Census, *United States Census of Agriculture*, Tennessee, County Table IV, 736–47. Very small plots of land can be used effectively to produce truck crops, but that was not common in the Upper Cumberland. In 1925 the acreage in the region devoted to vegetables raised for the market amounted to less than 1 percent of the total planted and harvested. According to the census, 434 of 514,892 acres were planted in truck crops for sale. It should be noted that this figure included only those acres specifically planted by farmers planning to sell the harvest. The figure does not include potatoes, of which Upper Cumberland farmers grew copious amounts both for home use and for sale. Of the crops grown, acreage per crop was as follows: cabbages 29, melons 231, onions 18, sweet corn 18, tomatoes 97, and lettuce 41. Note that melons—cantaloupes and watermelons combined—were the crops most often raised for market.

In the early 1920s University of Tennessee researchers did a survey of fifty-two farms near Livingston, the county seat of Overton. By that date Livingston was accessible by paved state highway. Of the farms surveyed, forty-nine were "general" farms, two produced mostly grain, and one was a dairy farm. The general farmers raised milk cattle; sold the calves, steers, and heifers; and consumed most of the meat they produced at home. See "The Farm Survey," *Livingston Enterprise*, February 13, 1924; "An Economic Analysis of Farming in Overton County," *Livingston Enterprise*, August 17, 1928.

The university surveyed the entire state and published its findings by region. The Upper Cumberland counties include areas in the Eastern Highland Rim and the Cumberland Plateau. In the Eastern Highland Rim only 3 percent of the cornmeal and 36 percent of the flour consumed was purchased. On the plateau, farmers bought 33 percent of the cornmeal and 71 percent of the flour they consumed. According to the survey the farmers of the Eastern Highland Rim were self-sufficient, ranking below other sections of the state in purchases of vegetables and starchy foods, although farm families' consumption of such foods compared favorably with that of their peers in other parts of the state. See Allred and Powell, "Meat Consumption in Rural Tennessee." See also Sanders, "Educational and Economic Survey of Pickett County, Tennessee," 30–35. The number of families surveyed was 140.

Gilbert Fite's description of agriculture in the mid-South in the 1920s could have been written with the Upper Cumberland in mind. According to Fite, farms in the region were small and unprofitable: "The basic problem in the region was the pressure of people on the land. Land resources were simply not sufficient to produce a decent living for so many people" (Fite, *American Farmers*, 22–23). As a result, farmers were slow to industrialize. In 1925 there were 146 tractors in the eleven Upper Cumberland counties.

See Allred and Robinson, "Significant Changes," 19; Department of the Interior, Census Office, *Report on the Statistics of Agriculture*, Tennessee, tab. 5, 180–83, and *Report on Population*, tab. 5, 317–28; Department of Commerce, Bureau of the Census, *United States Census of Agriculture*, Tennessee, County Table 1, 700–710, County Table V, 748–55.

Mining was an important source of work only in the plateau counties. In Fentress County approximately 15 percent of all employed males worked as miners, the largest percentage of miners working per population in the region. Throughout the region, men continued to work as loggers and also took jobs in sawmills. Small wood product factories dotted the region by the 1920s. Mills and factories, such as the Sparta Spoke Factory, which sometimes processed up to 2 million spokes a year, employed about 2,000 men in the region. The factories were also an important source of income for farmers. As a county historian noted in the 1930s, the Sparta factory had "been of great advantage to small farmers having a little timber and who in cutting their firewood could sell the saleable part of the trees to the spoke factory." Data on employment from U.S. Department of Commerce, Bureau of the Census, *Fifteenth Census, Occupation.* See also Seals, *White County,* 142; *Livingston Enterprise,* April 1, 1925; *Carthage Courier,* July 28, 1927.

10. "Does Our County Need a County Agent," *Carthage Courier,* December 6, 1923; "Putnam County Employs an Agricultural Agent," *Carthage Courier,* January 17, 1924; *Golden Age,* February 23, 1916; Krechniak and Krechniak, *Cumberland County's First Hundred Years,* 115–20; Seals, *White County,* 64. Bankers in Smith and Putnam Counties sponsored the adoption of better breeds of poultry. See "What One County Has Done," 2–3; "Attention Poultry Raisers," *Putnam County Herald,* March 2, 1922. In Overton County the Livingston Booster Club sponsored the agricultural fair and helped fund corn, pig, and poultry clubs for youth (under the supervision of the county agent). See "New Booster Club" and "A Very Wrong Impression," *Golden Age,* April 14, 1920. A recent study of the Rockefeller General Education Board's agricultural reform programs contends, "If there is a unifying theme to the G.E.B.'s programs in the southern countryside it is their goal of moving white yeoman away from a set of dependencies and interdependencies that progressive interests could not control to a set of dependencies in which class interests represented by the G.E.B. dominated and through which those interests could determine not just the direction of social reform, but also the terms of the debate." The authors contend that demonstration work taught individual farmers to go for profit. During the Progressive Era the General Education Board funded 625 farm agents in southern states and spent $2 million on farm demonstration programs, rural organization plans, and agriculture clubs. See Mitchell and Lowe, "To Sow Contentment," 317–40.

11. *Golden Age,* July 8, 1914, October 8, 1919. In 1910 the Cumberland County fair was held on the grounds of the courthouse and featured competitions in corn, hay, and garden crops. According to a county history, "Cattle were allowed free range and some difficulty resulted from exhibits being eaten by cattle, sheep and hogs." County agent Robert Lyons, who took office in 1927, regularized the fair competitions. See Krechniak and Krechniak, *Cumberland County's First Hundred Years,* 231. In Overton County the farm agent organized fairs in Livingston, the county seat, and Rickman. See also Seals, *White County,* 64.

12. "Carthage Is Slowly but Steadily Growing," *Carthage Courier,* July 3, 1923; Department of Commerce, Bureau of the Census, *United States Census of Agriculture,* Tennessee, County Table VI, 756–65.

13. "To the Farmers of the Third Civil District of Overton County," *Golden*

Age, August 26, 1914; "To the Citizens of Overton County," *Golden Age*, January 21, 1920; "To the Farmers of Overton County," *Golden Age*, February 4, 1920; "On Tobacco Growing," *Golden Age*, February 14, 1920. Similar efforts were made in Putnam County in 1920, when farm agent W. W. Ford and M. E. Newell, freight agent for the Tennessee Central Railroad, encouraged farmers to raise tobacco. See "Raise Tobacco," *Putnam County Herald*, January 8, 1920.

14. "A Money Crop," *Golden Age*, January 21, 1920. Burley tobacco, grown extensively in the region today, did not take hold as a money crop until the 1930s, when the federal government effectively guaranteed both market stability and a safe profit by setting production quotas for tobacco per farm. After that point tobacco production began to increase. For example, in 1925 DeKalb County reported 95 farms growing tobacco; in 1939, 1,143 farms had tobacco patches. See U.S. Department of Commerce, Bureau of the Census, *Sixteenth Census*, County Table VII, 220–27.

15. Census Survey, 1920. Percentages were rounded off. These figures are based on the entire 313-household survey. Only 25 households were located in towns. Judging from those 25 cases, people in town were more likely than their country cousins to live in extended households (perhaps because relatives working in town boarded with them) or in primary couple households.

16. See Chapter 2 for a discussion of family and household composition in 1890; 1920 information from Survey of Census, 1920.

17. Sanders, "Educational and Economic Survey of Pickett County, Tennessee," 35–36. A University of Tennessee survey of Jackson County in 1929 found that of 121 surveyed homes, only 2 had running water in the house. Four homes had electric lights (powered by Delco plants). Forty-six of the houses had screened windows. Many had no toilets. See Overton, "Educational, Economic and Community Survey of Jackson County, Tennessee," chap. 3.

18. Information about urban services is not available for all Upper Cumberland towns. However, by 1912 Crossville had electric lights, powered by a Delco plant owned by Reed Mercantile Company. In the 1920s the Tennessee Electric Power Company, a private firm, began to supply services for the town. In 1927 the city let a contract for the construction of a town water and sewage system. See Krechniak and Krechniak, *Cumberland County's First Hundred Years*, 115–20. By 1927 residents of Carthage were sufficiently accustomed to electricity to complain of the poor service provided by Tennessee Electric Power Company to that town and others in the region. See "This Section Entitled to Better Electric Service," *Carthage Courier*, June 16, 1927.

Cookeville emerged early as the region's progressive center. In 1905 the city organized a light and water department and built a steam plant; the town's first electric lights went on in 1906. The streets were paved in 1908. A municipal water system gradually replaced wells and springs in supplying the town's water. In 1921 the town built a dam on a nearby river and drew power from that plant until 1944, when the city electric company signed a contract with the Tennessee Valley Authority. Cookeville also led in cultural amenities (such as they were), having by the 1920s a circulating library founded by Clara Cox Epperson and the local women's club, a movie theater, and a wireless club. See DeLozier, *Putnam County*, 149, 230–31, 214–15, 240–42.

19. *Livingston Enterprise,* June 1, 1928, featured a typical lament about the decline of the timber industry and projections of doom unless alternative sources of income were developed. In the April 14, 1920, *Golden Age* a citizen of Livingston deplored that road bond issues had been voted down due to lack of interest in progress and a willingness to go on living as the forefathers had. See De-Lozier, *Putnam County,* 223; Seals, *White County,* 142; "Sparta Silk Will Be Sold at Public Auction," *Sparta News,* May 30, 1929; "Exchange Club Has Interesting Meeting," *Livingston Enterprise,* September 7, 1921.

20. E. F. Christian, "Ossification," *Golden Age,* February 23, 1916.

21. *Carthage Courier,* December 12, 1918; see also letters to the editor, *Carthage Courier,* January–June 1919; "Smith County Issues $75,000 in Bonds for Good Roads. Bond Election Called on August 23," *Carthage Courier,* July 10, 1919; *Carthage Courier,* July 17, 31, August 21, 1919; "Smith County Votes Bonds and Joins the Ranks of Progress," *Carthage Courier,* August 28, 1919.

On the creation of the state highway department, see Allred, Atkins, and Hendrix, *Human and Physical Resources of Tennessee,* chap. 14, and Macpherson, "Democratic Progressivism in Tennessee," 69–70, 117–18, 193–249. Peay's administration financed road building with a series of short-term loans paid by gasoline and auto registration taxes.

22. "To the People of Smith County," *Carthage Courier,* July 21, 1921; "About the Road Labor," *Carthage Courier,* July 28, 1921; "An Appeal to Reason by the Road Commissioners," *Carthage Courier,* August 11, 1921.

23. "Serious Difficulty at Road Working," *Alexandria Times,* July 31, 1918; "Blood Hounds in Livingston Again," *Livingston Enterprise,* March 25, 1925.

24. Letter from W. H. Peebles, superintendent of construction, State Department of Highways, to Governor A. H. Roberts, box 2, folder 5, Roberts Papers.

Chapter 10

1. See Chapter 3; McDowell, *Social Gospel in the South;* J. C. M'Quiddy, "Should Women Enter Politics and Hold Office?," *Gospel Advocate,* November 4, 1920; "Woman Suffrage," *Gospel Advocate,* July 22, 1920.

Records of the Lafayette Baptist Church; records of the Bledsoe Missionary Baptist Association; Minutes of the Enon Baptist Association; records of the First Baptist Church, Monterey, Tenn.; records of the Mount Union Baptist Church; minutes of the First Baptist Church, Cookeville, Tenn.; Minutes of the Thirty-third Annual Session of the New Salem Missionary Baptist Association; Minutes of the Riverside Association of Missionary Baptists; Minutes of the Salem Baptist Association; Minutes of the Stone Association of Baptists.

Porter, *Feminism,* 9–44; Vickers, "Woman's Place," chap. 3. Vickers notes that while Baptist leaders continually preached that woman's place was in the home, stating their message in the most conservative and limited terms, Southern Baptist women saw their role as being mothers to the community at large, did most of the denomination's social outreach work, and ran day care centers for the children of working mothers.

In a 1923 report on women's work in rural Baptist churches, the author complained that when Women's Missionary Societies collected funds for church work, their local churches forwarded the funds without acknowledging that the money had been raised by women. This, the author noted, made it hard for the women in those churches to be "buoyant" about further fund raising. See Alldredge, *Southern Baptist Handbook*, 267–68.

Historian Betty DeBerg argues that the roots of fundamentalism lie not in theological questions but in concerns over twentieth-century challenges to gender roles, and posits that fundamentalism provided a bridge by which Victorian gender roles could be carried into the twentieth century. DeBerg points out that fundamentalists defended biblical inerrancy and condemned Darwinism because both threatened "the family" and "the home"—as both were understood by nineteenth-century American Protestants. Having read through a large number of late nineteenth- and early twentieth-century conservative denominational papers, I am convinced that she is correct. The conservative obsession with the woman question is striking, especially given that when I began my research I was not looking for women's issues but for discussions of Darwinism. See DeBerg, *Ungodly Women*.

2. "J. E. Evans Writes on Woman Suffrage," *Carthage Courier*, July 6, 1916; DeLozier, *Putnam County*, 163–66; "The Dixon Springs Equal-Suffrage League," *Carthage Courier*, November 4, 1915; "Equal Suffrage Club in Carthage," *Carthage Courier*, April 5, 1917. Prior to World War I, local debating societies used woman suffrage as a topic; see *Sparta News*, March 25, 1915.

3. *Carthage Courier*, October 21, 28, 1920; "Smith County Remains in the Ranks of Democratic Party," *Carthage Courier*, November 4, 1920. According to the latter source, many of the women of Dixon Springs did not bother to vote; however, two eighty-year-old women came to the polls to cast their vote fór the Democrats. See *Putnam County Herald*, October 21, 28, 1920; circular urging women to vote in Smith County, written by James M. Cox, circuit court clerk, in Roberts Papers, box 18, folder 5.

4. "Is It Constitutional," *Carthage Courier*, March 16, 1922; "Peay and McKellar Win Nomination," *Carthage Courier*, August 10, 1922; DeLozier, *Putnam County*, 167; Graves, *Evins of Tennessee*, 22–23. Mary Denny, who became Putnam County trustee, found it necessary to defend herself for seeking office by saying that she supported a disabled husband.

5. Rolling Stone's choice of "new dispensation" to discuss the changes in women's roles he foresaw as a result of suffrage probably reflects his religious background. As understood by many religious people in the region, mankind's history was divided into different dispensations reflecting the relations of God to Man. There had been a patriarchal dispensation and a Mosaic dispensation. The new (religious) dispensation was that of the Gospel. The use of "new dispensation" is thus more highly charged than might be immediately obvious.

6. "The New Dispensation," *Carthage Courier*, April 8, 1920.

7. "The Old Dispensation," *Carthage Courier*, May 6, 1920.

8. A survey of fifty Overton County farms indicated that poultry sales accounted for one-half of all livestock receipts and one-third of all the money earned by the farm. See "The Farm Survey," *Livingston Enterprise*, February 13, 1924; "An Economic Analysis of Farming in Overton County," *Livingston En-*

terprise, August 17, 1928. In 1923 the editor of the *Carthage Courier* scoffed at the idea that women should be excused from paying their poll taxes because they held no property. In most cases, he said, wives were partners with their husbands in farming. "It is said that some men go to the extreme and say that all the house furnishings, chickens, eggs, etc. belong to him and that his wife owns nothing. You should be careful in making such an evasion" ("Should the Women Pay Their Polltax?," *Carthage Courier*, July 3, 1923). In the same paper, farmers were urged to supply their wives with cows and chickens so that the farm wife could make some money. In 1927, when the Overton County Fair had a poultry show for the first time, many of the exhibitors were women. See "Poultry Show First at Overton Fair," *Livingston Enterprise*, October 12, 1927.

9. U.S. Department of Commerce, Bureau of the Census, *Fifteenth Census*, tab. 20, 908–19.

10. In the 1890s male Tennesseans had been more likely to be literate than women. By the end of the 1920s the situation was reversed. In 1930, 11 percent of the state's male rural population was illiterate, compared with just over 7 percent of the female rural population, according to Allred, Atkins, and Hendrix, *Human and Physical Resources of Tennessee*, chap. 28. In 1930 the percentage of illiteracy in rural areas was twice the urban rate (8.8 to 4.3 percent of the population.) At that date the illiteracy rate in Upper Cumberland counties ranged from 7.7 percent in Smith County to 15.9 percent in Macon County. See Albert Williams, *Biennial Report of the State Superintendent, 1919–1920*, 50–51; Harned, *Annual Report of the Department of Education, 1931*, 34–35, 48–49, 76–77, 124–25.

11. "Carthage High School Opens with Largest Enrollment Ever," *Carthage Courier*, September 6, 1928; *Carthage Courier*, March 19, 1925.

12. Harned, *Annual Report of the Department of Education, 1931*, 82–83, 84–85. Most teachers in the region's systems, male or female, were high school graduates; some had completed one or two years of college work, but few were college graduates.

13. Tennessee, Department of Public Instruction, *Course of Study*.

14. Marie White, "A Challenge," 24–25. In 1922 a PTA meeting in Cookeville featured a demonstration of a new Victrola record player. See "City School Notes," *Putnam County Herald*, March 9, 1922.

15. See Don H. Doyle, *Nashville since the 1920s*, 34–42.

16. "Woman's True Place Is in the Home," *Putnam County Herald*, August 30, September 10, 13, 17, 24, 27, October 1, 11, 15, 25, 29, November 1, 5, 8, 15, 19, 1923. With a few exceptions the women employed pseudonyms, thus making it impossible to determine their class, age, or place of residence. Some of the letters are clearly from farm wives, making reference to farm chores.

In the following notes, summaries of the entire letter exchange will be cited as "Woman's True Place." Because the paper ran all the letters under the heading "Woman's True Place Is in the Home," quotes will be cited by the pseudonyms. See "A Serious Thinker," *Putnam County Herald*, August 30, 1923; "An Observer," *Putnam County Herald*, November 19, 1923.

Mary Denny's vote totals, *Putnam County Herald*, November 8, 1923.

17. "Woman's True Place": "Winifred Densmore," *Putnam County Herald*, September 17, 1923; "A Deep Thinker," *Putnam County Herald*, September 10, 1923; "An Observer," *Putnam County Herald*, November 19, 1923; "Brown Eyes," *Putnam County Herald*, October 11, 1923; "A Serious Thinker," *Putnam County Herald*, September 27, 1923.

18. "Woman's True Place": "M. J. F.," *Putnam County Herald*, November 1, 1923; "Not an Old Maid," *Putnam County Herald*, October 1, 1923; "Calfkiller Club," *Putnam County Herald*, November 19, 1923.

19. "Woman's True Place": "X," *Putnam County Herald*, September 19, 1923; "A Deep Thinker," *Putnam County Herald*, September 27, 1923; "A Single Christian Girl," *Putnam County Herald*, November 15, 1923; "A Serious Thinker," *Putnam County Herald*, September 27, 1923; "Inexperienced Girl," *Putnam County Herald*, October 25, 1923.

20. "Woman's True Place": unsigned letter, *Putnam County Herald*, November 1, 1923; "A Subscriber," *Putnam County Herald*, October 29, 1923; "A Happy Woman," *Putnam County Herald*, September 27, 1923; "A Serious Thinker," *Putnam County Herald*, November 19, 1923; "L. E. R.," *Putnam County Herald*, November 1, 1923; "Experienced Wife," *Putnam County Herald*, November 1, 1923.

21. "Woman's True Place": "Experienced Wife," *Putnam County Herald*, November 1, 1923; "R. I. M.," *Putnam County Herald*, October 11, 1923; Rhoda Bush, *Putnam County Herald*, November 15, 1923. Bush opposed woman suffrage, saying, "I believe we need more Christian women worse than we need more women voters."

22. Statistics on church membership comparable to those given in Chapter 3 are not available for the 1920s. However, numerous gospel meetings, singings, and other religious events reported in the county press indicate that organized religion in the region was experiencing a revival.

23. The *Livingston Enterprise* of the 1920s documents the existence of exchange and women's clubs, bridge clubs, teachers' associations, corn clubs, etc. See also *Carthage Courier* and *Putnam County Herald* for the decade, and *Tennessee Bulletin*, 12–14, for information on regional PTA activities.

24. Defeated Creek Missionary Baptist Church records; Lafayette Baptist Church records. In the Lafayette case the young woman accused "rose on the floor and made statement that she had done rong [sic] but did not say she was sorry for the rong doings and did not ask the church to forgive her." The pastor pleaded with the young woman to repent and be forgiven. When she stood mute she was excluded from the fellowship. Although some churches seem to have dropped their policing of members' conduct (First Baptist, Monterey, and First Baptist, Cookeville, for example, make no mention of disciplining members in the standard forms they filed with the Southern Baptist Convention), others continued to oust people for bad behavior in the 1920s. See minutes of the First Baptist Church, Cookeville, Tenn.; First Baptist Church, Monterey, Tenn.; and Mount Union Baptist Church. Some denominations, by maintaining old standards, differentiated themselves from their more adaptable neighboring churches. The Churches of Christ, in particular, frowned on modern fashions, mixed bathing, short hair, card playing, dancing, prize fighting, professional

sports, and movies. See "Symptoms of Moral Laxity," *Gospel Advocate*, July 29, 192; "Hindrances to Christian Living," *Gospel Advocate*, September 7, 14, 1922.

25. "Methodist Church," *Golden Age*, January 7, 1920; "Men's Big Bible Class," *Livingston Enterprise*, March 9, 1928.

26. *Carthage Courier*, May 26, 1927. Religious debates continued to be held in the Upper Cumberland in the 1920s; however, they do not seem to have been as prevalent or as popular as in earlier times.

27. Conversely, religious people used the language of progressive politics. When a cross-denominational revival was organized in Cookeville in 1924, the one local denomination that refused to cooperate (the Church of Christ) was denounced in the local press as a group of unpatriotic, un-American slackers. See *Putnam County Herald*, July 1924. The charge of "slacker" referred to the ambivalence Churches of Christ showed toward supporting the First World War. See also *Gospel Advocate*, July 31, 1924.

28. "Must Read Bible," *Alexandria Times*, June 16, 1915; Gailor, "Moral Training in the Public Schools"; Brandon, "President's Address."

29. "Some Things of Which All Teachers Should Be Mindful," *Carthage Courier*, December 6, 1923.

30. In the 1920s people in the region were violent in the same ways and for the same reasons as previous generations. They were disorderly, quick to resent slights, lacking in respect for authority, and vengeful. For a collection of miscellaneous mayhem, see "Soldier Murdered," *Golden Age*, March 31, 1920; "Two Men Killed and Two Badly Wounded" and "Shoots Sweetheart and Then Kills Himself," *Livingston Enterprise*, November 28, 1923; "Christmas Revelers Do Damage to Courthouse," *Carthage Courier*, January 3, 1924; "Finds Ford Car Cut to Pieces," *Carthage Courier*, October 27, 1921; "Blood Hounds in Livingston Again," *Livingston Enterprise*, March 25, 1925; *Clay County Courier*, September 21, 1928.

31. "To the Law and Order People of Smith County," *Carthage Courier*, February 28, 1924; *Carthage Courier*, May 26, June 23, 1927. The Klan seems to have been either exceptionally active or exceptionally open about its activities in Smith County. However, Klan units also apparently existed in Putnam County, Overton County, and Macon County. See DeLozier, *Putnam County*, 217–18; "Ku Klux Klan Meet Monday Night," *Livingston Enterprise*, July 21, 1926. The July 21 story in the *Enterprise* prompted a letter from G. A. Smith, a former county resident then living in Oklahoma. He warned his old neighbors against the Klan, which he said divided families, communities, and churches and destroyed social life. In the next issue of the paper the editor defended himself for printing the critical letter, saying that the paper kept itself open for any kind of discussion and that he would print any signed letter, but he warned, "We do not intend to let the Enterprise be used for a mouthpiece for an argument on this subject." See *Livingston Enterprise*, August 11, 18, 1926.

32. Music provides the most striking example of the resilience of the culture of the countryside and the ability of country folk to adapt their culture to new technologies. Radio might have allowed the masses exposure to high culture. However, radio stations like WSM in Nashville quickly found that their most popular programs were not broadcasts of symphonies but live performances by

musicians playing what was even then called "old-time country" music. The growing popularity of country music made it possible for a White County boy like Lester Flatt to become famous as part of the renowned Flatt and Scruggs bluegrass band. See Wolfe, "Folk Songs and Fiddles," and *Tennessee Strings*.

33. Holt, *Struggle for a State System*, chap. 13; Harned, *Annual Report of the Department of Education, 1925*, 17–24; "Progress of State System," 6–16.

34. Brister, *Biennial Report of the State Superintendent, 1911–1912*, 61. The school year in the 1890s lasted about three months. By 1900 the term ranged from 64 to 110 days (see Fitzpatrick, *Annual Report of the State Superintendent*, 59–61). The 1919–20 state statistics indicate a growing disparity between town and country schools. Country primary schools had 80-day terms, while town schools' terms lasted 180 days. By 1920 the state certified teachers in three grades: first, second, and temporary. In 1920 nine Upper Cumberland counties reported on the qualifications of their teachers. In those nine counties, 25 teachers were college graduates, 28 had normal school training, 96 were high school graduates, 268 had limited normal training (probably reflecting attendance at teachers' institutes), and 247 had no professional training at all. (The report omits teachers in the Upper Cumberland's town school districts.) In 1920, 64 students completed four years in public high schools in the Upper Cumberland. See Albert Williams, *Biennial Report of the State Superintendent, 1919–1920*, 80–81, 62–63, 58–59, 52–53.

35. Supt. E. L. Huffines, "The Smith County School Situation," *Carthage Courier*, April 10, 1924; "Lafayette Picked for High School Site," *Carthage Courier*, October 14, 1926.

36. Tennessee, Department of Public Instruction, *Course of Study*, 65–67.

37. "Smith-Hughes Vocational Agriculture Course in Livingston Academy," *Golden Age*, August 24, 1921. The federal government paid half of the agriculture teacher's salary, the state paid one-eighth, and the county paid three-eighths.

38. "Schools," *Macon County Times*, June 17, 1920.

39. DeLozier, *Putnam County*, 221.

40. Tennessee, Department of Public Instruction, *Course of Study*. John Bridgewater West, a pupil at Riddleton School in Smith County, in 1927 wrote an essay on good roads that was published in the local paper. According to the child, good roads would mean more social life and more progress: the farmer "no longer depends on what he can raise or make at home for his living for he can bring in things from other parts of our country. As roads improve, the country as a whole will improve, therefore, good roads are requisite to social progress" ("How Good Roads Help the Farmer," *Carthage Courier*, March 17, 1927).

41. Tennessee, Department of Public Instruction, *Course of Study*, 163–70; the sick body–sick mind quotation comes from a guide for a 1923 education week, planned and cosponsored by the American Legion, the National Education Association, and the U.S. Bureau of Education, outlined in the *Tennessee Educational Bulletin*, vol. 2, no. 8 (October 1923), 1–3.

In 1922 a public health doctor, invited to Cookeville by the PTA, examined children at the Cookeville City Schools. Of 444 examined, he found only 141 without "defects." Of the defective, 150 had bad teeth, and 144 were underweight. Other common problems included bad eyes, noses, and throats. See

"Results of the Health Examination of the Pupils of Cookeville City Schools," *Putnam County Herald*, April 27, 1922.

42. Butler interview. Huber Butler, J. W. Butler's oldest son and a retired barber, was nineteen years old in 1925 and remembered the events of that summer vividly, most especially because his father went to the Scopes trial in Dayton during the middle of the summer threshing season, leaving young Huber with the remainder of the work. According to Huber Butler, his family lived off the farm, growing ten acres of corn and "corn field beans," which were dried for winter consumption. They had an apple orchard and also raised peaches. Butler and his siblings were given land by their father when they married: "set up," as Huber Butler put it. See also Butler, Biographical Questionnaires.

43. "Prohibition to a Finish," *Macon County Times*, March 11, 1920. On the other hand, perhaps Butler was just ahead of his time.

44. J. W. Butler, "Schools," *Macon County Times*, June 17, 1920; "What Would I Do?," *Macon County Times*, January 26, 1922.

45. Butler interview; "What Would I Do?," *Macon County Times*, January 26, 1922.

46. Butler interview; Ginger, *Six Days or Forever?*, chap. 1. Butler's official committee assignment was to the House Committee on Charitable Institutions; see Tennessee General Assembly, *House Journal*, 1923.

47. Of the other delegates from the Upper Cumberland, only Senator W. A. Overton, representing Clay, Fentress, Jackson, Overton, Pickett, and Putnam Counties, voted against the bill. All representatives present voted for the bill, as did the other four state senators from the Upper Cumberland. Vote tallies on House Bill 185 from Tennessee General Assembly, *House Journal*, 1925; see 18, 21, 248, 648, 655, 741; Governor's message, 741–45; Tennessee General Assembly, *Senate Journal*, 1925; Bailey, "Enactment of Tennessee's Anti-Evolution Law," 472–90.

48. "Fights Evolution to Uphold Bible," *New York Times*, July 5, 1925. In an editorial July 7 the *Times* noted that Butler was not a fanatic and that, given his premise that the government and the home rested on the Bible, his antievolution law was completely logical.

49. "Fights Evolution to Uphold Bible," *New York Times*, July 5, 1925.

50. Butler interview; Ginger, *Six Days or Forever?*, 145–46. Huber Butler has a photograph of his father with Bryan at the trial.

51. Butler interview; DeLozier, *Putnam County*, 219–20; *Carthage Courier*, July 2, 23, 30, October 1, 1925; Minutes of the Enon Baptist Association, 1925; Minutes of Stone Association of Baptists, 1925.

52. George G. Webb, "Repeal of the Butler Act," 14–17.

53. Butler interview. The weekly newspapers in the region were still running "correspondents" from communities in Ohio and Michigan as late as the 1970s.

Epilogue

1. Based on data supplied by the Upper Cumberland Development District, Cookeville, Tennessee. The 1940 data is from U.S. Department of Commerce,

Regional Employment by Industry. The information about 1990 employment patterns is from an Upper Cumberland Development District survey, "Selected Labor Force and Commuting Characteristics."

2. Tennessee State Planning Commission, *Tennessee*, 89–90; *The Economy and People of Cookeville and Putnam County*, October 1964.

3. Tennessee State Planning Commission, *Tennessee*, 71–85. The report's analysis of the farmer's prospects applied to farmers throughout the state, not just in the Upper Cumberland. However, since the Upper Cumberland lost population at a faster rate than any other Tennessee region during the 1950s, one would assume that conditions for regional farmers were just as bad if not worse.

4. Ibid., 20, 94.

5. All statistics come from reports kindly furnished by the Upper Cumberland Development District and indicate conditions in 1990 unless otherwise noted: "1990 Population by Age Group"; "Various Social and Economic Indicators"; "Selected Labor Force and Commuting Characteristics: 1990" for each of the counties in the region; "Adult Population by Highest Educational Attainment"; "1989 Poverty Statistics." See also U.S. Department of Commerce, *Regional Employment by Industry*. The Upper Cumberland as a whole still has very few residents of color. Cumberland County has 42 black residents out of a population of 34,736; Fentress has 2 black residents. Putnam is the only county in the region to show racial or ethnic diversity, with 457 Asian, 294 Hispanic, and 873 black citizens in a population of 51,373. See Upper Cumberland Development District, "1990 Population by Race and Hispanic Origin."

6. Upper Cumberland Development District, "Selected Labor Force and Commuting Characteristics: 1990," "1989 Income Data," and "1989 Poverty Statistics." Note that the regional median family household income includes Cannon, Van Buren, and Warren Counties, which are included in the Upper Cumberland Development District but not in this study.

7. Upper Cumberland Development District, "Adult Population by Highest Educational Attainment." These statistics were produced by sampling the 1990 census; "adult" refers to individuals over twenty-five.

BIBLIOGRAPHY

The following abbreviations are used in the bibliography.

CCEML   Clara Cox Epperson Memorial Library, Cookeville, Tenn.
DCHS   Disciples of Christ Historical Society, Nashville, Tenn.
JWML   Jere Whitson Memorial Library, Tennessee Technological University, Cookeville
NA   National Archives, Washington, D.C.
NARC   National Archives and Record Center, East Point, Ga.
SBCHLA   Southern Baptist Convention Historical Library and Archives, Nashville, Tenn.
HLUT   Special Collections of the Hoskins Library, University of Tennessee, Knoxville
TSLA   Tennessee State Library and Archives, Nashville

Primary Sources

County Records

DeKalb County Circuit Court Clerk's Office, Minute Books. Civil and Criminal. Vol. 5, November 1893–May 1895. TSLA.
DeKalb County Will Books, 1890–1900. TSLA.
Estate Inventories, 1893–99, 1904, 1914. Putnam County Courthouse. Cookeville, Tenn.

Church Records

Alldredge, E. P. *Southern Baptist Handbook, 1923*. Nashville: Baptist Sunday School Board, 1924. SBCHLA.
Bledsoe Missionary Baptist Association. 1919–30. SBCHLA.
Defeated Creek Missionary Baptist Church. Smith County, Tenn. Records, 1837–1980. TSLA.
First Baptist Church. Cookeville, Tenn. 1873–1939. SBCHLA.
First Baptist Church. Monterey, Tenn. 1927–43. SBCHLA.
Lafayette Baptist Church. Lafayette, Tenn. 1849–1958. SBCHLA.
Minutes of the Enon Baptist Association. 1900–1935. SBCHLA.
Minutes of the Riverside Association of Missionary Baptists. 33rd Annual Session, September 30–October 1, 1920. SBCHLA.
Minutes of the Salem Baptist Association. September 15–17, 1920. SBCHLA.
Minutes of the Stone Association of Baptists. 60th Annual Session, October 15–17, 1925. SBCHLA.

Minutes of the Thirty-third Annual Session of the New Salem Missionary
 Baptist Association. September 28–30, 1920. SBCHLA.
Mount Union Baptist Church. Clarkrange, Tenn. 1870–1941. SBCHLA.
New Bildad Primitive Baptist Church of Jesus Christ. DeKalb County, Tenn.
 Records, 1857–1919. TSLA.
Old Bildad Baptist Church of Christ. Keltonburg, DeKalb County, Tenn. Rec-
 ords, 1812–1925. TSLA.
Pleasant Grove Methodist Church. Gentry, Tenn. Box 31, Putnam County Pa-
 pers. TSLA.
Spring Creek Baptist Church. Jackson County, Tenn. Records, 1845–1968. TSLA.

Interviews, Manuscripts, and Papers

Butler, Huber. Interview by the author. Carthage, Tenn. June 1987.
Butler, John Washington. 1875–1952. Biographical Questionnaires, 1922.
 TSLA.
Claxton, Philander Priestly. Papers. HLUT.
Hutchings family interviews. Alvin York Collection. JWML.
Langford, Polly Draper. Diary. September 26, 1888–May 1889. TSLA.
Roberts, Governor Albert H. Papers. TSLA.
Rye, Governor Tom. Papers. TSLA.
Tennessee Central Railroad Papers. TSLA.
Tinsley, Mary Kirkpatrick. Diary. 1891–94. TSLA.

Newspapers

Regional newspapers from the period studied are available on microfilm at the
Tennessee State Library and Archives. In most cases a complete set is not available. In some cases only one or two editions of a paper have been saved. The
author endeavored to look at all regional papers published from 1890 through
1925. Regional papers are listed by county.

Baptist and Reflector, 1890–1900. SBCHLA.
Gospel Advocate, 1890–1925. DCHS.
New York Times, July 1925.

Clay County
Bill Fiske's Bugle, 1912–14.
Celina Herald, 1906.
Clay County Tribune, 1899.

Cumberland County
Crossville Chronicle, 1894–1925.
Crossville News-Democrat, 1898–99.
Crossville Times, 1886–89.
Tennessee Times, 1889–94.

DeKalb County
Alexandria Times, 1894–1918.
Smithville Review, 1897–1925.

Fentress County
Allardt Gazette, 1891–95.
Fentress County Gazette, 1895–1916.

Jackson County
Gainesboro Sentinel, 1898–1914.
Jackson County Sentinel, 1914–25.

Macon County
Macon County News, 1908–16.
Macon County Times, 1920–25.

Overton County
Golden Age, 1914–21.
Livingston Enterprise, 1898–1925.

Putnam County
Cookeville Press, 1889–1914.
Putnam County Herald, 1903–25.

Smith County
Carthage Courier, 1913–25.

White County
Sparta News
White County Favorite, 1896–1916.

Reports and Proceedings

Many of the following reports, while published, are not easy to find. Researchers interested in Tennessee agriculture should begin at the University of Tennessee. For current information on the Upper Cumberland economy, the Upper Cumberland Development District, Cookeville, Tenn., is a reliable and helpful source. No publication dates are given for the Upper Cumberland Development District reports listed here, but the information is from the 1990 census.

Allred, Charles. "An Economic Analysis of Farming in Overton County." *Livingston Enterprise,* August 17, 1928.
Allred, Charles, Samuel W. Atkins, and William E. Hendrix. *Human and Physical Resources of Tennessee.* Knoxville: University of Tennessee Rural Research Monograph No. 63, 1939.
Allred, Charles, and J. C. Powell. "Meat Consumption in Rural Tennessee, with Regional Comparisons." Agricultural Economics and Rural Sociology. Agricultural Extension Report No. 18, University of Tennessee, 1936.
Allred, Charles, James L. Robinson, and B. H. Luebke. "Rural Credit in Tennessee." University of Tennessee Rural Research Series No. 82, 1938.
Allred, Charles, and A. C. Robinson. "Significant Changes in Agriculture of Northeast Highland Rim." Rural Research Series Monograph No. 61. Agricultural Economics and Rural Sociology Department, University of Tennessee, 1937.

Brandon, A. J. "President's Address." *Seventeenth Annual Session of Public School Officers' Association*. Clarksville, Tenn.: W. P. Titus, 1904.

Educational Conditions in Tennessee. Bulletin of the Southern Education Board. Vol. 1, no. 3, December 1902.

Historical World War Data. Compiled by Mrs. Rutledge Smith, 1931–32. TSLA.

Perry, Gene. "Eastern Part of Clay County, Tenn. Preliminary Farm Location Map Showing Geological Structure Contours." TSLA.

Proceedings of the Seventh Annual Public School Officers Association of Tennessee. Nashville: Marshall and Bruce, 1894.

"Progress of State System." *Bulletin of the Tennessee State Teacher's Association*. February 1926, 6–16.

Social Survey of Putnam County, Tennessee. Prepared under the Auspices of Putnam County Red Cross, under Direction of Miss Marguerite Thompson, Southern Division, American Red Cross. TSLA.

Tennessee State Planning Commission. *Tennessee: Population, Labor Force, and Employment Projections and Interpretations*. Publication No. 358, June 1967.

39th Annual Meeting of TSTA, Monteagle, Tennessee, July 25–27, 1905. Clarksville, Tenn.: W. P. Titus, 1905.

Upper Cumberland Development District. "Adult Population by Highest Educational Attainment."

——. "1989 Income Data."

——. "1989 Poverty Statistics."

——. "1990 Population by Race and Hispanic Origin."

——. "1990 Population by Age Group."

——. "Selected Labor Force and Commuting Characteristics: 1990."

——. "Various Social and Economic Indicators."

U.S. Department of Commerce. *Regional Employment by Industry, 1940–1970*. Decennial Series for United States, Regions, States, Counties. Washington, D.C.: Government Printing Office, 1975. Stock No. 003-024-01119-1.

Tennessee Department of Education Materials

Annual Reports of County Superintendents, 1891–92, 1901–2. Department of Education Records. Record Group 51. TSLA.

Brister, J. W. *Biennial Report of the State Superintendent of Public Instruction for Tennessee for the Scholastic Year Ending June 30, 1911–1912*. Nashville: Brandon, 1912. TSLA.

Fitzpatrick, Morgan C. *Annual Report of the State Superintendent of Public Instruction for Tennessee for the Scholastic Year Ending June 30, 1900*. Nashville: Gospel Advocate, 1901. TSLA.

Harned, P. L. *State of Tennessee. Annual Report of the Department of Education for the Scholastic Year Ending June 30, 1925*. Nashville: Ambrose, 1925. TSLA.

——. *State of Tennessee. Annual Report of the Department of Education for the Scholastic Year Ending June 30, 1931*. Jackson, Tenn.: Long, Johnson, 1931. TSLA.

Jones, Robert L. *Biennial Report of the State Superintendent of Public Instruction for the Scholastic Year Ending June 30, 1909–1910*. Nashville: Ambrose, 1911. TSLA.

Williams, Albert. *Biennial Report of the State Superintendent of Public Instruction for the Scholastic Year Ending June 30, 1919–1920.* Nashville: Ambrose, 1920. TSLA.

Local Histories

"Alpine Mountain History: The Old and the New." Pamphlet compiled by the Dale Hollow Larger Parish Youth, Overton and Pickett County, Tenn., ca. 1960. DCHS.

Blankenship, Harold G. *History of Macon County Tennessee.* Tompkinsville, Ky.: Privately published, 1986.

Dodge, Emma Florence. *Souvenir History of Pleasant Hill Academy, 1884–1924.* Kingsport, Tenn.: Privately published, 1924.

Foster, Austin P. *Counties of Tennessee.* Nashville: Department of Education, State of Tennessee, 1923.

"A History of the Tennessee Central Railway Company." Typescript. CCEML.

Hogue, Albert R. *History of Fentress County: World War Memorial Edition.* Nashville, 1916, 1920. Reprint, Baltimore: Regional Publication Co., 1975.

Rogers, E. G. *Memorable Historical Accounts of White County and Area.* Collegedale, Tenn.: College Press, 1972.

Seals, Rev. Monroe. *History of White County Tennessee.* Spartanburg, S.C.: Reprint, 1974.

Stratton, Lora S., and Nettie M. Stratton. *And This Is Grassy Cove.* Crossville, Tenn.: Chronicle, 1938. TSLA.

Books, Articles, and Newsletters

Allison, Judge John. *Notable Men of Tennessee.* 2 vols. Atlanta: Southern Historical Association, 1905.

Brown, J. B. *Course of Study, Elementary Grades, Public Schools of Tennessee.* Nashville: Ewing, 1921.

Douglass, H. Paul. *Christian Reconstruction in the South.* Boston: Pilgrim, 1909.

Du Bois, W. E. B. *The Autobiography of W. E. B. Du Bois: A Soliloquy on Viewing My Life from the Last Decade of Its First Century.* New York: International, 1968.

Gailor, Thomas Frank. "Moral Training in the Public Schools." *Tennessee Educator* 1 (1915): 1–7.

Gregory, Calvin. *Cal's Column.* Edited by Christine Spivey Jones. Privately published, 1986.

Grime, John Harvey. *History of Middle Tennessee Baptists.* Nashville: Baptist and Reflector, 1902.

——. *Recollections of a Long Life.* Privately published, n.d.

Hale, Will T., and Dixon L. Merritt. *A History of Tennessee and Tennesseans.* Chicago: Lewis, 1913.

Hooker, Elizabeth. *Religion in the Highlands: Native Churches and Missionary Enterprise in the Southern Appalachian Area.* New York: Polygraphic Co. of America for the Home Missions Council, 1933.

Hull, Cordell. *The Memoirs of Cordell Hull.* Vol. 1. New York: Macmillan, 1948.

Killebrew, J. B., and Herbert Myrick. *Tobacco Leaf: Its Culture and Cure, Marketing and Manufacture.* New York: Orange Judd, 1897.

Oakley, John T. "Fifty[-one, -two] Years in the Ministry." *Carthage Courier,* 1921–24.

Porter, J. W., ed. *Feminism: Woman and Her Work.* Louisville, Ky.: Baptist Book Concern, 1923.

Tennessee Bulletin. PTA Newsletter. February 1927.

Tennessee. Department of Public Instruction. *Course of Study, Elementary Schools, 1921.* Nashville: Ewing, 1921.

Tennessee Educational Bulletin. Vol. 5. Nashville: R. L. Polk, 1887.

Tennessee State Gazetter and Business Directory. Vol. 5. Nashville: R. L. Polk, 1887.

Wharton, May Cravath. *Doctor Woman of the Cumberlands.* Pleasant Hill, Tenn.: Uplands, 1953.

"What One County Has Done." *Tennessee Educators Bulletin* 4, no. 5 (October–November–December 1925): 2–3.

White, Marie. "A Challenge." *Bulletin of the Tennessee State Teacher's Association.* January 1924, 25–25.

Who's Who in Tennessee. Memphis: Paul and Douglass, 1911.

Young and Company's Business and Professional Directory of the Cities and Towns of Tennessee. Atlanta: Young and Co., 1906–7.

U.S. Census Publications

Although use of the federal census rolls is all but mandatory for social historians today, the published census contains a lot of pertinent information, sometimes giving statistics down to the county level. Most of the data in this book on crops, livestock, and tenancy was found in the published census and in related government publications. The published census can be confusingly catalogued, since publication has been the charge of different government departments over the decades.

Census Reports. *Twelfth Census of the United States, Taken in the Year 1900. Population.* Vol. 1, part 1. Washington, D.C.: U.S. Census Office, 1901.

Census Reports. *Twelfth Census of the United States, Taken in the Year 1900. Agriculture.* Vol. 5, part 1. Washington, D.C.: U.S. Census Office, 1901.

Department of Commerce and Labor. Bureau of the Census. *Religious Bodies: 1906.* Part 1. Washington, D.C.: U.S. Government Printing Office, 1910.

——. *Thirteenth Census of the United States. Abstract of the Census with Supplement for Tennessee.* Washington, D.C.: U.S. Government Printing Office, 1913.

Department of Commerce. Bureau of the Census. *United States Census of Agriculture, 1925.* Part 2, *The Southern States.* Washington, D.C.: U.S. Government Printing Office, 1927.

Department of the Interior. Census Office. *Report on Manufacturing Industries in the United States at the Eleventh Census: 1890.* Washington, D.C.: U.S. Government Printing Office, 1895.

——. *Report on Population of the United States at the Eleventh Census: 1890.* Part 1. Washington, D.C.: U.S. Government Printing Office, 1895.

———. *Report on Statistics of Churches in the United States at the Eleventh Census: 1890*. Washington, D.C.: U.S. Government Printing Office, 1894.

———. *Report on the Statistics of Agriculture in the United States at the Eleventh Census: 1890*. Washington, D.C.: U.S. Government Printing Office, 1895.

U.S. Department of Commerce. Bureau of the Census. *Fifteenth Census of the United States: 1930. Population.* Vol. 3, part 2. Washington, D.C.: U.S. Government Printing Office, 1932.

———. *Sixteenth Census of the United States, 1940. Agriculture.* Part 4, *East-South Central Division.* Washington, D.C.: U.S. Government Printing Office, 1942.

State and Federal Government Records

Manuscript of the 1880 agricultural and population census rolls for Smith County, Tenn., TSLA. Microfilm.

Manuscript of the 1900 census rolls for Clay, Cumberland, DeKalb, Fentress, Jackson, Macon, Overton, Pickett, Putnam, Smith and White Counties, Tenn., TSLA. Microfilm.

Records of the Council of National Defense. Record Group 62. NA.

Tennessee. General Assembly. House of Representatives. *House Journal.*

Tennessee. General Assembly. Senate. *Senate Journal.* 1925.

U.S. District Court, 1918–19. Records of the Middle District of Tennessee, Cookeville Division. Records of the Northeastern Division of Middle Tennessee. NARC.

U.S. Selective Service Act Enforcement Records, 1917–19. Draft Cards. NARC.

Secondary Sources

Books, Articles, Theses, Dissertations, and Collected Essays

Alstrom, Sidney E. *A Religious History of the American People.* New Haven: Yale University Press, 1972.

"American Rural and Farm Women in Historical Perspective," *Agricultural History* 67 (Spring 1993): 1–291.

Ammerman, Nancy T. "North American Protestant Fundamentalism." *Fundamentalisms Observed.* Edited by Martin E. Marty and R. Scott Appleby. Chicago: University of Chicago Press, 1991: 1–65.

Arnow, Harriette Simpson. *Seedtime on the Cumberland.* New York: Macmillan, 1960.

Ayers, Edward. *The Promise of the New South: Life after Reconstruction.* New York: Oxford, 1992.

———. *Vengeance and Justice: Crime and Punishment in the Nineteenth Century American South.* New York: Oxford University Press, 1984.

Bailey, Kenneth K. "The Enactment of Tennessee's Anti-Evolution Law." *Journal of Southern History* 16 (1950): 472–49.

Banfield, Edward C. *The Moral Basis of a Backward Society.* 1958. Reprint, New York: Free Press, 1967.

Baron, Hal. *Those Who Stayed Behind: Rural Society in Nineteenth Century New England.* Cambridge: Cambridge University Press, 1984.

Birdwell, Michael E. "The Making of the Movie *Sergeant York*: A Journey from Reality into Myth." Master's thesis, Tennessee Technological University, 1990.

———. *The Sterns Coal Company, 1902–1975.* Cookeville: Upper Cumberland Institute, Tennessee Technological University, 1989.

Bowles, Samuel, and Herbert Gintis. *Schooling in Capitalist America: Educational Reform and the Contradictions of Economic Life.* New York: Basic Books, 1976.

Braden, Kenneth S. "The Wizard of Overton: Governor A. H. Roberts." *Tennessee Historical Quarterly* 43 (Fall 1984): 273–94.

Breen, William J. *Uncle Sam at Home: Civilian Mobilization, Wartime Federalism, and the Council of National Defense, 1917–1919.* Westport, Conn.: Greenwood Press, 1984.

Burt, Jesse C., Jr. "Four Decades of the Nashville, Chattanooga, and St. Louis Railway, 1763–1916." *Tennessee Historical Quarterly* 9 (1950): 99–130.

Carter, Cullen T. *History of the Tennessee Conference and a Brief Summary of the General Conference of the Methodist Church from the Frontier to the Present Time.* Nashville: n.p., 1948.

Chambers, John Whiteclay, II. *To Raise an Army: The Draft Comes to Modern America.* New York: Free Press, 1987.

Chatfield, Charles. *For Peace and Justice: Pacifism in America, 1914–1941.* Knoxville: University of Tennessee Press, 1971.

Davidson, James West, William E. Gienapp, Christine Leigh Heyrman, Mark H. Lytle, and Michael B. Stoff. *Nation of Nations.* New York: McGraw Hill, 1990.

DeBerg, Betty A. *Ungodly Women: Gender and the First Wave of American Fundamentalism.* Minneapolis: Fortress, 1990.

Degler, Carl N. *At Odds: Women and the Family in America from the Revolution to the Present.* New York: Oxford University Press, 1980.

DeLozier, Mary Jean. *Putnam County, Tennessee, 1850–1970.* Cookeville, Tenn.: Putnam County, 1979.

Denning, Jeanette Keith. "A History of the Resort Business in Red Boiling Springs, Tennessee." Master's thesis, Tennessee Technological University, 1982.

Dickinson, Calvin. "Our Fathers' Houses: Architecture in the Upper Cumberland." In *Lend an Ear: Heritage of the Tennessee Upper Cumberland,* edited by Calvin Dickinson et al. Lanham, Md.: University Press of America, 1983.

Dorman, Robert L. *Revolt of the Provinces: The Regionalist Movement in America, 1920–1945.* Chapel Hill: University of North Carolina Press, 1993.

Douglas, Byrd. *Steamboatin' on the Cumberland.* Nashville: Tennessee Book Co., 1961.

Doyle, Don H. *Nashville in the New South.* Knoxville: University of Tennessee Press, 1985.

———. *Nashville since the 1920s.* Knoxville: University of Tennessee Press, 1985.

Eigelbach, William B. "The Rise and Fall of a Summer School." University of Tennessee, Knoxville. *Library Development Review,* 1987/88, 16–19.

Faragher, John Mack. *Sugar Creek: Life on the Illinois Prairie*. New Haven: Yale University Press, 1986.

Farish, Hunter Dickinson. *The Circuit Rider Dismounts: A Social History of Southern Methodism, 1865–1900*. Richmond: Dietz, 1938.

Fink, Deborah. *Agrarian Women: Wives and Mothers in Rural Nebraska, 1880–1940*. Chapel Hill: University of North Carolina Press, 1992.

Fite, Gilbert. *American Farmers, the New Minority*. Bloomington: Indiana University Press, 1981.

Flynt, Wayne. "One in the Spirit, Many in the Flesh: Southern Evangelicals." In *Varieties of Southern Evangelicalism*, edited by Samuel Hill. Macon, Ga.: Mercer University Press, 1981.

Folmsbee, Stanley J., Robert E. Corlew, and Enoch L. Mitchell. *Tennessee: A Short History*. Knoxville: University of Tennessee Press, 1969.

"Forum: The Origins of Public High Schools." *History of Education Quarterly* 27 (Summer 1987): 241–58.

Fredrickson, George. "Down on the Farm." *New York Review*, April 23, 1987, 36–39.

Friedman, Jean E. *The Enclosed Garden: Women and Community in the Evangelical South*. Chapel Hill: University of North Carolina Press, 1985.

Ginger, Ray. *Six Days or Forever?* Boston: Beacon, 1974.

Graves, Susan B. *Evins of Tennessee: Twenty-Five Years in Congress*. New York: Popular Library, 1971.

Greene, Lee Seifert, and Robert Sterling Avery. *Government in Tennessee*. Knoxville: University of Tennessee Press, 1962.

Hahn, Steven. *The Roots of Southern Populism: Yeoman Farmers and the Transformation of the Georgia Upcountry, 1850–1890*. New York: Oxford University Press, 1983.

Hahn, Steven, and Jonathan Prude. *The Countryside in the Age of Capitalist Transformation*. Chapel Hill: University of North Carolina Press, 1985.

Harrell, David E., Jr. "Religious Pluralism: Catholics, Jews, and Sectarians." In *Religion in the South*, edited by Charles Reagan Wilson. Jackson: University Press of Mississippi, 1985.

———. "The South: Seedbed of Sectarianism." In *Varieties of Southern Evangelicalism*, edited by Samuel S. Hill. Macon, Ga.: Mercer University Press, 1981.

Hart, Roger L. *Redeemers, Bourbons, and Populists: Tennessee 1870–1886*. Baton Rouge: Louisiana State University Press, 1975.

Hatfield, James Monroe. "A History and Educational Survey of Putnam County, Tennessee." Master's thesis, University of Tennessee, 1937.

Hewitt, Nancy A. "Beyond the Search for Sisterhood: American Women's History in the 1980s." In *Unequal Sisters: A Multicultural Reader in U.S. Women's History*, edited by Ellen Carol DuBois and Vicki L. Ruis. New York: Routledge, 1990.

Hill, Samuel S. *Southern Churches in Crisis*. New York: Holt, Rinehart and Winston, 1966.

Holt, Andrew David. *The Struggle for a State System of Public Schools in Tennessee, 1903–1936*. New York: Columbia University Press, 1938.

Howell, Benita J. *Survey of Folklife along the Big South Fork of the Cumberland River.* Knoxville: University of Tennessee, Department of Anthropology, 1981.

Huehls, Betty Sparks. "Life in the Coal Towns of White County, Tennessee, 1882–1936." Master's thesis, Tennessee Technological University, 1983.

Isaac, Rhys. *The Transformation of Virginia, 1740–1790.* Chapel Hill: University of North Carolina Press, published for the Institute of Early American History and Culture, 1982.

Jensen, Joan. *Promise to the Land.* Albuquerque: University of New Mexico Press, 1991.

Jones, Lu Ann, and Nancy Grey Osterud. "Breaking New Ground: Oral History and Agricultural History." *Journal of American History* 76 (October 1989): 551–65.

———. "'If I Must Say So Myself': Oral Histories of Rural Women." *Oral History Review,* Fall 1989, 1–23.

Jones, Robert B. *Tennessee at the Crossroads: The State Debt Controversy, 1870–1883.* Knoxville: University of Tennessee Press, 1977.

Katz, Michael B. *Class, Bureaucracy, and Schools: The Illusion of Educational Change in America.* New York: Praeger, 1971.

———. *The Irony of Early School Reform: Educational Innovation in Mid-Nineteenth Century Massachusetts.* Cambridge, Mass.: Harvard University Press, 1968.

Keith, Jeanette. "Lift Tennessee out of the Mud: Ideology and the Good Roads Movement in Tennessee." *Southern Historian* 9 (Spring 1988): 22–37.

Kemp, Homer. "To Humanize Local History: Folk Legend in the Upper Cumberland." In *Lend an Ear: Heritage of the Tennessee Upper Cumberland,* edited by Calvin Dickinson et al. Lanham, Md.: University Press of America, 1983.

Kennedy, David. *Over Here: The First World War and American Society.* Oxford: Oxford University Press, 1980.

Krechniak, Helen Bullard, and Joseph Marshall Krechniak. *Cumberland County's First Hundred Years.* Crossville, Tenn.: Centennial Committee, 1956.

Kulikoff, Allan. "Households and Markets: Toward a New Synthesis of American Agrarian History." *William and Mary Quarterly* 50, no. 2 (1993): 342–55.

Lee, David. *Sergeant York: An American Hero.* Lexington: University Press of Kentucky, 1985.

Lewis, Charles Lee. *Philander Priestly Claxton, Crusader for Public Education.* Knoxville: University of Tennessee Press, 1948.

Lewis, David Levering. *W. E. B. Du Bois: A Biography of a Race, 1868–1919.* New York: Holt, 1993.

Link, William A. *The Paradox of Southern Progressivism, 1880–1930.* Chapel Hill: University of North Carolina Press, 1993.

McDowell, John Patrick. *The Social Gospel in the South: The Women's Home Mission Movement in the Methodist Episcopal Church, South, 1886–1939.* Baton Rouge: Louisiana State University Press, 1982.

McMurry, Sally. "Women's Work in Agriculture: Divergent Trends in England and America, 1800 to 1930." *Comparative Studies in Society and History* 34 (April 1992): 248–70.

Macpherson, Joseph T. "Democratic Progressivism in Tennessee: The Administration of Governor Austin Peay, 1923–1927." Ph.D. diss., Vanderbilt University, 1969.

Mathews, Donald G. *Religion in the Old South.* Chicago: University of Chicago Press, 1977.

Mitchell, Theodore R., and Robert Lowe. "To Sow Contentment: Philanthropy, Scientific Agriculture, and the Making of the New South, 1906–1920." *Journal of Social History* 24 (Winter 1990): 317–40.

Montel, Lynwood William. *Don't Go up Kettle Creek: Verbal Legacy of the Upper Cumberland.* Knoxville: University of Tennessee Press, 1983.

Neth, Mary. "Gender and the Family Labor System: Defining Work in the Rural Midwest." *Journal of Social History* 27 (Spring 1994): 563–77.

Norton, Herman. *Religion in Tennessee, 1777–1945.* Knoxville: University of Tennessee Press, 1981.

Osterud, Nancy Grey. *Bonds of Community: The Lives of Farm Women in Nineteenth Century New York.* Ithaca: Cornell University Press, 1991.

——. "Gender and the Transition to Capitalism in Rural America." *Agricultural History* 67 (Spring 1993): 14–29.

Overton, Walter Bruce. "An Educational, Economic, and Community Survey of Jackson County, Tennessee." Master's thesis, University of Tennessee, 1929.

Ownby, Ted. *Subduing Satan: Religion, Recreation, and Manhood in the Rural South, 1865–1920.* Chapel Hill: University of North Carolina Press, 1990.

Owsley, Frank Lawrence. *Plain Folk of the Old South.* Baton Rouge: Louisiana State University Press, 1949.

Peterson, H. C., and Gilbert C. Fite. *Opponents of War, 1917–1918.* Madison: University of Wisconsin Press, 1957.

Reichard, Gary Warren. "The Republican Victory of 1920 in Tennessee: An Analysis." Master's thesis, Vanderbilt University, 1966.

Roach, Dewey. "Grime, John Harvey." In *Encyclopedia of Southern Baptists.* Nashville: Broadman, 1958.

Robison, Daniel Meritt. *Bob Taylor and the Agrarian Revolt in Tennessee.* Chapel Hill: University of North Carolina Press, 1935.

Sachs, Carolyn E. *The Invisible Farmers: Women in Agricultural Production.* Totowa, N.J.: Rowman and Allanheld, 1983.

Sanders, Charles H. "An Educational and Economic Survey of Pickett County, Tennessee." Master's thesis, University of Tennessee, 1924.

"Scopes Trial." In *The Readers Companion to American History,* edited by Eric Foner and John A. Garraty. New York: Houghton Mifflin, 1991.

Schulman, Steven A. "The Lumber Industry of the Upper Cumberland Valley." *Tennessee Historical Quarterly* 32 (Fall 1973): 255–64.

Seccombe, Wally. "Patriarchy Stabilized: The Construction of the Male Breadwinner Wage Norm in Nineteenth Century Britain." *Social History* 2 (January 1986): 53–96.

Shea, Jonathan P., and Stuart A. Rosenfield. "The Urbanization of Rural Schools, 1840–1970." In *Education in Rural America: A Reassessment of Conventional Wisdom,* edited by Jonathan Shea. Boulder, Colo.: Westview Press, 1977.

Stevens, Edward, Jr., Michael Katz, and Maris A. Vinovskis. "Forum: The Origins of Public High Schools." *History of Education Quarterly* 27 (Summer 1986): 241–58.

Sturgis, Cynthia. " 'How're You Gonna Keep 'Em down on the Farm?' Rural Women and the Urban Model in Utah." *Agricultural History* 60 (Spring 1986): 182–99.

Sulzer, Elmer G. "The Three 'Tennessee Centrals' of Tennessee." *Tennessee Historical Quarterly* 30 (Summer 1971): 210–14.

Thomas, Keith. *Religion and the Decline of Magic.* New York: Scribner's, 1971.

Thorogood, James E. *A Financial History of Tennessee since 1870.* Sewanee: n.p., 1949.

Tilly, Louise A., and Joan W. Scott. *Women, Work, and Family.* New York: Holt, Rinehart and Winston, 1978.

Tindall, George Brown. *The Emergence of the New South, 1913–1945.* Baton Rouge: Louisiana State University Press, 1967.

Ueda, Reed. *Avenues to Adulthood: The Origins of the High School and Social Mobility in an American Suburb.* Cambridge: Cambridge University Press, 1987.

Vickers, Gregory K. "Woman's Place: Images of Womanhood in The Southern Baptist Convention, 1888–1929." Master's thesis, Vanderbilt School of Religion, 1986.

Vinovskis, Maris A. *The Origins of Public High Schools: A Reexamination of the Beverly High School Controversy.* Madison: University of Wisconsin Press, 1985.

Webb, George G. "The Repeal of the Butler Act." *Journal of the Tennessee Academy of Sciences* 59 (January–April 1984): 14–47.

Webb, Thomas G. *DeKalb County.* Memphis, Tenn.: Memphis State University Press, 1986.

Wells, Robert V. *Uncle Sam's Family: Issues in and Perspectives on American Demographic History.* Albany: State University of New York Press, 1985.

Whitaker, Sarah. "A History of Livingston Academy from 1909 Through 1947." Master's thesis, Tennessee Technological University, 1964.

Whiteaker, Larry. "The Civil War in the Upper Cumberland." In *Lend an Ear: Heritage of the Tennessee Upper Cumberland,* edited by Calvin Dickinson et al. Lanham, Md.: University Press of America, 1983.

Williams, Samuel C. *General John T. Wilder, Commander of the Lightening Brigade.* Bloomington: Indiana University Press, 1936.

———. *The Political Economy of the Cotton South: Households, Markets, and Wealth in the Nineteenth Century.* New York: Norton, 1978.

Wolfe, Charles. "Folk Songs and Fiddles: Music of the Upper Cumberland." In *Lend an Ear: Heritage of the Tennessee Upper Cumberland,* edited by Calvin Dickinson et al. Lanham, Md.: University Press of America, 1983.

———. *Tennessee Strings: The Story of Country Music in Tennessee.* Knoxville: University of Tennessee Press, 1977.

Wood, Gordon S. "Inventing American Capitalism." *New York Review,* June 9, 1994, 44–49.

Woodward, C. Vann. *Tom Watson, Agrarian Rebel.* New York: Macmillan, 1938.

Wright, Gavin. *Old South, New South: Revolutions in the Southern Economy since the Civil War.* New York: Basic Books, 1986.

Wyatt-Brown, Bertram. *Southern Honor: Ethic and Behavior in the Old South.* New York: Oxford University Press, 1982.

Miscellaneous

Birdwell, Michael E. Hutchings manuscript. In possession of Mr. Birdwell.

The Davidson-Wilder Story. Documentary by Public Television Station WCTE, Cookeville, Tenn., 1987.

Cookeville Citizen, January 29, 1962; January 21, 1964; May 5, 1964.

Cookeville Herald-Citizen, December 24, 1986.

"Final Report, Fentress County." Architectural Survey Conducted by Upper Cumberland Humanities and Social Sciences Institute, Tennessee Technological University, 1983–1984, for the Tennessee Historical Commission.

Index

Dixon, W. L., 127–28
Dixon Springs (Smith County),
186
Dodge, Emma Florence, 125
Doss, Bertha, 33
Double Springs (Putnam County),
82
Douglas, Lee, 163
Douglass, H. Paul, 42–43
Doyle (White County), 59, 121
Draft evaders, World War I, 166–68
Draper, Fanny, 40–41
Draper, James W. and Lucy, 40–41
Draper, Jim (son), 40–41
Draper, Lucy (daughter), 40–41
Draper, Mourning, 40–41
Draper, Polly: diary, 40–41
Draper, Robert Garland, 120
Dunlap, Fred, 168

Economic development, postbellum,
9–10
Economy in Upper Cumberland in
1890s, 12–25
Education: county systems of in
1890s, 66–67; attitudes toward,
67–68, 126–30, 138; local control
as issue in, 68; progressive expectations for, 118–19; and progressive reform campaigns, 118–42;
and social mobility, 119–20; goals
of, 123, 127–28, 190–91; and
alienation, 125–26; and discipline,
127–28; funding issues, 133;
effects of school reform on, 134–
42; high schools, 138–41; urban
orientation of, 190–91, 204, 245
(n. 35); and religion in 1920s,
197–98; reforms in 1920s, 199–
202; in 1990, 214. See also Compulsory education; County board
of education; County superintendents; Schools; Teachers
Elam, E. A., 147
Elites: and education, 119–20;
and World War I, 152. See also
Conscription

Enon Baptist Association, 185, 206
Ensor, Pastor Simon M., 196
Epperson, Clara Cox, 156
Epperson, John A., 156

Fairfield Glade (Cumberland
County), 213, 214
Falling Water River, 5
Familism, 222 (n. 1)
Family: in 1890s, 26–44, 35; as
transmitter of political culture,
58–60, 62; as factor in public
order, 72–75; and progressivism,
106–7; and the Bible, 206–7. See
also Family economy; Household
composition
Family economy: in 1890s, 12–25;
effects of railroad on, 84–89; in
1920s, 174–76
Family limitation: in 1890s, 34, 225
(n. 19)
Family size: in 1890s, 34; in 1920s,
178–79
Farm agents, 177
Farmers' Alliance, 61–62
Farming: semisubsistence, 7, 10,
173–74, 178; as business, 13–14,
176, 178; as normative occupation, 119; and women's work,
188–89; culturally depreciated,
202–3
Farm size, 84; in 1920s, 175–76
Federal Aid Highways Act, 109
Federal Espionage Law, 159
Federated Women's Club, 156
Feminism, menace of, 185
Fentress County, 5, 7, 16, 36, 61, 78,
81, 83, 111, 113, 129, 130, 139,
144, 145, 146, 152, 162, 214; vote
on secession, 8, population and
racial composition, 9, tenancy rate
in 1890, 15, politics, 59. See also
York, Alvin
Fentress County Gazette, 111, 113
Fertility: in 1890s, 34, 225 (n. 19)
Fertilizer, 220–21 (n. 20)
Folk tales, 37, 38–39

Hull, William, 60
Hunting: as food source in 1890s, 18
Hutchings, Ransom I., 124, 205
Hygiene: in schools, 202–3

Independence: as a virtue, 12. *See
also* Debt
Inheritance practices, 32
Interstate 40 (I-40), 212
Isoline (Cumberland County), 116

Jackson County, 5, 7, 14, 34, 35, 52,
63, 69, 73, 81, 116, 120, 126, 127,
130, 133, 135, 151, 156, 159, 160,
211; vote on secession, 8; tenancy
rate in 1890, 15
Jacobs, J., 162
Jacques, Isaac, 73–74
Jamestown (Fentress County), 113,
163
Jared, Mrs. W. E., 144
Jennings Creek, 56, 63
Johnson, C. C., 32
Jones, R. L., 129, 131
Jones, Tom, 168

Key, C. S., 173
Kittrell, William, 35
Ku Klux Klan, 121, 195; as agents of
traditional morality, 198–99
Kuykendall, Malinda, 41

Lafayette (Macon County), 197, 205
Lafayette Baptist Church, 47, 186,
196
Lafever, Canzada, 35
Law enforcement in 1890s, 71–75
Lawyers, 81
Lee, George Ray, 147
Lemert, Milo, 152
Liberty Loans: drives, 159; analogies
between road bonds and, 180
Lipscomb, A. S., 147
Lipscomb, David, 49, 147
Literacy rates: in 1890s, 67; in
1920s, 175
Little, W. P., 129

Livestock: in 1890s, 16–18, 176; in
1920s, 176
Living conditions, 35–36, 257 (n. 9).
See also Household composition;
Housing
Livingston (Overton County), 82,
114, 115, 116, 117, 134, 138, 150,
152, 159, 179, 180
Livingston Academy, 121, 122, 124,
135, 171, 178, 202
Livingston Methodist Church, 196
Localism, 26; in politics, 59; in
education, 68–69, in road build-
ing, 113, 116, 180–82. *See also*
Churches
Logging. *See* Timber industry
Louisville and Nashville Railroad
(L&N), 79, 81

McClain, Mrs. Ova, 161–62
McDowell, L. L., 163
McGee, S. B., 150, 241 (n. 28). See
also *Golden Age*
McGlasson, G. Lee, 120
McKent, Elizabeth, 40
Macon County, 5, 7, 32, 81, 109,
122, 130, 133, 171, 197, 201, 204,
205; vote on secession, 8; tobacco
production in 1890s, 18; politics,
59
Macon County News, 109
Macon County Singing Convention,
197
Maggart, Oscar, 151
Malone, A., 54
Manufacturing, 10, 180, 213
Market, 21; as determinant in rural
history, 4–5, 13–15
Market opportunities, 18, 177
Marriage: attitudes toward, 23, 25,
27, 29–30, 192–95; weddings in
1890s, 30–31, 224 (n. 9); ages at,
31, 224 (n. 10); as transition for
women, 33. *See also* Gender; Men;
Women
Martin, J. C., 37
Martin, Mahulda, 35

Memphis to Bristol Highway Association, 109

Men: as household heads, 28; age at marriage in 1890s, 31, 224 (n. 10); and gender roles, 31–32; and religion, 37–40; as teachers, 130–31; as heads of household in 1920s, 174; and education in 1920s, 189–90; women's attitudes toward, 193; and employment patterns in 1950s and 1960s, 212–13. *See also* Gender; Marriage; Women

Merchants, 13, 21

Methodist Episcopal Church, South, 46

Methodists, 37, 46, 51, 54, 155, 196–97; and social activism, 48; and women's role, 48–49, 185; ministers, 52; running mission schools, 121

Methodists, Northern, 46

Milk, 20

Ministers, 50–51. *See also* Preachers

Missionaries, Protestant: attitudes toward family life, 42–43; attitudes toward community, 42–43, 123

Mission schools, 121–25; and work ethic, 124–25; and social mobility, 125

Mitchell, Isaiah, 39

Mitchell, John A., 152

Monkey Law. *See* Butler, John Washington; Tennessee Anti-Evolution Law

Monterey (Putnam County), 81, 110, 134

Mont Vale College, 123, 127

Moorman, Hugh B., 152

Morison, James H. S., 152

Mortgages, 33, 112

Moss (Clay County), 133

Mullinax, Dr. W. E., 148

Murphy, W. C., 177

Mynders, Seymour A., 131

Nard, John, 162

Nashville, 7, 8, 13, 23, 77

Nashville and Knoxville Railroad (N&K), 78, 79

Nashville, Chattanooga and St. Louis Railway, 78, 79

New Bildad Primitive Baptist Church of Jesus Christ, 50, 51

"New Dispensation." *See* Gender: in 1920s

New Hope Meeting House, 54

New South, 2, 9–10, 218 (n. 13)

Nineteenth Amendment, 184

North Carolina and St. Louis Railroad, 9–10, 24

North Springs (Jackson County), 56, 63, 211, 212

Oakley, John T., 30, 53

Obey River, 5

Obituaries. *See* Prescriptive literature

Old Bildad Baptist Church of Christ, 51

Old Kentucky Stock Road, 8

Outmigration, 14

Overton County, 5, 7, 81, 82, 83, 88, 111, 117, 121, 122, 130, 133, 150, 149, 151, 156, 159, 175, 177, 178, 180; and road bond controversies, 112–17

Overton County Road Improvement Association, 114

Oxen: in 1890s, 18

Ozone (Cumberland County) 86

Paine, Tom, 54, 215

Pall Mall (Fentress County), 113, 147

Parent-Teachers Association, 156

Patriarchy: as a labor system, 27, 222 (n. 2); in religion, 45, 48–50; and woman suffrage, 185; and woman's place in 1920s, 192–95

Paupers, 70

Peabody Foundation, 131

Peay, Governor Austin, 181, 199–200, 205

Peebles, W. H., 182

"Phebe" (trolley), 82

48; in 1920s, 195–99; religiosity,
197; and the state, 197–98; as
source of social order, 206–7. *See
also* Bible; Christian ideals for
family life; Churches; Redemption: as religious issue
Republicans, 59–60, 61, 64; and
election of 1920, 172–73; and
women voters, 186
Rickman (Overton County), 81
Road building: in 1890s, 69–70; and
progressives, 108–17; and bond
issue controversies, 112–17; in
1920s, 180–82. *See also* Corvée
Roads: quality in early twentieth
century, 110, 116
Roaring River, 5
Roberts, A. H., 116, 122, 171–72,
182, 243 (n. 9)
Roberts, Fate and Sarah, 35
Rodgers, John, 72
"Rolling Stone," 183, 187–88
Roy, Rob, 88
Rugby, 148
Rye, Governor Tom, 157

Savage, John, 61
School directors, 66
School reform campaigns, 131–34
Schools: conditions in 1890s, 66–69;
conditions in early twentieth cen-
tury, 126; enrollments in 1900,
127; attendance, 128; enrollments
in 1912, 137; enrollments in
1919–20, 138, 203; funding,
200–201; conditions in 1920s,
200–203; curriculum in 1920s,
201–2. *See also* Education; Pro-
gressive reform campaigns
Scopes, John T., 1, 206
Scruggs, W. A., 173
Sedition, World War I, 159–66
Self-sufficiency, 13–14
Sellers, S. B., 32
Sermons. *See* Prescriptive literature
Sewell, Elisha, 55
Sharecroppers, 19

Sheriffs, 71
Silver Point (Putnam County), 144
Singings, 196, 197
Smith, Charlie D., 150
Smith, John, 167
Smith, Rutledge, 144, 145, 148, 153,
159, 160, 168
Smith County, 5, 7, 54, 79, 111, 116,
133, 137, 151, 160, 173, 181, 186,
187, 196, 198; vote on secession,
8; black population, 9; tobacco
production in 1890s, 19; road
bond controversies, 113–17
Smithville (DeKalb County), 75,
168
Snodgrass, Judge C. E., 74
Snodgrass, Henry Clay, 74
Social life, 40–41, 195–96
Southern Baptist Convention, 48,
185–86, 207, 231–32 (n. 21)
Southern Education Board, 131
Southern Good Roads Association,
108
Southern Railway, 79
Sparta (White County), 10, 24, 61,
110, 116, 152, 205
Sparta-Welwood Silk Mills, 180
"Speakings," 59
Speck, Burr L., 115
Spivey (Clay County), 133
Spring Creek Baptist Church, 50, 52
Stafford, Henry, 163
Stagecoach, 77
State debt repudiation controversy,
61
State Highway Association, 113
Stepp, Si, 162
Stone Association of Baptists, 207
Stores: as trading posts, 21–22
Summer School of the South, 131
Sutton, Elizabeth, 35
Sutton, Martha, 35

Tariffs, 63–64
Taxes, 61, 66; in 1920s, 171–73
Taylor, Alfred, 172–73
Taylor, George, 72

Taylor, Robert L., 59
Teachers, 66–67; qualifications and training, 126, 128–29; hiring practices, 130, 135–36; women as, 130–31, 190; and certification, 134–35. *See also* Education
Telephones, 179
Tenancy: in 1890s, 14, 19; as function of age, 31, 32–33, 85–86, 179; railroads and, 84–86; in 1920s, 174–75. *See also* Men; Sharecroppers
Tennessee Anti-Evolution Law, 1–3, 184, 203. *See also* Butler, John Washington
Tennessee Central (TC), 79–89, 144; reports to Interstate Commerce Commission, 82–83; and wood products industries, 86–87; and poultry sales, 88–89
Tennessee Polytechnic Institute, 106, 143, 154, 173
Tennessee Technological University, 214
Terry, Roland, 39
Textile production: in 1890s, 18
Timber industry, 23–24, 86–87, 237 (n. 3), 257 (n. 9); fear of decline of, 87
Tinsley, Mary Malinda Kirkpatrick, 41–42
Tobacco, 16, 18–19, 220 (n. 16); promoted as market crop in 1920s, 177–78
Towns: as centers of progressivism, 106; aspirations toward urbanity, 179–80; boosterism, 180; populations in 1890, 218 (n. 13)
Traditionalists, 10, 14, 116
Transportation patterns, 81–82, 212. *See also* Automobiles; Railroads; Roads
Trisdale, Henry, 151
Turner, Charles, 72–73

United States Good Road Association, 108

University of Tennessee, 109, 173, 175, 176, 179
Upchurch, Rachel, 35
Upper Cumberland: 2, 217 (n. 5); as hinterland, 3; as farmer's world, 4; geography, 5–7; rivers, 5–7; ethnic composition, 7; early settlers, 7–8; slavery in, 7–8; Civil War in, 7–9; postbellum, 9–10
Upper Cumberland Development District, 214

Vengence, 73–75
Violence, 59, 71–75, 236 (n. 32); as retarding business development, 75; against railroad, 80

Walden, Rueben, 167
Walker, Claud, 32
Walker, S. H., 32
Walling, Thomas, 167
Walton Road, 7
War Work Drive, 159
Watson, Tom, 149
Wauford, Elder D., 54
Wharton, Dr. May Cravath, 108, 224 (n. 11)
Wheeler, J. T., 148
White, Marie, 191
White County, 5, 7, 36, 59, 78, 88, 116, 121, 124, 137, 139, 164, 167; vote on secession, 8; rail connections, 10; average acreage per farm in 1890, 15; bank, 24; Farmer's Alliance in, 61–62
Whitefield, H. A., 14
Whitlock, William, 139
Whitson, Jere, 105–6, 122, 213
Wilder, John, 60, 114, 237 (n. 4)
Willette Academy, 122, 205
Williams, James A., 120
Willow Grove (Clay County), 68, 133
Wills, Ophelia, 35
Wilson, Levy and Mary, 35
Wilson, Woodrow, 148, 162, 163
Wirt, Elmer, 158; and opposition to

World War I, 164–66, 254 (n. 68); runs for governor in 1920, 172. See also *Putnam County Herald*

Wolf River, 5, 113

"Woman's True Place is in the Home," newspaper debate in 1920s, 191–95

Women: legal status of in 1890s, 27; age at marriage in 1890s, 31, 224 (n. 10); and public work, 33, 180, 189–90, 213; and literacy, 33, 189–90; and religion, 37–38, 260 (n. 1); and farm produce, 87–88, 189; and egg money, 88–89, 189; as teachers, 130–31; and World War I home front mobilization, 156–59; occupations in 1920s, 174; suffrage issue, 184–88; changing roles of in 1920s, 184–95; and politics, 186–87; and farm work, 188–89; educated, 189–90; and conflicts over morality in 1920s, 192–95; bobbed hair, 193; employment patterns of in 1980s, 214; coverture removed, 223 (n. 2). *See also* Christian ideals for family life; Gender; Marriage; Religion; Work

Women's Christian Temperance Union, 156

Work: and gender roles, 15–16, 33, 87–88, 189–90; and social implications, 20; occupations in 1920s, 174, 189–90. *See also* Public work

"Workings," 20

World War I, 107; effects on region, 143–69; draft boards, 148–50; public attitudes toward, 149; soldiers' reactions to army life, 151–52; home front mobilization, 152–68; deserters and draft evaders, 166–68. *See also* Conscription

Wyatt, J. S., 140

Yeoman farmer: and worldview, 14

York, Alvin, 144, 147, 152

Young and Boles, 164

Plate 1. Satellite map of the Egyptian Sahara (produced in part using Google Earth).

Plate 2. Djedefre Water Mountain, central cartouche, east face.

Plate 3. Mahmoud Marai (left) and Mark Borda with the newly discovered Uwainat Inscriptions, November 2007.

Plate 4. Two views of the megaliths that were arranged on top of CSA before CSA was excavated. These appear to be shaped as if fitted together or symbolic of connection. Images taken October 2003. As of April 2008, one of these megaliths was removed, possibly to the Nubian Museum.

Plate 5. A human figure emerging from the head of a large animal, possibly a lion, in the midst of a group dance. This appeared to us to be reminiscent of modern shamanic imagery (in which a shaman enters the mind of a powerful animal as part of a ritual). Lower left, a large orb, possibly the sun or moon, with a single hand. Mester Kawai-Foggini cave, southwest Gilf Kebir.

Plate 6. Domestic scene with cattle at the Unwainat cave.

Plate 7. Human with cattle on a leash, Uwainat cave.

Plate 8. Robert Bauval with herder near Assiut.

Plate 9. Nubian boatman at Aswan. Behind the boatman can be seen the Island of Bigeh, near Phliae, and the remains of the entrance of a doorway built by Augustus that lead up a stairway to a temple, the pronaos, built by Ptolemy XII.

Plate 10. Elder at Siwa Oasis.

Plate 11. Elder at Siwa Oasis.

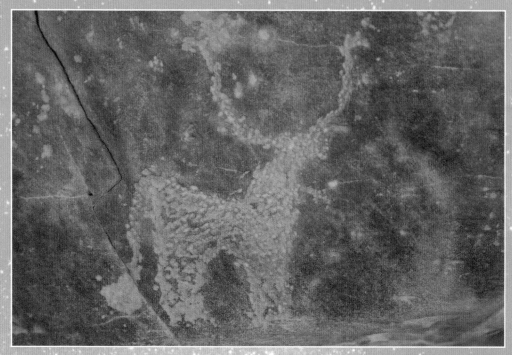

Plate 12. Prehistoric carving of cattle ca. 6000–8000 BCE, Gilf Kebir.

Plate 13. Prehistoric carving of cattle ca. 6000–8000 BCE,
Karkur Talh, Uwainat. Note how the cow is ornate with body brindles or perhaps a blanket.

Plate 14. Cattle, Borda Cave, north Uwainat, ca. 4000–6000 BCE. Note spotted cow.

Plate 15. Models of cows Eleventh Dynasty, ca. 2000 BCE. Courtesy of the Cairo Museum.

Plate 16. Cow goddess Mehet-Weret ("Great Flood") representing the yearly inundation of the Nile, ca. 1500 BCE. This goddess is sometimes linked to Isis.

Plate 17. The cow godess Hathor, New Kindom, ca. 1500 BCE. Note the stars on her body. Hathor's cult is attested from earliest times.

Plate 18. The goddess Isis with cow horns, suckling the child Horus.

Plate 19. The Step Pyramid at Saqqara.

Plate 20. The head of the Sphinx. Note "Negroid" features.

Plate 21. The Nilometer on Elephantine Island at Aswan.

Plate 22. The rock-cut tomb of Harkhuf at Aswan (west bank).

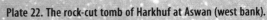

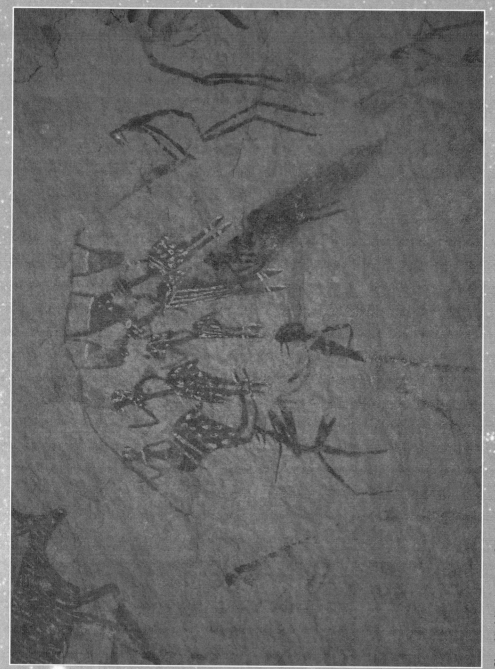

Plate 23. A hunting scene found in the Kifah cave. Photo courtesy of Mark Borda.

Plate 24. Rock painting of cattle, goats, and other animals found in the Kifah cave. Photo courtesy of Mark Borda

Plate 25. The temple of Hathor at Dendera.

BLACK GENESIS

BLACK GENESIS

The Prehistoric Origins
of Ancient Egypt

ROBERT BAUVAL AND THOMAS BROPHY, PH.D.

Bear & Company
Rochester, Vermont • Toronto, Canada

Bear & Company
One Park Street
Rochester, Vermont 05767
www.BearandCompanyBooks.com

Bear & Company is a division of Inner Traditions International

Library of Congress Cataloging-in-Publication Data
Bauval, Robert, 1948-
  Black Genesis : the prehistoric origins of ancient Egypt / Robert Bauval and
Thomas Brophy.
      p. cm.
  Includes bibliographical references and index.
  ISBN: 978-1-59143-114-5 (pbk.)
  1. Egypt—Civilization—To 332 B.C. 2. Egypt—Civilization—African
influences. 3. Blacks—Egypt—History. 4. Black race—History. I. Brophy,
Thomas G., 1960– II. Title.
  DT61.B38 2011
  932'.011—dc22

                                                                    2010053041

Printed and bound in XXXXX

10   9   8   7   6   5   4   3   2   1

Text design and layout by Virginia Scott Bowman
This book was typeset in Garamond Premier Pro with Gill Sans and Franklin
Gothic used as display typefaces

To send correspondence to the authors of this book, mail a first-class letter to the
authors c/o Inner Traditions • Bear & Company, One Park Street, Rochester, VT
05767, and we will forward the communication.

For my daughter, Candice, and my son Jonathan.
May you always remember your genesis.
—Robert Bauval

To my parents, in deepest gratitude for bringing me into
this amazing journey.
—Thomas Brophy

CONTENTS

ACKNOWLEDGMENTS

This book was not an easy one to research and to put together due to the vast and complex issues involved as well as the need to organize and undertake deep desert expedition to the Egyptian Sahara. Yet with perseverance, dedication, and enthusiasm, we plodded on, step-by-step, page-by-page, and we can now say that we are extremely proud and pleased with the result.

As always, our first thanks go to our respective families. Their support, love, and patience are greatly appreciated. We wish to pay special thanks and tribute to anthropologists Fred Wendorf and Romuald Schild of the Combined Prehistoric Expedition for opening the way to the study of Nabta Playa. We also thank astronomer Kim Malville for being the first to realize the importance of the megalithic alignments at Nabta Playa. Special thanks go to long-time colleague and friend Paul Rosen whose combination of scientific integrity and complete lack of bias or dogmatism has supplied immeasurably helpful collaboration. Thanks, too, to the Jet Propulsion Laboratory of Pasadena, California, for supporting the unusual project of further studies of Nabta Playa.

Our thanks and respect is also due to the desert explorers Mark Borda and Carlo Bergmann for their many discoveries in the Egyptian Sahara and for their kind efforts to share some of these with us. We also thank Mahmoud Marai for guiding us to the remote locations of Gilf Kebir and Jebel Uwainat and showing us the wonderful rock-art cave and the hieroglyphic inscriptions discovered at Uwainat in 2007. We extend thanks to our friend and desert guide Mahmoud (Tiger)

Nemr and geologist and desert guide Diaa Shehata for taking us safely to Nabta Playa, and we thank our friend Michael Ackroyd for delivering us to Nabta Playa in 2003 with necessary permits and with great panache. We thank Chance Gardner and Vanesse McNiel for making the fine graphic animations of the Calendar Circle.

Our thanks also go to the many colleagues and friends who, directly or indirectly, have help us put this book together: Linda and Max Bauval; Hoda and Camille Hakim-Taraboulsi; Sherif el Sebai of Tarot Travel Tours; Gouda Fayed; Angela Richards; Brian Hokum; Lyra Marble; Dustin Donaldson; John and Josette Orphanidis; Jean-Paul and Pauline Bauval; June and Jim Brophy; Geoffrey and Therese Gauci; Richard (Fuzzy) Fusniak; Ambassador Jean Paul Tarud-Kuborn and his lovely wife, Valentina Troni; William Horsman and Viviane Vayssieres; the lovely family of my late driver, Mahmoud El Kirsh; Arianna Mendo; Robert Schoch; John Anthony West; Lily Lee; the Helios family (you know who you are!); Khaled el Bary, owner of the wonderful Bary's Restaurant at the pyramids; Giulio Gallo; Mayumi Hashiyama; Carmen Boulter; and many others too numerous to name here, but who surely know that we are grateful for their friendship and support. We also thank our publisher, Inner Traditions, the lovely Cecilia Perugia at Corbaccio Edizione in Milan, and everyone at A. M. Heath Ltd. Last but definitely not least, we give thanks for having so many wonderful readers around the world who make all our efforts worthwhile.

ANCIENT EGYPT REBORN

No colors any more I want them to turn black . . .

MICK JAGGER AND KEITH RICHARDS,
"PAINT IT BLACK," 1966

This book is the product of a deep and strong desire to use the best of our intellect, knowledge, and abilities to put right an issue that has long beleaguered historians and prehistorians alike: the vexed question of the Black African origins of the ancient Egyptian civilization. In spite of many clues that have been in place in the last few decades, which strongly favor a Black African origin for the pharaohs, many scholars and especially Egyptologists have either ignored them, confused them, or, worst of all, derided or scorned those who entertained them. It is not our business to know whether such an attitude is a form of academic racism or simply the blinkered way of looking at evidence to which some modern Egyptology has become accustomed, but whatever the cause, this issue has remained largely unresolved.

We first came across this inherent bias and prejudice against African origins of the Egyptian civilization in the debate—more of an auto-da-fé really—against the Black African professor Cheikh Anta Diop, who, in 1954, published his thesis *Nation Négre et Culture,* which argued a Black African origin for the Egyptian civilization. Anta Diop was

both an eminent anthropologist and a highly respected physicist, and
as such, he was armed with an arsenal of cutting-edge science as well as
the use of the latest technology in radiocarbon dating and biochemistry
to determine the skin color of ancient mummies and corpses by analyzing their content of melanin, a natural polymer that regulates pigmentation in humans. Yet in spite of his careful scientific approach, the
Egyptian authorities refused to provide Anta Diop with skin samples
of royal mummies, even though only minute quantities were required,
and they pilloried and shunned him at a landmark symposium in Cairo
in 1974 on the origins of ancient Egyptians. Diop died in 1986, his
mission not fully accomplished. Fortunately, however, the debate on
African origins was quickly taken up by Professor Martin Bernal, who,
in 1987, published a three-volume opus, *Black Athena,* that flared even
further the already-heated debate. Bernal, a professor emeritus of Near
Eastern studies at Cornell University, was the grandson of the eminent
Egyptologist Sir Alan Gardiner, yet this did not prevent Egyptologists
from attacking him with even more vehemence than they had his Black
African predecessor Anta Diop.

Even though there is still much controversy surrounding the origins
of the ancient Egyptian civilization, we can now say with much evi-
dence-driven conviction that its origins have their genesis with a Black
African people who inhabited the Sahara thousands of years before the
rise of the pharaonic civilization. In this book we present hard scientific
evidence and cogent arguments that have been culled from the latest
findings and discoveries made in the Egyptian Sahara during the last
four decades. We have consulted the publications of eminent anthropologists, paleoanthropologists, paleoclimatologists, paleopathologists,
genetic scientists, archaeologists, archaeoastronomers, geologists, and
even reports from daring desert explorers such as Mark Borda, Carlo
Bergmann, and Mahmoud Marai, who have all contributed to showing
that this specific region of the world was the crucible of the ancient
Egyptian civilization. In researching this book, we have used the best
and latest research accredited to experts and scholars, and we have also

provided extensive notes in order for the reader to trace this source material for further reading. In addition, we have specifically used our own tool kit and method, which entails the application of the science of astronomy to interpret the alignments of complex megalithic structures, pyramids, and temples, as well extracting the astronomical content in ancient Egyptian texts and tomb drawings. To phrase it another way, we have coaxed the silent, ancient stones to reveal their secrets with the universal language of the sky.

Black Genesis is an intellectual time machine that takes you on a roller-coaster adventure into the beyond of recorded history. We have written it not for academic readership but for lay readers, those who wish to understand more regarding this debate on the origin of civilization, and perhaps who wish even to be part of the restoration of Black Africa to its rightful place at the genesis of the human journey. Although, in this book specialized topics such as anthropology and precession astronomy are reviewed, we have kept the discussion as easy and as entertaining as possible in order to achieve a text that is user-friendly and well within the grasp of anyone who has a thirst for knowledge and a sense of adventure. Our wish is to interest a wider audience in this fascinating research and, we hope, to encourage participation in the debate. With Internet communication and the instantaneous distribution of data and information as well as the now easy-to-use astronomy software accessible to all those with a home computer, the participation of the wider public in such debates has become a real and viable possibility, and, indeed, has quite often helped (*coerced* may be a better word!) experts to remove their blinkers and look at the wider picture.

There is still much work to do in bringing to the world a new vision of the Black African origins of civilization. Yet if we buttress the theory with solid, current research and exploration, and if we look at the evidence with open minds free of prejudice and bias, progress of this notion of origins is gaining momentum. For many centuries the Black race of the world has either been exploited by its White counterpart or looked upon as inferior. Although many in the Western world have advanced a great deal in curbing such an attitude, the truth is that racial prejudice is still very much rampant in other parts of the world, and it lingers even in uneducated or dark hearts in Europe and the New World. *Black Genesis* thus becomes not only a scientific thesis, but also a testament of respect and admiration of all whose skin happens to be Black, and who have a direct ancestral line to Black Africa.

Our research has taken us from Europe and the United States to Egypt, from the comfort of five-star hotels in Cairo to camping in the remote Sahara, and from the studious environment of public libraries to chaotic journeys along the entire stretch of the Egyptian Nile Valley. We have consulted with experts on the prehistory of the Egyptian Sahara and traveled in four-wheel-drive vehicles with intrepid explorers along large swathes of no-man's-land in southwestern Egypt. We have seen the dense, multiracial populations of large Egyptian cities as well as the sparsely inhabited oases of the Western Desert (Egyptian Sahara). In downtown Cairo, we have heard the cacophony of traffic, whose din reaches the brooding pyramids of Giza and the great temples of Luxor and Karnak, and we have experienced the deafening silence of Gilf Kebir and Jebel Uwainat. We have done all this because we believe in our cause and in our work and because we love the excitement and thrill of the chase and the challenge of the enterprise. Most of all, we have done all this because a huge intellectual dam has been breached, and we want to be part of the flood that will regenerate Egypt with a new and purer vision of itself.

1

STRANGE STONES

In Nabta there are six megalithic alignments extending across the sediments of the playa . . . . Like the spokes on a wheel, each alignment radiates outwards from a complex structure . . .

Dr. Mosalam Shaltout,
National Research Institute
of Astronomy and Geophysics, Egypt

[One of the] alignments points to the rising position of Sirius . . . the primary calibrator of the Egyptian calendar. . . .

Dr. Fred Wendorf and Dr. Romuald Schild,
The Megaliths of Nabta Playa

A LUCKY TURN OF THE SPADE

The phrase *a lucky turn of the spade* is well known in archaeology. It reminds us that many of the great discoveries have often been made not by intellectual ingenuity, as we would expect, but by pure chance. Moreover, it implies that the credit does not necessarily always go to the person who actually held the spade, but rather to his employer, the leader or financier of the archaeological project. For example, when, in 1873, a

Turkish worker plunged his rusty spade into the soil and discovered the legendary city of Troy, this was a lucky turn of the spade— not for him— but rather for the German adventurer Heinrich Schliemann. When, in 1922, an Egyptian peasant shifted the sand with his spade and discovered the entrance to Tutankhamun's tomb, this, too, was a lucky turn of the spade not for him, but for the English archaeologist Howard Carter. Schliemann and Carter became legends in their own time; the workers were given a small stipend and then departed into oblivion.

So when an unnamed student from Southern Methodist University of Texas (SMU) discovered Nabta Playa, his or her name was somehow lost and forgotten in the academic verbiage that followed. Admittedly, this time there was no lucky turn of the spade. In fact, there was no spade in the hand of the unnamed student. The leader of the expedition, Fred Wendorf, and the student as well as a few others with them had by chance stopped their Jeep in order to have a comfort break—a pee—after a long and tiring drive in the Egyptian Sahara. They were 100 kilometers (about 62 miles) due west of Abu Simbel in a nondescript, empty desert spot. During their rest, as they looked down around their feet, they slowly realized they were standing in a field of numerous artifacts, the remnants of finely made stone tools and potsherds. Those artifacts alone were intriguing enough to prompt Fred Wendorf to investigate further and begin an entirely new excavation site. What the explorers did not then realize was that the strange clusters of large stones all around them, half-buried in the sand, would eventually shock the world's concept of antiquity. At first, the members of the expedition assumed that these stones were just natural boulders sticking out of the ancient sediment—a common feature in this arid part of the world. In fact, for years, as they excavated in the midst of the boulders, searching for and finding the expected Neolithic artifacts, they assumed the large stones were natural bedrock outcrops. As they looked closer, however, it dawned on them that the stones were positioned in unnatural formations—strange geometrical clusters, ovals, circles, and straight lines—and they were sitting on the sediments of an ancient dry lake. Someone had taken the trouble to move these stones at great effort. Who had done this? When? More intriguingly, why? It would be no exaggeration to say from the outset of our story that Wendorf's findings and those of his team, which were published gradually from the mid-1970s until very recently, should have shaken to its very core the scholarly world and should have changed its perception of Egyptian history and even, perhaps, of civilization as a whole. This, however, didn't happen. Nabta Playa and its mysteries remained an undefused intellectual bomb, ticking away, remaining unexploded in the hallways of established knowledge.

Until now.

THE COMBINED PREHISTORIC EXPEDITION (CPE)

Fred Wendorf's fascination with the Egyptian Sahara started way back in 1960, when, in a desperate bid to save Egypt's ravaged economy, the Egyptian government decided to build a huge dam on the Nile just south of Aswan, 900 kilometers (about 600 miles) from Cairo. Egypt's population had burgeoned from a comfortable ten million at the turn of the nineteenth century to an unsustainable fifty million by 1960, and the country was now in dire need of cheap energy to service the ever-growing masses and sprouting agricultural and industrial projects. There were also new infrastructure projects planned for the delta region and all along the 1,000-kilometer (about 621 miles) Nile Valley—roads, pipelines, sewage plants, airports, hospitals, and schools—which President Gamal Abdel Nasser had promised the people after the so-called Free Officers Revolution of 1952. Unable to obtain funds for all this from the Western powers because of ongoing anti-Semitism in Egypt and the country's hostilities with Israel, Nasser was forced to seek help from communist Russia, which was eager to introduce socialism to Egypt and to gain a foothold in the Arab world. For infrastructure projects, Egypt provided cheap labor from its huge unemployed masses, while Russia provided the cash and the technology—and even threw a few Mig jet fighters and tanks into the deal.

When finished, the dam on the Nile was to form a giant lake, Lake Nasser, which not only would flood much of the inhabited Nile Valley upstream, but would also submerge many ancient temples, among them the great temple of Ramses II at Abu Simbel and the beautiful temple of Isis on the Island of Philae. The archaeological world communities were outraged. Not as well publicized at the time, but also slated to be lost were several prehistoric sites in the adjacent desert earmarked for new farming projects. At the eleventh hour, however, UNESCO World Heritage sounded the alarm, and funds were quickly raised from big donors across the world. A huge international rescue operation hastily worked to save the ancient temples. The effort involved experts and engineering contractors from Europe and the United States.

Yet while this sensational salvage operation grabbed all the headlines, another, more modest operation went relatively unnoticed. This was the scantily funded rescue mission started in 1962 and headed by Fred Wendorf, who was then curator of the Museum of New Mexico. Fred Wendorf had set himself the daunting task of salvaging or, at the very least, documenting in detail the prehistoric sites in the Egyptian Sahara before they were lost forever. Wendorf's rescue operation was at first funded by the National Science Foundation of America and the US State Department, and was made up of an informal team of anthropologists, archaeologists, and other scientists who were given the collective name of Combined Prehistoric Expedition, or CPE. Three institutions formed the core body of the CPE: (1) SMU, (2) the Polish Academy of Sciences (PAS), and (3) the Geological Survey of Egypt (GSE). In view of his credentials and seniority, Wendorf remained in charge of the CPE. In 1964, Wendorf resigned from his post at the Museum of New Mexico and joined Southern Methodist University (SMU) as head of the anthropological department—a move that allowed him to devote more time to the ongoing research in the Egyptian Sahara. In 1972, however, Wendorf handed the day-to-day operations to a Polish anthropologist, Dr. Romuald Schild. At this point, both Wendorf and Schild admitted, "Only a few signs suggested that a new archaeological dreamland is there buried in the sands and clays."[1] Barely a year later, however, in 1973, after Wendorf's fateful pee break 100 kilometers from Abu Simbel, and after they walked around the large, shallow basin and saw all the strange stone clusters and protracted alignments as well as a plethora of tumuli and potsherds strewn all over the ground, both men started to suspect that just maybe they had hit the anthropological jackpot—for this was no ordinary prehistoric site. It was a sort of unique Stone Age theme park in which mysterious events and occult ceremonies quite obviously took place. The local modern Bedouins called the region Nabta, which apparently meant "seeds." Borrowing this name and concluding that the wide, sandy-clay basin they stood on in the desert was the bottom of a very ancient lake, Wendorf and Schild christened the site Nabta Playa.

But what exactly is Nabta Playa, and what are the mysteries it conceals?

CIRCLE, ALIGNMENTS, AND TUMULI

The Egyptian Sahara—which is also known as the Eastern Sahara or Western Desert—is a vast, rectangular region that is bracketed on its four sides by the Mediterranean Sea in the north, the Nile Valley in the east, Libya in the west, and Sudan in the south. It is almost the size of France, and, apart from the five main fertile oases that run in a line from north to south, it is considered the most arid and desolate place in the world, especially the corner in the southwest, adjacent to Sudan and Libya. Because of this terrible aridity and also because some parts of it are so remote, the Egyptian Sahara remains largely unexplored. True, some archaeological research has taken place in and around the five major oases, but little, if any, explorations have been carried out into the deep desert or in that distant southwestern corner. This is especially the case for the two highland regions known as Gilf Kebir and Jebel Uwainat. These are composed of giant, rocky massifs that act as a natural barrier to Egypt's southwest frontier corner with Sudan and Libya. These almost surreal "Alps of the desert" emerge from the surrounding flat landscape like giant icebergs in a still ocean, and in daytime they loom in the haze like eerie mirages that can taunt, daunt, and terrify the most intrepid or placid of travelers.

As odd as it may seem, especially given our perspective of today's amazing technological advances in communication, no one in modern times or in the ancient past knew of the existence of Gilf Kebir or Jebel Uwainat until the early 1920s—or so it seemed, as we will see in chapter 2. The abnormally belated discovery of Gilf Kebir and Jebel Uwainat coupled with their remoteness and the harsh and extremely inhospitable climate of the region are the main reasons for the almost nonexistent archaeological exploration there. In addition, there has been a strange disinterest by Egyptologists who have insisted that it was impossible for the ancient Egyptians of the Nile Valley to have reached these faraway places through vast distances of open and waterless desert. Nonetheless, this belief is somewhat odd, because it has been known since 1923 that Gilf Kebir and Jebel Uwainat were once inhabited by a prehistoric people who left evidence of their presence there in an abundance of rock art on ledges and in caves and in the many *wadis* (valleys) skirting the massifs. Perhaps the greatest mystery of these strange places was that, in spite of the plentiful rock art and stone artifacts that attest to human presence, no actual human remains or even empty tombs have so far been found there. This was also the case at Nabta Playa.

The question surely begs asking: were Gilf Kebir, Jebel Uwainat, and Nabta Playa not places of permanent habitation but outposts for people who moved from place to place and who had their homebase elsewhere? For example, could the people of Nabta Playa, with their mysterious megalithic legacy, be the same people of Gilf Kebir and Jebel Uwainat, with their puzzling rock art legacy? If so, then how could such people traveling on foot—or, at best, on donkey—across such vast distances (there are 580 kilometers—about 360 miles—between Nabta Playa and the Gilf Kebir-Jebel Uwainat regions) in this totally waterless desert?

Before we attempt to answer such questions, we must look at an interesting and possibly very relevant geographical fact: Nabta Playa and the Gilf Kebir-Jebel Uwainat area are almost on the same east-west line that runs just north of latitude 22.5 degrees north, forming a sort of natural highway between the Nile Valley, Nabta Playa, and, at its western end, Gilf Kebir and Jebel Uwainat. From a directionality viewpoint, then, ancient travelers would easily have known how to journey to such distant locations simply by moving due east or due west—a direction that can be determined by the sun's shadow. Knowing, however, in which direction to move is one thing; making the long journey to an end point is quite another. Such a long stretch of desert crossing is impossible on foot or on a donkey unless there are watering holes or wells along the way. Yet there are no wells or surface water in this stretch of desert between Nabta Playa and Gilf Kebir, only bone-dry sand, dust, and rocks. Nothing can survive in this wasteland without adequate sources of water. Indeed, that Jebel Uwainat and Gilf Kebir were discovered so late shows how problematic it is to reach these regions without motorized four-wheel-drive vehicles that are fully equipped for rough terrain.

Because of this, as well as the hazards involved in such deep desert trekking, only a handful of people have ventured into this wilderness. The region is still a no-man's-land for tourists, and very few, if any, Bedouins that roam the Egyptian Sahara go there. In fact, so uninterested were Egyptologists in these remote areas that the places were—and still are—hardly mentioned in any but the rarest of Egyptological textbooks. Oddly enough, in 1996, it was left to Hollywood to generate some interest in Gilf Kebir and Uwainat through the academy-award-winning film *The English Patient* in which the hero supposedly crashes his single-engine plane on the western side of Gilf Kebir. Yet even then the scenes in the movie were shot not on location but in the more accessible desert of Morocco.* At any rate, whatever the reason, Gilf Kebir and Uwainat were not included in the Combined Prehistoric Expedition mandate. The CPE must have assumed, as most Egyptologists did in those days, that no one could have traveled such vast distances in the arid desert in ancient times and, therefore, there could not be a direct connection between the prehistoric people of Gilf Kebir and Uwainat and the people who built and occupied Nabta Playa. We will return to this important misjudgment in the next chapter.

In the later twentieth century, another misjudgment occurred: although, from 1973 to 1994, the site of Nabta Playa was the intense focus of anthropological and archaeological investigations by the CPE, it nonetheless failed to take notice of the very obvious megalithic alignments there, and it certainly did not have them checked by an astronomer. This was a rather curious oversight that even Fred Wendorf himself had trouble explaining: "The megaliths of Nabta were not recognized or identified for a long time. We began to realize their significance only in 1992. . . ."[2] and "It is not clear why we failed to recognize them previously, or rather why we failed to understand their significance during the first three field seasons 1974, 1975, and 1977 at Nabta. It was not that we did not see them because we did, but they were either regarded as bedrock or, in some instances where it was clear they were not bedrock, regarded as insignificant."[3]

As the author John Anthony West once remarked, archaeologists

---

The English Patient, 1996, features Ralph Fiennes and Kristen Scott Thomas. The so-called Cave of Swimmers (which is actually in Gilf Kebir's Wadi Sura), where the heroine, Lady Clayton, dramatically dies, was also filmed not on location in southwest Egypt but in Morocco. The real Lady Clayton actually died many years later in England by jumping from the open cockpit of her airplane and breaking her neck against a metal bar.

can have blinkered views and miss the obvious: "[I]f you are bent on looking only for potatoes in a field of diamonds, you will miss seeing the diamonds!"[4] To be fair to the CPE, though, the anthropological and archaeological evidence so far was in itself exciting stuff. Carbon-14 dating resulted in dates as far back as 7000 BCE and as recent as 3400 BCE, showing an on-and-off presence at Nabta Playa over an incredible span of years: more than three and a half millennia. The evidence at Nabta Playa also showed that at first, people came seasonally, when the lake was filled by the monsoon summer rains, arriving probably in July and staying until January, when the lake dried up again. Eventually, sometime around 6500 BCE, they figured out how to stay at Nabta Playa permanently by digging deep wells. Around 3300 BCE, however, the changes in climate made the region extremely arid, and Nabta Playa had to be abandoned. The mysterious people simply vanished, leaving behind their ceremonial complex that the CPE had discovered more than five millennia later. Its members were now at odds to understand the function and meaning of the complex.

First the CPE was baffled by the dozen or so oval-shaped tumuli at the north side of Nabta Playa. These looked like flattened igloos made of rock debris and covered with flat slabs of stones. More baffling still was when one of these tumuli was excavated by the CPE. I was found to contain the complete skeletal remains of a young cow, and other tumuli also contained scattered bones of cattle. Wendorf christened the area "the wadi of sacrifices" and concluded that these cattle burials and offerings appear to indicate the presence of a cattle cult. Radiocarbon dating placed these cow burials at around 5500 BCE, thus at least two thousand years before the emergence of the well-known cattle cults of ancient Egypt, such as those of the cow-faced goddess Hathor, the universally known goddess Isis, and the sky goddess Nut.[5]

There were also strange clusters of large stones at the western part of Nabta Playa—about thirty of them, which the CPE called complex struc-

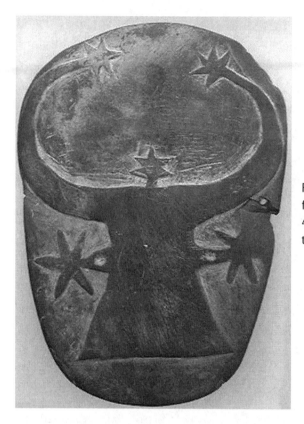

Figure 1.1. Prehistoric palette found at Gerzeh, ca. 3000–4000 BC, thought to represent the goddess Hathor.

tures. When some of these were excavated, the CPE found, to its great astonishment, that these structures had been deliberately placed over natural rock outcrops that were 3 to 5 meters (about 10 to 16 feet) below the surface of the earth. Furthermore, it seemed that these strange rock outcrops had actually been smoothed to "mushroom-like" shapes by human hands! The largest of these so-called complex structures was named Complex Structure A (CSA). When excavated, it was found to contain, at a depth of 3 meters, a large, rough stone sculpture carved to look something like a cow and placed above the sculpted rock outcrop. Moreover, emanating from Complex Structure A were a series of stone alignments that shot out like spokes from a bicycle wheel for several hundred meters, with some projecting toward the north and others toward the east.

There was more, however. The now-famous part of Nabta Playa, its pièce de résistance, was a small stone circle at the northwest part of the site, which looked a bit like a mini Stonehenge. The standing stones—twenty-nine of them—that formed the circle contained four gates, which created lines of sight that ran east-west and north-south. Placed in the center of the circle were two rows of three upright stones each (six stones in total), which gave the whole arrangement the appearance of the dial of a giant clock. Some of the stones had clearly been displaced, perhaps by vandals, and so the CPE invited a young and gifted anthropologist from the University of Arizona, Dr. Nieves Zedeño, to help them reconstruct the circle to its original form of millennia ago. Clearly, this was no ordinary prehistoric structure. At this stage, the CPE anthropologists were completely baffled as to what purpose it might have served. Wendorf and Schild were now beginning to suspect that the whole of Nabta Playa might have less to do with anthropology and more to do with astronomy. So, in 1997, they finally sought the help of an astronomer from the University of Colorado in Boulder, Dr. Kim Malville, who was known for his specialized studies on the astronomy of prehistoric sites. They were in for a big surprise.

Figure 1.2. Schild with Calendar Circle, Nabta Playa, winter 1999.

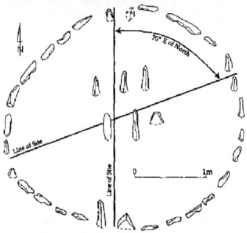

Figure 1.3. Artist's graphic depiction of the Calendar Circle, based on the
archaelogical reconstruction map of Applegate and Zedeño.
Graphics by Doug Thompson for Carmen Boulter.

Reconstructing the Calendar Circle

There has been a certain amount of controversy as to what exactly
happened during and after the reconstruction of the circle (called
the Calendar Circle) at Nabta Playa. In June 2008 the CPE contacted
Dr. Zedeño and asked her if, because there appeared to have been
much tampering with the Calendar Circle (especially in 2007–2008),
she might help work out what happened from the time the circle was
discovered (in 1974) to the publication of Malville's article in *Nature* in

1998. It was noted to Dr. Zedano that in February 2008 the Calendar Circle was removed from its original place at Nabta Playa and transported to the Nubian Museum in Aswan.

Dr. Zedeño replied in a personal corresponence to Robert Bauval: "I mapped the calendar in the winter of 1991–1992. I never saw it again, or before that date for that matter, so I don't know what happened to it. No idea what the cow stone is or where it was before it was removed. Some photos do not seem to be of the same site, in fact there seems to be a fake calendar photo here and there. . . . The only authoritative publication about the calendar I know of is a chapter in Wendorf, Schild, and associates. . . ." As Dr. Zedeño indicates, she mapped the circle in 1991 and 1992, whereas Schild said he made the first map in 1992. Also, Zedeño suggests that the only authoritative paper she knows is a chapter in the publication of Wendorf et al, which is in fact an article by Zedeño herself and a colleague, Alex Applegate, published in 2001. She ignores the 1998 publication in Nature by Wendorf and Malville. We are not sure what "fake calendar" she refers to. Furthermore, Zedeño says she never saw the Calendar Circle before 1991 or after 1992 and therefore does not know what happened to it. Yet in her 2001 article coauthored with Applegate, she writes: "However, one should note that since the time of the site's original discovery [1973], only eight of the presumed fourteen upright slabs remain in place, while the other six center slabs have fallen. In addition, the presumed outer ring suffered an even greater displacement with one of the stones deposited over 7 meters [about 23 feet] from its postulated position."[6] To confuse things even further, in an e-mail message we received from Romuald Schild on June 12, 2008, "The first field map of the calendar was made by Dr. Zedeño and Schild in February 1992, while the first hypothetical reconstruction of the devise, including directions and angles of the sights (gates), was drawn by myself, also in February 1992."

IN COMES ARCHEOASTRONOMY

In the last forty years or so there has been a growing interest in the new scientific field of archeoastronomy, which, according to one school of thought, is defined as the study of the astronomies, astrologies, and cosmologies, as well as the alignments of monuments and buildings of ancient cultures. This scientific discipline has emerged as a new tool for archaeology, because it has become more apparent in recent years that the cyclical motions of the stars, sun, moon, and planets were very much an integral part of the religious ideologies of ancient cultures, and that ancient peoples applied such ideas to the design and alignment of their monuments. It is thus imperative to bring in the science of naked-eye observational astronomy as a necessary instrument in order to understand fully the meaning of the design, alignments, and sometimes the choice of location of ancient temples, pyramids, and even whole cities. For example, according to E. C. Krupp: "The cosmos itself is what mattered to our ancestors. Their lives, their beliefs, their destinies—all were part of this bigger pageant. Just as the environment of their temples was made sacred by metaphors of cosmic order, entire cities and great ritual centres were also astronomically aligned and organised. Each sacred capital restated the theme of cosmic order in terms of its builders' own perception of the universe. Principles, which the society considered its own—which ordered its life and gave it its character—were borrowed from the sky and built into the plans of the cities."[7]

A sort of stillborn precursor of modern archaeoastronomy can be found in the turbulent intellectual milieu that swirled through the French intelligentsia at the turn of the nineteenth century, after Napoleon, in 1799, took a cadre of top scientists and scholars along with his army on their adventurous military campaigns through Egypt. Napoleon also took along artists to record the journeys in sketches. One such artist, Vivant Denon, was fascinated by a zodiac sculpted onto the ceiling of a temple at Dendera. In Paris, Denon published as a book his sketch of the Dendera zodiac along with an account of his travels, and it became a huge bestseller in both France and England. In the important scientific and scholarly societies of Paris there arose a protracted and very active debate focusing on attempts to date the Dendera zodiac. One camp was composed of scientific luminaries of the time, many of whose names are familiar to any student of science today. These scientists often gathered at the home of the Marquis de LaPlace. Particularly active in the Dendera zodiac debate were physicists Jean-Baptiste Biot and Joseph Fourier, astronomer Johan Karl Burckhardt, and his engineer partner Jean-Baptiste Coraboeuf. The approach that all in this camp followed in order to attempt to date the zodiac was to match calculations of the astronomical precession of the equinoxes with the images of constellations on the Dendera zodiac. They followed the reasoning of pre–French Revolutionary scholar Charles Dupuis, who had based his study of the origins of religion on interpreting religious mythologies in astronomical terms. As California Institute of Technology historian of science Jed Z. Buchald puts it, "Dupuis had located the birthplace of the zodiac in an Egypt older by far than any chronology based on textual arguments—and especially on the Books of Moses—could possibly allow. (Standard biblical chronology placed the origin of all things at about 4000 BC. . . .) According to Dupuis, the zodiac, and astronomy itself, was born near the Nile over 14,000 years ago. The Greeks, he insisted, were scientific children compared to the Egyptians, whose knowledge and wisdom underlay all of Western science and mathematics."[8]

The scientists competed fiercely, often disagreeing with each other. For example, Biot seems to have enjoyed pointing out that Fourier, famous for his mathematics, had miscalculated the heliacal rising of Sirius. Yet they all used precession calculations to date the Dendera zodiac. One thing that hampered them and that is still uncertain today was that it is not clear how much of the Dendera zodiac is representative of actual events in the sky, and how much of it is merely symbolic horoscope. This gets at the heart of the other camp in the zodiac-dating debates of the time: the philologists and linguists who argued that astrophysical calculations should not be applied because all ancient symbology is best understood as an expression of the cultural lives of the ancients, not as a representation of the physical world.

Stirring even more the turbulence of the debate was that many French intellectuals, such as Dupuis, had little use for biblical fundamentalism, while others believed all scholarship should be firmly based on interpreting biblical Mosaic (emphasizing the Books of Moses) chronology. One of these was the young Jean-Francois Champollion.

Meanwhile, a French antiquities collector named Saulnier had dispatched a master stonemason named Lelorrain on an expedition to Dendera to steal the zodiac. After using stone saws and chisels and finally dynamite, Lelorrain managed to cart the remains of the temple ceiling back to Paris. These remains, however, did not include the parts of the ceiling that ended up winning the Dendera zodiac debates. In September 1822, Champollion, after years of poverty-stricken excruciating efforts,[9] finally cracked the code for how to decipher hieroglyphs. Champollion first deciphered the cartouches that contain royal names. (A cartouche is an oval enclosure in which the name of a pharaoh is inscribed. Only a king's name can be written within a cartouche.) Among the first cartouches he deciphered were those next to the Dendera zodiac. There he read the ancient Greek word for "ruler," thus dating the construction of the zodiac ceiling to the Ptolemaic period and winning the debate for the side of the philologists, who could happily boot the physicists and astronomers out of the circle of those considered able to offer legitimate authority about antiquity.

Yet in what must be one of the great ironies of history, in 1828, when Champollion had the resources finally to mount his own expedition, and he arrived at Dendera to see his famous cartouches, he was horrified to find them empty. They had never had contained any hieroglyphs, no royal names at all. It seems the artists with Napoleon's army, who were often quite accurate in their depictions, in this case had been puzzled by the strange, empty cartouches and had sketched something in them simply for artistic reasons. By the time of Champollion's trip, however, the philologists had consolidated their authoritative hold on antiquities studies enough to keep the physical scientists at bay for some time. Further, as it turned out, Champollion's date was not far off anyway.*

Eventually, we would have a new mode of historical understanding stemming from neither the extreme philologists-linguists camp nor the extreme physicists-astronomers camp, but a synthetic approach including many forms of evidence—archaeological, artistic, linguistic, and astronomical—that would come into play.

Because he began to employ such a synthetic approach, the father of archaeoastronomy may legitimately be the British astronomer Sir Norman Lockyer. Lockyer was born in 1836 in Rugby, England. As a young man, he had worked for the War Office in London, and it was there that he first developed a keen interest in astronomy. In 1862, Lockyer was made a fellow at the Royal Astronomical Society, and, in 1868, while working at the College of Chemistry in London, he made his first major contribution to science by showing that the bright emissions from the sun during a total eclipse were caused by an unknown element he named "helium"—twenty-seven years before Sir William Ramsay would isolate this gas in the laboratory! In 1869, Lockyer made another important contribution to science: he founded the journal *Nature,* which was to become the most influential scientific periodical in the world. Further, in 1885, Lockyer became the world's first professor of astronomical physics. For his many discoveries and achievements, Lockyer was knighted in 1897.

At the age of fifty-three, toward the end of his academic career,

---

*As the historian of science Jed Z. Buchwald describes, the Dendera ceiling was constructed in the interregnum years after the death of Cleopatra's father, Ptolemy Auletes, in 51 BCE, when there was no king and therefore no royal name to put in the cartouches. We note, however, that is the date of the construction of the ceiling. There is still uncertainty regarding the date(s) to which the actual contents of the zodiac itself may refer. We caution the curious reader that before launching off to date the Dendera zodiac again, it is best to be aware that no less than the likes of LaPlace, Fourier, and Biot expended significant efforts at extracting dates, and their results remained inconclusive.

Lockyer indulged in his greatest passion: the study of the astronomies of ancient cultures and the alignments of their temples. He realized that archaeologists had not "paid any heed to the possible astronomical ideas of the temple builders,"[10] and, furthermore, that "there was little doubt that astronomical consideration had a great deal to do with the direction towards which these temples faced."[11] He had read of the magnificent pyramids and temples of ancient Egypt, and so, in November 1890, Lockyer went there to see them for himself. In Cairo, he was assisted by the German Egyptologist Heinrich Brugsch, an authority on astronomical inscriptions and drawings found in temples and tombs of pharaohs and noblemen. During a meeting with Lockyer, Brugsch explained that the rituals and ceremonies of ancient Egyptians clearly contained astronomical connotations. Encouraged by this, Lockyer sailed to Luxor. There he studied the alignment and symbolism of several temples, including the great temple of Amun-Ra at Karnak. Back in England, Lockyer published his findings in *The Dawn of Astronomy*. It was the first book of its kind, and, taking into account the incomplete and rudimentary knowledge of Egyptologists at that time, Lockyer's work is a remarkable achievement that brought to attention the importance of applying astronomy to the studies of ancient cultures. Yet even though Lockyer's approach was highly scientific and his arguments sound, nearly all Egyptologists either ignored or rudely derided his thesis. Like Galileo before him, who calmly told his inquisitors "but it [Earth] does move . . ." *(e pur si muove)*, poor Lockyer told the Egyptologists "of all the large temples I examined there was an astronomical basis . . ."[12] His words fell on deaf ears. In the years that followed, the Egyptologists took refuge in their belief that by having silenced Lockyer and having thrown him off their turf, they had shaken off all those pseudo-scientists, diletttantes, and hangers-on who dared to oppose their views. For a while it did seem that they had succeeded.

In 1963, however, another archaeoastronomer came to haunt them again with a vengeance: the American professor Gerald Hawkins of the Harvard-Smithsonian Observatories in Cambridge, Massachusetts.

Hawkins infuriated archaeologists by publishing in Lockyer's now highly influential academic journal *Nature* a series of articles on the vexed topic of the alleged astronomy of Stonehenge, and he followed the articles with the publication of his now-renowned book *Stonehenge Decoded*. Hawkins went much further than Lockyer: he claimed that the alignments at Stonehenge were definitely astronomical and had been deliberately aimed at the sun and moon *azimuths* (positions at rising and setting). He also asserted that the fifty-six holes of the so-called Aubrey Circle were representative of the fifty-six years of the moon's full eclipse cycle of three nodal revolutions of 18.61 years each. The implications were huge. This interpretation meant that the ancient builders of Stonehenge, far from being primitives and illiterate barbarians, were sophisticated astronomers who also knew that Earth was a sphere or globe. This, of course, was pure anathema to the archaeologists, and soon they were again up in arms. As our colleague and friend John Anthony West once remarked:

> There are few things in this world more predictable than the reaction of conventional minds to unconventional ideas. That reaction is always and invariably some combination of contempt, outrage, abuse and derision. . . . However, this standard reaction may be seriously muted or further enhanced by a potent new wild card, added to the deck only in the latter half of the twentieth century: the PR factor. If the unconventional idea attracts wide public interest, that is to say if it is easily understood and is "sexy" enough; especially if it results in bestselling books, extensive TV coverage or movie blockbusters, the attack gets ratcheted up. . . . As long as the public interest is there, Hollywood and television can be relied upon to keep stirring the pot no matter what the "experts" say. And sooner or later the cynics, skeptics and debunkers at the *New York Times*, *Scientific American* and *Skeptical Inquirer* will be forced to confront the offending idea.[13]

This time, however, they faced a less accommodating opponent than the passive Sir Lockyer. Hawkins's book became a bestseller, and, with his solid academic reputation, the archaeologists had much trouble quenching the huge interest and support Hawkins received from the public and media. Hawkins had singlehandedly forced the scholars out of their ivory towers and made them face up to the challenge. What made matters even worse for the skeptics was the support that he received from academic heavyweights such as Sir Fred Hoyle, who not only confirmed Hawkins's calculations, but also agreed that "a veritable Newton or Einstein must have been at work"[14] at Stonehenge three millennia ago.

Hawkins was soon followed by a Scotsman, Alexander Thom, an engineer with a keen interest in the ancient megaliths and prehistoric monuments of the British Isles. After years of meticulous investigation of the astronomical alignments of these ancient sites, Thom was convinced that all were the collective work of a pan-generation construction program that reached its pinnacle in 1850 BCE. He was able to show that many of the megalithic sites incorporated a common canon of geometry and mathematics that resembled what was supposedly invented by the Pythagoreans of ancient Greece—yet they appeared in the British Isles more than a millennium earlier! According to Thom, the dimensions of the prehistoric sites were determined by a common unit of measurement, about 2.72 feet in length, which he termed the *megalithic yard*. Thom proposed that these sites were meant to express magical ideas and symbolize important belief systems by making use of astronomical observations of the sun, moon, and stars.

This time, some archaeologists took notice with uneasy embarrassment, for it was becoming obvious that their elderly peers, in their zeal to defend their coveted turf, might have been too hasty in rejecting the research of Lockyer, Hawkins, and Hoyle. Alexander Thom's impeccable data and the razor-sharp mathematical logic in his book *Megalithic Sites in Britain* could not be ignored by unbiased archaeologists. Thom also managed to have articles published in the reputable and peer-reviewed *Journal of the History of Astronomy,* which gave much credence to his ideas. It seemed that, finally, the new science of archaeoastronomy had made a crack in the wall of archaeology.

Since Alexander Thom's days, the science of archaeoastronomy has gained much ground and popularity among the public and even with some Egyptologists and archaeologists of the new generation. Starting in the late 1960s, serious investigators began to feel more comfortable coming forward with their ideas on the astronomical alignments of ancient Egyptian temples and pyramids. The first major breakthrough came with the astronomer Virginia Trimble, who codiscovered the stellar alignments of the shafts in the King's Chamber of the Great Pyramid in 1963. This discovery opened the way for more research on the Egyptian pyramids and also encouraged others to come forth and brave the firewall of academic Egyptology.[15] Today, many new players have entered this fascinating field of research, mostly because computer and satellite technology such as Google Earth, GPS, and user-friendly astronomy software have allowed amateurs to investigate ancient sites on a screen in the comfort of their office or home. Further, with the arrival of the Internet coupled with the exponential growth of computer and digital technology and electronic communication with easy access to downloading scientific publications, research on ancient cultures is no longer the monopoly of closed-door archaeological institutions or university and museum departments. Even so, Egyptologists and archaeologists still pull rank when new ideas threaten to topple their coveted applecart. We speak from our own experience when we published *The Orion Mystery* in 1994 and, later, in 2002, *The Origin Map.* We, too, endured from Egyptologists and archaeologists the all-too-familiar war of words and the debunking that is passed off as criticism.

There are, nonetheless, signs of a growing acceptance that connections do exist between astronomy and the orientation, alignments, and location of ancient sites. In 1981, the First International Conference on Archaeoastronomy was held at Oxford, in England, where astronomical alignments of temples were discussed openly and seriously.

Then, in 1983, there took place the First International Conference on Ethnoastronomy at the Smithsonian Museum in Washington D.C. In 1993, the world's attention was galvanized by the German engineer Rudolf Gantenbrink and his daring exploration with a miniature robot of the star shafts in the Queen's Chamber of the Great Pyramid of Giza, and his stunning discovery of doors at their ends. Finally, in 2002, *National Geographic* staged a live television event in an attempt to open the Gantenbrink doors in the Great Pyramid. An estimated six hundred million viewers around the world saw the program. Thanks to the persistence of a new breed of archaeoastronomers such as Archie Roy of Glasgow University, Giulio Magli of Milano Politecnico, Edwin Krupp of the Griffith Observatory in Los Angeles, Anthony Aveni of Colgate University, Alex Gurstein of the International Astronomical Union, and Juan Belmonte of the Tenerife Observatory to name but a few, archaeoastronomy has now become an important aspect in the understanding of ancient cultures. Today, a few major universities around the world have added new chairs for archaeoastronomy, and more scholarly papers, articles, and books are being published by professional archaeoarstronomers and serious amateurs alike. All this has caused a a large crack in the wall of Egyptology—and archaeoastronomy has slipped in to stand beside conventional archaeology as a major tool to study the pyramids, temples, texts, and tomb drawings of the pharaohs.

So when Kim Malville, a professor emeritus of astrophysics and planetary sciences at the University of Colorado, arrived at Nabta Playa in late 1997, he was greeted not by the usual tongue-in-cheek reception, which might previously have been expected from Egyptologists and archaeologists, but with a genuinely collegial reception and a great hope that he could help solve the mystery of the stone alignments there. At this point, everyone working at Nabta Playa must have felt that under their feet was a potential intellectual and political time bomb, not only because of its great antiquity, but also because of what Malville was there to confirm. Before we go into this, however, we must understand better why the CPE made the mistake of leaving out of their research and investigation the regions of Gilf Kebir and Jebel Unwainat, for even with the problem of their great distance from Nabta Playa, it should have been obvious that they were in some way related to the ancient people who developed Nabta Playa. Let us review, then, where and when this intriguing story of the Egyptian Sahara really began. Surprisingly, it was not in Egypt, but in the dimly lit corridors of Balliol College, Oxford, England.

2
WANDERLUST

The journey of Hassanein Bey, graduate of Oxford University and now Secretary of the Egyptian Legation in Washington . . . a distance of 2200 miles, has been characterized by the Director of Desert Survey, Egypt, as "an almost unique achievement in the annals of geographic exploration."

Editor, "Crossing the Untraversed Libyan Desert," National Geographic Magazine, September 1924 To him who has the wanderlust, no other actuating motive for exploration is needed than the knowledge that a region is unknown to civilized man.

AHMED HASSANEIN BEY, "CROSSING THE
UNTRAVERSED LIBYAN DESERT,"
NATIONAL GEOGRAPHIC MAGAZINE, SEPTEMBER 1924

OXFORD GENTLEMAN, QUEEN'S LOVER, AND DEEP DESERT EXPLORER

When we think of the Arabian deserts and their rolling landscape of golden dunes, for most of us, what comes to mind are romantic figures such as Lawrence of Arabia, Omar Sharif, or even Rudolf Valentino.

Few will think of Ahmed Hassanein Bey* or even know who he was. It may come as a surprise to many, then, that according to the Royal Geographical Society of London, Hassanein Bey is ranked as the greatest desert explorer of all times, so much so that the director of the desert survey of Egypt at that time referred to Hassanein's desert exploration as "an almost unique achievement in the annals of geographic exploration."

So who really was Ahmed Hassanein Bey, and why is he important to our investigation into the origins of the pharaohs?

Ahmed Hassanein was born in Cairo in 1889. He was educated at an English private school, as was then customary for well-to-do families in Egypt. As a young man, he was sent to England to complete his gentleman's education at Balliol College, one of the most prestigious institutions of Oxford University. The very stiff-upper-lip education that he received there would serve Hassanein well for the diplomatic career he was destined to pursue in Egypt. Described by his peers and biographers as an exotic blend of court official, diplomat, Olympic champion (he represented Egypt in Brussels in the 1920 Olympics and in Paris in 1924), photographer, writer, politician, royal tutor (to the future king Farouk) and an incurable romantic (among his amorous conquests was the lovely queen Nazli), Hassanein was the last of the great desert explorers. He also had an excellent family pedigree: he was the son of an eminent scholar of Al Azhar Islamic University as well as the grandson of Egypt's last admiral and naval hero. Endowed with such impeccable breeding and education, as well as having wit, charm, and panache, Ahmed Hassanein was to become one of the most influential figures in Egypt, holding no less than the high ranks of chief of the Diwan and chamberlain to King Farouk. It is said that the young king was so dependent on Hassanein that the latter's untimely death in 1946 triggered the demise of King Farouk, which finally led to his abdication and exile in 1952. Tall, slender, romantic, charming, polite, and

---

*[Bey is a Turkish title for "chieftain." —. Ed.]

dashingly handsome, Hassanein's true passion, however, was not politics or glamorous women, but the open desert or, to be more specific, the great Egyptian Sahara. This passion would eventually drive him to undertake the most daring of desert expeditions and to discover one of the most mysterious places on earth.

He was always deeply loyal to the king of Egypt and a fervent believer in Egypt's sovereignty and independence—thus it is ironic that it was Hassanein's British education that would open doors for him and earn him a place of honor among famous explorers such as Burton, Stanley, and Livingstone. Oxford's Balliol College had—and still has—an illustrious reputation in molding promising young men into world leaders. It has an old boy's listing that reads like a who's who of famous men: it includes kings, national presidents, prime ministers, top authors, famous scientists, and Nobel laureates. Hassanein mingled comfortably in such elite company and was a sporting hero with the university's fencing team. During his stay at Oxford, he made friends with many future diplomats—in particular, with Francis Rodd, the son of Sir Rennell Rodd, Britain's ambassador to Rome and its representative at the League of Nations. Francis would later become a fellow of the Royal Geographical Society and serve as president from 1945 to 1948. This connection was to be extremely useful in bringing Hassanein's desert exploits to the attention of this prestigious society. Ironically, however, his friendship with Francis Rodd would also bring Hassanein into contact with a certain lady who was to cause him much public embarrassment, as we will soon see.

Hassanein returned to Egypt on the eve of World War I and was immediately recruited as private secretary to General Maxwell, British commander in chief of the Egyptian forces. When Maxwell left Egypt in 1916, Hassanein joined the Ministry of Interior, where, according to British intelligence, he was instrumental in squelching an anti-British riot in Upper Egypt during the so-called Revolution of 1919. Meanwhile, Hassanein maintained his sporting interests. In 1920 he was captain of the Egyptian Olympic fencing team and won for them a bronze medal.

It was during this time that King Fouad I appointed Hassanein personal tutor to the crown prince, the future and ill-fated Farouk, who, it was said, practically worshipped him. The king's mother, the lovely queen Nazli, fell deeply in love with Hassanein, and they eventually married secretly in later years.

Hassanein's fascination with the Sahara began in 1916, when, along with his old Balliol friend Francis Rodd, he was sent on a very delicate mission by King Fouad to pacify the Senussi Bedouins of the Libyan Desert. The Senussi were a confederation of Bedouin tribes in Libya who were deeply religious and had sided with the Ottoman Turks against the British in World War I. As such, they were a serious and nagging threat to Egypt's western borders with Libya. This threat had forced the Aglo-Egyptian army to mobilize thousands of troops to protect the western frontier—troops that should have been put to much better use in fighting the Turks elsewhere. Against all odds, Hassanein managed to persuade the Sennussi tribes to unite and adopt as their leader a pro-British chieftain, Sayed Idris (the future King Senussi I of Libya). The Senussi stronghold was the oasis of Kufra located nearly 800 kilometers (about 497 miles) inland from the Mediterranean coastline. In 1879, only a German explorer, Gerhard Rohlfs, had managed to reach it, but even he was not allowed to enter the oasis; he was chased away by the aggressive and fanatical Senussi. Hassanein made up his mind that he and Francis Rodd would be the first foreigners to enter Kufra:

> The inspiration for it [the journey to Kufra and beyond] dated from 1916, when I went . . . on a mission to Sayed Idris el Senussi, at Zuetina, a tiny port near Jedabya in Cyrenaica. One of the purposes of the mission was to effect an agreement with Sayed Idris, as head of the Senussi and the most influential chief in Cyrenaica, which should prevent in the future Badawi [Bedouin] raids across the western frontier of Egypt. At Zuetina I renewed acquaintance with Sayed Idris whom I had already met, through his friendship for my father, when he was returning from [a] pilgrimage to Mecca

in 1915. I told Sayed Idris of my ambition and desire to make the journey to Kufra, which had been visited only once by a stranger from across the desert's border, the intrepid German explorer Rohlfs in 1879. Sayed Idris was sympathetic with my desires, and asked me to let him know when I was ready to make the expedition. He promised to give me all the help he could in my undertaking. Early in 1917, in continuation of the same mission to the Senussi, I met their head again at Akrama, near Tobruk, and told him that I was still determined to make the journey. I proposed to go as soon as the end of the war should set me free. Sayed Idris again encouraged my determination and renewed his promise of co-operation. There was with me then on the same mission Mr. Francis Rodd, an old Balliol friend. We discussed the proposed expedition together, and agreed that we would be companions in it. At the close of the war Mrs. McGrath [a friend of Francis] brought me a letter of introduction from Mr. Rodd. She wanted to join us on the journey.[1]

Mrs. McGrath turned out to be none other than the notorious writer and traveler Rosita Forbes. When she was introduced to Hassanein in Cairo in 1920, she had already been divorced three years and had since traveled around the world. During the war she had been an ambulance driver in France and was awarded two medals for bravery, and she had also served as a journalist and informer for British intelligence in Damascus. In Cairo, Rosita moved in high circles and had befriended Colonel Lawrence Cornwallis, better known as Lawrence of Arabia. Rosita and Lawrence apparently met in secret, suggesting they had more than a casual friendship. Rosita also knew the celebrated author and adventurer Gertrude Bell.

It was Francis Rodd who introduced Rosita to Hassanein, and, according to some who knew them both, Rosita had an instant crush on the dashing and romantic Hassanein, but if there was any truth in this, neither Hassanein nor Rosita ever made it known to others. It seems that Hassanein and Francis Rodd decided to take Rosita along on their proposed expedition to the forbidden oasis of Kufra. At the last minute, however, Francis dropped out, and although Hassanein must have had second thoughts regarding taking along an unmarried foreign woman in these uncharted and dangerous parts of the Sahara, especially one as liberal and feisty as Rosita Forbes, Rosita somehow had her way. Amazingly, even Sayed Idris granted permission to Hassanein to take Rosita to Kufra—on the conditions, however, that Rosita wear Arab dress and be passed off as Hassanein's Muslim wife.

The journey to Kufra and back took three months. It was fraught with danger and drama, and, according to some, the alleged romance between Hassanein and Rosita had turned sour. No sooner had they returned to Cairo in January 1921, than Rosita and Hassanein parted company. Rosita returned to her notes and alone wrote a book, *The Secret of the Sahara: Kufara,* which was published a few months later in London. In the book, Rosita unabashedly presents herself as the leader of the expedition, and Hassanein is demoted to a glorified guide. Hassanein was too much of a gentleman to complain about this, and, to his credit, he always spoke highly of Rosita. In any case, any doubts that Rosita might have furthered about Hassanein's leadership and abilities as an explorer were soon to be dispelled, for he was already planning— this time, singlehandedly—his next expedition into the deep Sahara. This expedition would make the Kufra journey with Rosita look like a stroll in a London park.

THE LOST OASIS

In the winter of 1922, hardly a year after the events with Rosita Forbes, Hassanein headed for the small Egyptian port of Sollum near the Libyan border. From there, he set out on what later would be hailed as one of the greatest desert journeys of all time—and this time, there was no Rosita to steal his thunder. This time, too, Hassanein was under the full patronage of King Fouad I of Egypt and King Idris I of Lybia. This amazing and never-to-be-repeated journey is told in full in Hassanein's paper read at the Royal Geographical Society in London and also published in the society's journal in October 1924. Hassanein tells how he first led a camel caravan from the town of Sollum on the Mediterranean coast inland to the oasis of Siwa and from there to Kufra. After a short stay at Kufra, he took the caravan southward into totally unchartered and unexplored territory:

> There were also vague stories of the two "lost" oases of Arkenu and Uwainat lying well to the eastward of the trade route to Wadai. Those oases were almost mythical, situated as they are on no route that is travelled even by Badawi [Bedouins] or Blacks. I determined that I would go to the Sudan by way of the "lost" oases. If I could find my way to them and place them definitely on the map, it would be something worthwhile doing. . . . After leaving Kufra, the chief adventure of the expedition began. Here at last I was plunging into the untraversed and the unknown. What lay ahead? It was not the possible dangers of the journey, which made my nerves tingle and caused my spirits to mount with exhilaration—dangers are merely a part of the day's work in the desert. It was the realization that I was to explore hidden places; that I should go through a region hitherto untrodden by one of my own kind, and make, perhaps, some contribution, small though it might be, to the sum of human knowledge.[2]

Hassanein reached the first of the lost oases, Arkenu, after eight days of marching in blistering heat at daytime and bitter cold at night. This was a grueling trek, which he described as "the worst stretch of the entire journey."[3] After a few days in Arkenu, Hassanein set south toward the other lost oasis of Jebel Uwainat. He and his party traveled only at night due to the unbearable heat of day at this time of year. His Bedouin guide used the age-old tradition of night travel by navigating with the stars—which was, almost certainly, the same method used by the prehistoric people of Nabta Playa when they roamed the vast Sahara thousands of years earlier:

> The manner in which a Bedouin guide finds his way across the desert at night is a source of wonder to the uninitiated. In a region, which provides no familiar landmarks, he depends solely upon the stars. As we were proceeding in a southwesterly direction during most of our night trekking the polestar was at the guide's back. He would glance over his shoulder, face so that the polestar would be behind his right ear then take a sight to a star to the south in that line. He would march for perhaps five minutes with his eye riveted on this star, then turn and make a new observation of the polestar; for, of course, the star to the south was constantly progressing westward. He would then select a new star for guidance and continue.[4]

It took an overnight trek to reach the western flank of the lost oasis of Jebel Uwainat. There, he was confronted by a huge rocky massif sprouting out of the flat desert like a giant iceberg: "The range in that vicinity rose in a sheer cliff from the desert floor. Heaped against it were masses of boulders, which through the ages had been worn smooth by the grinding, polishing action of wind and sand. It was as if here were piled the arsenals of Stone-Age giants whose weapons had been gargantuan slings."[5]

At Jebel Uwainat, Hassanein "found ample supplies of water in the deep-shaded recesses of the cliffs."[6] Usually, in these parts of the remote desert, water is found in very deep underground aquifers that are often far too deep to be reached by simply digging wells. Here at Jebel Uwainat, however, the water was at the surface, coming from the occasional rain that trickled down the rocks and collected in natural pools. Hassanein found four such pools (called *uwyun,* literally "eyes" in Arabic, and hence the name Uwainat, meaning "many eyes"), which had water that was "cool and of good quality."[7] In the days that followed, Hassanein and his men circumnavigated the outer rim of the Uwainat massif, and at night, they camped in the dry wadis (valleys) and always assumed that they were completely alone in this strange wilderness. One morning, however, as Hassanein woke up, standing before him was a young Black woman holding a bowl of milk in offering. She was slender and very beautiful, and Hassanein at first thought he was having a dream. The woman spoke a strange language, which Hassanein's guide recognized as being of the Tebu people, pastoral nomads known to have once roamed this part of the Sahara. The young woman offered to take them to the king of Uwainat. He turned out to be a Black man called Herri who claimed to rule over some one hundred and fifty Tebu who lived there. King Herri spoke of mysterious rock carvings of animals and men not known in this part of the Sahara, and Hassanein was taken to see them:

> The animals are rudely drawn, but not, unskillfully carved. There are lions, giraffes, ostriches, and all kinds of gazelles, but no camels. The carvings are from a half to a quarter of an inch deep and the edges of the lines in some instances are considerably weathered. "Who made these?" I asked Malakheni, the Tebu. He expressed the belief that they were the work of the *jinn* [demons]. "For," he added, "what man can do these things now?" What man among the present inhabitants, indeed! Here is a puzzle, which must be left to the research of archeologists. Suffice it [is] to say that there are no giraffes in this part of Africa now, nor do they live in any similar desert country anywhere. Perhaps even more significant is the absence of camels from the drawings. If they had been native to the region at the time that the carvings were made, surely this most important beast of the desert would have been pictured. But the camel came to Africa from Asia not later [than] 500 BCE. Can these carvings antedate that event? Or has the character of this country undergone such astonishing modification to have converted into desert a fertile region in which the giraffe roamed, and the camel was not a familiar burden-bearer? With the inspection of these rock carvings, my hasty exploration of Uwainat was concluded.[8]

Figure 2.1. The tebu of the Sahara photographed by Ahmed Hassanein, 1923. Courtesy of SaharaSafaris.org/hassaneinbey.

Figure 2.2. King Herri of Unwainat photographed by Ahmed Hassanein, 1923. Courtesy of SaharaSafaris.org/hassaneinbey.

Hassanein turned down an offer by Herri to show him more of these rock carvings. He felt that it was not wise to linger too long in these uncertain circumstances. Hassanein did realize, nonetheless, the great importance of his discovery, for he later wrote: "[I]t was in Uwainat that I made the most interesting find of my 2,200-mile journey. I had heard rumors of the existence of certain pictographs on rocks . . . on the evening of our arrival I set out to find them."[9] As we will see, what Hassanein had discovered, although he himself never knew this, was the first irrefutable evidence of a prehistoric presence of humans in this remote part of Egypt. Many decades later, scholars would begin to see in them the origins of the pharaohs and, quite possibly indeed, of civilization as we know it.

Upon his return to Cairo several months later, Hassanein was received with honors and given the title of *pasha* (akin to "lord") by King Fouad I, as well as being hailed as a hero by the World Press. The Royal Geographical Society of England gave him the highly coveted gold medal, and he also received a knighthood. Hassanein deserved this admiration and honor. He was now also fully vindicated, and any doubts and misconceptions about his ability as a deep desert explorer were now removed. Rosita, however, was unrepentant. She still managed to cause further embarrassment at the Royal Geographical Society, where she claimed that she had been the second European, after Gerhard Rohlfs, to reach the oasis of Kufra—implying, of course, that Hassanein, being an Egyptian, did not really count. Many of the members of the Society took offense, and the usually restrained and friendly Gertrude Bell could not help remarking of Rosita: "[I]n matter[s] of trumpet-blowing she is unique. . . . I am sick of Rosita Forbes! And the thing that makes me sickest is that she scarcely ever alludes to that capital boy, Hassanein, who was with her, an Egyptian, without whom she couldn't have done anything . . .!"[10]

THE DESERT PRINCE AND
THE ENGLISH PATIENT

Another Egyptian of similar impeccable breeding immediately followed in the footsteps of Hassanein. This was the heir to the throne of Egypt, Prince Kemal El Din Ibn Hussein. Prince Kemal, who had received his education in Austria, refused the throne in order to pursue a career as a desert explorer and cartographer. Inspired by the recent exploits of Hassanein, Prince Kemal set about organizing and financing his own expeditions into the Egyptian Sahara—but this time not by camel caravan, as Hassanein had done, but with automobiles for off-road travel that were specially designed for him by Citroen and Ford. With these vehicles, Prince Kemal set out in 1926 from Cairo to Dakhla, and from there into the deep desert southwest toward Jebel Uwainat. Some 400 kilometers (249 miles) beyond Dakhla (and still 200 kilometes—124 miles—from Jebel Uwainat), Prince Kemal discovered an immense mountain range, which he christened Gilf Kebir. Amazingly, back in 1923 Hassanein had missed seeing it because he had traveled south from Kufra to Jebel Uwainat, and was thus 100 kilometers west of Gilf Kebir.

The mountain range of Gilf Kebir is 300 kilometers (186 miles) long and some 80 kilometers wide. It is almost the size of Switzerland, and, when approached from the west, seems to jut out of the flat desert like a monstrous tsunami in stone. Prince Kemal had much better scientific equipment at his disposal than Hassanein, and he was able to fix firmly all these new locations, including the peaks of Jebel Uwainat, on the ordinance map of Egypt. He missed seeing, however, the extensive prehistoric rock art that is found on the west side of Gilf Kebir. This was discovered later by another explorer whom Prince Kemal would actually sponsor: none other than the enigmatic and colorful Count Lazlo Almasy, a Hungarian aristocrat who, among many other things, is said to have been a secret agent for the Germans in World War II.

Almasy planned an expedition to Gilf Kebir with fellow travelers and sponsors Baron Robert Clayton and Robert's pretty wife, Lady

Figure 2.3. Early Egyptian desert explorers, clockwise from left: Ahmed Hassanein in 1922, Ralph Bagnold (see chapter 4) with desert vehicle in 1930, Prince Kemal el Din with tract vehicle in 1926, and Count Lazlo Almasy ca. 1930.

Clayton. The three were immortalized in the 1996 movie *The English Patient*. The trio proposed to get to Gilf Kebir by air with a single-engine Gipsy Moth airplane owned by the Claytons. Accompanying them were Patrick Clayton of the desert survey unit (and no relation to Baron Clayton) and wing commander H. S. Penderel, who was to pilot the airplane. Their objective was to search for the fabled lost oasis-city of Zarzora, a sort of Shangri-La of the desert, which Almasy believed was tucked away somewhere in the newly discovered Gilf Kebir. With their fantastic stories of an oasis lost to the world, Bedouins had long fantasized about the legend of Zarzora. They described it as having wonderful springs and being surrounded by a white wall that hid magnificent castles and gardens. They believed it was southwest of Dakhla, the farthest inhabited oasis in Egypt.

At Gilf Kebir, Almasy and his friends discovered the now-famous Caves of Swimmers at the mouth of a valley on the west side of Gilf Kebir. These two caves—more like deep ledges—contained a plethora of rock art that was actually drawn on the sandstone with vivid colors rather than carved. It depicted Black men, women, and children in social activities, some clearly enjoying swimming and diving in a river or lake. See chapter 5 for more description when we recount our own expedition to Gilf Kebir. Meanwhile, flying west from Gilf Kebir with the Gipsy Moth, Almasy and his colleagues spotted a group of lush valleys with unusual amounts of trees and vegetation, which they thought was the fabled oasis of Zarzora. Later, however, in 1932, when Almasy reexplored the region on the ground, he found no springs or white walls—not even the slightest signs of human habitation, let alone stone castles. Instead, he found typical wadis with the usual rugged acacia trees and a few shrubs here and there. In fact, there were three wadis (valleys) called Abdel Malik, Hamra, and Talh, which were already known to the ancient Tebu people of the region and which, at least according to Almasy's account, the Tebu also called Zarzora.

Yet, like the fabled lost oasis of Shangri-La or the mythical Atlantis, the legend of Zarzora still persists to this day, and, as we will see, it still lures eccentric explorers in search of adventure and glory. There is a strange irony about all these modern explorations and their claims of discovering of this or that lost oases, however: none of these places were lost at all. Instead, they were known to the ancients and were only rediscovered in modern times. Hassanein and Prince Kemal were definitely not the first Egyptians to reach Jebel Uwainat and Gilf Kebir, for the ancient Egyptians had in fact already beaten them to it by several thousands years.

THE EXPEDITIONS OF HARKHUF

About forty-two hundred years ago, on the very beautiful island of Elephantine near Aswan, a man of high rank named Iry and his eldest son Harkhuf were preparing for the most daring desert expedition ever to be attempted in antiquity or, indeed, even in modern times. On the command of the ruling pharaoh, they were about to leave their tranquil and lush island on the Nile and set out westward into the open and uncharted desert. In those days, this adventure would have been the equivalent of a first manned NASA mission to Mars. Indeed, the far-away region that they would eventually reach is so similar to the Martian landscape that the Egyptian scientist at NASA, Dr. Farouk El Baz, actually uses it as a model to study the geology of the Red Planet.[11]

Iry had been chief lector priest to the pharaoh Pepi I, and after the king's untimely death, Iry retained the same post under the new pharaoh, Merenre I (sixth dynasty, 2323–2150 BCE). Upon their return, and after Iry passed away, his son Harkhuf succeeded him as chief lector to Merenre I and also to this pharaoh's successor, the boy-king Pepi II. Harkhuf was also appointed governor of Aswan and Elephantine. It was under the orders of King Merenre I and then later King Pepi II that Harkhuf and his father Iry mounted several expeditions into the deep desert to "explore the way to the land of Yam."[12]

But where was Yam, and why was it so important for the pharaohs to send their most trusted advisors on such a dangerous mission . . . one from which they might never have returned? The location of the land or kingdom of Yam has long confounded Egyptologists. Some have believed it to be located south of Aswan, between the first and second cataracts of the Nile; others have thought that it was in the west, in the region of the inhabited oases such as Kharga or Dakhla.[13] These relatively accessible locations were proposed by Egyptologists because, until recently, scholars were convinced that the ancient Egyptians could not travel into the deep desert but could journey only southward along the Nile Valley or westward, but no farther than the habitable oases. Beyond these oases lies a seemingly endless and lifeless desert, a vast expanse of pure nothingness of sand, dust, and rocks, and so Egyptologists insisted that no one in their right mind would attempt to venture there without being sure they could return safely. The practical problem is that the maximum distance that anyone can travel into this waterless desert on foot (or by donkey, as Harkhuf did) is about 200 kilometers (about 124 miles), unless there are some water sources along the way. Any farther would mean a certain gruesome death by dehydration. Gilf Kebir and Jebel Uwainat, however, are a staggering 650 kilometers (400 miles) west of the Nile, and the journey to these places is theoretically impossible without a means to replenish the caravan with water and food.

In addition, it seems that another issue—one of a spiritual nature—troubled the ancient Egyptians: they apparently regarded the Sahara as the place of death and a place where evil spirits lived. Thus, according to the Egyptologists, they would certainly have refrained from venturing too far into it.

Finally, and more to the point, there was not a single shred of evidence that could attest to the presence of ancient Egyptians beyond the oases. Although, on the one hand there is much evidence of their presence in all five major oases of the Egyptian Sahara—Kharga, Dakhla, Siwa, Bahareya, and Farafra—in the form of temples, tombs, and an abundance of artifacts, there was for a long time absolutely no trace of them beyond the vicinity of these oases. Because of this lack of evidence, then, and also because of the forbidding geographical conditions, Egyptologists concluded that no one in ancient times had traveled into the deep desert. Indeed, it was not until relatively recent times—in 1879, to be more precise—that the likes of explorers such as Gerhard Rohls, and later, in 1920, Hassanein and Rosita Forbes, attempted such deep-desert journeys. The Egyptologists concluded that even if Yam was in the Egyptian Sahara, it must have been one of the habitable oases, either Kharga or Dakhla. As far as they were concerned, Gilf Kebir and Jebel Uwainat, let alone anywhere beyond these, were simply too far and out of reach for Harkhuf.

Nevertheless, some open-minded Egyptologists admitted that Yam's "location remains uncertain. . . . [O]nly new archaeological discoveries inscribed or otherwise, could resolve the issue."[14] This last statement—that ancient inscriptions could resolve the issue—was uncanny, for, as we will soon see, that is precisely what did happen in late 2007: ancient inscriptions were found that finally helped locate the lost kingdom of Yam. Before we go into this, however, let us re-examine the writings of Harkhuf (they are inscribed on the walls of his tomb at Aswan) and see for ourselves what can be derived from them. Here is the full text translated by French Egyptologist Claire Lalouette:

> His Majesty Merenre, my master, sent me, together with my father, Sole Companion and Lector-Priest, Iry, to the land of Yam to explore its ways. I carried out this mission in seven months, I brought back all sorts of tributes, beautiful and rare and I was praised for it very highly.
>
> His Majesty sent me a second time, alone. I went by way of the Elephantine road and returned via the land of Irtet, Makher and Teres of Irtet at the end of a voyage of eight months. I returned carrying tributes of this land in very great numbers, of a kind, which nobody had ever brought to Egypt before. I returned, coming from the camp of the chief of Setu and Irtet after having explored this land. You will find no other Sole Companion, Chief of interpreters who has reached [so far] into the land of Yam before.
>
> His Majesty sent me for a third time to the land of Yam. I went there from the Nome of Thinis by the oasis road and I observed that the chief of the land of Yam had left for the land of the Timhiu to chastise them, as far as the western corner of the sky. I followed his trail to the land of the Timhiu and I pacified him until he adored all the gods for the sake of the royal Sovereign. [I shall make haste . . . with a man from the land of Yam] . . . so that His Majesty Merenre, my royal Lord, shall know [that I went to the land of Timhiu] following the chief of the land of Yam. After having given satisfaction

to this celebrated chief . . . I returned with three hundred donkeys burdened with incense, ebony, hekenu perfume, grain, panther skins, elephant tusks, many boomerangs, and all kinds of beautiful and good presents. When the chief of Irtet-Setu-Wa-Wat saw how strong and numerous were the troops of the land of Yam returning with me towards the residence [marching] in the company of the army which had been sent with me, he handed over, to be given to me, bulls and goats and guided me through the ways of the hills of Irtet—because of the skill and the vigilance which I had shown, more than any other Companion, Chief of interpreters, former envoy to the land of Yam. Then, this servant followed the course of the river as far as the Residence; and it was arranged that the prince, Sole Companion, Steward of the two halls of libation [?] came to meet me with ships loaded with date wine, cakes, bread and beer.

THE PRINCE, TREASURER TO THE KING OF LOWER EGYPT, SOLE COMPANION, LECTOR-PRIEST, TREASURER OF THE GOD, SECRET COUNSELOR FOR THE DECREES, THE IMAKU, HARKHUF.[15]

In this inscription, Harkhuf claims that he "carried out this mission in seven months," and another in eight months. The Egyptologist James H. Breasted translated Harkhuf's statement thus: "I did it in only seven months!" Clearly this shows that Harkhuf was proud of his accomplishment of the time it took him to go to Yam and return, otherwise he would not have boasted about it.[16] We know, too, that Harkhuf used donkeys for these journeys (the camel was not known in Egypt until much later). Any experienced desert traveler knows that a donkey laden with a typical load of sixty kilograms (about a hundred and thirty pounds) can travel only 15 kilometers (about 9 miles) a day average (allowing for rest breaks) and even fewer kilometers if the terrain is rough and craggy.

In the ancient Egyptian calendar, seven months amounted to two hundred and ten days. Therefore, we can estimate the distance of Hakhuf's travel to Yam and back as 3,150 kilometers (1,957 miles).

Yet the distance from the Nile Valley to Kharga and back is only 400 kilometers (249 miles); and to Dakhla and back, the distance is 540 kilometers (336 miles) and would take only thirty-six days at the most. If either Kharga or Dakhla were Harkhuf's destination, as some Egyptologists have claimed, then surely Harkhuf would not have boasted to the pharaoh that he "did it in only seven months." The conclusion must be that Yam is much farther than either Kharga or Dakhla. Our estimate shows that it must have been at least some 1,500 kilometers (about 932 miles) from the Nile Valley at Aswan, most certainly in a southwestward direction. Most Egyptologists, however, have insisted that Harkhuf traveled south, albeit probably first going west to the Kharga oasis, but then turning south along the Darb El Arbaeen (the so-called Forty-Days Trail) parallel to the Nile to reach a place between the second and third cataracts in the Sudan, where, some say, Yam could also have been located.[17] Other than the fact that the distance to this location and back would be only 1,000 kilometers (about 621 miles), and thus 2,150 kilometers (1,336 miles) short of our estimate, we must also wonder why Harkhuf chose to travel in the desert parallel to the Nile to reach the second cataract when he could have much more easily sailed by boat on the Nile itself. To explain this, Egyptologists have speculated that perhaps the region on the Nile south of Aswan was in the hands of hostile tribes, and Harkhuf may have wanted to bypass them by traveling inland in the desert. In his inscriptions, however, Harkhuf makes it clear that Yam was somewhere very far. He started in Upper Egypt and traveled along the "oases road" and then westward "to the western corner of the sky"—and not, as Egyptologists claim, south toward the Sudan: "I went there from the Nome of Thinis [Upper Egypt] by the oasis road and I observed that the chief of the land of Yam had left for the land of the Timhiu to chastise them, as far as the western corner of the sky. I followed his trail to the land of the Timhiu." The Timhiu or Temehou are often said by Egyptologists to be the ancient dwellers of the Sahara in southern Libya. This belief prompted the

American Egyptologist Hans Geodicke of Johns Hopkins University to ask "where did the chief of Yam go in "the land of the Libyans" "to beat the Libyans"? The intention attributed to the chief of Yam "to beat the Libyans to the Western corner of heaven" makes it clear that the chief of Yam had gone in a westerly direction."[18]

Yet Hans Goedicke, like all Egyptologists before him, held firm that the ancient Egyptians could not travel into the deep desert beyond the oasis of Dakhla. He therefore concluded that Kharga was the land of Yam and that Dakhla was the land of the Timhiu (Libyans). But this is clearly incorrect, for we have already seen that if this was the case, Harkhuf's boast that it took only seven months to go to Yam and return does not make sense. Yet going farther due west does not make much sense either, because this direction would have taken Harkhuf directly into the Great Sand Sea, a formidable barrage of high dunes that even today cannot be crossed without specially equipped four-wheel-drive vehicles.

So which direction did Hakhuf take? The phrase "western corner of the sky" gives us a clue. The ancient Egyptians saw the sky as being held up by four pillars at each corner. In addition, at the time of Hakhuf, they defined the horizon as having two parts: east and west. The "western corner of the sky," therefore, implies the southwest corner—and it leads toward Gilf Kebir and, beyond it, to the Tibesti highlands in Chad. As we have seen, however, such a journey is not possible without adequate sources of water along the way, and no such water sources, either on the way or at Gilf Kebir itself, existed. The first available water is 200 kilometers southwest, at Jebel Uwainat. Interestingly, though, in a 1965 article by G. W. Murray, the director of the topographical survey of Egypt, Murray explains that he examined the inscriptions of Harkhuf, and he suggests: "The Land of Temeh [Timhiu/Libyans] was an Egyptian expression for the inhabited parts of the southern Libyan desert. They were widely scattered . . . [I]n the far south-west, the sandstone massif of the Gilf Kebir made up, to borrow a phrase from the Chief of Yam, 'the western corners of heaven. . . .'"[19]

Bearing this in mind, we can note another intriguing term found in the letter written to Harkhuf by the young King Pepi II. In this letter, Pepi II refers to Yam as *ta-akhet-iu,* which Egyptologists translate as "land of the horizon dwellers." In hieroglyphs it is written thus:

"Land of the horizon dwellers" implies that Yam was a very distant place—so distant that its people were deemed to live in the horizon. The historian A. J. Arkell even suggested that Yam was as far in the southwest as Darfur in the Sudan.[20] Where exactly was Yam, however, and who or what were the mysterious horizon dwellers?

We know with absolute certainty that, millennia before Harkhuf went to Yam, the southwest corner of the Egyptian Sahara either was inhabited or visited regularly by a Black people as attested by the rock art found at Gilf Kebir and Jebel Uwainat. Since 2003, we have known that these Black people were also in the Nabta Playa region, thanks to the CPE's discovery of a prehistoric cemetery only 20 kilometers (about 12 miles) from Nabta Playa near a large sand dune called Jebel Ramlah.

[The anthropological and forensic analysis] . . . show that two different populations—Mediterranean and sub-Saharan—co-existed here [at Gebel Ramlah near Nabta Playa] . . . [T]he people who inhabited the shores of the Gebel Ramlah lake were not cut off from the rest of the world. Their contacts sometimes stretched very far, as is evidenced by unearthed objects made of raw materials that were not to be found in the vicinity, and must have been brought in from outside. The best example of such long-distance imports is a nose plug made of turquoise, the closest sources of which are located 1000 km. to the north on the Sinai Peninsula. Shells were brought in either from the Nile, 100 km. away, or from the Red Sea much further to the east. . . . Ivory was brought from the south, since elephants, which belonged among the Ethiopian fauna, could not survive in such dry savanna. . . . The typical beliefs of the ancient Egyptians [to preserve the body so that the spirit could rest in peace in the after-world] may indeed have originated with the Neolithic peoples inhabiting the ever-drier savannah in what is today the Western Desert, only centuries prior to the emergence of ancient Egypt. In the basin of the dried-up Nabta Playa lake, located only 20 km. away, the same people who left behind the graveyards at the foot of Gebel Ramlah, erected gigantic clusters of stelae, extending over many kilometers. . . . Perhaps it was indeed these [prehistoric] people who provided the crucial stimulus towards the emergence of state organization in ancient Egypt.[21]

Here, at the foot of the dune, the CPE found three burial areas that contained human skeletons of sixty-seven individuals dated to six thousand years ago. According to Fred Wendorf and Romuald Schild of the CPE, "physical anthropology of rare skeletal remains . . . suggests racial association of the populations with the Sub-Saharan or Black groups."[22] In many burials, the bones of several individuals were placed together, thrown pell-mell, as if they had been brought to the grave in bags. This suggested to the anthropologists that the individuals may have died elsewhere in the Sahara, and their bones were brought back to their home settlement for burial near their ancestors. From this evidence, it seems that the Black people of Jebel Ramlah and Nabta Playa ventured far and wide in the Sahara when the climate was humid and the desert fertile. Could these people be the same as those of Jebel Uwainat and Gilf Kebir? Further, could they all have originated in the mysterious land of Yam?

If such thoughts were held by Fred Wendorf and Romuald Schild, then they kept them to themselves as far as we know. At this stage, we cannot help but recall that, in 1923, Ahmed Hassanein encountered a colony of black-skinned people at Jebel Uwainat, and we can also recall the Tebu man who claimed that the prehistoric art that was found there was his ancestors'. According to the Sahara historian J. L. Wright, these people that Hassanein encountered were Tebu refugees from the Goran tribe who originally had come from the Tibesti Mountains in northern Chad.[23] Hassanein was able to confirm this when he wrote, "The southern portion of the Libyan Desert is inhabited by tribes of blacks—Tebu, Goran, and Bidiat—who are rather more refined in features than the central African negroes."[24]

Unfortunately, before anyone could determine from where these Black people at Jebel Uwainat had originated, they left the region sometime after Hassanein's visit, never to be seen again. It is probable they returned to the oasis of Kufra, where, from time immemorial some of the ancient Tebu lived until the Arab conquest in the eighth century.[25] Were the ancestors of the Tebu, then, those people who were called Temenu by the ancient Egyptians and who, as Harkhuf reported, were chased by the "Chief of Yam" to the "western corner of heaven"? Further, could their true place of origin have been far in the southwest, into the highlands of northern Chad? Until recently, the answer from Egyptologists and anthropologists would have been a resounding no— that is, until there came another aficionado of the desert to join the ranks of Egyptian Sahara explorers such as Rohlfs Gerhard, Ahmed Hassanein, and Count Laszo Almasy.

FROM FORD COMPANY
TRAINEE TO CAMEL DRIVER

Carlo Bergmann arrived in Egypt in the mid-1980s. He was sent there by the Ford Motor Company to complete a management-training course. After a visit to the camel market in Cairo, Bergmann was so fascinated by these "ships of the desert" that he resigned from his job then and there and bought his first camel in order to become a desert explorer. He set up a base in the oasis of Dakhla, increased his camel fleet to twelve, and roamed the desert in search of lost oases. Bergmann was eventually solicited by Dr. Rudolf Kruper of the Heinrich Barth Institute to assist him in his explorations southwest of Dakhla. Carlo, however, was not impressed with the way the archaeologists explored from the comfort of their four-wheel-drive vehicles. He believed that moving by camel or on foot radically increases the chances of spotting something of value. With the desert's blinding sunlight and a landscape that is much the same everywhere, an explorer could easily miss seeing even the entrance to a cave unless he vigilantly checked every rock and mound along the way. Carlo Bergmann also had the advantage of a sixth sense regarding where to look for prehistoric artifacts—an ability he developed after years of exploring the desert on foot.

Bergmann knew that Bedouins in the past told stories about a lost temple in the open desert a few days march from Dakhla oasis. They told the British archaeologist Sir Gardner Wilkinson in 1835, "Some ruins of uncertain date [were] discovered about nine years ago by an Arab in search of stray camels . . . [and that their ancient] inhabitants are blacks."[26] Bergmann also knew that Wilkinson had not attempted to verify the story, probably because he discounted it as a tall tale told by imaginative Arabs. The same happened in 1910 to the British engineer and explorer W. J. Harding King, who was also told by Bedouins of a stone temple that existed "eighteen hours journey west of Gedida in Dakhla Oasis,"[27] but much like Wilkinson before him, Harding King dismissed the story as twaddle. Carlo Bergmann, however, took these stories seriously, and, in 2000, after six attempts to locate the alleged stone temple, he did, in fact, find something that matched the description and location given to Wilkinson and Harding King:

The "stone temple" revealed itself as a conical hill about 30 meters [about 98 feet] high and 60 meters [about 197 feet] in length. On its eastern side there is a natural terrace. This platform, which has an average width of 3 [about 10 feet] meters and a length of approximately 35 meters [about 115 feet] is about 7 meters [23 feet] above the ground and fenced by a dry wall of stone slabs. From the distance the place has some resemblance with the Nabataean rock-palaces and -tombs at Petra. When setting my foot onto the terrace my eyes glanced over a breathtaking arrangement of hieroglyphic texts, of cartouches of Khufu [Cheops] and of his son Djedefre, of short notes from stone-masons, of two figures of a pharaoh smiting the enemies and of enigmatic signs [water mountain symbols] evidently placed on the rock-face in wilful order. All these engravings were depicted in the midst of representations of animals and human figures from Prehistoric and Old Kingdom times. As pharaoh Djedefre's name first caught my eye, I christened the site Djedefre's water-mountain.[28]

There are hieroglyphic texts carved on the east face of the DWM which report that the pharaoh Khufu (fourth dynasty and builder of the Great Pyramid at Giza) ordered two "overseers of recruits" called Iymeri and Bebi to take an expedition of about 400 men (two regiments) into this "desert region" to collect an substance named "mefat," which, according to Egyptologists, was probably a mineral powder used for making red paint. The expedition took place in "the year of the thirteenth count of cattle," which Egyptologists reckon to be the twenty-sixth year of reign of Khufu. The inscription reads:

> "the year after the 13th occasion of the census of all large and small cattle of the North and the South of the Horus Medjedu (Khufu) given life eternally, the overseers of the recruits of the escort, Imeri and Bebi, they came with two regiments of recruits under their command, to make 'Mefat' from the pigments of the desert district."

The word "Mefat" (MfAt) was previously not know to Egyptologists, although the term "fat"or "fa" was known and generally taken to mean "powder" or "dust." This led many experts to propose that Mefat was probably red ochre (ferric oxide), which is used to make red paint. Since the pyramids of Giza and the sphinx are believed to have been originally painted red (partly at least), the suggestion that this expedition was for this purpose is a viable one, although far from being proved. Lending support to this connection with Giza is also several "seals" and "leather bags" dated to the fourth dynasty found at Giza; the "seals" mention expeditions of four hundred men sent to the desert to collect red ocre, and some of this substance was found in the leather bags. But the precise meaning of Mefat is still debated among experts, and Carlo Bergmann, the discoverer of the DWM, has proposed that it may not be "inorganic" but perhaps some organic substance. Here are Bergmann's views on Mefat:

> According to Kuhlmann, the translator of the fourth-dynasty inscriptions at DWM (Kuhlmann, K., "the Oasis bypath or the issue of desert trade in pharaonic times," in Tides of the desert, 2002), the Old Kingdom expeditions of Khufu and Djedefre had come to the site (and to Biar Jaqub) in order to produce powder (mefat) from SS'-pigments (?) taken from the "desert district." The term SS' has not been substantiated in hieroglyphic writing. Despite of scrupulous search for ancient pigment-quarrying activities, which (in a landscape where ancient relics have prevailed undisturbed over long periods of time) would remain conspicuous up to date, not the slightest indication of such works was found. Is, therefore, Kuhlmann's interpretation of SS' meaning "pigment" inconsistent with the findings of our investigation? Or was SS' collected merely from the ground, thence leaving no traces of its removal? Furthermore, is SS' really an unorganic pigment or is it of organic origin? A trial-trench at DWM has brought to light three hearths, seal impressions, potsherds of cups, bowls, and storage jars characteristic of the early Old Kingdom as well as shale-tempered pottery of the Sheikh Muftah group. In one of the hearths numerous parts of locusts and even complete specimens, which had been roasted

on the spot, were found. Most probably insects like these, the former having been radiocarbon dated to about 2600 BC, were part
of the daily diet of, at one time, some four hundred followers of
Khufu. For such purpose great amounts of locusts must have been
collected in the vicinity of DWM. Do their remains attest for sufficient vegetation in Biar Jaqub; "green land," by which the insects
once were attracted? If Biar Jaqub has to be envisaged as a florish-
ing oasis during Old Kingdom times, the probabilty of SS′ being
a much-esteemed organic substance should be estimated high. An
investigation of the hill in ½ kilometre distance to the stonecircle
settlement revealed no traces of ancient mining operations. If, in one
way or the other, SS′ was obtained from here (as a pigment incorporated in the sandstone or in layers of variegated shales fused into the
rock), would it then not have made sense for the ancients to errect
their settlement at the foot of the prominent landmark? During all
of the winter such considerations occupied my mind. Later, back in
Germany (in early summer of 2005), Friedrich Berger and Giancarlo
Negro called my attention to a press release, which reported the discovery of fourth dynasty seals and leather bags containing ferric
oxide. According to inscriptions on pieces of pottery belonging to
the find, the expedition, which consisted of more than four hundred
men, had been sent to the "desert district" in search of red paint to
decorate the pyramids. The discovery was made by Egyptian archaeologists in the region of the Giza pyramids."[29]

The Djedefre Water Mountain, as Bergamann now called it, is 80
kilometers (about 50 miles) southwest of Daklha oasis and is now under
the supervision of Egypt's Supreme Council of Antiquities (SCA). Until
recently, however, it was investigated by the German Archaeological
Institute in Cairo and the Heinrich Barth Institute of the University of
Cologne. The German team reported that the hieroglyphic inscriptions
found on the east side of the mound mention several expeditions during the twenty-fifth and twenty-seventh years of the reign of the pha-

Figure 2.4. Aerial view of Giza pyramids. Note the eastern offset of the third/smaller pyramid.

raoh Khufu, builder of the Great Pyramid at Giza (ca. 2450 BCE). They noted, too, that the name of Khufu's son and successor, Djedefre, is more prominent and appears alongside (and also within) the so-called water mountain sign, which Bergmann describes as "a pack of horizontal zig-zag lines framed by a sharply incised and slightly rounded rectangle, the upper corner of which ending in two small humps."[30]

The Djedefre Water Mountain also has engraved on its walls rock art, which is clearly prehistoric, for it depicts giraffes, elephants, and other creatures that since at least 4000 BCE could be found only thousands of kilometers farther south in Africa, but must have been here near Dakhla before that date when the Sahara was fertile. Most of the prehistoric rock art and the pharaonic inscriptions are high up on the east face and about 8 to 10 meters (about 26 to 33 feet) above ground level. They can be reached by an ancient man-made escarpment that leads to a platform cut into the mound. The platform itself faces due east, the direction of sunrise, and it is very evident that at dawn on this platform there is astronomical meaning to this orientation, as we will discuss in chapter 4. The most prominent inscription is found dead center of the east face and, inside a rectangle that has two protrusions or peaks at the top, bears the name of King Djedefre (see plate 2). This stylized hieroglyph denotes a mountain (⩊). The ancient Egyptians used a very similar sign, but with a sun disk between the two peaks. This (⩊) denoted the idea of a horizon and a sunrise.

It is thus perhaps relevant to note in passing that Djedefre was the first royal devotee of a new solar cult devised by the priests of Heliopolis, and he was also the first pharaoh to incorporate into his name the word Re (the sun god) and to add Son of Re to his royal titles.[31] His (now) truncated pyramid at Abu Ruwash, which stands some 7 kilometers (about 4 miles) north of the Giza plateau, is thought by some to have been the first sun temple and, like his mountain temple in the Sahara, was also made to face the rising sun due east. Clearly, the new symbolism brought into the royal cult by Djedefre is intensely solar and may have been the stimulus for his successors in the fourth dynasty, such as the pharaohs Khafre and Menkaure, builders of the second and third pyramids at Giza, also to add Re to their names. This new solar cult was even more prominent with the kings of the fifth and sixth dynasties, who built sun temples at Abu Ghorab, a few kilometres south of Giza. Oddly, it was the kings of the sixth dynasty whom Harkhuf and his father Iry had so diligently served by finding the way to the kingdom of Yam. At any rate, we will take a closer look at all this in chapter 6.

Meanwhile barely a few years after Carlo Bergmann's discovery of Djedefre Water Mountain, another chance discovery of a similar water mountain was made by a German team of anthropologists, but this time the site was a staggering 700 kilometers (over 400 miles) south of Dakhla and deep inside Sudan, adjacent to the town of Dongola. To everyone's surprise, this other water mountain contained prehistoric rock art perfectly matching that of the mysterious Djedefre Water Mountain. This rock art was studied by the German anthropologist Rudoph Kuper:

. . . [T]he isolated but identical presentation of the water ideograms [near Dongola] more than 700 kilometers south of the Dakhla area . . . bears implications for the question of early Egyptian relations with Sudanese Nubia. It suggests a line or a network of communication across the Eastern Sahara as late as the early third millennium BC. . . . The new evidence supports the scenario that even after 3,000 BC the Libyan Desert was not completely void of human activity. In its southern part, cattle keepers could survive as late as the second millennium BC. . . . Apparently, the Egyptian Nile Valley and the oases were connected with these regions and farther African destinations beyond by a network of donkey cara-van routes crossing southern Egypt. [32]

What Kuper seems to be saying is that prehistoric Black peo-ple living in the Egyptian Sahara not only were able to commu-nicate with others as far south as Dongola in Sudan, but also were probably still around when the pharaohs of the early dynasties (ca. 2500–2100 BCE), sent their emissaries, such as Harkhuf, into the Sahara. In 1990, German archaeologist G. Burkhard found a small rock mound 30 kilometers (about 19 miles) south of Dakhla which had on it prehistoric petroglyphs of wild animals and also an ancient Egyptian hieroglyphic inscription— "Regnal year 23, the steward Meri he goes up to meet the Oasis Dwellers"[33]—tentatively dated to the sixth dynasty (and thus contemporary with Harkhuf). This dis-covery prompted Rudolph Kuper to consider the possibility that the ancient Egyptians might have reached the extreme southwest region of the Egyptian Sahara, perhaps as far as Gilf Kebir.[34] The reason for Kuper's uncanny prediction was his awareness of the existence of a hill some 200 kilometers (about 124 miles) southwest of Dakhla known as Abu Ballas Hill (Father of Pots Hill or Pottery Hill), which had been discovered in 1918 by the British explorer John Ball. Strewn all along its base were hundreds of large clay pots dated to the Old Kingdom (ca. 2500–2100 BCE) as determined by the hieroglyphic engravings found on the hill. What was the purpose of this place? Why did it have all those large clay pots? Count Almasy had visited Abu Ballas Hill in the 1930s, and he had suggested that it was a very ancient water station or supply outpost, a sort of donkey filling station, along a long-forgotten route that may have linked the oasis of Dakhla to Gilf Kebir and perhaps beyond.[35] As it turned out, both Almasy and Kuper would be proved correct by none other than the indefatigable Carlo Bergmann.

THE ABU BALLAS TRAIL

The mystery of Abu Ballas Hill was finally solved in 1999 by Carlo Bergmann. In the course of a whole year, from March 1999 to March 2000, Bergmann explored on foot the region southwest of Dakhla oasis and discovered some thirty other water stations with similar large, clay pots set almost equidistant to one another, like a hop-skip-and-jump trail or, more poetically, a string of pearls along a 350-kilometer (217-mile) stretch of desert. The midpoint of this trail was Abu Ballas Hill, and the whole created an almost straight highway from Dakhla to Gilf Kebir. The conclusion was inevitable: this was the long forgotten ancient caravan trail predicted by Almasy.[36] This discovery amounted to an intellectual explosion for the academics, for here was hard, irrefutable evidence that the pharaohs did after all travel into the deep desert and probably even made contact with the descendants of the prehistoric people who lived there. Further, all this was happening forty-five hundred years before Prince Kemal el Din discovered Gilf Kebir. Here is how the pharaohs did it.

In ancient times, the essential commodities for such a trip were, of course, water and food, as well as water and fodder for the beasts of burden. It is well known that the camel was not introduced into Egypt before 500 BCE, so that the only other means of desert transport in the Old Kingdom was the donkey (*Equius asinus*). Harkhuf claimed to have taken three hundred donkeys for his journey to Yam,

Figure 2.5. Abu Ballas Pottery Hill discovered in 1918.

and donkey caravans are also attested on temple and tomb reliefs as early as the first dynasties. Also, on one of the large clay pots at Abu Ballas, there is a drawing of a donkey confirming that this animal had carried the pots and presumably other goods to this location in the desert. The donkey is an excellent desert traveler and can easily carry loads of sixty kilograms (about a hundred thirty pounds) and walk 15 kilometers (about 9 miles) per day and can go three days without water. A fully grown and healthy donkey will need about two to three liters of water and about three kilograms of fodder each day, which together will add five to six kilograms (about thirteen pounds) per day to the load he must carry. A one-way trip from Dakhla to the edge of Gilf Kebir will take a minimum of twenty days and thus will require a total load of a hundred twenty kilograms (about two hundred and sixty-five pounds) for each donkey, to which we must add another thirty kilograms (about sixty pounds) for the containers that carry the water and food as well as basic traveling equipment plus the food and water for the person leading the donkey (estimated at fifty kilograms—about a hundred and ten pounds—per load). Conservatively, then, each donkey must be able to carry, at the start of the journey at least two hundred kilograms (four hundred and forty pounds). This, of course, is impossible. A donkey walking at normal pace in such grueling conditions can carry only sixty to eighty kilograms without buckling under the load.

Theoretically, the payload can be reduced by taking extra donkeys, but there are an optimum number of donkeys for the trip, because each extra donkey will also require water and food. The optimum number of donkeys per person is three to four. Sharing the load makes the total load for each about a hundred and eighty-five kilograms, which is still not possible for a donkey to carry. It should be clear, then, that in order to undertake this journey, the donkey can start off with a load of only sixty to eighty kilograms, and then, when the water and food are used up, there must be refueling stations along the way—at least two spread equidistant along the way to Gilf Kebir. This assessment explains the need for the large Abu Ballas Hill watering station and also another large one that was discovered by Carlo Bergmann, which he named Muhattah Jaqub (Jacob's Station), located between Dakhla oasis and Abu Ballas Hill. These principal watering stations had to be kept fully supplied with water and food when a donkey caravan expedition was planned, which also explains the need for the thirty small stations that Bergmann discovered in between. In other words, the small stations along the trail were used only for the resupply of the Muhattah Jaqub and Abu Ballas Hill main stations. It was these last two that serviced the caravans and ensured that there was a supply of water and food all the way to the final destination. "But what was the final destination of the caravans?" asked the anthropologist Frank Förster.

> Certainly not Gilf Kebir. The nearest places with permanent water are the Kufra Oasis in modern Libya some 350 km [over two hundred miles]. to the northwest of the eastern fringes of the southern Gilf Kebir, and Gebel Uwainat some 200 km [about a hundred and twenty-four miles] to the southwest. Kufra, however, surrounded by seas of sand is rather isolated. . . . Therefore, and for other reasons, it is to be assumed that the next leg of the route led towards Gebel Uwainat, the islandlike most elevated feature in the whole of the eastern Sahara, which is provided with a number of rain-fed wells at its foot (in Arabic Uwainat means "the small fountains"). From here it would be possible to reach more southern regions in the territory of modern Sudan or Chad. To date, however, no evidence has been found in the Gebel Uwainat, nor in the Gilf Kebir proper, that attests to an Egyptian presence there.[37]

The German anthropologists Stefan Kröpelin and Rudolph Kuper had the same hunch as Förster, namely that the Abu Ballas Trail went on beyond Gilf Kebir, perhaps to Jebel Uwainat and also even beyond to Chad: "Its [the Abu Ballas Trails] final destination is still unknown . . . the nearest locality with permanent ground water lies at distances of 600 kilometers [373 miles] . . . in Jebel Uwainat, from where the trail might have continued to the ecologically superlative Ennedi Plateau or the outstanding lake region of Ounianga in Northeast Chad."[38]

Förster, Kröpelin, and Kuper wrote these words in early 2007. Little did they know that their hunch about Jebel Uwainat being a farther destination along the trail would be confirmed in just a few months. Such are the strange laws of synchronicity in human lives.

THE EGYPTIAN TEACHER
AND THE MALTESE BUSINESSMAN

Mahmoud Marai is an Egyptian chemistry lecturer who, like Carlo Bergmann, dropped his career in the classroom for a more adventurous career in the desert. He set up a tour operating business, taking tourists and adventurers into the deep desert, eventually specializing in trips dedicated to exploration. Mahmoud's infatuation with the desert began when he was stationed at the oasis of Siwa during his military service. There, roaming the golden dunes at the edge of the Great Sand Sea, he was hit by the explorer's bug, and his experience with the desert was love at first sight. Mahmoud just had to become involved with its barren beauty, its haunting and alluring isolation, and, of course, its many mysteries. Like others before him, he dreamed of finding the legendary lost oasis of Zarzora and going to places that were still unexplored. This strange pull that the desert has on some people is not uncommon. There is an inexplicable attraction to being alone in its vast emptiness where earth and sky seem to meet and become one. Somehow, the isolation from human habitation brings us closer to the essence of our humanity. There is an old Arab saying that God lives in the desert. To put it slightly differently, it feels as if it is not us but our soul that is alive when we roam the open desert, for it provokes a strange and very strong sensation that God is standing near us when we are alone in its vastness.

At any rate, Marai's enthusiasm for daring and challenging desert trips attracted the attention of many explorers. In the winter of 2007, a Maltese businessman, Mark Borda, hired Mahmoud Marai for a desert trek[39] to Uwainat. The permits for this expedition were issued via Mahmoud Marai as a registered tour operator by the Ministry of Interior and the Egyptian military authorities, who are responsible for the safety of travelers and tours in the Western Desert. Borda and Marai had met the previous year through the intermediary of Carlo Bergmann. Borda's objective was to search unexplored areas for anything that might be of scientific interest to scholars of geology, botany, archaeology, and anthropology. By carefully studying satellite imagery before the trip, Borda had drawn up an extensive list of targets. Upon his arrival at Jebel Uwainat, Borda immediately set about the task of surveying these targets systematically, very often with Marai accompanying him on his treks. They combed many areas in the lower slopes, wadis, and plateaus mainly southeast of the Uwainat massif. Each day they trekked about 15 to 20 kilometers (9 to 12 miles), checking every nook, crack, and cave they encountered. This method paid off, and they found the locations of dozens of unreported prehistoric works of art.

PHARAONIC INSCRIPTIONS!
A CARTOUCHE OF A KING!

By November 27, Marai and Borda had already been walking and searching for nine days. On that day, just as they were about to arrive back at camp for lunch, Borda scanned with his powerful binoculars the last remaining section of boulders that lay strewn on a slope. They were in a region at the southern rim of Jebel Uwainat—which is some 50 kilometers (about 31 miles) into Sudanese territory—an area into which it is dangerous to venture. (In September 2008, a group of Italian tourists was kidnapped at Jebel Uwainat by rebels, and they endured a two-week ordeal before they were freed after a gunfight between the rebels and the Egyptian military.) As Borda panned with his binoculars, he suddenly saw an unmistakable shape on the surface of one of the larger boulders some 100 meters from where he stood. It was a shape that he had seen many times before—but this time, he saw it only hundreds of kilometers from Jebel Unwainat.

He exclaimed to Marai in disbelief, "There is a pharaonic cartouche on that boulder!" As he moved closer, focusing his eyepiece with growing excitement, he began to see hieroglyphic inscriptions inside and outside the cartouche (see plate 3) The two men could barely contain their excitement, for there it was, after decades of speculation, incontestable evidence that the ancient Egyptians managed to reach this remote place after all! The whole geography of ancient Egypt suddenly changed before their eyes. They immediately took dozens of digital photographs and carefully recorded the coordinates of the location with GPS. After leaving Jebel Uwainat, Borda also decided to check various prominent hills and rocky outcrops and managed to discover a magnificent cave with exquisite prehistoric art in a region previously considered void of such work. The images were not engraved but painted in bright colors. There were scenes showing slender Black men and women tending cattle, performing daily chores, and dancing and acting out rituals. The details and colors were so vivid that it was difficult to accept that they were thousands of years old. These works and the pharaonic inscriptions were by far more than Marai and Borda had dreamed of finding. Now they could return to Cairo with this historical trophy and an amazing story to tell.

Upon their return, Mark Borda immediately flew to London to get a quick translation of the Uwainat Inscriptions, as they are now known. At the Institute of Archaeology, University College London, Borda showed the photographs to Maltese Egyptologist Aloisia de Trafford and British ancient languages specialist Joe Clayton of Birkbeck College. We can imagine how these scholars felt as they read the two lines of hieroglyphs, and their bewilderment and excitement upon seeing the words *land of Yam* in the ancient text . . . even more because, by a strange coincidence, Clayton had written a thesis on Yam.

PHARAOH MENTUHOTEP'S ENVOY TO YAM

The final translation of the Uwainat Inscriptions was a joint effort between Joe Clayton and Aloisia de Trafford, and their study and conclusions were published in an article coauthored with Borda in the July 2008 issue of the journal *Sahara*.[40] They refrained from giving the exact location of the inscriptions for fear of tourist guides taking clients there. The inscriptions are rather faint and cannot be seen from the plains below. Fate would have it that Mark Borda happened to aim his binoculars in that precise direction, a visual lucky turn of the spade (although, as Borda later explained to us, he quite methodically and thoroughly surveyed all likely surfaces in targeted areas, and the inscription is located on a conspicuous boulder that would have been difficult to overlook). The inscriptions form a rough rectangle 0.74 by 0.84 meters (about 29 by 33 inches). The left portion of the rectangle shows a king sitting on a throne under a canopy opposite a large cartouche bearing his name. Above and below the king's cartouche is written his royal title. The right portion of the rectangle has two lines of hieroglyphs, and beneath each there is a drawing of a man making offerings. Here is the translation by Clayton and de Trafford.

(Left side)
Son of Re, Mentuhotep [inside the cartouche]
King of Upper and Lower Egypt [above cartouche]
Horus living Forever [below cartouche]

(Right side)
Yam bringing incense [upper line]
[images: man kneeling, holding a bowl; another man lying face down, holding a bowl?]
Tekhebet bringing . . . [lower line]
[image: man kneeling, presenting a mountain goat]

Clayton and de Trafford dated the inscriptions from the Middle

Kingdom ca. 2000 BCE. This is, in any case, confirmed by the name of the king as well as the horizontal orientation of the hieroglyphs. The two proposed that the whole motif means that people from Yam and also from Tekhebet (a place of unknown location and, oddly, not mentioned in any other ancient Egyptian texts) came here to Uwainat to rendezvous with an Egyptian delegation sent by king Mentuhotep, probably Mentuhotep II, to present gifts to the pharaoh and also trade with his envoy. According to Clayton, de Trafford, and Borda: "This new find in Uwainat adds another startling piece to this puzzle by revealing evidence for Egypt's relations with two foreign lands and raises the possibility that these lands may have been located in sub-Saharan Africa, either south or southwest of Jebel Uwainat, possibly hundreds of kilometers further west of the Nile than previously thought."[41]

Oddly, Clayton, de Trafford, and Borda do not mention the Tibesti-Ennedi highlands in northern Chad as a possible location of the legendary kingdom of Yam and/or the mysterious kingdom of Tekhebet—although they imply this by suggesting sub-Saharan Africa hundreds of kilometers south or southwest of Uwainat. This can be only either Sudan (south of Uwanait) or the Tibesti-Ennedi highlands in northern Chad (southwest of Uwnainat). The latter are perhaps the most likely and most obvious place. Clayton, de Trafford, and Borda also avoided speaking of the Tebu or Goran people who originally came from the Tibesti Mountains, even though they presumably knew that Ahmed Hassanein had encountered a group of them at Jebel Uwainat in 1923. Although no one can tell for sure how long ago these black-skinned people inhabited the Tibesti-Ennedi highlands, these areas have an abundance of rock art similar to Uwainat that suggests a prehistoric origin. Today, some three hundred fifty thousand Tebu still inhabit the Tibesti Mountains, although they have now converted to Islam and therefore no longer live in their old ways. It is highly likely that prehistoric rock art of the Tibesti-Ennedi highlands and the art found at Uwainat have a common origin. It is also very likely that the Tibesti-Ennedi highlands were the final destination of the Abu

Ballas Trail. Surely, then, an expedition starting from Uwainat and heading to the Tibesti highlands would be the next logical step in the search for the fabled Land of Yam or Tekhebet. We will return to this intriguing issue in chapter 5. Meanwhile, we must examine the Uwainat Inscriptions regarding another issue, which was either not noticed or deemed unimportant by Clayton and de Trafford. This involves the form of the writing of the words Yam and Tekhebet. In both names is presented the same ideogram (⌐), which is usually translated as "hill land" or "foreign land" (that is, a place outside Egypt).

Although these translations are basically correct, we must now consider them alongside the quasi-similar ideogram of "water mountain" that is found at Abu Ballas Hill and Muhattah Jaqub (the two main water refueling stations between Dakhla and Uwainat). These main water stations can hardly be described as mountains: Abu Ballas Hill is only 30 meters (about 98 feet) high and Muhattah Jaqub is barely 25 meters (82 feet) high. On the other hand, the Tibesti-Ennedi highlands have the tallest mountains in the Sahara (3,450 meters; about 11,320 feet), and they are known to receive a 120 millimeters (about 5 inches) of rain each year. These highlands in Chad, which are directly southwest of Jebel Uwainat and which would define an extension of the Abu Ballas Trail, are clearly befitting of the name Water Mountain.

The ideogram for "mountain" is a two-peaked mound ( ), but we have seen that when a circle (solar disk) is placed between the two peaks ( ), it denotes the idea of "horizon," known as *akhet* in ancient Egyptian. Now the sign to denote "land" is a flattened ellipse ( ), so when it is combined with the akhet sign ( ), the meaning is "land of the horizon." Furthermore, by adding the sign for "people" ( ), the ideograms denote "the people of the land of the horizon," or, more simply, "the horizon dwellers."

We can now recall that King Pepi II, in his letter to Harkhuf, uses the word *akhet* in connection to the land of Yam so that he refers to it as *ta-akhet-iu* (literally, "the people of the land of akhet"). Although many Egyptologists also translate this as "the horizon dwellers," this is not actually correct, because in the letter of Pepi II, the word *ta-akhet* (the land of Akhet) is not written with the signs 𓇋𓇌, but with the combination of four signs: (1) crested ibis, (2) circle, (3) half circle, and (4) flattened ellipse ( ). Further, it is true that when these four sign are combined, they produce the phonetic sound *akhet,* but the meaning is quite different. However subtle, this difference provides a vital clue to the whereabouts of Yam. Let us see why.

The crested ibis sign ( ), *akh* in ancient Egyptian, is an ideogram that denotes a supernatural being or entity of light or, more simply, a "light spirit." So when *ta-akhet-iu* (people of the land of Akhet) is written with this *akh* sign coupled with the sign for "land" and the ideogram of three squatting divinities wearing an ostrich feather ( ), we must read it as "land of the akh" or "land of the light spirits," or, simply, "land of spirits." Indeed, both the American Egyptologist Henry Breasted and the British Egyptologist Wallis Budge, in their independent translations of Pepi II's letter to Hakhuf, rendered the term *ta-akhet-iu* as "land of spirits."[42] Even though "spirits" in this context implies inhabitants of a cosmic or imaginary land, the same cannot be said for the land of Yam, which is a geographical reality somewhere southwest of Egypt. Could the akh people also mean "ancestor spirits"? If so, who were these mysterious people whom Pepi II claimed populated the kingdom of Yam?

A detailed study of the letter of Pepi II was made by the French Egyptologist and philologist Charles Kuentz,[43] who reminds us that in Egyptian hieroglyphs the general idea of a divinity or spirit is given by the sign of a human figure donning the typical tress beard and squatting ( ). Yet this was not the case in Harkhuf's time, when a different sign—the falcon on a standard ( )—was used to denote "divinity." Thus, the sign used in the letter of Pepi II as the ideogram in "land of the akh/spirits" ( ) must therefore mean something else—something that should fit this geographical context of the region. One of Kuentz's colleagues, the German philologist A. Wiedemann, noted that this sign (𓈖𓂋)appears in the Pyramid Texts to denote an African people. This is also confirmed by Kuentz, who wrote: "The determinative 𓂋 which is placed *after* 𓂋 𓄿 𓊖, denotes in the Unas Inscriptions the names of *Negroes*."[44]

Kuentz also noted that in both the Harkhuf inscriptions and the letter of Pepi II, the names of African peoples are followed by the same determinative (𓈖𓂋) used in the name for "the people of the Ahket land" (that is, the people of Yam). There can be no doubt, therefore, that these people were regarded as black-skinned. We will discuss this issue in more detail in chapter 5. Meanwhile, let us see what Carlo Bergmann has to say about the newly discovered Uwainat Inscriptions of Marai and Borda.

THE ROAD TO YAM AND TEKHEBET

Bergmann agreed with the Egyptologists who studied the Uwainat Inscriptions: they revealed two geographical locations, Yam and Tekhebet. Here is what he says of the Yam location:

> . . . [I]ts geographical position has been misleadingly assigned to a "location between the first and second cataracts . . . further south than . . . Tumas, most likely also west of the Nile or . . . on either side of it . . . and south of the oases.[45] One reason for this misconception may be that, due to their social backgrounds, which are mainly upper or upper middle class, Egyptologists have for a century confused their own physically exhausting experiences in this region with the fitness levels of the ancients (e.g., Harkhuf or Weni and their followers) and have considerably underestimated the abilities of these people to travel to far away destinations even under unfavourable environmental conditions.[46]

Bergmann then asserts that the final destination of the Abu Ballas Trail he discovered in 1999,

. . . continues from Gebel Uweinat further to the southwest [a fact that] is already indicated by the geographical position of the Mentuhotep II inscription site which is located on the south of Gebel Uweinat. Where does it lead to? Most probably to Yam and/ or to Tekhebet! Although it is a prominent *muhattah* [water station] along the route, the pottery hill of Abu Ballas, from which the trail gets its name, must be viewed as just one amongst many of the road's way [water] stations. So in the light of the new discoveries, the current name of the ancient road is neither appropriate nor accurate. In fact, it has definitely become obsolete. Therefore, a more suitable name is suggested: "The Road to Yam and Tekhebet."[47]

With all this in mind, we must now return to Nabta Playa and review in greater detail what the astronomer Kim Malville discovered there. This is crucial to our investigation, because much hinges—indeed, perhaps everything hinges—on his interpretation of the alignments of the megaliths that are found there.

3

STONEHENGE
IN THE SAHARA

For the production of man a different apprenticeship was needed to sharpen the wits and quicken the higher manifestations of intellect—a more open veldt country where competition was keener between swiftness and stealth, and where adroitness of thinking and movement played a preponderating role in the preservation of the species.

RAYMOND DART,
AUSTRALOPITHECUS AFRICANUS,
THE MAN-APE OF SOUTH AFRICA

Ancient Stonehenge-style stones spotted in Egypt's Sahara Desert are the oldest megaliths yet discovered and probably served as both calendar and temple, researchers said on Wednesday.

REUTERS,
CABLE NEWS NETWORK,
APRIL 2, 1998

SAHARA CLIMATE CYCLES:
ANOTHER LINK TO THE STARS?

Before we look more closely at the initial discoveries at Nabta Playa, we must review the current knowledge of climate changes in the Sahara. In this process, we will see how yet another intriguing piece to the puzzle of early human's intimate association with the heavens links to Nabta Playa.

The climate in the Egyptian Sahara is harsh, sometimes even violent. The first night of our April 2008 expedition to Uwainat (told in more detail in chapter 5) was spent on an elevated pass somewhere in the deep, open desert. It was strangely cold at night, considering the extreme heat of daytime, and we shivered under our many layers of covers—from our cotton underwear to the padded sleeping bags—as the temperature plummeted to almost freezing during the late hours of the night. The reason for such huge temperature swings from day to night is due to the almost lunarlike conditions of the landscape and cloudless sky. The sun blazes in daytime, but after sunset, the heat begins to whoosh out into space, sending the thermometer down toward the zero-degrees-centigrade mark. From this lack of clouds also comes the hyperaridity of the region, which is considered by climatologists as the driest on Earth. In deserts such as California's Death Valley there is some life—sparse plants, cacti, insects, lizards, occasional foxes, and even coyotes—but in the Egyptian Sahara, especially around places such as Nabta Playa, there seems to be no life at all. There are no plants, no animals, not even insects—only sand and rocks, blowing dust, drifting sand dunes, fossils, loose pebbles and compacted desert pavement, loose boulders, and bedrock outcrops. In other words, the deep Egyptian Sahara is the Earth location most like the Martian landscape.

But it was not always so. In November 1981, the NASA space shuttle Columbia carried a radar-imaging camera from the Jet Propulsion Laboratory that was designed to view through the sands of the Sahara and "see" what was beneath. When the radar camera was trained on the Egyptian Sahara, it picked up the contours of dried-out ancient rivers and lakes beneath the sands.[1] This discovery jumpstarted a revolution in our understanding of the drastic climate changes of the ancient Sahara. We now know that the long-term climate of the Sahara has undergone violent swings.

Around 12,000 BCE, Earth's sea level rose suddenly more than 20 meters (about 66 feet) in less than two hundred years.[2] This was the direct result of catastrophic glacial melting that heralded the beginning of an eight-thousand-year period scientists call the end of the last ice age, when sea levels rose 120 meters (almost 400 feet) essentially to the level they are today. The Mediterranean Sea also rose, causing the climate of the Sahara to fluctuate and change. Around 9000 BCE, the monsoon rains moved north over what is now southwestern Egypt,[3] drawn up possibly by low pressure over the collapsing ice sheets in the distant north.[4] This ended a protracted dry period and brought in a humid period congenial to human and animal existence. Not surprisingly, soon thereafter the earliest human artifacts appear in the sediments at Nabta Playa. These sediments, which archaeologists are still digging through today, lie in and around the ancient *playa,* or seasonal lake (now permanently dry), and on top of much more ancient bedrock.

The surface of the now-covered bedrock was scoured by constant winds during many thousands of years of dry periods leading up to 9000 BCE. An area of softer bedrock was scoured more deeply by the winds, which created the depression that filled with water every summer season to become the playa during the monsoon season. This lasted to around 3500 BCE, after which the region became the hot, hyperdry place that it is today. The last humid period in the Egyptian Sahara, which lasted from about 9000 BCE up to 3500 BCE, seems also to have ended abruptly. Yet scientists also know that there have been several humid periods before this last one. Paleoclimatologists are finding that humid or wet periods in the Sahara occur with curious regularity, which suggests that these periods might be linked to Earth's cyclical geological changes. Paleoceanographer and marine geologist Peter B. deMenocal studied sediment cores from the eastern Atlantic Ocean to measure the past climate of the Sahara. These sediments, which were originally created by wind-carried dust and sand that then settled to the bottom of the ocean to form layers, act as graduations for measuring climate changes over long periods of time in the same way that rings in tree trunks can tell us of annual weather variations. The phases of the humid periods that deMenocal found in the ocean sediments matched those that the geologists found in the sediment layers at Nabta Playa. DeMenocal was able to show that the humid Sahara periods occurred regularly, about every twenty thousand years, and, furthermore, that they always began and ended suddenly. According to deMenocal, the cause of these sudden climate fluctuations from humid to dry were linked to the cyclical changes of Earth's motion with respect to the fixed stars.[5]

The basis of deMenocal's research relating climatic changes to the fixed stars began back in 1920. Interestingly, in that same year Ahmed Hassanein and Rosita Forbes undertook their fateful expedition to the Kufra oasis (which eventually led to the discovery, a few years later, of the massifs of Jebel Uwainat and Gilf Kebir), and in that year the Serbian mathematician Milutin Milankovich (1879–1958) published his controversial paper that would become a foundation in the science of climate change.[6] The Milankovich Curve, as his theory is known, was based on an elegant and simple notion: the small, gradual, annual changes in Earth's orbit around the sun as well as the spin of its axis when considered over many thousands of years will create sizeable recurring cycles causing Earth to receive sometimes more, sometimes less light and heat from the sun, which will cause significant climate changes. These changes are the result of three phenomena of Earth's movements: *precession, obliquity,* and *eccentricity.*

1. Precession is a gyrating motion of Earth's axis, which causes the planet to wobble like a spinning top, making a complete cycle every twenty-six thousand years or so.
2. Obliquity is the angle of tilt that Earth's axis makes with the

plane of its orbit around the sun. This angle moves up and down in a slow cycle of about forty-one thousand years, known as the obliquity of the ecliptic. Today, the angle is 23.4 degrees, but, for example, in 5000 BCE it was about 24.1 degrees. Like the precession cycle, astrophysicists today can calculate with a great deal of accuracy exact changes in past and future obliquity.[7]

3. Eccentricity is the elongatedness (that is, the *perihelion* and *aphelion*) of Earth's elliptical orbit around the sun, which changes in a complex cycle of about one hundred thousand years.[*]

Precession and the Zodiacal Belt

The sun at the equinoxes (March 21 and September 22) is located in the sky against a backdrop of a particular group of stars or constellations that lie along the so-called zodiacal belt. Every year, the position of the sun along the zodiacal belt at the equinoxes moves, or *precesses,* a tiny amount so that, in about twenty-six thousand years, the sun makes a complete cycle around the entire zodiac. Although the precise number of years per each full precession cycle always changing a bit, astrophysicists today can calculate the duration of precessional cycles, past and future, with a great deal of accuracy.[8]

These three effects—precession, obliquity, and eccentricity—when taken together, cause long-term climate change every twenty thousand to twenty-six thousand years—such as, for example, the great ice ages known to have occurred in the distant past. Around ten thousand years

---

[*]The eccentricity is currently about 0.017, meaning that Earth is 3.4 percent closer to the sun during closest approach compared to the farthest it is from the sun in the yearly orbital cycle. The gravitational pull from Jupiter, Mars, and the other planets causes the eccentricity of Earth's orbit to vary from a mostly round path (0.005) to a more elongated one (0.058) in a complex cycle of about one hundred thousand years. Also, the time of year when Earth is closest to the sun varies. Currently, Earth is closest to the sun on January 4 (perihelion).

from now, Earth will be closest to the sun in midsummer, as it was about ten thousand years ago. This approximate twenty thousand–year perihelion cycle is caused essentially by the precession of the equinox cycle, and it is shortened somewhat by the change in the eccentricity cycle.

This brings us back to Peter deMenocal, for while studying the sediment layers of the Eastern Atlantic Ocean bed, he found that specifically in the Sahara region the climate had switched from wet to dry every twenty thousand years or so over hundreds of thousands of years, and that such switches had taken place quite suddenly. Searching for the causes of these sudden switches, it occurred to deMenocal that the Milankovich Cycle matched very well the wet-dry cycle.[9] DeMenocal found that the most recent switch from wet to dry occurred around 3500 BCE[10] in a time frame that could be "felt within one lifetime."[11] Let us immediately highlight the fact that 3500 BC is when, according to anthropologists, the prehistoric people of Nabta Playa abandoned their ceremonial site and departed from the Sahara . . . and also when, according to Egyptologists the predynastic phase of the ancient Egyptian civilization is supposed to have begun.

TRACKING THE STARS

Living all their lives in the open desert under the clear, cloudless sky, the prehistoric people of the Sahara were highly tuned to changes in the position of the celestial bodies, and the evidence at Nabta Playa shows that they were not only aware of the long term motion of precession, but also that they must have placed great importance on this stellar cycle, because it seemed to affect the climate of the Sahara and, consequently, their ability to survive in this region that depended so much on suitable seasonal wet conditions.

We are fully aware, of course, that scholars and historians of astronomy attribute the knowledge of precession—and even the awareness of it—not to ancient cultures, but rather to the Greeks when Hipparchus of Nicaea supposedly discovered this phenomenon in 120 BCE. As we will see in chapter 6, however, this consensus no longer stands to close scrutiny, and the new evidence shows, if not proves, that the ancient pre-Hellenic cultures were aware of precession and may even have recorded its long effect in the astronomical alignments of their megalithic monuments. To put it more bluntly, Hipparchus did not discover precession; he *rediscovered* it. It is now a fact and not a theory that humid periods occurred every twenty thousand years or so during the past two hundred thousand years, which directly affected the movements and the culture of the people living in the Egyptian Sahara region. It is also a fact and not a theory that these humid periods were directly linked to precession and the apparent displacement of the stars during these twenty thousand years or so. In addition, it is a fact that the Sahara in Egypt is now generally regarded by paleoanthropologists as one of the crucibles, indeed if not the principal crucible, of civilization.

Is it possible, then, that the ancient megalith builders of Nabta Playa somehow knew that there was a correlation between the cycle of the climate and the cycle of the stars? It may seem to us that this is entirely possible for a people that lived for millennia in a region where the conditions forced them to perform daily and nightly observation of the sun and stars and develop a great knowledge of the celestial cycles and, eventually, incorporate this knowledge into the ceremonial complexes at Nabta Playa.

TEXTUAL EVIDENCE?

A curious verse from the Qur'an speaks of a primeval mind coping with climate changes over the millennia: "And [in] the variation of the night and the day, and [in] what Allah sends down of sustenance from the cloud, then gives life thereby to the earth after its death, and [in] the changing of the winds, there are signs for a people who understand (45:5).[12]

Although we cannot assume that ancient religious scriptures such as the one cited here can be taken as evidence of knowledge of precession and climatic changes by ancient people, they may be faint echoes of ancient memories that eventually found their way into religious records in this same region of the world. Another such example comes from the Russian mystic G. I. Gurdjieff, whose esoteric teachings attracted a wide following in Europe in the early part of the twentieth century. Gurdjieff journeyed extensively in Egypt, and he claimed that much of the inspiration for his teachings came from what he saw on a secret and very ancient map of "pre-sands Egypt" that he discovered in a remote Asian monastery. This map showed that the Egyptian Sahara was a lush and humid environment in very remote times.[13] Of course, such stories cannot be used to bolster the scientific argument for ancient knowledge of precession and cyclical climate changes in the Sahara, but perhaps we are now able to corroborate such stories with modern science. This is, indeed, one of the main objectives of our research: to show where this evidence is to be found and how to interpret it.

We start with a media event that stunned the academic community.

CNN: "SAHARA STONEHENGE!"

On April 2, 1998, the international media reported the news that "ancient Stonehenge-style stones [were] spotted in Egypt's Sahara desert."[14] In their report, CNN showed a graphic image of Egypt with huge stones placed on the southeast quadrant of the country. Needless to say, this was a gross exaggeration, because the actual size of each of the toppled megaliths is no more than 1 meter (about 3 feet). The original source of the reports was a press release from the University of Colorado, which was carefully timed to coordinate with a letter published that same day in the prestigious science journal *Nature* entitled "Megaliths and Neolithic Astronomy in Southern Egypt" and written by astronomer J. McKim Malville and anthropologists Fred Wendorf and Ali Majar of the CPE.[15]

Although the findings at Nabta Playa were worthy of international attention and respect, this sort of media sensationalism was misleading and confused the public. The impression given in the media prompted by the press release and the *Nature* letter was of a giant Stonehenge in the Sahara. When people eventually found out that the stones were much smaller and that they formed a rough circle only a few meters in diameter, there was general disappointment, and many people eventually lost interest. Furthermore, the letter in *Nature* contained some errors that were uncharacteristic for such a high-profile journal, as well as some significant omissions that would later make matters worse. All in all, the comparison to Stonehenge was a crude metaphor and amounted to a stillbirth for an otherwise very important discovery. In fact, it may have directly contributed to if not explained why the Egyptian authorities paid little heed to this important ancient artifact, why it was so mistreated and blantantly neglected by those who worked there, and why it was ultimately dismantled and taken away to a museum yard in Aswan (see appendix 3).

At any rate, most of the excitement on April 2, 1998, centered on the announcement of the discovery of a stone circle that was made with small stones that were each about 1 meter in height and that were placed in a ring 4 meters (about 13 feet) across. It was labeled the Calendar Circle by Fred Wendorf and his team. In reality, Wendorf and his team had known of the existence of this circle from the time they found the site of Nabta Playa in 1973, but nothing much was done about it until 1992, when the circle was reconstructed to its original form by Dr. Nieves Zedeño, an anthropologist from the University of Arizona, and her colleague Dr. Alex Applegate, who had recently joined the CPE.[16] Yet it took a further six years before the world was told about it. Oddly, it was the Applegate-Zedeño reconstruction map of the Calendar Circle that was used by Wendorf and Malville and the rest of the authors in the 1998 *Nature* letter. Also, even more oddly, in this letter, the authors give an interpretation of only four stones in the circle and totally ignore the possible meanings of the other stones, especially those within the circle itself. Nevertheless, this limited information was enough to spur the "older than Stonehenge" claim and to insure a massive media reaction.

Still, why did it take twenty-five years to inform the public of the oldest astronomical site in the world? What really happened to the stone circle between 1973 and 1998? First, we must emphasize that the Combined Prehistoric Expedition (CPE) was composed essentially of field anthropologists, archaeologists, and geologists, most of whom were unfamiliar with astronomy or, perhaps, simply reluctant to apply this science to their own professions. Thus, it took them from 1973 to 1992 to realize that the stone circle might be some sort of calendrical device. After the circle was reconstructed by Applegate and Zedeño in 1992, it quickly became apparent that an important feature of the circle were the so-called gates that created two alignments pointing to the rising sun at the summer solstice and also to the north-south meridian (which are both indicative of observation of the sun at important times of the year). At this stage, CPE director Fred Wendorf invited the American archaeoastronomer Kim Malville to come to Nabta Playa for the 1997 winter excavation season. Malville spent a few days at Nabta Playa in order to study the alignments of the stone circle and other features of the ceremonial complex, which resulted in the publication of the 1998 letter in *Nature*. In view of the importance of the claims made in *Nature* and the strong reputation and influence of *Nature*, we must now review in some detail what was reported in the letter.

GATES OF THE SUN

In the *Nature* letter, Malville and the other authors highlighted two sets of gates in the outer ring of stones of the Calendar Circle and deduced that these were deliberately intended to designate important directions: one set was directed north-south, clearly a cardinal direction; the other was directed northeast, clearly a summer solstice sunrise direction. In additon, according to Malville and the other authors, "The circle is too small to have functioned as a precise sighting device. The centre lines of the two windows have azimuths of 358° and 62°. Taking into account refraction, we estimate the azimuth of the first gleam of the summer solstice Sun 6,000 years before the present to have been 63.2°, which would have been visible through the slots of the circle."[17]

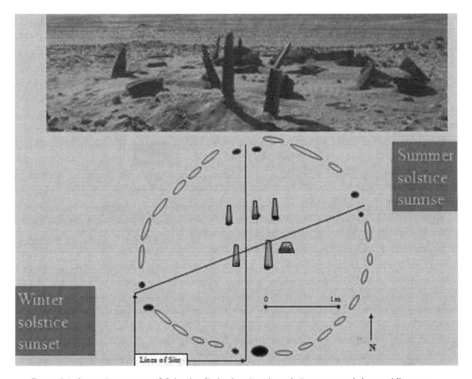

Figure 3.1. Approximate map of Calendar Circle showing the solstice gates and the meridian gates. Upper image is the Calendar Circle in its ruined state in 2008.

Although we can say that the ancient builders intended the circle's southeast gate to point to the rising sun on the longest day of the year, it is nonetheless an approximate alignment; the width of the gate varies 2 degrees in either direction and thus cannot be used for dating purposes with the sunrise because the changes in Earth obliquity over the past six thousand years is much less than 2 degrees. As a matter of fact, the approximate solstice alignment of the Calendar Circle is as valid today as it was six thousand years ago. It is also an exaggeration to call the stone circle a calendar simply because it has an alignment to the summer solstice. Indeed, neither the solstice gate nor the stone circle as a whole can be used as a calendar in the modern sense of the word. Further, although we, too, call it a Calendar Circle here, it seems that Malville's Nabta Playa tag of "six-thousand-year-old calendar" was more influenced by the nearby excavations that contained artifacts that could be radiocarbon analyzed and were dated to this epoch than by the astronomical alignments of the stones. Actually, the only real astronomy that can be derived from the 1998 *Nature* letter is that Nabta Playa is located near the Tropic of Cancer, implying that the standing stones would cast no shadows at noon on the summer solstice (June 21), a feature that modern achaeoastronomers often considered as significant to ancient cultures.[18] Thus according to Malville, et al, "At this latitude, the Sun crosses the zenith on two days, approximately three weeks before and after the summer solstice. Vertical structures cast no shadows under the zenith Sun, and within the tropics the day of the zenith Sun is often regarded as a significant event."[19]

Truthfully, the only actual astronomy reported in the *Nature* letter was that a small stone circle had an approximate solstice alignment and stood near the Tropic of Cancer. This fact, on its own, was not extremely impressive. As one prize-winning archaeoastronomer put it recently at the annual meeting of the American Astronomical Society, "you can be a primitive ape man and make a solstice alignment!" implying that scholars should start with the assumption that the people of Nabta Playa were simply primitive brutes. Yet all paleoanthropologists agree that the human brain ten thousand or more years ago was essentially identical to our own brain, and, as professor emeritus Archibald Roy of Glasgow University often remarks, "there were Einsteins and Newtons then," geniuses who were just as quick-thinking and astute as we are today, but who had to apply their intelligence without the science and technology that we have. It is true that setting a few stones in rough alignment to the summer solstice did not require the power of an Enstein or a Newton, so what were the anthropologists of Nabta

Playa really so excited about—as the 1998 *Nature* letter clearly implied? Apart from being perhaps the oldest astronomical site in the world, is it possible that something else at Nabta Playa had hinted to them that at the site there was much more there than meets the eye—which they were not yet ready to disclose?

INEXPLICABLE CONSTRUCTIONS

In addition to tumuli tombs of cattle (see chapter 1), the CPE anthropologists also found collections of large, oval-shaped megaliths on top of the playa sediments, which they called complex structures (also see chapter 1). They had hoped that these were the top parts of tombs belonging to high-status individuals or even kings, but when they excavated beneath these complex structures, they were surprised to find not human or animal remains, as they had hoped, but strange sculpted lumps of bedrock some 4 meters (about 13 feet) below the ground. The largest of these complex structures, which the CPE had labeled Complex Structure A, or simply CSA, also contained buried underneath it a huge human-sculpted megalith, which was placed over the sculpted lump of bedrock that lay 3 meters (about 10 feet) farther down! According to Fred Wendorf, et al, in CSA, ". . . [W]e found a sculptured rock, which has some resemblance to a cow. It was standing upright with its base 2 m [about 7 feet] below the surface, and its long axis was oriented a few degrees west of north. The rock had been blocked into place by two smaller slabs. Further beneath it, at a depth of 4 m [about 13 feet], the shaped table (bed) rock had a similar northward orientation."[20]

CSA consisted of a group of megalithic stones laid in oval formation on the surface of the ground. Below this oval structure, some 3 meters (about 10 feet) down, was buried the oddly shaped megalithic sculpture labeled the cow stone by the CPE. Directly beneath this cow stone sculpture there was a large, sculpted lump of bedrock that was still attached to the natural table rock strata that lay under the playa sediment. CSA was clearly the main feature of the whole ceremonial complex, for not only was it the largest megalithic structure at Nabta Playa, but it was also the focal point of several other megalithic stones alignments that had been placed upright in the playa sediments (but most of which people have toppled since). These aligned megaliths averaged 2 by 3 meters (7 by 10 feet) and were placed in rows running more than a kilometer (about .6 mile) toward the east and north horizons. They all radiated out of CSA like spokes of a bicycle wheel. The 1998 *Nature* letter gave the precise azimuths of five megalith lines, which seemed to imply some important symbolic meaning, although the CPE offered no suggestion as to what this might be. The only interpretation by Malville, et al was that "The megalithic complex may have been an expression of interconnections between the Sun, water, death, and the fertile Earth. . . ."[21]

The *Nature* letter also pointed out that "no star was visible at the north celestial pole during most of the occupation at Nabta,"[22] and

Figure 3.2. Excavation of the cow stone central sculpture from Comples Structure A at Nabta Playa.

Figure 3.3. Thomas Brophy with one of the megaliths that was arranged on the surface of the CSA.

made no mention of possible stellar orientation for the megalithic alignments. One of the megalithic alignments was reported to have an azimuth of 90.02 degrees, suggesting an incredibly high level of accuracy and knowledge of the cardinal direction east for observations without fine optical instruments.*

We were a bit apprehensive of the many inconsistencies in the 1998 *Nature* letter and also wondered why no suggestion was made for any possible alignments to stars. As it turned out, however, this was to come a few years later from the CPE.[23]

THE 2001 OFFICIAL SITE REPORT: RELUCTANT INTRODUCTION OF THE STARS

In 2001, two years after the *Nature* letter and twenty-five years after the discovery of Nabta Playa itself, the CPE finally published an extensive

---

*Oddly, in all subsequent publications on Nabta Playa by Malville, et al, there is no more mention of this highly accurate due-east alignment.

report of their excavations in book format edited by Fred Wendorf and Romuald Schild. It included the contributions of twenty-two articles by various participants in the archaeological work at Nabta Playa since its discovery.

One article in the book, titled "The Megalithic Alignments," was coauthored by Wendorf and Malville and gave a description of the various megalithic structures—and discussed stellar alignments at Nabta Playa. Indeed, the megalithic alignments that were now declared to have such stellar alignments were all those that radiated from CSA. Seen as a whole, CSA itself was the most elaborate member of a group of about thirty complex structures built in the playa silts and covering an area of about two football fields. This area was located some 2 kilometers (about 1 mile) south of the Calendar Circle and included the rows of megalithic alignments that emanated 2 kilometers from CSA to the northeast and southwest. With stellar alignments now identified at Nabta Playa, the site took on a completely new meaning and importance, which, even at this early stage, suggested there was some deep message—symbolic or practical—that had to be understood and interpreted. Before we investigate this message further, we must first familiarize ourselves in more detail with the thirty or so complex structures at Nabta Playa, which were the subject of another article in the CPE book written by Wendorf and Krolik.[24]

According to this article, each complex structure consisted of a cluster of megaliths arranged in an oval shape that measured some 5 to 7 meters (16 to 23 feet) long and 4 to 6 meters (13 to 20 feet) wide, with the longer axis oriented to a position slightly offset from the north-south meridian. The megaliths in each cluster were either placed on top of the playa silts or had been embedded in it. Some of the stones were still standing at the time of the article, but many have since fallen. The largest ones were placed in the center of the oval clusters, and although this was not mentioned by Wendorf and Krolik, we noted (when we finally traveled to see the megaliths for ourselves in 2003) that a few of the structures were partially sculpted with strange curves and angles that were clearly made by human hands.[25]

One of the odd aspects of these complex structures was that they were placed above the sculpted lumps of bedrock (about 3 or 4 meters under playa sediments, the exact depths are different for each complex structure). Only one complex structure (CSA) contained in addition a separate "cow stone" sculpture that were hidden about 4 meters (about 13 feet) beneath the ground. Two complex structures were fully excavated, and on another three, only borehole tests were performed—yet this was enough to confirm that all the structures had beaneath them sculpted bedrock, and the results also implied that all the remaining twenty-five or so complex structures had been built in the same way. We will later look at the possible meaning of these mysterious complex structures, but meanwhile, let us examine how and when they were built.

The CPE has established that the silt upon which the complex structures were built dates to 5100 BCE. This means that the visible part of these structures (the stone ovals) cannot be older than this date. Yet the bedrock that lies some 5 or 6 meters (16 or 20 feet) beneath the surface is surrounded by sediment that is dated from about 9000 BCE to 5100 BCE, which would indicate that the lumps of bedrock were sculpted by human hands at a time that was much earlier than the manufacture of the oval of stones that we see today on the surface. These sculpted lumps of bedrock are of hard quartzitic sandstone that remained in place after the softer surrounding sandstone was eroded by wind, long before 9000 BCE, and they were sculpted sometime before they were incorporated into the complex structures. How did the ancient builders who constructed the oval of stones on the surface know that deep beneath the spot they had chosen were these strange outcrops of bedrock? Wendorf and Krolik show their bafflement when they write: "How and why the builders of these [complex] structures located the buried bedrocks is not known. They may have used probes or dug pits. . . . Whatever technique was used to find the bedrock, when it was located, a large and deep

enough pit was dug to expose the entire circumference of the [bed]rock
. . . up to 5 meters [about 16 feet] in diameter at the base and 3.5 m
[about 11 feet] or more deep. . . . Dug through heavy silts and clays, the
pits required a major effort."[26]

According to Wendorf and Krolik, the ancient builders then
sculpted the bedrock and, in at least the case of Complex Structure A
(CSA), filled the pit partially, placed another megalithic sculpture, the
so-called cow stone, and then filled the pit completely to make it level
with playa silts. The final operation was then to make an oval of megaliths on the surface of the silts. We can note, however, another, more
natural solution to this mystery: "Wendorf and Krolik theorize that
CSA and thirty nearby similar Complex Structures were all constructed
entirely after the sediments were lay down, with the builders locating
subsurface bedrock lumps suitable for sculpting using some unknown
method for knowing what is under the sand. Given that parts of CSA
and the other Complex Structures consist of sculpted bedrock under
the playa sediments, it is reasonable to think that something was possibly constructed there before or during the playa sedimentation, and
only the final stage of construction occurred at or after the end of the
last major humid interphase.[27]

In other words, it is possible that whoever partially sculpted the
lumps of bedrock that lie about 4 meters (about 13 feet) below the surface were at Nabta Playa thousands of years before the final stage of the
complex structures was completed (that is, before the placement of the
oval of stones that lie on the surface of the earth today).

In 2007, after reading our paper ("Satellite Imagery Measures of the
Astronomically Aligned Megaliths at Nabta Playa"), Malville, Schild,
and Wendorf came to agree with the possibility that the bedrock sculptures of the complex structures were created much earlier than previously thought. Thus, accordingly, they wrote: "How or why the buried
table rocks were chosen remains a puzzle. It seems unlikely that the
rocks had been found accidentally during excavation for wells, as these
were in dunes at the edge of the playa and not in the playa sediments.

It is conceivable that these round, large quartzitic lenses were part of the symbolic landscape of the Middle Neolithic and became significant before the establishment of the complex ceremonial centre. Perhaps their locations had been marked by rock cairns before gradual burial by playa sediments."[28]

Not only did Wendorf and his coauthors come round to our way of thinking, but also, we made them aware in the paper we published in 2005 of a number of technical errors that the CPE had made in their previous publications.[29] Before reviewing these, let us recall that Complex Structure A (CSA) was the focal point of a series of megalithic alignments that radiated toward the horizon, and then look at how Wendorf introduced the discovery of these megalithic alignments with unusual candor:

> The discovery of the first alignment of large stones in 1990 came as a complete surprise. It is not clear why we failed to recognize them previously, or rather why we failed to understand their significance during the first three field seasons at Nabta [1974, 1975, and 1977]. It was not that we did not see them because we did, but they were either regarded as bedrock, or in some instances where it was clear they were not bedrock, regarded as insignificant. Perhaps the most embarrassing failure is the Group A alignment, which appears on one of our earlier published profiles as a somewhat fanciful steep sided hillock, buried under playa sediments. We were so sure it was bedrock that we failed to drill a borehole near the megalith. Our view of the Neolithic societies in the Sahara at that time was that the sites we were excavating represented small bands with simple social systems. Building [such] large stone monuments was not expected among such groups.[30]

Wendorf's candid words here show that even in the physical sciences, there is a tendency to find only what we set out to find and ignore or fail to notice other features that do not fall within our preset objective.

In other words, scientists have a tendency to discover what they expect. Important to note, at any rate, is that Wendorf and Malville in "The Megalithic Alignments" finally took notice of the mysterious megalithic alignments and structures and their possible astronomical meaning.

They were in for quite a surprise. In their 2001 report, Wendorf and Malville listed no fewer than twenty-five megaliths that were placed in six main alignments toward the horizon. Although most of the megaliths today are toppled and broken, as indicated earlier, origi-nally they stood upright and created impressive lines of sight. They were generally about 2 by 1 meters (about 7 by 3 feet) in height and about 0.4 meter (about one foot) thick. The biggest of these megaliths was a massive 3 by 2.5 meters (about 1 by 8 feet) in height and 0.7 meters (about 2.3 feet) thick, and is estimated to weigh more than ten tons. Yet this was by no means the largest block found at Nabta Playa. The larg-est, although not part of any apparent alignment, was labeled Megalith X-1 by Wendorf and measured 4 by 3.1 meters (about 13 by 10 feet) in height and 0.7 meter (about 2.3 feet) thick, and was estimated to weigh nearly 20 tons. Returning to the six megalithic alignments, the astronomer Kim Malville spent some time measuring their latitude and longitude to determine their precise azimuths, and he identified three of them going toward the north and the three others going toward the east.[31]

ALIGNMENTS TOWARD THE STARS: WHEN AND WHY?

Malville concluded that the megalithic alignments had been intended to point to the rising place of important stars on the horizon in the late Neolithic period. He proposed that the three alignments going north tracked the star Dubhe at 4742 BCE, at 4423 BCE, and at 4199 BCE. Of the set of three alignments going east, one was aimed at Sirius in ca. 4820 BCE and the two others tracked the stars of Orion's belt at 4176 BCE and 3786 BCE. What Malville had determined, even though he

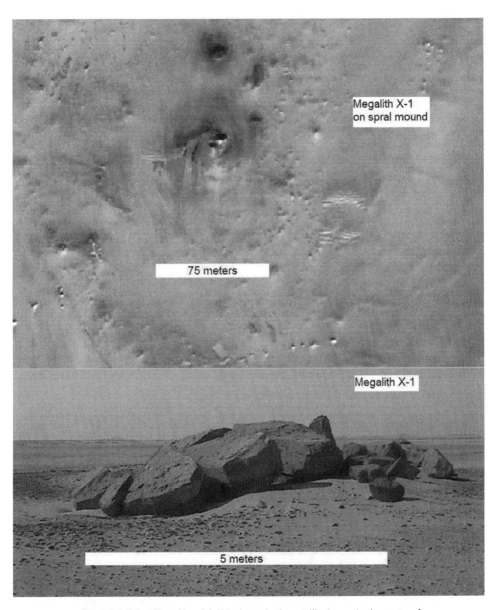

Figure 3.4. Nabta Playa Megalith X-1, shown in the satellite image in the center of an oval hill and large, low, spiral-armed feature. The broken or cut X-1 is on the ground. Scale in the two images is indicated by the lengths of the labeled white bars.

did not spell it out himself, was that the ancient builders were tracking the precessional shift of important stars over several centuries, perhaps even millennia.

At this stage, however, we must quickly point out that though one of the functions of the megalithic alignments was to act as trackers of

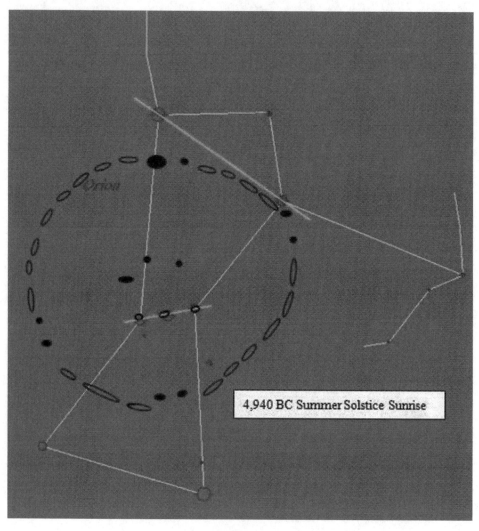

Figure 3.5. Orion's belt matching to a diagram of the central stones of the Calendar Circle in 4940 BCE.

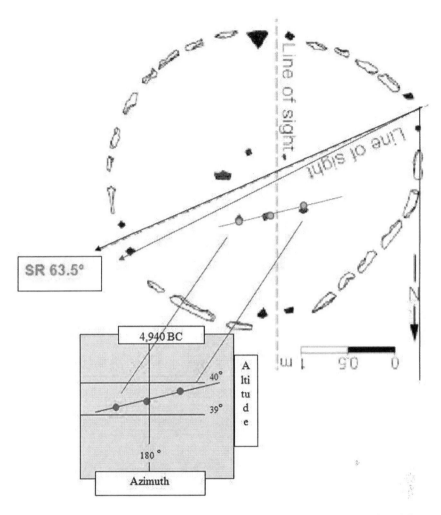

Figure 3.6. Diagram of Orion's belt matching Calender Circle stones at altitude, azimuth, and date.

the changing risings point of stars on the horizon across the epochs, it is important to note that the dates allocated by Malville to the alignments are in error due to the miscalculation of the azimuths made in the 2001 report[32]—errors that have since been corrected.[33] Further, although the 2005 corrected azimuths readings gave much earlier dates for the tracking of the stars, and although Malville agreed on the corrections, he did not then apply those dates, but instead proposed a set of different stars to fit his original (incorrect) dates. At this point, we and Malville parted directions in the interpretation of these alignments. We chose to retain the original stars proposed by Malville—Dubhe,* Sirius, and those of Orion's belt—for as we will see in chapter 4, these stars no doubt made far more sense to the prehistoric people of Nabta Playa. In addition, chapter 6 shows how this prehistoric star lore was eventually passed on to the ancient Egyptians, who built the pyramids, and how especially the bright star Sirius became the star par excellence of the pharaohs.

---

*As the primary member of a set of circumpolar stars.

4

SIRIUS RISING

We learn from the Pyramid Texts that Orion and Sirius occupied almost as important positions in the king's plans for his after-life as the circumpolar stars.

I. E. S. EDWARDS,
THE PYRAMIDS OF EGYPT

And He it is Who has made the stars for you that you might follow the right way thereby in the darkness of the land and the sea; truly We have made plain the communications for a people who know.

THE QUR'AN 6:97

The importance of Sirius for the Egyptians lay in the fact that the star's annual appearance on the eastern horizon at dawn heralded the approximate beginning of the Nile's annual inundation which marked the beginning of the agricultural year . . .

RICHARD WILKINSON,
*THE COMPLETE GODS AND GODDESSES
OF ANCIENT EGYPT*

CALENDAR CIRCLE REVEALED

Our own investigation of the astronomy of Nabta Playa began immediately after we had seen the 1998 *Nature* letter by the CPE and also the accompanying press release issued by the University of Colorado on behalf of professor Kim Malville. We were intrigued by the so-called Egyptian Stonehenge in the Sahara and the sensational claim that it was the oldest astronomical megalithic site in the world. Looking at the simple diagram and the few photographs of the Calendar Circle, as the CPE now called it, it was quite obvious to us that the much-touted Egyptian Stonehenge was substantially smaller than the famous one in England, but the true importance of this strange artifact is in its age and the information that we can derive from the monument. For example, we can recall that in late 1996 a small meteorite from Mars was found in Antarctica, which allegedly contained hydrocarbons and tiny globules formed by fossils of tiny primitive bacteria.[1] The photographs published in the press of the unimpressive ping-pong-ball-sized rock did not really have an impact on the general public—unlike, for example, the famous radio broadcast of October 30, 1938, when Orson Welles's sonorous voice read an adaption of H. G. Wells's science fiction novel *War of the Worlds,* in which Martians invade Earth and cause panic in several cities in the United States. Thousands mistook Welles's reading for a real news broadcast.

Regarding the Martian meteorite, it was not really its size or shape that could impress us, but rather the information it contained, which, if proved true, could completely change our perception of life in the universe and of who we really are. Likewise, the information locked in the arrangement and alignments of the Calendar Circle stones and its partner stone monuments could completely change our views on the origins and racial roots of the world's greatest civilization. The Calendar Circle of Nabta Playa, it turns out, is not an Egyptian Stonehenge, but instead, more of an Egyptian Mars meteorite with a rather special message for the story of humanity.

What first grabbed attention regarding the Calendar Circle, other than the two sets of gates on the outer ring of the circle reported by the CPE, were the six standing stones (actually two sets of three stones in rows) at the center of the circle. The CPE *Nature* paper focused on the so-called gates, explaining their astronomical alignments toward the summer solstice sunrise and toward the north-south (meridian) cardinal direction. No explanation at all was given for the two sets of standing stones inside the Calendar Circle. These were either ignored by the CPE or deemed unimportant. This seemed very strange, for if the Calendar Circle had meaning to the people who built it, then surely the primary feature of the arrangement—the two rows of stones standing at its center—must also have had meaning to the ancient builders. Perhaps the CPE simply had not been able to discern the meaning of the stones. We decided, therefore, to start our investigation by focusing on these mysterious stones. Our hunch was that they had some astronomical function that related not only to the gates of the Calendar Circle, but also, perhaps, to the whole ceremonial complex at Nabta Playa.

Yet we did not know how best to approach the meaning of these stone. We knew that one of the pitfalls of investigations of ancient cultures is first to entertain preconceived ideas about what their capabilities and knowledge were. We saw in chapter 3 how the CPE made this mistake ragarding the megalithic constructions at Nabta Playa, which they saw as natural outcrops of rock, because they had assumed that "building large stone monuments was not expected among such groups."[2] Further, although the CPE anthropologists did eventually realize their mistake, and understood that these megaliths were constructions that had been created by the prehistoric people of Nabta Playa, their preconceived ideas resulted in the delay of the advancement of knowledge by several decades.

How many times has this sort of obstinate blockage occurred in archaeology? Perhaps the most bald-faced one was when, in 1993, Rudolf Gantenbrink, an independent robotics engineer, explored one of the star shafts in the Great Pyramid and discovered at its end a small trap door with handles. "There is nothing behind this door!" cried German Egyptologist Rainer Stadelmann, who was in charge of the exploration. More than seventeen years later, the world is still waiting to know what might be hidden at the end of the star shaft. We were determined not to make the same blunder ourselves.

The *Nature* letter concluded that the Calendar Circle had an astronomical function of some sort. Thus, we approached those six stones in its center as a straightforward astronomy puzzle—that is, we determined not to presume to know in advance what the Neolithic people who built it could have been aware of or what they were thinking or why they were arranging the stones as they were. For the purpose of solving the puzzle of the Calendar Circle, we determined simply to consider human-made stones on the ground and astronomy in the sky.*

We decided that if we found a solution to the astronomy puzzle, then we could consider whether it fit in with the rest of the archaeological and anthropological evidence. It occurred to us that the first step toward solving the astronomy puzzle would be to assume that the six upright stones inside the Calendar Circle had been placed in position to work with the astronomical alignments of the gates. In other words, the two rows of central upright stones should somehow have been connected to the summer solstice sunrise and the north-south meridian directions when the Calendar Circle was built. Yet why would the ancient builders place six upright stones inside a circle that marked time with the summer solstice and that marked place with the meridian?

When we look at the Calendar Circle from directly above, the two sets of upright stones inside it appear analogous to the dials of a petrified giant clock. In the same way a police detective may examine the dials of a broken wristwatch or the pointers of a broken compass to

---

*Some scholars who emphasize the cultural approach, rather than the physical approach, to archaeology claim this method of analysis or puzzle-solving is invalid, because, they say, any proposed astronomy should be linked directly to ethnographic justifications— that is, we should have access to other evidence, including writings or stories, already proving that the specific people who built the structure in question were in fact interested in the proposed astronomy. We absolutely agree that ethnographic justifications greatly improve the validity of any archaeoastronomical finding, but we also note that considering astronomy first and then, subsequently, considering the ethnographics, is equally scientific.

determine the time and place of the crime, we decided to examine the two rows of upright stones in the frozen Calendar Circle to determine when and where in the sky the ancient astronomer-priests may have looked when they designed this astronomical stone instrument. What could they have seen on the meridian of the sky during the summer solstice that could be represented by these upright stones? We knew from our previous studies that much later, the ancient Egyptians of the nearby Nile Valley paid particular attention to the summer solstice, because it was during this time of year that the annual flood of the Nile irrigated the land and brought sustenance to the crops. We also knew that this yearly hydraulic miracle was marked by the appearance of three prominent stars at dawn—those we today call Orion's belt. We can recall how the monsoon rains that drenched the Sahara and refilled the dry lakes in midsummer were of vital importance to the prehistoric people of Nabta Playa. In fact, the very same monsoon rains also filled the great lakes of central Africa, which were the source of the Nile, and brought the annual flood to Egypt. Could the prehistoric people of Nabta Playa have seen the dawn appearance of Orion's belt as a marker of the annual rains, as did the ancient Egyptians later with the annual Nile's flood? More specifically, could the three stars of Orion's belt be correlated to one of the sets of three stones in the Calendar Circle? The three stars of Orion's belt were equidistance from each other, as were the three upright stones inside the Calendar Circle.*

This was, to say the very least, a tantalizing invitation to see a

---

*Of course, critics chime in at this point: "There is no reason to assume the Calendar Circle builders were interested in the stars of Orion's belt. Therefore it is pseudoscientific to consider such a solution to the Calendar Circle puzzle!" Our answer is that we we must not start with ethnographic associations or presumptions. In fact, for the moment, we exclude from the puzzle as we have defined them ethnographic assumptions in order to have a well-defined question that involves only simple physical astronomy and a man-made pattern of stones on the ground. Further, to isolate a problem by employing well-defined parameters is actually good scientific method. If we come up with a solution to the well-defined simplified astronomy puzzle, then we can consider whether there are or are not ethnographic justifications. This is at least as scientific a procedure as starting with ethnographic presumptions in the first place.

deliberate correlation between stars and stones. As we began to analyze the possibility, the puzzle of the Calendar Circle astronomy immediately began to yield.

We imagined using the Calendar Circle as an astronomical instrument, and we set our astronomical software to the earliest date possible for it: 4712 BCE, at the latitude of Nabta Playa. This was close to the date that the CPE had allocated to the Calendar Circle by radiocarbon analysis. We then looked at our computer simulation of the ancient sky. We imagined ourselves kneeling on the outside of the Calendar Circle and looking at the summer solstice sunrise through the set of gates that were directed northeast. We then imagined ourselves moving around the Calendar Circle and looking through the other set of gates toward the meridian in the sky. We set our computer screen to look at the south meridian—and there it was, close to the meridian: Orion's belt!

Our hypothesis at this stage was thus that the ancient astronomer-priests of Nabta Playa had designed a device that locked together the summer solstice sunrise and the culmination of Orion's belt for ritualistic purposes and also for the practical purpose of marking the coming of the monsoon rains. Yet could such a hypothesis be scientifically tested? Yes—it could be accomplished by working out at which epoch the pattern of the three stars of Orion's belt would have matched the pattern of the three stones in the Calendar Circle and then comparing this result to the one resulting from radiocarbon and other dating methods. If these dates matched, then the hypothesis would stand. We need not be bogged down here in details regarding how the position of Orion's belt can be worked out with precession calculations. This, in any case, can be verified easily on a home computer equipped with good astronomical software. Any keen observer of the night sky will know that Orion's belt forms a very noticeable *asterism* (small group of stars) in the southern sky. Indeed, so striking is this asterism that it was not only noticed but also used by many ancient cultures in their rituals and mythologies. The asterism is at the center of the great Orion constellation that today dominates the southern sky in the winter months.

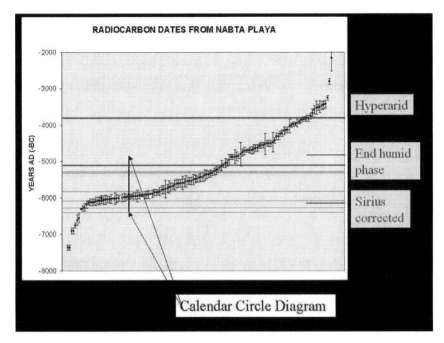

Figure 4.1. Plot of all the radiocarbon dates from Nabta Playa published by the CPE.

The current configuration of the constellation was formed about two million years ago* and will remain recognizable in the night sky for the next two million years or so, making it one of the longest observable-by-humans constellations, and its familiar pattern was recognized by many ancient people, although these cultures represented it differently. Most often, however, it was respresented as a giant human figure striding across the heavens. Thus, the ancient Egyptians saw Orion as a giant man representing the god of resurrection, Osiris. To the ancient Babylonians, the constellation was Mulsipazianna, the heavenly shepherd. The Greeks saw it as a giant hunter. Even the Bible speaks of Orion and Orion's belt in the books of Job and Amos.† Indeed, on a

---

*The constellations change shape very slowly over long periods of time, due to the so-called proper motions of stars. All the stars are moving with respect to each other, like billiard balls scattering on a pool table—though at extremely slow, angular rates.

†The Bible mentions Orion three times: Job 9:9, "He is the maker of the Bear and Orion"; Job 8:31, "Can you loosen Orion's belt?"; and Amos 5:8, "He who made the Pleiades and Orion."

clear, cloudless night, it is almost impossible not to be drawn to this bright and impressive asterism, especially to the obvious three-star asterism forming the belt—and likely this pull was stronger for the ancient people of the Sahara, who, every night, had the opportunity to watch the stars, unhindered by either obstacles or the light pollution of towns and cities.

Of course, it is important to note that the slow, twenty-six-thousand-years cycle of precession will change over time the angle that the Orion's belt asterism makes with the meridian. If we bear this in mind, it is relatively simple to verify by computer simulation of the sky what the angle of the three stars is relative to the meridian and then match it to that of the three upright stones at the center of the Calendar Circle. What epoch does the circle then resprent? The CPE concluded that the Calendar Circle must be dated to about 4800 BCE because organic matter found nearby was firmly fixed at that date by radiocarbon analysis and other archaeological methods. Clearly, then, it was worth checking the angle of the Orion's belt asterism around 4800 BCE in order to test our hypothesis. There was a hiccup at this point, however: our software went back only to Julian date zero, 4712 BCE. [3]

Scaliger's Julian Date Counting Method

We note that the commonly used astronomy programs (SkyMapPro and StarryNight) employ approximation methods to calculate the locations of stars. Because they approximate around the current date, they are extremely accurate for any dates within thousands of years of today, but for extremely ancient or extremely distant future dates, their accuracy begins to degrade. The program we used, SkyMapPro, cannot give readings earlier than 4712 BCE because it employs the so-called Julian date counting method, which is based on the Julian period proposed by Joseph Scaliger in 1583. This Julian period is a multiple of three time cycles: the nineteen-year Metonic cycle or synodic lunar cycle, times the twenty-eight-year solar cycle or leap year day counting cycle, times the fifteen-year indiction cycle used for tax accounting in medieval Europe. Scaliger intended his long period count to be useful for unifying the various measures of historical time with which scholars were then struggling, and he figured, interestingly, that 4712 BCE—the last time those three cycles were in their first year together—was a good enough place to start counting for a unified modern calendar system, because that date was earlier than all known historical dates at the time (that is, generally accepted historical dates known to European scholars at the time).

Like many figures in the past who have proposed important advances in knowledge and new ways of thinking about ancient history, he seemed to have ruffled many academic feathers in his time. As one writer on Scaliger puts it, he wanted to "revolutionize perceived ideas of ancient chronology—to show that ancient history is not confined to that of the Greeks and Romans, but also comprises that of the Persians, the Babylonians and the Egyptians . . ."[4] He wanted to push beyond the academically popular Eurocentric notions of Greeks and Romans being the source of all important modern knowledge in order to include more ancient roots, including sources from Egypt. Scaliger believed that much of the astronomical and calendrical knowledge that we tend to ascribe to discovery by ancient Greeks actually came from earlier Babylonian, Akkadian, and Egyptian sources that were transcribed, translated, and studied by Greek conquerors. That debate—rediscovery versus discovery—continues among scholars. As we will see later in this book, the earliest roots of discovery of that knowledge may keep moving back in time, past those pre-Greek sources toward even the people who built Nabta Playa. It is a curiosity that the dates of the Nabta Playa Calendar Circle turn out to be just a bit earlier than Julian date Zero.

CALENDAR CIRCLE RESOLVED

In order to accurately calculate ancient star locations, we were able to employ some methods related to our own doctoral dissertation work using computers to simulate certain planetary astrophysics motions.[5] We wrote a brief computer program to calculate very ancient star locations using the generally accepted mathematical equations for the long-term motions of Earth.[6] We then tested our method against the SkyMapPro astronomy software as far back in time as it could go in order to verify the accuracy of this method, which turned out to be very precise. Satisfied that we were well within the accuracy required for our purpose, we then examined the angle of the Orion's belt asterism with the meridian as seen from the latitude of Nabta Playa in epoch 4800 BCE, and we quickly realized that we had hit the bulls-eye with our hypothesis.

The natural place to stand when using the Calendar Circle as an observatory or observing diagram is at the north gate looking south—that is, toward the south meridian of the sky. By mentally registering the image of the nearest set of three upright stones inside the Calendar Circle and then looking up at the sky, the observer in ca. 4800 BCE would have seen the three stars of Orion's belt in almost exactly the same configuration. In other words, the three upright stones on the ground are a representation of the three stars of Orion's belt in the sky.

According to our calculations, the perfect match occurs in 4940 BCE, which is well within the margin of error obtained by the CPE's radiocarbon dating. This sky-ground correlation is unlikely to be a coincidence. What additionally supports this conclusion is the fact that the distance—that is, altitude—of the stars measured from the horizon matches the distance of the stones measured from the north rim of the Calendar Circle.

But there was more: Using our computer program and calculations, we established that in 4940 BCE, Orion's belt could be seen at meridian for approximately six months each year, from summer solstice sunrise to winter solstice sunset. These two extreme points in the sun's annual

cycle were in fact marked by the Calendar Circle with the line passing through the northeast gate and southwest gate, with one direction
pointing northeastward toward the summer solstice sunrise and the
opposite direction pointing southwestward toward the winter solstice
sunset. To put it more simply, the set of gates of the Calendar Circle, as
well as the set of upright stones inside it, worked together to delineate
the annual cycle of Orion's belt in ca. 4940 BCE. The ancient astronomer-priests had designed an extremely clever and very simple device to
track the cycle of this important stellar asterism throughout the year.
We also noted that although 4940 BCE was the best sky-ground fit
between the stones and the stars, a similar fit was visible from about
6400 BCE to 4800 BCE.* In practice, then, the Calendar Circle could
have been operational for this span of time.

We can note that we have now completed only half of our solution
to the Calendar Circle puzzle: we have identified the function of one of
the sets of three upright stones. Next, we turned our attention to the
other set, which was placed closer to the southern rim of the Calendar
Circle. Now that it was made clear to us that Orion's belt was the key to
this prehistoric machine, we could not help noticing that the stars that
make up the head and shoulders of the human figure of Orion can also
be correlated to these three stones, but at another, more ancient time
than 4940 BCE. We calculated that the best fit for the stars of Orion's
head and shoulders was in 16,500 BCE. What made this fit an unlikely

---

*One key aspect of this interpretation is the visibility of the stars on the meridian. Also,
given that solar zenith crossing was considered to be of significance to the Neolithic people and that at Nabta Playa the sun crossed the zenith two days per year—21 days after
and 21 days before the day of summer solstice—we can use this information to define
an operational window for the Calendar Circle (that is, those years when the Orion's
belt stars would have been visible on the meridian in the proper configuration any time
during those six weeks around summer solstice). Further, we estimate that the stars could
be seen in the sky up to about forty-five minutes before the sun rises above the horizon.
This gives an end date to the Calendar Circle operational window of about 4800 BCE.
The start of the window is when the configuration angle and altitude become a good
match, which we estimate to be about 6400 BCE. In actual practice, though, the device
may have been used after 4800 BCE, especially if its interpretation was known.

coincidence was also the fact the angle of the shoulder stars reached their maximum point during the autumnal equinox in the same epoch, and furthermore, in this interpretation, the brightest star in Orion, Betelgeuse, matched the position of the largest stone. Again, the distance (altitude) of these stars as measured from the horizon matched the distance of the corresponding stones measured from the rim of the Calendar Circle.

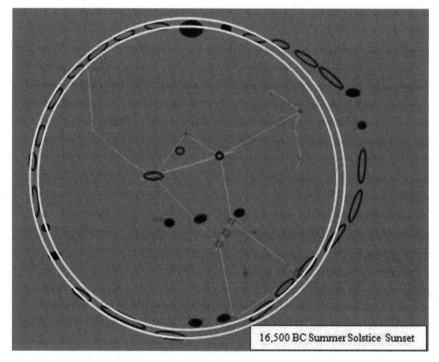

16,500 BC Summer Solstice Sunset

Figure 4.2. Orion's head and shoulders matching to the Calender Circle stones
at altitude, azimuth, and date.

If our conclusions are correct, then the Calendar Circle becomes far more than a snapshot of a single observation of Orion in the night sky. Instead, it is an elegant and profound device to show the change caused by precession on the stars of Orion over vast periods of time. In other words, the Calendar Circle becomes a teaching instrument that demonstrates the precession of the stars. We are not proposing that the Calendar Circle was constructed eighteen thousand years ago,* but rather that it commemorates two important dates in the precession cycle of Orion—4900 BCE and 16,500 BCE—with the former date being the actual date of its construction and use as indicated by the radiocarbon dating, and the latter date being some sort of memorial of an important event, perhaps a beginning in the history of those sub-Saharan herders who came to Nabta Playa in prehistoric times. In additon, the two dates bracket symbolically the two sides of the whole twenty-six-thousand-year precession cycle.

This, of course, presupposes an ability to predict the effect of precession on the stars, namely the cyclical changes in angular tilt and altitude of the constellations over the centuries and millennia. The usual opposition to this is the modern belief that ancient cultures were too primitive and did not have the knowledge or ability to accomplish these predictions. In fact, however, predicting the effects of precession—even without telescopes and sophisticated mathematical knowledge—is not as difficult as it seems to be. This is because the apparent motion of precession is essentially the same as the yearly apparent motion of the sun across the sky—except not in one year but over twenty-six thousand years. An intelligent mind of either today or thousands of years ago that was attuned to careful observation of the changes in the sky and privy to records kept over many generations need only have made a conceptual link in order to create such a device as the Calendar Circle at Nabta Playa and enable it to work with the yearly cycle as well as the precession cycle.

In other words, there are essentially two ways to grasp the effects of precession on constellations: (1) adding together incremental measures over many years and building up a mathematical model for how

---

*Though we do not see why it should be considered impossible, such an extremely ancient date would mean the Calendar Circle would have had to survive through thousands of years of wet Sahara conditions and through periods of heavy human use. Instead, we think the device was constructed and used during the recent epochs of significant human activity and then was abandoned when the area became hyperarid—and thus the construction survived mostly intact to modern times.

the sky moves gradually (as it is generally believed the ancient Greeks did), or (2) making a sort of vision-logic mental leap that suddenly grasps the geometric shifting of the whole cycle. Of course, such a conceptual mental leap required a particularly subtle and astute mind, but the Neolithic human's brain was perfectly able to perform such an intellectual task. Albeit, the design of the Calendar Circle involved a stroke of genius—indeed, probably many such strokes over many generations—but once constructed, the Calendar Circle was so user-friendly that all those who chanced upon it could easily have realized its meaning, especially those who had been avidly observing and study-ing the night sky, as did the ancient dwellers of the Sahara. In addi-tion, it is likely that as part of the whole ceremonial complex at Nabta Playa, the Calendar Circle was understood and used by generations of astronomer-priests not merely in isolation, but as part of a broader context of the other structures in the area. We can see that some of the stones, especially those from the north gate, are composed of finely worked and shaped hard stone, which further indicates a refined sense of design and significant effort on the part of the Calendar Circle builders. We can discern in the Calendar Circle the product of minds that were keenly attuned to the subtleties of annual cycles and the long-term cycles of the heavens, and to the ability to represent such awareness elegantly in a stone diagram. Indeed, after people today see animated graphics of how the Calendar Circle works, they immedi-ately understand and appreciate the plausibility of these conclusions. We have presented similar graphic animation[7] at meetings of profes-sional scholars in Atlanta, Georgia,[8] and Rhodes, Greece,[9] in 2004, as well as at meetings and public conferences in San Diego, California, in 2007; in Dubai, UAE, in 2008; and in Rome, Italy, in 2009—and the audiences immediately grasped how and why the Calendar Circle was used by the ancients. Regarding the scholars, however, although they easily grasp the idea, their academic conditioning often blocks them from changing their own preconceived beliefs about the Nabta Playa ancient people. Others who are more skeptical suggest that the data of field archaeologists, especially having to do with astronomy that matches the stones, may have been in error.*

We, however, have double-checked the source of the Calendar Circle data and have ourselves examined the remains of the circle. Further, with regard to the nearby megalithic structures, we also have undertaken measurements and have relied on both the field maps provided by archaeologists as well as very accurate satellite photography of Nabta Playa. What clinches our interpretation and conclusions that the ancient Nabta Playa astronomer-priests paid significant attention to Orion's belt as part of a unified system of tracking the changes in the sky is the fact that similar astronomical activities are also attributed to the other megalithic structures in the ceremonial complex.

SPACE AGE MEETS STONE AGE

In chapter 3 we saw how the ceremonial complex at Nabta Playa consists essentially of two major features: large stones, many of which are shaped and placed on the sediments of the ancient dry lake; and large, sculpted rocks and sculpted lumps of bedrock beneath the sediments. The 1998 *Nature* letter and other early CPE reports on Nabta Playa dealt only with the astronomy of the Calendar Circle; they did not attempt to interpret the astronomy of the megalithic alignments, although they did report some of these megaliths' various orientations. Finally, however, in 2001, the CPE published their report and in it gave their tentative interpretation of the megalithic alignments and the GPS coordinates of each megalith. They determined that the twenty-two megaliths formed

---

*Our interpretation does not require precision knowledge of astronomy or precision matching to the stone diagram, as some have objected. We did calculate the star locations with accuracy and precision only because there is no reason not to do so. Further, we noted that the astronomy matches the field archaeological reconstruction precisely, because it happens to, but the validity of our interpretation does not depend on such precision. If the field archaeology drawings turn out to be a bit incorrect, our case for this interpretation is not hindered in any way. Of course, however, certainly if these drawings are completely in error, then any interpretation based on them suffers.

six alignments that radiated out from Complex Structure A (CSA), and they proposed that these alignments were intended to designate the rising locations of two important stars, Dubhe and Sirius, and also the stellar asterism of Orion's belt. Three alignments (A1, A2, A3) pointing north aligned to Dubhe at three different dates in the fifth millennium BCE; a fourth alignment (C1) pointed, also in the fifth millennium BCE, toward Sirius; and two alignments (B1, B2) pointed toward Orion's belt at two different dates in the fourth and fifth millennium BCE.

Yet a serious problem with their data invalidated the dates they gave for these alignments. It is an understandable fact that most people do not question or verify the data and conclusions given in a technical or scientific publication by university professors of the caliber of Fred Wendorf, Kim Malville, and Romuald Schild of the CPE. Having already developed our own interpretation for the Calendar Circle before the CPE's 2001 site report was published, we were keenly interested in their alignment data for the megaliths. In order to verify the link among the alignments of the six rows of megaliths and the rising point of stars on the horizon, it was necessary to convert into azimuths the GPS coordinates of the megaliths given in the 2001 report and then to match them to the calculated azimuths of the proposed stars. Yet when we tried to convert these GPS readings into azimuths, we found that they did not match the published azimuths in the 2001 report! This meant that the dates for the stars' rising were also off. Only the azimuth given for Orion's belt was more or less the same as ours—but those given for Sirius and Dubhe differed radically from our calculations, which were in fact based on the GPS readings published in the 2001 report. Something clearly was not right. To make matters worse, the azimuths for the six megalithic alignments in the 2001 report were significantly different from those previously given in the 1998 *Nature* letter. Further, some of the CPE's calculations of ancient star locations differed from our calculations, even before they were matched to rising azimuths.

All this was very confusing, for it was impossible to tell from these reports whether the raw GPS readings taken on location were in error or that the CPE calculations to convert these into azimuths was in error. We determined that it was best to ask the CPE about this. The lead author replied that we should contact another author who was responsible for the data in the relevant 2001 report. While we waited for the response, as luck would have it, the Space Age provided us with another and better way to clear up this confusion: DigitalGlobe, a high-tech corporation, was in the process of developing the first high-resolution satellite imaging system for commercial use. In November 2000, they twice attempted to launch their Quickbird 1 satellites from Plesetsk Cosmodrome in Russia, but both rockets failed and the satellites were destroyed. On October 18, 2001, however, the Quickbird 2 satellite was successfully launched from Vandenberg Air Force Base in California, and after testing and calibration, DigitalGlobe began making commercially available 60-centimeter, high-resolution imagery from space. With this kind of resolution, we estimated that we could probably identify the Nabta Playa megaliths from space and obtain for ourselves the coordinates for our calculations. We thus sent in an order to Quickbird to task the satellite for us and obtain an image of Nabta Playa with their high-resolution data. As it turned out, we were likely the first to use Quickbird for archaeoastronomy. On December 31, 2002, Quickbird flew directly over Nabta Playa on a cloudless day and snapped the image with the coordinates we had supplied. After receiving and preparing the Quickbird data for analysis, we were thrilled to find that the Nabta Playa megaliths could be seen in the satellite image. Using the descriptions of individual megaliths given in the 2001 CPE report alongside some ground-based photographs published by Fred Wendorf, we were able to identify in the satellite image all the megaliths as well as Complex Structures A and B (and also other intriguing features, which we will discuss later). After georectifying the image and then correlating it to latitude and longitude, we were able to measure latitude and longitude coordinates for each of the megaliths. These coordinates were similar to those published by Wendorf and Malville in the 2001 report. This suggested, of course, that it was not the GPS readings obtained by them that were incorrect, but rather that the CPE had made errors in their calculations. Because there was still a shift in our satellite-determined measurements, in order to be absolutely sure of our results, we decided to go to Nabta Playa and take our own GPS measurements. The stakes were too high to rely only on the data we had thus far compiled, and we felt that a journey to Nabta Playa was well worth the cost and effort.

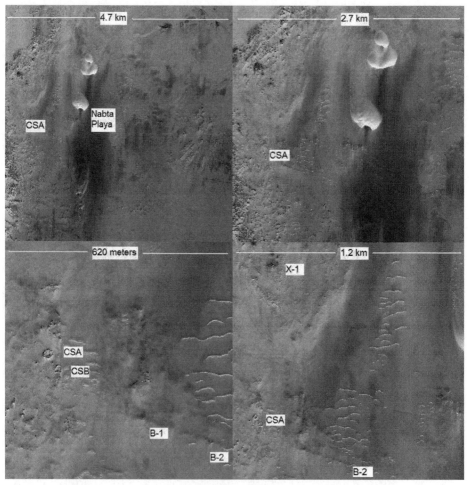

Figure 4.3. Zooming into the Nabta Playa satellite image (Digital Globe, Quickbird). Complex Structure A is labeled CSA. Also labeled are megalith lines B1 and B2, megalith X-1, and Complex Structure B (CSB). Note that that circular rings near CSA and CSB are the detritus left after excavation of these structures, not their original formation. The bright features in the center of the playa (seen in the upper two images) are actively moving sand dunes.

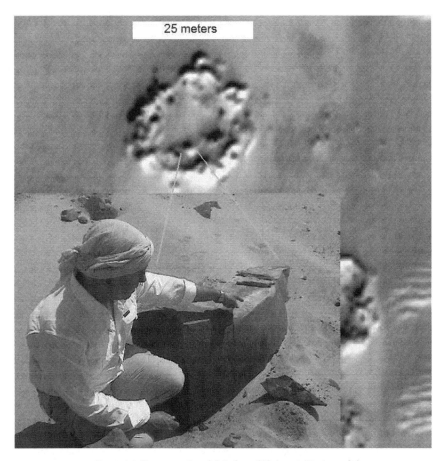

Figure 4.4. The excavation debris from CSA, in satellite image,
with one of the megaliths as seen on the ground in April 2008.

In October 2003, we used the service of a British safari tour company
to secure the necessary permits from the Egyptian government to visit
Nabta Playa, and we arranged for a very small safari tour to make a devia-
tion from their route and deliver us to the site. Egyptian regulations also
required that we be accompanied by an Egyptian military officer as well as
an inspector from the Egyptian antiquities department, a Supreme Council
of Antiquities (SCA) Egyptologist. After a long trek by jeep from Cairo via
the desert oases route, we arrived in the evening near Nabta Playa and set
up camp 5 kilometers (about 3 miles) away in order not to cause any environmental disturbance of the important archaeological site. Before leaving

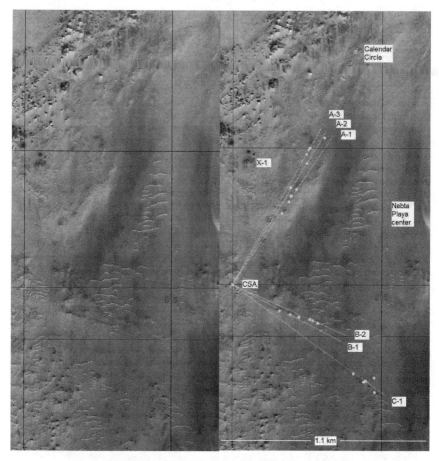

Figure 4.5. Satellite image of the area of Nabta Playa containing the megalith alignments. Left, satellite image with black gridlines for measuring; right, the magalith alignments and the Calendar Circle appear labeled, but the circle stones are too small to be seen in the satellite image.

from Cairo, we had coded into our hand-held GPS receiver the coordinates of the megaliths obtained from the Quickbird satellite data. Now, some two hours before dawn, we were ready to walk from camp to the Nabta Playa ceremonial complex. As we prepared to set out alone, however, the SCA Egyptologist who had come along asked if he could accompany us, perhaps out of curiosity but also to educate himself, because we were amazed to find that he knew nothing about Nabta Playa.

Wondering what the ancient people who had once lived there would have thought of us, on a chilly dawn, carrying a hand-held GPS, we set out on foot from our campsite to the world's oldest astronomical site. It seemed to us that the ancients would have been totally at ease moving around in the dark, using the stars for navigation, while we, with all our technological know-how, moved clumsily in the dark, clinging to our GPS tracking device in order not to get lost in this no-man's-land of empty desert. Five kilometers (about 3 miles) can seem a very long way to those trekking on foot and in the dark in one of the most vast and hostile environments on Earth. After a while, when we lost complete sight of our camp, and as we surveyed the horizon as a backup to our GPS navigation, the Egyptian inspector began to get somewhat nervous. He wrongly interpreted that we were totally lost, but we quickly reassured him that, with our GPS navigation, we knew exactly where we were. As we continued to trek in the dark, however, our reassurances failed to calm the inspector, and he began insisting that we should walk in a different direction. A serious dispute ensued. We stopped listening to the inspector's lament and decided to focus on our GPS indicator. We told him that he could go in a different direction if he wanted to or follow us with our GPS. After some deliberation, he decided to follow us, but with the caveat that his protest had been duly registered.

Finally, to our relief, the light from the growing dawn was strong enough for us to spot in the distance the first megaliths of Complex Structure A. The inspector beamed at us, and with a broad gesture of his hand to express his excitement and approval, he seemed to tell us that all the previous animosity toward us was quickly forgotten. We had at long last arrived at Nabta Playa, but our work was only just beginning. We estimated it would take all morning and several more kilometers of fast walking in this vast complex to get all the GPS readings and photographs needed for our purpose. Slowly and diligently, we recorded the GPS of all the megaliths, and we also had enough time before noon to investigate a mysterious feature beneath the largest megalith at Nabta Playa—labeled X-1—that had shown up on the Quickbird satellite image. The day was now becoming seriously hot, but we pressed on to visit the Calendar Circle and took some photographs for our own use. When we were satisfied that we had all the information and photographs we wanted, we rendezvoused with the jeeps, and after a quick sandwich break and refreshments, we headed south to connect with the new tarmac road that would take us to the city of Aswan on the Nile.

Back home in California, we carefully analyzed our GPS field measurements and compared the results to those obtained from the Quickbird image and found them to be in agreement (although we had to make a small correction for the very slight error in the satellite's pointing vector from space). We now had multiple corroborating coordinate readings for all the megaliths, and, armed with this data, we were able to determine their exact alignments, satisfied that at last we could do this with certainty. We found that the 2001 CPE report included raw GPS coordinates for the megaliths that were fairly accurate, but azimuth calculations derived from them were incorrect. Correcting this error yielded a completely new set of dates for the stellar alignments of the six rows of megaliths. Most significant was the alignment to the rising of Sirius. Malville and Wendorf had proposed that one of the megalith lines, C1, was directed toward the rising of Sirius in ca. 4820 BCE, but our calculations showed a much earlier date of ca. 6090 BCE. At this point we sought the support from a close colleague, Paul Rosen, from our previous interplanetary robotic space mission work, who was now a leader in spacecraft radar remote sensing technology. Together, in June 2005 we published the new results for the Nabta Playa megaliths alignments in a peer-reviewed academic journal.[10] Because our results showed that the megalith alignments given by Malville and Wendorf were substantially in error, we proposed a new set of dates around 6200 BCE for the stellar targets that fitted the corrected data.*

---

*As we suggested in our earlier book, *The Origin Map*. Essentially, the megalith alignments were consistent with the C1 line, indicating the stars of Orion's belt at the early dates ca. 6200 BCE; and the B1 and B2 lines of megaliths, indicating stars of Orion's head and shoulders as suggested by the Calendar Circle; and the three lines A1, A2, and A3, indicating the brightest star in the north, Vega, at simultaneous times with the Orion stars.

Although we were pleased to see that in 2007, Wendorf and Malville (with Schild and Brenmer of the CPE) formally acknowledged their errors and accepted our corrected calculations for the azimuths of the six lines of megaliths, they nonetheless rejected our earlier date of ca. 6200 BCE, because, they point out, some of the megaliths in the alignments were on top of playa sediment that was dated to ca. 5100 BCE, and also 6200 BCE is "about 1500 years earlier than our best estimates for the Terminal Neolithic."*

Even though we do accept that some of the megaliths were placed after the sedimentation of the playa's basin, we also note that in their 2007 article, Wendorf, Malville, and their coauthors suggested (as we also did earlier) that the original part of Complex Structure A, which is the center of all the megalith alignments and is part of the bedrock beneath the playa sediments, was "part of the symbolic landscape of the Middle Neolithic and became significant before the establishment of the complex ceremonial centre. Perhaps their locations had been marked by rock cairns before gradual burial by playa sediments."[11] This indicates that there was much activity at Nabta Playa during earlier epochs, which is in any case confirmed by many radiocarbon dates, with most clustered around 6000 BCE.[12] On this basis, and also on the dating of ca. 6200 BCE obtained from the corrected calculations, we reject the notion that none of the megaliths at Nabta Playa could have predated terminal Neolithic time, because most of the field evidence shows that

---

*J. M. Malville, R. Schild, F. Wendorf, and J. Brenmer, "Astronomy of Nabta Playa, *African Skies/Cieus Africains*, no.11 (July 2007). The authors further suggested that the B1 and B2 megalith alignments may have been intended to indicate Sirius on two different dates—ca. 3500 BCE and ca. 4500 BCE—and possibly also Orion's belt ca. 4200 BCE or Alpha Centauri ca. 4400 BCE. They also proposed a new target for the A1, A2, and A3 lines toward the bright star Arcturus at ca. 3600 BCE to 4500 BCE. In addition, they recommended that because many of the megaliths, which they determine stood as stele when they were intact, are now scattered and fragmented, an uncertainty of order of a half degree azimuth should be included when we try to ascribe star alignment dates to the megaliths. Finally, they abandoned one major alignment of megaliths, the C line, and chose not to interpret them, noting they they are in a more distant area that may have been removed from the playa.

parts of the ceremonial complex were indeed created before the terminal Neolithic.

SIRIUS, THE CIRCUMPOLAR STARS, AND ORION

We now felt that we were in a good position to integrate our and the CPE's field findings and derive from them the most robust interpretation that fits the context of Nabta Playa. The findings that emerge from this integrated analysis are:

1. There are at least nine megaliths that form the three lines—A1, A2, and A3—that point north. These track the star Dubhe in the Big Dipper over a considerable period of time.
2. There are at least six megaliths that form lines B1 and B2 pointing southeast. These track the bright star Sirius at two epochs.
3. Sirius also coordinated simultaneously with the star Dubhe in the Big Dipper so that their alignments formed an approximate 90-degree angle. (This curious connection had also been noted by Wendorf and Malville; they commented that the megalith builders of Nabta Playa had "a fascination with right angles.")[13]

This possible simultaneous observation of Sirius in the east and the star Dubhe in the north was of particular interest, because we know from our studies of ancient Egypt that the very same simultaneous observation of Sirius and Dubhe was performed in the alignment rituals of pyramids and temples since the beginning of the pharaonic civilization. This encouraged us to test for the simultaneous observation of Sirius and Dubhe at Nabta Playa, where we found a remarkably accurate and consistent repetition of this pattern of observation. Indeed, an observer at Nabta Playa in about 4500 BCE would have immediately noted that the stars Dubhe and Sirius could be aligned simultaneously with megalith lines A1 and B1, for precisely when Sirius appeared to rise on the eastern horizon and was thus aligned with megalith line B1, the star Dubhe could be seen in the northern sky, directly above megalith line A1 (at an altitude of 33 degrees).

Yet could this be a coincidence? We needed to find further evidence that this was the deliberate intention of the ancient astronomer-priests in order to eliminate the possibility that simple haphazard was at play in the observations. We found that the same simultaneous observation of Sirius and Dubhe with the same right-angle separation took place with two other megalith lines—A3 and B2. This not only confirmed the deliberate intent of the ancient astronomer-priests to delineate this particular simultaneous observation, but also proved that they tracked the stars across several generations, from at least 4500 BCE to 3500 BCE. Further, it meant that they were aware of precession and even tracked its effect more than three millennia before the Greeks were supposed to have discovered it. Clearly, the people of Nabta Playa were anything but primitive.

The simultaneous alignments of Sirius and Dubhe at Nabta Playa were amazingly precise for the context and conditions of that distant epoch.* Using our measures of the averaged azimuths of the megaliths lines, we found that today the angle made between lines B1 and A1 is 91.11 degrees, and the angle between lines B2 and A3 is 91.65 degrees. Precessing the sky back to 4500 BCE, we calculated that the azimuth difference between Sirius and Dubhe when the former was on the horizon was 91.2 degrees. Moving forward in time to ca. 3500 BCE, the azimuth difference became 91.5 degrees; so the stars matched the stones uncannily well at both dates, which were a thousand years apart. In addition, Dubhe, with a declination of 66.9 degrees ca. 3500 BCE, had

---

*For any extremely rigorously minded scholars, we note again that this correspondence of the megaliths to this interpretation of the stars happens to be rather precise—but our interpretation does not depend on such precision. For alignments such as these, even within a half-degree or so, correspondence would be considered a good match. It is possible that the Neolithic builders and the way the stones toppled over the millennia happened to produce such precision.

just become an eternal circumpolar star as viewed from Nabta Playa—which means that on its daily journey around the celestial pole, at its lowest point in the sky, Dubhe due north was just skimming the horizon before rising back into the sky to travel around the celestial pole again. This may be significant with regard to why the Neolithic builders monumentalized specifically this date in the alignment.

So far, we have explained four alignments of the six megalith lines—A1, A3, B1, and B2—and have found that they work in pairs so that A1 and B1, and A3 and B2 define simultaneous right-angle observations of Sirius and Dubhe in 4500 BCE and 3500 BCE, respectively. Still left to review, however, are lines C1 and A2. In their original reports, Malville and Wendorf claimed that line C1 had targeted Sirius in 4820 BCE and that line A2 had targeted Dubhe in 4423 BCE. Yet according to our corrected azimuths for these lines, we determined the date for Sirius to be 6100 BCE, which matched, at a simultaneous right angle at that date, not Dubhe but another bright star in the Big Dipper called Alkaid, located directly over line A2 at an altitude of 22 degrees, when Sirius would have appeared precisely on the horizon and in alignment to line C1. In other words, the megalith lines C1 and A2 worked in exactly the same way as the pairs B1 and A1 and B2 and A3, but at the much later date of 6100 BCE. We nonetheless asked ourselves why Sirius was observed simultaneously with Alkaid in 6100 BCE, but much later, in 4500 BCE and 3500 BCE, Alkaid was replaced with Dubhe. We will see in chapter 6 that part of the answer, as amazing as it might seem, can be found at the step pyramid complex of Djoser at Saqqara, near modern Cairo and some 1,000 kilometers (about 621 miles) away from Nabta Playa.

King Djoser and Alkaid

At the step pyramid complex is the so-called serdab monument in which is found a statue of King Djoser gazing through peepholes toward the star Alkaid in the north at the precise moment when the star Sirius rose in the east. Perhaps the correspondence at Nabta Playa may explain why King Djoser chose to monumentalize himself peering at Alkaid (with Sirius rising) rather than peering at Dubhe. At Djoser's complex in Saqqara (ca. 2650 BCE), Dubhe was at altitude 32.5 degrees and azimuth 22.5 degrees and at near a right angle from the rising Sirius, whereas Alkaid was 112 degrees from Sirius, too far off to be considered a representation of a right angle. Both Alkaid and Dubhe are of the Bull's Thigh constellation, Alkaid is at the hoof end and Dubhe is at the top of the thigh. One possible factor for why King Djoser chose Alkaid instead of Dubhe is that it was closer to the meridian, the most natural place in the sky to view and measure star transits. Now we know another reason. Perhaps King Djoser was monumentalizing the time when his distant ancestors at Nabta Playa ca. 6100 BCE initiated the ritual of using the Bull's Thigh constellation to track the rising of Sirius with Alkaid. Indeed, the step pyramid complex at Saqqara, built by Egyptian third-dynasty King Djoser and designed by the genius astronomer-priest Imhotep, is the first major gigantic monumental architecture project of the Old Kingdom and a natural place to expect to find that these Egyptians would have monumentalized the origin of the astro rituals which they had inherited from their distant ancestors.

Figure 4.6. Left, ancient Egyptian depiction of the Big Diper as the Bull's Thigh; middle, photo of constellation; right, constellation as sculpted on the Denderah zodiac ceiling.

For now, we could see that part of the answer for the 6100-BCE choice of the star Alkaid to mark the rising of Sirius can be found by considering the long-term astronomical changes in the sky. The precession cycle causes the equinox points (March 21 and September 22) to move along the zodiac at the rate of about 1 degree every seventy-two years and to occupy each zodiacal house or sign for about 2,166 years.*

This cycle also causes the north celestial pole to perform a large circle through a group of constellations in the northern sky. Today, the star Polaris in the constellation of Ursa Minor is our Pole Star around which the starry sky rotates every twenty-four hours. In 2500 BCE the Pole Star was Thuban in the constellation Draco. Going back further in time, ca. 12,000 BCE the Pole Star was the brilliant Vega in the constellation Lyra. As the millennia passed, the celestial pole migrated away from Vega in a circle centered on the neck of Draco, through the shoulders of the constellation Hercules ca. 9000 BCE. By 6100 BCE, there was no Pole Star, but the star Alkaid was some 17 degrees from the celestial pole and was thus a circumpolar star.†

Dubhe, on the other hand, which was 38 degrees from the celestial pole in 6100 BCE, was not circumpolar, because every day it traveled far beneath the horizon, into the underworld. It seems logical to conclude that for this very reason, the astronomer-priests at Nabta Playa in 6100 BCE used Alkaid to mark the rising of Sirius but later, around 4500 BCE, switched to the star Dubhe when it grew nearer the celestial pole.‡

The C1 megaliths line consists of at least six megaliths in a set that is plus-or-minus 1 degree around azimuth 130 degrees. Given that the Nabta Playa ceremonial complex was used and developed over many

*We can note that the precise rate of precession is variable with time, and we use in all our calculations the modernly calculated exact variable precession rate. The exactness of a number such as 2,166 for a zodiac age should not be overly emphasized.
†Nabta Playa is centered at 22.5 degrees north latitude, giving the horizon there a geometric declination of 90 − 22.5 = 67.5 degrees, but astronomers generally use the visual horizon, which is a half-degree lower due to atmospheric refraction of Earth's atmosphere bending starlight, or about 67 degrees for the declination of the visual horizon at Nabta.
‡Dubhe became an eternal star, always above the horizon, in around 3500 BCE, but perhaps it was considered circumpolar enough by around 4500 BCE.

centuries, perhaps even thousands of years, it is possible that the megaliths may have incorporated more than one meaning by being directed not only to Sirius, but also to other stars such as those of Orion's belt. This possibility was in fact suggested by Malville, Wendorf, and their coauthors in their 2001 report and was discussed in our previous publication[14] in which we showed that the C1 line may have targeted Orion's belt near the epoch of 6100 BCE. Interestingly, at that same date, the C1 line also marked a very special and unique occurrence for Orion's belt in the precession cycle: its heliacal rising at the spring equinox. This meant that Orion's belt rose together with the sun on the first day of spring (March 21). This is extremely significant, because it is perfectly consistent with the hypothesis that the Calendar Circle used Orion's belt as a sort of teaching device for the short- and long-term cycles of this special group of stars.

A Star's Vernal Equinox Heliacal Rising

The vernal equinox heliacal rising of a star is also essentially the halfway mark between the star's northern culmination when it is seen farthest north on Earth and the star's southern culmination about thirteen thousand years later, when it is seen furthest south on Earth. As the people of Nabta Playa used and constructed the playa basin to teach about, study, and employ in ritual ceremony the starry sky and heavens, there were certainly smaller, temporary stone constructions there all the time. When the primary asterism they used to conceptualize how the sky moves, Orion's belt, passed that special time in its cycle, vernal equinox heliacal rising, the time was best to create monumental megalithic alignments that would last through the ages. At the time of the height of the Calendar Circle at Nabta Playa, Orion's belt and Sirius were separated in declination, and so rising azimuth, by an angle of less than 2 degrees. Consequently, they passed horizon alignments separated by only a couple of hundred years.

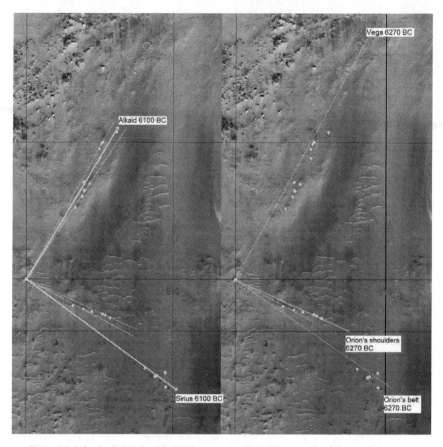

Figure 4.7. Left, the Sirius plus Alkaid alignment ca. 6100 BCE; right, the Orion stars and Vega depicted at one date ca. 6270 BCE. From that epoch, the Orion stars all move through vernal equinox heliacal risings, as the Vega rising line moves southeast over the megalith alignments.

Another association with the date of 6100 BCE is that the rising of the bright circumpolar star Vega was in line with the A2 megaliths as Orion's belt began rising over the C1 line.*

---

*The star Vega, on the opposite side of the sky from Orion, had its autumnal equinox heliacal rising ca. 5840 BCE, when it was in the center of the A megaliths—essentially, at line A2. In our previous publications, we have noted that the other alignments (B lines and A lines) were consistent with Vega in the north rising simultaneously with the Orion shoulder stars that are also indicated in the Calendar Circle. Yet we note here that those alignments, if represented by the present megaliths, must be re-creations of previous markers that are now beneath the playa sediments, because those particular Vega and Orion alignment dates precede the final heavy sedimentation period. Given that the complex structures also contain evidence of a much earlier symbolic landscape carved on the bedrock under the playa sediments, it seems the interpretation that the (A lines and

Figure 4.8. The star-studded ceiling in Tepi I pyramid at Saqqara (Sixth Dynasty).

In summary, at Nabta Playa in 3500 BCE and 4500 BCE there were megalith alignments (B1 and B2) oriented to the rising of Sirius that ran eastward (as suggested by Malville and his coauthors in 2007), and we have shown that these alignments were used simultaneously with—and formed right angles with—megalith alignments (A1 and A3) to the star Dubhe, which ran northward. It also seems that in 6100 BCE megalith alignment C1 was directed to the rising of Sirius, which was used simultaneously with the star Alkaid in the north. In addition, in 6200 BCE, line C1 may also have been associated with the heleical rising of Orion's belt at the spring (vernal) equinox. We have seen that these Orion's-belt alignments for C1 were consistent with the use of this stellar asterism in the Calendar Circle at that same epoch. It seems, then, that the C1 megaliths were either off the playa and thus not affected by the heavy

B lines megaliths) indicated Vega and Orion at the earlier dates (in addition to the later post-heavy sedimentation alignments) may still be viable. Indeed, as we will see, there is evidence of symbolic architecture involving these stars—Sirius, Orion's belt, and Vega— going back to the First Time, or Zep Tepi, at Giza, ca. 12,000 BCE.

playa sedimentation period, or were remnants of much earlier ceremonial structures (as was Complex Structure A).*

These findings and conclusions are perhaps better visualized in the table format below.

MEGALITH ALIGNMENTS AT NABTA PLAYA

MEGALITH LINE	MALVILLE AND WENDORF ET AL (2007)	OUR MEASUREMENTS (2005)	ASSOCIATION
AI	30.6 degrees	30.00 degrees	Dubhe simultaneous to Sirius risign ca. 4500 BCE
A2	28.1 degrees	27.68 degrees	Alkaid simultaneous to Sirius rising ca. 6100 BCE; also, Vega ca. 5840 BCE autumnal equinox heliacal rising; also, Dubhe simultaneous with Sirius rising ca. 4000 BCE
A3	26.3 degrees	25.86 degrees	Dubhe simultaneous to Sirius rising ca. 3500 BCE
BI	120.1 degrees	121.11 degrees	Sirius rising ca. 4500 BCE, with Dubhe at line AI
B2	116.6 degrees	117.49 degrees	Sirius rising circa 3500 BCE, with Dubhe at line A3
CI	125.4 degrees (2001)	130.1 degrees	Sirius rising ca. 6100 BCE. with Alkaid at line A2; also, Orion's belt at vernal equinox heliacal rising ca. same epoch

---

*If we assume that the Sirius–Big Dipper simultaneous star alignments extended back to 6100 BCE, we may logically ask why, if Sirius rising was tracked for as long as two millennia or more, there are not more alignments beyond the three major ones identified thus far. The geological sedimentation history of the playa may provide an answer. If the earliest line "C-line" is off the playa or on fossil dune hills not affected by the late

We can see from this table that the megalithic alignments at Nabta Playa represent a coherent and consistent ensemble that has meaning when it is deciphered with astronomy. Clearly, the alignments, instead of being random, are carefully made to target the rising of stars that were important ritualistically and also practically to the ancient people of Nabta Playa. The anthropologists of the CPE as well as other archaeoastronomers who have carefully studied this site are all in agreement: Nabta Playa was an important ceremonial center that required considerable complex social organization, physical effort, and resources to construct and maintain over a long period of time. It thus is sensible to conclude that embodied in the design of the ceremonial complex is some very high meaning that can be read with astronomy. As we will see later, this system of knowledge—we can perhaps call it star knowledge—at Nabta Playa was carried forward in time and space to the pharaonic civilization of the Nile Valley. Meanwhile, we'll take an initial look at a well-known star ritual from ancient Egypt that shows how and why Sirius and a star in the Big Dipper, Dubhe, were used simultaneously to align sacred megalithic monuments from earliest times harking back to 3200 BCE and perhaps even earlier . . . just as they were used at Nabta Playa.

A RIGHT ANGLE AND TWO STARS

The simultaneous observation of Sirius rising in the east and a star of the Big Dipper in the northern sky is a strong, nontangible piece of evidence that shows a direct link between the prehistory of the Sahara and the archaic period of ancient Egypt and the great civilization that ensued from it. At one end of this link is the ceremonial complex of

---

heavy playa sedimentation period, then possibly there were a sequence of alignments to Sirius rising as Sirius's location marched north via precession through the playa, from the C-line megaliths to the B-line megaliths. Those alignments would be gone or invisible now, covered by playa sediments. Only the 4500 BCE and 3500 BCE alignments survive because they were placed after the heavy sedimentation stopped.

Nabta Playa and at the other end is the earliest ceremonial complex in the Nile Valley on the Island of Elephantine near Aswan. In chapter 6, we will look directly at this link, but for now we will look at an important early Egyptian ritual known as *stretching the cord,* because it is likely that in this lies the very source of why and how the simultaneous observation of two stars was used by the Egyptians and, earlier, by the people of Nabta Playa in association with the astronomical alignment of megalithic structures.

The ancient Egyptian texts and temple reliefs explain that stretching the cord was carried out by a priestess, who represented a deity associated with the stars, and the pharaoh. Both the priestess and pharaoh held a rod and a mallet, and a rope or cord was looped between the rods. The priestess stood with her back to the northern sky and faced the pharaoh. This scene is depicted on many temples, and the texts alongside it tell us that the pharaoh observed the trajectory of the stars with his eye in order to establish the temple in the manner of ancient times. In the texts, we are unequivocally told that the king looked at a star in the Big Dipper (called Mesekhtiu, the Bull's Thigh). Some of the texts, however, mention the star Sirius and imply that it also was somehow involved in the ritual.

Exactly how was this stellar alignment ritual performed? Was the king aiming his gaze at a star in the Big Dipper while, simultaneously, the priestess announced the moment of the rising of Sirius, after which the cord between them was stretched and the rods were hammered into the soil, thus fixing the axis of the future temple? A further clue to the ritual is that the pharaoh observed carefully the motion of a star in real time. Inscriptions on the Temple of Horus at Edfu, accompanying portrayals of the ritual, quote the pharaoh, "I take the measuring cord in the company of Seshat. I consider the progressive movement of the stars. My eye is fixed on the Bull's Thigh constellation. I count off time, scrutinizing the clock…"[15] This is also what might have happened at the ceremonial center of Nabta Playa thousands of years earlier. An observer who was standing at Complex Structure A held a rod with a rope attached to it. Another observer, also holding a rod, stood some twenty paces north of the first observer with his or her back to the Big Dipper. This second observer then waited for Sirius to rise, and, at that precise moment, he or she gave the signal to the first observer to stretch the cord and aim it toward a star in the Big Dipper. Then, when the alignment was achieved, the first observer was to fix the rod in the soil. Later, a row of megaliths would be set along this alignment. On another day, this ritual was repeated to set an alignment toward the rising spot of Sirius on the horizon as seen from CSA. Thus the two lines of stone work together, one going north (line A) and the other southeast (line B). This interpretation is consistent with the ancient texts that describe that the Dubhe alignment required real-time observing of the star in the sky, whereas Sirius rising on the horizon is more easily set. These two lines also form a rough right angle, a feature that surely would have been noticed and intriguing.

The Relation of Dubhe and Sirius

We can go back in time to ca. 9000 BCE, when the north celestial pole is near the shoulders of the constellation Hercules, Dubhe rises many hours before Sirius and is very high in the sky when Sirius rises, and Dubhe's declination is so far from north that Dubhe and the whole Bull's Thigh constellation are far from being circumpolar stars. If we turn the clock forward to around 4500 BCE, the celestial pole has moved so that it is close to the Bull's Thigh constellation, Dubhe has moved north in declination to become a circumpolar star, and Dubhe is decreasing in altitude so that it is at only 33 degrees altitude when Sirius rises, as seen at Nabta. The low altitude of Dubhe when Sirius is on the horizon means that the angular separation of the two stars in the sky is essentially preserved in the angle of their alignments on the ground.

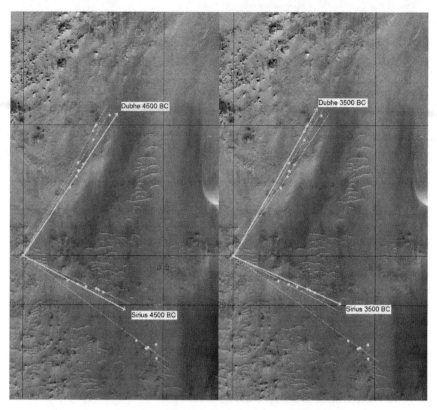

Figure 4.9. The right-angled megalith alignments of Sirius and Dubhe at 4500 BCE and at 3500 BCE as the stars moved through precession.

Indeed, any architect or designer will readily agree that right angles are universally recognized by humans not least because they define, among many other things, the four cardinal directions of Earth. Sirius rising may have been marked by the star Alkaid in the Big Dipper from the seventh millennium BCE to about 4800 BCE, but after that date and until 3500 BCE, the star Dubhe in the Big Dipper replaced Alkaid, and it was noticed that Dubhe and Sirius always formed a right angle. After that date, Nabta Playa and the ceremonial complex were abandoned*

---

*Today, the precise angular separation of Dubhe and Sirius is 93.4 degrees. Yet both Sirius and Dubhe are relatively close to our solar system, about 8.6 light years distant and 124 light years distant, respectively. Thus they have a fairly large proper motion (the apparent motion of individual stars against the backdrop of distant "fixed stars"). Combining the best recent measures of their proper motions, we can calculate that Sirius and Dubhe are moving away from each other at a rate of about 0.34 degree per thousand years. Ca. 4500 BCE, then, they were separated by 91.2 degrees, and they formed a perfect 90 degrees—a right angle—in the sky ca. 8160 BCE.

ONE YEAR OF ASTRONOMY
AT NABTA PLAYA

Now suppose you are viewing the various astronomical events during one year at Nabta Playa—say, 4500 BCE. You begin your observing year on the afternoon of the winter solstice. You intend to use the Calendar Circle that night, and so you observe that the winter solstice sun sets into the solstice gates of the circle and the sky begins to darken. You move to the north end of the circle to use the meridian gates as your sky-viewing guide, and over the next forty-five minutes, the sky becomes dark enough that the stars seem to pop out around you. Then, fifty-five minutes after sunset, directly on the meridian, you see the belt of Orion shining into the deepening dark, oriented very much like the three southerly stones inside the circle. Trailing Orion is the brilliant Sirius, which crosses the meridian an hour and forty minutes later. Two hours after that, the very bright star Canopus crosses the meridian, skimming low above the horizon. Perhaps, if you've learned your sky lessons, you know that when you travel north, Canopus drops even lower to the horizon. The starry show continues for eight more hours; then the sky begins to brighten, and the sun rises to make its low winter arc across the sky.

One month later, the nightly show is similar, except that the sun sets a bit north of the solstice gates of the circle, and when the sky darkens, you see that Orion has already passed the meridian and Sirius is already there. Two more months pass, and the sun rises due east and sets due west. It is the spring equinox, and now when the sky darkens after sunset, Orion's belt is gone—already set below the horizon—but Sirius is still visible, low to the southwest, for about forty-five minutes before it too sets. About ten days later, Sirius also disappears.* Another twenty-eight days later, just before dawn, Orion's belt reappears in the southeast.† After another twenty-nine days, Sirius

---

*Sirius is about 1 degree above the horizon as the sun is about 5 degrees below the horizon.

†When it is just under 3 degrees above the horizon and the sun is about 6 degrees below the horizon, before rising.

also reappears in the southeast, when you can glimpse it momentarily before dawn.* At Nabta Playa you have moved south of the Calendar Circle to view this heliacal rising of Sirius from Complex Structure A, the central megalithic construction which your society built to view stars rising over lines of megaliths. There, just before dawn, you see Sirius rise above a distant line of megaliths to the southeast, and when you look to the northeast, you see hovering there, above another line of megaliths, Dubhe of the Bull's Thigh constellation.

Of course, these alignments are just as you have expected, because this is in fact a year of heavy construction, when you are completing the building of those two lines of megaliths. It is now just four weeks before summer solstice, and in seven more days, it will be exactly three weeks before summer solstice, the time when, at noon, the sun passes directly overhead and the standing stones cast no shadow, which occurs only twice per year.

Now the annual rains have come, and if they are plentiful, the playa basin fills with shallow water. The Calendar Circle is located on a low mound just off the edge of the playa, so you can continue your star viewing from there even while the playa is full of water. On the night before summer solstice, you watch Orion's belt rising about an hour after midnight, followed, as always, by Sirius an hour and forty-five minutes later. Orion's belt moves toward the meridian and fades out of view about an hour before it reaches it, as the sky brightens and the sun rises in the solstice gates of the Calendar Circle. Three weeks after summer solstice, the noon sun again passes directly overhead and the standing stones cast no shadow, and the nightly show repeats. This time, you can see Orion's belt just approaching the meridian as the sky brightens with the sunrise. The sun now rises a bit south of the solstice gate, as the sunrise location moves toward winter, and the whole annual show will repeat.

---

*When Sirius is about 1 degree above the horizon and the sun is about 6 degrees below the horizon.

Figure 4.10. Photograph of Orion being followed by Sirius beneath the Milky Way.

MORE MYSTERIES AT NABTA PLAYA

When some important and new discovery such as Nabta Playa might put into serious question the established views about the origins of civilization, there is a tendency to wait until a suitable theory can be developed before releasing any data about the discovery. The problem with this is that sometimes the data that fits an established theory is regarded as more valuable than mysterious new data that contradicts it*

Others, like us, take an opposing view. We see the mysterious, unexplained data as more valuable, because if we try to understand the mystery, we might learn something new. To us, that is what scientific research is—or ought to be—all about. In this frame of mind, then, we will look in more detail at some mysterious aspects of Nabta Playa in the hope that such an approach might shed even more light on this mysterious place.

We recall that all the megalithic alignments at Nabta Playa radiate out from a central megalithic structure called Complex Structure A. CSA is composed of megaliths that lay on the surface; a large megalith carved by human hands (the so-called cow stone) buried 3 meters (about 10 feet); and finally, berneath the sculpted cow stone, a lump of bedrock, also partly carved by human hands. The megaliths on the surface are arranged in an oval shape, and some are partially sculpted. Two of these are partially sculpted into a curved geometric form, one into a convex form, and two into a concave form, giving the impression that they might have been chunks of a much larger structure that has now disappeared.[16] The cow stone that was buried beneath was 1.9 by 1.5 by 0.7 meters (6.2 by 4.9 by 2.3 feet) and composed of hard, quartzitic sandstone weighing about 2 tons.[17] Photographs of the cow stone immediately after it was excavated show that one part of the stone is finely shaped and smooth and another portion is either unfinished or

---

*This attitude perhaps harks back to premodernity, which was characterized, socio-culturally, by often prerational and fused (or predifferentiated) notions of the dualities of theory versus measurement, mind versus matter, inner versus outer, religion versus science. Modernity is characterized by a radical differentiation of these dualities. That differentiation is the wonderful essence of the Scientific Revolution and the Renaissance. Postmodernity, which is only beginning to activate in our culture, is characterized by fully rational operation, a complete appreciation for the modern and Renaissance differentiation of the inner and the outer, the spiritual and the material—and an awareness of the value of both aspects of those dualities and a movement toward a re-integration, at a fully differentiated level, into a new, whole conception of those dualities. Scholarly argument must still operate generally in terms of modernity, because this is how the majority culture operates . . . on a good day, that is. Obviously, vast portions of our culture still operate in the premodern and prerational modes.

was roughly flaked. According to Wendorf and Krolik, it "had a flat, possibly naturally smoothed, almost polished top. One side was convex and pecked smooth. At one end . . . there was a fan-like projection that might represent a head."[18] From photographs and video frames of the cow stone taken after its discovery and from taking measurements of the arching of its extended outer surface, we could see that it may have been shaped like a spherical section. As we have seen, the CPE concluded that this sculpture vaguely resembled a cow.*

As an integral part of an intensely astronomical construction linked to stellar alignments, this cow sculpture may be both bovine and supernal, both cow and star—that is, it may be symbolic astrologically. Because it was placed under CSA sometime around the start of the astrological Age of Taurus (the Bull constellation), usually assumed to be ca. 4500 BCE, then a symbolic connection to mark this age is a viable proposition.†

Of course, it is a widely held notion that the ancient Greeks invented the zodiac signs based on their knowledge of Babylonian-Chaldean star

---

*Initially, we were skeptical of the sculpture's cowlike appearance, and we suggested that because it was at the centerpiece of astronomically oriented megalithic alignments, it too may have astronomical meaning. [See Thomas Brophy, *The Origin Map: Discovery of a Prehistoric Megalithic Astrophysical Map of the Universe* (Bloomington, Ind.: iUniverse, September 20, 2002)].

†There is no agreement among astrologers or astronomers as to exact beginnings and endings of the zodiac Ages. A zodiac Age is when the vernal equinox sun resides in the sky against the backdrop of a given zodiac sign, or constellation of stars. The beginning of an Age depends on where in the starry sky we choose to draw a zodiac sign boundary. There may in fact be another curious correspondence to zodiac Age symbology in the Calendar Circle. We can recall that the window of applicability of our Calendar Circle interpretation was determined to be roughly 6300 BCE to 4800 BCE. That span of time is very similar to the zodiac Age of Gemini, which immediately precedes the Age of Taurus. Indeed, our interpretation of the circle is that it twice represents the figure of Orion, and the physical size of the circle is 4 meters (about 13 feet)—the size of two men. If we consider the sizes of the constellation Orion when it matched the stone circle, in the later date (ca. 4900 BCE), Orion is larger—when the stars are rising (north toward the pole) on their precession cycle—and in the earlier date (ca. 16,500 BCE) Orion is smaller—when the stars are falling (south away from the pole) on their precession cycle. Could a more subtle layer of symbology be present in the Calendar Circle also indicating the age of Gemini, with the burial of the cow stone marking the start of the Age of Taurus?

lore from the first millennium BCE. Yet there is significant dissent among historians as to the age of the zodiacal signs, with some proposing that they may be much older than we have generally presumed.[19] We can also note that several megalithic alignments emanating from CSA mark both the rising of Sirius and the Big Dipper—and the ancient Egyptians often identified the former with a cow and the latter with a bull's thigh. Indeed, the possibility of a cultural link between the cow stone at Nabta Playa and the ancient Egyptians was suggested by Wendorf when he proposed that this strange, sculpted megalith "may have been the origin of the ancient Egyptians' fascination with working large stones."[20] Many questions regarding this cow stone remain unanswered. How was the top surface so finely polished? How were the fine, sharp, and precise curvilinear edges made? What tools could have been used by ancient people who lived before the age of metal? Unfortunately, these questions may never be answered, for the cow stone was removed from Nabta Playa by the Egyptian antiquities authorities and today lies, broken, in the backyard storage area of the Nubian Museum in Aswan (see appendix 3). We can also recall that the cow stone itself was placed on top of another sculpture that was cut into the living bedrock of the site. This bedrock sculpture has the shape of a large, smooth disk that is about 3.5 meters (11.5 feet) across, with some of its parts and its edges carved by human hands. According to Wendorf and Krolik, "The north and west sides had been carefully shaped by removing one or two large sections that left a curved outline, following an arched bedding plane in the bedrock. The large sections removed during the shaping of the tablerock were most probably reused as the two large slabs placed in the center of the surface architecture. The top of the tablerock was flat and smoothed. It is possible this was natural smoothing . . . but this seems unlikely since none of the other tablerocks visible at the sourthern end of the Nabta Basin display similar smoothed surfaces. . . . Regardless of how the top was smoothed, the sides were clearly pecked and had a slightly re-curved outline."[21]

Surrounding this bedrock sculpture is a great mystery that has not been adequately investigated. How and why was it sculpted—and, more intriguingly, when was it fashioned? Wendorf initially proposed that it was created during the Late Neolithic—that is, around 5100 BCE, after the playa sediments were formed.[22] Yet if so, we may wonder how the ancient people of Nabta Playa could have known where this outcrop in the bedrock was located if they could not see it, for it was totally covered by a thick layer of sediment. Wendorf and Krolik had no explanation. According to them, however, the ancient people somehow knew where this outcrop was and thus dug through the sediments to expose it. They then sculpted it, covered it with sediment, placed the cow stone above it, covered the cow stone with more sediment, and finally arranged the megalithic architecture on the surface.

This seems quite implausible, and perhaps there is a simpler explanation: the bedrock sculpture long predates the Late Neolithic given by Wendorf.[23] How old is the bedrock sculpture, who built it, and why was it built? What could have been its true meaning? Clearly, it was important enough to be made the centerpiece of the Nabta Playa ceremonial complex when the Late Neolithic people placed the cow stone over it thousands of years later. Unfortunately, we could not investigate this matter further, for the sediment has been dumped back into the hole, and, as we have learned, some of the surface megaliths have been removed and taken to the Nubian Museum in Aswan while others have been moved on site, scattered randomly (see appendix 3). Whatever might be the solution to the unsolved mystery that lies behind the multilayered and pangeneration construction of the CSA, it is sure to fit into a very elegant astronomical scheme.*

---

*In Thomas Brophy, *The Origin Map: Discovery of a Prehistoric Megalithic Astrophysical Map of the Universe,* using purely astronomical puzzle-solving applied to the field data and drawings, we found, partly, that the CSA and the bedrock sculpture appeared consistent with a representative map of our Milky Way Galaxy and seemed to be an indication of Earth's location in the galaxy. We have noted that this solution was not connected with known cultural archaeological evidence. Further, we asked ourselves that if somehow this representation was the meaning of the sculpture, how could that knowledge have been acquired? It must have been attained in one of three ways: (1) through some very ancient possession of astronomical instrumentation, knowledge of which was totally lost over the ages; (2) through some way of perceiving the universe (such as remote viewing)

We must also remember that Complex Structure A, although the largest at Nabta Playa, is but one of thirty complex structures in the southwest part of the site. Only two of these structures, CSA and another, CSB, were fully excavated. The bedrock under CSB was also sculpted, but into a different shape described as an inclined oval disc; there was no imbedded sculpture above it. A third complex structure was also partially excavated, and two more complex structures had holes drilled into their sediment, confirming the presence of bedrock outcrops. This led Wendorf and his team to conclude that all the complex structures seen on top of the sediments probably contain a sculpted bedrock outcrop covered by 3 or 4 meters (10 or 13 feet) of sediment.

What could have driven the ancient people of Nabta Playa to sculpt all these outcrops of bedrock? Perhaps more intriguingly, when these outcrops were completely covered by sediment carried and compacted by wind and rainfall thousands of years later, how could they have been rediscovered by the people who built the megalith arrangements on the surface? Or, were they not rediscovered by the Late Neolithic people? Perhaps, instead, they were maintained over thousands of years by an even more ancient culture about which we know almost nothing.

Let us not forget, as well, the most provocative question that surrounds these mysterious complex structures. When the CPE, led by Wendorf, started their excavations at Nabta Playa in the 1970s, they

---

(continued from page 135) that was accessible to the ancients, though we are not now capable of this perception; (3) through receiving the knowledge from some outside source. These possible methods stimulated thought and questioning, as we had intended, but they also generatad some hysterical responses from both ends of the spectrum of thought. We did not, as Malville et al claim in their 2007 report, "propose that the nomads had contact with extra-galactic aliens."[24] Further, they go on to say, "Brophy proposes that the stones of the cromlech represent maps of the stars of Orion as early as 16,500 BC. These extremely early dates . . . are inconsistent with the archaeological record."[25] Yet we did not propose the cromlech (Calendar Circle) was built in 16,500 BCE. We suggested, however, that it represented the long-term precessional motion of the sky and was built and used ca. 5000 BCE. Generally, science is advanced by the exercise of imaginative problem-solving applied to accurate data and calculations, even if some speculations may not be upheld by more extensive data collection, and science is hindered by applying only conventional reasoning, especially to flawed data and incorrect calculations.

very much hoped that the many complex structures and tumuli were tombs that contained human remains of high-ranking individuals or even kings. Instead, excavators found the strangely sculpted outcrops of rock and the skeletons of cows in the tumuli. If we bear in mind that the complex structures and the tumuli are an integral part of a vast ceremonial complex that is intensely astronomical and stellar, we may wonder if the empty tombs and cow-bones burials are part of some mysterious star ritual related to some ancestral cult of rebirth. This provocative thought occurs because, as we will see in chapter 6, the same empty tombs have baffled Egyptologists when the Old Kingdom pyramids were explored and found to contain no human remains. Even more intriguingly, in some of the great pyramids of Giza only the bones of cows were found. Further, like the ceremonial complex of Nabta Playa, these pyramid complexes were intensely stellar in their orientation and symbolism. In chapter 6 we will return to this strange link between the empty tombs of Nabta Playa and those empty pyramids of ancient Egypt. Meanwhile, let us examine another mysterious feature at Nabta Playa: the largest megalith, which Wendorf called Megalith X-1.

Megalith X-1 consisted of a pair of giant stone, set on an oval-shaped mound of cretaceous bedrock.[26] The larger of the two stones measured 4 by 3.1 by 0.7 meters (13 by 10 by 2.3 feet), and was estimated to weigh some 20 tons. The oval-shaped mound on which the two stones stood seems to have been shaped by human hands.[27] When we looked at Megalith X-1 on the Quickbird satellite image, it was immediately apparent to us that it was in the middle of a large spiral arm feature, which was about 50 meters (164 feet) across.*

Upon examining this area during our 2003 expedition to Nabta Playa, we were able to discern clearly this strange, spiral-shaped mound that we had seen on the satellite image. We also found in its middle the fragmented remains of the two giant stones of Megalith X-1. How

---

*X-1 is indicated in a low-resolution version of the Quickbird image in Brophy and Rosen, "Satellite Imagery Measured of the Astronomically Aligned Megaliths at Nabta Playa," *Mediterranean Archaeology and Archaeometry* 5, no.1 (June 2005): 15–24.

were these massive stones moved? Why were they placed in the middle of the spiral mound? Was the mound man-made—and if so, by whom and when? We also considered the current condition of all the megaliths at Nabta Playa. Most of them were either toppled or broken or deliberately cut into parts. How did they get to this pitiful state? Closer examination showed that some of the megaliths had been cleanly cut, as if intentionally—but why? Was it, instead of the work of vandals, due to some ancient ritual or symbolic act, when the function of the megaliths became obsolete?[28]

Many of the remaining mysteries of the site involve understanding the bedrock sculptures, which are more ancient than the playa surface megaliths and are only slightly excavated. How extensive are the bedrock sculptures at Nabta Playa? Could there be a whole precursor ceremonial complex that is yet to be discovered? To begin to address these questions, it may be best to use ground-penetrating imaging methods that can see through the playa sediments to the bedrock beneath. Fortunately, launched are new synthetic aperture radar remote sensing satellites, and there are better ones in progress. With them, we have been able to start searching the subsurface at Nabta, and as a result, we have hints of intriguing new results.[29]

Though many mysteries at Nabta Playa still remain, those former mysteries that have come to be understood are more than enough to provide us with a vision of a social and cultural complexity that was not expected for such remotely prehistoric people. The level of skill, insight, and social organization, as well as the sophisticated astronomical observations that are incorporated into their megalithic ceremonial complex, should leave us with little doubt that we have in these mysterious ancient people the true precursors of the Egyptian civilization. We will look at this more closely in chapter 6. Meanwhile, we are now going to take a closer look at other prehistoric sites in the Egyptian Sahara that strongly indicate that such activity was not confined solely to Nabta Playa. Instead, it also seemed to extend hundreds of kilometers into the deep desert toward the north and west.

THE SUN TEMPLE OF
DJEDEFRE IN THE SAHARA

In chapter 2, we saw the important discovery of the so-called Djedefre Water Mountain (DWM) by the German desert explorer Carlo Bergmann. We recall that on this mountain (actually a small sandstone mound that is about 30 meters—98 feet—high), which is about 80 kilometers (50 miles) south of Dakhla oasis, were found hieroglyphic inscriptions of the names of the pharaohs Khufu and Djedefre alongside prehistoric petroglyphs that contained the water sign and depictions of fauna that no longer exist in this part of the world. Naturally, we might wonder, as Bergmann probably did, whether there could be a connection between the prehistoric site of DWM and that of Nabta Playa. True, nearly 400 kilometers (249 miles) separated the two places, but Bergmann's earlier discovery of the Abu Ballas Trail (see chapter 2) proved that ancient people could travel in such arid and waterless desert for much longer distances by creating watering stations along their route. At any rate, perhaps a connection between the two prehistoric sites could be established by the DWM containing evidence of astronomical knowledge that could be directly related to that incorporated in the ceremonial complex of Nabta Playa. The only way to resolve this issue was to examine DWM ourselves.

In early April 2008, the desert explorer Mahmoud Marai, a close colleague and friend of Carlo Bergmann, organized an expedition for us to visit the DWM, among other sites in the Egyptian Sahara. We started off-road near Dakhla oasis and headed south, and after a couple of hours of bumpy riding in Marai's well-equipped Toyota Landcruiser, we reached DWM late in the afternoon. Because it was fast growing dark, we decided to set up camp and wait until dawn to climb the small escarpment that led to the hieroglyphs and petroglyphs on the east side of the mound. We were up before the crack of dawn the next day, and after a swift breakfast of hot tea and biscuits, we made our way 10 meters (about 33 feet) up the man-made escarpment and reached a platform, also man-made, that brought us level with the inscriptions.

The most prominent of the inscriptions is at the center of the east face of the mound. As we saw in chapter 2, it consists of a royal cartouche that bears the name of the pharaoh Djedefre, which is enclosed in a rectangle with two protrusions at the top that Egyptologists have assumed to be a form of the hieroglyphic for "mountain." (See plate 2) As we have seen, a similar sign, but with a sun disk between the protrusions, was used to denote "horizon" or, more specifically, the Place of Sunrise. Because DWM faced east—the place of sunrise—it seemed to us more apt to regard this mound not as Water Mountain but rather as a sun temple. There was, however, one snag with this hypothesis: the view toward the eastern horizon was blocked by an elongated hill about 200 meters (about 256 feet) east of DWM.

This elongated hill or mesa is about 70 meters (230 feet) long and 12 meters (39 feet) high and has a flattened top with a very noticeable depression or notch in the middle. As far as we could tell, neither Bergmann nor the German scholars who studied DWM saw this hill as significant, but as we watched the sun rise over it, it became apparent to us that the hill was positioned in such a way that it would act as a sighting device for marking the yearly course of the sun and the two solstices and two equinoxes. We named this mesa Horizon Hill. Using our GPS and electronic compass, we determined that at the equinoxes, the sun would rest in the notch in the center of Horizon Hill, creating the hieroglyph $\bigcirc$.

We were at DWM on April 9. We established the location as 25.40 degrees north and that sunrise on that day would be 82.09 degrees on the horizon and 83.35 degrees when breaking at 7:06 A.M. over Horizon Hill (which we estimated to be at 2.75 degrees altitude above the geometric horizon). Figure 4.11 shows the view from DWM with the sun breaking over Horizon Hill. We calculated that at spring equinox (March 21), the sun will be at azimuth 91.2 degrees when it breaks over the notch on Horizon Hill, which matches the actual azimuth of the notch as seen from DWM.

We took GPS measures in front of the central cartouche on the sun

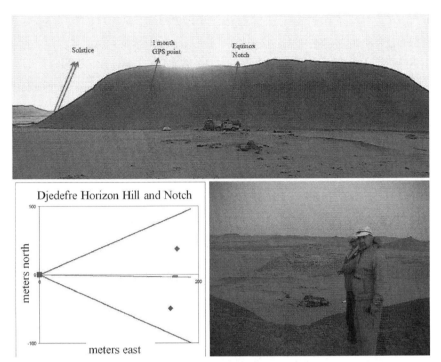

Figure 4.11. Sunrise over Horizon Hill at Djedefre sun temple, April 2008. Top: the rising azimuths at equinox over the notch in the hill and the approximate solstice rising azimuth. Lower right: Brophy and Bauval standing, before sunrise, at Horizon Hill notch and pointing to the east, facing the Djedefre cartouche. Lower left: the three GPS points taken at the top of Horizon Hill— at the notch and two central hilltop locations—the azimuths to sunrise over the notch from the Djedefre cartouche, and the solstice sunrises.

temple and also on top of Horizon Hill. On the hill, we took measurements on flat areas near the north and south ends of the hilltop and at the notch near the center. The measurements we took gave azimuths of 77.9 degrees, 91.1 degrees, and 106.7 degrees, respectively, as viewed from the central cartouche on the east face of the sun temple. We also measured the flat area of Horizon Hill and determined it to be 8 meters (26 feet) higher in elevation than the central cartouche on the sun temple, and it was positioned some 170 meters (558 feet) east of the sun temple. We thus estimated that the hypothesized solar notch was at altitude 2.7 degrees above the geometric horizon when viewed on Horizon Hill. We calculate that at equinox the sun would indeed be resting in the notch at 2.7 degrees altitude and azimuth 91.2 degrees when appearing over Horizon Hill. At the summer and winter solstices and at the same altitude of 2.7 degrees, the sun would be at azimuths 63.3 degrees and 117.7 degrees, respectively. Because we photographed the notch *in situ* as we took the GPS point there, our measure of the azimuth of the notch is very precise and accurately coincides with the equinox sun when it breaks over Horizon Hill. Yet we recognize that our azimuth measurements of the solstice sunrises at the north and south edges of Horizon Hill are less precise, because we did not have an independent calibrating marker. On a future visit, we hope to refine our measurement of the two edges of Horizon Hill with respect to the solstice paths of the sun.

It seems very unlikely that the emissaries of the sun king Djedefre, who had come to this place and probably stayed for extended periods of time, would have failed to note that Horizon Hill functioned as a natural solar calendar. If such a conclusion is correct, however, it would mean that, in all probability, the same was noted by the prehistoric people who had also stayed here. Was there any evidence of this? In light of this probability, we must re-examine some of the inscriptions and engravings on the mound.

Other than the Egyptian hieroglyphs and petroglyphs of fauna and other symbols, there are also arrows carved on the east face of DWM that conspicuously point upward, as if inviting an observer to look at the zenith of the sky. These arrows appear to be prehistoric rather than Old Kingdom Egyptian, because of their style of inscription and because near them are images of animals that could not have been present in Old Kingdom times. Today, the site is a little less than 2 degrees north of the Tropic of Cancer, but in ancient times it was a bit closer to the Tropic line, so that each year at summer solstice the sun would pass almost directly overhead at noon—that is, near the zenith. Could it be that ancient Egyptians of the Old Kingdom, during the reigns of Khufu and Djedefre, came here and rediscovered a prehistoric sun temple, which they then transferred to their own solar hieroglyphs? Judging from the evidence, this would seem the most likely scenario.

Within the central engraving, there is a finely rendered glyph found under the two peaks representing the horizon, or the Place of Sunrise. The lower part of that glyph appears like hieroglyphi deterinative S12 (by Gardiner's system,* which indicates gold/white gold/silver; the upper part of this glyph is composed only of three flag poles or standards, which we speculate may represent the three stations of the Sun on the eastern horizon: the two extreme stations marking the solstices and the mid-station marking the equinoxes. When we view the eastern horizon from DWM, these three stations are marked by the extreme ends and midpoint (the notch) of Horizon Hill. And visually this rendering of S12 seems reminiscent also of the cosmogonic solar barge, said th carry the sun across the sky, and usually carrying one or more deities, yet here it carries the three stations of the Sun—whether the original artists intended this visual metaphor, we don't know. Unfortunately, we could stay at DMW only a few hours before moving on to other destinations planned by our expedition. Still, we hope that our findings there will now encourage anthropologists and Egyptologists to look for more direct links between this mysterious place and Nabta Playa.

BAGNOLD CIRCLE

We next headed southwest into the deep, open desert. Our destination was a mysterious stone circle discovered in 1930 by Ralph Alger Bagnold and thus known as Bagnold Circle. The stone circle was poorly documented and very little was known about it, but photographs encouraged us to suppose that it, too, like the Calendar Circle at Nabta Playa, could be some sort of prehistoric astronomical device.

---

*http://en.wikipedia.org/wiki/List of hieroglyphs/german-Gardiner-list-translated#S-Crowns

Figure 4.12. Bagnold Circle in, top, 2008, and bottom, 1930.

It took us two days of grueling travel in some of the most desolate places we had ever seen to reach Bagnold Circle. We wondered how Ralph Bagnold, in those days with vehicles that must have been very primitive by comparison, managed to come here through this testing terrain. Bagnold, who was a veteran of trench warfare in World War I, became a pioneer of deep desert exploration—especially, of the Sahara—throughout the 1930s. During World War II, he was chosen to lead the British army's Long Range Desert Group. He was also a physicist who contributed valuable knowledge of the physics of blown sand, which is still used in planetary science research today.[30] He is credited with developing, for desert exploration, a sun compass that was not affected by magnetic anomalies. Bagnold's early expeditions in the Egyptian Sahara were in search of the fabled lost city of Zarzoura. It was on one such expedition in 1930, when he was traveling in the deep desert hundreds of kilometers southwest of Dakhla oasis, that he reported: "In a small basin in the hills we came the next day [October 27, 1930] upon a circle 27 feet in diameter of thin slabs of sandstone, 18 to 24 inches high. Half were lying prone, but the rest were still vertical in the sand. There was no doorway or other sign of orientation, and though we searched within and without the circle, no implements could be found.[31]

As we approached Bagnold Circle, we were keenly aware that no studies of its possible astronomical alignments had ever been conducted. As Wendorf, Schild, and Malville wrote in 2008, " . . . a well-known stone circle was discovered by Bagnold (1931 [sic.] in the Libyan Desert. . . . No evidence of astronomical orientations had been reported, and none is readily discernable in photographs of the circle.[32]

Because of its incredible remoteness, few people have actually seen Bagnold Circle, let alone studied it in detail on location.*

As far as we know, it was not visited until the 1990s, when four-wheel-drive vehicles became available in Egypt and the military authorities slackened their rules for tourists' deep desert travel. In a 1998 visit by Zarzoora Expeditions of the Egyptian Wael T. Abed, the group apparently placed a cairn (small pile of stones) in the center of the circle. In 2001–2002, the Fliegel Jezerniczky Expedition (FJE) also visited Bagnold Circle. Additionally, Mahmoud Marai

---

*In the article about his expedition published in *Geographical Journal,* Bagnold supplied only a rough mark on a map with a scale of 1:10 million units of scale. Due to the extreme remoteness of the area combined with the paucity of information about the circle's location, it was visited little or not at all at least until the 1990s, when four-wheel-drive jeep desert travel became readily available in Egypt. The first known visit was in 1998 by a small group calling themselves Zarzoora Expeditions of Wael T. Abed. We are lucky to have the very good black-and-white photograph taken by Ralph Bagnold when he discovered the site in 1930 and from which we can determine the original state of the stone circle.

brought small groups to Bagnold Circle a few times from 2004 to 2007. As we learned earlier, it was Marai who guided us to Bagnold Circle in April 2008. Yet neither the Zarzoora Expedition nor the FJE Expedition checked for any possible astronomical alignments at Bagnold Circle—nor had anyone else, as far as we could tell.*[33]

Bagnold Circle lies in a shallow basin, probably an ancient seasonal lake similar to the one at Nabta Playa.† The physical features we noted first were two prominent, upright, and elongated stones (very reminiscent of the gate stones of the Calendar Circle at Nabta Playa) that defined an east-west alignment. One of these stones on the west

---

*Both Bagnold in 1930 and the FJE in 2001–2002 say that no implements or artifacts were found in or near the circle. According to the FJE: "We could confirm Bagnold's observation that no stone implements were to be found in the vicinity. A kilometer (about 3.280 feet) away, near our campsite, a broken aterian biface [sic.] and some crude flake tools were noted, but no concentration of artifacts that would indicate any larger permanent settlement." In April 2008, however, we did, in fact, find a rather beautifully worked stone implement, a knife or perhaps the tip of a lance, at a place only 150 meters or so (about 492 feet) west of the circle, among numerous other man-made stone artifacts. In addition, to the south of the basin there is a gently sloping area, possibly the shore of the ancient playa, with adjacent lines and rows of small rectangular-shaped parcels divided by bits of stones and small upright slates that are still embedded in the sand. (These uprights could be the outlines of small agricultural plots near a prehistoric village, evidence of which was found in a circular gathering of stones that seemed to be the outline of a primitive habitation.) In light of finding the numerous man-made stone artifacts lying on the surface, similar to the initial finds at Nabta Playa, we considered other general similarities between Bagnold Circle and Nabta.

†Some kilometers to the west, as we later headed toward the northern edge of Gilf Kebir, we came across the remains of a prehistoric settlement, probably from the late Neolithic, where we found several circles of stones marking the outline of habitations, as well as many stone implements. There can be little doubt, in view of these findings, that there was much human activity in the area, some sedentary, some nomadic, and some perhaps even pastoralist (though no evidence of cattle or other bovine has been found yet near Bagnold Circle). We must be privy to further explortions to confirm this, and the site clearly seems suitable for an extensive survey by field archaeologists. Unfortunately, given that no traditional professional Egyptologists have even managed to visit Bagnold's site because of its remoteness from the Nile, it may continue to suffer from obscurity. Due to the flat, dry, playa sedimentlike conditions of the terrain, however, the site may be a good candidate for study by the new generations of high-resolution synthetic aperture satellite radar with remote sensing, which can see beneath the surface layers of sediments.

side was white, and the stone on the eastern side was black, which may indicate a symbolic significance of some sort. For our GPS we took readings of this alignment as well as readings for the north-south alignment, which also had, at each end, a very dark-colored stone, nearly black, and a very light-colored stone, nearly white. The conditions of the stones suggest extreme age: they have been deeply scoured by millennia of wind erosion. Some of the stones have suffered such extreme erosion that their tops have fallen off and are still on the ground where they fell. Notwithstanding this erosion, the circle is remarkably well preserved, considering its vast age. The two alignments—east-west and north-south—strongly imply an astronomical function for the Bagnold Circle.

Figure 4.13. Bagnold Circle north-south alignment.

Another clue are twenty-eight stones that form the circumference of the circle, which is not only implicit of the lunar phase cycle of 29.5 days but, more important for us, also brought to our attention a clear connection to the Calendar Circle at Nabta Playa, which also had twenty-eight stones around its circumference. We also noted that north of the circle there was an elongated low hill that suggests observation of the low northern sky, possibly for marking the passage of a circumpolar constellation or star.*

One of the most nagging questions that constantly comes to mind in this totally desolate and extremely remote place of the Egyptian Sahara is this: why build anything here at all? What could have influenced the ancient people who roamed the deep desert to go to the trouble of constructing a stone circle in the middle of nowhere and, furthermore, to align it to the four cardinal directions? The answer, ironically enough, may actually be that they did so because of the location itself—or, to be more specific, of the latitude of the place. Today, Bagnold Circle is approximately 23.5 degrees north and just a fraction north of the Tropic of Cancer.†

Using the circle's precise latitude and checking the earth's ancient obliquity at various epochs, we found out that from 13,110 BCE to 1490 BCE, the circle was located just south of the Tropic of Cancer. This means that within that range of epochs, the sun passed directly overhead exactly at the zenith a few days before and a few day after the summer solstice. This time of year was when the monsoon rains started drenching the desert, and may be a reason—though perhaps

---

*We also verified the north-south (meridian) alignment at night by aiming at the Pole Star, and in the daytime with a simple gnomon's noon shadow. In addition, in the distance directly north of the circle, there is visible a lone mountain peak that could have been ritually significant to the placement of the circle.

†We don't list the precise coordinates here because important sites in the Egyptian Western Desert have been left essentially unprotected. Even the extremely important and relatively accessible Nabta Playa is left unguarded, with nothing to protect it from damage but (we hope) the good sense of any visitors. The much more distant and remote Bagnold Circle is very unlikely to be protected.

not the only reason—for locating the stone circle here. We can recall from chapter 2 that, in 1999, Carlo Bergmann discovered the Abu Ballas Trail, an ancient donkey trail that ran across the 500 kilometers (311 miles) of waterless desert between the Dakhla oasis and Gilf Kebir. Although anthropologists and Egyptologists have agreed that this trail was used by ancient Egyptians of the late Old Kingdom, Bergmann believes it was used as early as the Late Neolithic, ca. 5500–3400 BCE. Bagnold Circle is located a bit west of this trail, and it is quite possible that it served as a point for a shortcut route to Gilf Kebir, perhaps by the same Neolithic people who once populated Gilf Kebir and Jebel Uwainat.

We also found more evidence of prehistoric astronomy in the region, when southwest of Bagnold Circle, 250 kilometers (155 miles) away, in the wadi Karkur Talh region on the north of Jebel Uwainat, at a latitude of 21.98 degrees north, we found an apparent solstice sunset marker. At a large rock face with western exposure, which contains glyphs of giraffes and human figures, there is an outcrop or mound on the cliff face about twelve feet high. Scrambling up the rock mound, we found on it a number of skillfully engraved marks, including an obvious arrow pointing toward the northwest horizon. Returning with our electronic compass, we measured the arrow as pointing approximately 26 degrees north of west, for an azimuth of 296 degrees, which marks the sunset on the day of summer solstice. This type of skillfully engraved rather than painted art tends to be on the more ancient end of the spectrum of rock art in the region. Given that the rock face also contained images of giraffes, we estimate that this solstice marker may predate 6000 BCE. In addition, when we were en route from Bagnold's Circle to the Gilf Kebir region, traveling not far from the Libyan border, we came across a large, isolated standing stone that protruded more than 1 meter (3 feet) out of the ground. Located in the middle of a long, narrow, flat basin, or wadi, that was convenient for our jeeps to drive on because of its featureless flatness, this stone was smooth,

Figure 4.14. Isolated standing stone north of Jebel Uwainat,
oriented slightly off zenith and possibly a prehistoric gnomon.

cylindrically shaped, and standing only a few degrees off vertical. It appeared likely to have been placed by humans, possibly as a gnomon with both solar and phallic allusions.

Bagnold Circle gives all indications of being from the Neolithic epoch. It is probably a vestige left by traveling pastoralists whose temporary settlements dot the desert region that lead from the circle to Gilf Kebir and, in all likelihood, had their permanent abode in the wadis and plateaus of the Gilf Kebir and Jebel Uwaiant mountains. The similarities of both the stones and the astronomical alignments of the Bagnold Circle and the Calendar Circle at Nabta Playa strongly suggest that we are dealing with the same Late Neolithic people whose images are present in the rock art of Gilf Kebir and, more prolifically,

Figure 4.15. Elevated horizontal rock face at the norther edge of Jebel Uwainat,
with engraved linear features and arrow pointing to the summer solstice sunset.

at Jebel Uwainat. Further, at Jebel Uwainat, the engraved arrow that
we discovered and that quite plausibly intended to mark the summer solstice sunset was probably associated with the same extended
cultural group. More explorations are necessary to find the human
remains of these astro-ceremonialists and navigators of the Egyptian
Sahara, but these findings contribute another important aspect to
our story of how their knowledge of astronomy, desert navigation,
rudimentary agriculture, and domestication of cattle were important

elements in the creation of the pharaonic state when, around 3400 BCE, the Sahara became superarid and forced these mysterious desert dwellers to migrate eastward into the Nile Valley.

So, with such thoughts in mind, we set out on what was a scorchingly hot and rugged drive to Gilf Kabir. We will pick up this story at the end of chapter 5. Meanwhile, we ask: who were these mysterious people that populated the Egyptian Sahara in such remote antiquity? How did they look? Can we refer to them as Egyptians? Perhaps most intriguing of all, where had they come from in the first place?

5

THE BIBLE, THE HAMITES, AND THE BLACK MEN

Now this is the genealogy of the sons of Noah: Shem, Ham, and Japheth. And sons were born to them after the flood. . . .The sons of Ham were Cush, Mizraim (the name of Egypt), Put, and Canaan.

GENESIS 10:1–8

Because Ham's name meant both 'black' and 'hot', Ham's descendants had to come from Black Africa.

DAVID GOLDENBERG,
*THE CURSE OF HAM: RACE AND
SLAVERY IN EARLY JUDAISM,
CHRISTIANITY AND ISLAM*

In practice it is possible to determine directly the skin color and hence the ethnic affiliations of the ancient Egyptians by microscopic analysis in the laboratory; I doubt if the sagacity of the researchers who have studied the question has overlooked the possibility.

CHEIKH ANTA DIOP

HAM, SON OF NOAH

In Egyptology, we frequently come across the term Hamites in connection with the origins of the ancient Egyptians. As we attempt to understand why and how the Hamites are associated with the ancient Egyptians, we are often led to the Bible and the story of Noah and his sons.

In the Book of Genesis, Ham is one of the sons of Noah. Ham's children are Mizraim, Cush, Put, and Canaan, but in the Bible the names of Ham's children are also used to denote geographical places: Egypt (Mizraim), Ethiopia (Cush), Libya (Put), and Palestine (Canaan). Many biblical scholars have proposed that the name Ham meant, in ancient Hebrew "black" and "hot," implying that the Land of Ham was a warm, tropical region populated by Black people. The Land of Ham is thus often said to be that part of the world we call Black Africa (what has been thought of as sub-Saharan Africa). Naturally, as has always been the case with the etymology of Hebrew words in the Bible, there is a heated debate over whether this interpretation is correct, because in Genesis 9:20–25 another story is told of how Noah, while tending his vineyard, became drunk and fell asleep naked in his tent, and then Ham did something unspeakable to him,* whereupon Noah cursed Ham through Ham's youngest son, Canaan. This so-called Curse of Ham (also known as the Curse of Canaan) has generated, as we might expect, all sorts of debate and various interpretations among fundamentalists of the Bible as well as racists. To confound the issue even further, in the Bible, the Land of Ham is also unequivocally associated with the land of the pharaohs—that is, Egypt, the traditional enemy of Israel: "Israel also came into Egypt, and Jacob dwelt in the land of Ham" (Psalm 105:23) and "They forgot God their Savior, who had done great things in Egypt, wondrous works in the land of Ham, awesome things by the Red Sea" (Psalm 106:21).

---

*The text simply says that Ham ". . . saw the nakedness of his father . . ." in private and implies that he did something unspeakable. Many scholars believe it was a sexual act or perhaps even castration. (The castration interpretation comes from the fact that Canaan is Ham's fourth son, and so Noah's banishing of Canaan from the family lineage could be revenge for Ham prohibiting Noah from having a fourth son himself.)

As we have just seen, in the Bible, the land of Egypt is also known as Mizraim, the name of one of Ham's sons. By implication, then, we can see how biblical literalists might conclude that the Egyptians were the descendants of Ham. At any rate, we can see all these biblical interpretations as fueling the neverending conflict between Israel and Egypt—a conflict that supposedly started with the Jews in captivity* in Egypt at the time of Rameses II (ca. 1290 BCE) and ended in 1979 with the fragile peace treaty between Israel and Egypt—the so-called Heskem HaShalom Bein Yisrael Le Mizraim.

We can note that even today Jews refer to Egypt as Mizraim. Indeed, the Egyptians themselves call Egypt Mizr, clearly a derivative of Mizraim. Of course, biblical stories are not scientific evidence for the ethnic origins of the ancient Egyptians, but we cannot ignore the possibility that such stories may be partially rooted in actual history. In any case, in these biblical stories, the term Hamites, for better or for worse, has often been adopted by scholars, particularly Egyptologists and anthropologists, in reference to the racial origins of the ancient Egyptians. Not surprisingly, this sort of labeling has generated much confusion and debate, not least by racists in Egypt and elsewhere, who are fearful of having Black Africa as the true origin of the ancient Egyptian civilization. A contemporary example of such fear is a description in a popular pocket travel guidebook: "Unfortunately, as in most developing societies, the world's population is usually categorized according to a cultural-racial hierarchy. White Westerners are at the top, Egyptians next, then Arabs, followed by Asians, and lastly Africans. While these attitudes are undoubtedly racist, they do not find violent expression toward poorer local Sudanese, for instance."[1]

Of course, such a racial hierarchy system is deplorable[2] to current sensibilities of modernity, and such a ranking is by no means universally

---

*Religious Jews and Arabs today both consider themselves sons of Ham's brother Shem through Abraham, who is considered to be a descendant of one of Shem's five sons, Arpachshad (eighth generation descendant, according to the Book of Genesis), via Abraham's two sons, Isaac and Ishmael. Further, according to the Exodus story, Moses is the fifth generation descendant of Isaac.

adhered to by the Egyptian people.* Yet evidence that the guidebook's point is somewhat accurate to many people's experience is the recurrent distribution of the guidebook and the fact that its reviewers do not seem to complain about the racial hierarchy description. And as we shall see, such cultural-racial value ranking has indeed played a role in shaping scholarly Egyptology.

THE HALF-HAMITES THEORY

A theory that was very popular in the late nineteenth and early twentieth centuries suggested that the Hamites were a Mediterranean people who had migrated to central or east Africa and interbred with the Negroes there to produce a Negroid-Hamitic race of black-skinned people with fine Caucasian-like features. Examples were thought to be the Tutsi and the Masai.[3] For example, in 1930, the British ethnologist Charles Gabriel Seligman even claimed that the Hamites were a subgroup of the Caucasian race and that all the major achievements of the African people were, in fact, the result of Hamites who had migrated into central Africa as Europeans and brought along with them all the know-how of civilization, which they then passed on to the inferior Black race.[4] In other words, the alleged Black Hamites were the product of a purer and superior Hamitic race. The conclusion was therefore that the Black Hamites should be regarded as superior to the "black negroes" by virtue of their alleged Mediterranean or Caucasian origins. According to C. G. Seligman, "Apart from relatively late Semitic influence . . . the civilizations of Africa are the civilizations of the Hamites, its history is the record of these peoples and of their interaction with the two other African stocks, the Negro and the Bushmen, whether this influence was

---

*In this chapter, we are focusing on the evidence regarding the color of the people who were the progenitors of the ancient Egyptian civilization. Regarding the term race, we note that contemporary specialists in human genetics, such as S.O.Y. Keita, point out that there are and have been human population groups with variation and fluent characteristics, such as skin color, but the genetic variabilities are such that the classical use of the term race has little scientific value.

exerted by highly civilized Egyptians or by such wider pastoralists as are represented at the present day by the Beja and Somali. . . . The incoming Hamites were pastoral 'Europeans'—arriving wave after wave—better armed as well as quicker witted than the dark agricultural Negroes."[5]

These false and rather blatantly racist views were finally challenged by many scholars in the 1950s and 60s, but so deep-rooted was the belief that Black Negroes were inferior to Black Hamites that such views are still entertained by some misguided and uneducated people, making it difficut to remove them once and for all. We must recognize, of course, that the Hamites controversy is not a simple one and that there are many gray areas in this debate that are far too complex to do full justice to them here. Suffice to say, however, that until very recently the very idea that an advanced Black race from sub-Saharan Africa was at the source of the ancient Egyptian civilization, and perhaps even of all civilization, was disturbing to many Western people and was pure anathema to those who held Eurocentric views. Thus we still find in textbooks the dubious Mediterranean or Levantine or Sumerian-Babylonian labels listed to explain the origin of the ancient Egyptians, while precious little is said of the far more plausible Black African influence. True, some Egyptologists do at times express their opinions that there could be a central African or east African origin of the ancient Egyptians, but such views are diluted by the use of such terms as Hamitic, Half-Hamitic, and Hamitic pastoralists that still imply a Mediterranean European origin. For example, Henry Frankfort, the renowned director of the prestigious Warburg Institute and professor of preclassical history, uses such terminology when he writes, ". . . somatic and ethnological resemblances, and certain features of their language, connect the ancient Egyptians firmly with the Hamitic-speaking people of East Africa. It seems that the Pharaonic civilization arose upon the north-east African Hamitic substratum"[6] and "The profound significance which cattle evidently possessed for the ancient Egyptians allows us to bring an entirely fresh kind of evidence to bear on the problem. . . . In the life of the Hamites or Half-Hamites, cattle played an enormous part . . ."[7] and " . . . that North and East African substratum from which Egyptian culture arose and which still survives among Hamitic and half-Hamitic people today."[8]

Even allowing that scholars tend to think that lexicological complexity is a requirement of academic writing, we note that the term Black African is clearly avoided by the otherwise very open-minded professor Henry Frankfort. It seems that such jargon is unfortunately still used to avoid directly stating that there is a Black African origin of the pharaohs' culture and race. In addition, after Champollion deciphered the hieroglyphs in 1822, scholars who monopolized Egyptology were not scientists but classicists, historians, linguists, and humanists, as we have seen in chapter 1. These academics held ancient Greece as the source of all cultural achievements. As such, Egyptologists of the nineteenth and early twentieth centuries were very different from those of today, who are, by and large, unbiased and more scientifically minded. In those early days of Egyptology, the tendency was to consider the first dynasty of pharaohs (ca. 3100 BCE) to be the actual origin of the ancient Egyptian civilization. No hard evidence suggested earlier or different origins for the so-called dynastic period.

Finally, however, in the 1920s, British Egyptologist Flinders Petrie began to cause a breach in this consensus. Petrie's excavations revealed evidence of what, at first, appeared to him as a completely different culture—in fact, so different from that of the dynastic Egyptians that he mistook it for the culture of a new race that had come from outside Egypt to cohabitate with more primitive people in the Nile Valley. Further investigations eventually showed that this was not a new race at all, but rather an older, prehistoric phase of the Egyptian culture. Petrie and his fellow Egyptologists were baffled by the distinct difference between this prehistoric or predynastic people and the early dynastic people of the Egyptian civilization. Unable to explain how the ancient Egyptians appeared to have started their civilization with a fully formed language, a complex system of writing, an advanced science, a very mature and sophisticated religion, artwork that nearly surpassed classical Greek art, monumental architecture that still astounded the world, and construction engineering and technology that would tax even modern contractors, Egyptologists theorized that some superrace of invaders had come into the Nile Valley and kick-started the civilization for the Egyptians. This alleged superrace was thought to have come from the east, fueling the popular view that it was in the Orient, especially in Mesopotamia, that we could find the birthplace of the Egyptian civilization. We can be thankful that this theory began to lose hold when evidence began to mount that pointed to, as a root for ancient Egypt, a homegrown civilization—probably one with some influence from the prehistoric pastoralists in the adjacent eastern and western desert regions. This is more or less the position of many Egyptologists today, even though the evidence, as we will see, is stacking up in favor of an origin outside the Nile Valley—somewhere in the far west, not east, of the river, and pointing toward the distant corner with Sudan and Libya that leads into sub-Saharan, Black Africa.

BLACK ATHENA

To be fair, it is also true to say that today there is an uneasy feeling among more open-minded Egyptologists about this racial origin issue—a sense that their older peers could have been wrong and that the notion of a Black African origin for ancient Egypt ought to be given serious consideration. In other words, Egyptologists today are hedging their bets and are also wary not to be drawn into a huge cultural blunder and fall into the same intellectual grave that their older peers dug with their own hands.

We can take, for example, the case of *Black Athena* of the late 1980s. Martin Bernal, a professor emeritus of Near Eastern Studies at Cornell University, developed a deep interest in Egyptology through the influence of his grandfather, the eminent Egyptologist Sir Alan Gardiner. Bernal's quest began when he was intrigued by a strange paradox in Egyptology: though many ancient Greek scholars insisted that the Greeks had received much of their knowledge from the Egyptians, Egyptologists insisted that it was the Egyptians who had received much of their knowledge from the Greeks. Bernal openly proposed that modern Egyptologists should let the ancient Greeks speak for themselves; they should take seriously their claims rather than see them as fanciful stories. In 1987, Bernal published *Black Athena,* a three-volume opus in which he argued in favor of an "Afro-Asiatic" origin for the Egyptian civilization and, by implication, the same for the Greek civilizations. He openly denounced the Eurocentrism of the late nineteenth and twentieth centuries, arguing that it was not supported by scientific evidence.[9] A heated academic debate ensued between the Eurocentrics and the Afrocentrics. Egyptologists pulled rank and accused Bernal of poor scholarship and lack of evidence to support his theory. Cambridge Egyptologist John Ray accused Bernal of confirmation bias, and Egyptologist James Weinstein claimed that Bernal was ignoring archaeological evidence by relying only on Greek reports—thereby implying that the reports of modern Egyptologists were somehow more reliable. So persistent and effective were these attacks on Bernal's scholarship that today the mere mention of *Black Athena* in academic circles is anathema, even heretical, and Afrocentrism is considered a pseudoscience and, to some, even a dangerous practice. One of the most zealous opponents of Afrocentrism is Clarence Walker, professor of Black American History at the University of California, Davis. Ironically, Walker is himself a Black American who was born in Texas. According to Walker, "Afrocentrism is a mythology that is racist, reactionary, and essentially therapeutic. . . . [It] places an emphasis on Egypt that is, to put it bluntly, absurd. . . . There is no evidence that the ancient Egyptians were black as we understand that term today."[10]

The born-and-bred-American Walker insists that he is not African, that he has never been to Africa and has no desire to go there. He sees himself as "an old-fashioned intellectual critic" and adds, "I don't like a lot of work being done in the field. . . . Just because you want to believe the world was created by black people doesn't make it so . . . "[11] Actually, though many may disagree with Walker about the ancient Egyptians, it is possible to find admirable the fact that he does not think his own Blackness should affect his scholastic conclusions. This may be a hopeful indicator that personal ethnicity should not affect our scientific or scholarly conclusions. Further, perhaps there is a problem of terminology—it may be accurate to label these commentators as Afrocentrists, for Afrocentrism is a pseudoscience, but only in the same way that Eurocentrism should be considered a pseudoscience. Both imply an attempt to fit data and observations into a box of preconceived notions. If the data, on balance, indicates that the people who originated the pharaonic civilization of Egypt were indeed Black Africans, then drawing such a conclusion need not be labeled Afrocentric or anti-Eurocentric—it may be thought of simply as accurate.

THE OUT OF AFRICA EVE

Ironically, in spite of views such as those of Clarence Walker, scientists in the field of genetics have been pointing out that it may actually be correct to say that the world was created by Black people. In 2009, more than a century after the exploration of darkest Africa by Livingstone, Burton, Stanley, and others, the BBC aired a documentary series entitled *The Incredible Human Journey*. In the series, introduced to a wide British public, was the notion that all human beings alive today have their origins in Africa—indeed, that these origins can be traced to a single Black African woman, the so-called Out of Africa Eve. This view is now widely held by scientists, and it is also called the Mitochondrial Eve hypothesis, because it traces the ancestral lineage of humans back through the mitochondrial DNA, which is passed on only from the mother. This hypothesis was first published by a team of University of California biochemists in *Nature* magazine in 1987.[12]

Mitochondrial Eve: Mitochondrial DNA exists in human cells outside of the cell nucleus in membrane-enclosed organelles called mitochondria, and contains a genome that is independent of the nuclear

DNA genome. At conception mitochondrial DNA is passed on separately from the nuclear DNA, with mitochondrial DNA transmitted only from the mother without combination from the father. Thus mitochondrial DNA passes from generation to generation with very little change, only infrequent mutations change the mitochondrial DNA over time. Genetic scientists realized if they could measure the variance (set of all differences) among currently living humans, and if they could estimate the mitochondrial DNA mutation rate, then they could estimate the "origin time" from which all of today's humans' mitochondrial DNA must have come. The logic is sort of similar to the way the "Big Bang" of creation of the universe was first discovered—astronomers observed that all distant galaxies were moving away from each other, and then measured the rate at which the galaxies are now moving apart and simply turned the clock backwards to when the galaxies would have all been in the same place, about 14 billion years ago, and called that the "Big Bang." For mitochondrial DNA, geneticists measured the currently existing variance in humans around the world, and they estimated the mitochondrial DNA mutation rate, and running the genetic clock back in time gave a human mitochondrial DNA origin date of about 200,000 years ago—this is called the "Mitochondrial Eve", and geographic details of the mitochondrial DNA variance point to that origin location as east-central Africa. Mitochondrial "Eve" is the most recent human woman from whom all living humans today have at least one unbroken matrilineal line. Eve was not alone though. There were many human women alive at the time who share ancestry to living people today, but for all of them other than Eve their descendent lineages contain at least one man (who did not pass the mitochondrial DNA). In fact nuclear DNA analyses indicate that human population never dropped below a few tens of thousands (e.g. Naoyuki Takahata, *Allelic Genealogy and Human Evolution*, Molecular Biology and Evolution [January 1993] Vol.10, N.1, pp.2-22.). As is the Big Bang in astrophysics, the Mitochondrial Eve is considered nearly settled science in genetics.

But controversies do remain, especially involving uncertainties in the DNA mutation rate (e.g. Christopher Wills, *When did Eve Live? An Evolutionary Detective Story*, Evolution, 1995, V. 49, pp.593-607.). Similar studies of male Y-chromosomes place the most recent common male lineage ancestor, or "Y-Chromosomal Adam", several tens of thousands of years more recent than Mitochondrial Eve (e.g. Yuehai Ke, et al, *African Origin of Modern Humans in East Asia: A Tale of 12,000 Y Chromosomes*, Science [May 11, 2001] Vol. 292, N. 5519, pp. 1151–1153). Interestingly, statistical genealogical studies separate from genetics indicate that the most recent common ancestor of all people alive today was much more recent than Mitochondrial Eve, and Y-Chromosomal Adam, probably within the past few thousand years (e.g. Douglas L. T. Rohde, Steve Olson, and Joseph T. Chang, "Modelling the recent common ancestry of all living humans," *Nature*, 30 Sept. 2004, Vol. 431, pp. 562-565.). Such a more recent common ancestor is consistent with the 200,000 year ago Mitochondrial Eve who was the most recent unbroken matrilineal ancestor.

In one of the BBC episodes, the presenter, Alice Roberts, who is also a lecturer in anatomy at the University of Bristol, explains that a "complex-looking DNA-based 'family tree' shows how twenty-first-century Europeans, Australians and the rest can all be traced back to the same black African population."[13] Roberts further explains, with refreshing candor, that "'Population'" . . . is the word we should be using instead of 'race.' I wouldn't use the word 'race.' Biologically, it doesn't make sense. It's a bizarre mismatch of concepts: culture, history. . . . Genetically, a white Scandinavian and someone from sub-Saharan Africa are very similar. In fact, humans have less variation genetically than chimpanzees. It makes you realize that all the historical attitudes towards different races are scientifically meaningless."[14]

The genetic evidence, bolstered by more recent refinements,[15] lends support to the Out of Africa Eve hypotheses for human migration, as opposed to the Multi-Regional hypothesis. In a book accompanying the BBC show, Roberts cites the work of the Oxford professor Stephen Oppenheimer, who describes the Out of Africa Eve story of humankind as going something like this:

> Homo Sapiens, modern humans, lived ca. 160,000 BC with the earliest mt-DNA and Y-chromosome ancestors found in East Africa. Four groups of hunter-gatherers travelled out southwest towards the Congo and west to the Ivory Coast, south towards the Cape of Good Hope, and northeast towards the Nile. Around 125,000 BC one group moved northwards down the Nile and into the Levant, but due to a climatic upheaval around 90,000 BC this group died out. A global freeze turned the Levant and North Africa into extreme desert. Around 85,000 BC another group crossed the entrance of the Red Sea in the south and into the Arabian Peninsula to reach the Indian sub-continent. They then spread to Indonesia and reached southern China by 75,000 BC. By ca. 65,000 BC they had spread to Borneo and Australia. Warmer climatic condition around 50,000 BC allowed a group to move again northwards through the Levant, cross the Bosporus and reach Europe. By 25,000 BC the ancestors of the Native Americans crossed the Bearing land bridge into Alaska and then spread into North America. By 10,500 BC they had spread also into South America. Between 10,000 and 8,000 years ago the Levant group moved back into the now-green Sahara.[16]

We can note that what remains to be explained is anomalous evidence for the later parts of that story, such as the fact that archaeological evidence for dating the earliest South Americans keeps moving back in time, which indicates that they may have crossed the oceans by boats, for example. In addition, Roberts's story is a mixture of the genetic, archaeological, and anthropological evidences, all of which are subject to new results and improvements. Yet some version of the basic Out-of-Africa-Eve view—that all humans alive today share one female ancestor from

Africa who lived roughly two hundred thousand years ago—is the currently prevailing notion among scientists. It is possible, then, that while this human journey was going on, the early modern humans of east Africa moved northward into Chad and settled in the Tibesti-Ennedi highlands. From there, perhaps around 9000 BCE, they started moving north again into the then-inviting, green Egyptian Sahara, probably going first to the Gilf Kebir and Uwainat mountain region, then slowly spreading east and northeast toward the Nile. Another group moved westward from central Africa into the green Tenere Sahara of Niger as well as into the fertile Aïr Mountains farther west. It is possible that around 8000 BCE, these black-skinned people in the Egyptian Sahara encountered an incoming Mediterranean group that had returned to North Africa from Europe via the Levant. This may perhaps explain why Romuald Schild and Fred Wendorf of the CPE found in the skeletal remains at the prehistoric cemetery of Gebel Ramlah near Nabta Playa two racial groups, one made up of sub-Saharan Black pastoralists and the other of Mediterranean or North African ethnology.[17] Then, starting around 5000 BCE, as the Sahara became drier, these people began moving out of the desertified regions. Finally, by 3500 BCE, the desert became superarid and forced them to migrate eastward into the Nile Valley. If this is true—and it does very much appear to be the case—then the origins of the ancient Egyptians are rooted in a black-skinned race of sub-Saharan pastoralists that had themselves likely come from the Tibesti-Ennedi highlands and, going further back in time, had their source in east Africa. In other words, the evidence is overwhelmingly in favor of a black-skinned African origin for the Egyptian civilization.

Yet is it possible to prove this via some sort of direct measurements?

IT IS ALL IN THE MELANIN

A great advocate of the African origins model as well as a believer in the Black African origins of the ancient Egyptians was the Senegalese anthropologist and radiocarbon physicist Cheikh Anta Diop. Hailed by many as one of the greatest African historians, Diop was studying for a physics doctorate in Paris in 1951 when he caused a huge stir at the university because his Ph.D. thesis on the Black African origins of ancient Egypt was rejected as unsuitable by his assessors. Not being easily discouraged, Diop boldly labored for nine more years to make the evidence in his thesis so airtight that, when he resubmitted the thesis again, this time it was grudgingly accepted. Hardened by those struggles and the bias he encountered against the African origins idea, Diop went further and published his thesis under the title *Nations Nègres et Culture*, and very soon he became a national hero and the major defender of the African origins theory. In his native country of Senegal, Diop founded the Radiocarbon Laboratory at the University of Dakar, became its first director, and used this cutting-edge technology to continue his research on the ethnic origins of the Egyptian civilization. Diop's argument was simple and straightforward: it was possible to know the skin color of an ancient corpse by microscopic analysis of the melatonin content in the body. His critics countered by saying that this method was not foolproof and that possible contamination of the embalming unguents and the deterioration of the corpse over the centuries made the result dubious, but these objections were in turn addressed by Diop. In 1974, Diop presented his findings to a large number of professional Egyptologists and anthropologists at the People of Ancient Egypt symposium in Cairo organized by UNESCO World Heritage. He was largely ignored. Diop died in 1986, leaving behind numerous publications as well as recorded interviews on radio and television. Here is a concise overview of Diop's thesis.[18]

Diop starts by recounting that in 1971, the Kenyan anthropologist Louis S. B. Leakey, in his final report at the Seventh Pan-African Congress of Prehistory at Addis Ababa, proved that more than one hundred fifty thousand years ago humans that were morphologically similar to us were living in central Africa around the great lakes that feed the Nile. Diop explains how this starling discovery opened a reappraisal

Figure 5.1. Cheikh Anta Diop. Diop and the
Cause of His Struggles

of the ethnology of the ancient Egyptians and humankind as a whole. Leakey even thought he had found the very spot where the adventure of modern man had begun: the beautiful, snow-capped Rwenzori Mountains between Uganda and the Democratic Republic of Congo, traditionally known as the Mountains of the Moon and discovered by Henry Morton Stanley in 1885. These mountains stand between Lake Albert and Lake Edward and are the highest source of the Nile River. Rwenzori means "rainmakers," a name inspired by the almost permanent rain clouds that cover the peaks of these mysterious mountains. According to Leakey, humans dispersed from here to inhabit the rest of Africa and, eventually, the whole planet. The implication was that modern humans, being from a warm and humid climate that caused the natural melanin in their pigmentation to darken, were originally black-skinned Africans. It was, therefore, from this Black stock that the other races of humans were formed. Other than migrating southward, eastward, and westward, these original humans coud also go northward to two main regions: the Nile Valley and the vast then-green Sahara.

Starting from the late Paleolithic age, the entire Nile Valley, from southern Sudan to northern Egypt, was populated by a Negroid people. Similarly, the northwest region of Africa that is today the Sahara was also populated by these same Negroid people. Diop rejected the claim by some anthropologists that ancient human skulls from Nagada in Lower Egypt and Abydos and El Amra in Upper Egypt exhibit not only Negroid but also Germanic features. He pointed out that similar skulls from well-known Black people such as the Ethiopians and Dravidians also exhibit the same characteristics, but are clearly not Germanic. Diop also pointed out that finding non-Negroid features in skulls does not necessarily mean that living individuals were white. In Egypt, some 1,787 skulls, dating from the predynastic period to the present day, were examined and found to be 36 percent Negroid, 33 percent Mediterranean, 11 percent Cro-Magnon, and the rest uncertain but most probably also Negroid. This shows, says Diop, that the original and pure Black Negroid race that first inhabited Egypt eventually merged with a Mediterranean race to create the Egyptians that we know today.

Diop also rejected Flinders Petrie's method of using symbolic images from ancient palettes to classify predynastic and protodynastic Egyptians into six racial types: an aquiline type, which he equated to white-skinned Libyans; a plaited-beard type, which he equated to originating on the Red Sea; a sharp-nosed type, which he equated to coming from central Arabia; a tilted-nose type, which he equated to coming from Middle Egypt; and a jutting-beard type, which he equated to coming from Lower Egypt. Diop points out that even if we accept such simplistic classifications, current Egyptology textbooks at best ignore the issue of racial origins or, at worst, flatly assert that the ancient Egyptians were white, leaving the lay reader with the false impression that such assertions are based on solid research—which, of course, they are not. Thus generations of readers have been misled to the false belief that the ancient Egyptian civilization owes little or nothing to Africa. Diop accuses Egyptologists of going "around the difficulty today by speaking of red-skinned and black-skinned whites without their sense of common logic being in the least upset."[19] He argues that in ancient times, the Greeks referred to all of Africa as Libya, which was a misnomer *ab initio,* because Africa contains many other peoples besides the so-called Libyans, who belong among the whites of the northern or Mediterranean periphery. Diop was justifiably repulsed by a textbook intended for middle and secondary school which explained that "a Black is distinguished less by the color of his skin than by his features: thick lips, flattened nose . . ."[20] Diop points out that many of the reliefs and murals from predynastic and early dynastic times in Egypt show

> . . . the native-born blacks subjugating the foreign intruders into the valley . . . wherever the autochthonous racial type is represented with any degree of clearness, it is evidently Negroid. Nowhere are the Indo-European and Semitic elements shown even as ordinary freeman serving a local chief, but invariably as conquered foreigners. The rare portrayals found are always shown with the distinctive marks of captivity, hands tied behind the back or strained over the shoulders. A protodynastic figurine represents an Indo-European prisoner with a long plait on his knees, with his hands bound tight to his body. The characteristics of the object itself show that it was intended as the foot of a piece of furniture and represented a conquered race.[21]

Diop argues that the two variants of the Black race—the straight-haired Dravidians in Asia and the Nubians and Tebu, and the kinky-haired humans from the Equatorial regions—are found in the modern Egyptian population. Diop's silver bullet, however, was the proven scientific method that can determine skin-color by the analysis of the melanin content in mummies from ancient Egyptians—and he insists that, contrary to the words of Egyptologists, it was entirely possible to determine the melanin content of ancient mummies by microscopic analysis in the laboratory. Melanin, or, more precisely, eumelanin, is a naturally produced polymer responsible for skin pigmentation. It is insoluble and can be preserved for millions of years, such as in the skins of fossilized creatures. Diop claimed that it can be measured in the skin of Egyptian mummies. Even though Egyptologists lament that the skin of mummies is tainted by embalming material and thus is no longer susceptible to such analysis, Diop rejected this by showing that although the outer epidermis is where the melanin is usually found, melanocytes are particles deeper in the skin where they are not destroyed by the mummification process. From samples of common Egyptian mummies from the Musée de l'Homme in Paris, Diop was able to show high melanin levels that are not found in white-skinned people. Diop wanted to apply the same analysis to royal mummies kept in Egypt, but the Egyptian authorities refused to give him any samples—not even the few millimeters of skin tissue that are required for such analysis.

Another criterion, which had proved successful in the past in determining racial origins, is the so-called Lepsius Canon. This entails examining the bones of mummies' bodies rather than their skulls. According to Diop, this method shows that the "bodily proportions of the ideal Egyptian was short-armed and of Negroid or Negrito physical type."[22] In addition, Diop suggests that blood groups could be used, for even today's modern Egyptians, especially those in Upper Egypt ". . . belong to the same Group B as the populations of western Africa on the Atlantic seaboard and not the A2 group characteristic of the white race prior to any crossbreeding. It would be interesting to study the extent of Group A2 distribution in Egyptian mummies, which present-day techniques make possible.[23]

Diop also reviewed the various statements made by ancient Greeks and Romans who visited Egypt, as did Martin Bernal later in *Black Athena*. Diop asserts that if we accept what the ancient Greek and Roman writers say—and frankly, there are no good reasons why we shouldn't—then we must conclude that the ancient Egyptians were black-skinned, for these writers leave us with no doubt that they saw the Egyptians as "dark" or "black" men. Egyptologists, on the other hand, insist that we should not take seriously these ancient writers. A few Greek and Roman writers make clear Diop's point.

Herodotus (ca. 450 BCE), the father of history, states that " . . . it is in fact manifest that the Colchidians are Egyptian by race . . . several Egyptians told me that in their opinion the Colchidians were descended from soldiers of Sesostris. I had conjectured as much myself from two pointers, firstly because they have black skins and kinky hair . . ."[24] Herodotus also used the fact that the Egyptians were Black in order to prove that the oracle of Dodoni in Epirus, which according to legend was founded by a Black woman, was Egyptian in origin: " . . . and when they add that the dove was black they give us to understand that the woman was Egyptian."[25]

In one of the works of Aristotle (ca. 320 BCE), the great philosopher and father of scientific thinking speaks rather derogatorily about the Egyptians, but nonetheless shows that he, too, regarded them as black-skinned: "Those who are too black are cowards like, for instance, the Egyptians and Ethiopians. But those who are excessively white are also cowards as we can see from the example of women . . . the complexion of courage is between the two i.e. (brown or tanned)."[26]

Aeschylus (ca. 480 BCE), in his play *The Suppliants,* has one of the protagonists, a certain Danaos, comment on an Egyptian ship: "I can see the [Egyptian] crew with their black limbs and white tunics."[27]

Apollodorus (ca. 70 BCE) affirms that "Aegyptos conquered the country of the black-footed ones and called it Egypt after himself.[28]

Another Greek writer, Lucian (180 BCE), presents a dialogue between two Greeks, Lycinus and Timolaus, discussing a young Egyptian boy. "Lycinus: This boy is not merely black; he has thick lips and his legs are too thin . . . his hair worn in a plait behind shows that he is not a freeman."[29]

Statements by many other ancient Greek and Roman writers provide similar confirmation, either directly or indirectly, that the ancient Egyptians were black-skinned.[30] Interestingly, before racial and cultural bias affected European scholars, many European travelers such as

Constantin-Francois Volney, who journey in Egypt in 1783–5, wrote honest statements: " . . . on visiting the Sphinx, the look of it gave me the clue . . . beholding that head characteristically Negro in all its features, I recalled the well-known passage of Herodotus which reads: 'For my part I consider the Colchoi are a colony of the Egyptians because, like them, they are black skinned and kinky-haired . . .'"[31]

Champollion-Figeac, the brother of the famous Champollion the Younger, who deciphered the hieroglyphics, wrote this bizarre response to Volney's observations: " . . . Volney's conclusion as to the Negro origin of the ancient population of Egypt is glaringly forced and inadmissible." [32]

Diop approaches the argument from a different and in some ways better perspective by asking how the ancient Egyptians viewed themselves. He notes that they referred to themselves as the Rmt-en-Km-t, which Egyptologists usually translate as People of the Black Land,[33] because, they say, the ancient Egyptians were not referring to themselves but rather to the color of the alluvial soil of the Nile Valley, which has a dark, almost black tint. Diop argues, however, that it makes far more sense to translate this term as Land of the Black People. Indeed, Km-t is perhaps the origin of the Biblical name Ham (hence Hamite), which also means "black." The *H* and *K* in the Semitic dialects are often mingled to create the guttural *Kh*. Thus the Hebrew *Kh-am* may be a derivative of the earlier Egyptian *Kh-em*. This would certainly explain why in the Bible, Egypt is often called the land of Ham or Khem. Diop also presents an array of epithets of divinities of ancient Egypt that associate them with the color black implicitly, if it's not explicitly stated that they were black-skinned,[34] and he also presents a variety of other arguments involving complex linguistic comparisons and word syntax of the ancient Egyptian language and other African languages, but such arguments are well outside the scope of our investigation.

At any rate, suffice to say that the evidence presented by Diop overwhelmingly supported a Black African origin for the ancient Egyptians. As we have said earlier, Diop's crowning moment was at the UNESCO Symposium in January 1974 in Cairo, where he and a colleague, Professor Obenga, carefully presented their scientific findings to a large audience of Egyptologists and anthropologists from all parts of the world. It was nevertheless stated in the conclusion of the report of the symposium: "Although the preparatory working paper sent out by UNESCO gave particulars of what was desired, not all participants had prepared communications comparable with the painstakingly researched contributions of Professors Cheikh Anta Diop and Obenga. There was consequently a real lack of balance in the discussions."[35]

The attending Egyptologists had not even bothered to prepare for a proper and balanced debate. Their biased conviction was so entrenched that they merely listened politely and then ignored the issue at hand. The UNESCO organizers, however, were clearly impressed by Diop and commissioned him to write the entry on the origins of the pharaohs in their *General History of Africa* published a few years later, in 1981. Yet the archaeologist Ahmed Mokhtar, who, ironically, was the editor of this UNESCO publication, could not prevent himself from adding a note in the introduction of the report: "The opinions expressed by Cheikh Anta Diop in this chapter are those which he developed and presented at the UNESCO symposium of 'The People of Ancient Egypt,' which was held in Cairo in 1974. The arguments put forward in this chapter have not been accepted by all the experts interested in this problem."

Notwithstanding Ahmed Mokhtar's odd remarks about a colleague and contributor to the UNESCO publication, what he said did not take into account the fact that some very senior French Egyptologists— notably Professors Jean Vercouter and Professor Jean Leclant—had been very impressed with Diop's professional presentation. In reality, the resistance to accept or even consider Diop's thesis came not from Egyptologists in general, but specifically from high Egyptian officials, as is well demonstrated by Dr. Zahi Hawass, the present chairman of Egypt's Supreme Council of Antiquities (SCA) and undersecretary of state to the Ministry of Culture. Hawass is well-known for his aggressive attitude toward those who oppose him so that even the normally discrete *Sunday Times* of London felt compelled to write: "He rules Egyptology with an iron fist and a censorious tongue. Nobody crosses Zahi Hawass and gets away with it. . . . Nobody of any standing in Egyptology will come out to help you . . . because they'd lose their jobs. Sadly, people are cowering round his ankles. . . . The hugged ankles belong to the most powerful man in archeology, Dr Zahi Hawass, aka Big Zee, secretary-general of Egypt's Supreme Council of Antiquities (SCA). It is Hawass who holds the keys to the pyramids, the Valley of the Kings, the Sphinx, Abu Simbel, everything. No Egyptologist gets in without his permission, and few will chance his anger . . ."[36]

More on Hawass

More recently, the *New York Times* was even more candid about Dr. Hawass's behavior to colleagues, students, and other researchers:

> Zahi Hawass, secretary general of the Supreme Council of Antiquities in Egypt, seems to get his name in the papers and his face on television every time anyone sticks a shovel in the ground there. The resulting fame—the man has become ubiquitous on history-heavy American cable channels—has apparently given Dr. Hawass, like many celebrities before him, the mistaken impression that any sort of personal behavior will be embraced by his adoring public, because he sure is obnoxious on "Chasing Mummies," an annoying new show that begins Wednesday night on History. Dr. Hawass has allowed a History crew to tag along as he does what he does, but, at least from the evidence of the premiere, this does not result in many revelations about the science of archaeology. It results instead in a fair amount of footage of Dr. Hawass verbally abusing those around him: the film crew, college-age interns who have come to worship at his feet, and so on. Any infraction, or no infraction at all, seems sufficient to warrant one of Dr. Hawass's tirades.[37]

We have experienced Hawass's anger since early 1994, when our first book, *The Orion Mystery,* was published. He branded Robert Bauval and his colleagues as liars, amateurs, pyramidologists, pyramidiots, and, befuddling as it may seem, even Zionists who were trying to steal the pyramids. In fact, when it comes to the ethnic origins of the ancient Egyptians or who built the pyramids, Hawass has issued some rather odd statements. For example, when, in 2002, a small robot was used to explore narrow shafts in the Great Pyramid of Giza, he told a bemused journalist of the popular *Al-Gomhoreya* newspaper: "The results of the robot's exploration refute the allegations reiterated by Jews and some Western countries that the Jews built the pyramids!"[38]

Hawass's superior, Egypt's Minister of Culture, Farouk Hosni, made a very similar bizarre statement: "Israeli allegations that they built the Pyramids abound, and we must face up to this even if it triggers a crisis with Israel! This is piracy! Our history and our civilization must be respected but the Israelis want to take over everything! We must counterattack with full strength because this is how they took Palestine. They keep on saying Palestine belongs to them and now they are doing the same with the Pyramids!"[39] Further, Hawass added to this: "A group of people are making an organized campaign. There are some people pushing them [Israel]. . . . These people are waging a big attack against us. I swore two years ago that I would not reveal their names, but I found out that I must mention them because it is becoming a threat . . . there is among us a bad person, a Jew . . . and I will tell the public that everyone who tries to talk against the Egyptians should shut their mouths!"[40]

According to Hawass, a member of the group allegedly waging a "big attack" backed by Israel against the Egyptians is Robert Bauval. Bauval is a Christian, not a Jew, and, ironically, he was born and raised in Egypt.*

---

*Thomas Brophy notes that from recent generations, he himself is a mix of European ethnicities, but he does consider himself a member of humanity, and thus, as we describe in this chapter, about two hundred thousand years ago, he was Black African. Brophy was raised mostly secular with some attendance at Christian churches, but after obtaining a Ph.D. in physics, he wrote a book that describes a view of the unity of all major religions within the context of modern physical science.[41]

In a more recent television interview in February 2009, Hawass unabashedly claimed that the Jews "control the entire world" and that ". . . for eighteen centuries they [the Jews] were dispersed throughout the world . . . they went to America and took control of its economy . . . they have a plan: Although they are few in number, they control the entire world . . . look at the control they have over America and the media!"[42]

Needless to say, with this type of display by the chief of the SCA, any claim, however scientific and scholarly, of a Black African origin for Egypt's ancient civilization will inevitably be met with indifference and, more likely, with opposition. Indeed, Hawass has already made this quite clear with his latest commentaries on this issue to the official Egyptian MENA News Agency: " . . . the portrayal of ancient Egyptian civilization as black has no element of truth to it! Egyptians are not Arabs and are not Africans despite the fact that Egypt is in Africa . . .!"[43]

According to this kind of logic, though Egypt is in Africa, Egyptians are not Africans. Such blatant contradiction most likely stems from the fact that Hawass probably equates Africans and Blacks. Therefore, any connection between the ancient Egyptians and Blacks or Africans must be rejected at all cost, even if it contradicts geographical realities. Perhaps this extreme view clarifies other, less blatant but still puzzlingly attacks that scholars have made in their academic publishing. Facts, however, are facts: Egypt is in Africa, Egyptians are Africans, and there is now overwhelming evidence that ancient Egyptians have a Black African origin.

Rejection of an Article

In early 2008, Thomas Brophy, together with another coauthor, submitted to an academic journal a paper about a small part of the proposed astronomy of Nabta Playa. The journal returned it with a critical review from an anonymous referee (perhaps from an Egyptian scholar) who, in the course of recommending that the journal reject the paper, actually referred to Brophy and his colleagues as "behaving like arrogant Westerners." We were puzzled by that strange comment. Why, we thought, would an accomplished scholar make such a personal attack within the formal review process? It seemed out of context. Then it dawned on us: perhaps he was speaking from a perspective formed partly by a racially hierarchical worldview. If this was true, it would be natural for him to have a sort of chip on his shoulder about Westerners. In Brophy's paper, as far as we were thinking at the time, we were simply proposing a solution to an astronomy puzzle. He and his colleagues made no mention of or concerned themselves with any contemporary racial-cultural implications of their paper. Yet we now understand why those innocent suggestions about astronomy at Nabta Playa may have been perceived as a threat.

At this point, we must state categorically that we are not trying to steal the pyramids, we are not claiming to have built the pyramids, and we are not claiming that our friends and family—or even our ethnic group—built them. We say this with tongue in cheek, of course—hoping that the SCA director will make room for some humor and a broader perspective. We must also acknowledge that Dr. Hawass, as a deputy minister of the Egyptian government, could well be under pressure from various contemporary sociopolitical sources. It is reasonable, then, to suppose that not all of his commentaries are motivated purely by dispassionate analysis of events from four or five thousand years ago, but may be colored in small part by contemporary sociopolitical concerns. Yet the modern Egyptian government has been a leader in the terribly difficult, indeed Herculean, contemporary efforts to transcend the ages-old rivalry between Egypt and Israel, as evidenced for example by the 1979 peace treaty for which Egyptian president Anwar Sadat shared the Nobel Peace Prize. If in some sense, therefore, there is a subliminal struggle going on among the various currently powerful ethnonationalist and subnationalist groups in Egypt today regarding claims of the origin of the civilization that built the pyramids, then it seems that the emerging answer should serve not to inflame but to defuse the situation—because the answer is that the origins stem not from any of these groups, but from Black Africans. Certainly, it was the Black Africans of Egypt who, over the subsequent ages, melded with a number of other colors and ethnicities, and thus essentially are today the same people of Egypt who should be extremely proud of the ancient accomplishments of their heritage.

CONSOLIDATING THE EVIDENCE

Other than the visual evidence of prehistoric rock art at Uwainat and Gilf Kebir, we will also see here and in chapter 6 that there is even more supporting evidence of a Black African origin in further analysis of the astronomical alignments at Nabta Playa and other prehistoric sites in the Egyptian Sahara. Meanwhile, in 2002, three decades after Nabta Playa was discovered, anthropologists Fred Wendorf and Romuald Schild published their overall views in the *Journal of the Polish Academy of Science* [*Archaeologia Polona*] affirming that:

> [t]he tumuli, calendar, stele alignments and megalithic construc-
> tions, all concentrated around western shores of the then already
> dried ancient Lake Nabta, indicate that this area was an important
> ceremonial centre in the late and final Neolithic. The complexity of
> the arrangements, and enormous amount of closely managed work
> put into the construction of the megalithic constructions, indicate
> that the cattle herders of the South Western Desert created an early
> complex society with the presence of a religious and/or political con-
> trol over human resources for an extended period of time. Common
> contacts of the Desert Dwellers with the Nile Valley inhabitants are
> indicated by frequent presence of raw material and ceramics origi-
> nating in the Nile Valley. These contacts of cattle pastoralists with

Predynastic, agricultural groups in the Nile Valley may have played an important role in the emergence of a complex, stratified society in the Great River Valley. . . . Physical anthropology of rare skeletal remains found in the late early, middle and late Neolithic suggests racial association of the populations with Sub-Saharan or black groups . . .[44]

Other eminent anthropologists were more categorical. In *National Geographic News* of July 2006, this article appeared:

The pharaohs of ancient Egypt owed their existence to prehistoric climate changes in the eastern Sahara, according to an exhaustive study of archaeological data that bolsters this theory.

Starting at about 8500 B.C., researchers say, broad swaths of what are now Egypt, Chad, Libya and Sudan experience a "sudden onset of humid conditions." . . . During this time the prehistoric people of the eastern Sahara followed the rains to keep pace with the most hospitable ecosystems.

But around 5300 B.C. this climate-driven environmental abundance started to decline, and most humans began leaving the increasingly arid region.

"Around 5,500 to 6,000 years ago the Egyptian Sahara became so dry that nobody could survive there." Said Stefan Kröpelin, a geo-archaeologist at the University of Cologne in Germany and study co-author. . . .

Among their finding, the researchers provide further evidence that the human exodus from the desert about 5,000 years ago is what laid the foundation for the first pharaoh's rule . . .

David Phillipson, a professor of African archaeology, directs the Museum of Archaeology and Anthropology at the University of Cambridge in England . . .

"As the Sahara dried and became less suited and eventually unsuited to habitation, people ultimately had to move out, whether it be southward or to the east into the Nile Valley," Phillipson said.

"And this [study] helps [us] to understand the apparent rather sudden development of intensive settlement by sophisticated societies in the Nile Valley 'round about five or six thousand years ago."[45]

Michal Kobusiewicz and Romuald Schild are both renowned anthropologists who have studied Nabta Plaja under the aegis of the Institute of Archaeology and Ethnology of the Polish Academy of Sciences. After pointing out that the ancient Egyptian pharaonic state was formed around 3300 BCE, they commented that "We already know that soon after this date, drought forced the [Nabta Plaja] herdsmen to abandon their lands . . . and so where might they have gone, if not to the relatively close Nile Valley? They brought with them the various achievements of their culture and their belief system. Perhaps it was indeed these people who provided the crucial stimulus towards the emergence of state organization in ancient Egypt."[46]

Schild and Kubusiewicz also call "these people" prehistoric herdsmen, prehistoric pastoralists, Neolithic cattle herders, and sub-Saharans. The term Black, however, is clearly avoided. As we have seen, the ancient sub-Saharan people were of the pre-Tebu Black race whose ancestors inhabited the Tibesti and Ennedi Mountains of northern Chad— but who really were the Tebu? How did they look? In the 1860s, the German explorer Gerhard Rohlfs was among the first Europeans who had made contact with the elusive Tebu people: "Their stature is svelte, their members fine, their disposition light and swift; they have lively eyes, their lips are a bit tough, their nose is small but not snubbed, and their hair is short but less wiry than the Negroes. . . . All other travelers who made contact with the Tebu have noted that their physical traits tend more towards the Negro . . . their customs and traditions are also nearer to that of the Negro . . . the land of the present day Tebu is located south of Fazan, in the north of Lake Chad . . ."[47]

When Rosita Forbes traveled to the oasis of Kufra with Ahmed Hassanein in 1921, she became the first European woman to encounter the Tebu—some two hundred of them still living in the Kufra region. Sir Harry Hamilton Johnston, the great British explorer and diplomat who wrote the introduction to Forbes's book, comments on that region and the Tebu people:

> It is one of the vestiges of a formerly well-watered country ten, twenty or more thousand years ago. To it [Kufra] came, long ago, when the intervening desert was much more traversable, clans of Tu, Tebu or Tibu people, nowadays the dominant population of Fazan and Tibesti. . . . They are seemingly of considerable antiquity, the Garamantes of Herodotus and the Romans, the Tedamansii of Caudius Ptolemeaus, the Alexandrian geographer of the second century. They represent one of the numerous races between the White man and the Negro, but in their purer and more northern extension they are a people with a preponderance of White man stock. The skin is dark-tinted and the hair has a kink, a curl about it. . . . They do not differ very much, facially, from the Hamitic people of Northeast Africa . . .[48]

It was a small contingency of Tebu people that Ahmed Hassanein had in fact encountered at Jebel Uwainat in 1923 (see chapter 2). He called them Goran, which is another name for these ancient people. There were one hundred fifty of them, ruled by a king called Herri. In Hassanein's words, here is what happened when he woke up one morning in Wadi Karkur Talh at Uwainat:

As I opened my eyes a figure stood near me that seemed to be part of a pleasant dream. She was a beautiful girl of the Goran, the slim graceful lines of whose body were not spoiled by the primitive garments she wore. She carried a bowl of milk, which she offered with shy dignity. I could only accept it and drink gratefully. . . . A Tebu appeared with a parcel of meat of the *waddan* or wild sheep. I gave him macaroni and rice and he went away happy. After we had eaten I went to see some relics of the presence of men in earlier times. . . . I had got talking with one of the Gorans, and having satisfied myself about the present inhabitants of Ouenat, I asked him whether he knew anything about any former inhabitants of the oasis. He gave me a startling answer. "Many different people have lived round these wells, as far back as anyone can remember. Even *djinns* have dwelt in that place in olden days." "Djinns!" I exclaimed. "How do you know that?" "Have they not left their drawings on the rocks?" he answered. With suppressed excitement I asked him where. He replied that in the valley of Ouenat there were many drawings upon the rocks, but I could not induce him to describe them further than saying that there were "writings and drawings of all the animals living and nobody knows what sort of pens they used, for they wrote very deeply on the stones and Time has not been able to efface the writings." Doing my best not to show anything like excitement, I inquired whether he could tell me just where the drawings were. . . . I gathered that Ouenat was the *pied-a-terre* of Tebus and Goran. . . . With these drawings in mind, then, I took Malkenni who had joined the caravan at Arkenu, and towards sunset he led me straight to them. They were in the valley at the part where it drew in, curving slightly with a suggestion of the wagging tail. We found them on the rock at the ground level. I was told there were other similar inscriptions at half a day's journey, but as it was growing late and I did not want to excite suspicion, I did not go to them. There was nothing beyond the drawings of animals, no inscriptions. It seemed to me as though they were drawn by somebody who was trying to compose a scene. . . . On their wall of rock these pictures were rudely, but not unskillfully carved. There were lions, giraffes and ostriches, all kinds of gazelle, and perhaps cows, though many of these figures were effaced by time . . . I asked who made the pictures, and the only answer I got came from Malkenni, the Tebu, who declared his belief that they were the work of the *djinn.*[49]

Djinns and the Rock Art at Jebel Uwainat

In chapter 2, we saw that Hassanein went on to speculate that the reason Malakenni and the Tebu thought the rock art was created by djinns was because it depicted giraffe and other animals that had not been in the area for thousands of years. We also saw that if the rock art scenes are taken as literal representations, some show strange activities, such as a human floating in thin air near the head of a giraffe. In one cave at Gilf Kebir, there are numerous images of a human form merging with or morphing out of animals—which is so reminiscent of modern shamanic ceremonialism that we started calling it the Cave of the Shamans. This, then, might be another reason why Malakenni and the modern Tebu attributed the rock art to djinns.

By 1932, however, the Tebu/Goran of Uwainat had completely disappeared. Thus, when Ralph Bagnold and his colleagues organized an expedition to Uwainat in 1938, under the sponsorship of the Egypt Exploration Society, they found only scant remains of these people at Karkur Talh: "Tibu [Goran] remains: In Karkur Talh many traces were found of the Guraan who formerly used to visit the wadi. Most of these were probably left by the band of fugitives who fled here after the French occupation of the Ennedi-Tibesti Highlands . . . there was no evidence that the Tibu had been in the region for a number of years."[50]

In addition, when Count Almasy was at Gilf Kebir and Uwainat in 1936, he took a Tebu man, Ibrahim, as his guide. Ibrahim recounted how a certain Tebu chief called Abdel Malik had been given permission by the Senussi of Kufra to graze his camels in the region. Abdel Malik discovered a lush valley at Gilf Kebir where he could graze his camels. He then left a written testimony that mentioned the origins of the Tebu people: "I, Abdel Malek, have the following to say concerning the valley I discovered: the Kufra oasis did not always belong to the Arabs. From time immemorial it was the land of the Tebu who owned all the places in the desert for ages. . . ."[51]

Ibrahim then told Almasy: "We, the Tebu, [are] the original inhabitants of this desert . . . "[52]

OUT OF THE SAHARA
AND INTO THE NILE VALLEY

For many years, a team of anthropologists headed by Rudolph Kuper and Stefan Kröpelin of Cologne University in Germany have been studying prehistoric sites and climatic changes in the Egyptian Sahara and the sub-Sahara in Chad, Sudan, and Libya. After analyzing radiocarbon samples from hundreds of prehistoric archaeological sites, they concluded that the climatic changes correlated with the movement of prehistoric people during the past twelve thousand years. The evidence also showed that there was a stable humid period from 8500 BCE to 5300 BCE, after which the people and their cattle—the same cattle people of Nabta Playa, Gilf Kebir, and Jebel Uwainat?—escaped the drying of the Sahara and spread pastoralism throughout the continent, and, perhaps, add Kuper and Kröpelin, "helped trigger the emergence of pharaonic civilization along the Nile."[53] This view is today shared by many anthropologists, including climatologists such as Professor Peter B. deMenorcal of Columbia University, who affirmed that "however fast the drying occurred, it pushed people out of north-central Africa, and that climatically forced migration might have led to the rise of the Pharaohs and Egyptian civilization."[54]

The speed at which the Sahara changed from a lush green savanna to the barren, arid, waterless desert that it is today has been a bone of contention among climatologists for many decades. In the early years, geoclimatologists were generally gradualists—that is, against the idea of any rapid changes. More recent measuring methods, however, have indicated very swift changes in some locations of the Sahara. Then, in 2005–2006, Kuper and Kröpelin studied deep core samples from Lake Yoa, in the Tibesti-Ennedi region of northeastern Chad, and found evidence there for a slow desertification that occurred over several millennia from ca. 10,000 BCE to ca. 3500 BCE. It seems, then, that there was a combination of very rapid change in some areas and more gradual regional change as the monsoon patterned moved and continuously reshaped itself. In any case, it seems the drying process eventually drove the prehistoric people out of the Sahara—meanwhile giving them ample time across many generations to develop animal domestication; basic agriculture; art; primitive sign writing; the knowledge of how to move large stones and construct complex megalithic structures; and knowledge of the simple principles of navigation, orientation, and timekeeping with the sun and stars. In other words, they acquired the practical and intellectual tools for building a civilization by the time they migrated into the Egyptian Nile Valley around 3500 BCE.

Let us now take a closer look at Lake Yoa near the Tibesti-Ennedi highlands. This region warrants a closer investigation, for it lies in the extended direction of Bergmann's Abu Ballas Trail, which has as its starting point Dakhla oasis and passes through the Gilf Kebir and Jebel Uwainat massifs.

THE SOURCE?

Lake Yoa is among the largest of a series of small lakes in the Ennedi that are located just 100 kilometers (62 miles) from the Tibesti highlands. All of these lakes total some 20 square kilometers (12 square miles) of surface water and were once part of a giant lake during the humid periods of the Sahara, between 13,000 BCE and 3500 BCE.

These lakes have a natural hydrological system that is unique in the world: because they are constantly fed with fresh water from underground aquifers and are also protected by a natural matting of reeds that reduces the evaporation effect, their water stays fresh in spite of the extreme heat and superaridity of the region that normally would lead to high evaporation and, consequently, high water salinity. In addition, the water from the higher lakes perpetually filters through the surrounding sand dunes and into the lower lakes, thus replenishing them with fresh water. Such conditions are ideal for human settlement in an otherwise inhospitable environment. As we have already seen, these lakes lie in the extended direction of the Abu Ballas Trail that runs southwest of Uwainat. The Tibesti-Ennedi region where these lakes are located is full of prehistoric rock art that resembles that of Uwainat, and there are also prehistoric tumuli or tombs that recall those of Nabta Playa. It seems almost certain, therefore, that the sub-Saharan people of the Tibesti-Ennedi highlands migrated north into the Sahara, perhaps during more humid phases, when the desert was green and fertile, which explains the sixty-seven human skeletons found at Gebel Ramlah, near Nabta Playa, in 2002 by Schild and Wendorf. These remains were declared to be those of a Black sub-Saharan people.

MEET THE ANCESTORS

In the autumn of 2000, a team of paleontologists led by Dr. Paul Sereno of the University of Chicago were exploring the western part of the Tenere Desert when they made a startling discovery at a place called Gobero, near the old Tuareg caravan village of Agadez. Here, partly buried in the sand, were dozens of human skeletons amid a proliferation of stone tools and potsherds. Many of the skeletons were in a fetal position, with legs tightly pulled up against their chest and hands tucked close to their chin. Near the human skeletons were animal bones, including those of antelope, giraffe, and hippopotamus. According to Sereno,

"Everywhere you turned, there were bones belonging to animals that don't live in the desert. . . . I realized we were in the Green Sahara."[55]

As we saw in chapter 3, for the past couple of hundred thousand years or so the Sahara has fluctuated between wet and dry phases caused by cyclical changes in Earth's motion, including the precession of the equinoxes, combined with other cyclical geologic processes. The most recent wet phase began after about 10,500 BCE, when the seasonal monsoons of central Africa again migrated north, bringing rain and fertility to a broad strip of land in the southern part of the Sahara running from the Nile in Egypt to the Atlantic coastline of Morocco. This wet phase brought into the Sahara fauna and people from the south, where, at first, they survived as hunter-gatherers, but then, with the change in climate, converted into pastoralists. In 2006, to find out more about what happened to these ancient people, Sereno teamed with the Italian archaeologist Elena Garcea of the University of Cassino, and together they re-examined the prehistoric skeletons of Gobero.

Garcea was very impressed by the large number of skeletons, which far outnumbered all others she had seen in the Sahara. She also directed her attention to the potsherds that were all around the skeletons and was quick to recognize on some of them the tiny dot marks that were typical of the Tenerian prehistoric herders that roamed the Sahara from 4000 BCE to 2500 BCE. What she found odd, though, was the pottery with wavy lines that Garcea attributed to the Kiffian, a fishing people who had lived in this same region thousands of years before the Tenerian, roughly from 6000 BCE to 4500 BCE. Garcea was baffled as to how the Kiffian and Tenerian peoples, whose presence here was separated by five hundred or more years, had used the same burial grounds. Garcea and Sereno also explored a dry lake nearby and found fishing hooks and harpoons made of bone and the remains of large Nile perch, crocodiles, and hippopotamus—all evidence of the Kiffian fishing people presence in this area. Yet what could have induced the Tenerian, centuries later, to bury their own people in the cemetery of the Kiffian? According to Garcea , ". . . perhaps the Tenerian found the Kiffian burials and recognized this place as sacred. It's possible they thought these bones belonged to their own ancestors."[56]

There were more than two hundred burials at Gobero, and only carbon dating could determine their true age. Garcea and Sereno had to act quickly, because the site was unprotected and open to looting by Tuareg nomads who were in search of artifacts to sell to tourists. Many prehistoric sites in Niger have been looted before they could be studied and excavated by archaeologists, and Sereno wanted to avoid this calamity at Gobero. He finally managed to ship bone samples to his laboratory in the United States and have them dated by radiocarbon analysis. The results showed that some bones were nine thousand years old, falling in the Kiffian epoch, while others were six thousand years old, falling within the Tenerian epoch.

A biochemist from Arizona State University, Chris Stojanowski, also went to Gobero to examine the prehistoric site, and his own study of bones and other prehistoric artifacts showed that the Kiffian men had huge leg muscles, implying a high-protein diet, and the wear and tear of their bones showed that they had arduous lives, consistent with the theory that they were hunter-gatherers and efficient fishermen. The Tenerian, on the other hand, had slender legs, and their bone structure showed that their lives were less strenuous than those of the Kiffian. This was consistent with the theory that they were herders and pastoralists. It seems that in the area there had been a hunter-gatherer phase as well as a later pastoralist phase, the former when the Sahara was very humid and rich with fauna, and the latter when the climate became drier and the fish and fauna became scarce, forcing the Kiffians to domesticate the wild cattle so that they could move their food supply to watering holes and fresh grazing grounds.

Of the hundreds of animal bones found at Gobero, none belonged to sheep or goats. They were the remains only of cattle. Yet the cattle bones were few, because the herders rarely slaughtered their cattle, but rather kept them for milk and blood. In other words, the cattle were living protein larders. As far as we know, no DNA tests have been performed to determine the origins of the Kiffian or the Tenerian, although, apparently, scientists in the United States are working on this. In 2007, there was trouble in Niger from antigovernment insurgents, and the authorities imposed emergency rules that prohibited foreigners from traveling into the Tenere Desert. Sereno and Garcea were obliged to abort their planned 2008 season at Gobero. As things stand now, this unique prehistoric graveyard may soon be lost forever.[57]

TWO GIANT GIRAFFES IN STONE

Another fact regarding the prehistoric people of Gobero attracted our attention. Many of the stone tools that were examined by Sereno and his team had come from the mysterious region known as the Aïr Mountains, located some 100 kilometers (62 miles) to the north of Gobero. A few years earlier, at the foot of the Aïr Mountains near a place called Dabous, there was discovered an abundance of prehistoric art, notably two life-sized giraffes that were exquisitely carved on a flat outcrop of sandstone. These engravings, according to the experts, probably belonged to the Kiffian and are tentatively dated to about 8000 BCE. The Dabous site contains more than eight hundred engravings, 50 percent of which are cows or other large bovines, and the rest of which are giraffes, ostriches, lions, rhinoceros, and even camels. There are also some sixty human figures. The two huge giraffes, a male and smaller female, are engraved on an 80-meters-long by 60-meters-wide (262-feet-long by 197-feet-wide) sandstone outcrop. The male giraffe is nearly 6 meters (20 feet) tall and the female about 3.5 meters (12 feet) tall. Albeit on a much larger scale, they resemble the giraffes engraved at Jebel Uwainat and Gilf Kebir in the Egyptian Sahara. More intriguingly, both at Gobero and Unwainat/Gilf Kebir, next to the giraffe's are carved human figures holding ropes attached to the mouths or heads of the animals—and this clearly shows a special connection between humans and giraffes, perhaps even an attempt at domestication.

It is unlikely to be a coincidence that such similar images are found at Gobero and at Uwainat. Could the Gobero people and the Uwainat/ Gilf Kebir people have a common ancestry or origin? Although the answer is still unclear, all the evidence points to the possibility that the Kiffian and Tenere of Niger, the Nabta Playa pastoralists, and the pre-cattle and cattle herders of Gilf Kebir and Uwainat all had a common ancestral source in the Tibesti-Ennedi region in Chad. The evidence to date compels us to conclude that the original sub-Saharan Black race that first settled in the Chad highlands subsequently gave rise to the cattle people of the lower Sahara, who, in turn, spawned the great Egyptian civilization when they finally migrated into the Nile Valley as the Sahara became superarid. All the evidence seems to point to a north-ward spreading of a Black African people from the Chad highlands into the green Sahara during the humid period that started ca.12,000 BCE. These people, it seemed, roamed the vast open spaces in search of water and grazing grounds as they gradually changed their habits from hunt-ers to pastoralists. This conversion caused them also to change their appearance and traditions, and it contributed to them acquiring an increasingly complex knowledge of astronomy and navigation—which were all imposed on them by the changing climate and the gradual dry-ing of the Sahara. Eventually, around 3500 BCE, they were forced to abandon the waterless desert and seek a new future in the Nile Valley. By then, these very ancient Black people had equipped themselves with a wealth of skills and knowledge that included domestication of cattle, basic agriculture, art, and, more important, the ability to devise time-keeping systems and to determine orientations with the stars in order to navigate in the deep, open desert. All these skills led them to develop a complex social system and perhaps even basic religious ideologies, which were finally taken into the Nile Valley and injected, like some massive cultural blood transfusion, into the more primitive dwellers there, thus planting the seeds that sprouted and eventually bloomed into the phara-onic civilization.

Unfortunately, at present, the Tibesti-Ennedi highlands are closed to foreign visitors due to political unrest in the region, but once they are accessible again, we hope to organize an expedition there. Yet the Egyptian part of the Sahara where we can find Gilf Kebir and Uwainat is still open to foreigners who acquire the necessary permits from the Egyptian authorities, and it is a very strong possibility that the people who left evidence there were the same as those who had constructed the ceremonial complex at Nabta Playa and, by extension, were the people who eventually migrated to the Nile Valley to kick-start the enlightened civilization of ancient Egypt.

DEEP DESERT JOURNEY

In December 2007, an old friend, Mark Borda (see chapter 2), contacted us while we were in Cairo. He lives on the island of Malta now and told us that he had recently been exploring the Egyptian Sahara with the services of an Egyptian, Mahmoud Marai. In 2006, Borda had been the main sponsor of Carlo Bergmann's camel expedition across the south of the Great Sand Sea in search of the Khufra Trail, which Bergmann believed linked the oases of Dakhla and Kufra in pharaonic times. For this expedition, Borda, together with other cosponsors, had hired Marai to provide vehicle back up. The next year, in November 2007, Borda again hired Marai for his own expedition to Uwainat. It was during this expedition that they had discovered irrefutable proof, in the form of hieroglyphic inscriptions, that the pharaohs had reached Uwaiant in earliest times.

Mark sent us photographs by electronic mail, and we agreed that we would help him get a second translation from one of the Egyptology institutes in Cairo. Meanwhile, Mark sought the help of British Egyptologists in London for another translation, reasoning that if both translations were the same, then he could be reasonably sure of the meaning of the hieroglyphs. He also put us in contact with Mahmoud Marai, who lived in Cairo.

We met Marai in January 2008 and immediately made plans for a deep-desert expedition to Gilf Kebir and Jebel Uwainat. Marai said he and his three Toyota Land Cruisers could be ready within a week. The problem, as usual, was raising the money to fund our expeditions, which, like other expeditions, could be a costly business. To defray some of the cost, we decided to invite a few paying guests in addition to putting up part of the money ourselves. By mid-March we had acquired all the funds necessary and fixed a date for the first week in April. The guests, which included Michele (Robert Bauval's wife), Bryan Hokum (a filmmaker from Los Angeles), Lyra Marble (who has a Pumpkin Patch* business in Hollywood), and Dustin Donaldson (a performance artist who also manages a Web site devoted to esoteric philosopher Manly P. Hall). We arrived in Cairo on April 5, and two days later we met Marai and his crew at the Bahareya oasis, the starting station for our deep-desert journey. After being delayed two days by local police till our permits were ready, and until we could be allocated a military escort (who was an unarmed soldier named Muhammad), we finally were ready to set off. We spent the third night at the Farafra oasis, and then we headed toward Dakhla oasis. Just before reaching Dakhla, we turned southwest and off the tarmac road to head into the open desert.

There is nothing more thrilling than traveling toward the unknown. Ahead of us was emptiness as far as the eye could see, and the more we pushed southwest toward the horizon, the more this emptiness engulfed us, reducing us, it seemed, to the size of ants. It is during moments such as these that we become aware of how vastly unpopulated our planet still is. If we are concerned about world population, then we ought to take a trek in the desert, where the gods will reassure us that all is not lost, after all.

We stopped for the night at Carlo Bergmann's Djedefre Water Mountain. It was too dark to explore it when we arrived, so we had to wait until dawn. As seen in chapters 2 and 4, we found solar solstice alignments, possibly prehistoric, and hieroglyphic evidence that added to our designation of the place as a sun temple revived from prehistoric times by expeditions under the reign of King Djedefre. After spending

---

*A franchize that sells evergreen trees at Christmas and pumpkins at Halloween.

a few hours around sunrise inspecting the site and its surroundings, we again set off southwest for another 100 kilometers (62 miiles), which, in these difficult off-road conditions, is the daily average distance that is reasonable to expect with heavily laden vehicles.

On the way, we inspected more prehistoric rock art, particularly on a strange castle-shaped mound where there were engravings of African fauna such as giraffes and elephants. On one such engraving, we identified a donkey, which reminded us that this was the only animal of burden available to desert travelers until the domesticated camel was introduced into Egypt in around 500 BCE. That evening, we camped at the foot of a large dune. It's difficult to find the right words to describe a night in such a remote and untouched place—*serene, peaceful,* perhaps even *close to the gods.*

On the third day, after we traveled for several hours along the edge of the Great Sand Sea and its massive golden dunes, we arrived at the mysterious stone circle that British explorer Sergeant Ralph Bagnold of the Long Range Desert Patrol discovered by chance in 1930. It was hard to believe that this strange artifact was thousands of years old and that most of the heavily eroded standing stones had remained undisturbed for all this time. Yet this is what is most curious about this particular desert: Explorers can find prehistoric stone artifacts simply lying in the sand, as if they had been placed there that same day. We examined Bagnold Circle and its possible astronomy and artifacts of the surrounding area (see chapter 4). We made camp for the night on a flat sandy area that was about 300 meters (985 feet) from the circle, which gave us a wonderful opportunity to check the alignments of the circle at sunset and at night with the stars. We also took measurements at sunrise.

The next day, we set off again, and after nearly a whole day's drive, we reached the edge of Gilf Kebir. The weather was scorching hot. We drove into a broad valley with a range of hills on both sides, and it was obvious that it had rained very recently, for the floor of the valley was covered with a fine duvet of green sprigs and a few wild flowers here and there. It was a beautiful site, so unexpected in this desert world of stark yellow and brown hues. Marai, who had been at Gilf Kebir many times before, said that he had never seen vegetation here, and would honestly not have believed it possible had he not seen it with his own eyes. According to weather statistics, it rains here only a few millimeters every twenty years or so.

We stopped the cars and stretched a tarpaulin between two of the vehicles to make a shaded area in order to have a light meal and sleep for a couple of hours, thereby avoiding the blistering heat of high noon. At last, when the sun was lower in the sky, we resumed our drive toward the so-called Aqaba Pass. We reached the pass a few hours before sunset and quickly drove through the massive gash that looks like a stone version of the parting of the Red Sea: It felt as if, at any minute, the high walls would come tumbling down upon on us like giant waves. While navigating the soft desert floor of the pass, we had some anxious moments when two of our three vehicles bogged down, stuck at the same time. If we had not been able to free at least one of them, our survival would have become precarious, but we managed to get them out, and we emerged safely on the west side of Gilf Kebir and then drove northward, our vehicles skimming the edge of the huge rocky cliffs like tiny cockroaches. The landscape is best described as Martian, with strange outcrops of brown and reddish rock and weird sand formations, and we felt as if we were on a lifeless alien planet.

Just as the sun was setting low, we reached the celebrated Wadi Sura, the location of the famous Cave of Swimmers discovered by Almasy in 1936. It was growing dark, and Marai gave orders to his crew to set up camp and prepare the evening meal. Sitting around a campfire, sipping hot tea, we talked of the rock engravings and drawings in the cave. We had seen photographs and the drawings of Almasy that showed black-skinned people diving and swimming (hard to imagine now in this arid region), and others in the art appeared to be dancing, hunting, playing games, and even perhaps performing religious rituals. Dustin, one of the American guests, was celebrating his fortieth birthday, so we decided to give him a treat by organizing a little celebration at the entrance of the cave. The spectacle seemed to be in a fairytale setting, with the stars twinkling brightly over the peaks of the cliffs in front of the cave and our flashlights bringing to life the prehistoric drawings. For a little while, we were all in an enchanted mood, as if time was standing still, as if we had perhaps been here before in some very distant time. It was amazing how well-preserved the drawings were, and we gazed at them for hours, entranced by the mood and the ancient art and talking to each other in whispers so as not to disturb the usual silence of this place. People had been here thousands of years ago, and now it was our turn to be here in this primordial world. As we watched the night slowly give way to day, a shooting star—a meteorite—streaked silently across the sky. We all knew in our hearts that we would never forget this starry night.

The next day at dawn we headed a few more kilometers north along the massif of Gilf Kebir to see a cave recently discovered by an Egyptian-Italian team in 2002, the Mestekawi-Foggini cave, named after its two discoverers. The cave was actually a deep ledge high up a rocky cliff that can be reached only by climbing up a steep sand dune that abuts the rocky cliff. It was very hot, and climbing up the dune took our breath away. We stood panting like marathon racers at the end of their run, but we forgot any physical discomfort as soon as we stood before hundreds of prehistoric drawings of men, women, cattle, and other fauna that filled the walls and ceiling of this large ledge. It was impossible to look at all of the drawings at once, so we each picked a spot where we could lie on our backs on the clean sand and admire the ancient art in segments. The Italian discoverer, Foggini, called this the Sistine Chapel of the Sahara, and no doubt a prehistoric Michelangelo must have been at work here.

The cattle, which comprised 90 percent of the drawings, were in all sizes and postures and were perfectly proportioned, running and being herded and milked by men and women. Clearly, cattle were the dominant interest of these ancient people. Were cattle sacred to them? There were, too, many prints of human hands with the palms and fingers fully spread, clearly created in the same manner as those at other ancient rock art sites: by blowing (spray painting) with the mouth over a hand. Was this to

Figure 5.2. Image of dancers at the Mestekawi-Foggini cave, southwest Gilf Kebir.

ward off evil or danger, or was it some sign of complex rituals? The cave also contained scenes of groups of people who seemed to be involved in ritual and images of a human emerging from or morphing into a powerful wild animal. This was so reminiscent of modern shamanic animal-spirit ritual that we called this the Cave of the Shamans. In addition, there were images of a large orb, possibly a sun or moon—but our sun was approaching noontime, and the heat became overbearing. It was time to resume our journey to Uwainat, the final destination of our expedition.

We had to travel another 130 kilometers (81 miles) of open flat desert to reach Uwainat. The sand, however, was quite compact and firm, so we could drive at a fairly high speed. On our way, we made a brief stop to examine a World War II vehicle that had been abandoned by the Italian army, and we were amazed that there was almost no rust on the metal parts. Halfway to Uwainat, we stopped again, this time to avoid getting too close to a large overloaded truck that was smuggling illegal contraband from Libya to war-torn Darfur in Sudan. The smugglers

Figure 5.3. Numerous prehistoric hand signatures and, lower left, people depicted as if reflected in a natural crack in the rock. The lower central group is possibly a depiction of a ritual. Mestekawi-Foggini cave, southwest Gilf Kebir.

simply waved at us, and, not knowing what to do, we waved back. Our single military escort, Muhammad, said, *"seebhom, homa nass ghalaba"* (they are poor people; leave them be). The border between Egypt and Sudan is totally unsupervised, and Muhammad told us that a constant flow of smugglers passed here totally unchecked. In fact, worn into the sand is a pair of truck tracks, which are followed by all the smugglers who angle across this corner of Egypt to Libya. Apparently, it was all very harmless, and both governments simply choose to turn a blind eye to this travel. We were told, however, that visitors had to watch for rebels from the Sudanese Liberation Army (SLA), who have been known to kidnap tourists in this region for ransom. As it turned out, we did not see any SLA rebels throughout our journey, although we cannot be sure whether they had not seen us! Finally, late in the afternoon, we could see the mountains of Uwainat. We still had some 40 kilometers (25 miles) to cover, but everyone was tired, and because we did not want to drive in the dark, we opted to make camp at the foot of a small dune and leave for Uwainat early the next morning.

We woke at the crack of dawn and drove southward until we reached the edge of Uwainat. There, we stopped to visit yet another cave with rock art that was discovered by Mark Borda in 2007. The cave is on the northern edge of Uwainat, and its entrance is tucked behind a ridge, which makes it almost invisible unless you know exactly where to look (which might explain why it was not discovered before 2007). We were, in fact, the first modern visitors to enter this cave since its original inhabitants had abandoned it millennia ago. The cave was half filled with sand up to one meter (3 feet) below the ceiling, which actually worked best for us, because most of the rock art was on the ceiling, like a prehistoric Sistine Chapel. The sand allowed us to see the rock art at very close range.

The drawings were of a much better quality than those we saw at

Figure 5.4. Bauval and Marai examine newly discovered cave art in April 2008.
Note that tha back wall of the cave appears to be constructed of megalithic blocks.

Gilf Kebir. Not only were the ancient scenes more elaborate and showed more detail, but the colors—blacks, browns, reds, yellows, and whites—were extremely vivid, as if they had been painted the day before (see plate 14). The cattle were clearly tame and domesticated, and some of them were even shown with bridles and leashes or with decorations on their bodies. The men were depicted as tall, slim, and agile. They were black-skinned and wore white ivory bands on their arms and thighs. They also had loincloths resembling those worn later by ancient Egyptians. On some of their heads were ornate hats, and many carried sticks, spears, and bows. The women wore skirts, necklaces, armbands, and earrings. A striking aspect of the renderings of the people was their heads, which were depicted either as wearing masks or symbolically as animal forms (long, rectangular snout, bright eyes, and ears near the top of the head). These animal-form heads, possibly cowlike, might have been representative of the central role that cattle played in the lives of these people. Some of them bore a striking resemblance to the early depictions of the Egyptian god Seth, a god of the desert regions whom the ancient Egyptians associated mythologically with the origin of dynastic Egypt itself. The Sahara scholar and rock art expert Dr. Jean-Loic le Quellec of the French CNRS (Centre National de Recherches Scientifique) is of the opinion that the "cave of swimmers" is a prehistoric precursor and probable influence of rituals found in the much later pharaonic Coffin Texts and Book of the Dead. He thinks the "swimmers" are performing an afterlife journey into the watery afterworld, which he relates to the mni.w (the dead who had sunk into the other world) and which confront a mythical Beast, which he related to the ancient Egypt beasts or monsters, mmyt, which swallow the dead in the so-called Judgement Scene of the Book of the Dead. According to Quellec the ancient Egyptians kept the memory of the origins in the Sahara and even may have periodically carried out pilgrimage to re-visit their ancestral lands:

> The memory of the ancient lands must have lasted for a long time,
> and was perhaps progressively mythified, following a process that has

been well documented in ethnology in many other places in Africa. Perhaps the rituals even demanded a periodic return to ancient cult places . . . like the great shelter of the Wadi Sura. In this way the memory of the ancient vision of the land of the dead, as well as the land of origins, would have been preserved."[58]

The recent finding of Bergmann and Borda fully support this hypothesis, and to which we also agree.

Central to the cave ceiling was a domestic scene, with bags or gourds, probably filled with milk or grain, hanging from the roof of a house. There were three types of cows: black and white, all white, and

Figure 5.5. Cattle and people at Uwainat cave.

white and brown with black spots. These were drawn in very realistic postures—walking, grazing, or being herded to a watering hole. We took photographs from every angle in order to have a detailed record for our own files. Oddly, outside the cave there were no visible signs of human presence as far as we could make out.*

It is likely that any such evidence lay buried under the sand that had filled the floor of the cave, drifting in and out over the millenia. Our imaginations ran wild: we conjured images of the hardy people who must have lived here thousands of years ago and who, perhaps, hailed originally from the Tibesti Mountains. The rock art they left behind made it easy for us to visualize their women milking cows or grinding seeds and cereals while their men went hunting or chipped stones to make knives and arrow or spear heads and the elderly sat outside at night, pondering the stars. The most thrilling part of this experience was finally to see with our own eyes those mysterious black-skinned ancestors that once navigated the desert, learned the art of husbandry, followed basic agriculture, practiced the rudiments of astronomy and timekeeping, and then finally moved eastward towards the Nile, toward Egypt, carrying their precious cargo: knowledge, which was to spawn a great civilization.

We resumed our journey, skirting the eastern flank of Uwainat Mountain, reaching the Sudanese border early in the afternoon. On our way south, we steered clear of a small sign fixed on a metal pole (we examined the sign and saw that it said, in Arabic, Misr (Egypt) on one side and Sudan on the other, and our handheld GPS indicated it was a few kilometers off the actual border.) Continuing south, we drove across the border and around the mountain and found ourselves on the south flank of Uwainat late in the afternoon. Here, the remoteness and utter

---

*In 1934, Enrico De Agostini discovered a prehistoric burial ground at Ain Doua on the Libyan side of southern Uwainat. It offered well-preserved pottery and two skeletons, which were apparently taken to Florence, Italy, but were very damaged during transportation and during the famous flood that hit the Florence area in 1966. The pots, however, are displayed today at Florence Archaeological Museum.

mystery of this strange place took hold of us. The landscape was other-worldly, and we felt as though we were astronauts landing on an alien planet for the first time. It was very tempting to start exploring, but night was falling fast, so we decided to camp in a sandy bowl set against a rocky mound some five kilometers (3 miles) from the mountain.

We hardly slept that night; the excitement was too great. We refrained from lighting a fire in order not to attract SLA rebels that may have been roaming the region. Just a few weeks before, a group of foreign tourists had been kidnapped in this area, and our unarmed military escort was extremely nervous about being here on the Sudanese side of the border. In the morning, at the first break of light, we quickly lifted camp, packed our gear, and set off toward the massif of Uwainat. We headed for the twin peaks that dominated the ridge and toward the place where Marai and Borda had seen the pharaonic inscriptions a few months before. As we drove there, one of the drivers suddenly let out a shout. He had apparently spotted part of a human skeleton sticking out of the sand. We stopped and rushed to examine the shallow burial. It was not prehistoric but was much younger, probably less than a century old. Likely, the skeleton belonged to a Tebu nomad or Bedouin. Our drivers could tell he was a Muslim from the way the body was laid. As Muslims themselves, our drivers uttered a brief prayer and covered the exposed part of the skeleton with more sand.

We resumed our drive toward the twin peaks and parked the vehicles at the foot of a rocky slope. Then, we all walked in silence, following Marai, still under the somber mood of seeing the lonely burial a few minutes before. After a trek of ten minutes or so, Marai stopped and pointed to a large boulder that rested precariously halfway up the rocky slope. We recognized the boulder from the photographs that Mark Borda had sent us in December. We quickly clambered up the slope, and finally, there they were: pharaonic inscriptions carved on the south face of the boulder.

After Marai and Borda, we were the first modern visitors actually to see them after some unknown ancient Egyptian scribe had crudely carved them thousands of years ago. It was a thrilling and rewarding feeling—perhaps a bit like Howard Carter must have felt when he discovered Tutankhamun's tomb. We knew from the translations that had been made by the Egyptologists in London that the inscriptions dated from ca. 2000 BCE and likely belonged to an envoy sent by King Mentuhotep II to rendezvous here with people from the kingdoms of Yam and Tekhebet. It was truly exciting to see with our own eyes this extremely ancient message carved thousands of years ago. It was rather like finding a message in a bottle in a vast ocean of sand. We felt privileged and, in a curious way, humbled. We knew the difficulty of such a trip from the Nile Valley, even in our well-equipped, four-wheel-drive

Figure 5.6. The April 2008 expedition team anticipating the first showers in eight days upon seeing the tarmac road again. Left to right: Robert Bauval, Dustin Donaldson, Michelle Bauval, Malmoud Marai, Bryan Hokum, Lyra Marbe, Thomas Brophy, and soldier Ahmed. Drivers Muhammad and Aziz are taking the photo.

vehicles, and we marveled at those unknown ancient Egyptians who had braved the journey on foot with their caravan of donkeys, traveling several months in such conditions.

They must have stayed here for some time, because, lower down the slope, we could see some stone rings that might be the leftover rims of habitations. How many ancient Egyptians had come here? Did the intrepid Harkhuf also come here? Who were the mysterious people from Yam and Tekhebet that they had met here, and from where had they come? Had they come from the Tibesti-Ennedi highlands of Chad some 700 hundred kilometers (435 miles) farther to the southwest? More important: did the ancient Egyptians know that they were meeting their own ancestors?

All these questions formed a tantalizing web of hints and clues in our minds, but we knew it was time to return to the Nile Valley to look more closely at the place where Egyptologists say the ancient Egyptian civilization supposedly began.

6

THE CATTLE AND
THE STAR GODDESSES

About the time the rains were falling off in the desert, the people in the Nile Valley suddenly started taking an interest in cows, building things with big stones, and getting interested in star worship and solar observatories. . . .

FRED WENDORF,
THE NEW SCIENTIST,
JULY 28, 2000

The . . . risings of Sirius had been observed on Elephantine throughout all periods of ancient Egyptian history.

RONALD A. WELLS,
SOTHIS AND THE SATET
TEMPLE ON ELEPHANTINE

The Egyptians . . . were the first to discover the solar year, and to portion out its course into twelve parts. They obtained this knowledge from the stars.

HERODOTUS,
THE HISTORIES,
BOOK II

TAMING THE AUROCH

In our modern world we take much for granted. One is the common domestic cow—one of the most gentle, most accommodating, and most useful animals on our planet. When we drive along a country road or walk past an open field and see these gentle and docile animals grazing or lazily walking about, we may give them a fleeting glance, but we soon forget about them. To ancient people, however, cattle were the main display of prosperity. The pharaohs of Egypt, for example, not only measured their wealth by the number of cattle they possessed, but also were themselves, as were many of their gods and goddesses, identified with cattle. Yet if cattle were of great importance to the ancient Egyptians, they were of crucial importance to the prehistoric people of the Sahara. Their very survival depended on cattle. Without cattle they simply could not have existed in the harsh conditions in which they lived. Indeed, it would not be an exaggeration to say that without cattle, there would have been no civilization, at least in the way we understand the word *civilization* today.

When and from where, however, did cattle come, and what did humans do before cattle were domesticated?

Scientists agree that the now-extinct *auroch,* or *Bos primigenius,* is the ancestor of domesticated cattle. The auroch, however, was a much larger and certainly a much more ferocious creature than our common farm cow. Its height was more than 2 meters (7 feet) and it weighed as much as 2 tons. The male auroch was black with faint stripes, and the female was reddish-brown. It is probable that the ancestor of the auroch itself existed in Africa some one million years ago and eventually spread to Asia and Europe around two hundred fifty thousand years ago. At first, and for many thousand of years that followed, the auroch was hunted for food by prehistoric man—a feat that must have been quite terrifying and very dangerous indeed, requiring many able hunters who could work together to bring down such a wild and powerful beast. Then, around 8000 BCE, the auroch was finally domesticated, although we don't fully understand where and how. Only a few years ago, scientists thought domestication of cattle had originally taken place in Turkey or southwest Asia and that, somewhere along the line, the domesticated breed spread into other parts of the world. Recent research in the mitochondrial DNA of cattle stock from Africa, Asia, and Europe, however, strongly suggests that there was not one domestication event, but several, which occurred independently in each continent in roughly the same epoch.

Normally, domestication of cattle and other animals follows the establishment of agriculture, but there are exceptions. In Africa, for example, domestication took place before agriculture or even without agriculture. The Masai of east Africa are well-known herders who do not practice agriculture, yet their lives are completely interwoven with cattle: their protein intake—milk, blood, and sometimes meat— is almost totally derived from their cattle. The Masai very rarely kill their cattle for food except on rare occasions, such as important feasts or celebrations. The evidence from Nabta Playa strongly suggests that the prehistoric people there treated their cattle in very much the same way. Furthermore, carbon-14 and other dating methods used by Fred Wendorf indicated that the cattle there were domesticated some ninety-five hundred years ago, making Nabta Playa the earliest known domestication center in the world. In view of this startling conclusion, let us take a closer look at the mysterious cattle people of Nabta Playa, for clearly they were far more sophisticated and resourceful than we previously thought.

BONES AND STONES

We can recall that at Nabta Playa, Fred Wendorf and his team discovered a dozen tumuli on the west side of the site, which contained dismantled bones of cattle and, in one particular case, the complete, articulated skeleton of a young cow. The heads of the cows were all directed south, implying a religious ritual. In addition, when they excavated the largest of the so-called complex structures, CSA was found to contain a huge boulder fashioned in the rough shape of a cow, the so-called cow stone. This stone was removed from its original burial place by anthropologists with a makeshift derrick and was taken to the city of Aswan, where it was placed in the yard of the Nubian Museum.*

We also have seen that it was from the cow stone tumuli and CSA that long lines of upright stones emanated like spokes from a bicycle wheel toward the north and the east—with the former lines directed toward the Big Dipper and the latter lines toward Sirius and Orion's belt. It should come as no surprise, therefore, to know that much later, these three stellar asterisms were also targeted by ancient Egyptians and were even given intense cow and bull symbolism. Indeed, according to most Egyptologists and archaeoastronomers, it is only these three stellar asterisms that can be identified with any certainty from ancient Egyptian texts and drawings.[1] The pharaohs knew the Big Dipper as Mesekhtyw, the thigh (of a bull or cow), and Sirius as Spdt, which was linked to the well-known cow goddesses Hathor and Isis.†

Orion was known as Sah, and this constellation was associated with Osiris and the pharaoh who, in turn, was also symbolized as a celestial bull and the celebrated Apis Bull of Memphis. Further, all of these clues involving cattle and megalithic astronomy specifically involving Sirius, Orion, and the Big Dipper strongly suggest a link across the centuries of religious ideologies between the prehistoric society of the Sahara and that of pharaonic Egypt. We will return to this and other links between the mysterious cattle/star rituals of Nabta Playa and the various stellar/cow goddesses and gods of pharaonic Egypt, but first we must understand why the ancients associated their cattle with the rising of these stars[2] and why this association was so important to the prehistoric black people of Nabta Playa.

---

*In 2001 Robert Bauval and John Anthony West went to examine the cow stone at the Nubian Museum and, sadly, found it damaged and broken into two pieces. Apparently, the accident happened during transportation from Nabta Playa.

†In the Dendera zodiac, Isis-Sirius is shown as a crouching cow, and elsewhere she, appears as a woman wearing a headdress with cow horns.

NAVIGATING THE SAND SEA

As we saw in chapter 2, when Ahmed Hassanein trekked at night to reach Uwainat, his Tebu guide used the stars to navigate in the featureless desert landscape, very much as some do on the open sea. When we travel in open desert conditions without a compass or GPS, especially at night, it is extremely easy to become confused and lost, with no way of telling direction. In the daytime, traveling is very different: the sun's shadow can be used to establish the cardinal direction at noon—but at night, and especially on a moonless night, only the stars can perform this role. As an example, we recall that on such a moonless night during our journey, we did not light any fires or lamps at our campsite in order not to advertise our position to SLA rebels or brigands. In such darkness, it was nearly impossible for our campsite to be seen beyond a hundred meters (328 feet) or so. The only way to mark its position, therefore, was to use the stars as the Bedouins did. In such open, barren spaces, in fact, it soon becomes second nature to use the stars for navigating at night. Almost certainly the ancient cattle herders of the Sahara did the same. Indeed, these ancient people had all the time in the world to study the night sky, because they were there in the desert, night after night, from generation to generation, from century to century, perhaps even from millennium to millennium. They could become fully familiar with all the observable star cycles, including precession. It is also probable that when they finally became sedentary and settled permanently at Nabta Playa, the need for navigation became obsolete, and thus their practical knowledge of the stars was converted into a star religion with rituals and symbolic structures that, in their minds, allowed them to communicate with the sky gods. The same star religion, but in a much more elaborate form, was later practiced by the ancient Egyptians, or, as we now are beginning to suspect, was inherited from the star cattle people of the Sahara and was further developed.

The immense importance of the stars, especially Sirius, to the ancient Egyptians is recognized by all Egyptologists. Sirius, as is well-known, marked New Year's Day and also served as a cosmic herald of the Nile's annual flood. More important, Sirius was directly associated with the rebirth of kings. Dr. Jaromir Malek, director of the Griffith Institute at Oxford, writes, "The Nile and its annual flooding were dominant factors in the newly formed Egyptian state";[3] and Dr. Richard Wilkinson, Egyptologist at the University of Arizona, adds that the great importance of Sirius to the ancient Egyptians "lay in the fact that the star's annual appearance on the eastern horizon at dawn heralded the approximate beginning of the Nile's annual inundation."[4] Likewise, Dr. Ian Shaw of Liverpool University and Paul Nicholson of Cardiff University write that "the Egyptian year was considered to begin on . . . the date of the heliacal rising of the Dog Star, Sirius."[5]

When we observe the daily cycle of Sirius, or indeed of any other star that rises and sets, the place of rising in the east will always be the same—that is, it will have the same azimuth.* By placing two or more markers in a straight line aimed at the rising place of a star, such as the upright stones placed at Nabta Playa, an observer can witness that same star rising at that same spot each day. Strictly speaking, however, this is not quite true, for the star has, in fact, moved a bit, but so minute is this movement in one day—about 0.000004 of a single degree—that it is not possible to notice except with the finest optical instrument. This slight progressive movement is due, as we have seen in previous chapters, to the precession of the equinoxes—that slow, gyrating motion of Earth, one full cycle of which takes about twenty-six thousand years. Yet although it is not perceptible on a daily or even yearly basis, we can notice it over the span of a human life. For each seventy-two years, the change in rising position will be about 1 degree—that is, about the thickness of of a thumb with the hand outstretched.†

Because the prehistoric star watchers of Nabta Playa observed the rising of stars over several generations and had originally marked

---

*Azimuth is measured in degrees all around the horizon: 360 degrees, with the Zero point being due north.
†Note that this change in rising azimuth depends on the starting azimuth of the star. Roughly about 1 degree applies, for example, to Sirius.

their rising points with straight lines of stones, they would surely have become aware that the rising position changed over time. As we have seen in chapter 4, there is even evidence they had a subtle and elegant concept of precessional motion. According to the latest estimates of Wendorf and Schild, Nabta Playa began functioning as a regional ceremonial center during the Middle Neolithic (6100–5500 BCE) and remained in use till about 3500 BCE—thus for at least two millennia of stellar observations. There is also evidence that the site was visited as far back as the early Holocene Period (9000–6100 BCE), thereby giving an even longer observation period. They further explain that "[f]ollowing a major drought which drove earlier groups from the desert, the Late Neolithic began around 5500 BC with new groups that had a complex social system expressed in a degree of organization and control not previously seen. These new people, the Cattle Herders (also known as Ru'at El Baqar people) appear to have been responsible for the ceremonial complex at Nabta Playa. The newcomers had a complex social system that displayed a degree of organization and control not previously seen in Egypt."[6]

We saw in chapter 4 that the people of Nabta focused their social system that displayed a degree of organization and contol onto creating a megalithic astro-ceremonial complex. One primary feature of that complex was repeated alignments to the rising of Sirius and to the circumpolar Bull's Thigh stars. We might ask, then, why the ancient astronomers of Nabta Playa also marked the rising of the star Sirius. What significance could this have had? In asking this, we are suddenly reminded that this star had its so-called heliacal rising at around the summer solstice, and that it was at this time of year that there began the monsoon rains that filled the lake at Nabta Playa. We can also remember that there was indeed such a summer solstice alignment at Nabta Playa defined by the so-called gate of the calendar circle. Was it possible that these alignments had been intended to work together in order to mark a direction as well as a specific time of year? In other words, could the astronomy of Nabta Playa have served as a point that gave a specific direction at a specific time of year? If so, what did it point to, and at what time of year?

MOVING EAST
TOWARD THE NILE VALLEY

Around 6000 BCE, the heavy monsoon rains began to come regularly during the summer solstice season to fill the large depression at Nabta Playa, turning it into a shallow, temporary lake and the region around it into lush prairies that were idyllic for grazing cattle. Further, it was this hydraulic miracle that attracted the so-called Ru'at El Baqar, or cattle people, every monsoon season. Year after year, the cattle people came around the time of the summer solstice to set up camp, graze their cattle on the thick, soft grass along the playa, and remain until the lake eventually dried up some six months later, in midwinter.

In this southern region of the Egyptian Sahara the summer nights are warm and crystal clear, and the starry firmament is a truly marvelous sight to watch. It looms above like a giant cupola or a canopy of twinkling lights that very slowly but perceptibly move majestically from east to west. The constellations appear to be so close that we might be tempted to ignore common sense and reach out to touch them. In these nightly displays, the cattle people had ample time to study the stars, perhaps even name some of the brighter ones and define the more striking of the constellations, such as Orion and the Big Dipper. Surely, they passed down their star lore over many generations. Because they were so dependent on their cattle, it was appropriate that they might have noticed that the seven-star asterism of the Big Dipper looked uncannily like the leg of a cow or bull, and that the large constellation of Orion appeared to be a striding giant herdsman holding a staff. Further, it was most likey apt that the heliacal rising of the brightest star of all, Sirius, that hung below Orion's foot, was seen as a sort of beginning or rebirth or, better still, the start of the year to mark the fertility of the coming lifegiving monsoon rains. Certainly, these assumptions occurred to

Wendorf and his team when they worked at Nabta Playa, for it was reported in *The New Scientist:*

By 1998, Wendorf's team had found megaliths scattered right across the western edge of the playa. Hoping to fathom what the nomads were up to, Wendorf invited University of Colorado astronomer Kim Malville to Nabta. Malville confirmed that the stones formed a series of stellar alignments, radiating like spokes from the site of the cow sculpture [Complex Structure A]. One of the alignments points to the belt of Orion, a constellation that appears in late spring. Three more indicate the rising points of Dubhe, the brightest star in Ursa Major [Big Dipper], which the Pharaohs saw as the leg of a cow. Most intriguing, though, is the parade of six megaliths marking the rising position of Sirius—the brightest star in the sky—as it would have appeared 6800 years ago. By that time, says Wendorf, the rains would have started their gradual retreat, and the alignments may have been an attempt to seek help from supernatural forces. To Malville, this seemed an incredible coincidence. Sirius was also of great importance to the civilisations of the Nile, which worshipped it as Sothis. The earliest known Egyptian calendars were calibrated to Sothis's appearance as a morning star, when the days were longest and monsoon rains flooded the crop fields along the Nile. Sothis was depicted as a cow with a young plant between her horns. To later dynasties, Sothis was known as Hathor—mother of the pharaohs.[7]

We have seen that around the fifth millennium BCE the cattle people worked out a way to stay permanently at Nabta Playa by digging deep wells to sustain them through the six months when the lake was dry from midwinter to midsummer. Now they could grow some basic cereal crops and hunt hare and gazelle that also came to the lake when it was full. They rarely, however, slaughtered their own cattle, for these were now considered sacred. They only used them for milk and perhaps blood, very much like the Massai herders of east Africa.*

With plenty of leisure time on their hands in the evenings and at night, their knowledge of the sky and its cycles increased, and the cattle people thus began to develop complex ideologies of life and death and to devise rituals and ceremonies to mark special days of the year. They gradually built the vast ceremonial complex we see today, using large stones quarried from the nearby bedrock. In the intellectual and spiritual sense, they moved a few steps up the cultural ladder to discard their cattle-people descriptor and become the Ru'at El Asam people, the megalith builders or, as we now prefer to call them, the star people.

Thus life for these people went on peacefully for generations until around 3300 BCE, when huge changes in the climate caused the lake to recede and the wells to dry up. It soon became obvious that they could not stay here much longer. For centuries they had heard of a wonderful river valley in the east, a cornucopia of plenty, with miles upon miles of banks of green pastures—a place where food and fresh water could be found in abundance. Indeed, their distant ancestors had trade relations with the people of the Nile Valley and even more distant regions. Therefore, forced out by the climate and lured by the legend of the great river, the people of Nabta Playa turned their attention east, toward the place of the rising sun, and dreamed of a new life in the green valley yonder. When they could stay in the desert no more, they rounded up their cattle, packed their meager belongings, and, leaving the ceremonial complex with its stone circle, tumuli, and alignments that their ancestors had raised, they started their march to a new promised land. According to one of the most prominent anthropologists of the Egyptian Sahara, Romuald Schild writes, "And where might they have gone if not to the relatively close Nile Valley? They brought with

---

*Like the Massai of Kenya and the Dinka of Sudan, the Nabta cattle people probably drank the blood of live cattle by inserting a straw into their jugular, and they likely only rarely slaughtered a calf for meat, perhaps only on special feast days or for ceremonial purposes.

them the various achievements of their culture and their belief system. Perhaps it was indeed these people who provided the crucial stimulus towards the emergence of state organization in ancient Egypt." Fred Wendorf echoes these words: "About the time the rains were falling off in the desert, the people in the Nile Valley suddenly started taking an interest in cows, building things with big stones, and getting interested in star worship and solar observatories. Is it possible that the Nabta nomads migrated up the Nile, influencing the great Egyptian dynasties?"[8] Fekry Hassan, professor of Egyptology at London University, adds: "It is very likely that the concept of the cow goddess in dynastic Egypt is a continuation of a much older tradition of a primordial cow goddess or goddesses that emerged in the context of Neolithic herding in the Egyptian Sahara."[9]

The modern town of Abu Simbel lies only 100 kilometers (62 miles) due east of Nabta Playa—three to four days' journey on foot. This would have been the most obvious route to take to reach the Nile Valley. We recall, however, that the central theme of the desert peoples' cosmological beliefs was fixated on the summer solstice sunrise—the time when both sunrise and the appearance of Orion and Sirius at dawn heralded the monsoon rains that brought life to the desert. Now that the rains came no more, however, did they still look toward the summer solstice for guidance? What propitious sign might the cattle people have taken? The Calendar Circle's summer solstice has an alignment to azimuth of about 62 degrees—that is, the place of sunrise at summer solstice. Was this a sort of prehistoric pointer for an exodus from Nabta Playa toward the Nile Valley? Was there among the star people of Nabta Playa a prehistoric Moses who led the way toward the rising sun and took his people toward a promised land in the east? At summer solstice, the sun remains at more or less the same place for about eight days, with a variation of azimuth as little as 2-arc minutes.[10] This means that the party of people leaving Nabta Playa had ample time to reach the Nile Valley by walking toward the sunrise. To where might this direction of azimuth 62 degrees have finally led them?

THE SACRED ISLAND OF ELEPHANTINE

The region of Aswan is some 250 kilometers (155 miles) northeast of Nabta Playa. A party traveling from Nabta Playa toward the rising sun at summer solstice would have reached Aswan after a journey of four to five days. This region is without doubt the choicest place to settle in the Nile Valley. The climate is perfect, with sunshine throughout the year, and at Aswan the river is at its very best—wide with clean, clear water dotted with beautiful islands, the most beautiful being the island of Elephantine.

Elephantine, as far as islands go, is rather small. It is 1.2 kilometers (.75 mile) long and 0.5 kilometers (.3 mile) wide, and is located down-river within sight of the first cataract* and opposite the modern town of Aswan. Today, half of the island has been developed into a tourist resort, but the remainder is an archaeological wonderland, which contains the great temple of Khnum and the lovely temple of the goddess Satis, as well as many other ancient vestiges from the entire age of ancient Egypt. There are no bridges that link the island to the mainland; it can be accessed only by boat or ferry. On the east of the island and across the river is the lush Nile Valley, to the west are high sand dunes, and beyond them is the open desert. The Nile here is at its widest, about 1 kilometer (.62 mile), and the water is clear, cool, and wonderfully refreshing. The banks are lined with palm and banana trees, and there are many color-ful bougainvillea and oleander trees. Sunset brings hundreds of white egrets to perch on the trees, and there they look like winged snowflakes or angels. At daybreak, the water buffaloes, Egypt's most ancient and strongest beasts of labor, graze in the shallows while local women do their laundry. Here, life is as it has always been for thousands of years: peaceful, serene, and timeless. An enthusiastic seventeenth-century English traveler, George Sandys, wrote of this place: " . . . than the waters whereof there is none more sweete: being not unpleasantly cold,

*A cataract is a change in the level of the river. In all, on the Nile there are six main cataracts, and the sixth is just north of Khartoum in Sudan.

and of all others the most wholesome. Confirmed by that answer of Pescenius Niger unto his murmuring soldiery, 'What? Crave you wine and have Nilus to drinke of?' . . . So much it nourisheth, as that the inhabitants thinke that it forthwith converteth into bloud. . . . Besides it procureth liberall urine, cureth the dolour of the veins, and is most soveraigne against that windy melancholy arising from the shorter ribs, which so saddeth the mind of the diseased."[11]

In very ancient times, Elephantine was the capital of the First Nome (district) of Upper Egypt. It was considered a place sacred to Khnum, the ram-headed creator god who is said to have fashioned humankind on his potter's wheel. Khnum's consort was the goddess Satet—also known as Satis. The notoriety of Elephantine rested on the belief that it was here where the floodwaters emerged from the underworld, or Duat, to rejuvenate the land of Egypt.[12]

The goddess Satis was regarded as the protector of Egypt's southern frontier, and as such she was depicted holding a bow and arrows. She was also the guardian of the source of the flood and, as such, was identified with the star Sirius, whose heliacal rising occurred in conjunction with the beginning of the flood season.[13] The goddess Satis is attested in ancient texts as early as 2700 BCE, and her name is found on pottery as far north as Saqqara, nearly 900 kilometers (559 miles) from Elephantine. We also find her name inscribed in pyramids of the fourth and fifth dynasties (ca. 2300 BCE), where she is said to purify the body of the dead king with the rejuvenating flood waters brought in jars from Elephantine.[14] Satis is depicted as a tall, slender woman wearing the White Crown of Upper Egypt with antelope horns. In Egypt, the antelope lives in the desert, which may symbolize the origins of Satis. On the crown is often drawn a five-pointed star, which represents Sirius. Her many epithets—Lady of Stars, Mistress of the Eastern Horizon of the Sky at Whose Sight Everyone Rejoices, The Great One in the Sky, Ruler of the Stars, Satis Who Brightens the Two Lands with her Beauty—are clearly allusions to her important identification with the star Sirius.[15] Her beautiful, small temple on Elephantine is just north of the much larger temple of her consort, Khnum. Excavation and restoration of the Satis temple by the German Archaelogy Institute of Cairo has been ongoing since 1969, and although the much-restored temple that is seen today dates from the Ptolemaic period,[16] beneath it are the remains of several earlier temples, stacked one atop the other like tiers on a wedding cake, going back to the predynastic period. In all, there are seven temples, the lowest being a simple shrine that dates from ca. 3200 BCE. Above it are two Old Kingdom shrines that date to ca. 2250 BCE, and above these are two Middle Kingdom temples that date to ca. 1950 BCE. These are surmounted by a New Kingdom shrine built by Queen Hatshepsut, ca. 1480 BCE, and finally, at the very top, is the restored Ptolemaic temple, which dates to the second century BCE.*[17]

In 1983, the American astronomer Ron Wells of the University of California took an interest in the alignments of the many superimposed Satis temples.[18] Working under the aegis of the Swiss Archaeological Institute in Cairo, Wells was permitted to take azimuth measurements of all the temples that were stacked on top of each other. It quickly became obvious to him that the azimuths of the temples differed slightly from one another, progressively changing in a counterclockwise direction. To a trained astronomer, this implied that the ancient builders were tracking the rising point of a celestial object, which changed azimuth proportionally. Ron Wells knew of the symbolic links between the goddess Satis and the star Sirius, and thus had a hunch that the changing azimuths of the temple's axes through the epoch may have something to do with the changing azimuths of the rising of Sirius. Making use of

---

*The first phase of the Satet (Satis) temple was an early-dynasty hut built into the corner of the three-boulders enclosure. In the third dynasty, this was enlarged and a forecourt was added. Further work took place in the sixth dynasty, and various new temples were constructed on top of the ruins of the earlier one during the eleventh and twelveth dynasties, especially by the pharaoh Sesostris I. In the New Kingdom, the eighteenth-dynasty queen-pharaoh Hatshepsut had the Satis temple completely rebuilt some 2 meters (7 feet) higher than the original three boulders. The eighteenth-dynasty edifice was then extended to the east during the Ramesside period and again in the twenty-sixth dynasty. Finally, a totally new temple was built over the ruins of the last one during the Ptolemaic period.

the pole star Polaris (Alpha Canis Minor) to establish true north, Wells calculated the azimuth of the topmost (Ptolemaic) temple and found it to be 114.65 degrees. He then calculated the azimuth of the earlier (New Kingdom) temple beneath it and found it to be 120.60 degrees. The 5.95-degree difference in azimuth exactly matched the difference in azimuth of Sirius for the same two epochs![19]

The azimuth changes of the axes of the temples implies an awareness of the precessional shift. Skeptics have argued that successive ancient surveyors were not aware that the older axis was no longer directed to Sirius, and they simply oriented a new temple's axis without being conscious of the change. This may perhaps be an explanation, however, if only one change had taken place; but the original axis was changed at least four times. The ancient surveyors surely must have known that the temple was dedicated to Satis, goddess of the flood linked to the heliacal rising of Sirius, and it seems inconceivable that they did not notice the change in azimuth of the axes of the various temples that were aligned to this star.

More recently, in 2004, the Spanish astronomer Juan Belmonte, along with the Egyptian astronomer Mossalam Shaltout, undertook a new study of the orientations of the superimposed Satis temples and confirmed Wells's measurements as well as the orientation of the lowest, and thus oldest, shrine: "The archaic sacred precinct of Satet [Satis] at Elephantine: this area was enclosed on three sides by three large boulders of granite and opened roughly towards the south-eastern area of the horizon, where the sun rises at the winter solstice and where Sirius rose heliacally in 3200 B.C. The shrine is preserved in a cellar below the concrete terrace where the temple of Satet, erected by Hatshepsut, has been reconstructed.[20]

Interestingly, Wells also determined that the topmost Satis temple had been aligned to other star systems. One set of alignments was toward Orion's belt and another set was toward the Big Dipper. These were the very same constellations and stars to which the various alignments of the ceremonial complex at Nabta Playa had been directed thousands of years before. This was too much of an actual coincidence to be merely accidental. We can recall that it was, indeed, from this location that the ancient Egyptian governor of Aswan and Elephantine, the explorer Harkhuf, launched his epic journeys to the kingdom of Yam. Harkhuf's tomb, where are inscribed the stories of his journeys, is located on the west bank of the Nile in the hills almost directly opposite Elephantine Island. It is very tempting to suppose that Harkhuf knew the location of Yam before he set off on his first expedition, because he knew that his ancestors had come from there. The earliest date for the Satis temple is ca. 3200 BCE, a date that uncannily coincides with the departure of the cattle people from Nabta Playa. Had the latter come here and brought along with them the astronomical ideas that were incorporated into the multileveled temples of Satis?

At Elephantine, in ca. 3200 BCE, it was not the monsoon rains that brought renewal and regeneration of the land but the Nile's flood, which was the direct result of the monsoon rains that no longer occur in this part of Egypt, but instead occur much farther south, in central Africa. In other words, the same system of astronomical knowledge that was developed in the Sahara in prehistoric times could have been used in the Nile Valley, because the time of arrival of the monsoon rains exactly matched the time of arrival of the flood, with both occurring at the summer solstice. To be more specific, the flooding of the Nile is caused by the same monsoon rains that flooded Nabta Playa every year, except that the monsoon wind pattern has moved south and is now inundating the great lakes at the source of the Nile, which sends the flood north to the lower Nile. In the light of this new evidence, we can therefore see why it was at about 3200 BCE that Elephantine began to acquire great religious importance as the source of the flood.[21]

In 1890, on the small island of Sahal a few kilometers upstream from Elephantine, the American traveler Charles Wilbour discovered hieroglyphic inscriptions on a large boulder protruding from the Nile. Today, the boulder is known as the Famine Stele, and the boulder's inscriptions speak of a terrible drought that struck Egypt for seven years due to a series of bad floods in the reign of the pharaoh Djoser, first ruler of the third dynasty (ca. 2650 BCE). In the text of the Famine Stele, King Djoser asks the high official of the region, Mater, from where rose the water of the Nile. Mater replied, ". . . the Nile flood came forth from the Island of Elephantine whereon stood the first city that ever existed; out of it rose the Sun when he went forth to bestow life upon man, and therefore it is also called Doubly Sweet Life, and that the very spot on the island out of which the flood waters rose from was the double cavern called Querti, which was likened to two breasts from which all nourishment poured forth; here the Nile God lay on a 'couch' and waited for the coming of Akhet [the season of inundation], after which he rushed out of the cavern like a vigorous youth and filled the whole country."[22]

From the Famine Stele at Aswan

Year 18 of Horns: Neterkhet; the King of Upper and Lower Egypt: Neterkhet; Two Ladies: Neterkhet; Gold-Horus: Djoser, under the Count, Prince, Governor of the domains of the South, Chief of the Nubians in Yebu, Mesir. There was brought to him this royal decree. To let you know: There is a town in the midst of the deep, Surrounded by Hapy [the Nile; the Nile God], Yebu by name [Elephantine]; It is first of the first, First nome to Wawat, Earthly elevation, celestial hill, Seat of Re when he prepares To give life to every face. Its temple's name is 'Joy-of-life, "Twin Caverns" is the water's name, They are the breasts that nourish all. It is the house of sleep of Hapy, He grows young in it in [his time], [It is the place whence] he brings the flood: Bounding up he copulates, As man copulates with woman, Renewing his manhood with joy; Coursing twenty-eight cubits high, He passes Sema-behdet at seven. Khnum is the god [who rules] there, He is enthroned above the deep . . . His sandals resting on the flood; He holds the door bolt in his hand, Opens the gate as he wishes. He is eternal there as Shu, Bounty-giver, Lord-of-fields, So his name is called. He has reckoned the land of the South and the North, to give parts to every god. It is he who governs barley, [emmer], Fowl and fish and all one lives on. Cord and scribal board are there, The pole is there with its beam. . . . His temple opens southeastward, Re rises in its face every day; Its water rages on its south for an iter, A wall against the Nubians each day. There is a mountain massif in its eastern region, With precious stones and quarry stones of all kinds, All the things sought for building temples In Egypt, South and North, And stalls for sacred animals, And palaces for kings, All statues too that stand in temples and in shrines."[23]

This tradition that the island of Elephantine was the source of the Nile and also the source of the annual flood was still current when Herodotus visited Egypt in the fifth century BCE. This is what the Father of History writes about Elephantine: " . . . [A]s to the sources of the Nile, no one that conversed with me, Egyptian, Libyan or Greek professed to know them, except the recorder of the sacred treasures of Athena [Satis] in the Egyptian city of Saïs. I thought he was joking when he said that he had exact knowledge, but this was his story. Between the city of Syene [Aswan] in the Thebaid and Elephantine there are two hills with sharp peaks, one called Crophi and the other Mophi.* The springs of the Nile which are bottomless, rise between these hills . . . "[24]

In the first century, some half-century after Caesar occupied Egypt and turned it into a Roman province, the chronicler Pliny the Elder reports:

Timaeus the mathematician has alleged a reason of an occult nature: he says that the source of the river [Nile] is known by the name of

---

*The Egyptologist Gaston Maspero explains that Krophi and Mophi are Qer Hāpi (Cavern of the Nile God) and Mu-Hāpi (Water of the Nile God).

Phiala [Philae, the island of Isis near Elephantine], and that the stream buries itself in channels underground, where it sends forth vapors generated by the heat among the steaming rocks amid which it conceals itself; but that, during the days of the inundation, in consequence of the sun approaching nearer to the earth, the waters are drawn forth by the influence of his heat, and on being thus exposed to the air, overflow; after which, in order that it may not be utterly dried up, the stream hides itself once more. He says that this takes place at the rising of Sirius, when the sun enters the sign of Leo, and stands in a vertical position over the source of the river, at which time at that spot there is no shadow thrown.[25]

On the latitude that passes near Elephantine, Aswan, and Philae, the sun at summer solstice is positioned nearly vertical at noon, and hence no shadows are cast. This latitude is, of course, the Tropic of Cancer, at 23 degrees 27' north. The famous Alexandrian scholar Eratosthenes knew this and also knew that on that very same day and time in his hometown of Alexandria (which is 900 kilometers, or 559 miles, north of Aswan) the sun would cast a pronounced shadow. He determined that the angle of the shadow at Alexandria was 1/50 of a full circle (that is, 7 degrees 12') from the zenith, and he thus reasoned that the distance from Alexandria to Aswan must be 1/50 of the total circumference of Earth. Because that distance from Alexandria to Aswan, was known to him as 5,000 stadia (some 500 geographical miles), he reckoned that the full circumference of Earth was 252,000 stadia, which is 16 percent more than the true value, but a solid result nonetheless, given the crude method he used. Eratosthenes went down in history as the first to have calculated Earth's size. The irony, however, is that it was the Egyptian priests who had informed Eratosthenes of this phenomenon, which, almost certainly, they had been aware of since time immemorial. Indeed, it may well be for that very reason that the location of Elephantine was regarded by the Egyptians as the first city that ever existed. It may also be the reason why the people of

Nabta Playa, who were guided by the summer solstice, came to settle in Elephantine in ca. 3200 BCE.*

At any rate, further inscriptions on the Famine Stele state that Hapy's temple "opens southeastward, and Re [the sun] rises in its face every day,"[26] which implies an alignment toward Sirius, a star that also rises southeast. This conclusion seems correct, and Ron Wells estimated that the entrance to the archaic temple of Satis was directed at azimuth 120.60 degrees, which matched the azimuth of Sirius in ca. 3200 BCE.[27†]

This date also corresponds to the date of the archaic temple given by Belmonte and Shaltout. Bearing this in mind, in 1981, the German Egyptologist and chronologist Rolf Krauss argued that the Island of Elephantine had been the principal site in all Egypt for observing the heliacal rising of Sirius since at least the time of the Middle Kingdom (ca. 2000 BCE),[28] a deduction with which many researchers agree.[29] All in all, there is much to suggest that the observation of Sirius at Elephantine harks back to the archaic period of ca. 3200 BCE—a date which dovetails with the time when the star people of Nabta Playa abandoned the Sahara.

At Elephantine is one of the oldest nilometers in Egypt. A nilometer is a simple but very effective device used to measure the rising and ebbing water level of the Nile. It basically consists of a stone well with steps that lead down into the river. The wall of this well has graduated marks to measure the level of the river. When the Romans first came to Elephantine in the 25 BCE, along with them came the geographer Strabo, the author of the famous *Geography,* who recognized correctly the function of the nilometer. He describes his visit to Elephantine and the nilometer:

---

*The latitude of Elephantine Island, 24.08 degrees north, precisely equaled the Tropic line circa 3760 BCE. By 3300 BCE, the Tropic line had moved down to 24.045 degrees, which was essentially the same.

†According to Ron Wells, Sirius had to be at an altitude of 10.48 degrees in order to be seen when observers took into account the high knoll that rises on the east bank of the river (today occupied by the Old Cataract Hotel).

Elephantine is an island in the Nile, at the distance of half a sta-
dium in front of Syene [Aswan]; in this island is a city with a temple
of Cnuphis [Khnum], and a nilometer like that at Memphis. The
nilometer is a well upon the banks of the Nile, constructed of close-
fitting stones, on which are marked the greatest, least, and mean risings of the Nile; for the water in the well and in the river rises and
subsides simultaneously. Upon the wall of the well are lines, which
indicate the complete rise of the river, and other degrees of its rising. Those who examine these marks communicate the result to the
public for their information. For it is known long before, by these
marks, and by the time elapsed from the commencement, what the
future rise of the river will be, and notice is given of it. . . .[30]

Although restored in Roman times, the nilometer of Elephantine is
probably much older. According to the Famine Stele inscriptions, King
Djoser (2650 BCE) is informed that "There is a town in the midst of
the deep surrounded by Hapy [the Nile], Yebu by name [Elephantine];
It is first [town] of the first nome to Wawat [Nubia], [it is known as]
'Earthly Elevation,' 'Celestial Hill,' and 'Seat of Re' when he prepares to
give life to every face. Its temple's name is 'Joy-of-life.' 'Twin Caverns'
is the water's name, they are the breasts that nourish all. It is the house
of sleep of Hapy. He grows young in it in [his time]. [It is the place
whence] he brings the flood . . . "[31]

The author of the texts was the high official of the region, Mater.
He duly informs King Djoser that the ideal flood is when the water level
reaches "twenty-eight cubits high at Elephantine [and that] he [the Nile]
passes [the town of] Sema-behdet at seven [cubits]."[32] The name Sema-
behdet is that of the Seventeenth Nome of Lower Egypt, which borders
the coastline of the Mediterranean, some 920 kilometers (572 miles)
downstream from Elephantine as the crow flies. Today, it is called Tell
Balamun. The difference in the level of the Nile between Elephantine
and Tell Balamun is about 85 meters (279 feet). This provides the natural fall from south to north, allowing the river to flow northward at

about 16 knots.[33] A sudden rise of 28 cubits, nearly 14 meters (46 feet), at Elephantine would bring about a rush of water, causing the banks to overflow and the water to flood the adjacent land. Even so, the flooding of the land could be somewhat controlled—but any higher water levels would cause overflooding and untold structural damage to the land and crops. Any flooding lower than necessary would cause a drought that could lead to food shortage and, eventually, famine. It was thus crucial that some sort of early warning system be installed, hence the nilometer.

Although the nilometer at Elephantine was far from being the refined hydraulic instrument that we would use today, it gave a good indication of what type of flood to expect. Part of the early warning system came from the stars. Around early June, as the sun approached its most northerly rising at the summer solstice, the constellation of Orion appeared again at dawn in the east, followed by Sirius. At this time of year, the nilometer was watched with great care. No wonder, then, that the temple of Satis, divine protector of the Nile and the flood, from where officials monitored the rising of Orion and Sirius, was located only a short distance away from the nilometer of Elephantine. Intriguingly, Ron Wells showed that the ancient designers of the temple seemed to have demarcated the two extreme variations of the Big Dipper constellation as it revolved around the north celestial pole. We can recall how the stars of this particular constellation, as well as those of Orion and Sirius, were specifically used by the star people of Nabta Playa. Yet can such astronomical similarities be regarded as evidence of a progressive cultural link between Elephantine and Nabta Playa?

A new trend in archaeology and cultural anthropology is open to what has been loosely termed *nontangible evidence,* which, as its name implies, cannot be physically evaluated—it does not, for instance, include artifacts. Nonetheless, conclusions are valid because they can be reasoned to be so—there is a sort of silent eyewitness account from the past. Astronomical evidence is nontangible regarding understanding ancient cultures, especially in the case of ancient Egypt. It has been known for some time that the ancient Egyptians performed a very important ritual for aligning their religious monuments toward the sun and stars. From earliest times, they performed a ceremony called stretching the cord to align royal pyramids and temples. This ceremony, which we have seen in chapter 4, required the participation of the pharaoh and a priestess, who assumed the role of a deity called Seshat.

The goddess Seshat was unique among all the other goddesses of ancient Egypt in that she was said to be supremely proficient in the sacred sciences, particular astronomy and sacred architecture. Depicted as a slender woman, Seshat was especially venerated by scribes, for she was also the patroness of the sacred hieroglyph writing and keeper of the royal annals.[34] Her companion-husband was Thoth, the god of wisdom and astronomy, and she often appears next to him on temple reliefs. Such a prestigious union gave Seshat enormous status and respect. Nonetheless, her most important role was participating with the kings in the stretching the cord ceremony to establish the four corners of temples and pyramids and to align them toward specific stars, usually the Big Dipper. In this capacity, Seshat is always shown in a leopard-skin dress with spots that are sometimes shown as stars, which is apparently symbolic of her ability to see in the dark, like the leopard.[35] On her head, Seshat is depicted wearing a golden tiara with a seven-pointed star or rosette. Her many epithets included Foremost in the Library, Mistress of Writing in the House of Life, Keeper of the Royal Annals, and Lady of the Stars.[36] The French scholar Anne-Sophie Bomhard, an expert on the ancient Egyptian calendar, writes, "The recognition of the annual cycle and its definition, the linking of celestial phenomena to terrestrial happenings, are essential preliminaries to establishing any kind of calendar. This enterprise requires long prior observations of the sky and the stars, as well as the recording, in writing, of these observations, in order to verify them over long periods of time. It is quite natural, therefore, that the divine tutors of Time and Calendar should be Thoth, God of Science, and Seshat, Goddess of Writings and Annals."[37]

Egyptologists have established that the stretching the cord ceremony was known since at least ca. 2900 BCE, and it was a "crucial part
of a temple foundation ritual."[38] Textual knowledge of this ceremony
comes mostly from inscriptions on the temples at Edfu and Dendera,
although much earlier evidence is found in drawings and reliefs depict-
ing the ceremony. Sir I. E. S. Edwards, the foremost expert on Egyptian
pyramids, writes that "[i]n spite of the relative late date of the inscriptions referring to the episodes of the foundation ceremonies, there is no
reason to doubt that they preserved an ancient tradition. Some indication that similar ceremonies were already current in the Pyramid Age is
provided by a fragmentary relief found in the Vth Dynasty sun-temple
of Niuserre, which shows the king and a priestess impersonating Seshat,
each holding a mallet and a stake to which a measuring cord is attached.
The scene is in complete agreement with the text in the temple at Edfu,
which represent the king saying: 'I take the stake and I hold the handle
of the mallet. I hold the cord with Seshat.'"[39]

During the stretching the cord ceremony, both the Seshat representative and the king carried a peg and a mallet and faced each other,
probably from some twenty paces apart. A cord was looped between
the pegs while the king and Seshat determined the alignment of the
axis of the future temple or pyramid by sighting a specific star in the
northern sky. Once the sighting was successfully made, they stretched
the cord and fixed the line by hammering the two pegs into the ground
with the mallets. From inscriptions at Edfu and Dendera we can read:
"[The king says]: 'I hold the peg. I grasp the handle of the mallet and
grip the measuring-cord with Seshat. I turn my eyes to the movements
of the stars. I direct my gaze towards the bull's thigh [the Big Dipper].
. . . I make firm the corners of the temple . . .'"[40] "[Seshat says]: 'The
king stretches joyously the cord, having turned his head towards the
Big Dipper and establishes the temple in the manner of ancient times.
[The king says]: 'I grasp the peg and the mallet; I stretch the cord with
Seshat; I observed the trajectory of the stars with my eye which is fixed
on the Big Dipper; I have been the god who indicates Time with the

Merkhet instrument. I have established the four corners of the temple. [Seshat says]: 'The king . . . while observing the sky and the stars, turns his sight towards the Big Dipper . . .'"[41]

In the many years that we have investigated the astronomical alignments of Egyptian pyramids and temples, it has often occurred to us that there may be more than just a religious purpose in fixing the axes toward the rising stars or the sun. If we attribute a knowledge of precessional astronomy to the ancient builders—and recent studies have shown that there is much reason to do so[42]—then it is quite possible that these ancient megalith builders may have used their monuments for long-term calendric computations in order to hark backward to distant epochs that had special significance to them. Further, this stretching the cord ceremony may well have been a ritual to verify, upon inauguration of a new temple building site, that the stars in the heavens were continuing to operate as the astronomer-priests expected they should, and so the earthly and heavenly events could be unified in the temple to maintain sacred order. Indeed, as we have seen in chapter 4, all the signatures of the precursor to the stretching the cord ceremony were present at Nabta Playa, even if it was not the same ritual itself.

Yet there is more evidence that Old Kingdom temples were in fact encoded with sophisticated calendar functions, but to verify this, we must first grasp the essential features of the ancient Egyptian calendar and how it may have been applied to such a lofty purpose.

THE TIME MACHINE OF THE ANCIENTS

Today, we need not have years of direct observations of the night sky to be initiated into this ancient system of astral knowledge, for with the use of sophisticated astronomy software such as StarryNightPro plus a common home computer, we can speed up the cycles of the celestial bodies to condense a year into a minute—or even, at the touch of a button, hop into the distant past or future. All it takes to operate such user-friendly software is basic knowledge of celestial mechanics and a keen interest in the sky. Nonetheless, we must consider the sky from the perspective of the ancient stargazers of Egypt, and for this we must understand how they computed short- and long-term cycles for their timekeeping needs.

A SENSE OF ETERNITY

The so-called civil calendar of ancient Egypt was a timekeeping device of elegant simplicity. It had the amazing benefit of requiring no adjustment as well as serving as a device for eternity. "The quest for Eternity," wrote the French scholar Anne-Sophie von Bomhard, "was the most essential preoccupation of the Egyptian civilization."[43] The ancient Egyptians sought eternity through understanding of the long-term cycles of the sun and stars. Everything the ancient Egyptians did—all monuments they built, all ceremonies and rituals they performed, all art and writings they created—were inspired by the idea of eternity and how they could become part of it. We need only look at the pyramids to feel their inspiration.

Yet if the pyramids are a monumental legacy to eternity, then surely the ever-flowing Nile and its annual flood are the living expression of it. Herodutus said that Egypt was "the gift of the Nile," and the Egyptians themselves saw the Nile as a sacred river, which had its source in heaven among the stars.[44] The Egyptologist Jean Kerisel writes, "the mystery of the distant sources of the Nile and the inability to explain the mechanism behind the flooding of the river which followed a regular calendar . . . must have nourished the image of divinity and the sense of eternity."[45]

The source of the Nile is the great lakes in the distant south, thousand of kilometers away, in central Africa and Ethiopia. As we have seen, the annual flood is the direct product of the heavy monsoon rains that occur in midsummer, which cause these great lakes to overflow and discharge their waters into the Nile. These very same monsoons once reached the south of Egypt and created temporary lakes such as the one at Nabta Playa. According to standard Egyptology, however, the ancient Egyptians never knew this. Indeed, the source of the Nile—and thus the cause of the annual flood—were not known to modern humans until the late nineteenth century. Given our new evidence, however, we can question to what extent we can say that the ancient Egyptians never knew that the monsoon flooding in the south was the source of the annual Nile floods. Perhaps the ancient Egyptians did not know as we today think of knowing, but in addition to the astronomical evidence, their origin stories suggest they did have some sort of awareness.

The ancient Egyptians represented the Nile as the god Hapy, a plump man with drooping breasts and a belly that implied contentment and fulfillment. They imagined that its source was a cave leading into the underworld, the Duat. Yet the Duat was also a starry world near the Milky Way. The Lord of the Duat was the god Osiris, with whom the dead pharaohs were identified. Thus according to the Egyptologist J. Gwyn Griffiths, "Osiris is especially associated with the Duat, a watery celestial region where he consorts with Orion and Sothis [Sirius], heralds of inundation and fertility. He is also Lord of Eternity . . ."[46] And Mark Lehner writes that "the word for 'Netherworld' was Duat, often written with a star in a circle, a reference to Orion, the stellar expression of Osiris in the underworld. Osiris was the Lord of the Duat, which, like the celestial world (and the real Nile Valley) was both a water world and an earthly realm."[47] The seemingly contradictory fact that there was a celestial Duat and an underworld Duat can be explained by the observation of what actually happens in the sky: the stars journey in the sky after they rise from east to west, and they journey in the underworld—that is, below the horizon from west to east, after they set. What added to this earth-sky connection for the Duat was the visible feature of a celestial Nile near Orion. As the historian and astronomer Alan Chapman aptly puts it: "was not the life-giving Nile itself reflected in the very heavens themselves, in the form of the Milky Way?"[48] The American Egyptologist Mark Lehner also points out that "the Milky Way was the 'beaten path of the stars,' although it was also a watery way. . . . In fact, the vision is that of the Nile Valley at inundation."⁴⁹ Further, the mythologist Lucie Lamy adds: "If Egypt is a reflection of the sky, then divine beings sail on the waters of the Great River which animate the cosmos: the Milky Way."⁵⁰ Robert Bauval had published the same idea in 1989 when he wrote, "a major feature of the After-world often mentioned in the Pyramid Texts is the 'Winding Waterway,' which was, in all probability, seen as a celestial counterpart of the Nile."⁵¹

THE SACRED YEARLY INUNDATION

Each year, the Nile started to swell in mid-June and spilled its water on the adjacent valley. Herodotus, who journeyed in Egypt in the fifth century BCE, commented: "about why the Nile behaves precisely as it does I could get no information from the priests nor yet from anyone else. What I particularly wished to know is why the water begins to rise at the summer solstice, continues to do so for a hundred days, and then falls again at the end of that period, so that it remains low throughout the winter until the summer solstice comes round again in the following year.⁵²

What Herodotus wanted to know, and what the Egyptians could not or would not tell him, was that the reason the Nile behaved in its mysterious way was because of the monsoon rains in the distant south, which, in a sense, regulate the flow and level of the river. Even after the monsoons receded south out of Egypt and the rains that had once drenched the dry Sahara each summer came to an end, much of the downpour of the rainwaters did, in fact, still reach Egypt via the Nile. Like the Nabta Playa prehistoric stargazers before them who experienced monsoon rains, the ancient Egyptian astronomers could not help but notice that the annual arrival of the flood occurred when the sun rose at its most northerly position on the eastern horizon—that is, at summer solstice. The common view among scholars is that this prompted the ancient stargazers of the Nile to count the number of days between each cycle, reaching the conclusion that it took 365 days*—a year—

---

*Actually, it is 365.242 days, to be exact.

which furthermore made the summer solstice their New Year's Day.

If we observe sunrise from the same place each day, we can notice that the sun changes position along the eastern horizon between two extreme points: the summer solstice to the far left (north) of due east, and the winter solstice to the far right (south) of due east. At these two extreme points, the sun appears to be stationary for a week or so, hence the term *solstice,* from the Latin, which means "stationary sun." In our modern Gregorian calendar, the summer solstice falls on June 21 and the winter solstice falls on December 21. The sun's journey from one solstice to the other and back takes 365 days, which we call one year. Most historians agree that this discovery was made first in Egypt in the fourth millennium BCE. As we have seen, however, the evidence now strongly suggests that the discovery was made much earlier, in the Egyptian Sahara, and was then imported into the Nile Valley by the Black people that traveled there from Nabta Playa. Admittedly, this discovery was probably refined a few centuries later—most likely, sometime around 2800 BCE—by the ancient Egyptians (by the sun priests of the Great Sun Temple at Heliopolis, near modern Cairo) to produce a sophisticated calendar with weeks and months.

Egyptian Calendar Divisions

The civil (Egyptian) calendar was divided in the following manner: twelve months of thirty days, with each month having three weeks, or decades, of ten days. The twelve months amounted to 360 days to which were added five days known as the Epagomenal Days, or Five Days upon the Year, thus making up the full 365-day year. The Egyptian year had only three seasons of four months each: the first season, called Akhet, meaning "inundation," from months 1 to 4; the second season, called Peret or Proyet, meaning "emergence" or "coming forth," from months 5 to 8; and the third season, called Shemu, meaning "harvest," from months 9 to 12. Originally, the months were not given names but were assigned only numbers

from one to twelve. The first day of the first month of the first season was known as I Akhet—that is, month I, season Akhet, day I.
Later in the New Kingdom, the months received official names: (1)
Thoth, (2) Phaopi, (3) Athyr, (4) Choiak, (5) Tybi, (6) Mechir, (7)
Phamenoth, (8) Pharmuti, (9) Pachons, (10) Payni, (11) Epiphi, and
(12) Mesore. Egyptologists and historians can never agree on the age
of the Egyptian calendar. There is, however, much evidence to support the conclusion that the calendar was already in place during the
Old Kingdom.

The solar (tropical) year is, in fact, longer than 365 days by a very
small fraction, almost a quarter of a day. The exact value of the year
is 365.2422 days. Today, to keep our modern Gregorian calendar
synchronized with the seasons, we add one day every four years to
the year, making the lengthened year what is known as a leap year.
Evidence suggests that even though the ancient Egyptians were aware
of this shift, they did not have a leap year but simply let their calendar
drift relative to the seasons. This, by necessity, created a long-range
cycle of 1,460 years—(365 × 4 = 1,460)—and can be seen as a Great
Solar Cycle. It so happens that the ancients also observed the rising
of stars, and they chose the heliacal rising of Sirius as a marker of the
New Year. This means that their civil calendar New Year also drifted
relative to the astronomical Sirius New Year at the rate of one day
every four years, creating the same cycle of 1,460 years, which scholars
call the Sothic cycle (because Sothis is the ancient name for Sirius).[53]
The peculiarity of the annual cycle of Sirius (or indeed any star that
rises and sets) is that it will seem to disappear for a period of time—
that is, it is hidden from view (because the star is up only in daylight).
This period was about seventy days in the case of Sirius in ancient
Egypt, after which it reappeared at dawn in the east. This first reappearance at dawn is known as the heliacal rising. The heliacal rising
of Sirius was significant to the ancient Egyptians for two reasons: it

took place near the summer solstice and also appeared at the start of the flood season.⁵⁴

The Heliacal Rising of Sirius

The rising time of stars is delayed by nearly four minutes each day. If we watch Sirius's rising in early August, the rising will be at dawn. In late October, the rising is at midnight. Sirius's rising in early January is at dusk. There is a period from late January to late May in which Sirius has already risen in daylight and seems to emerge out of sky as the dome darkens after sunset (that is, the sky becomes dark enough for us to see the spot of light that is Sirius). If we were at the Giza pyramids in early March and we looked due south at dusk, Sirius would emerge from the sky directly over the Great Pyramid. At one point in the year—in late May—Sirius can be seen hovering just over the western horizon after sunset. In the days that follow this, the star will not be seen anymore, because it is now too close to the sun's light for its own light to be seen. Sirius remains thus invisible for about seventy days, until August 5, when it rises anew before sunrise in the eastern horizon. This first dawn rising of Sirius is technically known as the heliacal rising of Sirius, and was seen by the Egyptians as the rebirth of the star.

BLACK GENESIS: YEAR ZERO

We in the modern world consider the Year Zero of our calendar to be the presumed birth of Jesus, which, today, is thought to have been 2,010 years ago.* This, however, is purely an arbitrary date. Indeed many other people—such as the Muslims, the Jews, the Chinese, and the Japanese— had (and some still have) other Year Zeroes for their own calendars.

---

*Some scholars suggest this date is also astronomical—occurring at the beginning of the zodiac Age of Pisces, and hence the reason why early Christians adopted the fish as the symbol of their age.

Usually, years are numbered from the date of a historical person, either an ancient person, as in the case of the Muslim, Jewish, and Christian calendars, or a sequence of emperors, as in ancient China or modern Japan, where legal documents are dated "year Heisei 22."

When was the Year Zero of the ancient Egyptians? How can we calculate its date? This is where we can note an interesting issue regarding study of the drift of the civil calendar relative to the heliacal rising of Sirius.

Sirius was known as the Sparkling One, the Scorching One, or, less flatteringly, the Dog Star or Canicula.* These epithets derived from the fact that the heliacal rising of this star occurred in midsummer, when the sun was at its hottest—the so-called dog days of the Roman year. The Greeks called this star Sothis, a name that perhaps derived from the ancient Egyptian Satis, the goddess of the Nile's flood at Elephantine whom the Egyptians identified with Sirius.[55]

Modern astronomers know it as Alpha Canis Major or by its common name, Sirius. It is the star that shines the brightest in the sky— its brightness in absolute terms is twenty-three times the brightness of our sun. It is also twice as massive as our sun and much hotter, and its 9,400-degrees-Kelvin temperature makes it appear to be brilliant white. The American astronomer Robert Burham Jr. tells us that it is "the brightest of the fixed stars . . . and a splendid object throughout the winter months for observers in the northern hemisphere."[56] The star Sirius, however, does not stand alone. It is, in fact, part of a bright constellation we call Canis Major, the Big Dog, which trails behind Orion the Hunter. As the brightest of all the visible stars, Sirius is almost ten times more brilliant than any other star and can be seen in broad daylight with the aid of a small telescope. Its color is a brilliant bluish-white. Quite simply, it is the crown jewel of the starry world.

When the very first pyramid in Egypt was built in ca. 2650 BCE, Sirius rose at azimuth 116 degrees near modern Cairo. In 6000 BCE, when the prehistoric astronomers of the Sahara also observed it, Sirius

---

*The Hebrew called Sirius Sihor, and the Romans called it Sirio or Canicula—the Dog.

rose at azimuth 130 degrees at Nabta Playa. As we can see in appendix 1, in the centuries around 11,500 BCE, Sirius rose almost due south at azimuth 180 degrees as seen from the Cairo area. It is a well-established fact that the Egyptians observed the rising of Sirius, especially its helia-cal rising, since at least 3200 BCE. Because of the effect of precession, the time and place on the horizon of the heliacal rising of Sirius will slowly change. Today, it takes place in early August. In 2781 BCE the rising occurred on June 21, the day of the summer solstice, when the Nile also began to rise with the coming flood. Of course, this propitious conjunction—the summer solstice, the heliacal rising of Sirius, and the start of the flood season—would have been so for the prehistoric people of the Sahara, except that it was the playa flood season that started with the monsoon season.

The Nile and the New Year

The summer solstice may have originally marked the first day of the civil calendar. This idea was first proposed in 1894 by the astrono-mer Sir Norman Lockyer. The German chronologist E. Meyer also proposed it in 1908. Recently, the Spanish astronomer Juan Belmonte revived this idea and further proposed that the summer solstice was the basis of the original calendar. According to the archaeoastrono-mer Edwin C. Krupp:

> In ancient Egypt this annual reappearance of Sirius fell close to the summer solstice and coincided with the time of Nile's inundation. Isis, as Sirius, was the "mistress of the year's beginning," for the Egyptian New Year was set by this event. New Year's ceremony texts at Dendera say Isis coaxed out the Nile and caused it to swell. The metaphor is astronomical, hydraulic, and sexual, and it parallels the function of Isis in the myth. Sirius revives the Nile just as Isis revives Osiris. Her time of hiding from Set is when Sirius is gone from the night sky. She gives birth to her son Horus, as Sirius gives birth to the New Year, and in texts Horus and the New Year are equated. She is

the vehicle for renewal of life and order. Shining for a moment, one morning in summer, she stimulates the Nile and starts the year. [57]

The British astronomer R. W. Sloley reminds us, and with good reason, that "ultimately, our clocks are really timed by the stars. The master-clock is our earth, turning on its axis relative to the fixed stars."[58] Further, the American astronomer and director of the Griffith Observatory in Los Angeles, Ed Krupp, points out that "celestial aligned architecture and celestially timed ceremonies tell us our ancestors watched the sky accurately and systematically."[59] What we may most want to know is whether Egyptians also used the stars for long-term computations of time, such as the Sothic cycle of 1,460 years. Perhaps this is why the ancient Egyptians deliberately opted not to have the leap year—so that their slipping calendar could also work for long-term Sothic dates.

Providence would have it that a Roman citizen named Censorinus visited Egypt in the third century CE and witness the festivities in Alexandria that marked the start of a new Sothic cycle. This is what he reported: "The beginnings of these [Sothic] years are always reckoned from the first day of that month which is called by the Egyptians Thoth, which happened this year [239 CE] upon the 7th of the kalends of July [June 25]. For a hundred years ago from the present year [139 CE] the same fell upon the 12th of the kalends of August [July 21], on which day Canicula [Sirius] regularly rises in Egypt."[60]

To put it more simply, the Egyptian New Year's Day (1 Thoth of the Egyptian calendar) recoincided with the heliacal rising of Sirius in the year 139 CE.* Egypt was at that time a dominion of Rome and was ruled by Emperor Antonius Pius. This calendrical-astronomical event was clearly regarded as having great importance and was commemorated on a coin at Alexandria bearing the Greek word *A ION,* implying the end or start of an era. At any rate, this information provided modern chronolo-

---

*The altitude of Sirius is taken as 1 degree above horizon and that of the sun 9 degrees below horizon. Sirius would have had an azimuth of 109 degrees 16'.

gists with an anchor date from which they could easily work out the start of previous Sothic cycles by simply subtracting increments of 1,460 years from 139 CE. Thus we know that Sothic cycles began on 1321 BCE, 2781 BCE, 4241 BCE, and so forth. Yet do the Sothic cycles hark back ad infinitum, or is there a Year Zero, as in other calendrical systems?

Even though the ancient Egyptians were obsessed with the idea of eternity, they also believed in a beginning of a secular time they called Zep Tepi, literally, the First Time. The British Egyptologist Rundle T. Clark comes tantalizingly close to the very heart of ancient Egyptian cosmogony when he writes that all rituals and feasts, most of which were linked to the cycle of the year, were "a repetition of an event that took place at the beginning of the world."[61] According to Clark, "This epoch—*zep tepi*—'the First Time'—stretched from the first stirring of the High God in the Primeval Waters. . . . All proper myths relate events or manifestations of this epoch. Anything whose existence or authority had to be justified or explained must be referred to the 'First Time.' This was true for natural phenomena, rituals, royal insignia, the plans of temples, magical or medical formulae, the hieroglyphic system of writing, the calendar—the whole paraphernalia of the civilization . . . all that was good or efficacious was established on the principles laid down in the 'First Time'—which was, therefore, a golden age of absolute perfection . . ."[62]

The start of Sothic cycles, as we have seen, can be computed simply by moving backward or forward in increments of 1,460 years using Censorinus's anchor point of 139 CE. At the resulting years of Sothic cycles, the heliacal rising of Sirius coincided with New Year's Day (1 Thoth) of the calendar of ancient Egypt, but can we track these cycles back to Zep Tepi, the First Time . . . to the Year Zero of this calendar?

THE GREAT PYRAMID AND ZEP TEPI

In 1987, Robert Bauval sent a paper to the academic journal *Discussions In Egyptology* presenting a new and controversial theory on the Giza pyramids. The theory had been developed when, in 1983, Bauval was working in Saudi Arabia in the construction industry. One night while there, in the open desert, he made an unusual discovery involving the stars of Orion's belt and the Giza pyramids. While looking at the three stars of Orion's belt, it struck him that their pattern and also their position relative to the Milky Way uncannily resembled the pattern formed by the three pyramids of Giza and their position relative to the Nile. This curious similarity did not seem a coincidence, for not only did the ancient Pyramid Texts identify Orion with the god Osiris, who in turn was identified with the departed kings, but the ancient Egyptians also specified Orion as being in the celestial Duat.[63] The correlation between the three stars of Orion's belt and the three pyramids of Giza was striking, if only for one reason: Orion's belt is made up of two bright stars and a less bright third star. This last is slightly offset to the left of the extended alignment created by the two other stars, much the same way that the third, smaller pyramid is slightly offset from the other two.

A fact that adds to this correlation was discovered in 1964 by two academics from UCLA, the Egyptologist Alexander Badawi and the astronomer Virginia Trimble, who proved that a narrow shaft emanating southward and upward from the King's Chamber in the Great Pyramid had once pointed to Orion's belt in ca. 2500 BCE, the date traditionally ascribed to this building of this monument. Later, in 1990, Bauval published another article in *Discussions in Egyptology* showing that from the Queen's Chamber is another shaft that points to the star Sirius at that same date. In 1994, Bauval published *The Orion Mystery*, which presented his theory to the general public.*

The book, which has been the subject of numerous television documentaries, caused quite a stir at the time of its publiction and is still the subject of much controversy. More recently, in his book *The Egypt Code,* Bauval puts forward the final conclusion that the Giza pyramids may have been modeled on an image of Orion's belt not at the time of their

---

*The Orion Mystery was first published by Heinemann in 1994. It was a bestseller in the United Kingdom and was an international bestseller. It has been translated into more than twenty languages.

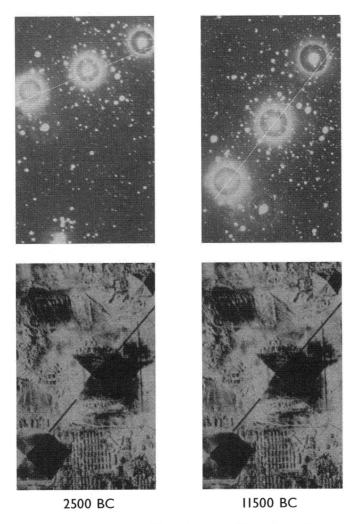

2500 BC   11500 BC

Figure 6.1. The pyramids of Giza and the stars of Orion's belt as they appeared in 2500 BCE and 11,500 BCE.

presumed construction in ca. 2500 BCE, but at a much earlier time, ca. 11,450 BCE. In other words, in deciphering the astronomy embedded in the design of the Giza pyramids, we can note the locking of two dates: 2500 BCE, which marks the time of construction, and ca. 11,500 BCE, which marks the significant time that might allude to the First Time—Zep Tepi. This is our reasoning: If today you observe from the location of Giza the star Sirius cross the meridian it will be at 43° altitude.

If you could see the same event in 2500 BC when the Great Pyramid was built, Sirius would have culminated at 39.5° altitude, which is where the south shaft of the Queen's Chamber was aimed at. Going even much further in time the altitude of Sirius would drop and drop until, at about 11,500 BC, Sirius would be just 1° altitude. Beyond this date Sirius would not been seen at all because it would not break above the horizon.

In appendix 1, we look in detail at the motion of Sirius and find that Giza was actually the place on Earth where Sirius went down to rest briefly exactly at the horizon at the lowest point of its twenty-six-thousand-year cycle, and that occurred basically in this same epoch, ca.12,280 BCE. Further, we find that the light of the Mother of All Pole Stars, Vega, shone down the subterranean passages at Giza and Dashur in the same epoch, 12,070 BCE. In appendix 1, we also review how the Orion's belt-to-pyramids layout dates are also in this same general epoch. It is now well accepted that in the Great Pyramid, the southern shaft of the Queen's Chamber marks the date of ca. 2500 BCE, around the construction date of the monument—but what other shaft elsewhere in the Great Pyramid marks Zep Tepi?

The internal design of the Great Pyramid has been the source of numerous theories, none of which have provided a satisfactory solution to the many questions it poses or solves the great mystery that has baffled generations of researchers. In spite of this, Egyptologists are nonetheless adamant that the Great Pyramid served a funerary purpose, and they point for evidence to the so-called King's Chamber and the empty and undecorated sarcophagus in this otherwise totally barren and totally uninscribed room. At first, this consensus appears convincing, but for the troublesome fact that there are two other chambers in the pyramid: the so-called Queen's Chamber, which lies some 21 meters (69 feet) beneath the King's Chamber, and also the so-called subterranean chamber that is 20 meters (66 feet) beneath the pyramid's base and cuts into the living rock. At a loss to explain why three sepulchre chambers would be needed for only one dead king, Egyptologists for a long time had assumed that the subterranean chamber and the Queen's

Chamber were abandoned and that the ancient architect had for some reason changed his design three times regarding where the burial chamber should be. Today, this abandonment theory has itself been abandoned. Most modern architects and construction engineers believe the entire monument was constructed according to a well-established plan, which was executed without any major alterations. There is, too, the nagging fact that no mummy or corpse was ever found in the Great Pyramid or, for that matter, in any other royal pyramid in Egypt. True, many pyramids contained empty sarcophagi, but this does not necessarily mean that these sarcophagi were meant for dead bodies. They could easily have served a ritual function rather a practical function as coffins. Perhaps the most convincing fact that the Great Pyramid was not a tomb—or at least, not only a tomb—is that its design contains detailed and accurate astronomical and mathematical data which, if properly understood and decoded, seem to suggest a completely different message than that claimed by Egyptologists.

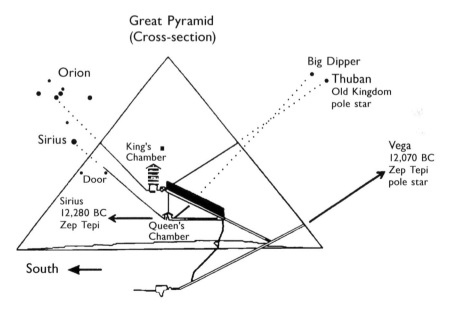

Figure 6.2. The Great Pyramid of Giza's subterranean passage and internal platform aligned to the North Star, Vega, and to Sirius at Zep Tepi. The star shafts built into the upper portions of the completed pyramid aligned to the same and related stars during the Old Kingdom fourth dynasty.

Returning to the question of the date of Zep Tepi and the internal design of the Great Pyramid, the fact that the southern shaft of the Queen's Chamber was aimed at Sirius in ca. 2500 BCE, when the star was at 39.5 degrees and was at essentially 0 degrees in the centuries around 12,200 BCE, when it rested on the horizon as seen from Giza, and the fact that the cycles of Sirius was used by the pyramid builders for both long-term and short-term calendric computations justifies a surmise that the horizontal passage leading to the Queen's Chamber was not intended to mark the 0-degree altitude of Sirius at its southern culmination. If the Great Pyramid was designed to symbolize one thing, it is, without question, the sky vault—for the perimeter of the pyramid's square base relative to its height represents the same ratio as the circumference of a circle to its radius. We are to think of the Great Pyramid, therefore, not as a pyramid at all, but as a symbolic hemisphere or as a reduced model of the hemispherical sky vault above it.

The southern shaft in the Queen's Chamber invites us to consider two altitudes of the star Sirius, one at 39.5 degrees and the other at 0 degrees, thus determining two dates: 2500 BCE, which is probably the actual construction date of the pyramid, and 12,000 BCE, which represents a date in the remote past that has to do with the beginning or first time of the ancient Egyptians' history defined with calendrical computations of the Sothic cycle and precession cycle of the star Sirius. But is there confirming evidence of such long-term date reckoning in Egyptian pyramid designs?

THE GREAT WALL OF TIME

In *The Egypt Code,* we demonstrated that evidence of both the Sothic cycle and precession involving the star Sirius could be found in the elaborate design of the step pyramid complex of King Djoser at Saqqara or, more precisely, in the design of the gigantic boundary wall that surrounds the complex (see figure 6.4 on page 248). The step pyramid complex is dated to ca. 2650 BCE and is said to be the very first major

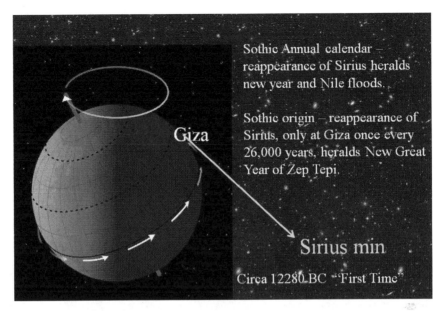

Sothic Annual calendar –
reappearance of Sirius heralds
new year and Nile floods.

Sothic origin – reappearance of
Sirius, only at Giza once every
26,000 years, heralds New Great
Year of Zep Tepi.

Giza

Sirius min

Circa 12280 BC "First Time"

Figure 6.3. Sirius culminated south so that it just met the horizon—
as seen from the latitude of the Great Pyramid at Giza.

architectural complex of ancient Egypt and, according to many, the oldest in the whole world. It is one of those curious facts of history that we actually know the name and function of the architect who was responsible for its design: his name was Imhotep and he was vizier to King Djoser. According to professor I. E. S. Edwards, "Imhotep's title 'Chief of the Observers,' which became the regular title of the high priest of Heliopolis, may itself suggest an occupation connected with astral, rather than solar observation. . . . It is significant that the high priest of the centre of the sun-cult at Heliopolis bore the title 'Chief of the Astronomers' and was represented wearing a mantle adorned with stars."[64]

In the recently built museum at the reception area at Saqqara, Imhotep is given a place of honor, and there are several statues representing this Leonardo da Vinci of the ancient world. His name, titles, and functions are attested on the pedestal of a statue of King Djoser. As we have seen, it seems certain that a calendar based on the heliacal rising of Sirius was used since earliest time in Egypt and was referred

Figure 6.4. Djoser step pyramid complex and Saqqara, showing the massive wall enclosing the compound. Inset: Detail of the reconstructed portion of the paneled wall around the main entrance.

to sometimes as the Sothic calendar. It also seems certain that this calendar was eventually formally adopted by the Heliopolitan priests, who pinned it to their own newly devised civil calendar, when a Sothic cycle was made to begin with the New Year's Day of 1 Thoth. It is thus quite possible that it was Imhotep who introduced the Sothic calendar based on the cycles of Sirius, or, as we now strongly suspect, merely formalized it from an earlier calendar that was already in place with the prehistoric star people of Nabta Playa. At any rate, much evidence supports the view that a Sothic calendar ran parallel to a civil calendar so that they both resynchronized every 1,460 years—that is, every Sothic cycle. According to the science historian Gerald J. Whitrow "there is reason to associate this with the minister of king Djoser of the Third Dynasty known as Imhotep."[65] Bearing this in mind and also recalling that Imhotep was the architect of the very first pyramid complex in Egypt, we would expect to find some indication of the Sothic cycle in the design of his masterpiece, the step pyramid complex at Saqqara.

In *The Egypt Code,* we discuss at length the design of the step pyramid complex and the intense astronomical and calendrical quality that it exhibits. Intriguing is a very curious architectural feature called a serdab that is linked to the north face of the step pyramid itself. The serdab consists of a small stone cubicle that is inclined against the slope of the lowest tier of the step pyramid at an angle of about 15 degrees and oriented about 4.5 degrees east of due north. The peculiarity of this cubicle is that inside it was a seated statue of King Djoser, which faces north and seems to look out of the cubicle through two peepholes cut into its north wall. The consensus among Egyptologists today is that the statue was meant to be gazing into the circumpolar region of the sky, where could be found the important constellation of the Big Dipper. Our calculations showed that circa 2650 BCE, when the step pyramid was constructed, the exact spot in the sky on which the gaze of the statue of Djoser seems transfixed was occupied once every twenty-four hours by the star Alkaid, the lowest star in the Big Dipper, which marked the hoof of the Bull's Thigh asterism of the ancient Egyptians. Perhaps the reason behind this alignment was to mark the rising time of the star Sirius in the east. In other words, precisely when the hoof star Alkaid aligned itself with the direction of gaze of the statue in the north, the star Sirius would be seen rising in the east. It is interesting to consider again, as we did in chapter 4, why Imhotep chose to orient Djoser's statue to gaze at the hoof star, Alkaid, instead of the brighter, upper thigh star Dubhe.

The tracking of the rising of Sirius with the Big Dipper would come naturally to an avid stargazer living in Egypt at the time of Imhotep, mainly because an interesting simultaneous alignment took place each day between the culmination of Sirius on the south meridian and the culmination of the brightest star in the Big Dipper, Dubhe, on the north meridian. We will recall from chapter 4 that two important stars tracked by the prehistoric stargazers of Nabta Playa were Dubhe and Sirius. Once such a conjunction is noticed, a person such as Imhotep, who was adept in geometry and astronomy, would realize very quickly that the perpetual circular trajectory of the Big Dipper around the north celestial pole could be used as a sort of dial to mark the rising, culmination, and setting of the star Sirius.

The Big Dipper contains seven bright stars, with the two brightest being Dubhe and Alkaid. These stars appear to revolve around a fixed point, the north celestial pole, in one full day—in other words, they travel in a circular, counterclockwise direction, a bit like the hand of a clock moving backward for twelve hours. If we observe the specific constellations night after night, month after month, and year after year, their cycles eventually become second nature to us and become ingrained in our memory. What Imhotep could not help but notice was that when Sirius rose in the east, the star Alkaid was at about 4.5 degrees east of the meridian. The important pieces for our arugument that Imhotep had to note were (1) when the star Dubhe was at north meridian, the star Sirius was at south meridian, and (2) when the star Alkaid was about 4.5 degrees east of north (and at altitude 15 degrees—the line of sight of Djoser's statue in the small stone cubicle at Saqqara), the star Sirius was rising in the east. If Imhotep was to have access to earlier observations such as, say, those made at Elephantine centuries before or even earlier ones made at Nabta Playa, he would have realized that the position of the star Sirius had changed due to the precession. As we saw in chapter 4, this may explain why Imhotep directed the serdab toward Alkaid rather than to Dubhe. Imhotep, as the designer of the first major architectural complex of Old Kingdom Egypt, may have been paying homage to his distant ancestors who originated this astral ritual at Nabta Playa when the hoof star Alkaid moved into place to initiate the Bull's Thigh constellation as the circumpolar star group that would herald the rise of Sirius. Had he known of an earlier, 365-day calendar, Imhotep would also have realized that New Year's Day had drifted from the heliacal rising of Sirius at the rate of about one day every four years and would synchronize again about every 1,460 years (every Sothic cycle). In addition, the fact that a Sothic cycle had begun in Imhotep's lifetime or just before would certainly have induced him to commemorate this event in his great architectural design of the step pyramid complex. It should come as no surprise, then, that the number 1,460, as we will see, comes up in the design of the massive boundary wall that surrounds the step pyramid complex.

The step pyramid complex of Djoser was named Horus Is the Star at the Head of the Sky,[66] which alone implies some cosmic function related to the principal or brightest star in the sky, which can be only Sirius. This is confirmed by the fact that the god Horus, in very early times, was also identified with this star.[67] The most impressive feature of the step pyramid complex other than the pyramid itself is the huge 10-meter-high (33-feet-high) boundary wall that once enclosed the entire complex. It is a rectangle 550 meters (1,804 feet) long and 220 meters (722 feet) wide, and even today, it would be considered a masterpiece of architecture. Rather than simply making the wall with a smooth face, Imhotep incorporated in its design an elaborate system of recesses and protrusions, massive bastions and false doors. There are no less than 192 recesses and protrusions, 14 false doors, 4 corner bastions, and a main monumental entrance. On all of these features there are vertical panels, each some 20 centimeters (8 inches) wide, 3 centimeters (about 1 inch) deep, and several meters high, some cut into the wall, others flush with it. The west wall contains 1,461 panels and the east side contains 1,458 or 1,459 panels. The south side and north sides each contain 732 panels, thus a total of 366 × 4 = 1,464. These numbers, to say the least, speak of calendrical meaning that is specifically related to Sirius, which is very near the Sothic Cycle duration (1460-1), and 366 imply the sidereal year* Let us see why.

---

*The number of days that a star takes to return to the same point, usually measure at the meridian transit. The rising of a star, such as Sirius, occurs about 4 minutes longer than sunrise each day, thus it "looses" 1 day in the solar year).

Sufi Tradition and the Wall

We can note that the design of this massive temple complex enclosure recalls the words of one of our teachers of the ancient medita-
tion technique of *sufi zikr*: the design of all Persian rugs harks back
to a very ancient spiritual tradition. If we look at the design of any
Persian rug, it always consists of a gardenlike complex enclosed by a
very elaborate wall with many recesses and complex meanderings.
This design, the sufi said, is a representation of the primordial garden
enclosed by a wall with one hundred twenty-five thousand doors—
and each door, it is said, represents a new way to enter the garden,
which opens up each time another human becomes fully enlightened
(through sufi or any other yogic practice). The sufi tradition, it is
claimed, originates from extremely ancient times. It is interesting to
speculate that the genius-priest Imhotep designed the giant Djoser
complex enclosure wall as astronomical-calendrical and developmen-
tal-spiritual—thus symbolizing the connection among humans, mind,
and cosmos on a both a subtle level and in enormous monumental
architecture that exists out in plain sight.

First, and most obviously, we consider the number 1,461. As we've
noted, the solar year is not exactly 365 days, but has an extra 0.242
day or, approximately, an extra quarter day (as does the Julian year we
use today—which is exactly 365.25 years). A peculiarity of the star
Sirius, which was apparently known to the ancient Egyptians, was that
its yearly cycle was nearly 365¼ days during Old Kingdom times, thus
making a Sothic cycle of 365¼ × 4 = 1,461,[68] the same length as the
solar-year return cycle and also the number of panels on the west side of
the boundary wall of the step pyramid complex.[69]

What, however, of the east wall of the step pyramid complex, which
has 1,458 or 1,459 panels, and the north and south walls, which each
have 732 panels? The answer emerges if we look in more detail at Sothic

cycles. Many historians of astronomy and Egyptian chronologists have often pointed out that the length of the true astronomical Sothic cycle for the heliacal rising of Sirius to return to the exact point in the sidereal year varies slightly, and, according to the British astronomer M. F. Ingham, it ranged during dynastic Egyptian times from 1,450 years to 1,460 years.[70] In appendix 2, we see the nature of Sothic cycles and calculate the length of the Sothic cycles in Old Kingdom times, independently testing Ingham's values by using a slightly different method: we set the year 2781 BCE, the day of summer solstice, as the starting point for a Sothic cycle and to constrain a definition for heliacal rising of Sirius. We then find that the Sothic cycle immediately preceding 2781 BCE was 1,459 Egyptian civil calendar years (1,458 Julian years), and the Sothic cycle starting at 2781 BCE was 1,457 Egyptian civil calendar years. Both those values essentially agree with Ingham's calculations. We conclude, then, that the east wall represents the exact Sothic cycle duration up to the design and construction of the complex, which itself commemorates or inaugurates the correspondence of the heliacal rising of Sirius with the summer solstice (an event that happens only once every twenty-six thousand years). Thus the 1,461-panel wall may reflect a standardized or general public knowledge cycle, and the 1,459–panel wall could reflect the esoteric knowledge of the exact natural cycle known only to initiates such as Imhotep.

Was the Calendar Secret?

Mathematician James Lowdermilk argues that there is evidence that an esoteric or secret tradition did exist:

> Evidence of knowledge of the workings of the calendar being held secret is also found in the Reisner papyrus, ca.1900 BC. If the Egyptian calendar year of 365 days is 10/39ths of a day short of a sidereal year, then it takes $39 \div 10 = 3.9$ years for the calendar to lose one day to the sidereal year, not exactly 4 calendar years. In the Reisner papyrus, a hired scribe wrote the approximation $39 \div 10 = 4$ even though

elsewhere in the papyrus he has correctly worked the problems 30 ÷ 10 and 9 ÷ 10, which when added together give the correct value of 39÷10, proving his ability (Gillings 1972: 221). Apparently the author of the Reisner papyrus knew or was told that the calculation 39 ÷ 10 was not to be performed in such a profane location as the official registers of a dockyard workshop. Furthermore, when the geographer Strabo (second century CE), wrote of Plato's and Eudoxus' studies in Egypt in the 4th century BC, he tells us that the Egyptian priests "did teach them the fractions of the day and the night which, running over and above the 365 days, fill out the time of the true year" (Strabo, Geography, p. 83–5). These priests understood that the "true year" contains 10/39ths of a day more than the 365-day calendar year they used, but they were "secretive and slow to impart" this knowledge." From, "Unit Fractions: Inception and Use," The Ostracon, Journal of the Egyptian Study Society, Vol.14, No.2, Summer, 2003. (Note that 365 days plus 10/39ths day gives the length of the sidereal day to within 4 seconds, whereas the crude approximation 365 days plus 1/4th day is off by more than 9 minutes).

The difference, then, of two years represented on the walls progressing in time from east to west could also reflect the changing Sothic cycle—the next one will be two years shorter. Further, the difference between the east and west wall representations, two years, appears to be reflected in the north and south walls, each of which has 732 panels. Two years equal 730 solar days or 732 sidereal days.*

Egyptologists agree that Imhotep lived in the reign of King Djoser during the third dynasty, which, they say, began in the year 2630 BCE.

---

*A sidereal day is the time it takes Earth to complete one rotation relative to the vernal equinox, which is essentially one full rotation with respect to the stars (hence the word *sidereal*). It is four minutes shorter than a solar day, which is a full rotation of Earth with respect to the sun. Thus there is one extra sidereal day in a standard solar year of 365 days, as we can see, because one solar-day rotation is taken up by Earth moving around the sun in one year.

They openly admit, however, that a margin of error of at least one hundred fifty years must be allowed for the early dynasties, thus placing Imhotep as living anytime between 2780 and 2480 BCE.[71] The date 2780 BCE, which could well have been the start of Djoser's reign, now also rings a bell, for it was the year when the summer solstice coincided with the heliacal rising of Sirius and also when, most chronologists strongly suspect, the official civil calendar was set in motion.[72] Therefore, we see that both the calculated value of 1,461 years and the actual value of 1,459 years of the Sothic cycle (which is a combination of the solar and stellar cycles) are expressed on the east and west sides of the boundary wall. Further, the precise difference between these two durations is expressed by the walls that connect them in terms of the number of sidereal days (or star days), which also is a combination of solar and stellar times. Finally, the whole step pyramid complex and the small stone cubicle/serdab are aligned with the Big Dipper to mark the reappearance of Sirius in the east at the one time in twenty-six thousand years that this occurs on summer solstice. All of these facts taken together cannot be a coincidence. The entire complex appears to announce the long-term cosmic cycles of Sirius—how they are measured and predicted and connected to the human-made cycles of the civil calendar, all constructed around the very special time when heliacal reappearance of Sirius coincided with the summer solstice. Of course, this interpretation addresses not only the elegant calendar and cosmic meanings of the wall panel design, but also the reason why the Step Pyramid complex was built at that precise time.

If we accept that Imhotep knew not only that an approximation to the Sothic cycle was 1,461 Egyptian civil years, but also the precise duration of the previous Sothic cycle and that this cycle is a combination of solar and sidereal motions, and if we also accept that he had a concept of the difference between the sidereal day and the solar day, then it is highly likely that he was informed by careful observations going back at least one Sothic cycle—that is, back to 4241 BCE, to the period of heavy activity at Nabta Playa.

OTHER EVIDENCE OF THE
LONG-TERM TRACKING OF SIRIUS

We have seen that as early as 3200 BCE, the star Sirius was tracked at Elephantine with the changing axes of the multitiered temple of Satis. Yet there are shrines in Egypt other than the step pyramid complex and the Giza pyramid complex that also tracked this special star.

In the area of ancient Thebes (modern Luxor) are the remains of a small temple commonly known as Thoth Hill. The temple was built on a high point in the Theban hills overlooking the Nile Valley below, with a clear view of the eastern horizon. Discovered by George Sweinfurth in 1904 and studied by Sir Flinders Petrie in 1909, the temple has been confirmed to have been built under the reign of King Mentuhotep of the eleventh dynasty. Extensive investigations between 1995 and 1998 by a Hungarian team from Eotvos Lorand University, under the directorship of Dr. Gyozo Voros, has led to the conclusion that this temple was sacred to the star Sirius. The structure stands on a terraced platform facing east. After excavating the foundations, the Hungarian team found that this eleventh-dynasty temple was actually built on top of the ruins of an archaic-period temple dating from probably ca. 3000–3200 BCE, which had a similar floor plan but had an axis 2 degrees farther south: "The Hungarian team that excavated these structures believes this difference may be attributed to the shift in astronomical alignments over the intervening centuries. Their research indicates that the later brick temple was aligned to Sirius. In the archaic period the same star would have appeared just over 2 degrees further south in the eastern sky—exactly the difference visible in the orientation of the earlier building. Thus, rather than simply follow the physical orientation of the earlier sacred structure, the Middle Kingdom architects had carefully adjusted the temple's orientation in order to align the new building once more precisely to Sirius . . ."[73]

We can recall from chapter 2 that the name of the pharaoh Mentuhotep (ca. 2010 BCE) was found in the inscriptions at Jebel Uwainat in the Egyptian Sahara, which were discovered by Mark Borda and Mahmoud Marai in 2007. If the Black prehistoric people of Nabta Playa were the same people that once occupied Uwainat, and if these people came to the Nile Valley in ca. 3200 BCE and brought along their astronomical knowledge of tracking the stars, especially Sirius, then it is not at all surprising to us now to find that King Mentuhotep knew of an archaic temple at Thebes, which was aligned with Sirius and, consequently, that he built his own temple above it and knew that its axis had to be 2 degrees farther north.

The whole historical puzzle seems slowly to be taking shape, revealing a remarkable scenario which flows from the astronomical alignments of Nabta Playa as mentioned in the 1998 *Nature* letter of Malville and Wendorf. Before we look at possible conclusions, however, let us examine further evidence that the tradition of the long-term tracking of the star Sirius persisted throughout the whole of pharaonic civilization until its closure in ca. 30 BCE, when it fell under the dominion of Rome.

THOSE WHO FOLLOWED THE SUN

One of the greatest and most magnificent temples of ancient Egypt is the temple of Hathor at Dendera, located on the west side of the Nile near the modern town of Qena, some 60 kilometers (37 miles) north of Luxor. The temple complex stands at the edge of the desert and is so well preserved that from a short distance, it looks as though it was built only a few years ago. In fact, the temple is more than two thousand years old, and its origins may even hark back to earliest times.

The cult of the cow goddess Hathor goes back to the archaic period and ranked very high in the Egyptian religion. Evidence of her cult has been detected from the very early dynasties, and many Egyptologists believe that it was even much older than this. Her name, Hat-Hor, literally means House of Horus* [74]

As such, Hathor was very closely associated with the goddess Isis, mother of Horus. Indeed, so closely identified with each other were

---

*The word *Hwt* ('Hat') . . . was used in the New Kingdom with the meaning "Temple."

these two goddesses that in Ptolemaic times, when the extant temple at Dendera was built, their names were often fused or interchangeable.[75] At Dendera there are tombs that date to the first dynasties, indicating that the site was sacred in very remote, perhaps even prehistoric, times. The temple we see today, however, was founded by Ptolemy XII Auletes in 54 BCE. It is known with certainty that at the same place stood an older temple built under Tuthmoses III in ca.1450 BCE. In additon, there are inscriptions at Dendera that refer to Pepi I of the sixth dynasty, ca. 2350 BCE. More intriguing still, there are inscriptions in a crypt that refer to the Shemsu-Hor or Followers of Horus,[76] whom the pharaohs regarded as their remote ancestors, although Egyptologists tend to consider these as mythical ancestors.[77] One of these inscriptions actually claims that the original blueprint of the temple was provided by the Shemsu-Hor and was later preserved on the temple walls by Pepi I: "King Tuthmoses III has caused this building to be erected in memory of his mother, the goddess Hathor, the Lady of Dendera, the Eye of the Sun, the Heavenly Queen of the Gods. The ground plan was found in the city of Dendera, in archaic drawing on a leather roll of the time of the Shemsu-Hor [Followers of Horus]; it was [also] found in the interior of a brick wall in the south side of the temple in the reign of king Pepi."[78]

According to the so-called Royal Papyrus of Turin, also known as the Turin Canon, Egypt was ruled in prehistoric times by the Shemsu-Hor kings (and Shemsu-Hor is commonly translated as the Followers of Horus). Horus was the solar deity par excellence of the Egyptians; he personified the sun, especially when it rose on the horizon. In this specific role, he was known as Hor-Akhti, Horus of the Horizon, and later, when the cult of Ra, the Heliopolitan sun god, came to power in the fourth dynasty, the two solar deities were united as Ra-Hor-Akhti—literally, Sun God Horus of the Horizon. This union was specific to the morning sun, leading Egyptologists such as Richard Wilkinson to assert that when Ra was "coalesced" with the more primitive Hor-Akhti, this caused the combined deities to become "Ra-Horakhti as the morning sun."[79]

From the many mentions of Hor-Akhti in the Pyramid Texts and other ancient texts, it is clear that the time at which this sun disk was most observed and venerated was not merely at sunrise, but especially at sunrise at summer solstice. This is confirmed in the Pyramid Texts, which say that Horakhti is in the "eastern side of the sky . . . the place where the gods are born [that is, the place where they rise]."[80] It was at the summer solstice, as we have already seen, that the flood season began. The very existence of Egypt depended on the flood—its agriculture, its ecology, and the survival of its people. It is therefore totally understandable that the sunrise at summer solstice would have a very special meaning to the ancient Egyptians—as it had thousands of years before to the prehistoric people of Nabta Playa, who lived by the monsoon rains. If the floodwaters were too low or worse, failed to come, strife and eventually famine would follow. The flood was, quite literally, the jugular vein of Egypt. Nothing frightened the pharaohs more than the possibility that the gods would fail to bring forth the flood. The early warning signal came from Elephantine, where the nilometer was carefully monitored at the time of the summer solstice. As Egyptologists Peter Shaw and Paul Nicholson explain: "Egypt's agricultural prosperity depended on the annual inundation of the Nile. For crops to flourish it was desirable that the Nile should rise about eight meters [26 feet] above a zero point at the first cataract near Aswan. A rise of only seven meters [23 feet] would produce a lean year, while six meters [20 feet] would lead to famine."[81]

There was, however, another factor that required careful observation: the heliacal rising of Sirius, which also occurred around the time of the summer solstice.*

The ancient astronomer-priests paid avid attention to the celestial events that took place at dawn at this important time of year, and they waited for the heliacal rising of Sirius. We get a glimpse of the impor-

---

*The heliacal reappearance of Sirius occurred before the day of summer solstice in early dynastic times, before about 2600 BCE, and it occurred after summer solstice in later years up to today.

tance of this event—the conjunction of the summer solstice, the heliacal rising of Sirius and the summer solstice—in some passages of the Pyramid Texts:

> The reed-floats of the sky are set in place for sungod *Ra* that he may cross on them to the horizon; the reed-floats are set in place for *Horakhti* that he may cross on them to *Ra*; the reed-floats of the sky are set in place for me that I may cross on them to *Ra*; the reed-floats are set in place for me that I may cross on them to *Horakhti* and to *Ra*. The Fields of Rushes are filled [with water] and I ferry across on the Winding Waterway; I [the Osiris-king] am ferried over to the eastern side of the horizon, I am ferried over to the eastern side of the sky, my sister is Sothis [Sirius] . . .[82]

> The king will be the companion of *Horakhti* and the king's hand will be held in the sky among the followers of the Sun god *Ra*. The fields are content, the irrigation ditches are flooded for this king today . . . receive this pure water of yours which issues from Elephantine . . . O King, your cool water is the Great Flood . . . [83]

> The reed-floats of the sky are set in place for me that I may cross to the horizon, to *Ra* and to *Horakhti*. The nurse-canal is open, and the Winding Waterway is flooded, that I may be ferried over to the eastern side of the sky, to the place where the gods were born . . . [84]

The above quotes clearly show the conjunction of the start of the Nile's flood and the appearance of Sothis (Sirius). Although the summer solstice is not specifically mentioned, it is definitely implied, because, of course, both the "birth" (rising) of Sirius and the start of the flood occurred at that time of year when the sun rose to its extreme northern position. Another passage in the Pyramid Texts does imply this by having the departed king say: "I ferry across [the river Nile] that I may stand on the eastern side of the sky when the Sungod Ra is in his northern region . . . [85]

With all this textual, astronomical, and archaeological evidence, we must include the Shemsu-Hor, Those Who Followed the Sun—those ancestral kings—as being the people who followed the direction of the summer solstice sunrise in ca. 3200 BCE . . . namely the prehistoric Black people of Nabta Playa (see chapter 5). Further, it could also be the Shemsu-Hor who brought with them an astronomical plan drawn on a leather roll, which was used for the layout of the temple of the cowgoddess Hathor. In spite of the obstinacy of Egyptologists who continue to see the Shemsu-Hor as mythical kings, the British Egyptologist Henri Frankfort says this of the Shemsu-Hor:

> The designation [Shemsu-Hor/Followers of Horus] was reserved for rulers of the distant past. The texts leave no doubt that the term referred to earlier kings. An inscription of a king Ranofer, just before the Middle Kingdom, contains the phrase "in the time of your forefathers, the kings, Followers of Horus [Shemsu-Hor]." Texts of Tuthmosis I and Tuthmosis III refer to them in the same manner. The first mentions fame the like of which was not "seen in the annals of the ancestors since the Followers of Horus"; the other states that, in rebuilding a temple, an old plan was used and proceeds: "The great plan was found in Denderah in old delineations written upon leather of animal skin of the time of the Followers of Horus." From these quotations it appears that "Followers of Horus" is a vague designation for the kings of a distant past. Hence the Turin Papyrus places them before the first historical king . . .[86]

From the Turin Papyrus we can work out that the Shemsu-Hor ruled for 13,420 years before the first historical pharaoh, who was identified as Menes. Egyptologists place the reign of Menes at about 3000 BCE. This means that the start of the Shemsu-Hor lineage was at about 16,420 BCE—which can be rounded to 16,500 BCE. Could it be a coincidence that this very date of 16,500 BCE is found in the astronomy of the Calendar Circle at Nabta Playa, as we have see in chapter 4.[87]

We now return to the alleged plans for the temple of the cow goddess Hathor at Dendera and the claim that the temple's original plans were from the time of the Shemsu-Hor. If we assume that the original plans were from Nabta Playa, then we would expect to find the same kind of astronomy at Dendera that was dominant at Nabta Playa. This, unquestionably, is the astronomy defined by the focal point of the ceremonial complex at Nabta Playa, CSA, which contained the cow stone. We recall that from CSA there emanate a series of megalithic lines toward the star Dubhe in the north and a series of lines toward the east, directed toward the rising of Sirius.

Could the same be found at Dendera?

HATHOR, ISIS, THE BIG DIPPER, AND SIRIUS

The entrance to the temple of the cow goddess Hathor at Dendera faces north. The huge gate is flanked by six imposing columns whose four-sided capitals are decorated with faces of Hathor, here a woman's face with cow's ears. Beyond the entrance is the hypostyle hall with a further eighteen similar columns, thus equaling a total of twenty-four columns. The whole temple is a maze of rooms, chapels, corridors, underground crypts, and stairs leading to the roof. On the roof, in one of the chapels, was found the famous Zodiac of Dendera, which we encountered in chapter 1, and which is now at the Louvre Museum in Paris.[88]

The Zodiac of Dendera

The main Hathor temple is famous for having housed the so-called round Zodiac of Dendera (as well as a lesser known rectangular zodiac located on the ceiling of the first hypostyle hall). The round Zodiac is really more a *planisphere*, or sky map, that shows the whole celestial landscape from the perspective of having the north celestial pole near its center. The actual zodiac, which was fixed on the ceiling of a chapel on the upper floor of the temple, is made from the twelve familiar Babylonian-Greek astrological signs, which are scattered in a rough loop around the celestial pole. In a larger loop are scattered the thirty-six decans of ancient Egypt, which were used for timekeeping and rebirth rites (because they contain Orion and Sirius). It is worth reminding ourselves that the decans were known from at least the pyramid age, which suggests that the Dendera planisphere has incorporated elements of great antiquity. Here, Orion-Osiris is represented by a striding man who wears the royal crown, and Sirius-Isis is shown as a recumbent cow with a five-pointed star above her horns. Interestingly, behind the Isis-Sirius cow is the figure of a woman holding a bow and arrow, almost certainly Satis of Elephantine, whom, as we have already seen, was also identified with Sirius (particularly with its heliacal rising and the Nile flood). Very near the center of the zodiac is the figure of a small jackal on what looks like a hoe. To its left is a large standing hippopotamus that represents the constellation Draconis, and to its right is the familiar bull's thigh that represents the Big Dipper. These last two constellations, as we have already seen, can be traced back to the pyramid age, again giving the Dendera planisphere links to the distant past.

The rounded planisphere that is seen today at Dendera is not the original one but a facsimile made in the 1920s. The original was taken to France after the Napoleonic invasion of Egypt in 1798, and it is now displayed at the Louvre Museum in Paris. Books and articles abound on the meaning and date of the planisphere of Dendera. It is well outside the scope of this investigation to review them all, but there is little doubt that the planisphere dates from the time when the temple was built—ca. 54 BCE. It is much less clear whether the planisphere represents the sky at that time or, as some have suggested, a much older sky. In other words, we may wonder if the Dendera planisphere is a copy of a much older one on which was incorporated the Babylonian-Greek astrological signs. If this is the case, then there is no question that this artifact is a symbol of the precession of the equinoxes, which sees the astrological signs transit the east-west axis of the planisphere in a neverending cycle of twenty-six thousand years. The first scholar to suggest that this indeed was the case was the French astronomer Jean-Batiste Biot, who argued that a careful study of the position of the constellations and planets on the Dendera planisphere indicates a much older sky and, by extension, knowledge of the precession. Such ideas are usually vehemently rejected by Egyptologists and historians of science.

Outside the temple on its west side are a series of *mammisi,* or "birth houses," built in Roman times, And farther still along the west side of the temple is a deep, artificial sacred lake, which is now dry and has palm trees growing in it. At the back of the temple is a small chapel known as the Birth Place of Isis, sometimes also called the temple of Isis.

This temple of Isis has its outer area aligned toward the east and its inner area aligned toward the north and parallel to the axis of the main temple of Hathor. The distinct impression it conveys is that observations toward east and north were carried out simultaneously. An inscription at the temple reads: "She [the star of Isis—that is, Sirius] shines into her temple on New Year's Day, and she mingles her light with that of her Father Ra on the horizon."[89]

This inscription clearly refers to the heliacal rising of Sirius.[90] Yet we have seen how the conjunction of the heliacal rising of Sirius with New Year's Day can take place only at the start of a Sothic Cycle. With this in mind, the astronomer Edwin Krupp pointed out, "some traditions preserved at Dendera are thousands of years old,"[91] and he goes on to say that the inscriptions "describe metaphorically the heliacal rising of Sirius . . . certainly this astronomical event was watched from the roof of Dendera temple . . ."[92]

The British astronomer Sir Norman Lockyer* first noted that the

---

*Lockyer actually took *in situ* measurements and concluded that the alignment of the Isis temple was 18 degrees 30' south of east; this was also roughly the average of the measurements obtained earlier by Lepsius and Mariette.

axis of the temple of Isis at Dendera had an azimuth of 108 degrees 30', which corresponded to the azimuth of Sirius when the temple was constructed, ca. 54 BCE.[93]

Figure 6.5. Cow head, probably Hathor, on the so-called Marmer Palette, First Dynasty ca. 300 BC.

Thus Lockyer concluded correctly, "the temple of Isis at Dendera was built to watch it [Sirius]."[94] On the other hand, inscriptions at Dendera confirm that the axis of the main temple of Hathor was aligned northward, toward the Big Dipper, using the traditional stretching the cord ceremony. Lockyer determined that it was aligned 18 degrees 30' east of north. According to Lockyer, the temple was aligned to the star Dubhe in the Big Dipper.*

It seems clear that the axes of both temples—that of Hathor and of Isis—were aligned simultaneously, the latter toward Dubhe in the north and the former toward Sirius in the east. Inscriptions at Dendera suggest this simultaneous sighting and, furthermore, that the observations were made at dawn.

---

*Lockyer's calculations that the main temple was aligned to Dubhe (Alpha Ursa Major), the brightest star in the Bull's Thigh constellation, were based on very early dates which do not apply to the existing temple.

[East alignment toward Sirius]: The great goddess Seshat brings the writings that relate to your rising, O Hathor [as Sirius], and to the rising of Ra [the sun at dawn] . . . [95]

[North alignment toward Dubhe]: The king joyously stretches the cord, having cast his gaze towards the Big Dipper [*Meskhetiu*] and thus establishes the temple in the manner of ancient times.[96]

So disdainful are most Egyptologists at possible astronomical alignments of temples and pyramids that one senior Egyptologist, Cathleen A. Keller of UCLA, even openly admits that "sometimes I think that the more resistant Egyptologists are more afraid that connections *do* exist between the orientation and plans of Egyptian temples and the heavens, than they do not."[97]

The fact is that no Egyptologists approved of Sir Lockyer's finding at Dendera, at least not until nearly an entire century later. In 1992, the French Egyptologist Sylvie Cauville, who is well-known for her extensive work on the inscriptions of Dendera, undertook a detailed study of the astronomical orientation of the temple of Isis.[98] She, too, felt that its alignments had been greatly ignored and that no one had given much currency to the findings of Lockyer. Cauville boldly solicited the collaboration of an astronomer, Professor Eric Aubourg, to examine again the orientations at Dendera, especially those at the temple of Isis.

As we see it today, the temple of Isis was erected in 30 BCE under the directive of the Roman emperor Augustus (Octavian) Caesar. It was built over the foundations of a much older temple, which are clearly visible even now. Recent excavations by the French team showed that there had been several interventions at vastly different epochs. In the foundations of the Roman temple, blocks belonging to the penultimate native pharaoh, Nectanebo I (ca. 350 BCE), were found. In addition, it would appear that the Ptolemaic kings Ptolemy VI Philometor (ca.150 BCE) and Ptolemy X Alexander I (ca. 20 BCE) had carried out innovations here. More intriguingly, Cauville discovered reused stone blocks from the Ramesside period (ca. 1250 BCE), which bore the name of Prince Kha-emouaset, a son of Ramses II. Aubourg calculated that the azimuth of the Roman temple built in 30 BCE was 108 degrees 40', which matched the azimuth of Sirius. He then determined the azimuth of the lower temple to be 111 degrees 11', which corresponded to the orientation of the rising of Sirius in the epoch of Ramses II, ca. 1250 BCE. Here again, exactly as at the Satis temple at Elephantine and the Thoth Hill temple in Thebes, the ancient surveyors had responded to the effect of precession on the star Sirius by changing the orientation of the axes accordingly—very much as their ancestors had done at Nabta Playa several millennia before.

THE SUN TEMPLES OF
THE SUN KINGS

In the fourth dynasty, immediately after the reign of King Khufu, builder of the Great Pyramid, there seems to have been a sudden shift in religious ideologies. For reasons that have not yet been properly understood, a new solar cult seems to have been introduced to the pyramid builders. This seems to have happened in the reign of King Djedefre, a son of Khufu. For example, Khufu's immediate sucessors, Djedefre, Khafra, and Menkaure, incorporated the name of the sun god Re (or Ra) into their names. They also took on the title Son of Re. Indeed, according to Egyptologist Mark Lehner, "Djedefre is the first pharaoh to take the title 'Son of Re.'"[99]

Djedefre chose a promontory some 8 kilometers (5 miles) northwest of the Giza pyramids to build his own pyramid complex in a region known today as Abu Ruwash. No adequate explanation was given by any of his contemporaries as to why this king chose to move so far away from Giza. Not even Djedefre himself explained. Being thus at a loss for a good explanation, Egyptologists have invented a reason: they theorize that there was a family feud—that Djedefre quarreled with his father, Khufu, and was banished from Giza, thus inducing him to build his own complex at Abu Ruwash.*

Needless to say, there is not one shred of textual evidence to support this theory. With Carlo Bergmann's recent discovery, in 1999, of Djedefre Water Mountain in the Sahara, however, a new theory backed by evidence can now be proposed. An observer at Abu Ruwash who looked east at sunrise at the summer solstice would have witnessed the sun rising directly over the sun temple of Heliopolis,† a fact that can hardly be a coincidence in view of the circumstances surrounding Djedefre and the solar ideologies introduced in his reign. We can recall that the summer solstice marked the birth of Re, when the civil calendar was inaugurated, and could be a reason why Djedefre chose the title Son of Re.

We also now know, thanks to Carlo Bergmann, that during Djedefre's reign an expedition was sent into the deep Sahara and reached at least 80 kilometers (50 miles) south of Dakhla oasis and that the name of Djedefre is found inscribed on a mound called now Djedefre Water Mountain (DWM). We can recall from chapter 4 that when we witnessed the sunrise at DWM in April 2008, we noted that the mound was facing east, directly toward another flat-topped mound whose midpoint and ends marked the two solstices and the two equinoxes. The midpoint also had a small depression that seemed to have been cut by human hands, so that when the sun filled the depressed space, it formed the hieroglyphic sign "sun disk between two peaks" (⊙) which stood for "horizon" and "sunrise." Yet we are aware that this sign was not known before Djedefre's reign, but instead appeared in the fifth dynasty, which immediately followed his own.

---

*Evidence of an earlier presence at Abu Ruwash is attested by found objects that bear the names of kings of the first dynasty, Aha and Den.
†The azimuth of the rising sun at summer solstice was nearly 28 degrees north of east. If we allow for 2 degrees altitude for the full disk to be seen over a mound or obelisk from Abu Ruwash, the azimuth is nearer to 27 degrees north of east.

All Egyptologists agree that the fifth dynasty was intensely solar and had a very special connection to the sun temple at Heliopolis and its high priest. In the so-called Westcar Papyrus there is a story that tells us how a priestess named Rudjdjedet, the wife of the high priest of Heliopolis, gave birth to male triplets, whom she claimed had been conceived by the sun god Re himself.[100] All three were destined to become kings. Two of them, Sahure and Neferikare, incorporated the name Re into their own, and the third, Userkaf, made the unprecedented decision of commissioning a sun temple for himself, which was modeled on the great sun temple of Re at Heliopolis.[101] Five other sun kings that followed him also built for themselves sun temples near Userkaf's, at a place called Abu Ghorab.*[102]

So far, only two of the six sun temples—Userkaf's and Niussere's—have been found. The other four are known only by their names on contemporary inscriptions. The six are: The Stronghold of Re, The Offering Fields of Re, The Favorite Place of Re, The Offering Table of Re, The Delight of Re, and The Horizon of Re.

The Sun Temple
and Heliopolis

The connection of these temples to the sun god of Heliopolis was not merely spiritual, according to a new theory by British Egyptologist David Jeffreys about the exact location where they were placed relative to Heliopolis. In the 1990s, David Jeffreys conducted a survey in the area of Memphis on behalf of the Egypt Exploration Society. He noted that from the vantage point of the sun temples of Userkaf and Neussera, he had an unobstructed line of sight to Heliopolis, but if he moved just a bit farther south toward the Abusir pyramids, his view was cut off by the Muqattam hills. The sun temples were

---

*According to Miroslav Verner, the name Abusir derives from the Greek Busiris, which was taken from the ancient Egyptian Per Usir, meaning the Realm of Osiris.

built some distance north of their corresponding pyramids in order to have a direct line of sight toward Heliopolis. "A re-examination of the location of Pyramids whose owners claim or display a special association with the solar cult betrays a cluster pattern for which a political and religious explanation suggests itself. . . .The Giza pyramids could also be seen from Heliopolis. . . . It is therefore appropriate to ask, in a landscape as prospect-dominated as the Nile Valley, which sites and monuments were mutually visible and whether their respective locations, horizons and vistas are owed to something more than mere coincidence."[103]

Could it be that the discovery of the Water Mountain in the Sahara by Djedefre was the underlying cause that brought about the new solar religion to the pharaohs? Was this a natural temple in the desert, which was behind design of artificial temples at Abu Ruwash and Abusir? We can recall that on DWM there was also found prehistoric artwork next to the Egyptian hieroglyphic inscription of Djedefre's expedition. Were a prehistoric people still occupying the area when Djedefre's expedition arrived in ca. 2500 BCE? Were they the same people that also occupied Nabta Playa—the Black star people or cattle people that we encountered throughout the Egyptian Sahara, those followers of the sun and the star Sirius?

On the east face of Djedefre Water Mountain is a most telling inscription or, more specifically, a strange glyph that now, with all that we know of these very ancient star and cattle people, we can easily decipher. The glyph is composed of three rows of signs. The top row shows a five-pointed star, a cow's head, and a rope with a shape reminiscent of an ankh sign. The middle row depicts a flat plate with four lines extending vertically below it. The bottom row shows the same flat sign, but with only one line extending down crookedly, and with two prongs at its end and, on each side, zigzagging lines.

All the signs are recognizable Egyptian hieroglyphs.[104]

N14 = ⭐ star *(sba)*

F5 = 🐇 isdom, knowledge

V7 = 𓍵 rope *(shen)*

N4 = 𓏲 sky *(pet)* and rain (?)

N2 = 𓇯 lighting from the sky?

The two other glyphs in the bottom row, a lightning bolt and a human figure running or jumping, probably imply a rain-dance or storm-dance ritual.

Perhaps the entire glyph could thus read: "the star of wisdom which heralds in the rainy season/monsoon is greeted with joy." Perhaps Djedefre Water Mountain was a sort of natural sun temple to mark the summer solstice, and perhaps the star people or cattle people told the Egyptians of their knowledge and tradition, which linked the summer solstice, the monsoon, and the heliacal rising of the star Sirius.

There are so many water signs (〰) on Djedefre Water Mountain that we must recall heavy downpours (the monsoons). Yet climatologists are adamant that the monsoons stopped coming this far north around 5000 BCE—but how else could the Egyptians have known of these heavy downpours if not from a people who had actually experienced them? Further, could these people have traveled such a vast distance—from Nabta Playa to Djedefre Water Mountain, which, as the crow flies, is 360 kilometers (224 miles)?

In chapter 2, we briefly saw that in 2006 the Sahara anthropologists Stefan Kröpelin and Rudolph Kuper discovered another water mountain located 700 kilometers (435 miles) south of Nabta Playa, within Sudan, just west of a place called Dongola. The water mountain, which Kröpelin and Kuper described as a rock shelter, very much resembles Djedefre Water Mountain. Kröpelin and Kuper called the location Gala El Sheikh, and apparently it will soon be part of a protected national park. Also found were many petroglyphs—and, amazingly, there was the same water emblem as the one found by Bergmann at Djedefre Water Mountain (the slightly bulging rectangle with two peaks and within it zigzag lines).[105]

Unlike Bergmann's site, however, at Gala El Sheikh there were no ancient Egyptian hieroglyphs or drawings, suggesting that not only was the site of prehistoric origin, but also that the people who once occupied this place had cultural connections to those who once occupied the region near Dakhla oasis. If this was so, then both were clearly also connected to the Nabta Playa people, for that site lies directly in the middle of a trail that could have joined Gala El Sheikh and Djedefre Water Mountain. As Carlo Bergmann strongly suspected about these mysterious water emblems, a thorough study of them, as well as further explorations in the Egyptian Sahara and along the possible trail that leads to northwest Chad and the Ennedi Mountains, may prove that a vast network of communication existed in prehistoric times among Black sub-Saharan Africans, and this eventually led them to migrate into the Nile Valley, where they, with their millennia-old knowledge of astronomy, husbandry, and even perhaps basic writing and a religious system, hastened the civilization which we call Egyptian. Much work remains to be done, but the evidence is convincing that the pharaohs were the descendants of these Black prehistoric people from the Egyptian Sahara, and that the pharaohs knew about these people even in early dynastic times.

For more than twenty-five years, we have been on the quest for the origins of the ancient Egyptian civilization, yet we never suspected that it would be such a thrilling and rewarding intellectual adventure. We have tried our very best to pass the barrage of entrenched interests and to tell the general public of the many scattered clues that we have found in the alignments of pyramids and temples, all of which have lead us to piece a giant historical puzzle. Slowly but surely, a completely new picture of our past emerges, revealing a lost and forgotten world, which extended from the Nile to the borders of Sudan and Chad ,and which told a very different story of the origins of ancient Egypt—a tale much more thrilling than that which any Egyptologist or anthropologist had previously led us to believe. We now can look with even greater awe at the wonderful legacy of ancient Egypt—especially, at those imposing pyramids and temples—and see in them a very ancient message that was written in the stars, a message that directed us to faraway places in the desert and to a time when hardy and intelligent black-skinned men planted a seed that grew in the Nile Valley to give rise to a wonderful civilization. We know that from now on, Egypt will never be the same for us, for when a Black Nubian or African passes us by, we will see in him or her, as surely as we see in ourselves, the reflection of a common Black genesis.

DISCOVERY OF THE KIFAH CAVE

On the November 26, 2010, while this book was receiving the final editing at our publishers, we got news from Mark Borda (the Maltese desert explorer who back in 2007 had found the hieroglyphic inscriptions at Gebel Uwainat) that he had just returned from one of his daring solo expeditions in the Sahara and had made a new and stunning discovery, this time at Gebel Arkenu, the "sister-mountain" of Gebel Uwainat (located within the Libyan border some 50 kilometers northwest of Uwainat): *a massive prehistoric rock art site, perhaps the largest known in Libya!*

The reader will note that the main events discussed in our book occurred in the vast eastern segment of the Sahara Desert known as the Libyan Desert. The area is bounded on the west by various mountain ranges that extend down the center of Libya, in the east by the river Nile, in the north by the Mediterranean Sea, and in the south by the Tibesti and Ennedi mountains. Measuring some 1,100,000 square kilometers, this area is ten times dryer than the rest of the Sahara, and is the world's largest hyper arid hot desert. Harsh, inhospitable, and waterless, its dune belts, sand sheets, bare rocky plateaus, and mountains are almost completely void of life of any kind, and the little of it that exists is mostly concentrated into a handful of oasis scattered throughout the region. The reader will also recall that in the early to mid-Holocene period (roughly ten to five thousand years ago) the picture was very different. The area was relatively moist with plants, wild animals, and human settlements in considerable abundance. Today this vast area is teeming with prehistoric remains that date from this period. The Sahara has long been noted for its rock art, primarily in the more accessible and thus more explored Western Sahara. But in recent years a handful of modern day explorers, equipped with GPS devices and satellite maps are now also penetrating the less accessible wastes of the Eastern Sahara. From their numerous discoveries over the past ten years it now appears that the area contains an immensely rich treasure trove of prehistoric paintings, engravings, and other archaeological remains, ranking it as one of the most important rock art regions in the world. The distinctively different rock art styles at the various sites, without the need for tedious and lengthy archaeological excavations, immediately impart a wealth of information about the distribution and movements of the ancient cultures that created them. The ever-growing inventory of sites is gradually building up a map that is revealing the geographical extent of the areas occupied in various ages. It is hoped that more detailed scientific investigation of the rock art sites will eventually establish the chronological movements of the various groups of people as their populations expanded, contracted, mixed, and migrated, and thus providing a clearer picture of why, how, and when these mysterious desert people impacted the area of the Nile valley and the later Pharaonic civilization. These discoveries, therefore, have a direct bearing on the various themes discussed in our book.

The "Kifah Cave" is a most dramatic and impressive example of these ongoing recent discoveries and was found by Borda in a previously unexplored area of Mount Arkenu. Mr. Borda, who, as we have seen, had already impressed the archaeological world in 2007 by finding Pharaonic hieroglyphs at Gebel Uwainat, the "sister mountain" of Arkenu, found the cave on the morning of November 13, 2010, while exploring the chasms and spires of the much broken sandstone plateau that straddles the northeast of Arkenu. The cave, which is 28 meters wide and only a little more than a meter high at the opening, has the appearance of a horizontal slit sitting atop a series of ledges at the base of a cliff face. The Kifah cave is the most conspicuous of a group of shelters that attracted Borda's attention from a considerable distance. Being on the highest part of the ridge, where the shelters are located, the Kifah site was one of the last he inspected. The shelters lower down had proved to contain some rock paintings but in spite of the large size of these shelters, as well as the good headroom, light conditions, and ideal and ample rock surfaces on the ceiling, the rock art there consisted only of three cows and a single human figure. Based on this, Borda did not hold much expectations of finding anything more substantial as he proceeded further up the ridge. When he got onto the final ledge, he could see from a distance of about 20 meters, many dark markings on the ceiling of the cave, and within a few moments he was stunned to note that across its entire width, the shelter was filled with painted rock art! His immediate reaction was one of astonishment at the existence of such a large site at Arkenu, mixed with wonderment at the quality and details of the paintings he was seeing!

Borda describes the paintings in the Kifah Cave as being from "the Uweinat Pastoralist period." It is concentrated in the front ceiling area of the cave to a depth of around four meters, yielding a continuous painted area of roughly 100 square meters, which makes it one of the largest, if not the largest rock art shelter in Libya. The evenness of the ceiling and the unbroken progression of paintings give the impression of a single vast mural. The many hundreds of motifs mainly portray cattle, goats, and other animals such as giraffes (see image of an aardvark above). Hundreds of humans are also depicted in many different types of scenes such as hunting, herding, domestic, ritual, and so forth (see plates 23 and 24). The fine state of preservation of the images reveals many interesting details about adornment, shoes, clothing, implements, weapons, homes, furnishings, and items used by the prehistoric people. Although the cave extends inward about eight meters, the deeper reaches are not painted, probably because the ceiling there is too low and dark. Mr. Borda plans to return to the site with a professional photographer to make a composite high-resolution digital montage of the entire painted rock ceiling. A pictorial article will then appear in the *SAHARA* journal in the middle of

A rock painting of an aardvark.

2011. Mr. Borda wished us to also note that Kifah is the name of the first daughter of the Tuareg Salem Ben Yahya, one of Libya's most renowned desert guides, who Borda has traveled with on several of his expeditions. A day before Borda found the cave, Ben Yahya greeted Borda with the words "your mother was praying you" instead of the usual "good morning." Ben Yahya then promptly showed Borda a five-inch yellow scorpion that had scurried out from under Borda's mattress whilst Ben Yahya was gathering up the sleeping gear. The species is known as the Death Stalker (*Leiurus quinquestriatus*). Ben Yahya then related the harrowing story of how, at the tender age of just three months, Kifah was killed in the oasis of Rebbiana after the same species of yellow scorpion had crept into her bed while she slept. With the tragic story still ringing in his ears when he found the cave, Borda was moved to dedicate his discovery to the memory of Kifah.

We wish to thank Mark Borda for kindly allowing us to report this discovery and also for providing us with some photographs, which he took at the time of the discovery. Mr. Borda has been exploring the Libyan Desert since 2005, his main objective being to seek out possible remains of ancient Egyptian presence in its vast wastes and beyond. Apart from the discovery mentioned above, he has made a number of significant discoveries. We were among the first to visit one of these in 2008, a site that is now rather dryly referred to in the archaeological world as CC21, but which we prefer to call the "Borda Cave" in this book. It is unusually located between Gilf Kebir and Gebel Uweinat, an area previously thought to be devoid of rock art. The cave contains magnificent prehistoric rock paintings, now considered to be one the very finest and best preserved prehistoric rock art sites of Egypt. Also the now-famous "Uwainat Inscriptions" that Borda found in the southern part of Gebel Uwainat proved that the ancient Egyptians of the early Middle Kingdom (ca. 2000 BC) somehow managed to travel the vast distance from the Nile across the totally arid desert without camels to meet the mysterious "people of Yam and Tekhebet," yet unidentified kingdoms perhaps located in the once fertile sub-Saharan regions of Africa.

Thomas Brophy (left) and Robert Bauval at the Uwainat Inscriptions, April 2008.

BACK TO
THE FIRST TIME

Vega, Sirius, and Orion Agree at Giza

One day our descendants will think it incredible that we paid so much attention to things like the amount of melanin in our skin or the shape of our eyes or our gender instead of the unique identities of each of us as complex human beings.

Franklin Thomas I refuse to accept the view that mankind is so tragically bound to the starless midnight of racism and war that the bright daybreak of peace and brotherhood can never become a reality. I believe that unarmed truth and unconditional love will have the final word.

MARTIN LUTHER KING JR.

In the main chapters of this book we have seen that there is a connection between the astro-ceremonial culture of the people of the Nabta region in Late Neolithic times and the earliest proto-dynastic and dynastic Nile astro-symbolism. The tracking of the rising of Sirius with the stars of the circumpolar Bull's Thigh constellation leads directly from Nabta to the Nile, as does attention to the motion of Orion's belt.

Here, in more detail, is the evidence for continuous astro-ceremonial culture in the other direction, back in time to the Middle Neolithic* and perhaps earlier. We can now trace the astro-ceremonial evidence back before 5000 BCE.

So far, in this journey back in astro-ceremonial time, we have the Sirius-plus-Bull's Thigh-Alkaid megalithic alignment of 6100 BCE and alignments to the vernal equinox heliacal risings of Orion's belt stars plus the autumnal equinox heliacal rising of Vega—and all are within a few hundred years of that same epoch. In addition, the Calendar Circle Orion's belt observing feature stretches back to about 6300 BCE—and the Calendar Circle suggests a method for imagining the entire precession cycle of the sky. The circle draws our attention to two time periods—ca. 5000 BCE and, half a precession cycle before this, ca. 16,500 BCE. That cycle brackets the time circa 12,000 BCE, which was the era referred to by the ancient Egyptians as Zep Tepi, or the First Time. The pyramids at Giza refer back to that time via their reflection of the Orion's belt stars in the layout of the Giza monuments. In terms of the precession cycle of a star, if Zep Tepi is the First Time, it is logical that it refers to the culmination time of the star when it is either farthest south or farthest north on its twenty-six-thousand-year cycle. Nabta seems to have been built during the half time or middle time to the Zep Tepi cycle or the precession cycle, and also reflects representations

---

*Actually, the term Neolithic was originally devised by anthropologists in 1865 to refer to a stage of human cultural development defined by the types of tools used (*lithos* is stone in Greek), rather than to refer to dates. Over the decades, as scholars developed a sort of canonical view, the actual dates believed to apply to the various cultural developmental stages (Early Neolithic, Middle Neolithic, Late Neolithic, Terminal Neolithic) gathered an air of certainty, though the dates of each stage were believed to be different for different geographic regions of the planet. Over time, terms such as Late Neolithic became almost interchangeable with actual dates, rather than cultural type. At Nabta, however, Wendorf himself notes that, regarding the megalithic constructions there, "[b]uilding large stone monuments was not expected among such groups."[1] These very findings have changed the concept of what is Neolithic and are changing our understanding of the time period to which the term will apply. To avoid confusion, then, we refer mostly to actual dates rather than conventional terms such as Middle Neolithic.

from the sky of the earlier time as well as the time when Nabta was built. (Thus if Giza is the place of the First Time, Nabta may be the place of the center of time.) If there is a symbolic connection between Nabta and Giza, it may be possible to find more representation of the First Time at Giza by digging deeper into the findings at Nabta, which might tell us what to look for at Giza.

VEGA AND THE SUBTERRANEAN PASSAGE

As we have seen, the primary stars that were tracked ceremonially at Nabta are Sirius, the stars of Orion' belt, and the circumpolar stars, including Vega (Alpha Lyrae), which is a very bright star. At visual brightness magnitude 0.0, Vega, since Hellenistic times, defined the brightest portion of the stellar brightness scale. It is essentially equal to the variable star Arcturus as the brightest star in the northern hemisphere.* Further, it is by far the brightest star that is ever near the long-term path of the celestial pole, and so for several centuries around 12,000 BCE, Vega was the brightest North Star ever. In the Great Pyramid at Giza, the two internal chambers, the King's Chamber and the Queen's Chamber, are connected to shafts oriented up and out along the meridian, the north-south line in the sky. Though they were previously determined to be air shafts, a number of authors have discussed that they probably indicate stars. Today, it is generally accepted that the shafts were, in fact, associated with stars—and that specifically the King's Chamber southern shaft was oriented to Orion's belt and the Queen's Chamber southern shaft was oriented to Sirius during the fourth-dynasty era completion of the pyramid.

Yet the pyramid complex contains another major shaft that is oriented along the meridian: the subterranean passage that cuts in a straight line from the original entrance of the pyramid, down through the

---

*Sirius is the brightest star of all. At visual magnitude −1.46, it is significantly brighter than Vega, but Sirius is in the Southern Hemisphere.

bottom courses of masonry on the north side of the pyramid, then deep underground into the bedrock to the subterranean chamber beneath the center of the pyramid. This other major meridianal shaft of the pyramid has never been successfully associated with a star. The subterranean passage is 1.2 meters (about 4 feet) high and 1.04 meters (3.4 feet) wide and runs 105 meters (344 feet) down into the bedrock. It is surprisingly uniform and straight, descending at an angle of 26.52 degrees.[2] Given the latitude of the Great Pyramid, the subterranean passage points to a declination of 86.54 degrees in the sky, 3.46 degrees directly south of the celestial pole. It is precisely aligned over its entire length, "without deviating more than a centimeter in angle or orientation," as Mark Lehner puts it.[3] The meticulous pyramid surveyor Sir Flinders Petrie notes for 2/5 of its length an even greater precision, requiring "readings to 1/100th inch or to 1" [one arcsecond] on the longer distances."[4] It is one of the most astonishingly precise features of the whole Great Pyramid complex, which itself is a wonder of precision—and it points to the sky, for what could be more of an intended orientation than a star? The passage is cut so consistently straight, and other aspects of the Great Pyramid, such as its cardinal orientation, are so accurate that it is likely that whoever cut the subterranean passage probably did not intend it to align with the celestial North Pole, because if that were indeed the target, it surely would have been hit more accurately.

To what, then, could the subterranean passage have been oriented? Given Nabta's megalith alignments toward Vega, we decided to test Vega against the Giza subterranean passage. Employing the most recent measures for Vega's proper motion[5] into the long-term calculations for its motion in the sky, we see that Vega achieved its highest declination of 86.54 degrees ca. 12,070 BCE. Vega matched the subterranean passage not simply at some passing date, but exactly when the star was at its northern culmination, the closest it comes to the celestial pole in its twenty-six-thousand-year precession cycle. In addition, the precision with which Vega seems to have matched the center of the shaft is surprising. Given the height and length of the shaft, its viewing angle actually includes a range of declination angles from 86.22 degrees to 86.87 degrees, centered on 86.54 degrees, and Vega appears to have hit it directly in the middle,* exactly at culmination. Therfore, if these calculations and measures for Vega prove to be accurate,† Vega began shining down to the bottom of the subterranean passage ca. 12,320 BCE, when Vega's declination rose above 86.22 degrees, and in ca. 12,070 BCE, Vega shone down the center of the shaft until ca. 11,820 BCE, when Vega sank below 86.22 degrees declination again and no longer shone to the bottom of the shaft.‡

These Vega-subterranean passage dates are consistent with the general Zep Tepi we can estimate from the fact that Orion's belt matches the layout of the three pyramids on the Giza plateau.§

It is important that Sirius culminated at about the same time. In *The Egypt Code,* Bauval notes that around Zep Tepi, Sirius would have been just visible on the horizon, as seen from the Giza plateau. In light

---

*Atmospheric refraction affects the apparent viewing angle of a star significantly only when very close to the horizon—by up to about 0.56 degrees on the horizon. At an altitude of 26.5 degrees, the altitude of the subterranean passage, the atmospheric refraction would be very small, less than 2 arc minutes.

†Of course, we believe our calculations are accurate according to the current knowledge of the long-term motion of the celestial pole and Vega's currently measured proper motion, which is quoted in the SIMBAD database as having small uncertainty. It is always possible, however, that new information might be measured or discovered about the long-term apparent motion of a star.

‡In addition, if we were to consider only the part of the passage that descends through the bedrock, which is about two thirds of its length, the Vega-shinning-down time would be extended by a couple of hundred years.

§In *The Origin Map,* Brophy estimates around 11,770 BCE for the match of Orion's belt and the pyramids, and in *The Egypt Code,* Bauval estimates 11,450 BCE. For a number of reasons, these matching dates should be considered estimates to within a few hundred years. For example, some date variation may arise from the choice between matching the line connecting the end stars (to the end pyramids) or matching the first two stars (to the first two pyramids). In addition, there may be some differences as to whether more recent, proper motions measurements were used for the stars and slight differences in approximations in the methods of celestial pole motion calculations. We do not, therefore, view the Orion's-belt-to-pyramids layout match as a highly precise date, though it definitely occurred within this era. The subterranean passage star shafts, however, offer more precise dating.

of this new information of the bright pole star, Vega, shining down the subterranean passage when it was at precessional culmination, we can now look in even more detail at the astrophysics of the Sirius connection. Again, employing the latest measures for Sirius's proper motion,[6] as we did for Vega, we see that Sirius reached its southern culmination ca. 12,280 BCE at a declination of −60.43 degrees. That declination is noteworthy because the declination of the geometric horizon at Giza looking south is −60.02 degrees, and the visual horizon is thus −60.5 degrees,[7] essentially identical to the southern culmination of Sirius. The Giza plateau, then, is the place on Earth (the only latitude) where Sirius, at the southernmost point of its twenty-six-thousand-year precession cycle, just barely eclipsed the earth.

Visual Horizon versus Geometric Horizon

The visual horizon is about 0.5 degrees lower than the geometric horizon, because the light from a star is bent when it passes through Earth's atmosphere. It is thus possible to see starlight from slightly below the geometric horizon. The precise amount of refraction depends on atmospheric temperature and humidity, but, generally, it averages a bit more than 0.5 degrees.

TAKE A WALK AT THE FIRST TIME WITH SIRIUS

Sirius is so bright that it is the only star that can sometimes be seen during daylight, and under good conditions at night, it can be seen even when the star is just barely above the visual horizon.*

We can imagine that we are living in the region (that is now Egypt)

---

*Dimmer stars cannot be viewed when they are just barely above the horizon, because of atmospheric extinction. As they rise farther above the horizon, often to a degree or more altitude, the light from the star passes through less of Earth's atmosphere and obscuring dust, and the star becomes visible to the eye.

ca. 12,250 BCE and are so highly attuned to the night sky that we are especially oriented to the brightest star of all, Sirius. It is the time of year that is near the summer solstice, and it is millennia before the monsoons move north to bring life again to the desert—we are near the life-sustaining waters of the Nile, but we are nomadic, moving north and south each year, following the best conditions for survival. We are traveling north for several days during a hot summer, and we travel about 55 kilometers (34 miles) per day—a long but feasible day's walk for a well-conditioned wanderer. This distance is half of one-degree latitude on Earth's surface. We are five-days' walk south of the place that is now known as Giza. We are aware that the always-easy-to-spot three-star asterism of Orion's belt will rise early evening in the far southeast, and it will culminate south, hanging in the sky at a low altitude of around 15 degrees two hours before midnight. We also know that just after Orion's belt transits the meridian to the south, at 110 minutes before midnight, Orion's trailing companion, the starry ruler of the night sky, Sirius, will crack the horizon just 12 degrees east of due south, and Sirius will skim the southern horizon at a very low arc, reaching an altitude of just more than 2 degrees before descending again below the horizon. We know that Sirius is so bright that if we have an unobstructed view of the south horizon, perhaps if we are on a low hill or sand dune in the desert, we will be able to view our old friend in the sky for a couple of hours around midnight. To the north, the brilliant Vega is always up, always visible whenever the sky is dark. Less than 3.5 degrees from the celestial pole in the north, Vega is a restless North Star that cycles up down and around the pole each night in a small circle which is 7 degrees across, and when Sirius is high, Vega is low, reaching the bottom part of its circle around the celestial North Pole at just more than an hour after Sirius reaches its height in the south.

As we trek farther north each day, the familiar starry show in the sky each night repeats itself, but Sirius skims the horizon on an even lower and shorter arc each night as we move north. By the time we arrive, a few days walk farther north, at the place now known as Giza,

Sirius makes such a low, brief arc on the horizon that viewing it requires perfectly clear conditions, and we must stand on a platform to catch any glimpse of the star. In one more day's walk farther north, it will be impossible to glimpse Sirius at all. The tracking of the star is a deeply ancient part of our ancestral lore and our annual life. During the days, the angle of the sun in the sky informs us what time of year it is, and during nights, the appearance of Sirius tells us the same information. In this way, our ancestors have kept in tune with the seasons for a very long time. What's more, we know that in the region just a couple of days farther north, at the place we now know as Alexandria, we used to be able to glimpse Sirius only a few generations ago before it disappeared entirely from the night sky. Our ancestors have been studying the sky for so long that they were able to teach us how the sky changes over a very long time. Thus we know that Sirius will again return to the northern regions, and the brilliant Vega will move down, away from the celestial pole, and Sirius will climb higher again in the southern regions. That is why the place in which we are standing now is the place of the First Time, Zep Tepi: Giza.

DUAL DATING AND VEGA RECONFIRMED

The ancient name of the Great Pyramid at Giza, the name used by the ancient Egyptians, was Akhet Khufu, The Horizon of Khufu.[8] Is it possible that the sacred place where Khufu marshaled his kingdom to build the Great Pyramid was already known simply as Akhet, The Horizon, the place on Earth where the ruler of heaven, Sirius, briefly comes down exactly to the horizon every twenty-six thousand years? Khufu built his great pyramid on the Place of The Horizon in order to make it The Horizon of Khufu.*

We have seen that the standard date for the building of the pyramids is the fourth dynasty, and we have seen that the layout of the pyramids

---

*The ancient names of its two sister structures were less poetic and seemingly less informative: Great is Khafre, and Menkaure is Divine.

that matches the stars of Orion's belt is an allusion to a distant past, a symbolic reference to Zep Tepi described in inscriptions. Similarly, the Calendar Circle at Nabta Playa was likely constructed and used ca. 5000 BCE, and it teaches about much earlier times—actually, about the entire precession cycle. In light of our findings regarding the subterranean passage and Vega, and our more detailed study of the motion of Sirius, we must consider again the possibility that the pyramids at Giza were indeed built during the fourth dynasty, but were built on top of a location where there was some preexisting, symbolic, much older architecture. Constructions at sacred sites around the world, including those in ancient Egypt, have been built and rebuilt on locations of earlier constructions, often over millennia. Many people have suggested that the Giza plateau complex itself is one such site. Probably, the most stunning evidence for this has come from Boston University geologist Robert Schoch, who, together with inspiration from independent Egyptologist John Anthony West, measured the weathering of the Great Sphinx and the Sphinx enclosure. Schoch essentially proved that from a geophysical standpoint the Sphinx was weathered by long-term heavy rainfall and thus predates 5000 BCE. Schoch notes that we cannot determine precisely when the Sphinx was carved into the living bedrock, but rigorous geophysical analysis gives the epoch ca. 5000 BCE as a minimum age.[9]

Like all things that challenge a reigning dogma in an academic field, Schoch's dating of the Sphinx has generated voluminous polemical argumentation, but he is well supported by the geophysical evidence. In the Sphinx, then, there is monumental architecture on the Giza plateau that predates the fourth dynasty by more than two millennia. Our study of the Vega and Sirius signatures suggests there was some symbolic architecture on the Giza plateau as far back as the actual Zep Tepi and that Giza is the place of Zep Tepi. It has long been suggested that the subterranean chamber at the end of the subterranean passage of the Great Pyramid appears to be much more ancient than the fourth dynasty. Schoch has also suggested that the central subterranean chamber of the Red Pyramid of fourth-dynasty founder Pharaoh Sneferu at

Dashur shows geological weathering that is evidence of a much more ancient date.[10]

It's possible that the symbolic architecture existent at Zep Tepi included the subterranean passage down to the subterranean chamber, beneath a mound topped by a flat platform, possibly to the level where the Queen's Chamber exists today. Indeed the Great Pyramid is known to be built over a bedrock mound platform that is, in its interior, about 8 meters (26 feet) high and extends to approximately where the subterranean passage emerges from the bedrock.[11] In this view, the Great Pyramid was completed in the fourth dynasty on top of the then-ancient subterranean passage and platform. The Zep Tepi platform was symbolically preserved in the completed architecture of the pyramid by the horizontal passage that leads to the Queen's Chamber. The horizontal passage basically has the same dimensions (1.2 meter—3.9 feet—in height) as the subterranean passage, and conceptually, the horizontal passage is another star shaft directed exactly along the horizon—symbolically preserving the much more ancient horizontal platform used to represent and probably to view Sirius at the First Time, Zep Tepi, and preserving the place on Earth that demarcates the parts of Earth from where Sirius never disappears and the parts of Earth where Sirius does disappear.

Further suggestive of symbolic unity is the ascending passage that now connects the subterranean passage and the horizontal passage of the Queen's Chamber. It is of the same dimensions (1.2 meters—3.9 feet—in height), and it is sloped upward at an almost identical angle to the downslope of the subterranean passage—much like a reflection off the horizon plane. If there was a Sirius platform at Zep Tepi and if the subterranean passage did exist then, it would have been possible for a single priest or priestess to view, by employing a simple flat reflector or still pool of water where the subterranean passage enters the earth, and connect the light of Vega from the north shining down the passage at the same time as the light of Sirius from the south just skimmed the horizon. Thus two great rulers of the starry sky—Sirius, the crown jewel of the night, and Vega, the ruler of all the circumpolar stars—were viewed and symbolized simultaneously at both of their twenty-six-thousand-year precessional culminations (with Sirius culminating south and Vega culminating north). Their precise culminations were 180 years apart, but for centuries they demonstrated simultaneous shining along the horizon platform and into the subterranean passage, and ca. 12,020 BCE their lights shone simultaneously and directly from the south and the north onto the place of the First Time. Significantly, this starry drama occurred around midnight, when the sky was dark, only on the days of the year around summer solstice. Further, the Great Pyramid and subterranean passage are located on the Giza plateau in such a way that the plateau slopes down and away to the southeast, giving an unobstructed view of the southern horizon in order to accommodate viewing the starry show.

Throughout ancient Egyptian history, the heliacal reappearance of Sirius marked the New Year as well as the imminent arrival of the Nile floods, much as the appearance of Sirius marked the New Year and the playa-filling monsoons at Nabta Playa. Monuments simultaneously marking the rising Sirius and the circumpolar stars represented the bounteous measure of the New-Year cycle. We can see that at the place of the First Time, Zep Tepi, the start of the new Great Year of precessional motion of Sirius, ruler of the heavens, is monumentally indicated, together with the Great Year cycle of the celestial pole around the invariant point ruled by the greatest pole star of all, Vega. There is an elegant similarity in this use of stellar symbology (Sirius rising simultaneous with the circumpolar star) to mark both the annual cycle of the seasons and the Great Year cycle of the Ages.

At this point, traditional-minded archaeoastronomers would raise an objection that the Vega-to-subterranean passage alignment is only one star in one alignment and therefore is not significant. Yet we can now see that this single alignment is part of a symbolic system repeated again and again, and that it occurs not simply in any time in the star's cycle, but at the special time of culmination. Still, objectors would say that other examples of the same alignment are needed for verification. To honor this, we can examine other subterranean passages.

Actually, there are only two extensive subterranean passages associated with the six giant pyramids:[12] third-dynasty Djoser's step pyramid at Saqqara, fourth-dynastry founder Sneferu's Bent Pyramid and Red Pyramid at Dashur, the great pyramids of Khufu and Khafre at Giza, and the fourth-dynasty Unfinished Pyramid at Zawiyet el-Aryan. Besides Khufu's Great Pyramid, the other subterranean passage is beneath Sneferu's Bent Pyramid at Dashur. Located 21 kilometers (13 miles) south of the Great Pyramid of Khufu, the giant Bent Pyramid of Sneferu is at latitude 29.79 degrees. We learn from Egyptologist I. E. S. Edwards[13] that the subterranean passage of the Bent Pyramid starts at the entrance to the pyramid on its north face, about 12 meters (39 feet) aboveground. It continues down through the masonry for 25 meters (82 feet), first at an angle of 28.36 degrees, and then shifts to an angle of 26.33 degrees before moving from the masonry down into the bedrock after another 48 meters (157 feet). The passage continues, precisely directed at a constant angle through the bedrock to a chamber under the center of the pyramid, and the entire subterranean length of the passage into the bedrock is at a constant angle of 26.33 degrees. This angle, combined with the latitude of the Bent Pyramid, points to a location in the sky with a precise declination of 86.54 degrees—identical to the subterranean passage of the Great Pyramid of Khufu at Giza. So if the subterranean passage that is now under the Bent Pyramid existed at Zep Tepi, plunging into the bedrock beneath a horizon viewing platform on the surface, essentially the same starry drama as at Giza could have been observed at Dashur—with the only difference being that at Dashur, Sirius would rise to a slightly higher altitude by about 20 arc minutes.

The ancient name of the Bent Pyramid was The Southern Shining Pyramid.[14] Perhaps, when Sneferu marshaled his kingdom to build the Bent Pyramid, the location was already known and revered as The Southern Shining—the place on Earth, and especially south, where the ruler of the heavens, Sirius, shines eternally and never disappears beneath the horizon. Sneferu built three large pyramids. The first, at Meidum, bears an exalted personal ancient name: Sneferu Endures. The last, about 2 kilometers (1.2 miles) north of The Southern Shining Pyramid, had the ancient name of The Shining Pyramid. Sneferu's son, Khufu, built the pyramid called The Horizon of Khufu. The Bent Pyramid and its subterranean passage are also located topographically so that the distant southern horizon was nearly perfectly flat and unobscured.

The subterranean passage under the Bent Pyramid has not been surveyed as extensively and repeatedly as has the subterranean passage under the Khufu Great Pyramid, thus we don't know whether the Bent Pyramid passage may also be as precisely wrought as the Khufu Pyramid passage.* We do know, however, from measuring the structures that the builders of both of these giant pyramid complexes were capable of and in fact implemented great precision over long distances. If it can be shown, then, that the only two subterranean passages under the two key true giant pyramids were oriented to the same declination in the sky with the same high precision, then that alone would contribute evidence that the builders indeed had astronomical intent—whether or not that intent was Vega. In light of these findings, perhaps another survey of this aspect of the Bent Pyramid could further illuminate the origins of these two subterranean passages.

We also note that the two other great pyramids on the Giza plateau, the Menkaure and Khafre pyramids, have shorter, less surgically precise subterranean passages that don't extend down all the way under the center of their structures. Menkaure's bedrock passage descends 31 meters (102 feet), about half of that length through the lower courses of masonry and the rest down into the bedrock at an angle of 26.03

---

*As we have said, there is a significant spread of half a degree or so in the viewing angle of these subterranean passages, due to their 1.2 meter- (3.9 feet-) shaft heights, so the possible association of the precessional culmination of Vega does not depend on the fact that it seems to have hit directly the middle of the viewing angle—that amount of precision could be happenstance.

degrees, and Khafre's passage descends a much shorter distance at an angle of 25.92 degrees. These yield declinations to the sky of about half of one degree lower than their Great Pyramid partner, and the broader angular spread of their openings means that they would have captured the light of the culminating Vega during the same times as did the passage under Khufu's pyramid.*

Finally, we must look at the dual nature of many aspects of the Bent Pyramid. First there is the bend in the slope of the pyramid itself. Further, the north descending entrance passage is bent, within the masonry of the lower part of the pyramid that is not bent, and the west entry passage is bent (from 30.15 degrees to 24.28 degrees),[15] also entirely within the lower courses of masonry that are not bent. Many Egyptologists believe that the Bent Pyramid was bent due to a series of accidents and poor planning of the construction, but there seems to be ample evidence that it was planned in its structure. As Schoch puts it: "I suspect strongly that the Bent Pyramid was meant to be bent from the beginning. Unlike any other Egyptian pyramid, it expresses duality—two angles, two geometries, two tunnel and chamber complexes. There is something ritualistic and symbolic in this shape, a meaning we now find elusive. The Egyptians clearly found this meaning to be important. The craftsmanship of the Bent Pyramid achieves a high level, and the entire structure is beautifully wrought. Clearly Sneferu and the Egyptians of his time were using architecture to express something of great importance, and they were giving this work their all."[16]

The Bent Pyramid is the first true giant pyramid created by the ancient Egyptians† under the reign of Sneferu the founder of the fourth dynasty. Evidence suggests that it was located on a site that included

---

*If we wanted to interpret the half-degree difference as precise to Vega, the central alignment would be about three hundred years later than for Khufu's subterranean passage. Alternatively, they may be considered as less precise versions of the same alignment to Vega.

†Djoser's and Imhotep's step pyramid complex at Saqqara was the first major pyramid complex construction, but it contained a step pyramid, not a true pyramid.

preexisting symbolic architecture, such as the Zep Tepi Vega shaft that was revered and extremely ancient even in the time of Sneferu. The duality symbolism repeatedly built into the Bent Pyramid may represent the dual times—Zep Tepi (the First Time), and the second time of the revival of monumental astro-ceremonial architecture in Sneferu's fourth dynasty. This dual astro-ceremonial architecture is also present at Giza and was present at Nabta Playa. We can note that these two monumentalized epochs—Zep Tepi and the initiation of giant pyramid complex construction in Old Kingdom times—also represent two stations of the Great Year cycle of the ages: the southern culmination of Sirius at summer solstice midnight and the heliacal reappearance of Sirius at summer solstice dawn.

We can note that when we find a new interpretation, one that will endure the test of time, for an ancient monument or set of monuments, there tends also to be found some bits of folklore, mythology, or story from the past, often ignored or dismissed by moderns, that points toward the same interpretation. Thus, once these alignments to Vega at Zep Tepi were determined, we searched the literature and indeed found that Manly P. Hall writes in 1928, "In the light of the secret philosophy of the Egyptian initiates, W. W. Harmon, by a series of extremely complicated yet exact mathematical calculations; determines that the first ceremonial of the Pyramid was performed 68,890 years ago on the occasion when the star Vega for the first time sent its ray down the descending passage into the pit."[17] W. W. Harmon, an esoteric Theosophist, seems to have claimed to have received somehow, from an ancient initiatory tradition, the basic idea of Vega shining down the subterranean passage as the first use of the Giza complex for ritual initiatory purposes. He then attempts to calculate a date on his own. It is interesting that he seems to have been correct about Vega and the subterranean passage but is completely wrong about the date. (Even going back to earlier precession cycles does not yield Harmon's date.) Quite opposite Harmon, we first suspected Vega for purely astronomical reasons based on calculations, then we researched the cultural and contextual evidence in order to find that an intended Vega alignment does indeed fit into the historic-cultural sequence.

There seems to be mounting evidence that there was some symbolic architecture at Giza and Dashur during Zep Tepi and that it referenced Vega and Sirius, because these stars represented the First Time, the beginning of the Great Year of precession. At this point, defenders of the orthodox view may object along the traditional line of thinking that there was nothing at Giza before the Old Kingdom and that, therefore, it is not plausible that several millennia earlier there was monumental architecture. As Zahi Hawass, director of the Supreme Council of Antiquities, states, "But no single piece of material culture, not a single object nor piece of an object, has been found at Giza that can be interpreted as coming from a lost civilization [before the Egyptian Dynasties]."[18] The Great Sphinx, however, must qualify as a piece of material culture. Further, though the Sphinx may not have been in existence as far back as Zep Tepi, and perhaps it was, or is, only seven thousand years old, the minimum age required by geophysical weathering. In either case, the Sphinx is strong evidence that there was monumental symbolic architecture at Giza long before the pharaonic Old Kingdom times. In the orthodox view, of course, the physical evidence for the ancient Sphinx could be dismissed on the basis that it is an anomaly—the only piece of evidence—and, therefore, it doesn't count. The Vega shafts and Sirius platform Zep Tepi findings can also be dismissed by some as anomalies based on the fact that this evidence is astro-ceremonial, rather than proved by radiocarbon or other traditional dating methods. At some point, however, enough anomalies from enough different disciplines add up to an overwhelming body of evidence.* [19]

---

*Recent discoveries in Turkey, at a site called Gobekli Tepi, involve finely carved megalithic pillars and rings that have been firmly radiocarbon dated to the tenth millennium BCE. In a submission to an academic journal, we mentioned Gobekli Tepi as evidence that man was making fine megalithic constructions much earlier than the Late Neolithic to support our contention that some of the megalithic constructions at Nabta Playa may also predate the orthodox view of the Late Neolithic. The anonymous academic referee objected to our reference on the grounds that "authors remarks on megalithic

So the developmental sequence may have been thus: The Black African star people of the Sahara developed the forerunner of the Egyptian civilization and, in the process, built the astro-ceremonial complex at Nabta Playa. When the extreme dryness of the region finally set in, they moved to the Nile Valley and developed the archaic temple of Satis at Elephantine Island. They then spread throughout the Nile Valley, assimilating the existing populations into dynastic Egypt and increasing their megalithic building activities. By the third dynasty, King Djoser, with his astronomer-priest Imhotep, built at Saqqara the first major monumental complex of dynastic Egypt. Then fourth-dynasty founder King Sneferu, and Sneferu's son, King Khufu, built the Bent Pyramid at Dashur, followed by the Great Pyramid at Giza, both constructed on top of much more ancient sacred subterranean passages and platforms from Zep Tepi. Thus, all the truly monumental pyramid architecture of the dynastic period (with the exeption, perhaps, of the fourth-dynasty Unfinished Pyramid at Zawiyet el-Aryan) is associated with Zep Tepi. The Great Sphinx at Giza already existed in some form, and was probably modified by fourth-dynasty refurbishments. The Zep Tepi architecture was likely abandoned for a long time before the protodynastic and dynastic Egyptians arrived to build on it—or at least it was little used and clearly was not in a location of a major habitation or city.

The question then becomes: Can we draw a line back through time from the dynastic Egyptian architects to the Nabta Playa megalith builders and back even further to Zep Tepi builders? We can recall that ca. 5000 BCE, the Black African star people at Nabta Playa built their astro-ceremonial complex on top of a preexisting symbolic landscape

---

(continued from page 290) pillars found in Turkey are totally irrelevant. I reject any idea of possible contacts between Turkish site and Nabta assuming both sites were independently constructed." In our paper, we neither claimed nor disclaimed contact between Nabta and Gobekli Tepi. We did claim that recent evidence pushed much farther back in time the dates of ceremonial megalithic architecture at other sites, and that this evidence should lessen the resistance to consider new evidence, which might similarly push back dates at Nabta.

carved onto the bedrock that they knew to be much more ancient. Further, when they moved to the Nile and up to Giza, they again built on top of much more ancient star monuments. All these constructions display a knowledge of the stars that would seem to have taken a very long time to develop. Surely, the Nabta Playa star people who became the protodynastic ancient Egyptian builders were aware of and perhaps somehow connected to the more ancient Zep Tepi people. Perhaps they were the Shemsu Hor, who migrated from the Nile to the Sahara when the monsoons moved north and made the Sahara green, and it is their very distant progeny who we can track back through Nabta Playa to the Nile as the monsoons again moved south.

SOTHIC CYCLES AND ZEP TEPI

We must next consider how the calendar-based Sothic cycle from the Old Kingdom may relate to Zep Tepi. We can recall how 11,541 BCE would have been the start of a Sothic cycle if it was reached by measuring in increments of the 1,460-year calendar counting method, starting from the one recorded Sothic cycle end in 139 CE. Yet the precise interval between heliacal risings of Sirius, as with any star, varies somewhat if we consider it over an entire precession cycle. Around 12,000 BCE, when Sirius was very low on the southern horizon, the idea of heliacal rising at Giza was problematic, because Sirius didn't even reach the 1-degree altitude normally considered for heliacal reappearance. Simple geometry, however, shows us a very interesting fact: when Sirius was at its southern culmination, it was highest in the sky at midnight on the day of summer solstice. At Giza, then, the place of Zep Tepi, the precise year around 12,000 BCE that marked the southern culmination of Sirius was by definition the heliacal rise of the entire Sirius precession cycle—the origin of the supercycle of all the cycles. Further, at essentially the same time, the king of all North Stars, Vega, culminated shining down into the subterranean passage and the pattern of the three stars of Orion's belt matched perfectly the pattern of the three pyramids of Giza.

Another Way to Think of
the Southern Culmination of a Star

Those inclined to think geometrically can easily visualize this: the southern culmination of a star, in this case Sirius, occurs when the south pole of Earth points as nearly toward the star as is possible during the twenty-six-thosand-year precession cycle. This orientation is similar to the Earth-to-sun orientation at winter solstice, which occurs every year. On the day of summer solstice, then, the sun and a south-culminating star (in this case, Sirius) are directly opposite each other relative to Earth. We can then imagine the sun shining on Earth and creating a shadow (night time) on the far side of the planet. Thus the south-culminating star is viewed at midnight on the day of summer solstice and on the meridian (due south, just at the horizon—in the case of Sirius, at Giza) at the darkest time of night. We can also see that in some sense the geometrical heliacal rising of a south-culminating star occurs at vernal equinox, because that is the day of the year when an observer on spinning Earth moves from dark into light, just as the south-culminating star is on the meridian, but in actual viewing conditions, the sky is probably too bright to see the star at that moment.

EXACT DATE OF ZEP TEPI?

Astronomy in isolation can give precise dates, but we must make the cultural connection. In summary, the astronomically determined dates related to Zep Tepi are these: (1) The layout of the Great Pyramids at Giza, referring back to the centuries around 11,700 BCE; (2) The southern culmination of Sirius ca. 12,280 BCE, marked by the location of the Giza monuments and the Queen's Chamber horizontal passage; (3) Vega located as North Star at its northern culmination, in 12,070 BCE, marked by the subterranean passage of Khufu's Great Pyramid at

Giza and Sneferu's Bent Pyramid at Dashur. Yet we may want to know what was the exact date of Zep Tepi. It's important to remember that Zep Tepi is an astro-ceremonial concept: it is a combination of astronomical measurement and cultural-religious meaning. It is the origin of long-term human cultural cycles and is a calendrical origin to long-term astronomical cycles. Here, we have hammered away at the purely astronomical parts of an exact date. The astronomy seems to point to Zep Tepi being in the era around 12,000 BCE. Further, the date is associated conceptually with the culminations of Sirius and Vega, which mark the starting point of the long-term precession cycle, or Great Year, of about twenty-six thousand years, and with Orion's belt,* which provides the sky asterism for tracking that Great Year. If Zep Tepi did refer to a more specific date, we must make more progress on understanding culturally the specific aspect of astronomy to which it was tied. We don't seem to have a complete answer at this time—but we have suggested some clues. Specifically, this cycle is what we also know as the cycle of Zodiac Ages and has also been correlated to the Vedic Yuga cycle, and both of those originated in the same general epoch.[20] Further, we have suggested that the northern culmination of the center of our galaxy, which visually is located in the Dark Rift in the Milky Way, occurs in the same epoch,† may also be monumentally referenced, and can provide a less variable calibration point, because, unlike stars, it has no proper motion. We have seen that the Great Sphinx at Giza, gazing east to the rising sun in its namesake constellation, Leo, also comes from around the same epoch.[21]

As we have seen in chapter 6, British Egyptologist Rundle T. Clark concluded this about Zep Tepi: "[A]ll that was good or efficacious was established on the principles laid down in the 'First Time'—which was, therefore, a golden age of absolute perfection."[22] If the Vedic Yuga cycle is properly calibrated to the precession cycle in the same way, then

---

*Orion's belt also culminated south during the same epoch, ca. 10,650 BCE.
†In *The Origin Map* it is shown to be 10,909 BCE.

we can conclude that Zep Tepi was coincident with the center of the Satya Yuga, which the Vedas identified as the perfect time or golden age of humanity. Here, we trace the physical archaeological and astro-ceremonial evidence to identify that the ancients themselves placed that golden age in the epoch around 12,000 BCE. The question of whether or not there could be some mechanism that actually does connect the astrophysical cycle to the cultural development of humans is a subject beyond the scope of this book.

SOTHIC CYCLES AND IMHOTEP'S CALENDAR WALL

The Sothic cycle is the duration of synchrony between a 365-day Egyptian civil calendar and the heliacal rising of Sirius. A difficulty with calculating this cycle lies in defining *heliacal rising*. The basic concept of heliacal rising is the day of the year on which Sirius first seems to reappear on the eastern horizon just before the sun rises. Obviously, it would be problematic if we were to apply this purely visual definition. If the weather happened to be cloudy or the sky was filled with dust, an otherwise viewable reappearance would be missed, perhaps for many days. A more sensible definition could be the day on which Sirius would be visible, if the viewing conditions were optimal, and *optimal* is defined as a specific angular relationship of sun, Sirius, and horizon.

In order to understand the Sothic cycle, we must first look at two related cycles. Today, the length of the tropical year is 365.2422 days, so that a 365-day civil calendar would return the day of summer solstice to the same calendar date every 1,507.1 years. (We can call this the solstice-to-civil cycle.) Today, the length of the sidereal year (with respect to the distant stars) is 365.2564 days, so that a 365-day calendar would return a star sign or zodiac constellation date to the same calendar date every 1,423.8 years. (We can call this the sidereal-to-civil cycle.) This difference between the sidereal-to-civil cycle of 1,423.8 years and the solstice-to-civil cycle of 1,507.1 years is due to the precession of Earth's pole, the precession of the equinox. If Earth did not precess, then the sidereal-to-civil cycle would be the same as the solstice-to-civil cycle. Further, those sidereal and solstice rates are as measured today, while the actual precession rate varies slightly over time, which means these cycle durations also vary. Because the heliacal rising is a combination of sidereal and solar measurements—essentially, a complex addition of the two—we would expect the Sothic cycle, to first approximation, to be the average of the sidereal and solstice cycles, which, given today's rates, would be 1,465.4 years. This is remarkably close to the purely calendar-based cycle of 1,460 years—the cycle between two types of civil calendar systems (one that adds a day every four years, like our leap year, and a fixed, 365-day calendar such as the Egyptian civil calendar).

Yet we would expect an actual Sothic cycle to vary from our rough estimate, due to several factors. First, the precession rate varies with time; the rate has been steadily increasing since roughly 8000 BCE. Today, the precession rate is about 50.29 arc seconds per year, while ca. 4000 BCE the rate was roughly 1 arc second per year slower. Due to this effect alone, almost half of one year would be added to the Sothic cycle over the span of about two Sothic cycles. A second factor is that the tropical year itself also changes over time—but this effect is orders of magnitude smaller. A third factor, more difficult to estimate but which has a greater effect, is due to the change in declination of the star and its drift in right ascension relative to the vernal point—the day relative to solstice moves steadily through the year so that the angular relationship of star to sun to horizon is altered.

Still, we can fairly easily use SkyMapPro to measure the Sothic cycles. First, we set the latitude to that of Djoser's step pyramid (29.871 degrees north) and we set the year to 2781 BCE and we set the day to summer solstice. The result is that on that day, when Sirius is at altitude 1 degree, the sun is at altitude −8.96 degrees 45 minutes before the center of the sun disk passes the horizon. This is clearly a good reference for heliacal rising, because Sirius is certainly bright enough to be seen briefly under such conditions. We call this summer solstice day, the first day of Thoth (1 Thoth) on the Egyptian civil calendar, and we note that SkyMapPro calls this day July 16, 2781 BCE. We make this the definition of Sirius heliacal rising—the day of the year when Sirius is at altitude 1 degree and the sun is simultaneously at altitude −8.96 degrees or lower. Next, we search for the previous year when Sirius rose heliacally on a first day of Thoth (1 Thoth) according to the Egyptian civil calendar. We know that SkyMapPro uses Julian years (365.25 days per year), so we note that what SkyMapPro calls July 16, 4241 BCE is a first day of Thoth on the Egyptian civil calendar. When we look at that date, we see that when Sirius was at 1 degree altitude, the sun was at −9.41 degrees altitude just below the horizon, and the day before 1 Thoth, the sun was only −8.70 degrees below the horizon—less than our criterion of 8.96 degrees—so in that year the first day of Thoth was indeed the day of reappearance of Sirius.

We must remember, however, that a given date for heliacal rising of Sirius should persist for about four years in a row on the Egyptian civil calendar, so in order to nail down the exact Sothic cycle, we must check the following years. We see, then, that two years later, 4239 BCE, on the first day of Thoth with Sirius at altitude 1 degree, the sun was −9.05 degrees altitude, which still satisfies heliacal rising (and this time, eleven days before summer solstice). In later years, all the way up until 2781 BCE, the first day of Thoth was not the heliacal rising date. So this Sothic cycle extended from 4239 BCE to 2781 BCE (in Julian years), which is 1,459 Egyptian civil calendar years.

By a similar method, we find that the next first day of Thoth-Sirius heliacal rising was 1325 BCE (twelve days after summer solstice) which is 1,457 Egyptian civil calendar years. These cycles agree with Ingham's calculations[1]—he calculated the cycles before and after 2769 BCE and came up with 1,458 and 1,456 Julian years, which equal 1,459 and 1,457 Egyptian civil calendar years. Ingham's date of 2769 BCE* came from

---

*Ingham calculated four cycles: 1,458 years ending in 2769 BCE; 1,456 years ending in 1313 BCE; 1,453 years ending in 141 CE; and 1,450 years ending in 1,591 CE.

stepping back in time and using a definition of *heliacal rising* that is slightly different from ours. As our definition, we chose whatever the condition was on 2781 BCE summer solstice, so clearly the twelve-year difference in our starting dates is not a discrepancy and we agree on those cycle durations.*

Now we can reconsider the panels on the Djoser complex monument wall. The eastern wall, with 1,459 panels, may in fact reflect the 1,459 Egyptian civil years of the Sothic cycle preceding its construction. The 1,461 panels on the western wall may reflect the average duration since the last time that the first day of Thoth coincided with Sirius heliacal— a period that lasted for four years, yielding a cycle time of from 1,463 to 1,459 years, which averages 1,461. In addition, the 1,461-panel wall may reflect a standardized or general public knowledge cycle (the cycle if the Sirius year was exactly 365.25 days, which would be the first estimate immediately when they noticed that a given Sirius appearance date lasts about four years—similar to how the general public today are aware of the simple 4-year "leap year" cycle, but few are aware of the more esoteric exact year cycle that needs to be adjusted over the millenia). The 1,459-panel wall could reflect the esoteric knowledge of the exact natural cycle known only to initiates such as Imhotep. In either case, the difference of two years represented on the walls progress in time from east to west could also reflect the changing Sothic cycle—the next one will be two years shorter. Further, the difference between the eastern and western wall representations—two years—appears to be reflected in the northern and southern walls, each of which has 722 panels. Two years equal 720 solar days or 722 sidereal days (we can remember that a sidereal day is the time it takes Earth to complete one rotation relative to the vernal equinox, which is essentially one full rotation with respect to the stars), and it is four minutes shorter than a solar day, which is a full rotation with respect to the sun. Thus there is one extra sidereal day

---

*One problem: we don't know how the ancient Egyptians defined the heliacal rising of Sirius. All we know is that they considered it very important and called it the reappearance of Sirius or, simply, the rising of Sirius.

in a standard solar year of 365 days, as we can also see because one solar day rotation is taken by Earth moving around the sun in one year. The Sothic cycle is essentially a combination of stellar and solar cycles.

Imhotep seems to be informing us that the ancient Egyptians knew this—and they knew the cycle durations very accurately, for they show this in symbolizing human's unity with the cosmos by synchronizing the human civil calendar with cosmic astro-calendars in their monumental architecture. If we accept that Imhotep knew not only that an approximation to the Sothic cycle was 1,461 Egyptian civil years, but also the precise duration of the previous Sothic cycle, then we can believe that he knew that this cycle is a combination of solar and sidereal motions and that he had a concept of the difference between the sidereal day and the solar day. If he did, it is highly likely that he was informed by careful observations going back at least one Sothic cycle, which brings us back to the period of heavy activity at Nabta Playa.

We can also note that this interpretation for the step pyramid complex wall, which otherwise would appear as a needlessly convoluted design, addresses not only the elegant calendar and cosmic meanings of the wall panel design, but also the reason why it was built when it was. It was fashioned to mark the correspondence of the summer solstice and the heliacal rising of Sirius, something that happens only once every twenty-six thousand years, and to calibrate that with the first day of Thoth on the Egyptian civil calendar.

Clearly, then, some time around the building and design of the step pyramid complex, a heliacal rising of Sirius occurred simultaneous with the summer solstice and the first day of Thoth. We cannot get to the precise date without knowing the exact way in which the ancient Egyptians determined the heliacal rising or by some other constraint. The Djoser serdab may give us this other constraint. We can remember that the serdab was probably not meant as a precision device—it shows us the king gazing at the area of the sky where Alkaid was at the time of Sirius's rising. Finding a best fit for that alignment may help constrain our date. Somewhere around 2680 BCE may be a good estimate. On that date, on the day of summer solstice, Sirius was at 1 degree above the horizon, the sun was 8.16 degrees below horizon (suitable for a reappearance of Sirius) and Alkaid was at 13.4 degrees altitude and 3.14 degrees azimuth—within the viewing range of the serdab.[*]

We can almost hear the massive calendar wall announcing, "We now monumentalize in stone our transition from the good old days of acting as nomads around Nabta Playa to a more settled existence in monumental cities, which means that we're going to have to rely more on that civil calendar that nobody much likes because it drifts with respect to the wondrous natural astro-calendar of our ancestors. We're going to have to keep the civil calendar in use for collecting taxes and enforcing legal contracts—but here, in great splendor, is a monument that shows how the two types of time, human time and godly cosmic time, work together."

---

[*]There are two types of uncertainties regarding the serdab view angle. First is the spread of angles due to the aperture of the peepholes, and second is any remaining uncertainty as to the basic measures of its angles. Mark Lehner lists the altitude of the serdab as 13 degrees without reference, and the layout survey gives an azimuth of about 4.5 degrees for the whole complex. We then used a protractor and plumb bob at the site to estimate about 16 degrees for the serdab box. In any case, the serdab gazes generally in the correct region of the sky to view Alkaid simultaneous with Sirius rising heliacally on the day of summer solstice.

APPENDIX 3

SAVING NABTA PLAYA

Will the Oldest Prehistoric Astronomical Complex in the World be Destroyed?

In July 1998, a short letter published in the highly respected scientific journal *Nature* sent a huge wave of interest across scientific communities worldwide. Professor Fred Wendorf, an American anthropologist, and his colleagues, astronomer Kim Malville and fellow anthropologist Romuald Schild, made a startling announcement: they had discovered in Egypt's Western Desert, at a location 100 kilometers (62 miles) west of Abu Simbel, the oldest astronomical megalithic site in the world, predating Stonehenge by at least one thousand years. They called the site Nabta Playa. Wendorf and his team then concluded that the African-origin prehistoric people of Nabta Playa were most probably the ancestors of the pharaohs, and it was them, with their well-developed knowledge of astronomy, agriculture, and cattle-herding, who provided the impetus that inspired the great civilization of ancient Egypt.

The news went around the world like wildfire, and soon many academics were becoming convinced that it was, indeed, in the Western Desert of Egypt (also called the Eastern Sahara or Egyptian Sahara) that civilization began and, eventually, in the fourth millennium BCE, spread to the adjacent Nile Valley, where it then spawned the pharaonic culture. In view of this realization, Nabta Playa acquired immense importance for the study of the origins of civilization as well as other elements of early humans, such as astronomy, the domestication of cattle, the development of agriculture, and early religious ideologies. A team headed by Fred Wendorf, calling itself the Combined Prehistoric Expedition (CPE) was allocated a concession by the Supreme Council of Antiquities of Egypt (SCA) to study and excavate at Nabta Playa.

In fact, Nabta Playa was discovered in 1974 by Wendorf and his team, but it was not until the early 1990s that they realized that the many megaliths strewn about the site were not in their natural place but instead had been deliberately placed by humans. Gradually, the team became aware that this was no ordinary prehistoric Neolithic site, but instead was a ceremonial complex of unique value. In 1991–1992, the anthropologist Maria Nieves Zedeño, of the University of Arizona, and her colleague Alex Applegate of Southern Methodist University (SMU) joined the Combined Prehistoric Expedition (CPE) under the guidance of Fred Wendorf and Romuald Schild and were assigned the reconstruction of a stone circle—the so-called Calendar Circle. In 1997, the archaeoastronomer Kim Malville of the University of Colorado in Boulder was invited to join the CPE at Nabta Playa. Malville, who had much experience in the study of ancient astronomical alignments, quickly realized that not only did the Calendar Circle have solar alignments to the summer solstice and equinoxes, but also that several of the nearby megalithic alignments that emanated from a conglomerate of large stones (called Complex Structure A, or simply CSA) were astronomically aligned to the rising point of important stars: Alpha Canis Major (Sirius), Alpha Ursa Major (Dhube), and the three bright stars of Orion's belt.

Knowing that these stars had also been important to the ancient Egyptians in their sky religion (as expressed in the Pyramid Texts and other funerary literature, such as the Coffin Texts, the Book of the Dead, and the so-called Carlsberg Papyrus) Wendorf, Schild, and Malville published a series of articles (their most recent in 2007) in which they expressed their strong suspicion that the evidence found at

Nabta Playa (the stellar and solar alignments, the cow cult, the burial customs) shows a direct connection to the pharaonic civilization of the nearby Nile Valley. This hypothesis was further fortified by the fact that radiocarbon dating at Nabta Playa showed that the presence of the people who had populated this desert region ceased to exist at around 3400 BCE, when the southwestern desert of Egypt became superarid— a date, which, most tellingly, coincided with the emergence of the pharaonic civilization in southern Egypt along the Nile. It very much seemed that the more ancient people of Nabta Playa migrated to the nearby Nile Valley, bringing along their body of astronomical knowledge and domesticated cattle that kick-started the pharaonic civilization.

In view of the immense cultural importance of Nabta Playa, however, the supervision and protection of the site during the periods when the CPE team was not there was practically nonexistent. The CPE was generally present on the site from around January to the end March, but before and after this, the high temperatures of the region made any work very difficult if not impossible, and thus Nabta Playa was left without any security system or guards. When the astrophysicist Thomas Brophy visited Nabta Playa in October 2003, there was no one on the site, and he noted the lack of any sign or fencing or official notice that indicated that this was an archaeological site. Brophy took extensive photographs of the megaliths, which he eventually published in magazines and scientific journals. Along with the Calendar Circle, Brophy visited the remains of the excavation of Complex Structure A, where he found several megaliths strewn about the site where the central cow stone sculpture had been removed.

Directly from Nabta Playa, Brophy went to the Nubian Museum in Aswan and met with its director, who is also the SCA official in charge of archaeology in the region. Brophy was told the cow stone sculpture was being held in the back of the museum, in a closed storage area, awaiting the construction of a pedestal so that it could be displayed prominently at the front of the museum. Brophy asked to see the sculpture and was escorted by an AK-47-armed guard, at night, to the location where he found the megalithic sculpture damaged and broken.

In 2007, Robert Bauval also decided to visit Nabta Playa, and he duly informed Dr. Schild, who replied that he, too, planned "to be at Nabta Playta in January and early February, 2008." On November 18, 2007, Bauval and some of his friends and colleagues (Dr. Carmen Boulter of Calgary University, professional cameraman Eric Phillips-Horst, Michele Bauval, and the photographer Joanne Cunningham) arrived at Nabta Playa. With them were an officer from the Egyptian military and a local guide, Muhammad Nemr, as well as two drivers provided by Nemr, who had been responsible for obtaining all the necessary permits from Egyptian National Security. Dr. Boulter had also applied for a filming permit from the Ministry of Information and the Supreme Council of Antiquities. Upon arriving at Nabta Playa in the early part of the afternoon, they found a group of tourists with the British Egyptologist Dr. Nicole Douek. This group had arrived earlier that morning and were now about to leave for Gilf Kebir, a mountainous region that was several hundred kilometers to the west of Nabta Playa. Dr. Douek invited Robert Bauval to give a short talk to her group on the astronomy of Nabta Playa. She also agreed to give an on-camera joint interview with Bauval. After Dr. Douek and her group departed, Bauval and his colleagues examined the Calendar Circle and other artifacts in the area, taking many photographs and much video footage.

A few months later, in April 2008, Thomas Brophy came to Cairo to join Robert Bauval in an expedition to Gilf Kebir and Jebel Uwainat. It was after this expedition that, on April 17, 2008, Thomas Brophy revisited Nabta Playa. The required permits were obtained for him by the local guide, Muhammad Nemr, who also took Brophy and an officer from the Egyptian military to Nabta Playa. Upon arrival at the site, Brophy noticed that the Calendar Circle had been severely disrupted: many of its stones had been dispersed and moved. It also seemed that there were some stones missing, especially a beautifully shaped stone, which he had photographed in 2003. Brophy also noted that a large megalith from Complex Structure A was missing. When he returned to Cairo, Brophy visited Bauval, and they compared photographs taken in November 2007 (by Bauval) and those taken in April 2008 (by Brophy). It was quite evident that the Calendar Circle in the November 2007 photos was very different from the one in the April 2008 photos. More troubling still, when he was at Nabta Playa, Brophy noted that much rubbish had been dumped on the eastern side of the area, at the foot of a sand dune where the CPE team usually camped.

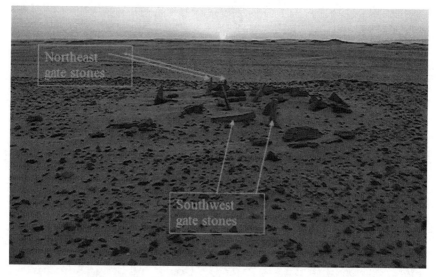

Figure A1. Calendar Circle, sunrise, October 2003. Since the 1999 image was taken, some stones have been removed, toppled, and possibly replaced.

Figure A2. Rubbish dumps in the central area of Nabta Playa, 2008.

Figure A3. Top: Calendar Circle, November 2007.
Bottom: Calendar Circle, April 2008. The arrangement has been
altered yet again and has been partially reconstructed.

Bauval decided to return to Nabta Playa on May 8, 2008, to assess the situation. He was thus able to confirm that the Calendar Circle had, indeed, been much tampered with and that there were signs of other disruption on the site. A prehistoric stone sundial that he had photographed in November 2007 was badly ravaged. In addition, there were heavy vehicle tracks around the megaliths and several open rubbish dumps near the sand dunes. Elsewhere, a prehistoric grinding block was missing and another was broken in two. Bauval decided to go to the Nubian Museum at Aswan the next day to ask the director what had happened at Nabta Playa between November 2007 and April 2008. In the afternoon of May 9, 2008, Bauval met Deputy Director Dr. Ragheb of the Nubian Museum. He informed Bauval that, upon instructions from Dr. Schild, three large megaliths from Nabta Playa had been brought to the Nubian Museum in February 2008. Dr. Ragheb showed Bauval the three megaliths, which were in the yard of the museum. Dr. Ragheb also showed Bauval a large megalith known as the cow stone, which had been brought from Nabta Playa several years before. This cow stone, which had been buried several meters beneath CSA, had unfortunately been damaged (broken into two parts). When Bauval inquired about the Calendar Circle, Dr. Ragheb insisted that the stones had not been removed and were still in their original position on site. Dr. Ragheb knew nothing of the rubbish dumps.

Soon after, Bauval contacted Romuald Schild. In a series of e-mails received from Dr. Schild between May 15 and June 12, 2008, Bauval was informed that the CPE had been aware that unauthorized visits to Nabta Playa by tourists had taken place over the years. According to Schild, an estimated one thousand unauthorized tourists had come to Nabta Playa in the last decade, and there was evidence that they had tampered with the Calendar Circle several times and had even made a reconstruction and built a New Age stone circle around an upright prehistoric marker near C-group house. Schild added that the original Calendar Circle was removed from its place in February 2008 to be reconstructed in the Nubian Museum. In its place, the CPE had added a modern reconstruction of this monument. Apart from this, Schild stated that he did not know of any very recent, serious damages except for some bulldozer work around the stele that were removed in February to be re-erected at the Nubian Museum in Aswan. As to why Dr. Ragheb denied that the Calendar Circle had been moved to the Nubian Museum, Schild

Figure A4. Top: Robert Bauval and the director of the Nubian Museum with the broken cow stone scupture, April 2008. Bottom: Bauval and John Anthony West examine a piece of the broken cow stone at the Nubian Museum in 2003.

Figure A5. Left: Prehistoric grinding block seen near Nabta Playa in 2007.
Right: A similar grinding block used as an ashtray at a hotel.

offered that either Dr. Ragheb did not want to disclose the information to Bauval or that he had misunderstood Bauval's question. Schild
insisted that "The calendar, and other selected Nabta monuments, had
been removed from their original place on February 18, 2008, in my
presence as well as in the presence of a number of the members of the
Expedition and a Special High Committee of the Supreme Council of
Antiquities headed by an Undersecretary of State. The entire removal
was filmed and intensively photographed. The antiquities were immediately taken to the Nubian Museum in Aswan in a separate convoy
escorted by the police. Dr. Osama, Director of the Museum, received
the convoy and its load at the Museum."[1]

As for the rubbish on the site, Schild at first offered that it had
been left by tourists. When Bauval, however, said that the evidence
pointed to the rubbish being from the CPE, Schild offered that perhaps
it had been interred in a pit and now, for some unknown reason, someone had excavated the pits and exposed the rubbish. On June 12, Bauval
received an e-mail from Dr. Schild in which Schild stated that "since
May 2007 I am not heading the CPE any more, although, I have been
responsible for some of the projects carried out by the CPE, like the
archaeological operations undertaken in conjunction with the Egyptian

Supreme Council of Antiquities, i.e., salvage of Nabta monuments." It was also at this stage that Dr. Schild informed Bauval, "Nabta has been earmarked for an extensive reclamation, i.e., total destruction, as a part of the Tushka project."

Since 1997, the Egyptian government has launched a series of large civil engineering projects to reclaim the arid Western Desert and turn 1.5 million acres into agricultural land. The projects are broadly divided into two parts: (1) to build a canal fed by Lake Nasser that will deliver billions of cubic meters of water to irrigate various regions of the desert as far north as the Qattara Depression, and (2) to extract groundwater from natural aquifers, mostly from the east Uwainat region, a few hundred kilometers west of Abu Simbel. To date, the first phase of the canal project, known as the Sheikh Zayed Canal, has been completed. It involves a 70-meter-wide (230-feet-wide) concrete-lined canal that is fed by a huge pumping station (the Mubarak Pumping Station). At its terminus, the canal splits into four branches, each about 50 kilometers (31 miles) long, which will be used to irrigate the adjacent desert lands. The whole region where the canal and its branches run is known as the Tushka Depression or Basin, and these projects are collectively known sometimes as the Tushka Project. (The official name of the collective project is the Southern Egypt Development Project.) The project that most threatens the Nabta Playa area is the east Uwainat groundwater project, which, according to the Egyptian government, would irrigate 200,000 feddans (acres) in the region. Nevertheless, as Schild himself admits, "recent financial problems facing the project brought a temporary stop to these plans, although all the planning work, designs, drilling for water, survey, soil assessments, etc., of the area have been finished."[2] In addition, according to Schild, "exempting Nabta from these governmental plans by the SCA has not yet been successful." It is because of this, says Schild, that "the CPE has been very intensively recording all the megaliths and related monuments at Nabta, e.g., we have just finished mapping, in the scale of 1:50, all the megaliths and their fragments, together with the associated quarries, in the entire Nabta Basin."[3]

We felt it was important that UNESCO World Heritage be consulted on this matter. Communications were sent to both the UNESCO World Heritage headquarters in Paris and its offices in Cairo. UNESCO funded the creation and operation of the impressively built Nubian Museum of Aswan. No reply, however, has yet been received. We also contacted Dr. Malville, the astronomer who was a member of the CPE and who had been responsible for the study of the Calendar Circle and the megalithic stellar alignments at Nabta Playa in 1997–1998. Oddly, Dr. Malville had not been consulted or even informed of the removal of the Calendar Circle. We also communicated with the Egyptian astronomer Dr. Mosalam Shaltout, who had been involved with the study of Nabta Playa. Dr. Shaltout had also not been informed of the removal of the Calendar Circle. We hope that with the publication of this text, an alarm bell will be heard by the archaeological and anthropological communities in the hope of salvaging the Nabta Playa prehistoric site as well as other monuments that may be threatened by ongoing desert reclamation projects.

April 2010 update: unauthorized visits to Nabta Playa are still taking place. To our knowledge, no security system has been put into place, and the site still remains unprotected. We are given to understand that no official announcements have been made by the Nubian Museum in Aswan or the Supreme Council of Antiquities as to what is planned for the Calendar Circle and other monuments that were removed from the site. On April 7, 2010, Robert Bauval discussed the matter with professor Salima Ikram of the American University in Cairo. She offered to look into this matter.

NOTES

CHAPTER I. STRANGE STONES

1. Romuald Schild and Fred Wendorf, "Forty Years of the Combined Prehistoric Expedition," *Archaeologia Polona* 40 (2002): 11.
2. Fred Wendorf and Romuald Schild, "The Megaliths of Nabta Playa, Focus on Archeology," *Academia* 1, no. 1 (2004): 11.
3. Fred Wendorf, *Holocene Settlement of the Egyptian Sahara,* vol. 1, in Fred Wendorf, and Romuald Schild, eds., *The Archaeology of Nabta Playa* (New York: Kluwer Academic/Plenum, 2001).
4. *The Mystery of the Sphinx,* NBC documentary, November 10, 1993.
5. Ian Shaw and Paul Nicholson, *The Illustrated Dictionary of Ancient Egypt* (Cairo: American University in Cairo Press, 2008), 82–3. See also Richard H. Wilkinson, *The Complete Gods and Goddesses of Ancient Egypt* (Cairo: American University in Cairo Press, 2005), 139.
6. Wendorf, Schild et al., *Holocene Settlement of the Egyptian Sahara,* vol. 1.
7. E. C. Krupp, *Echoes of the Ancient Skies* (New York: Oxford University Press, 1983), 259.
8. Jed Z. Buchwald, "Egyptian Stars under Paris Skies," *Engineering and Science Magazine* 66, No. 4, California Institute of Technology (2003).
9. E. G. Lesley and Roy Adkins, *The Keys of Egypt* (New York: HarperCollins, 2000).
10. Norman Lockyer, *The Dawn of Astronomy* (London: Cassel and Co. Ltd., 1894) Preface.11. Ibid.
12. Ibid.
13. Thomas Brophy, *The Origin Map: Discovery of a Prehistoric Megalithic*

Astrophysical Map of the Universe, afterword by John Anthony West (Bloomington, Ind.: iUniverse, 2002), 118.

14. John Michell, *A Little History of Astro-Archaeology* (London: Thames and Hudson, 1977), 68.

15. Virginia Trimble, *Astronomical Investigation Concerning the So-called Airshafts of Cheop's Pyramid, Mitteilungen der Institut Fur Orientforschung* 10, no. 2/3 (1964): 183–87. See also Robert G. Bauval, "The Seeding of the Star-gods: A Fertility Rite inside Cheop's Pyramid?" *Discussion In Egyptology* 16 (1990), 21–25; Robert G. Bauval, "Cheop's Pyramid: A New Dating Using the Latest Astronomical Data," *Discussions In Egyptology* 26 (1993): 5–6; Dr. Mary T. Bruck, "Can the Great Pyramid be Astronomically Dated?" *Journal of the British Astronomical Association* 105, no. 4 (1995): 161–64.

CHAPTER 2. WANDERLUST

1. A. M. Hassanein Bey, "Through Kufra to Darfur," *Geographical Journal* 64, no. 4 (Oct., 1924): 273–91.

2. Ibid.

3. Ibid.

4. Ibid.

5. Ibid.

6. Ibid.

7. Ibid.

8. Ibid.

9. Ibid.

10. www.scribd.com/doc/21432876/Rosita-Forbes-Bio.

11. Hans Goedicke, "Harkhuf's Travels," *Journal of Near Eastern Studies* 40, no. 1 (January 1981): 1–20.

12. J. H. Breasted, *Ancient Records of Egypt,* Part I (Chicago: University of Chicago Press, 1906), 328.

13. David B. O'Connor, and Stephen Quirke, *Mysterious Lands* (London: University College, Institute of Archaeology, 2003), 10.

14. Ibid.

15. Claire Lalouette, *Textes sacrés et textes profanes de l'ancienne Egypte* (Paris:

Gallimard, 1984). 16. Breasted, *Ancient Records of Egypt,* Part I, 328.

17. Bill Manley, "Where was the Kingdom of Yam?" in *The Seventy Great Mysteries of Ancient Egypt* (London: Thames and Hudson, 2003), 135.

18. Goedicke, "Harkhuf's Travels," 10.

19. G. W. Murray, "Hakhuf's Third Journey," *Geographical Journal* 131, no. 1 (March 1965): 72–75.

20. A. J. Arkell, *A History of the Sudan: From Earliest Times to 1821,* 2nd ed., rev. (London: n.p., 1961), 43.

21. M. Kobusiewicz and R. Schild, "Prehistoric Herdsmen, Focus on Archaeology," *Academia* 3, no. 7 (2004): 20–23.

22. R. Schild, and F. Wendorf, "Forty Years of the Combined Prehistoric Expedition," *Archaeologia Polona* 40 (2002): 18.

23. J. L. Wright, *Libya, Chad and the Central Sahara* (London: Hurst and Co., 1989), 22. See also R. F. Peel, "The Tibu Peoples and the Libyan Desert," *Geographical Journal* 100, no. 2 (August 1942), 73–87.

24. Ahmed Hassanein, "Crossing the Untraversered Libyan Desert," *National Geographic Magazine,* vol. XLVI, no. 3, September 1924.

25. Wright, *Libya, Chad and the Central Sahara,* 22; Peel, "The Tibu Peoples and the Libyan Desert," 73–87.

26. G. Wilkinson, *Topography of Thebes and General View of Egypt* (London: John Murray Publishers, 1835), 358–59.

27. W. J. Harding King, *Mysteries of the Libyan Desert* (London: Century, 1925), 145.

28. www.carlo-bergmann.de/Discoveries/discovery.htm. Accessed August 10, 2010.

29. www.carlo-bergmann.de/ex2004-5/expedition2004-5-2.htm.

For more on the issue of 'Mefat' see: C. Bergmann and Kl. P. Kuhlmann, "Die Expedition des Cheops", GEO Special 5, 2001, p. 120-127; Kl. P. Kuhlmann, "The 'Oasis Bypath' or The Issue of Desert Trade in Pharaonic Times", in T. Lenssen-Erz, U. Tegtmeier, St. Kröpelin et al. (eds.), "Tides of the Desert. Contributions to the Archaeology and Environmental History of Africa in Honour of Rudolf Kuper, Köln," 2002, pp.133–138. Also R. Kuper and Fr. Forster, "Khufu's 'mefat' expeditions into the Libyan Desert," *Egyptian Archaeology* 23, 2003, p. 25-28.

30. Ibid.

31. Mark Lehner, *The Complete Pyramids* (London: Thames and Hudson, 1997), 120.

32. Stefan Kropelin, and Rudolph Kuper, "More Corridors to Africa," *Cripel* 26 (2006–2007), 219–29. 33. G. Burkhard, "Inscriptions in the Dakhla Region," *Sahara* 9 (1997), 152–53.

34. Zahi Hawass and Lyla Pich Brock, *Egyptology at the Dawn of the Twenty-first Century: History, Religion* (Cairo: American University in Cairo Press, 2004), 374.

35. Richard A. Bermann, "Historic Problems of the Libyan Desert," *Geographical Journal* 83, no. 6 (June 1934): 456–63.

36. Ibid.

37. Frank Förster, "With Donkeys, Jars and Water Bags into the Libyan Desert: The Abu Ballas Trail in the late Old Kingdom/First Intermediate Period," *British Museum* SAES 7 (September 2007): 7.

38. Stefan Kropelin and Rudolph Kuper, "More Corridors to Africa," 220.

39. Joseph Clayton, Aloisia De Trafford, and Mark Borda, "A Hieroglyphic Inscription Found at Jebel Uweinat Mentioning Yam and Tekhebet," *Sahara* 19 (2008).

40. Ibid.

41. Ibid.

42. Breasted, *Ancient Records of Egypt,* Part 1, 351, and Wallis Budge, *An Egyptian Hieroglyphic Dictionary* (Mineola, N.Y.: Dover Publications, 1978), 1050 a.

43. Charles Kuentz, *Bulletin de L'Institut Francais d'Archeologie Orientale* 17 1(920): 121–90. 44. Ibid., 137. See also A. Weidemann, *Recuil de Travaux,* tome XVII, 4, note 1.

45. K. P. Kuhlmann, "The Oasis Bypath or the Issue of Desert Trade in Pharaonic Times," in Tilman Lenssen-Erz, Ursula Tegtmeier, and Stefan Kröpelin, *Gezeiten der Wüste* (Köln: Heinrich Barth Institut, 2001), 141–42.

46. www.carlo-bergmann.de/ . Result of Winter 2007/08 Expedition, Advance Report

47. Ibid.

CHAPTER 3. STONEHENGE IN THE SAHARA

1. J. F. McCauley, G. G. Schaber, C. S. Breed, et al, "Subsurface Valleys and Geoarcheology of the Eastern Sahara Revealed by Shuttle Radar," *Science* 218, no. 4576 (December 3, 1982): 1004–1020.

2. Vivien Gornitz, Springerlink Online Service, *Encyclopedia of Paleoclimatology and Ancient Environments* (Dordrecht, Netherlands: Springer, 2009).

3. Fred Wendorf and Romuald Schild, *Holocene Settlement of the Egyptian Sahara,* vol. 1: *The Archaeology of Nabta Playa* (Dordrecht, Netherlands: Kluwer Academic, 2001).

4. The Fezzan Project: Geoarchaeology of the Sahara, www.cru.uea. ac.uk/~e118/Fezzan/fezzan_home.html. Accessed April 16, 2007.

5. P. B. DeMenocal, J. Ortiz, T. Guilderson, J. Adkins, M.Sarnthein, L. Baker, and M. Yarusinski, "Abrupt Onset and Termination of the African Humid Period: Rapid Climate Response to Gradual Insolation Forcing. *Quaternary Science. Review* 19 (2000), 347–361.

6. Milutin Milankovitch, *Théorie Mathématique des Phénomènes Thermiques produits par la Radiation Solaire* (Paris: Gauthier-Villars, 1920).

7. Details of this calculation are referenced in, for example, Thomas Brophy, *The Origin Map: Discovery of a Prehistoric Megalithic Astrophysical Map of the Universe* (Bloomington, Ind.: iUniverse, September 20, 2002).

8. Ibid.

9. DeMenocal, Ortiz, Guilderson, et al, "Abrupt Onset and Termination of the African Humid Period: Rapid Climate Response to Gradual Insolation Forcing," 347–61.

10. P. B. DeMenocal, "Cultural Responses to Climate Change during the Late Holocene," *Science* 292 (2001): 667–73.

11. History Channel documentary: *How the Earth was Made: Sahara,* December 15, 1999.

12. Qur'an, trans. M. H. Shakir (Elmhurst, N.Y.: Tahrike Tarsile Qur'an Inc., 1983).

13. G. I. Gurdjieff, *All and Everything: Meetings with Remarkable Men* (New York: E. P. Dutton and Co. Inc., 1963. 14. CNN, April 2, 1998.

15. J. McKim Malville, Fred Wendorf, Ali A. Mazar, et al, "Megaliths and Neolithic Astronomy in Southern Egypt," *Nature* 392 (April 1998): 488–91.

16. Alex Applegate and Nieves Zedeño, *Holocene Settlement of the Egyptian Sahara,* vol. 1 (New York: Plenum, 2001), 463–67. 17. Malville, Wendorf, Mazar, et al, "Megaliths and Neolithic Astronomy in Southern Egypt," 490.

18. A. F. Aveni, "Tropical Archaeoastronomy," *Science* 243 (1981): 161–71.

19. Malville, Wendorf, Mazar, et al, "Megaliths and Neolithic Astronomy in Southern Egypt," 490.

20. Ibid.

21. Ibid.

22. Ibid.

23. Fred Wendorf and Romuald Schild, eds., *Holocene Settlement of the Egyptian Sahara,* vol. 1: *The Archaeology of Nabta Playa* (Dordrecht, Netherlands: Kluwer Academic, 2001).

24. Ibid.

25. Thomas Brophy and Paul Rosen, "Satellite Imagery Measures of the Astronomically Aligned Megaliths at Nabta Playa," *Mediterranean Archaeology and Archaeometry* 5, no. 1 (2005): 15–24.

26. Wendorf and Schild, *Holocene Settlement of the Egyptian Sahara,* vol. 1: *The Archaeology of Nabta Playa.*

27. Brophy and Rosen, "Satellite Imagery Measures of the Astronomically Aligned Megaliths at Nabta Playa."

28. J. M. Malville, R. Schild, F. Wendorf, and J. Brenmer, "Astronomy of Nabta Playa," *African Skies/Cieus Africains,* no. 11 (July 2007).

28. Brophy and Rosen, "Satellite Imagery Measures of the Astronomically Aligned Megaliths at Nabta Playa."

30. Wendorf and Schild, *Holocene Settlement of the Egyptian Sahara,* vol. 1, Introduction to the chapter "The Megalithic Alignments," 489.

31. Brophy and Rosen, "Satellite Imagery Measures of the Astronomically Aligned Megaliths at Nabta Playa."

32. Wendorf and Schild, *Holocene Settlement of the Egyptian Sahara,* vol. 1, "The Megalith Alignments" by Wendorf and Malville. In the chapter, Wendorf writes, "There are two parts to this chapter. The first, by Wendorf, describes the megaliths and the other unusual features that may be related to the megalith phenomena. The second, by Malville, documents the relationships of the alignments with the positions of several stars . . . " So

comments from the later part of that chapter are referenced "by Malville" and the Introduction to that chapter is "by Wendorf."

33. Ibid.

CHAPTER 4. SIRIUS RISING

1. David S. McKay, et al, "Search for Past Life on Mars: Possible Relic Biogenic Activity in Martian Meteorite ALH84001," *Science* magazine (August 16, 1996).

2. Wendorf and Schild, *Holocene Settlement of the Egyptian Sahara,* vol. 1: *The Archaeology of Nabta Playa,* 489.

3. http://en.wikipedia.org/wiki/Joseph_Justus_Scaliger. Accessed January 2010.

4. Ibid.

5. Related, though not identical, planetary dynamics calculations were employed in T. G. Brophy, L. W. Esposito, G. R. Stewart, et al, "Numerical Simulation of Satellite-ring Interactions: Resonances and Satellite-ring Torques, *Icarus* 100 (1992): 412–33.

6. From A. L. Berger, "Obliquity and Precession for the Last 5,000,000 Years," *Astronomy & Astrophysics* 51 (1976): 127–35.

7. We thank professional animator and producer Chance Gardner for producing these animated graphics.

8. Annual Meeting of the American Astronomical Society, Historical Astronomy Division, January 5, 2004, Atlanta, Georgia.

9. International Conference on the Archaeology of World Megalithic Cultures, University of Rhodes, Greece, October 28, 2004.

10. Brophy and Rosen, "Satellite Imagery Measured of the Astronomically Aligned Megaliths at Nabta Playa," *Mediterranean Archeology and Archaeometry* 5, no. 1 (June 2005): 15–24.

11. J. M. Malville, R. Schild, F. Wendorf, and J. Brenmer, "Astronomy of Nabta Playa," *African Skies/Cieus Africains*, no. 11 (July 2007).

12. See chart in Brophy and Rosen, "Satellite Imagery Measured of the Astronomically Aligned Megaliths at Nabta Playa."

13. J. M. Malville, R. Schild, F. Wendorf, and J. Brenmer, "Astronomy of Nabta Playa."

14. Thomas Brophy, *The Origin Map: Discovery of a Prehistoric Megalithic Astrophysical Map of the Universe* (Bloomington, Ind.: iUniverse, September 20, 2002).

15. E. C. Krupp, *Echoes of the Ancient Skies* (New York: Oxford University Press, 1983), 26.16. We published a photo of them in Brophy and Rosen, "Satellite Imagery Measured of the Astronomically Aligned Megaliths at Nabta Playa."

17. Wendorf and Schild, et al., *Holocene Settlement of the Egyptian Sahara,* vol. 1: *The Archaeology of Nabta Playa,* 510.

18. Ibid.

19. See, for instance, G. De Santillana, and H. von Dechend *Hamlet's Mill* (Boston: Gambit Inc., 1969).

20. Discovery Channel documentary: *Egypt Uncovered: Chaos and Kings,* 1998.

21. Wendorf and Schild, et al., *Holocene Settlement of the Egyptian Sahara,* vol. 1: *The Archaeology of Nabta Playa,* 510.

22. Ibid.

23. Brophy and Rosen, "Satellite Imagery Measured of the Astronomically Aligned Megaliths at Nabta Playa."

24. J. M. Malville, R. Schild, F. Wendorf, and J. Brenmer, "Astronomy of Nabta Playa," *African Skies/Cieus Africains,* no.11 (July 2007).

25. Ibid.

26. Wendorf and Schild, et al., *Holocene Settlement of the Egyptian Sahara,* vol. 1: *The Archaeology of Nabta Playa,* 495.

27. F. Wendorf, A. E. Close, and R. Schild. "Megaliths in the Egyptian Sahara," *Sahara* 5 (1992–1993): 7–16.

28. For example, P. A. Rosen, T. Brophy, and M. Shimada, "Satellite Observations of Archaeoastronomical Structures at Nabta Play, Egypt," proceedings of the IEEE International Geoscience and Remote Sensing Symposium, Boston Massachusetts, 2008.

29. R. A. Bagnold, *The Physics of Blown Sand and Desert Dunes* (London: Methuen, 1941).

30. R. A. Bagnold, "Journeys in the Libyan Desert 1929 and 1930," *Geographical Journal* 78, no. 1 (July 1931).

31. J. McKim Malville, Romuald Schild, Fred Wendorf, et al, "Astronomy of

Nabta Playa," in J. Holbrook et. al, eds., *African Cultural Astronomy— Current Archaeoastronomy and Ethnoastronomy Research in Africa* (New York: Springer, 2008), 133.

32. See, for example, Rosen, Brophy, and Shimada, "Satellite Observations of Archaeoastronomical Structures at Nabta Play, Egypt."

32. See, for example, Rosen, Brophy, and Shimada, "Satellite Observations of Archaeoastronomical Structures at Nabta Play, Egypt."

33. Fliegel Jezerniczky Expeditions website (6 Jan 2009): http://www.freere-public.com/focus/f-chat/2160254/posts.

CHAPTER 5.
THE BIBLE, THE HAMITES, AND THE BLACK MEN

1. Jailan Zayan, *Egypt—Culture Smart!: The Essential Guide to Customs and Culture* (London: Kuperard, 2007), 60.

2. A description of this view can be found in a letter published in the *American Journal of Human Biology* 13 (2001): 569–75 referencing S. O. Y. Keita, and A. J. Boyce, *Race: Confusion about Zoological and Social Taxonomies, and Their Places in Science* (Chicago and Oxford, England: Field Museum and Institute of Biological Anthropology, Oxford University).

3. Peter Rigby, *African Images* (Oxfor, England: Berg Publishers, 1996), 68.

4. C. G. Seligman. *Races of Africa* (London: T. Butterworth, 1930).

5. Ibid., 96.

6. Henri Frankfort, *Kingship and the Gods* (Chicago: University of Chicago Press, 1978), 16.

7. Ibid., 163.

8. Ibid., 70.

9. Martin Bernal, *Black Athena: The Afroasiatic Roots of Classical Civilization,* vols. 1, 2, and 3 (Piscataway, N.J.: Rutgers University Press 1987).

10. See Clarence Walker, *We Can't Go Home Again: An Argument about Afrocentrism* (New York: Oxford University Press, 2004).

11. Ibid. Also see http//www.egyptsearch.com/forum/HTML/001646.html.

12. Rebecca L. Cann, Mark Stoneking, and Allan C. Wilson, "Mitochondrial DNA and Human Evolution," *Nature* 325 (1987): 31–36.

13. Michael Deacon, "Interview with Alice Roberts: The Incredible Human Journey," *Daily Telegraph,* May 5, 2009.

14. Ibid.

15. Pedro Soares et al, "Correcting for Purifying Selection: An Improved Human Mitochondrial Molecular Clock." *American Journal of Human Genetics* 84, no. 6 (June 4, 2009): 740–59.

    We note that more recent research (see note 14) pushes that back to about 200,000 BCE.

16. See Bradshaw Foundation at http://www.bradshawfoundation.com/journey/

17. Ibid.

18. Anta Diop, "Origin of the Ancient Egyptians" (see http//www.africawithin.com/diop/origin_egyptian.htm).

19. Ibid.

20. Ibid.

21. R. Schild and F. Wendorf, "Forty Years of Combined Prehistoric Expedition," *Archaeologia Polona* 40 (2002): 18.

22. Taken from an article by Cheikh Anta Diop in "Egypt Revisited," *Journal of African Civilization* 10 (Summer 1989): 9–39.

23. Ibid.

24. Herodotus, *The Histories,* II, 104.

25. Ibid., 22.

26. Aristotle, *Physiognomy,* 6.

27. Aeschylus, *The Suppliants,* verses 719–20. See also verse 745.

28. Apollodoros, Book II, "The Family of Inachus," paragraphs 3 and 4.

29. Lucian, *Navigations,* paragraphs 2 and 3.

30. Strabo, *Geography*, Book I, chapter 3, paragraph 10; Diodorus of Sicily, *Universal History*, Book III; Diogenes, *Laertius,* Book VII, verse i; Ammianus Marcellinus, Book XXII, paragraph 16: 23.

31. M. C. F. Volney, *Voyages en Syrie et en Egypte* (Paris: n.p., 1787), vol. I, 74–77.

32. Jean-Jacques Champollion-Figeac, *L'Egypte Ancienne,* Didot ed., Paris: 1839, pp. 26–7

33. Adolf Erman, Hermann Grapow, *Deutsche Akamemie, Worterbuch der Aegyptischen Sprache,* vol 5 (n.p., 1971), 122, 127.

34. Ibid., 123–28.

35. UNESCO Symposium on the Peopling of Ancient Egypt and the Deciphering of the Meroitic Script, January 1974, Cairo. Proceedings of the Conference published in 1978.

36. Richard Girling, "King Tut Tut Tut," *Sunday Times* of London, May 22, 2005.

37. Neil Genzlinger, "Chasing Mummies—The Pharaoh of Egyptian Antiquities," *New York Times,* July 13, 2010.

38. http://findarticles.com/p/news-articles/jerusalem-post/mi_8048/is_20070402/war-pyramid-theorist/ai_n47369584/.

39. Ibid.

40. Jerusalem Post, April 2, 2007, "War of the Pyramid Theorists," by Yaniv Salama-Scheer: http://findarticles.com/p/news-articles/jerusalem-post/mi_8048/is_20070402/war-pyramid-theorists/ai_n47369584/.

41. Thomas Brophy, *The Mechanism Demands a Mysticism* (Blue Hill, Maine: Medicine Bear Publishing, 1999).

42. Memri TV, Arabic video, English transcript, broadcast February 11, 2009. See www.memritv.org/clip/en/2049.htm. Accessed August 20, 2010.

43. http://www.liveleak.com/view?i=f50_1279175755.

44. Romuald Schild and Fred Wendorf, "Forty Years of the Combined Prehistoric Expedition," *Archaeologia Polona* 40 (2002): 3–22.

45. Sean Markey, "Exodus from Drying Sahara Gave Rise to Pharaohs, Study Says," *National Geographic News,* July 20, 2006, http://news.nationalgeographic.com/news/2006/07/060720-sahara.html. (Accessed August 20, 2010.)

46. Romuald Schild and Michal Kobusiewicz, "Prehistoric Herdsmen, Academia," *Focus on Archaeology* 3, no. 7 (2005).

47. Gerhard Rohlfs, *Voyages et Explorations au Sahara,* tome 2 (n.p.,1865–67).

48. Rosita Forbes and Sir Harry Johnston, *The Secret of the Sahara: Kufara* (London: n.p., 1923), Introduction.

49. Ahmed Hassanein, "Crossing the Untraversered Libyan Desert," *National Geographic Magazine,* vol. XLVI, no. 3, September 1924.

50. R. A. Bagnold, O. H. Myers, R. F. Peel, and H. A. Winkler, "An Expedition to the Gilf Kebir and 'Uweinat, 1938," *Geographical Journal* 93, no. 4 (April, 1939), 281–312. See also Major R. A. Bagnold, "Journeys in the

Libyan Desert, 1929 and 1930," *Georgaphical Journal* 78, no. 1 (1931): 13.

51. From L. E. Almasy. *Recentes Explorations dans le Desert Libyque, Royal Geographical society of Egypt,* 1936, p. 36. Quoted in Wael T. Abed's book *The Other Egypt* (Cairo: n.p., 1998), 108.

52. Ibid.

53. Rudolph Kuper and Stefan Kröpelin, "Climate-Controlled Holocene Occupation in the Sahara: Motor of Africa's Evolution," *Science Journal AAAS* (July 2006).

54. Kenneth Chang, "In Lake, Signs of Slow Shift from Savannah to Sahara," *New York Times,* May 9, 2008.

55. Peter Gwin, "Lost Tribes of the Green Sahara," *National Geographic,* September 2008.

56. Ibid.

57. Ibid. Sponsors and funders for the Gobero expeditions are: *National Geographic,* Island Fund of the New York Community Trust, the National Science Foundation, and the Wenner-Gren Foundation for Anthropological Research. See also "Stone Age Graveyard Reveals Lifestyles of a 'Green Sahara': Two Successive Cultures Thrived Lakeside," http://news.uchicago.edu/news.php?asset_id=1424 (accessed August 20, 2010), and P. C. Sereno, E. A. Garcea, C. M. Stojanowski, et al. "Lakeside Cemeteries in the Sahara: 5000 Years of Holocene Population and Environmental Change," www.plosone.org/article/info%3Adoi%2F10.1371%2Fjournal.pone.0002995 (accessed August 20, 2010).

58. Jean-Loic Quellec, "Can One 'Read' the Rock Art? An Egyptian Example." In Paul Taylor, ed., *Iconography without Texts* (London: Warburg Warburg Institute Colloquia 12), 2008, p. 25–42. http://cnrs.academia.edu/documents/0097/7841/Le_Quellec_2008-k.pdf.

CHAPTER 6.
THE CATTLE AND THE STAR GODDESSES

1. Richard Parker, "Ancient Egyptian Astronomy," Department of Egyptology, Brown University, Philosophical Transaction of the Royal Society of London, 1974, A 276, 51–65. See also Professor Jiro Kondo, *Ancient Egyptian Astronomy* (Tokyo: Waseda Universtiy, 2008), www.yomiuri.co.jp/

adv/wol/dy/opinion/culture_081006.htm. Accessed August 23, 2010.

2. For a very early, possibly even prehistoric, representation of a star-cow god-dess of ancient Egypt see Donald B. Redford, ed., "Predynastic Star-studded Cow Goddess," *Oxford Guide to Egyptian Mythology* (New York: Berkley Books, 2002), 157–61.

3. Jaromir Malek and John Baines, *The Cultural Atlas of the World: Ancient Egypt* (Richmond, Va.: Stonehenge Press, 1991), 14.

4. Richard Wilkinson, *The Complete Gods and Goddesses of Ancient Egypt* (Cairo: American University in Cairo Press, 2003), 167.

5. Ian Shaw and Paul Nicholson, *Dictionary of Ancient Egypt* (London: British Museum Press, 1995), 58.

6. J. McKim Malville, R. Schild, F. Wendorf, et al, "Astronomy of Nabta Playa," *African Skies/Cieux Africains,* no. 11 (July 2007): 21.

7. Jeff Greenwald, "Moo Age Travellers: Were cattle-worshipping nomads the predecessors of the Pharaohs?" *The New Scientist* 2249, July 29, 2000.

8. Fred Wendorf and Romuald Schild, "The Megaliths of Nabta Playa," *Academia, Focus on Archaeology,* no. 1 (2004): 11.

9. Quoted in Richard H. Wilkinson, *The Complete Gods and Goddesses of Ancient Egypt* (London: Thames and Hudson, 2003), 15.

10. Juan Belmonte, "Some Open Questions on the Egyptian Calendar: An Astronomer's View," *Trabajos de Egiptología* (TdE) 2003, p. 24.

11. Quoted by Peter Ackroyd, "Afloat on the Nile," *New York Times,* October 2, 1988.

12. Richard Wilkinson, *The Complete Temples of Ancient Egypt* (New York: Thames and Hudson, 2000), 165.

13. Ron Wells, "Sothis and the Satet Temple on Elephantine," *Studien Zur Altagyptischen Kultur* 12 (1985), 258. See also Gunther Roeder, "Sothis und Satis," *Zeitschrift fuer Aegyptische Sprache,* Band 45, Leipzig 1908, pp. 22–30.

14. Wilkinson, *The Complete Temples of Ancient Egypt,* 165.

15. Wells, "Sothis and the Satet Temple on Elephantine," 258.

16. From the declaration of Ptolemy I as pharaoh of Egypt in 305 BCE to the death of Cleopatra in 30 BCE.

17. Data from the *in situ* information board by the German and Swiss Archaeological Team. See also Wilkinson, *The Complete Temples of Ancient*

Egypt, 212; Wells, "Sothis and the Satet Temple on Elephantine: A Direct Connection," 255.

18. Wells, "Sothis and the Satet Temple on Elephantine," 258–62.

19. Ibid.

20. J. A. Belmonte and M. Shaltout, "On the Orientation of Ancient Egyptian Temples I: Upper Egypt and Lower Nubia," in *Journal of the History of Astronomy* (Pre-print series: PP 03/2005), 21, figure 8.

21. Wilkinson, *The Complete Temples of Ancient Egypt,* 211.

22. Adapted from E. A. Wallis Budge, *Legends of the Egyptian Gods: Hieroglyphic Texts and Translations* (New York: Dover, 1994).

23. Ibid.

24. Herodotus, *The Histories,* Book II, chapter 28.

25. Pliny the Elder, *The Natural History,* Book V, chapter 10.

26. Budge, *Legends of the Egyptian Gods.*

27. Wells, "Sothis and the Satet Temple on Elephantine," 262.

28. Rolf K. Krauss, "Probleme des Altagyptischen Kalendars und der Chronologie des Mittleren und Neuen Reiches in Agypten," Ph.D. dissertation, Freie University, Berlin, 1981. See also R. Krauss, "Sothis, Elephantine und d. Altagypt Chronologie," *Gottinger Miszellen* 50 (1981): 71–81.

29. L. Rose, "The Astronomical Evidence for Dating the End of the Middle Kingdom of Ancient Egypt to the Early Second Millennium: A Reassessment," *Journal of Near Eastern Studies* 53 (1994): 246.

30. Strabo, *Geography,* Book XVII.

31. Budge, *Legends of the Egyptian Gods.*

32. M. Lichtheim, *Ancient Egyptian Literature: A Book of Readings,* vol. 3 (Berkeley: University of California Press, 1973), 94–100.

33. Norman Lockyer, *The Dawn of Astronomy* (London: Cassell and Co. Ltd., 1894), 236.

34. G. A. Wainwright, "Seshat and the Pharaoh," *Journal of Egyptian Archaeology* 26 (1941): 30–40.

35. E. C. Krupp, *Echoes of the Ancient Skies* (New York: Oxford University Press, 1983), 212.

36. Wainwright, "Seshat and the Pharaoh."

37. Anne-Sophie Bomhard, *The Egyptian Calendar: A Work for Eternity* (London: Periplus, 1998), 4.

38. George Hart, *A Dictionary of Egyptian Gods and Goddesses* (London: Routledge and Kegan Paul, 1988), 193.

39. I. E. S. Edwards, *The Pyramids of Egypt* (London: Penguin, 1982), 249–250.

40. Martin Isler quoting R. W. Stoley, "Primitive Methods of Measuring Time with Special Reference to Egypt," *Journal of Egyptian Archaeology* 17 (1931), 170.

41. Z. Zaba, *L'Orientation Astronomique Dans L'Ancienne Egypte et la Precession de l'Axe du Monde* (Prague: n.p., 1953), 58–59.

42. See R. Bauval, *The Egypt Code* (London: Century Books, 2006) and T. Brophy, *The Origin Map* (Bloomington, Ind.: iUniverse, 2002).

43. Anne-Sophie Bomhard, *The Egyptian Calendar: A Work for Eternity*, 2.

44. R. A. Schwaller de Lubicz, *The Temples of Karnak*, (Rochester, Vt.: Inner Traditions, 2001), 1.

45. Jean Kerisel, *The Nile and Its Masters: Past, Present, Future Source of Hope and Anger* (Rotterdam: A. A. Balkema, 2001), 37.

46. Donald B. Redford, ed., *The Ancient Gods Speak* (Oxford: Oxford University Press, 2002), 254.

47. Mark Lehner, *The Complete Pyramids* (New York: Thames and Hudson, 1997), 29.

48. A. Chapman, *Gods in the Sky: Astronomy from the Ancients to the Renaissance* (London: Channel 4 Books, 2002), 32–33.

49. Lehner, *The Complete Pyramids*, 28.

50. Lucie Lamy, *Egyptian Mysteries* (New York: Thames and Hudson, 1981), 48.

51. R. Bauval, "A Master Plan for the Three Pyramids of Giza Based on the Configuration of the Three Stars of the Belt of Orion," *Discussions in Egyptology* 13 (1989), pp.7-19.

52. Herodotus, *The Histories*, Book II: 18-24.

53. Wilkinson, *The Complete Temples of Ancient Egypt*, 45.

54. See also Richard Parker, *The Calendars of Ancient Egypt* (Chicago: University of Chicago Press, 1950). For a recent discussion on the Sothic Cycle, see Paul Jordan, *Riddles of the Sphinx* (New York: New York University Press, 1998), 35–37.

55. Robert Burnham Jr., *Burnham's Celestial Handbook*, vol. 1 (New York: Dover Publications, 1978), 387.

56. Ibid.

57. E. C. Krupp, *Echoes of the Ancient Skies* (New York: Oxford University Press, 1983), 22.

58. R. W. Sloley, "Primitive Methods of Measuring Time, with Special Reference to Egypt," *Journal of Egyptian Archaeology* 17 (1930): 167.

59. Krupp, *Echoes of the Ancient Skies,* 23.

60. Censorinus, *De Die Natali,* translated by Holt N. Parker (Chicago: The University of Chicago Press 2007).

61. Rundle Clark, *Myth and Symbol in Ancient Egypt,* Thames and Hudson, London 1978, p. 27.

62. Ibid., 263.

63. Lehner, *The Complete Pyramids,* 29.

64. Edwards, *The Pyramids of Egypt,* 284, 286.

65. G. J. Whitrow, *Time in History: View of Time from Prehistory to the Present Day* (New York: Oxford University Press, 1988), 26.

66. Stephen Quirke, *The Cult of Ra* (London: Thames and Hudson, 2001), 116.

67. Nathalie Beaux, "Sirius Étoile et Jeune Horus," *Hommages a Jean Leclant, Insitute Français D'Archéologie Orientale, Biblitheque D'Etude* 106, no. 1 (1993).

68. Francis A. Cunningham, "The Sothic Cycle Used by the Egyptians," *Journal of the American Oriental Society* 34 (1915): 369–73.

69. Ibid.

70. M. F. Ingham, "The Length of the Sothic Cycle," *Journal of Egyptian Archaeology* 55 (1969): 36–40.

71. Jaromir Malek and John Baines, *The Cultural Atlas of the World: Ancient Egypt* (Alexandria, Va.: Stonehenge, 1991), 36.

72. Juan Belmonte, "Some Open Questions on the Egyptian Calendar: An Astronomer's View," *Trabajos de Egyptologia,* no. 2 (2003): 10.

73. Wilkinson, *The Complete Temples of Ancient Egypt,* 37.
    Jaroslav Cerny, "The Temple as an Abtriviated Name for the Temple of Medinet Habu," in *JEA* 26 (1940), p. 127.

74. Krupp, *Echoes of Ancient Skies,* 258.

75. Baines and Malek, *Atlas of Ancient Egypt* (New York: Facts on File Publications, 1980), 112.

76. For a full discussion on the Followers of Horus, see Bauval and Hancock, *Keeper of Genesis* (London: Heinemann, 1996).

77. H. Brugsch, *Egypt* (n.p., 1891), 189, quoted by Lockyer, *The Dawn of Astronomy*, 204–205.

78. Lockyer, *The Dawn of Astronomy*, 204–5

79. Wilkinson, *The Complete Temples of Ancient Egypt*, 205.

80. Pyramid Texts, line 351.

81. Ian Shaw and Paul Nicholson, *The Illustrated Dictionary of Ancient Egypt* (Cairo: American University in Cairo Press, 2008), p. 112.

82. Pyramid Texts, Utterance 263.

83. Ibid., line 865.

84. Ibid., lines 351–53.

85. Ibid., lines 1000–1001.

86. Henri Frankfort, *Kingship and the Gods* (Chicago: University of Chicago Press, 1978), 90.

87. Thomas Brophy, *The Origin Map* (Bloomington, Ind.: iUniverse, 2002), 15–18.

88. A. Mariette, *Denderah: Description Generale du grand temple de cette Ville*, vol. 1, Paris-Cairo: n.p., 1875) 142, 263.

89. Beaux "Sirius, Etoile et Jeune Horus," 64, note14.

90. Krupp, *Echoes of the Ancient Skies*, 257.

91. Ibid., 258.

92. Ibid.

93. Lockyer, *The Dawn of Astronomy*, 193.

94. Ibid., 200.

95. Mariette, *Denderah,* 206. See also Lockyer, *The Dawn of Astronomy,* 194.

96. Z. Zaba, *L'Orientation Astronomique dans L'Ancienne Egypte et la Precession de l'axe du monde* (Prague: n.p., 1953), 59.

97. Private correspondence with Robert Bauval, October 8, 1986.

98. Sylvie Cauville-Colin, "Le Temple D'Isis a Dendera," *Bulletin de la Societe Francaise d'Egyptologie* 123 (March 1992): 31–48.

99. Lehner, *The Complete Pyramids*, 120.

100. The story is told in the *Westcar Papyrus* (Berlin Museum). See Miroslav Verner, *Abusir: Realm of Osiris* (Cairo: American University in Cairo Press, 2002), 70.

101. Malek and Baines, *The Cultural Atlas: Ancient Egypt*, 154.

102. Verner, *Abusir: The Realm of Osiris*.

103. David G. Jeffreys, "The Topography of Heliopolis and Memphis: Some Cognitive Aspects," in R Stadelmann, H. Guksch, and D Polz, eds., *Stationen: Beitrage zur Kulturgeschichte Agyptens* (Mainz: von Zabern, 1998), 63–71.

104. For hieroglyphic signs and allocated code, visit: http://pagesperso-orange. fr/hieroglyphes/Hieroglyphica%20=%20A.htm

105. Stefan Kröpelin and Rudolph Kuper, "More Corridors to Africa," in B. Gratien, ed., *Mélanges offerts à Francis Geus* (Villeneuve-d'Ascq: Université Charles-de-Gaulle, 2007), 219–29.

APPENDIX I. BACK TO THE FIRST TIME:
VEGA, SIRIUS, AND ORION AGREE AT GIZA

1. Wendorf, *Holocene Settlement of the Egyptian Sahara*, vol. 1, 489.

2. W. M. F. Petrie, *The Pyramids and Temples of Gizeh* (London, n.p., 1883).

3. Lehner, *The Complete Pyramids*.

4. Petrie, *The Pyramids and Temples of Gizeh*.

5. RA = 201.03, Dec = 287.47 milliarcseconds per year. From SIMBAD Astronomical Database, http://simbad.u-strasbg.fr/simbad/sim-id?protocol=html&Ident=vega (accessed February 2010).

6. RA = -546.05, Dec = -1223.14 milliarcseconds per year. From SIMBAD Astronomical Database, http://simbad.u-strasbg.fr/simbad/sim-id?Ident= Sirius&NbIdent=1&Radius=2&Radius.unit=arcmin&submit=submit+id (accessed February 2010).

7. An online calculator is available at http://wise-obs.tau.ac.il/.

8. Lehner, *The Complete Pyramids*, 17.

9. See R. M. Schoch, "Geological Evidence Pertaining to the Age of the Great Sphinx," *New Scenarious on the Evolution of the Solar System and Consequences on History of Earth and Man*, Emilio Spedicato and Adalberto Notarpietro, editors, Proceedings of the Conference, Milano and Bergamo, June 7–9, 1999, Universita degil Studi di Bergamo, Quaderni del Dipartmento di Matematica, Statistica, Informatica ed Applicazion, Serie

Miscellanea, Anno 2002, N.3, pp. 171–203. (also available online at http://www.robertschoch.com/geodarasphinx.htm.

10. R. M. Schoch, *Voyages of the Pyramid Builders* (New York: Tarcher and Putnam, 2003).

11. Alberto Siliotti, *Guide to the Pyramids of Egypt* (New York: Barnes and Noble Books, 1997).

12. Lehner, *The Complete Pyramids.*

13. Edwards, *The Pyramids of Egypt.*

14. Lehner, *The Complete Pyramids,* 17.

15. Edwards, *The Pyramids of Egypt,* 86.

16. R. M. Schoch and R. A. McNally, *Pyramid Quest* (New York: Penguin, 2005), 27.

17. Manly P. Hall, *The Secret Teachings of All Ages* (Radford, Va.: Wilder, 2007).

18. Siliotti, *Guide to the Pyramids of Egypt,* preface by Zahi Hawass.

19. Klaus Schmidt: *Sie bauten die ersten Tempel. Das rätselhafte Heiligtum der Steinzeitjäger* (München: n.p., 2006).

20. Brophy, *The Origin Map: Discovery of a Prehistoric Megalithic Astrophysical Map of the Universe*; Thomas G. Brophy, *The Mechanism Demands a Mysticism* (Blue Hill, Maine: Medicine Bear), 1999.

21. G. Hancock and R. Bauval, *The Message of The Sphinx* (New York: Crown, 1996).

22. Rundle Clark, *Myth and Symbol in Ancient Egypt* London: Thames and Hudson, 1978).

APPENDIX 2. SOTHIC CYCLES AND IMHOTEP'S CALENDAR WALL

1. M. F. Ingham, "The Length of the Sothic Cycle," *Journal of Egyptian Archaeology* 55 (1969): 36–40.

APPENDIX 3. SAVING NABTA PLAYA

1. E-mail from Schild, May 26, 2008.

2. Ibid.

3. Ibid.

BIBLIOGRAPHY

Abed, Wael T. *The Other Egypt.* Cairo: n.p., 1998.

Ackroyd, Peter. "Afloat on the Nile." *New York Times,* October 2, 1988.

Aeschylus. *The Suppliants.*

Applegate Alex, and Nieves Zedeño. *Holocene Settlement of the Egyptian Sahara,* vol. 1.

New York: Plenum, 2001.

Apollodoros. Book II, "The Family of Inachus."

Aristotle. *Physiognomy.*

Arkell, A. J. *A History of the Sudan: From Earliest Times to 1821,* 2nd ed., rev.

London: n.p., 1961.

Aveni, A. F. "Tropical Archaeoastronomy." *Science* 243 (1981): 161–71.

Bagnold, R. A. "Journeys in the Libyan Desert 1929 and 1930." *Geographical Journal* 78, no. 1 (July 1931).

Bagnold, R. A., O. H. Myers, R. F. Peel, and H. A. Winkler. "An Expedition to the Gilf Kebir and 'Uweinat, 1938." *Geographical Journal* 93, no. 4 (April, 1939), 281–312.

———. *The Physics of Blown Sand and Desert Dunes.* London: Methuen, 1941.

Bauval, Robert G. "Cheop's Pyramid: A New Dating Using the Latest Astronomical Data." *Discussions In Egyptology* 26 (1993).

———. "A Master Plan for the Three Pyramids of Giza Based on the Configuration of the Three Stars of the Belt of Orion." *Discussions in Egyptology* 13 (1989), 7–19.

———. *The Egypt Code.* London: Century Books, 2006.

———. "The Seeding of the Star-gods: A Fertility Rite inside Cheop's Pyramid?" *Discussion In Egyptology* 16 (1990), 21–25.

Bauval, Robert, and Graham Hancock. *Keeper of Genesis.* London: Heinemann, 1996.

Beaux, Nathalie. "Sirius Étoile et Jeune Horus." *Hommages a Jean Leclant, Insitute Français D'Archéologie Orientale, Biblitheque D'Etude* 106, no. 1 (1993).

Belmonte, Juan. "Some Open Questions on the Egyptian Calendar: An Astronomer's View." *Trabajos de Egiptologia,* 2003, 24.

Belmonte, Juan, and M. Shaltout. "On the Orientation of Ancient Egyptian Temples I: Upper Egypt and Lower Nubia." in *Journal of the History of Astronomy* (Pre-print series: PP 03/2005), 21, figure 8.

Berger, A. L. "Obliquity and Precession for the Last 5,000,000 Years." *Astronomy & Astrophysics* 51 (1976): 127–35.

Bergmann, C., and Kl. P. Kuhlmann. "Die Expedition des Cheops." GEO Special 5, 2001.

———. "The 'Oasis Bypath' or The Issue of Desert Trade in Pharaonic Times." in T. Lenssen-Erz, U. Tegtmeier, St. Kröpelin et al. (eds.), *Tides of the Desert. Contributions to the Archaeology and Environmental History of Africa in Honour of Rudolf Kuper, Köln,* 2002.

Bermann, Richard A. "Historic Problems of the Libyan Desert." *Geographical Journal* 83, no. 6 (June 1934): 456–63.

Bernal, Martin. *Black Athena: The Afroasiatic Roots of Classical Civilization,* vols. 1, 2, and 3. Piscataway, N.J.: Rutgers University Press, 1987.

Bomhard, Anne-Sophie. *The Egyptian Calendar: A Work for Eternity.* London: Periplus, 1998.

Breasted, J. H. *Ancient Records of Egypt* Part I. Chicago: University of Chicago Press, 1906.

Brophy, Thomas. *The Mechanism Demands a Mysticism.* Blue Hill, Maine: Medicine Bear Publishing, 1999.

———. *The Origin Map: Discovery of a Prehistoric Megalithic Astrophysical Map of the Universe.* Bloomington, Ind.: iUniverse, 2002.

Brophy, Thomas, L. W. Esposito, G. R. Stewart, et al. "Numerical Simulation of Satellite-ring Interactions: Resonances and Satellite-ring Torques." *Icarus* 100 (1992): 412–33.

Brophy, Thomas, and Paul Rosen. "Satellite Imagery Measures of the Astronomically Aligned Megaliths at Nabta Playa." *Mediterranean Archaeology and Archaeometry* 5, no. 1 (2005): 15–24.

Bruck, Dr. Mary T. "Can the Great Pyramid be Astronomically Dated?" *Journal of the British Astronomical Association* 105, no. 4 (1995): 161–64.

Brugsch, H. *Egypt*. N.p., 1891.

Buchwald, Jed Z. "Egyptian Stars under Paris Skies." *Engineering and Science Magazine* 66, No. 4, California Institute of Technology (2003).

Budge, E. A. Wallis. *An Egyptian Hieroglyphic Dictionary*. Mineola, N.Y.: Dover Publications, 1978.

———. *Legends of the Egyptian Gods: Hieroglyphic Texts and Translations*. New York: Dover, 1994.

Burkhard, G. "Inscriptions in the Dakhla Region." *Sahara* 9 (1997), 152–53.

Burnham Jr., Robert. *Burnham's Celestial Handbook*, vol. 1. New York: Dover Publications, 1978.

Cann, Rebecca L., Mark Stoneking, and Allan C. Wilson. "Mitochondrial DNA and Human Evolution." *Nature* 325 (1987): 31–36.

Cauville-Colin, Sylvie. "Le Temple d'Isis a Dendera." *Bulletin de la Societe Francaise d'Egyptologie* 123 (March 1992): 31–48.

Censorinus. *De Die Natali*. Chicago: The University of Chicago Press, 2007.

Cerny, Jaroslav. "The Temple as an Abtriviated Name for the Temple of Medinet Habu." in *Journal of Egyptian Archaeology* 26 (1940), 127.

Champollion-Figeac, Jean-Jacques. *L'Egypte Ancienne*. Paris: Diot, 1839.

Chang, Kenneth. "In Lake, Signs of Slow Shift from Savannah to Sahara." *New York Times,* May 9, 2008.

Chapman, A. *Gods in the Sky: Astronomy from the Ancients to the Renaissance*. London: Channel 4 Books, 2002.

Clark, Rundle. *Myth and Symbol in Ancient Egypt*. London: Thames and Hudson, 1978.

Clayton, Joseph, Aloisia De Trafford, and Mark Borda. "A Hieroglyphic Inscription Found at Jebel Uweinat Mentioning Yam and Tekhebet." *Sahara* 19 (2008).

Cunningham, Francis A. "The Sothic Cycle Used by the Egyptians." *Journal of the American Oriental Society* 34 (1915): 369–73.

Deacon, Michael. "Interview with Alice Roberts: The Incredible Human Journey." *Daily Telegraph,* May 5, 2009.

DeMenocal, P. B. "Cultural Responses to Climate Change During the Late Holocene." *Science* 292 (2001): 667–73.

DeMenocal, P. B., Ortiz, J., Guilderson, T., Adkins, J., Sarnthein, M., Baker, L., and Yarusinski, M. "Abrupt Onset and Termination of the African Humid Period: Rapid Climate Response to Gradual Insolation Forcing." *Quarterly Scientific Review* 19, 2000, 347–361.

De Santillana, G., and H. von Dechend. *Hamlet's Mill.* Boston: Gambit Inc., 1969.

Diogenes. *Laertius,* Book VII.

Diop, Cheikh Anta. "Egypt Revisited." *Journal of African Civilization* 10 (Summer 1989): 9–39.

——. "Origin of the Ancient Egyptians." http//www.africawithin.com/diop/origin_egyptian.htm.

Diodorus of Sicily. *Universal History,* Book III.

Edwards, I. E. S. *The Pyramids of Egypt.* London: Penguin, 1982,1993.

Erman, Adolf, and Hermann Grapow. *Deutsche Akamemie, Worterbuch der Aegyptischen Sprache,* vol 5. N.p., 1971.

Forbes, Rosita, and Sir Harry Johnston. *The Secret of the Sahara: Kufara.* London: n.p., 1923.

Förster, Frank. "With Donkeys, Jars and Water Bags into the Libyan Desert: The Abu Ballas Trail in the late Old Kingdom/First Intermediate Period." *British Museum* SAES 7 (September 2007): 7.

Frankfort, Henri. *Kingship and the Gods.* Chicago: University of Chicago Press, 1978.

Genzlinger, Neil. "Chasing Mummies—The Pharaoh of Egyptian Antiquities." *New York Times,* July 13, 2010.

Girling, Richard. "King Tut Tut Tut," *Sunday Times* of London, May 22, 2005.

Goedicke, Hans. "Harkhuf's Travels." *Journal of Near Eastern Studies* 40, no.1 (January 1981): 1–20.

Gornitz, Vivien. *Encyclopedia of Paleoclimatology and Ancient Environments.* Dordrecht, Netherlands: Springer, 2009.

Gratien, B. *Mélanges offerts à Francis Geus.* Villeneuve-d'Ascq: Université Charles-de-Gaulle, 2007.

Greenwald, Jeff. "Moo Age Travellers: Were cattle-worshipping nomads the predecessors of the Pharaohs?" *The New Scientist* 2249, July 29, 2000.

Gurdjieff, G. I. *All and Everything: Meetings with Remarkable Men.* New York: E. P. Dutton and Co. Inc., 1963.

Gwin, Peter. "Lost Tribes of the Green Sahara." *National Geographic,* September 2008.

Hall, Manly P. *The Secret Teachings of All Ages.* Radford, Va.: Wilder, 2007.

Hancock, Graham, and Robert Bauval. *The Message of The Sphinx.* New York: Crown, 1996.

Hart, George. *A Dictionary of Egyptian Gods and Goddesses.* London: Routledge and Kegan Paul, 1988.

Hassanein, Ahmed. "Crossing the Untraversered Libyan Desert." *National Geographic Magazine,* vol. XLVI, No.3, September 1924.

———. "Through Kufra to Darfur," *Geographical Journal* 64, no. 4 (Oct., 1924): 273–91.

Hawass, Zahi, and Lyla Pich Brock. *Egyptology at the Dawn of the Twenty-first Century: History, Religion.* Cairo: American University in Cairo Press, 2004.

Herodotus. *The Histories,* Book II.

Ingham, M. F. "The Length of the Sothic Cycle." *Journal of Egyptian Archaeology* 55 (1969): 36–40.

Isler, Martin. "Primitive Methods of Measuring Time with Special Reference to Egypt." *Journal of Egyptian Archaeology* 17 (1931), 170.

Jordan, Paul. *Riddles of the Sphinx.* New York: New York University Press, 1998.

Keita, S.O. Y., and A. J. Boyce. *Race: Confusion about Zoological and Social Taxonomies, and Their Places in Science.* Chicago and Oxford, England: Field Museum and Institute of Biological Anthropology, Oxford University.

Kerisel, Jean. *The Nile and Its Masters: Past, Present, Future Source of Hope and Anger.* Rotterdam: A. A. Balkema, 2001.

King, W. J. Harding. *Mysteries of the Libyan Desert.* London: Century, 1925.

Kobusiewicz. M., and R. Schild. "Prehistoric Herdsmen, Focus on Archaeology." *Academia* 3, no. 7 (2004): 20–23.

Kondo, Jiro. *Ancient Egyptian Astronomy.* Tokyo: Waseda Universtiy, 2008. www.yomiuri.co.jp/adv/wol/dy/opinion/culture_081006.htm. Accessed August 23, 2010.

Krauss, Rolf K. "Probleme des Altagyptischen Kalendars und der Chronologie des Mittleren und Neuen Reiches in Agypten." Ph.D. dissertation, Freie University, Berlin, 1981.

———. "Sothis, Elephantine und d. Altagypt Chronologie." *Gottinger Miszellen* (GM) 50 (1981): 71–81.

Kropelin, Stefan, and Rudolph Kuper. "More Corridors to Africa." *Cripel* 26 (2006–2007), 219–29.

Krupp, E. C. *Echoes of the Ancient Skies.* New York: Oxford University Press, 1983.

Kuentz, Charles. *Bulletin de L'Institut Francais d'Archeologie Orientale* 17 1(920): 121–90.

Kuhlmann, K. P. "The Oasis Bypath or the Issue of Desert Trade in Pharaonic Times." in Tilman Lenssen-Erz, Ursula Tegtmeier, and Stefan Kröpelin, *Gezeiten der Wüste.* Köln: Heinrich Barth Institut, 2001.

Kuper, Rudolph, and Frank Förster. "Khufu's 'mefat' expeditions into the Libyan Desert." *Egyptian Archaeology* 23 (2003): 25-28.

Kuper, Rudolph, and Stefan Kröpelin. "Climate-Controlled Holocene Occupation in the Sahara: Motor of Africa's Evolution." *Science Journal AAAS* (July 2006).

Lalouette, Claire. *Textes sacrés et textes profanes de l'ancienne Egypte.* Paris: Gallimard, 1984.

Lamy, Lucie. *Egyptian Mysteries.* New York: Thames and Hudson, 1981.

Lehner, Mark. *The Complete Pyramids.* London: Thames and Hudson, 1997.

Lesley, E. G., and Roy Adkins. *The Keys of Egypt.* New York: HarperCollins, 2000.

Lichtheim, M. *Ancient Egyptian Literature: A Book of Readings,* vol. 3. Berkeley: University of California Press, 1973.

Lockyer, Norman. *The Dawn of Astronomy.* London: Cassel and Co. Ltd., 1894.

Lucian. *Navigations.*

Malek, Jaromir, and John Baines. *Atlas of Ancient Egypt.* New York: Facts on File Publications, 1980.

———. *The Cultural Atlas of the World: Ancient Egypt* Richmond, Va.: Stonehenge Press, 1991.

Malville, J. McKim, Fred Wendorf, Ali A. Mazar, et al. "Megaliths and Neolithic Astronomy in Southern Egypt." *Nature* 392 (April 1998): 488–91.

Malville, J. McKim, Romuald Schild, Fred Wendorf, and J. Brenmer. "Astronomy of Nabta Playa," *African Skies/Cieus Africains*, no.11 (July 2007).

———. "Astronomy of Nabta Playa," in J. Holbrook et. al, eds., *African Cultural Astronomy—Current Archaeoastronomy and Ethnoastronomy Research in Africa*. New York: Springer, 2008.

Manley, Bill. *The Seventy Great Mysteries of Ancient Egypt*. London: Thames and Hudson, 2003.

Marcellinus, Ammianus. *Book XXII*.

Mariette, A. *Denderah: Description Generale du grand temple de cette Ville*, vol. 1. Paris-Cairo: n.p., 1875.

Markey, Sean. "Exodus from Drying Sahara Gave Rise to Pharaohs, Study Says." *National Geographic News*, July 20, 2006.

McCauley, J. F., G. G. Schaber, C. S. Breed, et al. "Subsurface Valleys and Geoarcheology of the Eastern Sahara Revealed by Shuttle Radar." *Science* 218, no. 4576 (December 3, 1982): 1004–1020.

McKay, David S., et al. "Search for Past Life on Mars: Possible Relic Biogenic Activity in Martian Meteorite ALH84001." *Science* magazine (August 16, 1996).

Michell, John. *A Little History of Astro-Archaeology*. London: Thames and Hudson, 1977.

Milankovitch, Milutin. *Théorie Mathématique des Phénomènes Thermiques produits par la Radiation Solaire*. Paris: Gauthier-Villars, 1920.

Murray, G. W. "Hakhuf's Third Journey." *Geographical Journal* 131, no.1 (March 1965): 72–75.

O'Connor, David B., and Stephen Quirke. *Mysterious Lands*. London: University College, Institute of Archaeology, 2003.

Parker, Richard. "Ancient Egyptian Astronomy." Providence, R.I.: Department of Egyptology, Brown University, Philosophical Transaction of the Royal Society of London, 1974.

———. *The Calendars of Ancient Egypt*. Chicago: University of Chicago Press, 1950.

Peel, R. F. "The Tibu Peoples and the Libyan Desert." *Geographical Journal* 100, no. 2 (August 1942), 73–87.

Petrie, W. M. F. *The Pyramids and Temples of Gizeh*. London: n.p., 1883.

Pliny the Elder. *The Natural History*, Book V.

Pyramid Texts.

———. Utterance 263.

Quirke, Stephen. *The Cult of Ra.* London: Thames and Hudson, 2001.

Redford, Donald B. *The Ancient Gods Speak.* Oxford: Oxford University Press, 2002.

———. *Oxford Guide to Egyptian Mythology.* New York: Berkley Books, 2002.

Rigby, Peter. *African Images.* Oxford, England: Berg Publishers, 1996.

Roeder, Gunther. "Sothis und Satis, Zeitschrift fuer Aegyptische Sprache." Band 45, Leipzig (1908): 22–30.

Rohlfs, Gerhard. *Voyages et Explorations au Sahara,* tome 2. N.p., 1865–67.

Rose, L. "The Astronomical Evidence for Dating the End of the Middle Kingdom of Ancient Egypt to the Early Second Millennium: A Reassessment." *Journal of Near Eastern Studies* 53 (1994): 246.

Salama-Scheer, Yaniv. "War of the Pyramid Theorists." *Jerusalem Post,* April 2, 2007, http://findarticles.com/p/news-articles/jerusalem-post/mi8048/is_2000402/war-pyramid-theorists/ai_n47369584/.

Schwaller de Lubicz, R. A. *The Temples of Karnak.* Rochester, Vt.: Inner Traditions, 2001.

Schild, Romuald, and Fred Wendorf. "Forty Years of the Combined Prehistoric Expedition." *Archaeologia Polona* 40 (2002).

———. *Holocene Settlement of the Egyptian Sahara: The Archaeology of Nabta Playa* vol. 1. New York: Kluwer Academic/Plenum, 2001.

———. "The Megaliths of Nabta Playa, Focus on Archeology." *Academia* 1, no. 1 (2004): 11.

Schild, Romuald, and Michal Kobusiewicz. "Prehistoric Herdsmen, Academia." *Focus on Archaeology* 3, no. 7 (2005).

Schmidt, Klaus. *Sie bauten die ersten Tempel. Das rätselhafte Heiligtum der Steinzeitjäger.* München: n.p., 2006.

Schoch, R. M. "Geological Evidence Pertaining to the Age of the Great Sphinx." *New Scenarious on the Evolution of the Solar System and Consequences on History of Earth and Man.* Proceedings of the Conference Milano and Bergamo: 1999.

———. *Voyages of the Pyramid Builders.* New York: Tarcher and Putnam, 2003.

Schoch, R. M., and R. A. McNally. *Pyramid Quest.* New York: Penguin, 2005.

Seligman, C. G. *Races of Africa.* London: T. Butterworth, 1930.

Shakir M. H., Translator. Qur'an. Elmhurst, N.Y.: Tahrike Tarsile Qur'an Inc., 1983.

Shaw, Ian, and Paul Nicholson. *The Dictionary of Ancient Egypt*. London: British Museum Press, 1995.

———. *The Illustrated Dictionary of Ancient Egypt*. Cairo: American University in Cairo Press, 2008.

Siliotti, Alberto. *Guide to the Pyramids of Egypt*. New York: Barnes and Noble Books, 1997.

Sloley, R. W. "Primitive Methods of Measuring Time, with Special Reference to Egypt." *Journal of Egyptian Archaeology* 17 (1930): 167.

Soares, Pedro, et al. "Correcting for Purifying Selection: An Improved Human Mitochondrial Molecular Clock." *American Journal of Human Genetics* 84, no. 6 (June 4, 2009): 740–59.

Stadelmann, R., H. Guksch, and D Polz, eds. *Stationen: Beitrage zur Kulturgeschichte Agyptens*. Mainz: von Zabern, 1998.

Strabo. *Geography*, Book I.

———. *Geography,* Book XVII.

Taylor, Paul. *Iconography without Texts*. London: Warburg Warburg Institute Colloquia 12), 2008. http://cnrs.academia.edu/documents/0097/7841/Le_Quellec_2008-k.pdf.

Trimble, Virginia. *Astronomical Investigation Concerning the So-called Air-shafts of Cheop's Pyramid, Mitteilungen der Institut Fur Orientforschung* 10, no. 2/3 (1964): 183–87.

Verner, Miroslav. *Abusir: Realm of Osiris*. Cairo: American University in Cairo Press, 2002.

Volney, M. C. F. *Voyages en Syrie et en Egypte,* vol. I. Paris: n.p., 1787.

Wainwright, G. A. "Seshat and the Pharaoh." *Journal of Egyptian Archaeology* 26 (1941): 30–40.

Walker, Clarence. *We Can't Go Home Again: An Argument about Afrocentrism*. New York: Oxford University Press, 2004.

Weidemann, A. *Recuil de Travaux,* tome XVII.

Wells, Ron. "Sothis and the Satet Temple on Elephantine." *Studien Zur Altagyptischen Kultur* (SAK) 12 (1985), 258.

Wendorf, Fred, A. E. Close, and R. Schild. "Megaliths in the Egyptian Sahara." *Sahara* 5 (1992–1993): 7–16.

Wendorf, Fred, and Romuald Schild. "The Megaliths of Nabta Playa." *Academia, Focus on Archaeology,* no.1 (2004): 11.

Westcar Papyrus. Berlin Museum.

Whitrow, G. J. *Time in History: View of Time from Prehistory to the Present Day.* New York: Oxford University Press, 1988.

Wilkinson, G. *Topography of Thebes and General View of Egypt.* London: John Murray Publishers, 1835.

Wilkinson, Richard H. *The Complete Gods and Goddesses of Ancient Egypt.* Cairo: American University in Cairo Press, 2005.

———. *The Complete Gods and Goddesses of Ancient Egypt.* London: Thames and Hudson, 2003.

———. *The Complete Temples of Ancient Egypt.* New York: Thames and Hudson, 2000.

Wright, J. L. *Libya, Chad and the Central Sahara.* London: Hurst and Co., 1989.

Zaba, Z. *L'Orientation Astronomique Dans L'Ancienne Egypte et la Precession de l'Axe du Monde.* Prague: n.p., 1953.

Zayan, Jailan. *Egypt—Culture Smart!: The Essential Guide to Customs and Culture.* London: Kuperard, 2007.

INDEX